REPORT OF MAJOR GENERAL WILLIAM T. SHERMAN

KRAUS REPRINT CO.

Millwood, N.Y.

1977

Extracted from:
U.S. Congress. Joint Committee on the Conduct of the
War. Report of the Joint Committee on the Conduct of
the War. 1863-1866.

ISBN 0-527-17566-8
LC 76-43555

KRAUS REPRINT CO.
A U.S. Division of Kraus-Thomson Organization Limited
Printed in U.S.A.

INTRODUCTION

In the summer of 1861 the cry heard in Washington was, "On to Richmond." The citizens of the north, as well as the Congress itself, believed that a single decisive battle would end the new-born Confederacy once and for all.

On July 21, President Lincoln, under pressure from Congress and his War Department, allowed General McDowell to advance against General Beauregard's forces at Manasas Junction—about thirty miles south of the capital—in the hope of claiming "one decisive battle." Under the horrified watch of spectators who had driven out to enjoy a picnic lunch and watch their boys "whip the rebels," a fierce and bloody battle ensued along a little creek called Bull Run. The resulting fight appeared at first to be a Union victory, but the tide quickly turned. Inexperienced federal troops first retreated and then panicked into a desperate race for the safety of Washington, leaving thousands of their dead and wounded behind.

Within three months federal troops again faced a Confederate force, this time on Harrison's Island—a day's march northwest of Washington—and again met bloody defeat in the Battle of Ball's Bluff. Killed during the battle was a United States Senator from Oregon, Colonel Edward E. Baker.

Congress, now under intense pressure to investigate the military disasters, attempted to develop a uniform war policy. On December 5, 1861, Senator Zachariah Chandler, a leader of western radicalism, presented a motion to create a joint Senate and House committee to determine the causes of the Union defeats at Bull Run and Ball's Bluff.

The Joint Committee on the Conduct of the War, under the chairmanship of Senator Benjamen F. Wade, held hearings and meetings from December 20, 1861, through the final days of the conflict some four years later. Although political infighting, personal prejudices, and regional differences often prevented a common understanding of military strategy, the detailed testimony and reports from the military officers and personnel directly involved with the day-to-day conduct of the war provide a unique picture of the Union's action during each critical phase of the conflict.

This monograph, extracted unedited and unabridged from the eight-volume *Report of the Joint Committee on the Conduct of the War, 1863-1866*, published by the U.S. Congress, makes available the individual reports, testimony, individual communiques, maps, and accompanying correspondence that resulted from the Committee's work. This unique monograph provides scholars and Civil War buffs with an opportunity to study and evaluate one individual segment of the Civil War.

Benedict A. Leerburger
Kraus Reprint Company

February 1977

REPORT

OF

MAJOR GENERAL WILLIAM T. SHERMAN

TO THE

HON. COMMITTEE ON THE CONDUCT OF THE WAR.

COMMITTEE ROOM, CONDUCT OF THE WAR,
Washington, D. C., May 22, 1865.

GENERAL: The Committee on the Conduct of the War have found it impossible to take testimony heretofore in regard to the many important campaigns in which you have been engaged since the commencement of the rebellion.

In order to place upon record some reliable account of those campaigns, the committee have decided that the best way was to submit to you some questions in writing which are herewith enclosed, and request you to prepare answers to them, and forward the same to the chairman at any time prior to the next session of Congress, for publication.

The committee desire that you will make your statement as full and detailed as may be necessary to a clear understanding of the subject of inquiry in every respect, and for that purpose they would like to have you submit copies of the enclosed interrogatories, with such others as may suggest themselves to you, to those of your subordinates in any campaign whom you may deem best qualified to furnish information; their statements to be forwarded with your own.

I remain, yours, respectfully,

B. F. WADE,
Chairman of Committee.

Major General W. T. SHERMAN.

Questions.

No. 1. Please state what positions you have held and what commands you have exercised since the commencement of the rebellion, giving the periods during which those commands respectively have been exercised by you.

No. 2. Please state such particulars as you may deem necessary to a proper understanding of the several campaigns in which you have been engaged; setting forth the orders and instructions under which those campaigns were conducted, and the principal orders and instructions given by you, with such incidents and circumstances as you consider will be of interest to the public; appending to your statement copies of your reports and those of your principal subordinates, and keeping the account of each campaign by itself as far as convenient.

Answers.

No. 1. On the first day of June, 1861, I was a citizen of St. Louis, Missouri, residing there with my family, and engaged in business as president of the Fifth street railroad. On a summons from my brother, John Sherman, I proceeded to the city of Washington, and, on the eighteenth day of June, received from the Secretary of War, Simon Cameron, an appointment as colonel of the 13th regiment United States regular infantry, reported for duty, and by Special Orders No. 105, of June 20, 1861, was assigned to duty at the headquarters of the army, Lieutenant General Scott commanding.

On the 30th of June, was ordered to report for duty to Brigadier General McDowell, commanding department northeast Virginia, and by Special Order No. 16 from those headquarters was ordered to relieve Colonel D. Hunter in command of Fort Corcoran; relieved him same day, and proceeded to prepare the troops there for field service.

On the 21st July, commanded a brigade in General Tyler's division at the battle of Bull Run, official report of which, dated July 25, 1861, is on file in the Adjutant General's office, Washington, D. C.

About the middle of August, 1861, General Robert Anderson, about to be assigned to command the department of the Cumberland, sent for me to meet him at Willard's hotel, when he notified me he had applied for myself, Brigadier Generals Thomas, Burnside, and Buell, to act under him in his new command. I then expressed to him, and also to President Lincoln, that I did not wish to be placed in any conspicuous position, but would attempt any amount of work.

On the 15th of August, received an appointment of brigadier general of United States volunteers. August 28, 1861, was relieved of command at Fort Corcoran by General Fitz John Porter, pursuant to Special Order No. 11, August 28, 1861, of Major General McClellan, and ordered to Cincinnati, Ohio, to report in person to General Robert Anderson; by him was sent on a tour to the governors of Indiana and Illinois, and to confer with Major General Frémont, at St. Louis, and summoned back to Louisville, Kentucky, in time to take command of a detachment of volunteers and militia sent out to Muldroagh Hill to check the advance of the rebel army on Louisville; remained out in command of that force until summoned back to Louisville to be placed in chief command of the department, by reason of General Anderson's health compelling him to return east. Earnestly remonstrated against being placed in chief command, and, considering the President pledged not to put me in any prominent command, urged it with earnestness, and was relieved pursuant to Special Orders No. 305, Adjutant General's office, Washington, D. C., November 13, 1861, and ordered to report to Major General Halleck for duty in the department of Missouri. Reported at St. Louis, November 24, 1861, and by Special Order No. 8 was assigned to special inspection duty, as therein defined; and subsequently, by Special Order No. 87, of December 23, 1861, put in command of the post of Benton barracks. Remained there in command until February 17, 1862, when I was sent, by a telegraphic order from General Halleck, to Paducah to control the movement of supplies and troops for General Grant, then operating up the Tennessee river. Remained there until about the 9th of March, 1862, when, by General Halleck's order, I made up a division of twelve (12) new regiments, just arrived, with which to take the field.

March 10, 1862, moved in transports up the Tennessee river, and reported for duty to Major General C. F. Smith, at Savannah, Tennessee; was sent up the Tennessee to break the Memphis and Charleston railroad at or near Burnsville, Mississippi. Failed, by reason of the high water, and, by verbal order of Major General Smith, still in command at Savannah, Tennessee, landed at Pittsburg Landing, March 16, 1862. Marched out to Monterey, ten (10) miles, and, by orders, drew back and made camp at Shiloh meeting-house.   Remained there, drilling and organizing, and, April 6 and 7, 1862, took part in the battle of Shiloh, under command of Major General U. S. Grant, and afterwards moved on Corinth, Mississippi, with the grand army commanded by Major General H. W. Halleck, (April 29, 1862.)

May 1, 1862, promoted to major general of United States volunteers.

May 30, 1862, entered Corinth, and, by order of Major General Halleck, moved my own and Major General Hurlbut's division to Chewalla, Mississippi, thence along the Memphis and Charleston railroad, repairing it, until July 21, 1862, we entered Memphis, Tennessee; assumed command and remained there until September 24, 1862, when, by Major General Grant's Order No. 83, took command of the first district of West Tennessee.

November 25, 1862, pursuant to orders of General Grant, moved out of Memphis, for Tchulahoma, to report to him at Holly Springs, to attack and drive the enemy, then in force along the line of Tallahatchie river; December 3, 1862, crossed the Tallahatchie at Wyatt's, and December 5, 1862, met General Grant at Oxford, Mississippi.   By his order, returned to Memphis, Tennessee, December 12, 1862, leaving all my command but one division.   Organized out of the new troops there and at Helena, Arkansas, a special command, to move by water, and by a sudden coup de main carry Vicksburg.   Embarked December 20, 1862, and from December 25, 1862, to January 1, 1863, made repeated attacks on the bluffs between Vicksburg and Haines's Bluff, but failed.   January 4, 1863, was relieved of the command of the expedition by Major General John A. McClernand, and assumed command of the 15th army corps, January 13, 1863, then first organized out of the troops with me, in compliance with General Orders, No. 210, War Department.   Had taken part under General McClernand in the capture of Arkansas Post, January 11, 1863, and returned with that expedition, January 22, 1863, to Young's Point, Louisiana, opposite the city of Vicksburg, where, soon after, General Grant assumed immediate command of the entire army operating against that place.   Was in command of the 15th army corps during all the operations against Jackson and Vicksburg.

Vicksburg was surrendered to General Grant July 4, 1863, and the same day I was ordered to push back Joe Johnston's rebel army, that was near us for the purpose of relieving the garrison of Vicksburg; drove him into Jackson, and beyond, and by General Grant's orders dropped back to the Big Black, and went into camp for the summer months.   July 4, 1863, appointed brigadier general in the regular army.   September 22, 1863, in camp on Big Black, received orders from General Grant to send one of my divisions to Memphis, Tennessee, thence to go east, to the assistance of General Rosecrans; next day received orders, in person, to go myself with the 15th corps, and such of the 16th corps about Memphis as could be spared; left Memphis October 11, 1863; en route, at Iuka, Mississippi, October 24, 1863, received orders assigning me the command of the department and army of the Tennessee; reached Chattanooga November 15, 1863, in advance of my troops; conferred with General Grant, got his orders, and returned to Bridgeport, Alabama, to meet my command.   November 17, conducted them as rapidly as possible to the points assigned me, and took part in the battle of Missionary Ridge, November 24 and 25, 1863, and pursued the retreating enemy to Greyville, Georgia, and sent a detachment to Red Clay, Georgia, between Dalton and Cleveland, to break the railroad.   November 28, 1863, at Greyville, Georgia, General Grant consented that I might conduct my command up to the Hiawassa river for forage, and afterwards, December 1, he sent me orders to assume command of all troops moving north, and hasten to Knoxville to relieve General Burnside, then hard pressed by the rebel General Longstreet.   Moved rapidly, and entered Knoxville December 6, 1863; gave General Burnside the re-enforcements he needed, and returned by easy marches to Chattanooga and Bridgeport, where, on December

19, I put in motion my corps (the 15th) for their winter camps along the railroad from Stevenson to Decatur, Alabama, and in person proceeded to Nashville, Tennessee, where General Grant had made his headquarters. Thence, with his consent, proceeded via Cairo to Memphis and Vicksburg to inspect that part of my department, and to drive the enemy back and out of Mississippi.

February 4, 1864, having collected at Vicksburg the necessary forces, marched to Jackson the 6th and Meridian 14th February, destroyed all the railroads thereabouts, and drove the enemy's infantry beyond the Tombigbee river; remained at Meridian until February 20, and returned to Vicksburg, reaching there February 28; and to assist Major General Banks in a similar move west of the Mississippi, I hastened to him at New Orleans for conference, and left him March 3, 1864, with the promise to put ten thousand (10,000) infantry for him at Alexandria, Louisiana, March 17. This was done.

I proceeded up the river to Memphis, where I received General Grant's letters of March 4, 1864, calling me to Nashville, notifying me that he had been nominated Lieutenant General of the armies of the United States, which would take him east, and that he designed to devolve on me the command of the military division of the Mississippi. Reached Nashville March 17, 1864, and next day assumed command of the military division of the Mississippi, of which I have had command, with changed boundaries, ever since.

August 12, 1864, before Atlanta, Georgia, received notice of appointment as major general in the regular army on that day, my present commission.

Of all the above events the most minute official details have been given and are now on file in the Adjutant General's office, Washington, District of Columbia, and are too voluminous to repeat; but the campaign of Atlanta, Savannah, and the Carolinas having proven so conclusive, I hereto subjoin complete details, composed mostly of the correspondence between myself, the Secretary of War, General Halleck, Lieutenant General Grant, and my subordinate commanders, which will form rather the crude material for history than history itself.

Answer No. 2. To give all the orders made and all the details of events prior to the Atlanta campaign would be more voluminous than the committee can possibly expect, and I venture to confine myself purely to matters illustrative of the campaigns where I was in chief command. In pursuance of which, I send a printed copy of my orders since assuming command of the military division of the Mississippi, and the compilation of letters and instructions during the same period. To give matter illustrative of other times when I was not in chief command, would doubtless confuse rather than throw light on those events.

LETTERS.

HEADQUARTERS DEPARTMENT OF THE TENNESSEE,
Vicksburg, March 4, 1864.

GENERAL: By an order this day issued you are to command a strong well appointed detachment of the army of the Tennessee sent to reinforce a movement against the Red river line, but more especially the fortified positions of Shreveport.

You will embark your command as soon as possible, but little encumbered with wagons or wheeled vehicles, but well supplied with fuel, provisions and ammunition. Take with you the twelve (12) mortars with their ammunition and all the thirty (30) pounder Parrots the ordnance officer will supply. Proceed to the mouth of the Red river and confer with Admiral Porter; confer with him, and in all the expedition rely on him implicitly, as he is the approved friend of the army of the Tennessee, and has been associated with us from the beginning. I have undertaken with General Banks that you will be at Alexandria, Louisiana, on or before the 17th day of March, and you will, if time allows, co-operate with the navy in destroying Harrisonburg, up Black river, or the Washita; but as I passed Red river yesterday I saw Admiral Porter, and he told me he had already sent an expedition to Harrisonburg, so that I suppose that part of the plan will be accomplished before you reach Red river, but in any event be careful to reach Alexandria about the 17th of March.

General Banks will start by land from Franklin, in the Teche country, either the fifth or seventh, and will march *via* Opelousas to Alexandria. You will meet him there, report to him, and act under his orders. My understanding with him is, his forces will still move by land *via* Natchitoches, &c., to Shreveport, whilst the gunboat fleet is to ascend the river with your transports in company. Now Red river is very low for the season, and I doubt if the boats can pass the falls or rapids at Alexandria. What General Banks proposes to do in that event I do not know, but my own judgment is that Shreveport ought not to be attacked until the gunboats can reach it. Not that a force marching by land cannot do it alone, but it would be bad economy in war to invest the place with an army so far from heavy guns, mortars, ammunition and provisions, which can alone reach Shreveport by water.

Still I do not know about General Banks's plans in that event; but whatever they may be, your duty will be to conform in the most hearty manner.

My understanding with General Banks is that he will not need the co-operation of your force beyond thirty days from the date you reach Red river. As soon as he has taken Shreveport, or as soon as he can spare you, you will return to Vicksburg with all despatch, gather up your detachments, wagons, tents, transportation, and all property pertaining to so much of the command as belongs to the 16th army corps, and conduct it to Memphis, where orders will await you. My present belief is, your division entire will be needed round with the army of the Tennessee about Huntsville or Bridgeport; still I will have orders with General Hurlbut at Memphis for you on your return.

I believe if water will enable the gunboats to cross the rapids at Alexandria, you will be able to make a quick, strong and effective blow at our enemy on the west, thus widening the belt of our territory and making the breach between the confederate government and its outlying trans-Mississippi department more perfect.

It is understood that General Steele makes a simultaneous move from Little Rock on Shreveport or Natchitoches with a force of about 10,000 men. Banks will have seventeen thousand (17,000) and you ten thousand (10,000.) If these can act concentrically and simultaneously, you will make short work of it, and then General Banks will have enough force to hold as much of the Red river as he deems wise, leaving you to bring to General Grant's main army the seven thousand five hundred (7,500) men of the 16th corps.

Having faith in your sound judgment and experience, I confide this important and delicate command to you, with certainty that you will harmonize perfectly with Admiral Porter and General Banks, with whom you are to act, and thereby insure success.

I am, with respect, your obedient servant,

W. T. SHERMAN,
Major General, Commanding.

Brigadier General A. J. SMITH,
Commanding Expedition up Red river, Vicksburg, Miss.

HEADQUARTERS DEPARTMENT OF THE TENNESSEE,
Vicksburg, March 6, 1864.

SIR: By my order of to-day it is provided that your present command be moved by water to Cairo, thence up the Tennessee river to some convenient point, and thence by land to join General Dodge's command, near Athens, Tennessee.

To enable you to fulfil these orders you can take passage by regiments and detachments in steamers bound up the Mississippi and disembark at Cairo. There the quartermaster will be instructed to charter a sufficient number of boats to carry your command at one trip up the Tennessee river, and in selecting boats he will be governed by the stage of water in the Tennessee.

If the stage of water be low you will disembark your command at Savannah and march for Pulaski, and report in advance by courier to General Dodge; but should there be a good stage of water, and should Colbert shoals be passable, you may proceed up to Florence and disembark there; but if there be the least doubt on this subject it will be better to land at Savannah, or Waterloo, opposite Eastport. Draw your supplies at Cairo, and so calculate the quantity that your wagons will be able to haul everything belonging to you from the point of disembarkation to Pulaski and Athens.

Report by telegraph and mail your progress to my headquarters at Huntsville, Alabama.

On arrival at your destination you will assume command of your entire division, subject to the command of General Dodge, till the corps headquarters are removed from Memphis to that army in the field.

Impress on your colonels and subordinate officers the importance of preserving good discipline, cleanliness and a soldierly appearance on board the boats at Cairo, or wherever the command may be.

Leave no men behind, but reduce your camp and garrison equipage to the smallest, as the weather is now moderate and winter is past.

I am, with respect, your obedient servant,

W. T. SHERMAN,
Major General, Commanding.

Brigadier General J. C. VEATCH,
Commanding 4th Division, 16th Army Corps.

HEADQUARTERS DEPARTMENT OF THE TENNESSEE,
Vicksburg, Mississippi, March 7, 1864.

DEAR ADMIRAL: I received last night the despatches, and was delighted at the result. Taking the guns at Trinity, the burning at Harrisonburg, and general driving away the force there, gives you the initiative, and if you only had water enough you could alone follow it up to Shreveport. But in a day or two I will have with you General A. J. Smith, with ten thousand good infantry, which can land and act in concert with you.

The lowness of water in the Mississippi and Red rivers is most extraordinary, and will embarrass us; but at all hazards, and at whatever cost, we should meet General Banks at Alexandria on the 17th instant. I will instruct my quartermaster to use small boats as far as possible, and suggest that you put some of your light iron-clads up as far as Alexandria *anyhow*, and wait there for a rise. General Banks will move so as to turn the position at De Russey, so that a mere display of force on its water front will, connected with the movement of our troops on land, lead to an evacuation of the fort, and, it may be, the surrender of its armament and garrison. At all events, I think we should not let General Banks arrive at Alexandria without finding our Red river party there. You have bounced them from the Washita, and, conjointly with my infantry, which will join you in a day or two, can also open up the Red river as far as Alexandria. Beyond that point, I agree with you, and authorize you to use my name with General Banks, that a further move ought not to be attempted above Alexandria, unless the Red river admits the navigation by your first-class ironclads and large transports, viz: seven (7) feet water on the "rapids" of Alexandria.

I must hurry around to my command in the field at Huntsville, but send A. J. Smith to co-operate with you in Red river and leave General McPherson here on the Mississippi. With these I know you will take pleasure in conferring and co-operating harmoniously.

I am, with great respect,

W. T. SHERMAN,
Major General, Commanding Department.

Admiral D. D. Porter,
Commanding Mississippi Squadron, Red River.

Headquarters Department of the Tennessee,
Vicksburg, Mississippi, March 7, 1864.

General: I think it important I should hasten somewhat to my command at Huntsville, Alabama; I am therefore compelled again to leave you to the exercise of this most important command, but assure you I do so with absolute confidence. You may rely on my cordial support at all times.

You know the plans and purposes of your superiors for some months to come, but, to be more certain, I will repeat their leading points. The river Mississippi must be held sacred, and any attempt of the enemy to make a lodgement anywhere on its banks must be prevented by any and all means. Also its peaceful navigation must be assured; any firing on boats or molestation of them when engaged in a legitimate and licensed traffic should be punished with terrible severity. I believe that our expedition, in which we destroyed absolutely the Southern railroad and the Mobile and Ohio, at and around Meridian, will prevent the enemy approaching the river with any infantry or heavy artillery, but he will, of course, reoccupy Mississippi with his marauding cavalry, that can in no wise influence the course of the grand war. I would heed this cavalry but little; still it may unite and threaten Memphis, in which event I want you to act promptly, by embarking as heavy a force as you can spare to ascend the Yazoo as far as Greenwood or Sidon, and strike at Grenada. This would take Forrest in the rear, and compel him to fall back on Pontotoc. I cannot believe cavalry will ever trouble you at or near Vicksburg, but may attempt to reach the river at some point above or below. An expedition up the Yazoo is the remedy for the river above; and if we could garrison Harrisonburg and operate up Washita and Tensas, it would have a similar effect on that side; but this is not in our command, and we have not the force to spare.

Encourage by all means the packet and through trade on the river as auxiliary to its defence, and also encourage trade with the interior not contraband of war. Such trade will keep the people dependent on the luxuries and conveniences of life, and to that extent shake their love for the impoverished rebel concern. Let the treasury agents manage this trade, and keep your officers aloof from all interest in it. I think the attempt to cultivate plantations premature, and all the protection we can promise is to buy their corn, facilitate their supplies, and give incidental protection; we cannot try to guard their estates.

The Red river expedition is designed to last but thirty days. Manage your veterans as to furlough so that this detachment of yours may return before all the veterans are spared.   Nearly the whole of General Hurlbut's corps will be needed over on the Tennessee river, so that, in fact, your corps will have to look to the whole river.

The gunboats and General Ellett's fleet can do all ordinary patrolling, and you will only be called on when the enemy attempts some more extended operation than he has hitherto done.   Make the regular reports to my headquarters, and when you have no special instructions, act with the full confidence of a separate commander.   I know you want to be in the field, and I will accomplish it if possible, but this command is of vital importance to our cause.

I am, &c.,

W. T. SHERMAN,
Major General Commanding.

Major General McPHERSON,
Commanding District of Vicksburg.

HEADQUARTERS DEPARTMENT OF THE TENNESSEE,
En route for Memphis, March 8, 1864.

GENERAL: I had the honor to receive, at the hands of General Butterfield, General Grant's letter of February 18.   I had returned from Meridian by the time I had appointed; but the condition of facts concerning the Red river expedition being indefinite, I took one of the marine boats, the Diana, and went down to New Orleans to confer with General Banks.   En route I saw the admiral, and learned he was ready, and a large and effective gunboat fleet would be at the mouth of Red river for action March 5.   At New Orleans I received the general's (Grant's) letter, with enclosures, and was governed by it in my interview with General Banks.

General Banks is to command in person, taking with him seventeen thousand (17,000) of his chosen troops, to move by land from the end of the Opelousas railroad, *via* Franklin, Opelousas, and Alexandria; Steele is to move from Little Rock on Natchitoches; and he (Banks) asked of me ten thousand (10,000) men in boats to ascend Red river, meeting him at Alexandria the 17th of March.   I enclose copies of General Banks's letter to me, and my answer, which are clear and specific.

I have made up a command of ten thousand (10,000) men—seven thousand five hundred (7,500) of Hurlbut and two thousand five hundred (2,500) of McPherson.   General A. J. Smith goes in command of the whole, and will be at the mouth of Red river by the 10th, and at Alexandria on the 17th.   These ten thousand (10,000) men are not to be gone over thirty (30) days, at the expiration of which time General McPherson's quota will return to Vicksburg, and General Hurlbut's come to Memphis, whence, if all things remain as now, I can bring them rapidly around to Savannah, Tennessee, and so on to my right flank, near Huntsville.   I think this will result as soon as the furloughed men get back.

Inasmuch as General Banks goes in person, I could not with delicacy propose that I should command; and the scene of operations lying wholly in his department, I deem it wisest to send General A. J. Smith, and to return to Huntsville in time to put my army in the field in shape for the coming spring campaign.

I have ordered five regiments, under General Veatch, to join General Dodge at once, and I feel sure I can safely draw General A. J. Smith's division, of full five thousand men, to the same point in April.

General McPherson and General Hurlbut are both instructed to furlough their veterans at once, and many regiments are already off.   I have inspected Natchez and Vicksburg, and feel sure they can now be held safe with comparatively small garrisons, and the river is patrolled by gunboats and the marine brigade.

I will inspect Memphis, and in a few days will hasten to Huntsville to put myself in command of my troops in that quarter, and will be ready for work at once, as I am in no manner fatigued. Indeed, the men I took with me to Meridian are better fitted for war now than before we started.

I send by General Butterfield my official report, with copies of orders, letters, &c., giving you full information of all matters up to date.

I am, with much respect, your obedient servant,

W. T. SHERMAN,
Major General Commanding.

Brig. Gen. JOHN A. RAWLINS,
Chief of Staff of General Grant, Nashville, Tennessee.

HEADQUARTERS MILITARY DIVISION OF THE MISSISSIPPI,
Nashville, February 18, 1865.

Enclosed I send you copy of despatches between General Halleck and myself relative to a movement up Red river on your return from your present expedition. Whilst I look upon such an expedition as is proposed as of the greatest importance, I regret that any force has to be taken from east of the Mississippi for it. Your troops will want rest for the purpose of preparing for a spring campaign, and all the veterans should be got off on furlough at the very earliest moment. This latter I would direct, even if you have to spare troops to go up Red river.

Unless you go in command of the proposed expedition, I fear any troops you may send with it will be entirely lost from further service in this command. This, however, is not the reason for my suggestion that you be sent. Your acquaintance with the country, and otherwise fitness, were the reasons.

I can give no positive orders that you send no troops up Red river, but what I do want is their speedy return if they do go, and that the minimum number necessary be sent. I have never heard a word from Steele since his department has been placed in the military division. Do not know what he proposes nor the means he has for executing. The time necessary for communicating between here and Vicksburg being so great, you will have to act in this matter according to your own judgment, simply knowing my views.

I send this by special messenger, who will await your return to Vicksburg, and who will bear any letters you may have for me.

U. S. GRANT, *Major General.*

Major General W. T. SHERMAN,
Commanding Expedition against Meridian.

HEADQUARTERS DEPARTMENT OF THE TENNESSEE,
Steamer Diana, (under way,) March 4, 1864.

GENERAL: I had the honor to receive your letter of the 2d instant yesterday at New Orleans, but was unable to answer except verbally, and I now reduce it to writing.

I will arrive at Vicksburg the 6th instant, and I expect to meet there my command from Canton, out of which I will select two divisions of about ten thousand (10,000) men, embark them under a good commander, and order him—

1. To rendezvous at the mouth of Red river, and, in concert with Admiral Porter, (if he agree,) to strike Harrisonburg a *hard* blow.

2. To return to Red river and ascend it, aiming to reach Alexandria on the 17th of March to report to you.

3. That this command, designed to operate by water, will not be encumbered with much land transportation—say two wagons to a regiment, but with an ample supply of stores, including mortars and heavy rifled guns to be used against fortified places.

4. That I calculate, and so have reported to General Grant, that this detachment of his forces is in no event to go beyond Shreveport, and that you spare them the moment you can, trying to get them back to the Mississippi in thirty days from the time they actually enter Red river.

The year is wearing away fast, and I would like to carry to General Grant at Huntsville, Alabama, every man of his military division as early in April as possible, as I am sure we ought to move from the base of the Tennessee river to the south before the season is too far advanced—say April 15 next.

I feel certain of your complete success, provided you make the concentration in time, to assure which I will see in person to the embarcation and despatch of my quota, and I will write to General Steele conveying to him my personal and professional opinion that the present opportunity is the most perfect one that will ever offer itself to him to clean out his enemies.

Wishing you all honor and success, I am, with respect, your friend and servant,

W. T. SHERMAN,
Major General.

Major General N. P. BANKS,
 Commanding Department of the Gulf, New Orleans.

HEADQUARTERS DEPARTMENT OF THE TENNESSEE,
Vicksburg, March 6, 1864.

GENERAL: I am just arrived. My troops are all in, and I shall embark ten thousand (10,000) men for Red river to-morrow and next day.

General Banks will surely march from Franklin on Opelousas, reaching Alexandria by the 17th instant. My force will meet him there at that date. He expects you to co-operate from Little Rock, and you certainly will never again have so good a chance to clear your front as now. Besides, your forces are deemed an essential part of the programme. Mine ought to hasten round to General Grant at once, and I only can spare them for thirty (30) days. I saw Captain Dunham on his way down, and read your letter to him, and must confess I feel uneasy at your assertion that you can only move with seven thousand (7,000) infantry, and that you prefer to wait until after the election of the 14th. If we have to modify military plans for civil elections we had better go home.

I repeat that General Banks will surely move on Shreveport via Alexandria, reaching that point March 17, expecting you to co-operate from the north in time.

Admiral Porter has now a magnificent fleet up Red river, and his guns were at work on Harrisonburg as I passed up the river. He too will meet General Banks at Alexandria, March 17. Colonel Woodroe comes to you with despatches, and I send by him my former letter and this.

Nearly all our command is of re-enlisted veterans, but they cheerfully defer their furloughs to enable us to make these blows, and I feel assured yours would also.

I am, with respect, your obedient servant,

W. T. SHERMAN,
Major General Commanding.

Major General FREDERICK STEELE,
 Commanding Department of Arkansas.

On the 10th of March I reached Memphis. En route I met Captain Badeau, of General Grant's staff, and the following letters passed:

HEADQUARTERS DEPARTMENT OF THE TENNESSEE,
ON BOARD STEAMER WESTMORELAND,
Near Memphis, March 10, 1864.

GENERAL: Captain Badeau found me yesterday on board this boat and delivered his despatches.

I had anticipated your orders by ordering General Veatch's division of General Hurlburt's corps at once to General Dodge, via the Tennessee river, and had sent General A. J. Smith up Red river, with ten thousand (10,000) men, to be absent not over thirty (30) days, when I designed General Smith's division of about six thousand (6,000) men also to come round.

We must furlough near ten thousand (10,000) men, and by the time they come back the Red river trip will be made, and I can safely re-enforce my army, near Huntsville, with fifteen thousand (15,000) veterans.

I send by General Butterfield full details of all past events and distributions, which I hope will meet your approval.

As to the negroes, of course, on my arrival at Memphis, I will cause your orders to be literally executed. A clamor was raised by lessees by my withdrawal of Osband's four hundred (400) men from Skipwith's and General Hawkins's brigades, and two thousand one hundred (2,100) men from Goodrich's. I transferred them to Haines's Bluff, to operate up the Yazoo, and the effect was instantaneous. Not a shot has been fired on the river boats since. I also designed to put a similar force at Harrisonburg, Louisiana, to operate up the Washita, which would secure the west bank from Red river to the Arkansas line.

Admiral Porter has already driven the enemy from Harrisonburg, so that project is immediately feasible. I assert that three thousand (3,000) men at Haines's Bluff, and three thousand (3,000) at Harrisonburg, would more effectually protect the plantation lessees than fifty thousand (50,000) men scattered along the shores of the Mississippi. You know the geography so well that I need not demonstrate my assertion.

I understand General Lorenzo Thomas has passed down to Vicksburg, and am sorry I did not see him, but as soon as I reach Memphis to-day I will send orders below, and show him how much easier it will be to protect the Mississippi by means of the Yazoo and Washita rivers than by merely guarding the banks of the Mississippi.

After awaiting to observe the effect of recent changes I will hasten round to Huntsville to prepare for the big fight in Georgia. Fix the time for crossing the Tennessee, and I will be there.

Your friend,

W. T. SHERMAN,
Major General.

Major General U. S. GRANT,
Comd'g Division of the Mississippi, Nashville, Tenn.

HEADQUARTERS MILITARY DIVISION OF THE MISSISSIPPI,
Nashville, March 4, 1864.

You will be able better than I to judge how far the damage you have done the railroads about Meridian will disable the enemy from sending an army into Mississippi and West Tennessee, with which to operate on the river, also what force will now be required to protect and guard the river. Use the negroes, or negro troops more particularly, for guarding plantations, and for the defence of the west bank of the river. The artillerists among them, of course, you will put in fortifications, but most of the infantry give to Hawkins, to be used on the west bank. Add to this element of your forces what you deem an adequate force for the protection of the river, from Cairo down as far as your command goes, and extend the command of one army corps to the whole of it. Assemble the balance of your forces at or near Memphis, and have them in readiness to join your column on this front in their spring campaign. Whether it will be better to have them march, meeting supplies sent up the Tennessee to Eastport, or whether they should be brought round by steamers, can be determined hereafter. Add all the forces now under Dodge to the two corps or to one of the two corps you take into the field with you.

Forces will be transferred from the Chattanooga and Nashville road to guard all the roads now protected by your troops. If they are not sufficient, enough will be taken from elsewhere to leave all yours for the field.

I am ordered to Washington, but as I am directed to keep up telegraphic communication with this command, I shall expect, in the course of ten or twelve days, to return to it.

Place the marine brigade under the command of the corps commander left on the Mississippi river. Give directions that it be habitually used for the protection of leased plantations, and will not pass below Vicksburg, nor above Greenville, except by order of the corps commander or higher authority.

U. S. GRANT, Major General.

Major General W. T. SHERMAN,
   Commanding Department Tennessee.

[Private.]

NASHVILLE, TENNESSEE, March 4, 1864.

DEAR SHERMAN : The bill reviving the grade of lieutenant general in the army has become a law, and my name has been sent to the Senate for the place.

I now receive orders to report to Washington immediately, in person, which indicates either a confirmation or a likelihood of confirmation

I start in the morning to comply with the order, but I shall say very distinctly, on my arrival there, that I accept no appointment which will require me to make that city my headquarters. This, however, is not what I started out to write about.

Whilst I have been eminently successful in this war, in at least gaining the confidence of the public, no one feels more than me how much of this success is due to the energy, skill, and the harmonious putting forth of that energy and skill of those who it has been my good fortune to have occupy a subordinate position under me.

There are many officers to whom these remarks are applicable to a greater or less degree proportionate to their ability as soldiers, but what I want is to express my thanks to you and McPherson, as the men to whom, above all others, I feel indebted for whatever I have had of success. How far your advice and suggestions have been of assistance you know. How far your execution of whatever has been given you to do entitles you to the reward I am receiving you cannot know as well as me. I feel all the gratitude this letter would express, giving it the most flattering construction.

The word you I use in the plural, intending it for McPherson also; I should write to him, and will some day, but starting in the morning, I do not know that I will find time just now.

   Your friend,

U. S. GRANT, Major General.

[Private and confidential.]

NEAR MEMPHIS, *March* 10, 1864.

DEAR GENERAL: I have your more than kind and characteristic letter of the 4th. I will send a copy to General McPherson at once.

You do yourself injustice, and us too much honor, in assigning to us so large a share of the merits which have led to your high advancement. I know you approve the friendship I have ever professed to you, and will permit me to continue, as heretofore, to manifest it on all proper occasions.

You are now Washington's legitimate successor, and occupy a position of almost dangerous elevation; but if you can continue, as heretofore, to be yourself— simple, honest, and unpretending—you will enjoy through life the respect and love of friends, and the homage of millions of human beings, that will award you a large share in securing to them and their descendants a government of law and stability.

I repeat, you do General McPherson and myself too much honor. At Belmont you manifested your traits; neither of us being near. At Fort Donelson also you illustrated your whole character; I was not near, and General McPherson in too subordinate a capacity to influence you.

Until you had won Donelson, I confess I was almost cowed by the terrible array of anarchical elements that presented themselves at every point, but that admitted the ray of light which I have followed since.

I believe you are as brave, patriotic, and just as the great prototype, Washington; as unselfish, kind-hearted, and honest as a man should be; but your chief characteristic is the simple faith in success you have always manifested, which I can liken to nothing else than the faith a Christian has in a Saviour. This faith gave you victory at Shiloh and Vicksburg. Also, when you have completed your best preparations, you go into battle without hesitation, as at Chattanooga—no doubts, no reserves; and I tell you it was this that made us act with confidence. I knew, wherever I was, that you thought of me; and if I got in a tight place you would come if alive.

My only points of doubt were in your knowledge of grand strategy and of books of science and history; but I confess your common sense seems to have supplied all these.

Now as to the future. Don't stay in Washington. Halleck is better qualified than you to stand the buffets of intrigue and policy. Come west; take to yourself the whole Mississippi valley. Let us make it dead sure, and I tell you the Atlantic slopes and Pacific shores will follow its destiny as sure as the limbs of a tree live or die with the main trunk. We have done much, but still much remains. Time and time's influences are with us. We could almost afford to sit still and let these influences work. Even in the seceded States your word now would go further than a president's proclamation or an act of Congress. For God's sake and your country's sake come out of Washington. I foretold to General Halleck before he left Corinth the inevitable result, and I now exhort you to come out west. Here lies the seat of the coming empire, and from the west, when our task is done, we will make short work of Charleston and Richmond, and the impoverished coast of the Atlantic.

Your sincere friend,

W. T. SHERMAN.

General GRANT.

HEADQUARTERS DEPARTMENT OF THE TENNESSEE,
Memphis, March 11, 1864.

GENERAL: I arrived here yesterday. En route I met Captain Badeau, of General Grant's staff, who bore me two letters, copies of which I enclose herewith.

I answered both fully by General Butterfield, who left in a swift packet last evening, and will find General Grant in Washington, or wherever he may be.

I think General Grant is making a mistake in taking all the negro troops and marine brigade to cover plantations; or, in other words, that the plan of distributing these troops along the west bank of the river will be less effective than the plan I had initiated of defending the Yazoo and Washita rivers, which would cover the plantations from the rear. But this will manifest itself in time.

Please order General Hawkins and his brigade of blacks to reoccupy the west bank of the Mississippi in such manner as he deems best to protect the plantations and replace his troops at the bluff, or leave it vacant, as you may judge best.

I suppose Adjutant General Thomas is with you; and if so, confer with him and let him have the blacks, *i. e.*, all such as are not in actual occupation of the forts at Vicksburg and Natchez.

When the marine brigade returns from Red river, it also should receive orders as indicated by General Grant. In the meanwhile such of the marine boats as have not gone up Red river can cover the plantations from Vicksburg up as high as Greenville. I enclose herewith a letter for General Thomas, which you can read and cause to be delivered.

I have reflected on the proposition you made me before leaving Vicksburg, and will adopt it substantially. After you have satisfied yourself that no force but Jackson's cavalry followed us back to this side of Pearl river, you may furlough all your veterans and dispose the remainder as garrisons for Vicksburg and Natchez. Place good commanders at each place, then in person come to Memphis and give minute returns of each to General Hurlbut, whom we will leave to command the district of the Mississippi, embracing that of Memphis and Vicksburg, then proceed to Cairo, where you can leave some of your staff to receive and organize your veteran regiments as they return, when you may take a twenty (20) days' leave, getting back to Cairo in time to make two divisions of about ten thousand (10,000) men, which I will order up the Tennessee, and across from Savannah to Pulaski and Huntsville. I will give you four No. 1 divisions, and if times out here justify it, I will draw further to embrace General A. J. Smith's division.

I will leave Hurlbut here until you come up, and if the garrisons left at Vicksburg and Natchez seem small, I will instruct General Hurlbut to stop General Tuttle's division at Vicksburg, and bring General A. J. Smith here when the Red river trip comes out. I send this by a bearer of despatches, who will bring me your answers. I await them here. Make the figures as exact as possible.

I think General Hurlbut will be required, as commander on the river, to make his headquarters at Vicksburg. I want your opinion on this. I dislike to break up corps, but can't help it.

Truly your friend,

W. T. SHERMAN,
Major General Commanding Department.

Major General J. B. McPHERSON,
Commanding Vicksburg.

HEADQUARTERS DEPARTMENT OF THE TENNESSEE,
Memphis, March 11, 1864.

DEAR GENERAL: I have a letter from General Grant of date March 4, a copy of which I send by bearer of despatches to General McPherson, and which is subject to your perusal. I have ordered General McPherson accordingly. I wanted to see you, and am sorry I missed you. I fear you think

I do not protect lessees of plantations. I know my action inland and the move up the Yazoo more effectually covered the east bank of the Mississippi river above Vicksburg than could have been done by ten thousand troops on its very banks.

I know also a similar disposition up the Washita would in like manner cover the west bank from Red river up to the Arkansas. I shall still advise the perfection of the plan. Osband's force at Skipwith's, and Hawkins's at Goodrich's, may have protected a radius each of say ten or fifteen miles, but no more; whereas by putting Hawkins's brigade at Haines's Bluff, with facilities for operating up Yazoo, and a similar brigade at Harrisonburg to manœuvre up Washita and Tensas, you can cover the river perfectly.

But I have ordered McPherson to put Hawkins's brigade west of the river to be disposed of according to your wishes, and he can add to Hawkins's command any other black troops not actually employed in the forts at Vicksburg and Natchez. He will also direct such of the marine brigade as are not up Red river to protect the river between Vicksburg and Greenville, to protect the planters and lessees, and when all the brigade of Ellet's is back, which will be in a month, they also will be devoted to the same end. As a speculation, this is a bad one. Every pound of cotton raised will cost the United States five hundred dollars, and so far as effect is concerned, it will not have one particle of effect on the main war.

As a matter of course I dislike to see such a mistake made at this period of the war, when we should at least have learned something by experience of our own. It would be far wiser to pension the lessees of the plantations.

In the end we must defend the Mississippi from the Yazoo and Washita, and if you agree with me, I will promise seven thousand (7,000) men on those rivers to cover and protect the plantations more perfectly than fifty thousand (50,000) could distributed along the banks of the Mississippi.

Since I sent up Yazoo not a shot has been fired from the east bank of the Mississippi; and now that Admiral Porter has taken Trinity and Harrisonburg, the same could be done west. Transfer the fighting to the Yazoo and Washita, and you have peace on the Mississippi; but leave them uncovered, and twenty guerillas will break up any plantation you establish. Nevertheless, I have instructed General McPherson to execute General Grant's orders, and when I meet General Grant I will explain to him what I was about.

I will await the return of this courier, and should like to hear from you. Then I must hasten to Huntsville to resume command of the army in the field. I will leave Hurlbut to command on the river with three (3) full divisions and the local garrisons of Memphis, Vicksburg and Natchez.

I am, &c.,

W. T. SHERMAN,
Major General.

Brigadier General LORENZO THOMAS,
Adjutant General U. S. A., Vicksburg, Mississippi.

HEADQUARTERS DEPARTMENT OF THE TENNESSEE,
Memphis, March 11, 1864.

SIR: I venture to address you on a point in which you may be disposed to differ from me.

Before marching from Vicksburg for Meridian, I detailed an expedition up the Yazoo to take advantage of the opportunity to inflict on that country a punishment merited for the connivance of its inhabitants in the attacks on the steamboats navigating the Mississippi river.

I ordered the commanding officer to bring to Vicksburg one thousand (1,000)

2*

bales of cotton, to be deposited with your special agent at Vicksburg, coupled with the request that its proceeds should be applied to indemnify owners of steamboats in whole or part damaged by the public enemy.

I had no power over such agent, and I also knew that he had no right to make such a distribution, and only used the language to assure steamboat owners of my earnest desire to remunerate them, so far as it lies in my power, for damages sustained when in pursuit of a lawful commerce, and one which aids us materially in the exercise of the war power. The one thousand bales of cotton have been taken and are now in the hands of your special agents at Vicksburg, and I ask you to appropriate the proceeds of its sale to the purposes I have indicated. I know that such prompt indemnification will do good, more good than to throw the parties on Congress by way of petition for relief.

I contend that as a military commander I have a right by the laws of war, in no wise qualified by acts of Congress, to make similar acts of restitution in kind, but not in money. Thus, if a good, worthy Union man is robbed of his horse or his cotton because he is our friend, I contend I have a perfect right to take another horse or equivalent quantity of cotton from a confederate or accomplice of the robber or enemy and make immediate restitution. I have done so, and will continue to do so, for *that* is war.

Again, although the orders are that, when practicable, we shall aid the treasury agents to collect abandoned or enemy's property, when I find it resorted to to influence military movements, or to corrupt wagon-masters, steamboat agents, and even officers, I must check it, for the reason that war is the main object of our army, and anything that tends to corrupt it does more public harm than is compensated by the thing obtained. I make these general points because I know some of your agents regard me as hostile to their office. It is not so. My orders are clear and specific that officers and soldiers must leave all matters of trade to your agents. I don't want them to exercise a supervising or concurrent action. I want the army to be far above the contaminating influences of trade and gain. Let the merchant count his gain, but the soldier is lost if he dreams of a cent beyond his pay.

We are getting along well and fast enough in this quarter. Peace and prosperity exist wherever our foothold is secure, and each point is becoming the centre of an extending circle. I am willing to use commerce as a means to war, to corrupt and demoralize an enemy, to make him dependent on us, and to loosen his affection for the impoverished section to which he clings with a love which we should emulate. But our army must keep hands off. No fees, no gain, no association with contaminating trade, till war is over and peace supreme.

With great respect,

W. T. SHERMAN,
Major General.

Hon. S. P. Chase,
Secretary United States Treasury, Washington.

Headquarters Department of the Tennessee,
Memphis, March 14, 1864.

Dear General: I wrote you at length on the 11th by a special bearer of despatches, and now make special orders to cover the movements therein indicated. It was my purpose to await here your answer, but I am summoned by General Grant to be in Nashville on the 17th, and it will keep me moving night and day. I must rely on you. You understand that we must re-enforce the great army at the centre as much as possible, at the same time not risk any point on the Mississippi fortified and armed with heavy guns. I want you to push matters as rapidly as possible, and do all you can to put two handsome divisions of your own corps at Cairo, ready to embark up the Tennessee by the 20th or 30th of April at the very furthest. I wish it could be done quicker, but these thirty-days furloughs in the States of enlistment, though politic, are very unmilitary. It deprives us of our ability to calculate as to time. But do the best you can. Hurlbut can do nothing until Smith returns from Red river and matters settle down, when I will order him to occupy Grenada temporarily, to try to get those locomotives that we need here. I may also order him with cavalry and infantry towards Tuscaloosa at the time we move from the Tennessee.

I don't know as yet the grand strategy, but on arrival at Nashville I will soon catch the points and advise you. Steal a furlough and run to Baltimore *incog.*, but get back and take part in the next move.

Write me fully and frequently of your progress. I have ordered the quartermaster to send as many boats as he can get to facilitate your movements. Mules, wagons, &c., can come up by transient boats.

I am truly your friend,

W. T. SHERMAN,
Major General Commanding.

Major General McPHERSON,
Commanding, &c., Vicksburg, Mississippi.

HEADQUARTERS DEPARTMENT OF THE TENNESSEE,
Memphis, Tenn., March 14, 1864.

GENERAL: I am somewhat suddenly called by General Grant to Nashville. I must leave at once; and after full reflection on the state of affairs in the department since our Meridian trip, I am sure we can safely spare fifteen thousand (15,000) men from the river to re-enforce the army in the field, headquarters at Huntsville. I have, therefore, ordered General McPherson to assemble two divisions of his corps at Cairo, Illinois, ready for embarcation up the Tennessee, to join me at Huntsville; and, as you know, the fragment of Veatch's division is also in motion for the same destination. I leave you to command on the river, and, without disturbing the corps organizations, I give you command of all my troops on the river. You can make your headquarters anywhere you choose on the river, from Memphis to Natchez; but it may be Memphis, for the present, is best, on account of its proximity to Cairo, through which point all communications must pass.

I know, and you know, that the enemy cannot now maintain an army in Mississippi, and we also believe that the movement up Red river, now in progress, will extend our empire to the west.

I want you to make sure the defence of Memphis, Vicksburg, and Natchez against any possible contingency; to encourage and protect the navigation of the river; and lastly, to encourage the change in feeling towards us and our government by the citizens of West Tennessee and Mississippi. I do not mean by political combination and conciliation, but by the exercise of that power, strength, and confidence that indicates a permanent change in the affairs in this region.

Truly yours,

W. T. SHERMAN,
Major General Commanding.

Major General HURLBUT, *Memphis.*

I reached Nashville March 17, and found General Grant there busy in closing up his business preparatory to going to Washington. I accompanied him as far as Cincinnati, on the 19th, in order to confer with him fully on many points he had not had time to write of. We parted at Cincinnati on the 22d, he for Washington and I for Nashville, where, on the 25th, I began a rapid inspection of our lines, beginning with Decatur, Alabama, and extending up to Knoxville, Tennessee. General McPherson had reached Huntsville, and had assumed command of the army of the Tennessee—right wing. Major General George H. Thomas was at Chattanooga, in command of the army of the Cumberland—centre; and General J. M. Schofield was at Knoxville, in command of the army of the Ohio—left wing. Returned to Nashville April 2, and the following letters passed:

[Original by mail; copy by telegraph, in cipher.]

HEADQUARTERS MILITARY DIVISION OF THE MISSISSIPPI,
Nashville, Tenn., April 2, 1864.

Lieutenant General U. S. GRANT, *Washington, D. C.:*

After a full consultation with all my army commanders, I have settled down to the following conclusions, to which I would like to have the President's consent before I make orders:

1st. Army of the Ohio, three divisions of infantry, to be styled the 23d corps, Major General Schofield in command, and one division of cavalry, Major General Stoneman, to push Longstreet's forces well out of the valley; then fall back, breaking railroad, to Knoxville; to hold Knoxville and Loudon, and be ready by May 1, with twelve thousand (12,000) men, to act as the left of the grand army.

2d. General Thomas to organize his army into three corps; the 11th and 12th to be united under General Hooker, to be composed of four divisions. The corps to take a new title, viz: one of the series now vacant. General Slocum to be transferred east, or assigned to some local command on the Mississippi. The 4th corps, Granger, to remain unchanged, save to place General Howard in command. The 14th corps to remain the same. Thomas to guard the lines of communication, and have, by May 1, a command of 45,000 men for active service, to constitute the centre.

3d. General McPherson to draw from the Mississippi the divisions of Crocker and Leggett, now *en route*, mostly of veterans on furlough, and of A. J. Smith, now up Red river, but due on the 10th instant out of that expedition, and to organize a force of thirty thousand (30,000) men to operate from Larkinsville or Guntersville as the right of the grand army; his corps to be commanded by Logan, Frank Blair, and Dodge.

I propose to put Newton, when he comes, at Vicksburg.

With these changes, this army will be a unit in all respects, and I can suggest no better.

I ask the President's consent, and ask what title I shall give the new corps of Hooker, in place of the 11th and 12th corps, consolidated. The lowest number of the army corps now vacant will be most appropriate.

I will have the cavalry of the department of the Ohio reorganize under Stoneman, at or near Camp Nelson, and the cavalry of Thomas, at least one good division, under Garrard, at Columbia.

W. T. SHERMAN,
Major General.

––––––––––

[Cipher telegram.]

HEADQUARTERS MILITARY DIVISION OF THE MISSISSIPPI,
Nashville, April 2, 1864.

Major General SCHOFIELD, *Knoxville:*

Am back at Nashville. Telegraph me daily any matters of interest. I have asked the President the necessary authority to announce you as the commander of the 23d corps. As soon as you can spare Stoneman, order him to go to Kentucky and assemble all the cavalry, mounted and dismounted, of your department at or near Lexington, and to put it in fine order, drawing supplies from Cincinnati and the country. Hovey marches to-morrow, and will report to you his progress. As soon as you can spare Thomas's troops, let them go below the Hiwassee, and keep yours above.

W. T. SHERMAN,
Major General.

[Cipher telegram.]

HEADQUARTERS MILITARY DIVISION OF THE MISSISSIPPI,
Nashville, April 2, 1864.

Major General THOMAS, *Chattanooga :*

Am at Nashville. Have telegraphed to Washington for authority to make the changes we agreed on. To-night the railroad superintendent, (Anderson,) Colonel Donaldson, and I, will meet and arrange about the railroad management. I will also compel the beef contractor to drive cattle. Unless we devote the railroad solely and exclusively to the use of dead freight, we cannot accumulate the surplus required for our plans. Watch Joe Johnston close. Your weak point is Cleveland. As soon as Schofield can ascertain, certain, that Longstreet is no longer in force in East Tennessee, he will let your troops come below the Hiwassee. I will make the order the moment I hear from Washington.

W. T. SHERMAN,
Major General.

[Cipher telegram.]

HEADQUARTERS MILITARY DIVISION OF THE MISSISSIPPI,
Nashville, Tenn., April 2, 1864.

General McPHERSON, *Huntsville :*

Am back to Nashville. Telegraph me daily anything of interest. I will give my personal attention to the question of accumulation of supplies. Have you made up your mind which is your best point—Huntsville or Decatur? I want to send Corse down the Mississippi to give life to Hurlbut's movements against Forrest. I want the regulars here as headquarters guard. I will assign Newton to you, with a view to his assignment to Vicksburg. I would not give orders about Forrest, who is in your department, only the matter involves Kentucky also. As soon as he is disposed of, I will leave all matters in your department to you. Veatch is posted near Purdy to cut off escape by the head of Hatchee. Hurlbut, with infantry and cavalry, will move towards Bolivar with a view to catch Forrest in flank as he attempts escape. Brayman will stop a few veteran regiments returning, and will use them out as far as Union City. If you will control the movements I will desist.

W. T. SHERMAN,
Major General.

HEADQUARTERS MILITARY DIVISION OF THE MISSISSIPPI,
Nashville, April 2, 1864.

ADJUTANT GENERAL, *Washington, D. C.:*

Inform the commander-in-chief that Schofield's infantry occupies Bull's Gap, and his cavalry is scouting beyond. The enemy is all beyond Jonesboro' and probably beyond the Wautauga, having burnt both railroad and other road bridges, and carried off telegraph wire, but otherwise have not destroyed the railroad. I will not advance the infantry beyond Bull's Gap, as our line is now pretty long and weak.

General Schofield thinks Longstreet is gone to Virginia, leaving about three thousand five hundred cavalry to protect the salt works.

W. T. SHERMAN,
Major General Commanding.

HEADQUARTERS MILITARY DIVISION OF THE MISSISSIPPI,
Nashville, April 3, 1864.

Colonel S. G. HICKS, *Paducah :*

Your defence of Paducah was exactly right. Keep cool and give the enemy a second edition if he comes again. I want Forrest to stay just where he is, and the longer the better. Don't credit any of the foolish and exaggerated reports that are put afloat by design. I know what Forrest has, and will attend to him in time. Whenever you get a chance, strike any small detachments.

W. T. SHERMAN,
Major General.

[General Memoranda.]

HEADQUARTERS MILITARY DIVISION OF THE MISSISSIPPI,
Nashville, April 3, 1864.

1. The posts of Columbus, Cairo, and Paducah to be held in force, and mere excursions sent out to occupy the attention of Forrest.

2. General Veatch to occupy a point near Purdy and to strike Forrest in flank as he attempts to pass out.

3. General Hurlbut to operate from Memphis with his infantry and cavalry, guarding the passes of Big Hatchie and communicating with General Veatch.

4. General A. J. Smith to return from Red river, pause at Vicksburg to replenish supplies, and to push up Yazoo to Greenwood and Sidon, disembark, march rapidly on Grenada, and operate in Forrest's rear.

If Forrest is escaped, broken up or captured, all the troops to resume the *statu quo*, and General Smith to conduct his force by steady marches across to the Tombigbee and up to Decatur, Alabama, whence General Dodge will move out to meet him. General Smith to send word round by Cairo, giving his route of march and indicating the probable time of his arrival. This column to move light as to wagons and artillery, depending for forage, corn, meal and meat on the country, reckoning for supplies only at Vicksburg and Decatur; General Smith taking with him the two tried generals, Corse and Mower. If General Smith calls for cavalry, General Hurlbut will send as much as he can spare from Memphis, to meet him at some point of the Tallahatchie, and General Smith may call on the commanding general at Vicksburg for enough cavalry to serve as advance guard.

5. General Corse may order in my name any subordinate details to carry out these plans and the instructions of the commanding general.

Copies of this to be sent to Generals McPherson, Veatch, Brayman, Hurlbut and McArthur, and to the commanding officers at Paducah and Columbus, with express orders of secrecy.

W. T. SHERMAN,
Major General Commanding.

[Cipher telegram.]

HEADQUARTERS MILITARY DIVISION OF THE MISSISSIPPI,
Nashville, April 4, 1864.

Major General McPHERSON, *Huntsville:*

I will order the balance of Garrard's division of cavalry to rendezvous at Columbia. I wish you would keep scouts and mounted detachments well out to the Tennessee river, towards the mouth of Duck river. I don't care if Forrest does cross to this side, only we should have timely notice. I have sent down General Corse to communicate with Paducah, Cairo, Memphis and Vicksburg, and then to go on to Red river and bring A. J. Smith's command, by a route that will be indicated to you by a confidential messenger. This will divert from Vicksburg a part of your command which you may have designed to form a part of McArthur's command. If this be so, please arrange McArthur's division, so that the men now up Red river will belong to Crocker and Leggett. One division of the 16th and one of the 17th corps, with the black troops, must suffice to protect Memphis and Vicksburg, and the gunboats must keep the river clear. Forrest is supposed to be at Jackson, Tennessee, but I think he will try to get south as soon as possible.

W. T. SHERMAN,
Major General Commanding.

———

HEADQUARTERS MILITARY DIVISION OF THE MISSISSIPPI,
Nashville, Tennessee, April 4, 1864.

General BURBRIDGE, *Louisville:*

I do not believe the enemy will move far into Kentucky, through Pound Gap, unless as a cavalry raid. You should concentrate all your troops at Lexington, with cavalry well out to give notice. Grant designs a move in southwest Virginia which will check any such move, and by way of East Tennessee we can get to the rear of Pound Gap. Longstreet is reported as going back to Virginia, and would naturally send a small force through the gap to cover the movement. Forrest is now reported at Jackson, Tennessee. I have an infantry force at Purdy, and if Hurlbut acts with energy, Forrest will have trouble in getting out. You may send that Ohio regiment of cavalry to re-enforce General Sturgis. As soon as certain things are done in East Tennessee, General Stoneman will come to Kentucky. In the mean time you must collect all your detachments at some point near Lexington. In case of any formidable invasion of east Kentucky, we can call down from Ohio, Indiana, and Illinois a large force of furloughed veterans, who could reach the threatened points sooner than troops could come from the front, where they are needed.

W. T. SHERMAN,
Major General Commanding.

———

HEADQUARTERS MILITARY DIVISION OF THE MISSISSIPPI,
Nashville, Tennessee, April 4, 1865.

GENERAL: Since my return to Nashville I have made the complete circuit, going with McPherson to Decatur, Larkin's Ferry, Chattanooga, and Knoxville This enabled me to see all my corps and division commanders, and to learn the actual state of affairs. I have made few or no changes, but have suggested some by telegraph, a copy of which I enclose, as it is yet unanswered. I am sending all of Hovey's infantry to Schofield, to enable him to return to Thomas

Granger's troops that are properly his. I am assembling Garrard's division of cavalry on the right flank near Columbia, and will give Stoneman all the cavalry of Schofield's department, to organize in Kentucky, say near Lexington to move to the front when there is grass, and when I have forage enough at the front. At present the railroads supply bountifully the troops there, but make no surplus. I am making troops march, cattle do the same, and am cutting down sutlers, and private business, so as to gain cars for surplus stores and forage. I am endeavoring to persuade the railroad superintendent to run the cars in a circuit, so as to work as an endless chain, but the habit of running by a time-table is so strong that I find him disinclined. If I could see McCallum I could convince him that his present stock could do double the present work by making the round circuit by Stevenson and Decatur, all the cars running one way loaded, and bringing in the empty cars. I want to have on the line of the Tennessee by May 1 enough stores to enable me to move on, if General Grant so orders it.

To do this I calculate that Schofield should have twelve thousand (12,000) men; Thomas, forty-five thousand (45,000;) and McPherson, thirty thousand (30,000,) besides the railroad guards and depot garrisons. I propose that Schofield should be prepared to move from Cleveland, Thomas from Chattanooga, and McPherson from Gunter's Landing, on the Rome road; all my plans are subordinate to these general ideas.

Forrest got a severe rebuff by Hicks at Paducah, and still lingers somewhere between the Tennessee and Mississippi, and above the Hatchee. I want to keep him there awhile, when I hope to give him a complete thrashing. I order Paducah, Cairo, and Columbus to be held secure; have placed Veatch, with five regiments of infantry, at Purdy, and ordered Hurlbut, with all of Grierson's cavalry, and two thousand four hundred (2,400) infantry, to watch the line of the Hatchee, and to catch Forrest in flank as he attempts to pass out.

Last night I sent General Corse down the river in a steamboat, to touch at Paducah, Cairo, and Columbus, with orders and verbal explanations to all these commanders. He is then to push on to Memphis, explain the same to Hurlbut, and then hurry up the Red river to General A. J. Smith, and bring him with all despatch to Vicksburg, and up the Yazoo, and rapidly occupy Grenada. His appearance there with ten thousand (10,000) men, now hardened by our march to Meridian, and recent marching up the Red river, will be a big bombshell in Forrest's camp, should he, as I fear he will, elude Hurlbut. At Grenada Smith will do all the mischief he can, and then strike boldly across the country by Aberdeen, to Russelville and Decatur, there making his junction with McPherson. This with Crocker and Leggett's divisions, to rendezvous at Cairo after their furloughs, will make a large decrease of our Mississippi river forces, but I order McPherson to keep one white division at Vicksburg, and another at Memphis, which, with the black troops, the marine brigade, and the gunboats, should suffice to protect the river commerce; especially since we have so ruined Meridian that the enemy cannot supply an army near the river with either ammunition or provisions.

It is all nonsense about their repairing the break at Meridian. It is a simple impossibility. I would like to have General Grant's opinion as to this move of Smith's across from Grenada. I deem it safe, and its effects will in a measure compensate for the ill effects of Forrest's recent raid. With ten thousand (10,000) men, and two such dashing officers as Corse and Mower, A. J. Smith can whip all the cavalry and infantry (if any) in north Mississippi.

General Banks positively agreed with me that our troops should form a junction at Alexandria on the 17th of March. Mine were there on time, capturing Fort De Russey en route, and since it is reported they are up at Natchitoches, which is all right; but it seems Banks did not leave New Orleans till March 22. This is not right. This failure in time in conjoint operations is wrong, because it endangers the troops that punctually obey orders. I suppose that Steele is moving on Shreveport with seven thousand (7,000,) and Banks with seventeen thousand (17,000.) These are enough to co-operate with the gunboats, and therefore I rightfully claim my ten thousand (10,000) with General A. J. Smith at the time agreed on, viz: thirty days after the time they entered Red river, which expires April 10, at which time General Corse should find them at Alexandria, and conduct them to their new field of operations. I will move heaven and earth to have my command ready for war as early in May as the furloughed men return, and this you can better expedite from Washington than I can from here. I will not bother the general at all, but will keep him well advised of all real movements. He must not be disturbed by the foolish rumors that will get into the newspapers, spite of all precautions.

Write me answers to my inquiries as early as possible, even if they have been answered by telegraph.

I have the honor to be, &c.,

W. T. SHERMAN,
Major General Commanding.

Brigadier General J. A. RAWLINS,
Chief of General Grant's Staff, Washington, D. C.

[Cipher telegram.]

HEADQUARTERS MILITARY DIVISION OF THE MISSISSIPPI,
Nashville, Tennessee, April 4, 1865.

General SCHOFIELD, *Knoxville:*

Your despatch received. I don't want your infantry to go beyond Lick creek. Our line is already too much drawn out, but with cavalry you can demonstrate as far as you please. If you can force the enemy to destroy Wautauga bridge, it will be a good thing. Don't destroy the railroad till I give you notice. I will arrange to give you plenty of time. Let Thomas have his troops as soon as you can safely do so, as I regard Cleveland as our weak point.

Hovey is marching to you with five thousand (5,000) infantry, and I will put five (5) new regiments of cavalry at Lexington for Stoneman as soon as possible.

W. T. SHERMAN,
Major General.

[Confidential.]

HEADQUARTERS MILITARY DIVISION OF THE MISSISSIPPI,
Nashville, Tennessee, April 5, 1865.

DEAR COLONEL: Your letter of March 26 came to me on the 2d instant, and the mail brought me the map yesterday. The parcel had evidently been opened, and the postmaster had marked some additional postage on it. I will cause inquiries to be made lest the map has been seen by some eye intelligent enough to read the meaning of the blue and red lines. We cannot be too careful in these matters.

That map, to me, contains more information and ideas than a volume of printed matter. Keep your retained copies with infinite care, and if you have occasion to send out to other commanders any more, I would advise a special courier. From that map I see *all*, and glad am I that there are minds now at Washington able to devise; and for my part, if we can keep our counsels, I believe I have the men and ability to march square up to the position assigned me, and to hold it. Of course, it will cost us many a hard day, but I believe in fighting in a double sense—first to gain physical results, and next to inspire respect on which to build up our nation's power.

Of course General Grant will not have time to give me the details of movement east, and the *times*. Concurrent action is the thing. It would be wise if the general, through you or some educated officer, should give me timely notice of all contemplated movements, with all details that can be foreseen. I now know the results aimed at; I know my base, and have a pretty good idea of my lines of operation. No time shall be lost in putting my forces in mobile condition, so that all I ask is notice of time, that all over the grand theatre of war there shall be simultaneous action. We saw the beauty of time in the battle of Chattanooga, and there is no reason why the same harmony of action should not pervade a continent.

I am well pleased with Captain Poe, and would not object to have half a dozen thoroughly educated young engineer officers.

I am, with respect, your friend,

W. T. SHERMAN,
Major General Commanding.

Colonel C. B. COMSTOCK,
General Grant's Staff, Washington, D. C.

[Private and confidential.]

HEADQUARTERS ARMIES OF THE UNITED STATES,
Washington, D. C., April 4, 1864.

GENERAL : It is my design, if the enemy keep quiet and allow me to take the initiative in the spring campaign, to work all parts of the army together, and somewhat towards a common centre. For your information I now write you my programme as at present determined upon.

I have sent orders to Banks by private messenger to finish up his present expedition against Shreveport with all despatch; to turn over the defence of the Red river to General Steele and the navy, and return your troops to you, and his own to New Orleans; to abandon all of Texas except the Rio Grande, and to hold that with not to exceed four thousand men; to reduce the number of troops on the Mississippi to the lowest number necessary to hold it, and to collect from his command not less than twenty-five thousand (25,000) men. To this I will add five thousand (5,000) from Missouri. With this force he is to commence operations against Mobile as soon as he can. It will be impossible for him to commence too early.

Gilmore joins Butler with ten thousand (10,000) men, and the two operate against Richmond from the south side of James river. This will give Butler thirty-three thousand (33,000) men to operate with ; W. F. Smith commanding the right wing of his forces, and Gilmore the left wing. I will stay with the army of the Potomac, increased by Burnside's corps of not less than twenty-five thousand (25,000) effective men, and operate directly against Lee's army wherever it may be found.

Sigel collects all his available force in two columns—one, under Ord and Averill, to start from Beverly, Virginia; and the other, under Crook, to start from Charleston on the Kanawha, to move against the Virginia and Tennessee railroad. Crook will have all cavalry, and will endeavor to get in about Saltville and move east from there to join Ord. His force will be all cavalry, while Ord will have from ten to twelve thousand men of all arms.

You I propose to move against Johnston's army, to break it up and to get into the interior of the enemy's country as far as you can, inflicting all the damage you can against their war resources.

I do not propose to lay down for you a plan of campaign, but simply to lay down the work it is desirable to have done, and leave you free to execute in your. own way. Submit to me, however, as early as you can, your plan of operations

As stated, Banks is ordered to commence operations as soon as he can. Gilmore is ordered to report at Fortress Monroe by the 18th instant, or as soon thereafter as practicable. Sigel is concentrating now. None will move from their places of rendezvous until I direct, except Banks. I want to be ready to move by the 25th instant if possible. But all I can now direct is that you get ready as soon as possible. I know you will have difficulties to encounter getting through the mountains to where supplies are abundant, but I believe you will accomplish it.

From the expedition from the department of West Virginia I do not calculate on very great results; but it is the only way I can take troops from there. With the long line of railroad Sigel has to protect he can spare no troops, except to move directly to his front. In this way he must get through to inflict great damage on the enemy, or the enemy must detach from one of his armies a large force to prevent it. In other words, if Sigel can't skin himself, he can hold a leg whilst some one else skins.

I am, general, very respectfully, your obedient servant,

U. S. GRANT,
Lieutenant General.

Major General W. T. Sherman,
Commanding Military Division of the Mississippi.

[Private and confidential.]

Headquarters Military Division of the Mississippi,
Nashville, Tennessee, April 10, 1864.

Dear General: Your two letters of April 4 are now before me, and afford me infinite satisfaction. That we are now all to act on a common plan, converging on a common centre, looks like enlightened war.

Like yourself you take the biggest load, and from me you shall have thorough and hearty co-operation. I will not let side issues draw me off from your main plans in which I am to knock Joe Johnston, and do as much damage to the resources of the enemy as possible. I have heretofore written to General Rawlins and Colonel Comstock, of your staff, somewhat of the method in which I propose to act. I have seen all my army, corps, and division commanders, and have signified only to the former, viz., Schofield, Thomas, and McPherson, our general plans, which I inferred from the purport of our conversations here and at Cincinnati.

First. I am pushing stores to the front with all possible despatch, and am completing the organization according to the orders from Washington, which are ample and perfectly satisfactory.

It will take us all of April to get in our furloughed veterans, to bring up A. J. Smith's command, and to collect provision, and cattle to the line of the Tennessee. Each of these armies will guard by detachments of its own their rear communications.

At the signal to be given by you, Schofield will leave a select garrison at Knoxville and Loudon, and with twelve thousand (12,000) men drop down to Hiwassee and march on Johnston's right by the old Federal road. Stoneman, now in Kentucky organizing the cavalry forces of the army of the Ohio, will operate with Schofield on his left front—it may be, pushing a select body of about two thousand (2,000) cavalry by Ducktown or Elijay and toward Athens, Georgia.

Thomas will aim to have forty-five thousand (45,000) men of all arms and move straight on Johnston, wherever he may be, fighting him cautiously, persistently, and to the best advantage. He will have two divisions of cavalry to take advantage of any offering.

McPherson will have nine divisions of the army of the Tennessee, if A. J. Smith gets in, in which case he will have full thirty thousand (30,000) of the best men in America. He will cross the Tennessee at Decatur and Whitesburg, march toward Rome and feel for Thomas. If Johnston falls behind the Coosa, then McPherson will push for Rome; and if Johnston then fall behind the Chattahoochee, as I believe he will, then McPherson will cross and join with Thomas. McPherson has no cavalry, but I have taken one of Thomas' divisions, viz., Garrard's, 6,000 strong, which I now have at Columbia, mounting, equipping and preparing. I design this division to operate on McPherson's right, rear or front, according as the enemy appears. But the moment I detect Johnston falling behind the Chattahoochee, I propose to cast off the effective part of this cavalry division, after crossing the Coosa, straight for Opelika, West Point, Columbus, or Wetumpka, to break up the road between Montgomery and Georgia. If Garrard can do this work good, he can return to the Union army; but should a superior force interpose, then he will seek safety at Pensacola and join Banks, or, after rest, act against any force that he can find east of Mobile, till such time as he can reach me.

Should Johnston fall behind Chattahoochee, I would feign to the right, but pass to the left and act on Atlanta or on its eastern communications, according to developed facts.

This is about as far ahead as I feel disposed to look, but I would ever bear in mind that Johnston is at all times to be kept so busy that he cannot in any event send any part of his command against you or Banks.

If Banks can at the same time carry Mobile and open up the Alabama river, he will in a measure solve the most difficult part of my problem—*provisions*. But in that I must venture. Georgia has a million of inhabitants. If they can live, we should not starve. If the enemy interrupt my communications I will be absolved from all obligations to subsist on our own resources, but will feel perfectly justified in taking whatever and whenever I can find.

I will inspire my command, if successful with my feeling that beef and salt are all that is absolutely necessary to life, and parched corn fed General Jackson's army once on that very ground.

As ever, your friend and servant,

W. T. SHERMAN,
Major General.

Lieutenant General U. S. GRANT,
Commander-in-Chief, Washington D. C.

HEADQUARTERS MILITARY DIVISION OF THE MISSISSIPPI,
Nashville, April 11, 1864.

GENERAL: Since my interview with you I have a letter from Grant, full, clear and explicit, which I well understand, but cannot now impart to you, but will in due time. The arrangements are begun, and the organizations are in exact accordance with the part assigned us, only the general fixes the time a little earlier than I did; yet I will risk my judgment that the time I named to you will be as soon as others will be ready.

Get your three corps well in hand, and the means of transportation as ready as possible. When we move we will take no tents or baggage, but one change of clothing on our horses, or to be carried by the men and on pack animals by company officers. Five days' bacon, twenty days' bread and thirty days' salt, sugar, and coffee. Nothing else but arms and ammunition in quantity proportioned to our ability. Even this will be a heavy incumbarnce, but is rather the limit of our aim, than what we can really accomplish. Draw your forces down from the direction of Knoxville, so as not to attract attention.

I read the reports of your scouts with interest. I usually prefer to make my estimate of the enemy from general reasoning, than from the words of spies or deserters. We will get prepared for the maximum force possible of the enemy. We must not be led aside by any raids. We will be much aided by a diversion in a different quarter, of which I prefer not to write, but may communicate by the first confidential opportunity.

Look well to our supply of beef cattle on the hoof and salt in large excess of the rations. Encourage drills by brigades and divisions, and let the recruits practice at the targets all the time.

Newton is still detained by sore eyes; keep a division for him, but in all else make up your organization to suit yourself and corps commanders. R. S. Granger wants a leave—do you object? I suppose Rousseau could do district and post duty both.

Your friend,
W. T. SHERMAN,
Major General Commanding.

General GEORGE H. THOMAS,
Commanding Department of Cumberland.

HEADQUARTERS MILITARY DIVISION OF THE MISSISSIPPI,
Nashville, Tennessee, April 11, 1864.

GENERAL: Yours of April 8 is received. Slocum's assignment to Vicksburg was made at Grant's suggestion. I did name Newton, having in mind his engineering qualities, but General Grant feared Newton might entertain a natural prejudice against the negro element which will hereafter enter so largely into the means of defence to the river.

Veatch's withdrawal from Purdy makes Forrest's escape from the trap in which he caught himself easy and certain; but if you have at Cairo anything that could go up the Tennessee, and move inland on Jackson or Paris even, it would disturb Forrest more than anything Hurlbut will do from Memphis. I take it Forrest is now scattered, some of his men on furlough, and at mischief, stealing horses and recuperating. He may cross over the Tennessee into Kentucky or Tennessee, but I don't care if he does. Should he break the railroad between this and Louisville it would not bother us, for we have vast supplies here; and if he comes over to the neighborhood of Pulaski or Columbia, we will give him more than he expects.

As our great problem is to whip Joe Johnston, we want a surplus of our best troops on the line of the Tennessee. When that is done, we can give more attention to the Mississippi as against the small bands that threaten it. Surely there is now nothing there that can touch Memphis, Vicksburg or Natchez, and it will not be long before Banks will turn against Mobile, when the confederates must look to the safety of their own lines on the Alabama.

Give your chief thoughts to the making up of your army of the Tennessee and getting everything necessary to make the move from your present line on Rome and the Coosa. You will have the longest marches, and it may be the hardest knocks, but you have the elements of the best kind. You will have nine (9) divisions, averaging from four to five thousand (4 to 5,000,) viz: Harrow's, Smith's (Morgan L.,) Osterhaus' (in which is Chas. R. Wood, a magnificent officer,) and Jno. E. Smith, composing the 15th corps, (Logan's,) Veatch, Sweeny, and A. J. Smith, under Dodge, and Crocker and Leggett under Frank Blair.

I am told that Blair will soon leave Washington. I wrote him he would be wanted by April 20, at Cairo; you may telegraph him.

You had better begin moving up to Clinton your regiments and wagons as fast as they accumulate at Cairo. You can get steamers plenty at Cairo and St. Louis.

Grant says he will be all ready April 25, and when he moves we must. Thomas and Schofield are progressing well in their preparations.

Your friend,

W. T. SHERMAN,
Major General Commanding.

Major General JAMES B. McPHERSON,
Comm'dg the Department of the Tennessee, Huntsville, Ala.

HEADQUARTERS MILITARY DIVISION OF THE MISSISSIPPI,
Nashville, Tennessee, April 12, 1864.

DEAR GENERAL: Yours of March 30, from Natchez, is received, and I take pleasure in answering. I confess I fear to enunciate any plan that can reconcile all objections; but am willing to say that I will use all my official power and influence to carry out yours or that of the War Department. My objections to the plantation scheme are purely military. The Mississippi is a long, weak line, easily approached from the rear. Plantations of, say, three whites and fifty blacks to a mile of river, can be broken at any point by a guerilla band of one hundred with perfect impunity. You and I know the temper of the whites in the south.

I heard a young lady in Canton, educated at Philadelphia, who was a communicant of a Christian church, thank her God that her negroes, who had attempted to escape into our lines at Big Black, had been overtaken by Ross's Texas brigade, and killed. She thanked her God, and did so in religious sincerity. Now, a stranger to the sentiment of the south would consider this unnatural, but it is not only natural but universal. All the people of the south, old and young, rich and poor, educated and ignorant, unite in this, that they will kill, as vipers, the whites who attempt to free their slaves, and also the "ungrateful slaves" who attempt to change their character from slave to free.

Therefore, in making this change, which I regard as a decree of nature, we have to combat not only the organized resistance of the confederate forces, but the prejudices of the entire people of the south. I would prefer much to colonize the negroes on lands clearly forfeited to us by treason, and for the government to buy or extinguish the claims of other and loyal people in the districts chosen. I look upon the lands bordering the Mississippi, Steele's bayou, Deer creek, Sunflower, Bogue Phaliah, Yazoo, &c., in that rich alluvial region lying between Memphis and Vicksburg, of which Haines's Bluff, Yazoo City, and Grenada are the key points, as the very country in which we might collect the negroes, and where they will find more good land already cleared than in any district I know of, and it would enable the negroes at once to be useful.

If, however, the government prefer the "lessee" system, then I shall favor the occupation, by a black brigade, of Harrisonburg, and cover as well as may be the Mississippi country lying between the Washita and Yazoo. General Slocum will soon come down, and we believe he will co-operate with you with his whole heart. Of course, the possession of Vicksburg is a *sine qua non*. We don't want the task of taking it again; but if he can spare troops he will be instructed, in connexion with Natchez, to hold Harrisonburg, with one or more gunboats up the Washita and Tensas.

Steele is ordered to hold the line of Red river, but I must have Smith's command, which I loaned for but thirty (30) days, and I have reason to know that Banks must swing over against Mobile, so Steele will have only his Arkansas command, and that may be insufficient; of this we cannot judge until we know what is already done. If Shreveport be taken before these orders reach Steele, he may hold that point; otherwise, all he should attempt would be Alexandria, in connexion with the gunboats.

We have, sure enough, a big job on hand, and the only way is to go on trusting to consequences, following naturally grand results. Lee and Johnston must be whipped, and it should not be deferred an hour beyond the first possible practicable moment.

I necessarily write in some haste, but you will catch the drift of my argument.

With respect, your friend and servant,

W. T. SHERMAN,
Major General Commanding.

General LORENZO THOMAS,
Adjutant General U. S. A., Vicksburg, Mississippi.

HEADQUARTERS MILITARY DIVISION OF THE MISSISSIPPI,
Nashville, Tennessee, April 14, 1864.

DEAR GENERAL : I send you a parcel of papers of the latest dates from the south. You will find them interesting. One set of my former scouts is just in from Memphis; having come from Memphis, Holly Springs, Pontotoc, Aberdeen, Columbus, Mississippi,; Selma Montgomery, Opelika, West Point, and Columbus, Georgia; thence back to Selma, and up the railroad to Talladega, Jacksonville, and Blue mountain. The enemy is collecting at a place near Centreville, a camp to which Loring's division is to come from Demopolis. This force will be behind the Coosa, and is clearly designed by Johnston to watch McPherson as he advances against Rome. Forrest still is up between the Tennessee and the Mississippi, and is reported to-day crossing the Tennessee at Hamburg, also attacking Columbus. I admire his great skill, but he can't do all that. I am willing he should continue to attack our forts, and he may also cross the Tennessee. We have plenty of stores here; also we are pushing them to the front as fast as possible. I will not let Forrest draw off my mind from the concentration going on.

Longstreet is represented still up about Bristol and Abingdon, but I don't believe he will move into Kentucky by Pound Gap—road too bad and long. He may send some cavalry in, but he doesn't probably know that he can't interrupt our communications; because if the Louisville road is reached by a dash, we are not disturbed; and then for him to get out would be a question.

All well with us. I await McPherson's two divisions on furlough, and A. J. Smith from Red river.

Yours,

W. T. SHERMAN,
Major General.

General RAWLINS,
Chief of Staff, Washington.

HEADQUARTERS MILITARY DIVISION OF THE MISSISSIPPI,
Nashville, Tennessee, April 13, 1864.

General THOMAS, *Chattanooga :*

Continue to send me reports of scouts and rebel newspapers. Yours are most interesting. Two (2) of mine are in from Memphis, having come from Holly Springs, Pontotoc, Aberdeen, Columbus, Selma, Montgomery, West Point, back to Selma, up to Talladega and Blue mountain. The enemy is collecting a cavalry force at Blue mountain, which is about twenty-five miles from Gadsden, on account of forage which comes up the railroad from Selmaan d Talladega; and it is believed that Loring's division is ordered to the same point from Demopolis. Johnston doubtless is trying to make up a force to watch that flank, which he must observe is being threatened by McPherson. Forrest is reported again to be attacking Columbus, Kentucky, and also trying to cross the Tennessee near Hamburg. He seems to be omnipresent, but I think his cavalry is scattered over between the Mississippi and the Tennessee stealing horses and feeding them. I would as lief have him there as anywhere else now. Newton is here and will come forward to-morrow. Keep a good division for him.

Keep on collecting your command, as we arranged, and unload your cars as fast as possible. I will push forward stores as fast as possible.

W. T. SHERMAN,
Major General.

HEADQUARTERS MILITARY DIVISION OF THE MISSISSIPPI,
Nashville, April 18, 1865.

General Grant has made the following orders:

He has ordered three regiments from St. Louis to Cairo, with which to re-enforce Paducah, Cairo, and Columbus, and to feel out to Union City. Union City must not be garrisoned, but simply visited by scouts and patrols.

As soon as possible, a division or strong brigade of McPherson's command, due from furlough about the 20th instant, General Gresham, if possible, will hasten up the Tennessee, leave its wagons and incumbrances at Clifton, but proceed to Savannah and scout across by Purdy to the head of the Hatchee.

General Slocum has gone to Vicksburg to assume command there, and General Sturgis has started this morning to assume command of all the cavalry at and near Memphis, with which he will sally out and attack Forrest, wherever he may be. General Grierson may seize all the horses and mules in Memphis to mount his men, and be ready for the arrival of General Sturgis; and Buckland's brigade of infantry should be ready to move.out with the cavalry. Mower's division, now at Red river, will be detained at Memphis on its way up the river, and A. J. Smith will come, as ordered, up the Tennessee. General C. C. Washburne is ordered to Memphis, and General Hunt to Columbus. General Hurlbut will take post for the present at Cairo, and Hicks remain in command at Paducah.

All the troops along the Mississippi must act with vigor against any portion of the enemy within reach. Paducah, Cairo, Columbus, Memphis, Vicksburg, and Natchez must be held, and all minor points exposed should be evacuated.

The troops at Memphis should act by land; those at Vicksburg should operate up Yazoo, at Yazoo city, and threatening Grenada.

All former orders will be modified to suit this general plan.

W. T. SHERMAN,
Major General Commanding.

General McPHERSON, Huntsville.
General HURLBUT, Memphis.
General BRAYMAN, Cairo.
General SLOCUM, Vicksburg.

HEADQUARTERS MILITARY DIVISION OF THE MISSISSIPPI,
Nashville, Tennessee, April 19, 1865.

GENERAL: I have read with interest General Geary's report and your indorsements. With all the facts before me, especially the complete details of the facts given by your scouts, I have no doubt that Johnston's main army is on the railroad at or near Dalton; that it is about forty thousand (40,000) strong, well commanded, and in good order, but it cannot move many days' march, except along the line of that road, front and rear; that he has a good force of cavalry, one part of which is kept to his right rear for food, and that another part, say four thousand (4,000) men, are on his left, over about the Blue Mountain depot, for the same purpose, and to watch the assemblage of the army of the Tennessee, which he knows threatens his left flank, and which has two good bridges with which to pass the Tennessee at pleasure. This cavalry, with some infantry supports, are seen often at Larkins's and at Decatur, and some skirmishing has been carried on with them, but we want to mask our force by the Tennessee till the right time. Of course, then, McPherson can sweep them from his front as a cob-web.

At Blue Mountain depot this cavalry gets corn, which is sent up from the line of the railroad and Selma, and this point is the present terminus of that railroad.

It is ten (10) miles south of Jacksonville, which is twenty-two (22) miles east by south of Gadsden, which is full forty-five (45) miles from Guntersville, the nearest point of the Tennessee. I have no apprehension of a raid on our right, for the reason that the enemy cannot pass the Tennessee, save at isolated points, and then only in small parties; besides, the stream of troops soon to come up the Tennessee from Cairo, and across to Huntsville, from Savannah and Clifton, will serve to cover that flank. Still we must push our measures to accumulate a surplus of all essentials to the front, so that a temporary interruption will not cripple us or delay our general plans, which remain unchanged.

The only real move I see for Joe Johnston is to strike your line at his nearest point, about Cleveland or Ooltewah, but this he cannot reach without first fighting the Ringgold force. I advise you to group your commands so as to admit of easy and rapid concentration at such point as your judgment approves, and be careful not to accumulate stores anywhere but inside of Chattanooga.

The season is now mild, and even surplus tents and all useless baggage should thus be placed, that the troops in camp could pack up and move at the shortest notice. Study all means to save wagons and transportation at all events till our advance passes the Coosa.

Please continue as heretofore the scout reports. I have two smart girls who have just come in from Memphis via Okalona, Columbus, Selma, Montgomery, West Point, back to Selma, up the railroad to Talladega, and Blue mountain, whence they crossed on foot by way of Gadsden, Black river, Will's creek, Tower creek, and Larkin's. They saw little or no infantry, and the only cavalry they saw was at the Blue mountains, and close up to the Tennessee river.

I am, &c.,

W. T. SHERMAN,
Major General Commanding.

Major General THOMAS,
    Commanding Department of the Cumberland, Chattanooga.

HEADQUARTERS MILITARY DIVISION OF THE MISSISSIPPI,
Nashville, April 19, 1865.

GENERAL: I received a despatch from General Grant asking me if the report that Johnston was sending off Hardee's corps was true. I have answered that Thomas thinks not. You know how easy such reports get currency. I have read every official report from all quarters very carefully, and the only one which even hints at such a thing is one from Thomas, the words of a deserter taken down by the usual provost marshal, under date of April 15, that there

3*

was a camp rumor in Johnston's camp when he left that Hardee's corps was to be sent to Virginia, but subsequent reports describe minutely the position and strength of the rebel army as unchanged since you left, save that a heavy cavalry force is being collected near the Coosa, abreast of Guntersville, evidently for the purpose of watching McPherson; although I have daily the reports of thousands and tens of thousands marching and raiding all round the compass, yet I have now scouts in from Memphis who bring in passes and papers from Selma, Montgomery, West Point, Opelika, and Talladega, and from them I learn that things remain as above.

Thomas is gradually drawing down his command to a common focus, Chattanooga. Schofield has infantry force at Bull's Gap and a small cavalry force beyond, but is preparing to have about twelve thousand (12,000) infantry near Hiawassee at the time appointed, May 1, with his cavalry under Stoneman, remounting and refitting as fast as possible, near Lexington, Kentucky, whence at the right time I will move them to the Hiawassee.

McPherson has Decatur well fortified, and is examining the river carefully to ascertain the best point to cross over. He is still in doubt whether Guntersville or Whitesburg be the place. But one or the other is, and our bridges at Larkin's can on a short notice drop down. This will give him two good points of invasion. I am doing all I can to get forward the necessary stores, and more still to diminish the useless mouths that eat up our substance,

I enclose you two orders which are preliminary, but I am resolved, when General Grant gives the word, to attack Johnston in the manner I have heretofore described, if our men have to live on beef and salt. They will do it, if necessary, we know. As long as cavalry officers can let their horses run down to get a remount by a mere requisition, they will bankrupt any government. Grierson had seven thousand (7,000) horses when I made up the Meridian count, and Smith and he reported the capture of some four thousand (4,000) animals, and yet now the reason for not attacking Forrest is, that he can only mount two thousand four hundred (2,400) men. Even with that he should have attacked the enemy at Somersville, as it was then known Forrest was up about Paducah with a considerable part, and what was at Somersville was of course only a part, and should have been fought at all odds. At Memphis are Buckland's full brigade of splendid troops, (2,000;) three other white regiments, one of black artillery, at Fort Pickering, 1,200 strong; about one thousand (1,000) men floating, who are camped in the fort; near four thousand (4,000) black troops, three thousand (3,000) enrolled and armed militia, and all Grierson's cavalry, ten thousand nine hundred and eighty-three (10,983) according to my last returns, of which surely not over three thousand (3,000) are on furlough. Out of this a splendid force of about two thousand five hundred (2,500) well mounted cavalry and four thousand (4,000) infantry could have been made up, and by moving to Bolivar, could have made Forrest come there to fight or get out.

I have sent Sturgis down to take command and whip Forrest, and, if necessary, to mount enough men to seize any and all the horses of Memphis, or wherever he may go.

The forces of Fort Pillow are not on my returns. I broke it up, and the garrison was composed of a regiment of Tennesseeans, enlisting, and four companies of blacks, of which I have no satisfactory report as yet, but have sent for full details.

I think everything hereabouts is working as well as I can promise, and if A. J. Smith is coming, and McPherson's two furloughed divisions reach us, I will be ready at the drop of a hat to cross the Tennessee and pitch in.

I sent for the governor of Kentucky, and he is well satisfied with all the steps taken, and undertakes by his militia and the troops now controlled by Burbridge to catch the wandering guerillas and keep peace in his State. But we are independent of Kentucky, for there are here now all the essentials for an army of eighty thousand (80,000) men for six months. Railroad accidents are still happening, but as seldom as we could expect.

I am, &c.,

W. T. SHERMAN,
Major General Commanding.

General JOHN A. RAWLINS,
Chief of Gen. Grant's Staff, Washington, D. C.

[Cipher telegram.]

HEADQUARTERS MILITARY DIVISION OF THE MISSISSIPPI,
Nashville, Tennessee, April 20, 1865.

Lieutenant General GRANT, *Washington:*

These are copies of my latest despatches from Chattanooga and Knoxville:

[From Knoxville, April 19, 1865.]

Major General SHERMAN:

I have information this evening that Longstreet's three divisions of infantry have gone east as far as Lynchburg ; the last left Bristol on Wednesday, the 13th instant. My informant is a man who was employed on the railroad, and went from Bristol to Lynchburg on the 13th and returned on the 14th. He is believed to be loyal and truthful. Reports from other sources also corroborate this statement. Vaughn's cavalry brigade, from eight hundred to fifteen hundred strong, moved, at about the same time, from Kingsport towards North Carolina, by the road leading up the Wautauga. This leaves the force in southwest Virginia little more than that which was recently driven through Pound Gap by Colonel Gallop. From all the information obtained while in command here, I estimate the effective strength of Longstreet's three divisions at twelve thousand five hundred (12,500.) General Foster's estimate was somewhat larger. I state this as it may be of importance to General Grant in Virginia at this time.

J. M. SCHOFIELD, *Major General.*

[From Chattanooga, April 19, 1865.]

Major General SHERMAN:

There is no foundation for the report that Johnston is re-enforcing Lee. One of my most reliable men reports as follows : Dalton, April 12.—No change at Dalton. Resaca, April 15.—No change at Resaca or Dalton. Trains full of soldiers going and coming on furlough. Resaca, April 18.—No change in Dalton. Wash. Johnson and command left here for Dalton at 10 a. m. this morning ; four hundred (400) Florida troops took their places. A large number of wagons, loaded with crackers at Calhoun, have been waiting orders some few days.

Besides the above-mentioned man, I have by the way of others who visit Dalton at least once a week each. They all confirm what he says regarding the position of the enemy there.

GEORGE H. THOMAS,
Major General.

W. T. SHERMAN,
Major General Commanding.

[Cipher telegram.]

HEADQUARTERS MILITARY DIVISION OF THE MISSISSIPPI,
Nashville, April 23, 1865.

General MCPHERSON, *Huntsville:*

We must make calculations, leaving A. J. Smith out. Banks cannot spare him, as I feared.

Hurry up the two divisions from Cairo, and get ready as soon as possible, for I think Grant is pushing matters. I have news from Dalton to the 20th. A part of Polk's troops have arrived there.

We must not allow our chief attention to be drawn towards Mississippi, as that is what the enemy wants.

W. T. SHERMAN, *Major General.*

[Cipher telegram.]

HEADQUARTERS MILITARY DIVISION OF THE MISSISSIPPI,
Nashville, April 23, 1865.

General MCPHERSON, *Huntsville:*

Colonel Comstock is here from General Grant, and we may have to move sooner than we are ready, but we can go as far as the Coosa. I will throw forward provisions enough to load your wagons, and they can be replenished at Ringgold.

If we move before Crocker gets up I will require you to move by Lebanon and Chattooga, to communicate with Thomas at Lafayette and Villanow. But I will write at length. If we move by May 1, the divisions at Scottsboro,' Larkin's, and Woodville should cross at Larkin's. Dodge's force and Garrard should cross at Decatur and move to Guntersville, and a junction made at Lebanon. I do not propose to cross the Coosa till all are up, but we will gain time by a move in concert with Grant.

W. T. SHERMAN,
Major General.

HEADQUARTERS ARMIES IN THE FIELD,
Culpeper C. H., Va., April 19, 1864.

GENERAL: Since my letter to you I have seen no reason to change any portion of the general plan of campaign, if the enemy remain still and allow us to take the initiative. Rain has continued so uninterruptedly until the last day or two that it will be impossible to move, however, before the 27th, even if no more should fall in the mean time. I think Saturday, the 30th, will probably be the day for our general move.

Colonel Comstock, who will take this, can spend a day with you, and fill up many a little gap of information not given in any of my letters.

What I now want more particularly to say is, that if the two main attacks, yours and the one from here, should promise great success, the enemy may, in a fit of desperation, abandon one part of their line of defence and throw their whole strength upon a single army, believing that a defeat with one victory to sustain them is better than a defeat all along their line, and hoping, too, at the same time, that the army, meeting with no resistance, will rest perfectly satisfied with their laurels, having penetrated to a given point south, thereby enabling them to throw their force first upon one and then on the other.

With the majority of military commanders they might do this. But you have had too much experience in travelling light and subsisting upon the country to be caught by any such ruse. I hope my experience has not been thrown away. My directions, then, would be, if the enemy in your front show signs of joining Lee, follow him up to the full extent of your ability. I will prevent the concentration of Lee upon your front if it is in the power of this army to do it.

The army of the Potomac looks well, and, so far as I can judge, officers and men feel well.

Yours, truly,

U. S. GRANT,
Lieutenant General.

Major General W. T. SHERMAN,
Commanding Military Division of the Mississippi.

[Cipher telegram.]

HEADQUARTERS MILITARY DIVISION OF THE MISSISSIPPI,
Nashville, April 23, 1864.

General SCHOFIELD, *Knoxville :*

Colonel Comstock is here from General Grant. We may have to begin quite as soon as I first estimated, May 1. You will commence at once to break up railroad above Bull's Gap and either bend and twist the bars or carry them to Knoxville, and move down the infantry force about the Hiwassee. Stoneman will be able to overhaul us before we will need the flanking force.

W. T. SHERMAN,
Major General.

[Cipher letter.]

HEADQUARTERS MILITARY DIVISION OF THE MISSISSIPPI,
Nashville, April 24, 1865.

General THOMAS, *Chattanooga :*

You may be as severe as possible with citizens who smuggle themselves into the cars. All are prohibited from going. I have more than doubled the number of cars per day. Yesterday we got off one hundred and ninety-three cars.

If you send a staff officer I will send you copies of General Grant's letters. They embrace the points of mine. Time is nearly up, and you cannot have your preparations too far advanced. For the first week out we will need but few wagons.

As McPherson will not have A. J. Smith's division, and some of his furloughed regiments will be late, you had better make ready with every man you can take along, and as McPherson's detachments come up your surplus forces can be sent back. I will come down as soon as possible.

W. T. SHERMAN,
Major General.

HEADQUARTERS MILITARY DIVISION OF THE MISSISSIPPI,
Nashville, April 25, 1865.

GENERAL : I have received your several despatches and letters touching the check on railroad travel. I have ordered the quartermaster to check the tendency of our military railroads sliding into a public convenience, but to keep it just as he would a train of army wagons. Nobody should travel in the cars save officers and soldiers under orders entitling them to transportation. I left him to ease off by sending only such as were caught away from home by the change. I think it will in time come out all right. If we allow conductors to collect money we know they will little by little pick up way-travellers for their own profit. We have not the system of checks that would enable us to detect peculation and fraud. The officers of the army of the Tennessee have complained bitterly that in all matters pertaining to the railroad they were slighted, and there were some grounds, not intentional on your part, but calculated to raise a prejudice, that after they had come to the relief of the army of the Cumberland they were denied bread or any facilities from the road. Some even thought you shared this feeling, and had refused them even a passage to or from Nashville.

This resulted from the fact that the conductors and your guards were familiar with your passes, and were not with those of Logan or other commanders of that wing. This made my transportation order manifestly just, putting all department commanders on a just equality.

We have increased the daily cars from about eighty (80) to from one hundred and thirty (130) to one hundred and ninety (190.) If I can get the average to one hundred and fifty (150) the road will supply us, and make an accumulation. I wish you to increase the facilities for throwing stores forward to Ringgold, as McPherson, Schofield, and you will have to draw from that common depot. All I can now hope for is to get McPherson to Lafayette, or thereabouts, with twenty (20) days' bread, salt, &c., from Guntersville.

McPherson's two divisions are not yet at Cairo, and in many cases the furloughs were dated after a long delay in the State waiting for payment, so that I can't even tell when they will be up to Clifton; but we are pushing as hard as possible. I want McPherson to have thirty thousand (30,000) men, independent of Garrard's cavalry; but if we can't get these two divisions in time, his force will fall far short. As he and Schofield cover your flanks, I want to make your force as heavy as possible as far out as Dalton, Resaca, and Kingston. By that time we will have a better knowledge of what we will need, and can trim down and send back such as should remain to guard your rear. The only danger I apprehend is from resident guerillas, and from Forrest coming from the direction of Florence. I did want A. J. Smith on the Tennessee, about Florence, to guard against that danger, but Banks cannot spare him, and Grant orders me to calculate without him. General Corse is here from Red river. The battle up Red river resulted thus wise: The advance cavalry, incumbered with wagons, met the enemy in position four miles from Mansfield, where the road forks to Texas. Lee, who commanded the cavalry, sent back for supports. A brigade of infantry was sent, but both cavalry and infantry were driven back in disorder. Another brigade sent forward shared the same fate, and the enemy pursuing struck Franklin, who held them till night. Next day A. J. Smith got up, and a hard fight ensued on the 9th, extending into night. Our troops had the advantage, but in the night both armies retired—ours forty miles back to Grand Ecore; and the enemy discovering first our retrograde, took advantage of it. So they have the victory. They took all the wagons of the cavalry, over two hundred, (200,) and some eighteen guns, two of which were recovered.

Banks was refitting on the 14th at Grand Ecore, preparing to advance. Nothing from Steele, who, at that date, should have been near Shreveport, on the north and east bank of the river.

I am quite uneasy about Steele, as the movement up Red river has been so slow that all the Texas and Louisiana forces are assembled, and having defeated Banks, may turn against Steele; but still I hope Banks will not pause, but resume his march, and prevent Kirby Smith from crossing to the north side of Red river. Our joint forces are far superior to those of the enemy, and we have also the gunboats and transports in Red river.

The best fighting was evidently done by my troops, and Admiral Porter writes me that A. J. Smith's command saved Banks's army from utter rout. Banks should have seventeen thousand, (17,000,) Steele seven to nine thousand, (7 to 9,000,) and Smith ten thousand, (10,000.)

The joint force of the enemy is reckoned at twenty-five thousand, (25,000.) Grand Ecore is the river town of Natchitoches, a little back from Red river, but on one of the roads leading to Shreveport, and about forty (40) miles from Natchitoches.

I will be with you by May 1.

> Truly, yours,
>
> W. T. SHERMAN,
> *Major General.*

Major General GEO. H. THOMAS,
Commanding Department of the Cumberland, Chattanooga.

[Confidential.]

HEADQUARTERS MILITARY DIVISION OF THE MISSISSIPPI,
Nashville, April 16, 1864.

GENERAL: I telegraphed you last night that Colonel Comstock had come from General Grant with a letter, that he, General Grant, would be ready by the 27th to take the initiative, if in the mean time Lee did not, and, of course, he wants me to act at the same time; but Colonel Comstock tells me he does not think General Grant can do anything till May 2.

Of course the movement in Virginia is the principal, and ours is secondary, and must conform. We must be as far ready as possible.

First. Give Generals Slocum and Washburne orders to seem most active, to hold there all the enemy possible, even at a small risk to the river, for if we whip Joe Johnston good, everything lying west will feel the blow.

Second. Do all that is within the power of mortal to get up your two divisions from Cairo, with wagons, beef cattle, &c. I will write to Lieutenant Commander Shirk, United States navy, to watch the Tennessee, all that is possible, to prevent any damage to our roads from that quarter.

Third. You should at once move your effective force of the 15th corps to the neighborhood of Larkin's, or wherever you propose to cross the Tennessee, to be ready to move on Lebanon. Dodge's command should cross at Decatur, and brush away that cavalry, and move on Guntersville and Lebanon. From Lebanon your army should move as light as possible by Summerville or other good route toward Lafayette or Villanow, to communicate with Thomas. From Lafayette you can renew your supply of bread, salt, sugar, and coffee from Ringgold, to which point we have cars. We are accumulating stores as fast as possible at Chattanooga. If you can start with twenty days' supply, it is all that I now expect. I will explain to Comstock, and send word to General Grant how important it is that we should have the two divisions now at Cairo, and on furlough, and have him correspond by telegraph with them at Cairo, and judge when they can reach your right flank *via* Clifton.

You should have a force of about thirty thousand, (30,000,) exclusive of Garrard's cavalry, which will remain with your extreme right till we are beyond the Coosa, when it must strike for the Montgomery and Atlanta roads.

I think I understand the cavalry force in front of Dodge; it is a detachment from Joe Johnston, sent there to watch your operations; but the moment you cross the Tennessee in force, it will hasten to cover Rome and watch Johnston's left flank and rear.

The worst that we have to apprehend is, Forrest may come across to act against our right flank; but this would be prevented if Washburne and Slocum threaten Grenada. I take it for granted that, unless Banks gets out of Red river and attacks Mobile, (which is a material part of General Grant's plan,) we will have to fight Polk's army as well as Johnston's. General Corse has returned. Banks would not spare Smith; indeed, it appears that Smith's force is the real substance of his army. He was whipped near Mansfield and retreated to Grand Ecore, forty miles, though Banks claims a victory; but from what General Corse tells me he might have made it a victory by going ahead, but by retreating he left the enemy in possession of wounded, dead, artillery, and trains; and worse, leaves Steele in danger. General Banks writes me that all is well there, but facts do not sustain him.

General Prince will go to Columbus, and you had better give Washburne command of all the river from Cairo down, to include the Memphis district. Grant thinks him a man of action. I will send your pontoon train down, and I think you had better have it at Scottsboro', with orders to follow as soon as facts demonstrate that Johnston will not fight us this side of the Coosa. Until that fact is demonstrated we should be as little encumbered as possible.

> Yours, &c.,
>
> W. T. SHERMAN,
> *Major General Commanding.*

Major General J. B. McPHERSON,
 Commanding Department of the Tennessee, Huntsville.

[Confidential.]

HEADQUARTERS MILITARY DIVISION OF THE MISSISSIPPI,
  Nashville, Tennessee, April 24, 1864.

GENERAL: I now have a messenger out from General Grant, which convinces me that the army of the Potomac, from its shorter lines and superabundant supplies, will be ready sooner than we; but let come what may, we must attack Joe Johnston in position, or force him back of Coosa, at the moment the initiative is made in the east. I prefer that Johnston should not move at all, but receive us on his present ground. But I do not propose rushing on him rashly until I have in hand all the available strength of your, Thomas's, and McPherson's armies.

Supplies are the chief trouble; but if the worst comes to the worst, we can live on beef and salt, with such bread as our road ought to carry for us to Ringgold.

Of course there remains now in East Tennessee no rebel force that can come down on our flank that could seriously endanger us moving forward from Chattanooga; but I wish you to dispose your command to guard against that chance. Destroy a considerable section of the railroad above Bull's Gap, bending and twisting the rails or carrying them to Knoxville.

Leave Knoxville and Loudon well guarded, and assemble your effective force near Charleston on the Hiwassee, prepared by May 1, if possible, to move in concert with Thomas down by way of Varnell's station direct on Dalton.

Order Stoneman to move by the best route available to him so as to report to you. If Johnston refuses us battle, this cavalry will be sent by way of Spring Place, or it may be higher up by the copper mines, to threaten the enemy's right rear.

Order all your forces in Kentucky to be most active, even to feel out through Pound Gap into the valley beyond. I have no apprehension of the enemy interfering with our lines of communication in Kentucky, because we have here in Nashville the essential supplies for six months. Those in the western part of Kentucky ought to watch well the line, and to arrest all suspicious men hanging about who have no honest employment; precaution may save us temporary annoyance. Such men are not prisoners of war, but simply men held by us rather than incur the risks of their mischievous acts.

It is useless for us to expect the new cavalry from Indiana. We cannot mount even the veteran cavalry, which should, of course, have precedence.

I will be at Chattanooga about May 1.

Truly yours,

W. T. SHERMAN, *Major General Commanding*.

Major General J. M. SCHOFIELD,
 Commanding Department of the Ohio, Knoxville.

[Confidential.]

HEADQUARTERS MILITARY DIVISION OF THE MISSISSIPPI,
 Nashville, Tennessee, April 24, 1864.

GENERAL: I now have, at the hands of Colonel Comstock, of your staff, the letter of April 19, and am as far prepared to assume the offensive as possible. I only ask as much time as you think proper, to enable me to get up McPherson's two divisions from Cairo. Their furloughs will expire about this time, and some of them now should be in motion for Clifton, whence they march to Decatur to join on to Dodge.

McPherson is ordered to assemble the 15th corps near Larkin's, and to get Dodge and Blair at Decatur at the earliest possible moment; and from these two points he will direct his forces on Lebanon, Summerville, and Lafayette, where he will act against Johnston if he accept battle at Dalton, or move in the direction of Rome, if he give up Dalton, and fall behind the Oostanaula or Etowah. I see there is some risk in dividing our forces; but Thomas and Schofield will have forces enough to cover all the valley as far as Dalton; and should Johnston turn his whole force against McPherson, the latter will have his bridge at Larkin's, and the route to Chattanooga *via* Wills's valley and the Chattanooga creek; and if Johnston attempt to leave Dalton, Thomas will have force enough to push on through Dalton to Kingston, which would checkmate him. My own opinion is, Johnston will be compelled to hang to his railroad, the only possible avenue of supply to his army, estimated at from forty-five to sixty thousand (45 to 60,000) men.

At Lafayette all our armies will be together, and if Johnston stands at Dalton we must attack him in position. Thomas feels certain that he has no material increase of force, and that he has not sent away Hardee, or any part of his army. Supplies are the great question. I have materially increased the number of cars daily. When I got here they ran from sixty-five (65) to eighty (80) per day. Yesterday the report was one hundred and ninety-three (193,) to-day one hundred and thirty-four (134,) and my estimate is one hundred and forty-five (145) per day will give us daily a day's accumulation.

McPherson is ordered to carry in wagons twenty (20) days' supplies, and rely on the depot at Ringgold for the renewal of his bread ration. Beeves are now being driven to the front, and my commissary, Colonel Beckwith, seems fully alive to the importance of the whole matter.

Our weakest point will be from the direction of Decatur, and I will be forced to risk something from that quarter, depending on the fact that the enemy has no force available with which to threaten our communications from that direction.

Colonel Comstock will explain much that I cannot commit to paper.

I am, with great respect,

W. T. SHERMAN, *Major General.*

Lieutenant General GRANT,
 Comm'dg Armies of the United States, Culpeper, Va.

[Confidential.]

HEADQUARTERS MILITARY DIVISION OF THE MISSISSIPPI,
Nashville, Tennessee, April 24, 1864.

GENERAL: I had the honor to receive yesterday, at the hands of General Corse, your letter of April 14, from Grand Ecore, and was glad to hear the specific account of your affairs up Red river.

We had become quite anxious from confused and conflicting accounts sent by the busy correspondents who always exaggerate things, good or bad.

I was and am disappointed, as I do sadly need that command of General A. J. Smith's, but I see that you could not spare it at that moment. I hope you pushed on at once, as otherwise the enemy must surely have availed themselves of the tempting opportunity to fall on Steele.

We have no later dates of any of our Red river forces than those brought by General Corse. I had a message from General Grant last night, and we must all soon pitch in, and, for weal or woe, battles must ensue more bloody than any which have heretofore characterized this war.

I hope you will soon finish up that job, and turn your attention to a more important work; but you are so far away that I can make no calculation upon your forces.

I am, with respect, your obedient servant,

W. T. SHERMAN,
Major General Commanding.

Major General N. P. BANKS,
Commanding Department of the Gulf, Red River.

[Confidential.]

HEADQUARTERS MILITARY DIVISION OF THE MISSISSIPPI,
Nashville, Tennessee, April 24, 1864.

DEAR GENERAL: General Corse has returned. He brought no letter from you, but gave good accounts of you and your troops. I had hoped, from the rapid work you did up to Alexandria, that the whole expedition would go on in like manner. I want your command, but of course you could not leave under the circumstances by which you were surrounded on the 14th of April. General Corse says that in the second day's fight at Pleasant Hill the enemy were beaten and were retreating. I cannot understand why our army retraced its steps to Grand Ecore, when it was so important in time, in distance, more especially as Steele was known to be approaching from the north. But all will be explained in time. I have simply ordered that when you do come out of Red river, that Mower's division remain at Memphis, and yours come round by Cairo, and up the Tennessee to Clifton, and thence across to Decatur; but as time and circumstances may change, I will have orders meet you at Memphis. General McPherson now commands the department, and all our attention is engaged in the awful responsibilities that rest on us here. General Grant has ordered that Steele command on Red river, and he must order things according to the result of your expedition. I was in hopes it would have been made more rapidly, so that those troops could have taken part with us in the events soon to transpire.

You will, as soon as you can possibly be spared, come to Memphis, where orders will meet you.

I am, with respect, your obedient servant,

W. T. SHERMAN,
Major General Commanding.

Brigadier General A. J. SMITH,
Commanding Detachment on Red River.

[Cipher.]

CULPEPER, *April 25—11.30 a. m.*

Major General SHERMAN :

Will your veterans be back to enable you to start on the second of May? I do not want to delay later.

U. S. GRANT,
Lieutenant General.

[Cipher telegram.]

HEADQUARTERS MILITARY DIVISION OF THE MISSISSIPPI,
Nashville, April 25, 1865.

General THOMAS, *Chattanooga :*

General Grant telegraphs me to be ready May 2. Make dispositions accordingly. McPherson is least ready.

W. T. SHERMAN,
Major General.

[Cipher telegram.]

HEADQUARTERS MILITARY DIVISION OF THE MISSISSIPPI,
Nashville, April 25, 1864.

General MCPHERSON, *Huntsville :*

General Grant telegraphs me to be ready by May 2. We cannot wait for the veterans. It may be well for your whole column to move from Scottsboro'. They could be moved to that point by rail. The two divisions expected up from Cairo would cover that flank and guard the roads, or join you *via* Chattanooga. Make every possible preparation.

W. T. SHERMAN,
Major General.

[Cipher telegram.]

HEADQUARTERS MILITARY DIVISION OF THE MISSISSIPPI,
Nashville, April 25, 1864.

General SCHOFIELD, *Knoxville :*

General Grant telegraphs me to be ready by May 2. Make preparations accordingly. Order Stoneman forward with all the cavalry that is ready ; the rest can follow.

W. T. SHERMAN,
Major General.

[Cipher telegram.]

HEADQUARTERS MILITARY DIVISION OF THE MISSISSIPPI,
Nashville, April 27, 1864.

Lieutenant General GRANT, *Culpeper :*

In view of the fact that I will have to take the initiative with twenty thousand less men in McPherson's army than I estimated, I intend to order all

McPherson's disposable force, twenty thousand, (20,000,) and Garrard's cavalry, five thousand, (5,000,) to Chattanooga, to start from a common centre. I go forward to-morrow.

W. T. SHERMAN,
Major General.

Headquarters Military Division of the Mississippi,
Nashville, April 27, 1864.

GENERAL: General McPherson is now here, and on consultation, taking into consideration all the facts known to me of the strength and position of the enemy, we have concluded that McPherson's troops can reach their position at and near Lafayette more expeditiously by Chattanooga than by the contemplated road by Decatur, Gunter's, and Lebanon.

It is very desirable that the whole army should be at and in front of Chattanooga by May 5th. You may therefore put in motion your cavalry that is mounted and equipped, with the wagons needed for efficient action, and the rest as fast as horses are received, leaving, as heretofore arranged, your dismounted men at Columbia and along the road.

General Rousseau will send a regiment to hold the road down as far as Pulaski. Enough horses are now on hand to increase your mounted force to five thousand (5,000.) With these I want you at Chattanooga about the 5th of May; and as there is no necessity of your moving with Dodge, you can select your own route, and move by brigades and regiments as you please. On arrival at Chattanooga, take position near the extreme right of the whole army.

General McPherson will see you to-morrow. These orders may seem to you a little sudden, but are made necessary by orders from General Grant.

I am, &c.,

W. T. SHERMAN,
Major General.

Brigadier General GARRARD,
    Commanding 2d Division Cavalry, right wing.

Culpeper, Va., April 28, 1864.

Major General SHERMAN :

Get your forces up so as to move by the fifth (5th) of May.

U. S. GRANT,
Lieutenant General.

[Cipher telegram.]

Headquarters Military Division of the Mississippi,
Chattanooga, Tennessee, April 29, 1864.

General GRANT Culpeper, Va.:

I am here. Thomas is already in position. Schofield will be by May 2d; and McPherson is marching for Lafayette via of this place. All my effective cavalry is heading for Dalton, and I will be all ready by May 5th. I will write you fully to-night.

W. T. SHERMAN,
Major General.

[Cipher telegram.]

HEADQUARTERS MILITARY DIVISION OF THE MISSISSIPPI,
In the field, Chattanooga, April 29, 1864.

General McPHERSON, *Huntsville, Ala.:*

Put everybody in motion at once for Chattanooga by roads north of the Tennessee, according to the figures we agreed on, viz: ten thousand of the 15th corps and ten thousand of the 16th corps and Garrard's cavalry.   I have a despatch from General Grant wanting me to be all ready by May 5th   You know how I like to be on time.   A steamboat has gone to Larkins' for the bridges. Make your orders for the two divisions at Cairo and Clifton as full as possible, and when all things are working well, come up.

W. T. SHERMAN,
Major General Commanding.

[Cipher telegram.]

HEADQUARTERS MILITARY DIVISION OF THE MISSISSIPPI,
In the field, Chattanooga, April 29, 1864.

General SCHOFIELD, *Knoxville, Tenn.:*

General Grant gives me to the 5th to be ready.   I will expect your quota at or near Charleston by May 2d, where I will come to see you or get you to come here in person.   Keep your movements from the press as much as possible.   Let the enemy find out our movements through their own spies, not ours.   Thomas is all right and McPherson is coming.

W. T. SHERMAN,
Major General Commanding.

[Cipher telegram.]

HEADQUARTERS MILITARY DIVISION OF THE MISSISSIPPI,
In the field, Chattanooga, April 29, 1864.

General McPHERSON, *Huntsville, Ala.:*

General Grant wants me to be all ready by the 5th of May.   To accomplish this the 15th corps could March here by that date, but we would have to push up Dodge's command in cars, leaving the wagons to follow and overtake them at some point to be hereafter fixed.   Therefore order Dodge's march by roads that will carry them near the railroad.   The cavalry must of course come all the way by the common road.

W. T. SHERMAN,
Major General Commanding.

[Cipher telegram.]

HEADQUARTERS MILITARY DIVISION OF THE MISSISSIPPI,
In the field, Chattanooga, April 29, 1864.

General McPHERSON, *Huntsville, Ala.:*

I approve your suggestion as to the evacuation of Decatur, but it should only be as an alternative at the last moment.   If it be possible to get any of the

Clifton force I would prefer to hold Decatur, as it is a constant threat to "north Alabama."

It is desirable to keep the rebel cavalry there as long as possible, and I would risk something. It is there merely to watch you.

W. T. SHERMAN,
Major General.

[Cipher telegram.]

HEADQUARTERS MILITARY DIVISION OF THE MISSISSIPPI,
In the field, Chattanooga, April 30, 1864.

General GRANT, *Culpeper:*

I have news from Atlanta 24th, and Dalton 27th.   Some of Polk's troops have arrived. By the fifth all of Thomas's and Schofield's troops will be within one march of Dalton, and I doubt not McPherson will be on time. All things working as smoothly as I could expect.

Rosecrans holds some of the Memphis dismounted cavalry to guard against some secret plot in St. Louis. I think the city police and militia could attend to all such machinations and leave us all our troops at this critical time.

W. T. SHERMAN,
Major General.

[Cipher telegram.]

HEADQUARTERS MILITARY DIVISION OF THE MISSISSIPPI,
In the field, Chattanooga, May 1, 1864.

General SCHOFIELD, *Charleston, Tennessee:*

Make all the preparations for your command to move to Cleveland and Red Clay. Run down to see me for a few hours, and we will go over all the maps and papers. Send orders for Stoneman and all your detachments to follow you, and get all your fighting force close in hand to move *via* Cleveland, Red Clay, &c.

W. T. SHERMAN,
Major General Commanding.

[Cipher telegram.]

HEADQUARTERS MILITARY DIVISION OF THE MISSISSIPPI,
In the field, Chattanooga, May 1, 1864.

Hon. JAS. GUTHRIE,
President Louisville and Nashville Railroad, Louisville, Kentucky:

I am aware of the diminution of your stock, and only ask that you do all that is possible: the next ten (10) days will be the test. We have enough stores at Nashville. We prefer veterans to new troops. Allen might send some of the latter around by boats up the Cumberland.

I ask that you do the best possible with your facilities to forward veterans, whose absence breaks up regiments and brigades. I think the emergency would warrant the stoppage of all civil business for ten (10) days. Every car and every locomotive south of Nashville is busy. I think you should keep your repair shops busy night and day. The business of your road will double and quadruple as the Cumberland falls, and your road can well profit by the fact by enlarging its capacity.

McCallum is doing all that is possible to increase the stock, but the numerous smashes-up of trains consume cars and locomotives faster than he can get new ones.

A long pull and a strong pull may carry us over this tide; after which I hope all will be well.

W. T. SHERMAN,
Major General Commanding.

[Cipher telegram.]

HEADQUARTERS MILITARY DIVISION OF THE MISSISSIPPI,
In the field, Chattanooga, May 1, 1864.

General GRANT, *Culpeper, Virginia:*

Schofield is now at Charleston, and will move to Cleveland. Thomas will concentrate at Ringgold, and McPherson's troops are all in motion towards Chattanooga, and by May 5th I will group them at Rossville and Gordon's Mills. The first move will be: Thomas, Tunnel Hill; Schofield, Catoosa Springs, and McPerson, Villanow. Next move will be battle.

I have Atlanta dates 29th of April. Enemy has a general idea of our plans, and are massing about Richmond and Dalton. Nothing new in the papers, except that General Polk reports, under date Demopolis, 23d April, that Wirt Adams had captured and burned a gunboat at Yazoo City, taking on shore eight 24-pounder guns. Weather fine; roads very good.

I leave John E. Smith's division at Huntsville and Decatur till Blair gets there with the 17th corps, when I will bring forward more men, according to the issues of our first battle. A good deal of the enemy's cavalry is hanging about north Alabama, and McPherson is uneasy about Decatur; but we must risk something. I have removed the bridge at Larkin's, and will try and get one of the new gunboats to patrol the river from Bridgeport down.

Thomas is here, but we will all go out on the 5th. I will expect further notice from you, but will agree to draw the enemy's fire within twenty-four hours of May 5th.

W. T. SHERMAN,
Major General.

[Cipher telegram.]

HEADQUARTERS MILITARY DIVISION OF THE MISSISSIPPI,
In the field, Chattanooga, May 2, 1864.

General McPHERSON, *Huntsville, Alabama:*

Colonel McCallum is now here. I have arranged for him to bring forward Sweeny's command of five thousand (5,000) men from Larkinsville, at eight (8) a. m., on Wednesday, 4th instant, and Veatch's command of five thousand (5,000) from Woodville at the same hour. Let them be there accordingly. Bring by cars one (1) battery per division and one wagon per regiment, if possible; also, horses for field officers; five (5) days' rations. All else to follow by the road.

W. T. SHERMAN,
Major General Commanding.

CULPEPER, *May* 2, 1864—3 p. m.

Major General SHERMAN, *Chattanooga, Tennessee:*

Move at the time indicated in my instructions; all will strike together.

U. S. GRANT, *Lieut. General.*

[Cipher telegram.]

HEADQUARTERS MILITARY DIVISION OF THE MISSISSIPPI,
In the field, Chattanooga, May 2, 1864.

General GRANT, *Culpeper, Virginia:*

Despatch of to-day received; all right; we will be on time.

W. T. SHERMAN,
Major General Commanding.

———

[Cipher telegram.]

HEADQUARTERS MILITARY DIVISION OF THE MISSISSIPPI,
In the field, Chattanooga, May 4, 1864—8.45 a. m.

General GRANT, *Culpeper, Virginia:*

Thomas has just started for Ringgold; all his command will be there to-night. Schofield is at Cleveland, moving down to Red Clay, and closing on Thomas's left. McPherson is here, and by night three divisions will be at Rossville; the other two will be there to-morrow, and all move to Thomas's right.

Thomas will have forty-five thousand (45,000;) Schofield thirteen thousand (13,000;) McPherson twenty thousand (20,000.)

W. T. SHERMAN,
Major General.

———

CLEVELAND, *May 4, 1864.*

Major General SHERMAN:

I go to Red Clay this afternoon. Will have my troops all there to-morrow, except those from Kentucky, and will be ready to move on the morning of May 6, 1864.

J. M. SCHOFIELD,
Major General.

———

[Cipher telegram.]

HEADQUARTERS MILITARY DIVISION OF THE MISSISSIPPI,
In the field, Chattanooga, May 4, 1864.

General THOMAS, *Ringgold, Georgia:*

Dodge's two divisions are coming in by the cars. Logan's three divisions are closed up on Geary, who is crossing the mountain at Whitesides, the Coal Mines, Trenton, and Dug Gap, to Lafayette, there to join McPherson.

We are one day behind time, but I will get McPherson to Gordon's Mills before we make any real demonstration. In the mean time get your troops well into position.

W. T. SHERMAN,
Major General Commanding.

———

RINGGOLD, *May 4, 1864.*

Major General SHERMAN:

Your two despatches of this evening are received. My troops are all in position now, with the exception of Geary's division, and that will be up to-morrow.

GEO. H. THOMAS, *Major General.*

[Telegram.]

HEADQUARTERS MILITARY DIVISION OF THE MISSISSIPPI,
In the field, Chattanooga, May 5, 1864.

A. LINCOLN, *President of the United States, Washington, D. C.:*

We have worked hard with the best talent of the country, and it is demonstrated that the railroad cannot supply the army and the people too. One or the other must quit, and the army don't intend to, unless Joe Johnston makes us. The issues to citizens have been enormous, and the same weight of corn or oats would have saved thousands of the mules, whose carcasses now corduroy the roads, and which we need so much.

We have paid back to Tennessee ten for one of provisions taken in war. I will not change my orders, and I beg of you to be satisfied that the clamor is partly humbug, and for effect; and to test it, I advise you to tell the bearers of the appeal, to hurry to Kentucky, and make up a caravan of cattle and wagons and come over the mountains by Cumberland Gap and Somerset, to relieve their suffering friends, on foot, as they used to do before a railroad was built. Tell them they have no time to lose. We can relieve all actual suffering by each company or regiment giving of their savings. Every man who is willing to fight and work gets a full ration, and all who won't fight or work should go away, and we offer them free passage in the cars.

W. T. SHERMAN,
Major General Commanding.

[Cipher telegram.]

HEADQUARTERS MILITARY DIVISION OF THE MISSISSIPPI,
In the field, Chattanooga, May 5, 1864.

General THOMAS, *Ringgold, Georgia:*

I will be out to-day; Schofield is at Red Clay; McPherson's head of column will be at Gordon's Mills to-night; everything is moving well.

W. T. SHERMAN,
Major General Commanding.

[Cipher telegram.]

HEADQUARTERS MILITARY DIVISION OF THE MISSISSIPPI,
In the field, Ringgold, Ga., May 5, 1864—7½ p. m.

General HALLECK, *Washington, D. C.:*

Telegraph to General Grant that I am here, and we have advanced our lines three (3) miles to-day. McPherson is one day behind. I will attack Tunnel Hill on Saturday, and in the mean time will occupy Johnston's whole attention.

W. T. SHERMAN,
Major General Commanding.

[Cipher despatch.]

HEADQUARTERS MILITARY DIVISION OF THE MISSISSIPPI,
In the field, Ringgold, Ga., May 5, 1864—7½ p. m.

General McPHERSON, *Chattanooga, Tenn.:*

Am here. Thomas has advanced his line three (3) miles. I want you all up at Gordon's Mills by to-morrow night. Don't leave Chattanooga till I give you full orders.

W. T. SHERMAN, *Major General.*

4 *

CHATTANOOGA, *May 5, 1864.*

Major General SHERMAN, *Ringgold, Ga.:*

Despatch received. Dodge's command, I presume, is well down towards Gordon's Mills to-night. I have not heard from him yet. Harrow's division is encamped near Rossville. Morgan L. Smith is in Lookout valley, and Osterhaus just behind him.

J. B. McPHERSON,
Major General.

HEADQUARTERS MILITARY DIVISION OF THE MISSISSIPPI,
In the field, Ringgold, Ga., May 5, 1864.

SIR: The position of our troops to-morrow night, the 6th instant, will be: Schofield at Red Clay, you at Ringgold, and McPherson at Gordon's Mills.

The plan of action will be: You move in force on Tunnel Hill; secure it and threaten Dalton in front, but do not attack its defences until further orders, unless the enemy assume the offensive against either of our wings, when all must attack directly in front towards the enemy's main army, and not without orders detach to the relief of the threatened wing. At the time you move against Tunnel Hill, McPherson will move to Ship's Gap and Villanow, and secure possession of Snake Creek Gap, from which he will operate vigorously against the enemy's flank, or line of communications between Tilton Station and Resaca. I want you with cavalry or infantry to feel well up Dog Wood valley, and communicate with McPherson at Villanow.

Trains likely to embarrass our movements should not be taken east of Taylor's ridge till we have observed the effect of these first movements.

I expect to be all ready to move on Saturday, and wish you to make all preparations accordingly.

I am, &c.,

W. T. SHERMAN,
Major General Commanding.

Major General THOMAS,
Comd'g Army of the Cumberland, Present.

HEADQUARTERS MILITARY DIVISION OF THE MISSISSIPPI,
In the field, Ringgold, Ga., May 5, 1864.

GENERAL: The enemy still lies about Dalton, seemingly on the defensive, his preparations being mostly against our approach from the north and west. I wish to give him little time for preparations and to assume the offensive on Saturday.

Thomas will move straight on Tunnel Hill; McPherson will move from Gordon's mills, via Rocky Spring, to Ship's Gap and Villanow; thence he will occupy Snake Creek Gap, and from that point operate on the enemy's flank if in motion, or against the railroad at some point between Tilton and Resaca.

I want you to keep up communication with Howard, and as he moves toward Tunnel Hill you move on Varnell's Station, inclining to your right so as to hold the road between Varnell's and Catoosa Springs. If you have reason to apprehend encountering a force superior to your own, you can cross the hills to your right and make for Catoosa. As you perceive I do not propose to attack Dalton from the north, but the west and south, therefore the movements should continue to Varnell's except with almost a certainty of the case I make of a superior force there.

Keep your columns as light as possible, your wagons over towards Parker's Gap, till the issue of the first battle is determined.

As soon as Tunnel Hill is secured to us, I shall pause to give McPherson time for his longer march, but we must occupy the attention of all the enemy lest he turn his whole force on McPherson, which must be prevented. Therefore on the sound of heavy battle always close up on Howard and act according to circumstances. We will not be able to detach to McPherson's assistance, but can press the enemy so close from this direction that he cannot detach but a part of his command against him.

I have reason to believe Johnston has sent most of his cavalry to north Alabama; but still you should guard against a cavalry sweep on that flank, which can best be done by keeping your columns compact.

I am, with much respect, yours truly,

W. T. SHERMAN, *Major General Commanding.*

Major General SCHOFIELD,
Commanding the Army of the Ohio, Red Clay, Georgia.

HEADQUARTERS MILITARY DIVISION OF THE MISSISSIPPI,

In the field, Ringgold, Georgia, May 5, 1864.

SIR: The enemy still lies about Dalton, and from all appearances is on the defensive, guarding approaches mostly from the north and west. He occupies in some force the range of hills known as the Tunnel Hill.

By to-morrow night our forces will be about as follows: Schofield at Red Clay; Thomas at Ringgold, his left at Catoosa Springs, centre at Ringgold, and right (Hooker) near Wood's Station, and you at Gordon's Mills.

If you are all ready, I propose on Saturday morning to move against the enemy—Thomas directly on Tunnel Hill; Schofield at Varnell's, and the gap between it and Catoosa Springs, feeling towards Thomas. Hooker will move through Nickajack Gap on Trickum and threaten the road which runs from Buzzard Roost to Snake Creek Gap. As these are in progress, I want you to move via Rock Spring and Tavern road to the head of Middle Chickamauga, then to Villanow, then to Snake Creek Gap, secure it, and from it make a bold attack on the enemy's flank, or his railroad, at any point between Tilton and Resaca.

I am in hopes that Garrard's cavalry will be at Villanow as soon as you, for you know I have sent General Corse to meet him at Shell Mound and conduct him across the mountain to Lafayette and to you. But in any event his movement will cover your right rear, and enable you to leave all encumbrances either at Ship's Gap or at Villanow, as you deem best. I hope the enemy will fight at Dalton, in which case he can have no force there that can interfere with you; but should his policy be to fall back along his railroad, you will hit him in flank. Do not fail in that event to make the most of the opportunity by the most vigorous attack possible, as it may save us what we have most reason to apprehend, a slow pursuit, in which he gains strength as we lose it. In either event you may be sure the forces north of you will prevent his turning on you alone. In the event of hearing the sounds of heavy battle about Dalton, the greater necessity for your rapid movement on the railroad. If broken to an extent that would take them some days to repair, you can withdraw to Snake Creek Gap and come to us, or await the development according to your judgment, or the information you may receive.

I want to put this plan in operation, beginning with Saturday morning if possible.

I am, with great respect,

W. T. SHERMAN, *Major General Commanding.*

Major General J. B. McPHERSON,
Commanding Army of the Tennessee.

[Cipher.]

HEADQUARTERS MILITARY DIVISION OF THE MISSISSIPPI,
In the field, Ringgold, Georgia, May 6, 1864—8½ a. m.

Meet one of my staff officers at Gordon's Mills this evening at sundown. I will send written orders and want a written reply.

Get your troops to Gordon's to night and be ready to move via Rocky Spring and the Tavern road to-morrow. I am not afraid of your not having wagons enough—I fear too many.

I have just heard that Steele's trains in Arkansas have been captured, and now I hope he will go ahead.

W. T. SHERMAN,
Major General Commanding.

General McPHERSON,
Chattanooga, Tennessee.

HEADQUARTERS MILITARY DIVISION OF THE MISSISSIPPI,
In the field, Ringgold, Georgia, May 6, 1864

General McPHERSON, *Commanding Army of the Tennessee:*

GENERAL: I have been to Catoosa Springs and have seen all of Thomas's command. It will move on Tunnel Hill to-morrow. General Schofield will move down to near Varnell's.

I want you to-morrow night about the head of Middle Chickamauga, near the word "Gordon," on the Tavern road, about the intersection of the Gordon Spring Gap road with the main road lying along the west base of Taylor's ridge. Next day at Villanow and Snake Creek Gap. Hooker to-morrow will be through Nickajack Gap, about Trickum, and will control the road from Buzzard Roost to Villanow. Thomas will have Tunnel Hill. I have dates from Dalton of the 4th. Johnston is there expecting our attack from the north. Let me hear from you as often as possible.

Yours,

W. T. SHERMAN,
Major General Commanding.

HEADQUARTERS MILITARY DIVISION OF THE TENNESSEE,
In the field, Ringgold, Georgia, May 6, 1864.

GENERAL: The general commanding directs me to say to you that he has sent Major McCoy, A. D. C., to General Schofield, with instructions similar in general design as those given you under date of last night, and also has sent Captain Audenreid to General McPherson at Gordon's Mills with like general instructions, and that he wants you to move with your force against the enemy upon Tunnel Hill at sunrise on the 7th, (to-morrow.)

He will accompany you during the operations.

Respectfully, yours,

L. M. DAYTON, *A. D. C.*

Major General GEO. H. THOMAS,
Commanding Army of the Cumberland, Ringgold, Georgia.

HEADQUARTERS MILITARY DIVISION OF THE MISSISSIPPI,
In the field, Ringgold, Georgia, May 6, 1864—9¾ p. m.

GENERAL: The general-in-chief directs me to say that he has received full and satisfactory replies from General McPherson and General Schofield, in answer to his letters of instruction given this day and last night, and given substantially to you verbally and otherwise to-day. Both are in the positions indicated for them and are fully ready to take the positions assigned for them to-morrow, viz: General McPherson near Ship's Gap, and General Schofield between Catoosa Springs and Varnell's.

I am, general, with much respect, yours truly,

L. M. DAYTON, *A. D. C.*

Major General GEO. H. THOMAS,
Commanding Army of the Cumberland, Ringgold, Georgia.

HEADQUARTERS MILITARY DIVISION OF THE MISSISSIPPI,
In the field, Tunnel Hill, Georgia, May 7, 1864—11¼ a. m.

Major General SCHOFIELD, *Near Catoosa Springs:*

We are in possession of Tunnel Hill with little or no resistance. I do not propose any more to-day, as we must give time to McPherson. Hooker should be at Trickum. Let your men bathe and rest. If your cavalry can hold Varnell's it is well, but don't risk much on that flank. The tunnel is not injured. I will send you orders for to-morrow later in the day. Study well the lay of the country and roads; especially see if Rocky Face ridge can be reached from your position.

Yours, &c.,

W. T. SHERMAN,
Major General Commanding.

HEADQUARTERS MILITARY DIVISION OF THE MISSISSIPPI,
In the field, Tunnel Hill, May 7, 1864—2 p. m.

General SCHOFIELD, *Near Catoosa Springs:*

Thomas took Tunnel Hill with scarcely any opposition. I have been all over it. It is a strong ridge, not as high as Taylor's, and looks right towards the break of Rocky Face ridge, through which pass the rail and common roads In this gorge is the Buzzard Roost, which is the place where Johnston expects to fight us. To-night McPherson will be at Ship's Gap, and next day should strike or threaten the railroad. To-morrow I want to occupy all of Johnston's attention. Thomas will threaten in front. I want you to hold well the gap towards Varnell's, and reconnoitre up the point of Rocky Face, near Lee's, on the ridge towards Buzzard Roost.

If possible, get some point where you can see Dalton, and I want to guard against the possibility of Johnston's turning on McPherson. Hooker is about Trickum. Reconnoitre the ridge to-night, and make a lodgement to-morrow morning, but don't be drawn into a battle.

Yours, &c.,

W. T. SHERMAN,
Major General Commanding.

Memorandum of movements for May 8, 1864.

HEADQUARTERS MILITARY DIVISION OF THE MISSISSIPPI,
In the field, Tunnel Hill, Georgia, May 7, 1864.

General Thomas to threaten the Buzzard Roost Pass; to occupy in force the Tunnel Hill ridge, the roads leading from Buzzard Roost towards Trickum and Catoosa, also to keep up communication with Villanow; the threats on Buzzard Roost not to lead to a battle unless the enemy comes out of his works; to get, if possible, a small force on Rocky Face ridge.

General Schofield to occupy the gap at Lee's and Varnell's, and to feel from Lee's along down Rocky Face to the enemy's signal station, if possible.

General McPherson to move through Villanow and to occupy Snake Creek Gap to its strongest point, and to get up Garrard's cavalry, if possible, for the next day's work.

If the enemy leave Buzzard Roost Gap, General Thomas will follow direct, and General Schofield through Lee's Gap towards Dalton, on the east side of Rocky Face ridge, viz., by Crow's Valley.

W. T. SHERMAN,
Major General Commanding.

———

[Cipher.]

HEADQUARTERS MILITARY DIVISION OF THE MISSISSIPPI,
In the field, Tunnel Hill, Georgia, May 8, 1864.

Major General HALLECK, *Washington, D. C.:*

Despatch of to-day received. Am delighted at the arrangement, and it shall receive my most hearty concurrence. I will telegraph very full to General Canby to-day at Cairo.

I have been all day reconnoitring the mountain range, through whose gap the railroad and common road pass. By to-night McPherson will be in Snake Creek Gap threatening Resaca, and to-morrow all will move to the attack. Army in good spirits and condition. I hope Johnston will fight here, instead of drawing me far down into Georgia.

W. T. SHERMAN,
Major General.

———

[Cipher.]

HEADQUARTERS MILITARY DISTRICT OF THE MISSISSIPPI,
In the field, Tunnel Hill, Georgia, May 8, 1864.

Major General CANBY,
Commanding Division of West Mississippi, Cairo, Illinois:

I am rejoiced that you are to command west of the Mississippi, and will heartily concur in anything that you may undertake.

A. J. Smith has his own division and the fragments of two others. I am willing you should have Smith permanently, but the other fragments should be sent to McPherson as soon as you can spare them. The garrisons of Columbus, Kentucky, Memphis, Tennessee, Vicksburg and Natchez, Mississippi, will be instructed, through General McPherson, commander of that department, to co-operate in anything you may undertake.

I can give you but little information, as Steele's reports are very meagre, and Banks does not report to me. Arkansas is the field of danger, and you should hasten there to see General Steele. His wagons having been captured by the enemy, he will need more ; but unless you have the control of the resources of Missouri and Kansas, you may not be able to cover them against raids. The firm possession of Alexandria and Little Rock would prevent the passage of the enemy to Missouri, but each point should be strong enough to act offensively. I would have no hesitation in seizing any horses and mules in the country and subsisting on the country, unless the people prevent raids and small guerilla operations. We must, of course, provide against organized armies, but can hold the country people responsible for the acts of guerillas. Such towns as Monroe, Alexandria, and Natchitoches should be held responsible for attacks on boats ; for if they fire on boats with women and children in, we can fire and burn houses with women and children.

At Memphis and Helena you will get all the information possible of the state of affairs since I left.

W. T. SHERMAN,
Major General.

[Cipher telegram.]

HEADQUARTERS MILITARY DIVISION OF THE MISSISSIPPI,
In the field, Tunnel Hill, Georgia, 8 p. m., May 9, 1864.

General HALLECK, Chief of Staff, Washington, D. C.:

We have been fighting all day against precipices and mountain gaps to keep Johnston's army busy, whilst McPherson could march to Resaca to destroy the railroad behind him. I heard from McPherson up to two (2) p. m., when he was within a mile and a half of the railroad. After breaking the road good, his orders are to retire to the mouth of Snake Creek Gap, and be ready to work on Johnston's flank in case he retreats south. I will pitch in again early in the morning. Fighting has been mostly skirmishing, and casualties small. McPherson has the army of the Tennessee, twenty-three thousand (23,000,) and only encountered cavalry, so that Johnston did not measure his strength at all.

W. T. SHERMAN,
Major General.

[Cipher telegram.]

HEADQUARTERS MILITARY DIVISION OF THE MISSISSIPPI,
In the field, Tunnel Hill, Ga., May 10, 1864—7 a. m.

Major General HALLECK, Washington, D. C:

I am starting for the extreme front in Buzzard Roost Gap, and make this despatch that you may understand Johnston acts purely on the defensive. I am attacking him on his strongest fronts, viz., west and north, till McPherson breaks his line at Resaca, when I will swing round through Snake Creek Gap and interpose between him and Georgia. I am not driving things too fast, because I want two columns of cavalry that are rapidly coming up to me from the rear—Stoneman on my left and Garrard on my right; both due to-day. Yesterday I pressed hard to prevent Johnston detaching against McPherson, but to-day I will be more easy, as I believe McPherson has destroyed Resaca, when he is ordered to fall back to the mouth of Snake Creek Gap and act against Johnston's flank when he does start. All are in good condition.

W. T. SHERMAN,
Major General.

HEADQUARTERS MILITARY DIVISION OF THE MISSISSIPPI,
In the field, Tunnel Hill, May 10, 1864.

GENERAL: I think you are satisfied that your troops cannot take Rocky Face Ridge, and also the attempt to put our columns into the jaws of Buzzard Roost would be fatal to us.

Two plans of action suggest themselves:

1st. By night to replace Schofield's present command by Stoneman's cavalry, which should be near at hand, and to rapidly move your entire army, the men along the base of John's Mountain by the Mill Creek road to Snake Creek Gap, and join McPherson, while the wagons are moved to Villanow. When we are joined to McPherson, to move from Sugar Valley on Resaca, interposing ourselves between that place and Dalton. Could your army and McPherson's surely whip Joe Johnston?

2d. I cast loose from the railroad altogether and move the whole army on the same objective point, leaving Johnston to choose his course.

Give orders for all your troops to be ready with three days' provisions, and to be prepared to march to-night. I expect to hear from McPherson and Schofield as to their situation, also as to the near approach of Stoneman. He was at Charleston yesterday, and is apprized of the necessity for haste. Do you think any danger to McPherson should make us delay one day?

Please give me the benefit of your opinion on these points.

Yours, &c.,

W. T. SHERMAN,
Major General Commanding.

Major General THOMAS, *Present.*

HEADQUARTERS MILITARY DIVISION OF THE MISSISSIPPI,
Tunnel Hill, Ga., May 10, 1864.

GENERAL: Keep your entire command ready to move to this place. McPherson did not break the railroad, although he reached Resaca, which he found fortified and manned. I may make one or two moves, and either or both very sudden, take up my whole command and move to Resaca, or leave you here with Stoneman's cavalry at the point now occupied by you, to cover this narrow outlet, and with Thomas to issue on the east of Rocky Face, at Sugar Valley, and interpose between Johnston and his base. The latter I prefer. If possible, hurry Stoneman, and write me your opinion.

Yours, &c.,

W. T. SHERMAN,
Major General Commanding.

Major General SCHOFIELD,
Rocky Face, &c.

HEADQUARTERS MILITARY DIVISION OF THE MISSISSIPPI,
In the field, Tunnel Hill, May 10, 1864.

GENERAL: I propose to leave hereabouts one (1) of your corps, say Howard's, the cavalry of Colonel McCook, and the cavalry of General Stoneman, to keep up the feint of a direct attack on Dalton through Buzzard Roost, as long as possible, and with all the remainder of the three armies to march to and through Snake Creek Gap, and to attack the enemy in force from that quarter.

You may at once commence the necessary preparations, and give orders that the force left here is to be under the command of the senior officer, who will strip his command light, sending all spare wagons to Ringgold; that the cars run daily to this point with daily supplies, but the main stores to be at Ringgold; that the cavalry watch well the passes north of Tunnel Hill, and at Ray's Gap, and that in case the enemy detect the diminution of the force and attack, it gradually withdraw in the direction of Ringgold, but defend that point at all costs; that a locomotive and construction train be kept here with orders, and prepared, if this retrograde movement be made necessary; that the party shall take up at intervals rails, so as to make a repair train necessary to replace them; this that the enemy may not have the track to facilitate his movement in pursuit. A few rails should at once be removed at some point east of the tunnel that can again be put down when we want it done.

The pass at Snake creek is represented as very narrow. Please instruct a division to be there to-morrow, provided with axes and spades, so to widen the road as to enable the passage of wagons; also to facilitate the march of troops by roads and paths outside the wagon track.

General Stoneman will be at Varnell's to-night, and by to-morrow night all his command will be in, so that we will calculate all to go to Snake Creek and close up on General McPherson during the day after to-morrow. As soon as General Stoneman comes, I will cause him to relieve Colonel McCook on that flank, so that you may send him to replace General Geary at Ray's road. Let the troops move as much under cover as possible; wagons going round by Villanow, and the troops by the Mill Creek road. General Schofield will either go round by Villanow or follow General Newton.

I am, &c.,

W. T. SHERMAN,
Major General Commanding.

Major General THOMAS,
Commanding Army of the Cumberland.

HEADQUARTERS MILITARY DIVISION OF THE MISSISSIPPI,
In the field, Tunnel Hill, Georgia, May 10, 1864.

GENERAL: I shall attack Johnston through Snake Creek Gap. I will take your three infantry divisions along, but for the time will have to leave General Stoneman to guard the point now occupied by you, and to keep up a delusion as long as posssible. I propose to leave General Howard here so light and so familiar with the ground that Johnston cannot strike him. I have made some orders accordingly, and without attracting too much attention you may prepare to move about the day after to-morrow by Villanow and the gap.

It may be necessary to start in the night to avoid being seen. Get all your wagons in the best order possible, and send for Stoneman to come over to see me. I want to give him some personal instructions.

I regret I cannot, under the circumstances, relieve General Hovey, because I know General Grant esteems him, and gave him the promise of this division. He was peculiarly noted in the affair at Champion Hills, and had quite a name as brigadier.

I do not propose to keep any supplies here, but to send all that are not issued back to Ringgold, and if the enemy are drawn here, we will make short work of them at Dalton. I propose to take McPherson, twenty-three thousand (23,000;) General Thomas, thirty thousand, (30,000,) and you twelve thousand, (12,000,) with Garrard's cavalry at Villanow; McCook between this and Villanow, and General Stoneman north of the tunnel. On the contrary, I am glad to have you at all times give me your unqualified opinion freely and fully.

Call in the regiment at Red Clay, and continue the force at Charleston to keep on the north bank and guard the bridge. General Thomas will instruct the Cleveland garrison, and I will have a construction train run down to Var nell's and take up a train load of iron, and run it into Chattanooga, so that the enemy cannot use the road whilst we are south of them.

Chattanooga cannot be taken by Johnston with us on his heels. I will risk that.

I think all the chances are in favor of the move. General McPherson is already there; General Hooker has gone in support, and the defences of Dalton will not avail Johnston if we interpose between him and Georgia. Buzzard Roost is as hard to pass out as in.

Yours, &c.,

W. T. SHERMAN, *Major General Commanding.*

Major General SCHOFIELD,
Commanding Army of the Ohio.

I wish you would have Stoneman come to see me the moment you can. He can bring his cavalry near you and send here for corn.

W. T. S.

HEADQUARTERS MILITARY DIVISION OF THE MISSISSIPPI,
In the field, Tunnel Hill, May 10, 1864.

GENERAL: The Buzzard Roost Gap is so well defined, and naturally is so strong, that I will undertake to attack Johnston through Snake Creek Gap in this manner:

General Hooker's corps is ordered already to support you; his troops will arrive to-morrow and next day, and will be instructed to widen and improve the road through the gap, so that wagons may pass going and coming, and troops may march by paths alongside. You had better do this at your end of the gap at once. Another corps of General Thomas's (Palmer's) will follow and then General Schofield's. We expect all to be in motion the day after to-morrow, and to mask the movement as much as possible. General Howard will remain here with his corps, and will keep up the feint till the last moment, and if forced back will be prepared to do so, having sent back in advance all his supply wagons, and all incumbrances. He will have a small division of cavalry to watch the road between this and Snake Creek Gap, the same where General Geary now is, and Stoneman with two brigades of cavalry to his north and east.

This force will cover us to the north; Garrard's newly arrived cavalry will guard to the south and west, and we must take care of ourselves.

Once through the gap, I would interpose between Johnston and Resaca, and may, if it can be done quick, attack Resaca or Johnston. In the mean time, mask your own force as much as possible, but hold your own, and look well to secure the mountain range to the east and north. A single peak held by a regiment becomes a key to the whole range. I wish you to calculate to have ten days' supplies, and to send your wagons to the rear, not to come up till the time expires, or you order them.

I have a note from General Schofield, who says that one brigade of General Stoneman got to Cleveland to-day, and another will to-morrow, so that we may not be able to put our project in operation by the day after to-morrow, but we will get all ready. We can give you supplies here. If you think it practicable you may order General Kilpatrick to make a strike at the railroad. If Johnston passes down, can't you hit him in flank, or has he too many roads? Can't you get a road or find a way from the mouth of the valley across three or four miles north of Resaca? Do you think Johnston has yet discovered the nature of your force? Write me fully.

Yours, &c.,

W. T. SHERMAN, *Major General Commanding.*

Major General McPHERSON,
Commanding Army of the Tennessee.

[Cipher.]

HEADQUARTERS MILITARY DIVISION OF THE MISSISSIPPI,
In the field, Tunnel Hill, Georgia, May 10, 1864.

Major General HALLECK, *Washington, D. C.:*

General McPherson reached Resaca but found the place strongly fortified and guarded, and did not break the road. According to his instructions, he drew back to the débouche of the gorge, where he has a strong defensive position and guards the only pass into the valley of the Oostanaula available to us. Buzzard Roost Gap, through which the railroad passes, is naturally and artificially too strong to be attempted. I must feign on Buzzard Roost, but pass through Snake Creek Gap and place myself between Johnston and Resaca, where we will have to fight it out. I am making the preliminary move. Certain that Johnston can make no detachments, I will be in no hurry. My cavalry is just approaching from Kentucky and Tennessee, detained by the difficulty of getting horses and even now it is less than my minimum.

W. T. SHERMAN, *Major General Commanding.*

HEADQUARTERS MILITARY DIVISION OF THE MISSISSIPPI,
In the field, Tunnel Hill, Georgia, May 11, 1864.

GENERAL: I received by courier, in the night, yours of 5 and 6.30 p. m. of yesterday. You will also during the night have come to the same conclusion.

You now have your twenty-three thousand, (23,000,) and General Hooker is in close support, so that you can hold all Joe Johnston's army in check should he abandon Dalton. He can't afford to abandon Dalton, for he has fixed it up so well for us, and he observes we are close at hand waiting for him to quit. He can't afford a detachment strong enough to fight you, as his army will not admit of it.

Strengthen your position, fight anything that comes, and threaten the safety of the railroad all the time. But to tell the truth, I would rather he would stay in Dalton two more days, when he may find a larger party than he expects in an open field. At all events we can then choose our ground, and he will be forced to move out of his works. I do not intend to put a column into Buzzard Roost Gap at present.

See that you are in easy communication with me and all headquarters. After to-day the supplies will be at Ringgold.

Yours,

W. T. SHERMAN,
Major General Commanding.

Major General McPHERSON,
Commanding Army of the Tennessee, Sugar Valley, Georgia.

HEADQUARTERS MILITARY DIVISION OF THE MISSISSIPPI,
In the field, Tunnel Hill, Georgia, May 11, 1864.

GENERAL : The indications are that Johnston is evacuating Dalton. In that event, Howard's and the cavalry will pursue, and all the rest will follow your route. I will be down early in the morning.

Try to strike him if possible about the forks of the roads.

Hooker must be with you now, and you might send General Garrard by Somerville to threaten Rome and that flank. I will cause all the lines to be felt at once.

W. T. SHERMAN,
Major General Commanding.

General McPHERSON, *Sugar Valley.*

HEADQUARTERS MILITARY DIVISION OF THE MISSISSIPPI,
In the field, near Resaca, May 13, 1864—2¼ p. m.

General THOMAS, *Commanding Army of the Cumberland:*

Until I hear that Joe Johnston is south of the Oostanaula, I would not cross at Lay's; we must first interpose between Dalton and Resaca, threatening the latter all the time. I want Hooker right and McPherson left strong until we encounter Johnston, who has not yet got below Resaca I think. If he retreat east we have the advantage. I want the pontoons up and to secure the railroad on Hooker's right. Palmer should join on to Hooker and Hooker should be strong.

W. T. SHERMAN,
Major General Commanding.

HEADQUARTERS MILITARY DIVISION OF THE MISSISSIPPI,
In the field, Snake Creek Gap, May 13, 1864.

Major General THOMAS, *Commanding, &c.:*

I want the pontoon bridge laid at the best point near Lay's ferry, near the mouth of Lick or Snake Creek. I enclose a sketch made to-day by a seemingly intelligent officer.

As soon as I know the pontoons have started down the road, I will send all the cavalry here to cross the bridge and will order all of General Schofield's army to move as soon as it is demonstrated Johnston has actually retreated.

In the mean time turn the train toward the mouth of Snake Creek, and after an hour's work about daylight we can discover whether the rebel army proposes to fight us or not at or near Resaca.

Contemporaneous with laying the double bridge, I will order Garrard to move down to all the passes towards Rome to disturb them in flank.

Please give the necessary directions that the pontoon be carried down Snake Creek valley under a good escort, and to be held about a mile back of view till it be ordered to the bank. The sketch indicates Tanner's.

At daylight I want you from the extreme left of your army (General Palmer's) to swing into the railroad and General Hooker hold pretty strong on his own ground, and the instant my mind is clear that Johnston will not do his fighting here, I will turn General Schofield toward the pontoon at Lay's or Tanner's. Let your engineer copy this sketch and return it.

Send orders round to General Howard to pass down the valley, keeping his main force down by the Rome road and the cavalry down by the railroad.

W. T. SHERMAN,
Major General Commanding.

HEADQUARTERS MILITARY DIVISION OF THE MISSISSIPPI,
In the field, Snake Creek Gap, May 13, 1864.

General STONEMAN, *Commanding Cavalry:*

Your note of to-day was received; very good indeed. Press down the valley strong and communicate with me. Your messenger will find me where there is most noise of artillery or near Resaca. You can safely move on parallel roads by brigades. Let your packs follow on the heels of the column. Pick up whatever of provisions and plunder you can.

W. T. SHERMAN,
Major General Commanding.

HEADQUARTERS MILITARY DIVISION OF THE MISSISSIPPI,
In the field, near Resaca, May 13, 1864—11 p. m.

GENERAL: At daybreak send a regiment of infantry towards Dalton, about three (3) miles to the point near Swamp creek, where the Rome and Calhoun roads come together, and where General Palmer is ordered to send a regiment from this quarter. At the same time let a good staff officer with a regiment make a road across to us from the head of your column, to the left of our present line of battle, which you may estimate as on this (the Calhoun) road, two miles north of Resaca. In case of heavy battle, and your picket at the Swamp creek end reports no heavy force of infantry, come across to support General Thomas. In case you hear no sounds of heavy battle, get all ready to move with celerity down Snake Creek Valley to its mouth, near which, to-morrow, I will lay the double pontoon bridge. I propose you shall pass the Oostanaula first with your three divisions.

W. T SHERMAN,
Major General Commanding.

General SCHOFIELD,
Commanding Army of Ohio.

HEADQUARTERS MILITARY DIVISION OF THE MISSISSIPPI,
In the field, near Resaca, May 14—1864.

GENERAL: As I wrote you last night, I intended to cross the Oostanaula, south by your left, but Schofield has swung round so far to the north or left that time will be lost.

The pontoons will be in an hour or so at a point on Snake creek, near its mouth, with Captain Merrill, United States engineers, in charge. Send one division immediately with the necessary artillery, to effect a lodgement on the other side, under direction of your engineer, and as the day develops send other divisions in order, so as to march out from the Oostanaula, from about Lay's ferry on Rome, keeping the right. You may begin the march at once, and follow it up as fast as it is demonstrated that Johnston has retreated *in fact*. He left nothing at Dalton, and moves in too much order for a retreat. Therefore be duly cautious, but prompt to engage. If a part of your command gets into Resaca, withdraw it to General Thomas, who will continue to follow substantially the railroad to Kingston.

A division of cavalry under General Corse has already gone down along the Oostanaula to hold all the crossing places. I will send General Garrard from Villanow, by Dirt town and Dry creek, to cross the Oostanaula above Rome. All this cavalry will be on your right. Howard and Stoneman were last night close on the rear guard, about Swampy.

W. T. SHERMAN,
Major General Commanding.

General McPHERSON,
Commanding Army of Tennessee.

HEADQUARTERS MILITARY DIVISION OF THE MISSISSIPPI,
In the field, near Ressaca, Ga., May 14, 1864—8¼ a. m.

GENERAL: Your despatch of this 7 a. m. is received. Your position is a good one and you may retain it, connecting strong with General Palmer or General Thomas.

I suppose General Howard will come on to your rear as support, in conse quence of our line having swung around to the right.. I will move south by the right flank. I have sent Captain Poe to explain, so you will remain as now, and General McPherson will secure a crossing at Lay's and operate on the enemy's line of retreat. All well here.

W. T. SHERMAN,
Major General Commanding.

Major General SCHOFIELD,
    Commanding Army of Ohio.

HEADQUARTERS MILITARY DIVISION OF THE MISSISSIPPI,
In the field, near Resaca, May 14, 1864.

GENERAL: By the flank movement on Resaca we have forced Johnston to evacuate Dalton, and we are on his flank and rear, but the parallelism of the valleys and mountains does not give us all the advantage of an open country, but I will press him all that is possible. Weather fine and troops in fine order. All is working well and as fast as possible.

I have announced in orders Mr. Stanton's despatch as to the victory of Spottsylvania. Let us keep the ball rolling.

W. T. SHERMAN,
Major General Commanding.

General HALLECK,
    Washington, D. C.

[Cipher.]

HEADQUARTERS MILITARY DIVISION OF THE MISSISSIPPI,
In the field, near Resaca, May 14, 1864—8 p. m.

Major General HALLECK, Washington, D. C.

We have had hard fighting all day. Johnston purely on the defensive. The place has small detached redoubts and an immense amount of rifle trenches. We have closed the enemy well in, gaining ground slowly, but surely, all day. The country is very rough and woody. I will renew the attack at all points to-morrow, and continue till Johnston retreats, and then shall follow. General Sweeney's division, 16th corps, with a pontoon train tried to cross the Oostanaula at Lay's ferry, below Calhoun, but was stoutly opposed by a heavy force in the dense timber, on the opposite bank. General Howard's corps followed the enemy down from Dalton, and his right now joins to our main line, and my forces are all united, the line extending from the Oostanaula above to below the town. General Stoneman's cavalry division is on the east of the river, and General Garrard's division of cavalry is sent round by the right to cross the Oostanaula above Rome, if possible, and break the railroad north of Kingston.

W. T. SHERMAN,
Major General Commanding.

HEADQUARTERS MILITARY DIVISION OF THE MISSISSIPPI,
In the field, near Resaca, May 14, 1864.

GENERAL: Your despatch of $6\frac{1}{2}$ p. m. is received, and the general-in-chief is well satisfied. If you can move your force to-morrow over on to the Coosa-wattee into a strong position, and send a force sufficient to break the railroad below Resaca, you will please the general very much. He says not to risk your command too much, nor too much of it, but break the railroad good, if possible, and do the enemy all the damage you can.

L. M. DAYTON, Aide-de-Camp.

Major General STONEMAN,
Commanding Cavalry.

[Cipher.]

HEADQUARTERS MILITARY DIVISION OF THE MISSISSIPPI,
In the field, near Resaca, May 15, 1864.

Major General HALLECK, Washington, D. C.:

We have been fighting all day, pressing the enemy, and gaining substantial advantage at all points. We will strengthen the line of circumvallation so as to spare a large force to operate across the Oostanaula, below Resaca. Two pontoon bridges are over at Lay's ferry. The enemy attacked the brigade thrown across to cover the bridge, but was handsomely repulsed, leaving forty (40) dead. I cannot estimate our dead and wounded, up to this hour, but it will not fall much short of three thousand, (3,000.) The cars now run down to within seven (7) miles of us, and we have every facility to provide for the wounded.

The troops fight well, and everything works smoothly. We intend to fight Joe Johnston until he is satisfied, and I hope he will not attempt to escape; if he does, my bridges are down, and we will be after him. The country is mountainous and heavily wooded, giving the party on the defensive every advantage, and our losses result mostly from sharpshooters and ambush firing.

W. T. SHERMAN,
Major General Commanding.

[Cipher.]

HEADQUARTERS MILITARY DIVISION OF THE MISSISSIPPI,
In the field, near Resaca, May 16, 1864.

GENERAL: Despatch a good division down the old Rome road, which passes down the west of the Oostanaula, four (4) miles west of this, to Farmer's bridge, which is eight (8) miles north of Rome. There will be found General Garrard's train of artillery, which he will leave there while he operates against the flank of Johnston's retreating army.

Order the division to leave its train to follow its corps, and to cross the Oostanaula and move towards Kingston till it rejoins its own corps, whose route of march will be on Kingston. Take the division from that corps—say Palmer's, Baird's, or Jeff. Davis's—which will, I suppose, be your right flank as you move south, and can most easily effect its junction.

I want this division to move at once, and rapidly. The bridge is standing.

W. T. SHERMAN,
Major General Commanding.

General THOMAS,
Commanding Army Cumberland, Present.

[Cipher.]

HEADQUARTERS MILITARY DIVISION OF THE MISSISSIPPI,
In the field, Resaca, May 16, a. m.

Major General HALLECK, *Washington, D. C.:*

We are in possession of Resaca. It is a strongly fortified position, besides being a strong natural position. We saved the common road bridge, but the railroad bridge is burned. The railroad is good to this point, and our cars will run here to-day. Our columns are now crossing the Oostanaula—General McPherson at Lay's ferry, General Thomas here, and General Schofield about New Town.

We will pursue smartly to the Etowah. Generals Stoneman's and Garrard's cavalry are trying to get in rear of the enemy, and I hope will succeed. Our difficulties will increase beyond the Etowah, but if Johnston will not fight us behind such works as we find here, I will fight him on any open ground he may stand at. All well and in high spirits. We have about a thousand prisoners and eight (8) guns.

W. T. SHERMAN,
Major General Commanding.

HEADQUARTERS MILITARY DIVISION OF THE MISSISSIPPI,
In the field, Resaca, May 16, 1864.

GENERAL: I will attend General Thomas's army to-morrow, and expect to be at or beyond Adairsville to-morrow night. I wish you to push somewhat, and to be as near abreast as possible. I expect you will cross Coosawattee by one or the other of the fords about Field's, and to move *via* Big Spring to near the point where so many roads seem to centre, about four (4) miles east of Alexandria.

Yours, truly,

W. T. SHERMAN,
Major General Commanding.

Major General SCHOFIELD,
Commanding Army of Ohio

HEADQUARTERS MILITARY DIVISION OF THE MISSISSIPPI,
In the field, Resaca, May 16, 1864.

GENERAL: I will attend General Thomas's army to-morrow, and hope to reach Adairsville. You had better mass your men a little in front of Calhoun, and when you know Thomas is advancing south of Calhoun, keep abreast or a little ahead of him. I presume you are all across the Oostanaula. You may order the pontoon train to take up the bridges and follow you to the Etowah. General Thomas has a trestle-bridge here, one pontoon, and one made on the wreck of the railroad bridge, yet the passage has been slower than I estimated. I will push the column to-morrow. General Hooker is off to the left, somewhere, but not at New Town.

The road laid down on the cloth map by McGuire's and Woodland is your true course, provided the enemy has, on my theory, retreated on Alatoona. Bear in mind that General Garrard's cavalry is in your front, and that General Jeff. Davis's division of the 14th corps is on the west bank of the Oostanaula, approaching a bridge eight (8) miles above Rome. His route will bring him by McGuire's and Woodland.

Be sure to communicate your position to-morrow night, and if you fire signal-guns, with five minutes intervals, I will understand it as your head of column.

I am, &c.,

W. T. SHERMAN,
Major General Commanding.

General J. B. McPHERSON,
Commanding Army of Tennessee.

[Cipher.]

HEADQUARTERS MILITARY DIVISION OF THE MISSISSIPPI,
In the field, Resaca, May 17, 1864.

Major General HALLECK, *Washington, D. C.:*

Get Captain Merrill's map at the chief engineer's office, as I use it in my despatches.

General McPherson is all across the Oostanaula, at Lay's ferry, and is out abreast of Calhoun.

General Thomas is across here, where we have improvised three (3) bridges, and General Schofield has passed the Connasauga at Fite's ferry, and will pass the Coosawattee near Field's. To-night I propose my three heads of columns to be abreast of Adairsville. Johnston will be compelled to fight on this side of the Etowah, or be forced to divide his army, or give up either Rome or Alatoona. If he attempts to hold both, I will break the line at Kingston. If he concentrates at Kingston, I will break his railroads, right and left, and will fight him square in front. My belief is he will abandon Kingston and Rome, and retire on Alatoona, beyond the Etowah, in which case I will fix up my roads to Kingston, and then determine in what manner to advance beyond the Etowah. It will take five days to repair the railroad bridge here. We are abundantly supplied, and our animals are improving on the grass and grain fields, which now afford good pasture.

I start in person now for Adairsville. I think everything has progressed and is progressing as favorably as we could expect, but I know we must have one or more bloody battles such as have characterized General Grant's terrific struggles. Johnston has Hardee's, Hood's, and Polk's corps, with irregulars and militia on his lines of communication.

His cavalry outnumbers ours, but acts on the defensive.

W. T. SHERMAN,
Major General.

HEADQUARTERS MILITARY DIVISION OF THE MISSISSIPPI,
In the field, near Adairsville, May 17, 1864.

GENERAL: It is probable, on reaching Adairsville in the early morning, we will find the enemy has retreated, *via* Cassville. If such be the case, I want you to put your head of column after him as far as Cassville, when I will determine whether to continue the pursuit as far as Cartersville, or let him go. I prefer he should divide between Rome and Cartersville, in which event you will march directly on Kingston. I will be with you in the morning, and only mention these points that you may instruct your leading division. I wish you would put one of your boldest division commanders to lead to-morrow, and explain to him that General McPherson is close on his right, and General Schofield on his left, and that two heavy columns of cavalry, Garrard's and Stoneman's, have

5*

orders to strike the road; the one between Kingston and Rome, and the other between Kingston and Cartersville.

Instead of skirmishing only with the rear guard, it should be attacked promptly by his whole division, deployed in whole or part, according to the ground, but it should be preceeded by the usual skirmish line.

A real battle to-morrow might save us much work at a later period.

Yours, &c.,

W. T. SHERMAN,
Major General Commanding.

Major General THOMAS,
Commanding Army and Department of Cumberland.

HEADQUARTERS MILITARY DIVISION OF THE MISSISSIPPI,
Near Adairsville, evening, May 17, 1864.

GENERAL: I send my aid, Captain Audenreid, to you, who will tell you all you wish to know. I fear you have got your cavalry too far east to do much good at this time. Instead of going up the Selahquat, the Pine Log would have been better. I want you to-morrow night to strike the enemy in flank, between Cassville and Cartersville, or Etowah bridge, (railroad;) a small section of the road should be broken, enough to take a couple of days to mend.

It is also important that you should measure your fighting qualities with the enemy's cavalry about Cassville. I am sure you can beat them, but it should be done suddenly, so as to produce a salutary effect, and be a moral force to you in after operations. If you need it, General Schofield will give you McCook's cavalry, but whatever is done should be done to-morrow.

W. T. SHERMAN,
Major General Commanding.

Major General STONEMAN,
Commanding Cavalry.

HEADQUARTERS MILITARY DIVISION OF THE MISSISSIPPI,
In the field, evening, May 17, 1864.

GENERAL: Captain Poe is here, and has explained your difficulties. I want your head of column up at the intersection of the roads, about four (4) miles east of Adairsville, as early as possible, always with the standing order, that if you hear the sounds of serious battle you turn toward it; otherwise, shape your course towards Kingston.

General Thomas's head of column is against a pretty stubborn rear guard, which fights at every point, and as he can present nothing but a head of column, the enemy delays us, and saves the time he needs to remove his stores and army. It may be to-morrow I will turn your column to Cassville, and the railroad due south of Cassville, with a view to strike the flank of a retreating army; but unless you get such orders from me, incline towards Kingston with your infantry, but send McCook's cavalry to Cassville and the railroad, giving him always your head of infantry as a *point d'appui* in case he encounters a very superior force; but tell McCook that it is all-important to the cavalry arm to impress the enemy with a fear of him, as it will be an element of strength in our future operations.

Kingston is our present objective point, and from there I will make new dispositions.

Yours, &c.,

W. T. SHERMAN,
Major General Commanding.

Major General SCHOFIELD,
Commanding Army of Ohio.

HEADQUARTERS MILITARY DIVISION OF THE MISSISSIPPI,
Near Adairsville, May 17, 1864—12 m.

General McPHERSON, *Commanding Army of the Tennessee:*

Come *via* Adairsville, but try and keep on some road west of the railroad. This road now is almost blocked with men, wagons, &c. I am not surprised that you were in doubt whether we were in battle or skirmish. Our troops will fire away so much powder; but it was pretty smart skirmishing, and has cost us over a hundred wounded, though I still believe it was a rear guard covering the movement of trains.

Yours, &c.,

W. T. SHERMAN,
Major General Commanding.

HEADQUARTERS MILITARY DIVISION OF THE MISSISSIPPI,
In the field, near Adairsville, May 17, 1864—6¼ p. m.

General McPHERSON, *Commanding Army of the Tennessee:*

Direct your march early to-morrow to Adairsville, and order Garrard and the cavalry of Colonel Murray to make a dash on the railroad between Rome and Kingston (if not already done) *to-night.*

General Stoneman is on the other flank, and will attempt to break the road between Kingston and Etowah bridge. If not done to-night there will be no use of doing it at all, as I take it the enemy is trying to make time to save his material from his army and from Rome. I take it for granted General Garrard is near you. We wont go into Adairsville to-night.

W. T. SHERMAN,
Major General Commanding.

[Cipher.]

HEADQUARTERS MILITARY DIVISION OF THE MISSISSIPPI,
In the field, Adairsville, Georgia, May 18, 1864.

Major General HALLECK, *Washington, D. C.:*

Johnston passed last night here. We overtook him at sundown yesterday, and skirmished heavily with his rear till dark. In the morning he was gone, and we are after him. By to-night all the heads of column will be near Kingston, whither Johnston is moving. Whether he proposes to fight there or not we cannot tell, but to-morrow will know, for I propose to attack him wherever he may be. Our cavalry has not yet succeeded in breaking the railroad to his rear.

I now have four heads of column, all directed on Kingston, with orders to be within four miles by night. Weather fine, roads good, and the country more open and less mountainous.

W. T. SHERMAN,
Major General.

HEADQUARTERS MILITARY DIVISION OF THE MISSISSIPPI,
In the field, 3½ miles from Kingston, May 18, 1864—10½ p. m.

GENERAL: Yours of 1 p. m. is at hand. I was in hopes you would be further ahead by to-night, but the roads are not suited to a concentric movement on Kingston, and we must approach the game as near as the case admits of.

All the signs continue of Johnston's having retreated on Kingston, and why he should lead to Kingston if he designs to cover his trains to Cartersville I do not see, but it is probable he has sent to Alatoona all he can by cars, and his wagons are escaping south of the Etowah by the bridge and fords near Kingston. In any hypothesis our plan is right.

All of General Thomas's command will follow his trail straight; let it lead to the fords or towards Alatoona. You must shape your course to support General Hooker and strike the line of railway to his left. As soon as you can march in the morning, get up to General Hooker and act according to the developments. If we can bring Johnston to battle this side of Etowah we must do it, even at the hazard of beginning battle with but a part of our forces. If you hear the sounds of battle, direct your course so as to come up to the left of General Thomas's troops. If Johnston has got beyond Etowah, we will take two days to pick up fragments from Rome to Etowah. You will, in that event, still bear to the left and help General Stoneman, who should now be on the railroad somewhere between Cassville and Cartersville. I will be at Kingston.

> Yours,

W. T. SHERMAN,
Major General Commanding.

General SCHOFIELD,
> *Army of the Ohio, Montiller's Hill.*

HEADQUARTERS MILITARY DIVISION OF THE MISSISSIPPI,
In the field, near Kingston, Georgia, May 18, 1864—10½ p. m.

GENERAL: Early in the morning drop your wagons under escort, and move your entire command ready to deploy forward for battle on Kingston, and it may be to one or more of the crossing-places of the Etowah near that place. General Thomas will continue to follow the broad, well-marked trail of Johnston's army, and you must act on his right, according to our general plan. Johnston may get his wagons across Etowah, and fight us this side, trying to fall on one or other of our columns. General Hooker is now within three miles of Cassville, and General Schofield is to his rear, with orders to come up on his left. Until we ascertain the course of the enemy after reaching Kingston, we cannot do better. The rear of Johnston's infantry could not have reached Kingston before one (1) p. m. to-day.

W. T. SHERMAN,
Major General.

General McPHERSON,
> *Commanding Army of the Tennessee, on Barnsley Creek.*

HEADQUARTERS MILITARY DIVISION OF THE MISSISSIPPI,
In the field, near Kingston, May 18, 1864—10½ p. m.

GENERAL: Until we know exactly the course taken by Johnston from Kingston, I cannot make orders more exact than those already existing. You are now on the plain, well-marked trail of the enemy. You will early in the morning renew the pursuit, following this trail till it leads beyond the Etowah or gets to the eastward of Cassville, when you will relinquish pursuit unless otherwise ordered. General Schofield now is behind General Hooker, and is ordered early in the morning to close up and come up on his left. Let all your troops be in advance of all wagons, save ambulances and a moderate number of ammunition wagons, and order the enemy to be attacked if found. General

McPherson should now be at Woodland, and General Hooker about Two Run creek, and can easily join you at Kingston by eight (8) or nine (9) a. m.   I hope Generals Garrard and Stoneman have done good work to-day.   I will attend your column to-morrow.   Order up the pontoons, and ascertain the whereabouts of General Jeff. C. Davis as soon as possible.

Yours, &c.,

W. T. SHERMAN,
Major General Commanding.

Major General THOMAS,
Commanding Army of the Cumberland, Present.

HEADQUARTERS MILITARY DIVISION OF THE MISSISSIPPI,
In the field, near Kingston, May 18, 1864—12 m.

GENERAL: I despatched a courier to you at 10½, ordering you early in the morning to move on Kingston, to which point General Thomas will also move, and where I will meet you.   I now have General Garrard's report, and hope he is right in his conclusion that many locomotives and cars are west of the break in the railroad.   Let General Garrard send a detachment of about one hundred (100) men to Rome and to hunt up General Jeff. Davis; also, in case of Rome being in our possession or evacuated, to scour the country west of Barnsley's creek as far as Oostanaula for prisoners, deserters, wagons, horses, &c.

Let General Garrard with all his cavalry, a section of guns, but no wagons, move at the same time with you on the point of Etowah river about two (2) miles west of Kingston, just below the mouth of Connasene creek, where a bridge or ferry is represented; then in succession the other bridges and ferries supposed to be south of Kingston, and as far east as the road leading from the Saltpetre cave to Euharlee mill, and as much further as he thinks he can achieve anything, trying at all those points to make captures and boats if possible.   He may count on our attacking Kingston, if not already abandoned, as also Cassville and its railroad station.

General Stoneman should to-day have struck the same railroad near Cartersville, by which we cannot fail to make many captures of men and material to-morrow.

Tell General Garrard to ride hard and do much to-morrow, with the promise of a two days' rest, and plenty of forage up by the cars by the day after to-morrow. In the mean time, the pastures are all he could ask.

I am, &c.,

W. T. SHERMAN,
Major General Commanding.

General McPHERSON,
Commanding Army of Tennessee, Barnsley Creek.

HEADQUARTERS MILITARY DIVISION OF THE MISSISSIPPI,
In the field, Kingston, Georgia, May 19, 1864.

GENERAL: General Thomas is passing through Kingston to the east, and will put the head of his column four miles east of the town, where a mill is represented on Two Run creek.   General Hooker will join him at that point. I want you to put the head of your column at Cassville depot, your line facing east, and if you are in communication with General Stoneman put him toward Etowah bridge, (Pettit's creek.)   General Garrard will move south of the railroad, and will come up on your right.   General McPherson will halt here on Connasene for the present.   Report to me your arrival, and also the distance to Pettit's creek, to Cartersville, and Etowah bridge.

Yours, &c.,

W. T. SHERMAN,
Major General Commanding.

General SCHOFIELD, *near Cassville.*

HEADQUARTERS MILITARY DIVISION OF THE MISSISSIPPI,
In the field, Kingston, May 19, 1864.

GENERAL : I feel certain that Johnston, after the affair at Resaca, does not want to fight us in the comparatively open ground this side of Cartersville.

I send with this, orders for General Schofield, which are a repetition of orders heretofore sent him by courier, to press down to the road, and to order General Stoneman to secure the passage of Pettit's creek this side of Cartersville.   General Garrard's cavalry is now at the bridge across Etowah, and Murray is coming to you to connect with General Hooker.   Do you want General McPherson forward ?   He has his troops so he can advance by two roads.   Send me word. I will come forward in that event.   Connect with General Hooker, and, if possible, crush or capture any force that is, as I think, caught between General Stoneman and you.

Yours, truly,

W. T. SHERMAN,
Major General Commanding.

General THOMAS,
Commanding Army of Cumberland.

HEADQUARTERS MILITARY DIVISION OF THE MISSISSIPPI,
In the field, Kingston, Georgia, May 20, 1864—1 a. m.

GENERAL : My instructions for you to move toward Cassville depot were based on my theory, or supposition, that after passing " the Divide," or Gravelly plateau, the roads would divide naturally, one set leading to Kingston and one to Cassville depot.   Knowing that General Hooker would take the one to Kingston, I wanted you to take the one toward Cassville, with some rapidity of movement, to increase the chances of interposing between the Etowah bridge and the enemy, falling back before General Thomas's head of column.   Yesterday I was very anxious that General Stoneman or yourself should reach the road from Kingston to Etowah, for I saw by the singular manœuvring of the enemy, and the confusion of his wagon trains, how uneasy he was at fear of our capturing a part of his forces.

Had ten thousand (10,000) men reached the railroad any time after 10 a. m. yesterday, we should have had a signal success ; whereas, Johnston will now encourage his men by his skilfully saving his army and baggage in the face of such odds.   I know the difficulties of the roads and country, and merely mean to explain what I aimed to accomplish.

I did expect to catch a part of the army retreating before us, but I take it for granted that it is now impossible, and therefore wish simply to be assured that he has crossed Etowah, and that he there awaits our attack through the difficult pass of Alatoona.

I do not propose to follow him through that pass, but rather to turn south from here, leaving Alatoona to the north and east.   I wish, therefore, that to-day (the 20th) you move so as to strike the railroad east of Cassville, and then turn east and push the enemy past Cartersville and across Etowah or High Tower bridge.

I left General Thomas's head of column on the skirts of the village of Cassville. He is ordered to support your attack. I have no doubt the ground is very difficult between Cassville and the bridge, and that you can alone push back any force of the enemy remaining this side of the bridge. Still, you may call on Generals Thomas and Stoneman, of course, for support.

I will have the cars into Kingston and Cassville to-day. Shall replenish the wagons, and then on.

Yours, &c.,

W. T. SHERMAN,
Major General Commanding.

Major General SCHOFIELD,
Commanding Army of Ohio.

[Cipher.]

HEADQUARTERS MILITARY DIVISION OF THE MISSISSIPPI,
In the field, Kingston, Georgia, May 19, 1864.

Major General HALLECK, *Washington, D. C.:*

We entered Kingston this morning without opposition, and have pushed a column east as far as Cassville, skirmishing the latter part of the day with Hardee's corps. The enemy has retreated south of the Etowah. To-morrow cars will move to this place and I will replenish our stores and get ready for the Chattahoochee. The railroad passes through a range of hills at Alatoona, which is doubtless being prepared for us, but I have no intention of going through it. I apprehend more trouble from our long trains of wagons than from the fighting, though of course Johnston must fight hard for Atlanta.

W. T. SHERMAN,
Major General.

[Cipher.]

HEADQUARTERS MILITARY DIVISION OF THE MISSISSIPPI,
In the field, Kingston, Georgia, May 20, 1864.

Major General HALLECK, *Washington, D. C.:*

We have secured two good bridges and an excellent ford across the Etowah. Our cars are now arriving with stores. I give two days' rest to replenish and fit up. On the 23d, I will cross the Etowah and move on Dallas. This will turn the Alatoona Pass. If Johnston remain at Alatoona I shall move on Marietta, but if he fall behind the Chattahooche, I will make for Sandtown and Campbelton, but feign at the railroad crossing.

General Davis's division occupies Rome, and finds a good deal of provisions and plunder, five iron-works and machinery. I have ordered the 17th army corps, General Blair's, to march from Decatur to Rome. My share of militia should be sent at once to cover our lines of communication. Notify General Grant that I will hold all of Johnston's army to busy too send anything against him.

W. T. SHERMAN,
Major General.

[Circular.]

HEADQUARTERS MILITARY DIVISION OF THE MISSISSIPPI,
Kingston, Georgia, May 20, 1864.

Inasmuch as an impression is afloat that the commanding general has prohibited the mails to and from this army, he takes this method of assuring all, officers and men, that on the contrary he encourages them, by all his influence and authority, to keep up the most unreserved correspondence with their families and friends wherever they may be. Army, corps, and division commanders should perfect their arrangements to receive and transmit mails, and all chaplains, staff officers, and captains of companies should assist the soldiers in communicating with their families.

What the commanding general does discourage is the maintenance of that class of men who will not take a musket and fight, but who follow the army to pick up news for sale, speculating on a species of information dangerous to an army and to our cause, and who are more used to bolster up idle and worthless officers than to notice the hard-working and meritorious, whose modesty is generally equal to their courage, and who scorn to seek the cheap flattery of the press.

W. T. SHERMAN,
Major General.

[Cipher.]

HEADQUARTERS MILITARY DIVISION OF THE MISSISSIPPI,
In the field, Kingston, Georgia, May 22, 1864.—8.30 p. m.
General HALLECK, *Washington, D. C.:*

Weather hot, *very*, and roads dusty. We nevertheless by morning will have all our wagons loaded and be ready for a twenty days' expedition. I will leave a good brigade at Rome, a strong good point, about a thousand men to cover this point, but will keep no stores here to tempt an enemy, until I have placed my army about Marietta, when I will cause the railroad to be repaired up to that point.

I regard Resaca as the strong head of my line of operations till I reach the Chattahoochee. I have ordered the 17th corps to march from Decatur to Rome and to this point, to act in reserve till I call it forward. Returned veterans and regiments have more than replaced all losses and detachments, and we move to-morrow with full eighty thousand (80,000) fighting men.

General McPherson crosses the Etowah at the mouth of Connasene creek on a bridge, and moves for Dallas *via* Van Wert.

General Thomas crosses by a bridge four miles southeast of Kingston and moves for Dallas, *via* Euharlee and Huntsville. General Schofield crosses near Etowah cliffs on pontoons, and takes position on Thomas's left. I allow three (3) days to have the army grouped about Dallas, whence I can strike Marietta or the Chattahoochee, according to developments.

You may not hear from us in some days, but be assured we are not idle or thoughtless.

W. T. SHERMAN,
Major General.

HEADQUARTERS MILITARY DIVISION OF THE MISSISSIPPI.
In the field, Kingston, Georgia, May 23, 1864.

General BLAIR, *Huntsville, Alabama :*

We are now all in motion for the Chattahoochee. Colonel Long telegraphs from Pulaski and should overtake you at Decatur or soon after leaving. Although you must move on Rome and Kingston by the direct road, still you can make believe you have designs on Gadsden and Talladega. Keep silent and the enemy will exaggerate your strength and purposes. Johnston has called to him all the infantry of the southwest and also the cavalry of Mississippi; so you must watch out for them. If they hang around you keep Long close in and watch the opportunity for him to charge with sabres.

W. T. SHERMAN,
Major General Commanding.

HEADQUARTERS MILITARY DIVISION OF THE MISSISSIPPI,
In the field, near Dallas, Georgia, midnight, May 26, 1864.

GENERAL: Yours of to-day with Corse's is received, and is highly satisfactory. I have personally reconnoitred the ground, and am satisfied the enemy hold by hastly constructed rifle-pits the line of a creek, which is a branch of Pumpkin Vine creek and parallel with it. Your direction in the morning will be substantially down that creek, while General Howard's and Cox's will be up it. We find no trouble in fording it, and you will have less, as you must be near its head. The valley seems clear and cultivated.

Colonel McCook struck a column in flank about five miles northeast of this this p. m , broke it in two, and at night was pressing the fraction toward Ackworth. He reports quite a fight and the capture of fifty-two (52) prisoners. Our skirmishing to-day has been comparatively harmless. I doubt if we find the enemy here to-morrow; but if we do, my orders herewith will govern. I will expect to hear of you on General Hooker's right by ten (10) a. m.

Yours, &c.,

W. T. SHERMAN,
Major General Commanding.

General McPHERSON, *Dallas, Ga.*

HEADQUARTERS MILITARY DIVISION OF THE MISSISSIPPI,
In the field, near Dallas, Georgia, May 27, 1864.—11 a. m.

GENERAL: If you can't drive the enemy from his position, work to the left, so as to connect with General Hooker.

We are working on the left of the line in front of us, and as soon as you are in connexion with General Hooker I will strengthen the left and work round in that direction, so we may, if we choose, march round their extreme right, and reach Marietta or Ackworth.

Yours, &c.,

W. T. SHERMAN,
Major General Commanding.

General McPHERSON, *Dallas, Ga.*

HEADQUARTERS MILITARY DIVISION OF THE MISSISSIPPI,
In the field near Dallas, May 27, 1864.—1.15 p. m.

GENERAL: General Corse is here; we are pressing in front and General Thomas is working round by the left. We don't want to turn the enemy's left flank, but his right, so as to put our concentrated army between him and the railroad, of which we want to make use. Therefore, instead of compassing the enemy's left, I wish you to work up so as to connect with General Hooker, when I will strengthen our movement to our left, the enemy's right. Use the Marietta road as far as possible, and then reach for General Hooker's right. We have two divisions to the right of the road, Geary's and Butterfield's, and Williams's in reserve. All the rest of this is north of this road.

Yours, &c.,

W. T. SHERMAN,
Major General Commanding.

General McPHERSON, *near Dallas, Ga.*

HEADQUARTERS MILITARY DIVISION OF THE MISSISSIPPI,
In the field, near Dallas, Ga., May 27, 1864—5 p. m.

General SCHOFIELD :

Take position in front of the mill, facing south, and connecting with General Thomas's troops, holding one-third of your force in reserve, and concealing your flanks in the timber. I understand General Howard is moving off on your left. He is ordered to move in to connect with you. I will re-enforce that flank as soon as General McPherson makes his junction, which is expected this evening. It is useless to look for the flank of the enemy, as he makes temporary breastworks as fast as we travel. We must break his line without scattering our troops too much, and then break through.

See that General Stoneman is in close connexion with you, but you had better leave General Hovey to cover that point for the present.

Yours, &c.,

W. T. SHERMAN,
Major General Commanding.

HEADQUARTERS MILITARY DIVISION OF THE MISSISSIPPI,
In the field, near Dallas, sundown, May 27, 1864.

GENERAL : We have been busy with the enemy all along our front line. From description I think the hills in your front are stronger than the ground to our left, by which we can move toward Alatoona and Ackworth, or pound away till we find a weak place. We should have our army united, and therefore I think it best you should send your trains back across the Pumpkin Vine by moonlight, and let them park up to our rear, where General Palmer has a division ; then by moving by the left flank you can put yourself in connexion with us, and we can act against some one point, or turn his right flank. No doubt Johnston's whole army is present, as we have felt him for four miles to the north and east. I don't think there is more than a mile from General Davis's left to General Hooker's right. General Corse is with you, and has been back and forth twice.

Yours, &c.,

W. T. SHERMAN,
Major General Commanding.

General McPHERSON, *near Dallas, Ga.*

[Cipher.]

HEADQUARTERS MILITARY DIVISION OF THE MISSISSIPPI,
Near Dallas, May 28, 1864.

General HALLECK, *Washington, D. C. :*

The enemy discovered my move to turn Alatoona, and moved to meet us here. Our columns met about one mile east of Pumpkin Vine creek, and we pushed them back about three miles, to the point where the road forks to Alatoona and Marietta. Here Johnston has chosen a strong line and made hasty but strong parapets of timber and earth, and has thus far stopped us. My right is Dallas, centre about three miles north, and I am gradually working round by the left to approach the railroad anywhere in front of Ackworth.

Country very densely wooded and broken; no roads of any consequence. We have had many sharp, severe encounters, but nothing decisive. Both sides duly cautious in the obscurity of the ambushed ground.

W. T. SHERMAN,
Major General.

HEADQUARTERS MILITARY DIVISION OF THE MISSISSIPPI,
In the field, May 29, 1864.

GENERAL: I suppose General Blair to be now near Rome. I wish you to send a good staff officer to meet him there or at Kingston, and order him to replenish his stores and march for Alatoona Pass, east of the Etowah, to gain, if possible, its eastern terminus and then intrench his position. He had better march from Kingston four (4) miles southeast to the Free Bridge, cross the Etowah, and move for Alatoona, via Euharlee and Stilesboro'. This route will deceive the enemy as to his purposes till the latest moment possible. Once in possession of Alatoona, I wish him to order the railroad superintendent, who is already at Resaca, to repair the railroad up to Alatoona, including the Etowah or Hightower bridge. General Blair should also construct on the dirt road a trestle bridge at the same crossing.

I am, with great respect, yours truly,

W. T. SHERMAN,
Major General Commanding.

General McPHERSON,
Commanding Army of Tennessee.

HEADQUARTERS MILITARY DIVISION OF THE MISSISSIPPI,
In the field, near Dallas, May 29, 1864.

General HALLECK, Washington, D. C.:

Yesterday we pressed our lines up in close contact with the enemy, who has covered his whole front with breastworks of timber and earth. With the intention of working to my left, towards the railroad east of Alatoona, I ordered General McPherson, who is in advance of Dallas and forms my right, to send his trains to a point on Pumpkin Vine, about four miles north of his present position, and to withdraw his army and take General Thomas's present position, whilst all of General Thomas's and General Schofield's armies will be moved further to the east, working round the enemy to the left. The enemy, who had observed the movement of the train from his higher position, massed against General McPherson and attacked him at $4\frac{1}{2}$ p. m. yesterday, but was repulsed with great slaughter and at little cost to us.

The enemy fled back to his breastworks on the ridge, leaving in our hands his dead and wounded. His loss twenty-five hundred, (2,500,) and about three hundred prisoners. General McPherson's men being covered by log breastworks, like our old Corinth lines, were comparatively unhurt, his loss not being over three hundred (300) in all. I give him to-day, Sunday, to gather in the wounded and bury the dead of both sides, and to-night and to-morrow will endeavor to gain ground to our left two or four miles.

General Blair is now supposed to be near Rome; I will order him to march straight for Alatoona, which I infer the enemy has abandoned altogether, or left in the hands of militia. That point gained, I will move to the left and resume railroad communication to the rear. I have no doubt Johnston has in my front every man he can scrape, and Mobile must now be at our mercy if General Canby and General Banks could send to Pascagoula ten thousand men.

W. T. SHERMAN,
Major General.

HEADQUARTERS MILITARY DIVISION OF THE MISSISSIPPI,
In the field, May 30, 1864.

GENERAL: General McPherson made several attempts to draw off his troops, but as often was assaulted so as to put him on the defensive. It is utterly impossible that our enemy can hold all his line in strength, and we must work to the left. There is no absolute necessity for undue haste, as time will soon give us the advantage of General Blair's troops. I will go in person to Dallas, and after inspecting the ground will begin the movement and see if the enemy will attempt to sally, and then judge whether we had not better draw him out and fight him. We must not remain on the defensive. Therefore, in this connexion, I wish you to have your troops well disposed, the skirmishers well out; the lines full, and the reserves well disposed to be removed. Judge of the best point or points to assault in case that you hear us more than usually engaged at Dallas.

I will bring Davis and McPherson up if possible to-day, so that your command may occuppy all the front embracing the several Alatoona and Ackworth roads. I wish you to see that the high and commanding grounds near Picket's mill, which ought to overlook Leverett's, be occupied in force, and let the cavalry patrol the road up as far as possible. I will repeat my orders to General Stoneman to be active on that flank.

I will probably be absent all day, and in my absence you can command all in this part of the field, but preserve the general plan.

Yours, &c.,

W. T. SHERMAN,
Major General Commanding.

Major General THOMAS,
Commanding Army of the Cumberland.

[Cipher.]

HEADQUARTERS MILITARY DIVISION OF THE MISSISSIPPI,
In the field, near Dallas, May 30, 1864.

General HALLECK, Washington, D. C.:

To move General McPherson up to the centre he has to make a retrograde of a mile or so owing to difficult ground. Every time he attempted to withdraw division by division the enemy attacked his whole line; it may be on the theory that we wanted to draw off altogether. These assaults were made in the night, and were all repulsed with comparatively small loss to us, but seemingly heavy to the enemy. If we can induce the enemy to attack us it is to our advantage.

Don't expect us to make much progress towards the Chattahoochee till Blair comes up and moves into Alatoona Pass.

If General Banks and Admiral Porter are all out of Red river, instead of acting offensively on West Louisiana, I advise that the same command that General A. J. Smith took with him, re-enforced by two or three thousand from Memphis and Vicksburg, be sent to Pascagoula to act against Mobile in concert with Admiral Farragut, according to the original plan of the campaign. If this is feasible, I wish the orders to go direct from the general-in-chief to General A. J. Smith, giving him authority to make up his command to ten thousand (10,000) men, and at once proceed, *via* Pontchartrain, to Pascagoula.

I know that all of Polk's army and all the garrisons of Alabama and Florida are with Johnston, as we have prisoners who have been for two (2) years on local duties in those States, as well as from their active divisions, viz : Loring's, French's, and Maury's.

The movement of General Grant on Hanover Court House appears to me admirable, and it seems to me General Grant can force Lee to attack him in position or to move away towards Gordonsville and Lynchburg.

W. T. SHERMAN,
Major General.

HEADQUARTERS MILITARY DIVISION OF THE MISSISSIPPI,
In the field, near Dallas, May 31, 1864.

GENERAL : You will observe that after full reflection and due observation, I have concluded to make the movement by the left. To effect this, so far as you are concerned, I advise you to-night to place one brigade of Dodge on the parapet of Jefferson C. Davis immediately opposite the mountain, and another at the new parapet in the large field this side of Dallas. Then, at daylight, draw off division by division of the 15th army corps, and let them march direct for this road by the most convenient route, and proceed at once to General Hooker and relieve him. The other division of General Dodge should then move by the road from Dallas toward Burnt Hickory, and halt at or back of Owen's mill.

After the movement is past the new parapet in the cleared field, the brigade first posted there should be moved to the Marietta road where General Davis's battery is. This will leave General Dodge to watch that flank, and the 15th corps to occupy General Hooker's present ground. As General Blair cannot be expected as soon as I had contemplated, I must use the cavalry to secure Alatoona Pass.

It should move by a road outside of the one first travelled by General Dodge's division, which goes to Owen's mill. If the enemy follows he will do so cautiously, and I feel no doubt will be easily repulsed.

I want General Hooker relieved as early in the day as possible, to give General Schofield time to attack on our extreme left.

As soon as the cavalry secures Alatoona Pass, I will relieve them by infantry, and recall the cavalry to our flanks.

Yours, truly,

W. T. SHERMAN,
Major General Commanding.

Major General McPHERSON,
Commanding Army of the Tennessee.

HEADQUARTERS MILITARY DIVISION OF THE MISSISSIPPI,
In the field, near Dallas, May 31, 1864.

General GARRARD, *Commanding Division of Cavalry, Dallas:*

I did intend that General Blair's troops, expected from Decatur, should take the Alatoona Pass, but he will not be up in time. You should start your wagons for Burnt Hickory this evening, and, when General McPherson gives the word, move your cavalry by any road across Pumpkin Vine creek and outside the infantry up to the same point. Then start your wagons for Stilesboro' and

Kingston direct for forage and supplies. At Burnt Hickory take the road towards Cartersville, till it intersects the Alatoona road, and follow it briskly. If you find the pass occupied, attack the cavalry with cavalry, and the infantry with dismounted men, and force your way into and through the pass along the railroad till you secure some commanding position. Then report back to me what is done, and your supply train can come up to the Etowah bridge to your rear. Do not be deterred by appearances, but act boldly and promptly. The success of our movement depends on our having Alatoona Pass. After it is secured, I will recall you to General McPherson.

General Stoneman approaching from the front will shake any force in the pass.

      I am yours, truly,

W. T. SHERMAN,
Major General Commanding.

HEADQUARTERS MILITARY DIVISION OF THE MISSISSIPPI,

In the field, June 2, 1864.

GENERAL: Your note of last evening did not reach me till this morning at 7 o'clock, but I heard from a scout in the night that you were in Alatoona. Get a very strong position, and feel forward across Alatoona creek, toward Ackworth. Send to Kingston word that you are in Alatoona, and that I want the railroad finished up to that point at once. General Garrard can come up to you from the rear, if necessary; otherwise he had better be about Stilesboro', to cover the road from the south. I apprehend no serious trouble from the north, nor do I suppose Johnston will try to dispossess you so long as we are working toward Marietta.

Spare your horses as much as possible, and let them feed on grass. The cars can bring you corn to Etowah bridge. Send me to-night the best topographical sketch of the country between you and us. There is a high and valuable trestle-work somewhere about Alatoona, that I want to save; look to it also.

      Yours, &c.,

W. T. SHERMAN,
Major General Commanding.

General STONEMAN,
    Commanding Division of Cavalry, Alatoona.

HEADQUARTERS MILITARY DIVISION OF THE MISSISSIPPI,

In the field, near Dallas, June 3, 1864.

GENERAL: I received your note in the night, and am not astonished that you could not hear the sounds of battle in the midst of the storm yesterday.

General Schofield felt forward from the position Burnt Church, steering due east, and found cavalry dismounted all through the woods. He advanced until about dark, when he encountered infantry and artillery, posted behind finished breastworks. To-day I will still work by the left, and get to the railroad without weakening my line too much. All I ask is, that when we do come in contact with the enemy, on anything like fair terms and proportions, we whip them more fully.

I now hold Alatoona, and shall aim to work across to the railroad as far east and south as I can, without too heavy a loss. If you do hear sounds of battle you will know that Johnston will naturally draw from his left (to your front) on the theory that we are there on the defensive. Therefore, when you do hear sounds of battle, hold the enemy there, or take advantage of his weakening that flank. In my judgment, the point that furnishes you most advantages and cover is about where Butterfield's centre was, where a small stream comes from the east and crosses our line near where a cabin stood, and from which there is an open field, with dead timber to the front. If we can carry a single point and hold it, thereabouts, we gain advantage. General Dodge should intrench the main part of his command at the two points designated, but patrols and skirmishers should fill the woods to the south, especially where General Jeff. C. Davis was, in front of that hill. You should give great attention to the browsing of all animals, where there is a leisure moment, and empty wagons and caissons should be sent for growing wheat, barley, oats or rye, as well as grass, or such bushes as horses and mules eat. I may send a brigade of General Thomas up towards Alatoona, but I want General Blair to march up and through that pass, and on as far as he can. In the mean time I will hold it with cavalry.

Should any specific attack be required of you, I will send special orders; but in their absence act promptly, and with confidence on these general principles. Keep your pioneers at all times opening and improving roads from your rear up towards Alatoona and Burnt Hickory.

Yours, truly,

W. T. SHERMAN,
Major General Commanding.

Major General McPHERSON,
Commanding Army of the Tennessee.

[Cipher.]

HEADQUARTERS MILITARY DIVISION OF THE MISSISSIPPI,
In the field near head of Alatoona Creek, fourteen miles
West of Marietta, June 4, 1864.

Major General HALLECK, *Washington, D. C:*

My left is now well around, covering all roads from the south to the railroad about Ackworth. My cavalry has been at Ackworth, and occupies in force all the Alatoona Pass, and I have ordered the railroad to be finished across the Etowah up to Alatoona bridge. General Blair is not yet at Rome, but is hourly expected, and I await him to push on to Marietta and the Chattahoochee.

It has been raining for three days, making roads bad and swelling all the small mountain creeks, which, however, are easily bridged, and run out very soon. It is still raining. As soon as I hear of General Blair, I will swing east by north over to the railroad, leaving Johnston to my right. He is in force occupying blind and difficult ground, and we continue skirmishing along the whole front, each party inviting the other to attack.

W. T. SHERMAN,
Major General.

HEADQUARTERS MILITARY DIVISION OF THE MISSISSIPPI,
In the field, Alatoona Creek, June 5, 1864.

GENERAL: General McPherson reports the enemy gone from his front; he has advanced his skirmishers half a mile east of New Hope church, capturing a lieutenant and thirty men. If you feel your front, it too will be found abandoned, save by a small guard. The movement indicated in yesterday's orders will therefore be executed, and I have so instructed General McPherson. After feeling your front prepare to move your whole command by McCook's former headquarters, northeast across Alatoona creek towards Andersonville or Kenesaw Station, connecting by pickets with General McPherson about Ackworth. I propose then to complete our line of railroad, replenish and prepare to follow the enemy to and beyond the Chattahoochee, according to the point Johnston selects for defence. General Schofield can remain where he now is until you have passed, and then join your right. The only thing that requires despatch is the bridge at the Etowah where the railroad crosses, and I wish you to get your pontoons there as soon as possible. I consider the road from the Burnt Church to Alatoona more safe than that by Burnt Hickory.

Yours truly,

W. T. SHERMAN,
Major General Commanding.

Major General THOMAS,
Commanding Army of the Cumberland.

[Cipher.]

HEADQUARTERS MILITARY DIVISION OF THE MISSISSIPPI,
In the field, Alatoona Creek, June 5, 1864.

Major General HALLECK, *Washington, D. C:*

The enemy discovering us creeping around his right flank, abandoned his position and marched off last night. We captured about thirty of their pickets at daylight. General McPherson is moving to-day for Ackworth—General Thomas on the direct Marietta road, and General Schofield on his right. It has been raining hard for three days, and the roads are very heavy. The construction party is at work on the Etowah bridge, and should repair it in five (5) days, when I will move on to Marietta. I expect the enemy to fight us at Kenesaw Mountain, near Marietta, but I will not run head on his fortifications. An examination of his abandoned line here shows an immense line of works, all of which I have turned with less loss to ourselves than we have inflicted on him. The wheat fields of the country are our chief supply of forage, and we have in camp bread, meat, sugar, and coffee for many days, ample until the railroad will be complete to Ackworth.

W. T. SHERMAN,
Major General.

HEADQUARTERS MILITARY DIVISION OF THE MISSISSIPPI,
In the field, Alatoona Creek, June 6, 1864.

GENERAL: Captain Poe brought me late in the evening a sketch made by Colonel Asmussen, copy of which he says you have. This sketch clearly marks the strategic points in our advance. The place marked "court-house" must be the Golgotha of our map. I wish you to put your centre anywhere between the court-house and Mrs. Hall's, with your wings up the road towards Dr. Elliott's and Big Shanty, "Shandy Hotel," and toward the "Hard Shell church." Have a small picket at Peters's, the "White House," and General McPherson will connect with you there and about Dr. Elliott's.

Should the enemy be in force about Dr. Elliott's, we must strengthen the connexion by the road by J. McClain's, White House, Durham's, Davenport's, Chastine, &c.

I will go myself to-day to Ackworth and have the telegraph opened there, and give all orders for making Alatoona a strong fortified depot, with a place of issue at Ackworth. I think in three days we should be all ready to go to Marietta. I will have the main force of General McPherson on Proctor's creek about Fitzgerald's and W. J. Phillips', with pickets and patrols forward to Dr. Elliott's.

I think General Schofield had better stay where he is until you get in a better position, when we can place him about the Hard Shell church or Williams', according to the developments of the enemy. He will be instructed to come at your call, or on the sound of battle.

Be careful to shift everything on our back track across to the Alatoona road.

I want to spare our cavalry as much as possible to get ready for the move on Opelika, if Johnston has gone beyond the Chattahoochee.

Yours truly,

W. T. SHERMAN,
Major General Commanding.

Major General THOMAS,
Commanding Army of the Cumberland.

———

HEADQUARTERS MILITARY DIVISION OF THE MISSISSIPPI,
In the field, Ackworth, Ga., June 3, 1864—12 m.

Major General HALLECK, *Washington, D. C:*

I am now on the railroad at Ackworth Station and have full possession forward to within six (6) miles of Marietta. All well. Telegraph me all items of news to date. Has the movement on Mobile been ordered? General Canby telegraphs me that he can spare General A. J. Smith. All I ask is the co-operation of Farragut's fleet.

W. T. SHERMAN,
Major General.

———

HEADQUARTERS MILITARY DIVISION OF THE MISSISSIPPI,
In the field, Ackworth, June 1, 1864.

Major General BLAIR, *Kingston, Georgia:*

Instead of marching *via* Euharlee and Stilesboro' march direct for this place, *via* Cartersville and Alatoona. There is a pontoon bridge at the railroad crossing; leave a regiment at that bridge, and relieve General Garrard's cavalry, and the balance of a brigade at Alatoona, relieving General Stoneman's cavalry.

I want you to have ten (10) days' supply on arrival, ready for the Chattahoochee. Now is the time for big licks, so be alive night and day. At the pontoon try and manage that your command crosses between midnight and daylight, when it is not occupied by the supply trains. I want to go to Marietta on Wednesday or Thursday, and feel down to the Chattahoochee next day. Order the brigade left at Alatoona to be provided with tools, and to intrench both ends of the pass very strong. General McPherson is here with his command.

W. T. SHERMAN,
Major General Commanding.

———

[Cipher.]

HEADQUARTERS MILITARY DIVISION OF THE MISSISSIPPI,
Ackworth, June 7, 1864.

Major General HALLECK, *Washington, D. C.:*

I have been to Alatoona Pass, and find it admirable for our purposes. It is the gate through the last or most eastern spur of the Alleghanies. It now becomes as useful to us as it was to the enemy, being easily defended from either

6*

direction. My left, General McPherson, now lies on the railroad, in front of Ackworth, seven miles southeast of Alatoona; centre, General Thomas, three miles south, on a main Marietta road; and right, General Schofield, two miles further, a little refused.

The cars now come to the Etowah river, and we have sent back to replenish our supplies for a ten days' move, to commence on Thursday, the 9th instant. Colonel Wright reports it will take him ten days, eight of which yet remain, to have cars come to Ackworth.

General Blair was at Kingston last night, and will be across the Etowah to-night, and will be up with us to-morrow. We have three pontoon bridges at Etowah. I will leave a brigade in the pass, covering the bridge and its eastern debouche, and have sent Captain Poe, United States engineers, to lay out the works. The roads here into Georgia are large and good, and the country more open.

The enemy is not in our immediate front, but his signals are on Lost mountain and Kenesaw. I have had the cavalry at Alatoona Pass to get forage, but on the 9th will bring it forward. Colonel Long's brigade is with Blair, and will re-enforce our cavalry by two thousand horses.

I send you by mail to-day copies of my orders up to date, with Atlanta papers of the 5th.

W. T. SHERMAN,
Major General Commanding.

HEADQUARTERS MILITARY DIVISION OF THE MISSISSIPPI,
In the field, Ackworth, June 8, 1864,

Major General HALLECK, Washington, D. C.:

General Blair arrived to-day with two divisions of the 17th army corps, about nine thousand (9,000) strong, having left about fifteen hundred (1,500) in the Alatoona Pass to fortify and hold it. Colonel Wright, railroad superintendent, reports he will have the Etowah bridge done by the 12th instant.

To-morrow I will feel forward with cavalry, and follow up with infantry the moment the enemy develop his designs.

If he fight at the Kenesaw mountain, I will turn it; but if he select the line of the Chattahoochee, then I must study the case a little more before I commit myself.

W. T. SHERMAN,
Major General Commanding.

[Cipher.]

HEADQUARTERS MILITARY DIVISION OF THE MISSISSIPPI,
In the field, Ackworth, June 10, 1864.

Major General HALLECK, Washington D. C.:

Our cavalry yesterday developed the position of the enemy in a line along the hills from Kenesaw to Lost mountain. We are now marching by three roads, all towards Kenesaw, and shall feel the position in force to-day, prepared to attack or turn it to-morrow. All well.

W. T. SHERMAN,
ajor General Commanding.

HEADQUARTERS MILITARY DIVISION OF THE MISSISSIPPI,
In the field, Big Shanty, June 11, 1864.

General HALLECK *Washington, D. C.:*

Johnston is intrenched on the hills embracing Lost mountain, Pine Hill, and Kenesaw. Our lines are down to him, but it has rained so hard, and the ground is so boggy, that we have not developed any weak point or flank.

I will proceed with due caution, and try and make no mistake. The Etowah bridge is done, and the construction train has been to our very camps. Supplies will now be accumulated in Alatoona Pass, or brought right up to our lines.

One of my chief objects being to give full employment to Joe Johnston, it makes but little difference where he is, so he is not on his way to Virginia.

W. T. SHERMAN,
Major General.

[Cipher.]

HEADQUARTERS MILITARY DIVISION OF THE MISSISSIPPI,
In the field, Big Shanty, June 13, 1864.

Major General HALLECK, *Washington, D. C.:*

We have had hard and cold rains for about ten days. A gleam of sunshine this evening gives hopes of a change. The roads are insufficient here, and the fields and new ground are simply impassable to wheels. As soon as possible I will study Johnston's position on Kenesaw and Lost mountain, and adopt some plan to dislodge him, or draw him out of his position. We cannot risk the heavy losses of an assault at this distance from our base. Cars now come to our very front camps. All well.

There are troops enough in Kentucky to manage Morgan, and in Tennessee to watch Forrest, should he make his appearance, as Johnston doubtless calculates.

W. T. SHERMAN,
Major General.

LEXINGTON, KENTUCKY,
June 13, 1864—9.10 p. m.

Major General SHERMAN:

Morgan entered Kentucky with nearly three thousand (3,000) men, through Pound Gap, June 4. June 7 I started in pursuit from the mouth of Beaver or Big Sandy; attacked him at Mount Sterling at daylight June 9. Rebel loss nearly six hundred (600) prisoners, ours about twenty-five (25) killed, and one hundred wounded. I drove him *via* Lexington to Cynthiana, where I attacked at daylight yesterday a. m., gaining a complete victory. Rebel loss three hundred (300) killed and four hundred (400) prisoners, besides wounded. I captured over one thousand (1,000) horses, and recaptured most of General Hobson's command taken by Morgan the day before. Our loss about one hundred and fifty (150) killed and wounded. The rebel force is scattered, and small squads without arms or ammunition, and wholly demoralized, are being pursued and picked up in every direction.

S. G. BURBRIDGE,
Brigadier General United States Volunteers.

[Cipher.]

HEADQUARTERS MILITARY DIVISION OF THE MISSISSIPPI,
In the field, Big Shanty, June 14, 1864.

Hon. E. M. STANTON, *Secretary of War :*

I have just received the news of the defeat of our party sent out from Memphis, whose chief object was to hold Forrest there and keep him off our road. Of course, it is to be deplored, but we must prepare for all contingencies. I have ordered A. J. Smith not to go to Mobile, but to go out from Memphis and defeat Forrest at all costs. I know positively that all of Polk's command is here from Mississippi, viz : Loring's and French's divisions, and three (3) brigades of cavalry—Ferguson's, Ross', and Stark's. Forrest has only his own cavalry, which had started for North Alabama, and the militia under Gholson. I cannot understand how he could defeat Sturgis with eight thousand (8,000) men. Our troops must resume the offensive from Memphis.

W. T. SHERMAN,
Major General.

HEADQUARTERS MILITARY DIVISION OF THE MISSISSIPPI,
In the field, Big Shanty, Ga., June 15, 1864.

DEAR GENERAL : In further explanation of my orders of the day, I will add, I will be with General McPherson up to near noon ; after that with General Thomas's troops, near Howard's left, on Palmer's right, on the Burnt Hickory road. Of course, if an assault must be made on the enemy's lines, it devolves rightfully on the strongest army, and where it will do most good. A breach sufficient for me to pass the head of two columns about midway between Kenesaw and Pine mountains will be best ; although, if possible, one near the Sand Town road would be very good. Of course, the enemy is strongest on his right, and I doubt whether his left exceeds one division, and some cavalry. I infer from an intercepted despatch that Jackson's cavalry is sent, or will be to-day, on an errand to our rear. Now if you can mask a column anywhere about Cox's left, as near the Sand Town road as possible, and post it under cover, and secure some hill that will enable you to approach nearer the enemy than you now are, will be a great point gained, and I prefer you should work in your own way, but try and draw to your extreme right flank as much of the enemy as you can first. A brigade passing over the barricade near General Davis's house, half seen to the enemy, and deploying well off to your right towards Lost Mountain, taking all the cover possible and moving about with considerable eccentricity, would have the desired effect, while the rear column, as also that of General Stoneman, should act as much under cover as possible. A couple of brigades could hold your lines against any probable attack.

Although I did not clearly see the ground yesterday, I inferred that the skirmishing party you sent out the first day had crossed the main Alatoona creek. The lodgement, unless made across east of Alatoona creek, would not improve your present position ; but it is manifest your lines, where they now are, do not threaten the enemy.

He must regard them as precautionary or defensive, and, therefore, is at liberty to draw off from that quarter everything but skirmishers. To lessen the force in front of General Thomas you should, before two (2) p. m., force the enemy to strengthen that part of his line at the expense of his centre.

Of course, the position at Hard Shell church is your chief aim, but as that may be and is doubtless impossible now, I prefer one anywhere about the head of one of the branches of Alatoona creek, between Hard Shell and Hart.

I have just learned that General Howard is in possession of Pine Hill. This makes our movement more easy and necessary.

Yours, &c.,

W. T. SHERMAN, *Major General.*

General SCHOFIELD, *Mt. Olive Church.*

HEADQUARTERS MILITARY DIVISION OF THE MISSISSIPPI,
In the field, Big Shanty, June 15, 1864.

GENERAL: After the long storm had cleared away I examined carefully our whole front, and found the enemy occupying the series of broken ridges and hills which form the water-shed between the Etowah and Chattahoochee, embracing three prominent peaks—Kenesaw, Pine Hill, and Lost Mountain. Pine Hill is about four (4) miles southwest of Kenesaw, and was the apex of the triangle, the salient of the enemy's position. All seemed well fortified and connected by lines of breastworks in the midst of dense chestnut woods. I first ordered Thomas to push Palmer's and Howard's corps in the interval between Kenesaw and Pine Hill until they occupied a certain road, the batteries in front of Pine Hill occupying the attention of the enemy; one of the shots killed Bishop Polk. The movement was perfectly successful, and this morning Pine Hill was abandoned to us, strongly fortified. This morning I ordered Schofield, on the right, to threaten Lost Mountain, and McPherson to turn Kenesaw by the left, while Thomas pushed his whole army to break the centre. Schofield carried the first line of the enemy's works, left exposed by the loss of Pine Hill, and has some fifty prisoners. McPherson carried a hill to his left front, taking the fourteenth Alabama regiment entire, three hundred and twenty (320) strong, and Thomas has pushed the enemy back about a mile and a half, and is still moving. I hope he will pass the dividing ridge, in which case the enemy's position will be untenable. I left him about sundown, but the ground was so obscured by bushes that we could not discern whether the enemy had a second line of earthworks connecting Kenesaw and Lost Mountain, and I don't want to give them time to form one. From Pine Hill we can see Marietta. Losses to-day very small, it having been one grand skirmish extending along a front of eight miles. An intercepted despatch reports the death, by a cannon shot, of Bishop Polk, and is confirmed by the prisoners.

W. T. SHERMAN,
Major General Commanding.

Major General HALLECK,
Washington, D. C.

HEADQUARTERS MILITARY DIVISION OF THE MISSISSIPPI,
In the field, June 16, 1864.

GENERAL: Continue to work toward the lower Marietta road, aiming to reach nearly the same point that Thomas heads for, viz., Hart's; but with small detachments and skirmishers keep all the time feeling over about Lost Mountain; it is not necessary to keep up connected lines. We are not on the defensive, except as to our wagons and supplies, and should invite the enemy out. Send word to General Stoneman and have him to feel well around Lost Mountain. The enemy have had no signal on it for some days; still I know they are sensitive about that flank. Get all your guns to the front, where they can converge on some point of the enemy, knock away the obstructions and make a breach. I will try the same at General Thomas's front.

W. T. SHERMAN,
Major General Commanding.

General SCHOFIELD, *Present.*

[Cipher.]

HEADQUARTERS MILITARY DIVISION OF THE MISSISSIPPI.
In the field, Big Shanty, June 16, 1864.

General HALLECK, *Washington, D. C.:*

General Thomas did not make the progress last night I expected. He found the enemy strongly intrenched on a line slightly advanced from a straight line connecting Lost Mountain and Kenesaw. I have been along it to-day, and am pressing up close; shall study it, and am now inclined to feign on both flanks and assault the centre. It may cost us dear, but in results would surpass an attempt to pass round. The enemy has a strong position and covers his road well, and the only weak point of his game is in having the Chattahoochee to his rear. If by assaulting I can break his line, I see no reason why it should not produce a decisive effect. I know he shifts his troops about to meet our supposed attacks, and thereby fatigues his men, and the woods will enable me to mask our movements.

W. T. SHERMAN,
Major General Commanding.

[Cipher.]

HEADQUARTERS MILITARY DIVISION OF THE MISSISSIPPI,
In the field, Big Shanty, June 17, 1864.

General HALLECK, *Washington:*

By last night we had worked our way so close to Johnston's centre that he saw that the assault must follow. He declined it, and abandoned Lost Mountain and some six miles of as good field-works as I ever saw. My right and centre are, in consequence, swung forward, so that my right now threatens his railroad to Atlanta. I worked hard to-day to get over to that road, but the troops seem timid in these dense forests of stumbling on a hidden breastwork. I therefore simply report good progress to-day—some hundred prisoners, and but few lives lost. We begin to find more fields and cleared land. McPherson still faces Kenesaw, covering our railroad. General Thomas is on a curve line from Kenesaw around to where the Sandtown road forks off from the lower road from Dallas to Marietta; and Schofield is massed on the Sandtown road, head of column at Nose's creek.

Enemy still holds Kenesaw in force, and lies back of Nose's creek, near the Atlanta road.

W. T. SHERMAN,
Major General Commanding.

HEADQUARTERS MILITARY DIVISION OF THE MISSISSIPPI,
In the field, Big Shanty, June 18, 1864.

GENERAL: As soon as the weather will permit, I propose to operate against the enemy's left from the position on the Sandtown road near the Darby Place, which is near Nose's creek, and where a main Marietta road makes off with a right angle from the Sandtown road.

General Schofield will move substantially by the Sandtown road, varying his direction eastwardly if he finds the enemy's flank. General Thomas will move directly against the enemy's left flank. Hooker is on his right, Howard centre, and Palmer left.

I will instruct General Thomas to push Palmer's line forward, close up to

Kenesaw, and then draw off by his right flank in case his whole corps is called on, but to leave a division or brigade to cover his lines; but if the enemy meets it with his whole force, it may be necessary to draw out all Palmer's corps. But this will demonstrate that the enemy's lines are weak, and no apprehension need be felt of their assuming the offensive against you. Still the contingency may arise that will compel your command, also, to move by the right flank, following, as it were, the movement of Palmer; although I should prefer you to advance by the direct road to Marietta.

I want you, by your staff officers, to examine the ground from your right around to the place I have described as Darby's, as also to watch closely the movements of the enemy, and at the earliest possible moment to secure a position forward on the ridge over which the railroad and main Marietta road pass, and pursue always in case of retreat. In any event, should you hear heavy fighting off to the right of Kenesaw, make the strongest possible demonstration on your whole front, and break through if our operations on that flank weaken the enemy.

I am, &c.,

W. T. SHERMAN,
Major General Commanding.

Major General McPHERSON,
Commanding Army of the Tennessee.

HEADQUARTERS MILITARY DIVISION OF THE MISSISSIPPI,
In the field, Big Shanty, June 18, 1864.

GENERAL: As soon as the weather will permit, I propose we shall attack and drive the enemy's left flank. I propose that General Schofield shall move in strong column down the Sandtown road, and vary his course to the right or left until he finds the flank; that you move, as it were, on a grand left wheel in the order your troops now stand. Draw from Palmer division by division, giving, if possible, McPherson notice when the last division (Davis's) is called out of position, that he may dispose accordingly. McPherson has orders to watch well the effect on the enemy, and at the first possible chance to push forward on the line of the railroad and main Marietta road, break through the enemy, and pursue him or secure a position on the commanding ridge over which these roads pass. It is barely possible that McPherson may be called on also to re-enforce your movement by covering by his right flank, and I have instructed him to study the ground with that view; though, if it can possibly be obviated, I do not wish to uncover Big Shanty and our railroad.

I have just received Howard's report by signal, that he has carried two lines of the enemy, and has his batteries up within two hundred yards of his main line. I am very anxious to ascertain, at the earliest possible moment, if the enemy has any part of his main line this side of Nose's creek, and would like Palmer to feel forward with a very heavy line of skirmishers and supports until he finds the earthworks along the base of Kenesaw south of the railroad. Dodge and Osterhaus are up close to the base north of the railroad; but last night I followed Davis's pickets, and, though advanced during yesterday, they appeared to me still a long distance back from Kenesaw.

I suppose Hooker to be west of Mud creek and near its mouth, and that Howard is near brother Ballinger's or widow Ballinger's, and Palmer is from Britt's to Jack Smith's; what we want, then, is the ground from Cheatham's to Latimer's, Brand, and Wallace.

My impression is, the enemy's best forts will be found where the rail and main Marietta roads pass around the north end of Kenesaw, along the north base of Kenesaw, to some point behind Nose's creek, and then along back of Nose's creek indefinitely. Until Schofield develops the flank, we should move with due caution; but the moment it is found, or we are satisfied the enemy has lengthened his line beyond his ability to defend, we must strike quick and with great energy.

The weather is villanously bad; but I hope to-morrow will be clear. Send me word if you can define on our map Hooker's and Howard's positions, assuming Schofield's to be on the Sandtown road near the forks.

Yours, truly,

W. T. SHERMAN,
Major General Commanding.

Major General THOMAS,
Commanding Army of the Cumberland.

[Cipher.]

HEADQUARTERS MILITARY DIVISION OF THE MISSISSIPPI,
In the field, June 20, 1864.

General ROUSSEAU, *Nashville.*

The division of John E. Smith is ordered up from Huntsville to Kingston; it will leave the brigade of Dodge at Decatur for a short time, to wait and see what Forrest will do. I propose to keep him occupied from Memphis. He whipped Sturgis fair and square, and now I will put against him A. J. Smith and Mower and let them try their hand. But you should at all times have things so arranged that you are prepared for his appearance about Florence and Waterloo. You should keep scouts and parties out all the time to break up his posts in the centre to the west and south side of the Tennessee.

W. T. SHERMAN,
Major General Commanding.

HEADQUARTERS MILITARY DIVISION OF THE MISSISSIPPI,
In the field, June 20, 1864.

GENERAL: It is manifest the enemy is manœuvring on our communications, and is reaching as far back as Dalton and Cleveland. I have ordered General McPherson to call up the division of John E. Smith from Huntsville, to take post at Kingston. That will give General Steedman three good detachments along the Etowah—Rome, Kingston, and Alatoona. I have instructed him to send to Rome a regiment of Alabama cavalry that is hanging round here of no use, with orders to scout across the Tennessee to Guntersville, towards Gadsden, &c. Now, as soon as these changes can be made—and they will be initiated at once—you had better give Lowe all cavalry back of the Etowah, and keep him off along the old Tennessee road, from Cartersville, Spring Place, &c., with orders, at his discretion, to venture out to Ellijay, Dahlonega, Cumming, &c.

General Steedman was here last night, and has returned. He wants train guard, and I have also ordered you to supply him a thousand men, which is the equivalent of present garrison of Kingston, which will be relieved by John E. Smith's division as soon as it can come from Huntsville.

W. T. SHERMAN,
Major General Commanding.

Major General THOMAS,
Commanding Army of the Cumberland.

HEADQUARTERS MILITARY DIVISION OF THE MISSISSIPPI,
In the field, June 20, 1864.

GENERAL : General Blair's application for a mounted force of two companies is received. During our operations here, where infantry and artillery alone can act, our cavalry must all be kept on the grand flanks and on our communications ; as it is, our cavalry is liable to be absorbed in orderly and courier duty, leaving our flanks and rear at the mercy of our enemy. This I must prevent. I insist on all organized cavalry being massed on our flanks and rear, at present, where it can act to accomplish some military result. I know there are plenty of officers and men mounted in all the corps and divisions, that can be collected and made into orderlies and couriers. I wish you to make this rule general in your army. The two companies ordered from General Blair to their regiment was at the earnest appeal of the cavalry officers.

I am, &c.,

W. T. SHERMAN,
Major General Commanding.

Major General McPHERSON,
Commanding Army of the Tennessee.

NASHVILLE, *June* 20, 1864.

Major General SHERMAN :

On recently leaving Washington, to organize colored troops in Kentucky, the Secretary of War desired me to proceed to Chattanooga and put myself in communication with you, and he expressed his strong desire that you would give facilities for organizations within your command. I request that you will send the negroes, who may come in or be gathered in by your forces, to this place, where they can the more readily be organized and provided for. If you desire to form regiments with your army, do so, and send me the roster of the officers appointed. I have seen your recent order respecting the enlistment of negroes, the practical working of which, it seems to me, will almost altogether stop recruiting with your army. I know not under what circumstances it was issued, but the imprisonment of officers for disobedience seems to me a harsh measure. Would it not be better to organize the negroes, and from them make the necessary details for the staff departments ?

Of course, I do not wish to deprive you of any negroes you may require for service with your army, and have sent a copy of the order to the Secretary of War. I leave for Chattanooga this evening, where I shall be glad to hear from you.

L. THOMAS,
Adjutant General United States Army.

HEADQUARTERS MILITARY DIVISION OF THE MISSISSIPPI,
In the field, Big Shanty, June 21, 1864.

Major General HALLECK, *Washington, D. C.:*

This is the nineteenth day of rain, and the prospect of clear weather as far off as ever. The roads are impassable, and fields and woods become quagmires after a few wagons have crossed. Yet we are at work all the time. The left flank is across Noonday, and the right across Nose's creek. The enemy holds Kenesaw, a conical mountain, with Marietta behind it, and has retired his flanks to cover that town and his railroad. I am all ready to attack the moment the weather and roads will permit troops and artillery to move with anything like life.

W. T. SHERMAN, *Major General Commanding.*

HEADQUARTERS MILITARY DIVISION OF THE MISSISSIPPI,
In the field, June 22, 1864.

GENERAL : The rain having ceased, and a prospect of roads drying up, I have to instruct that you cause your cavalry to be most active down to the Sweetwater, both on the Powder Spring road and the factory road. Hold the place on your map called " Cheny's," and turn your head of column up the Marietta road until you support Hooker's right, and then act according to circumstances. If Johnston fights for Marietta, we must accept battle ; but if he give ground, we must be most active, and for that reason I want you as long as possible to control the Sandtown road.

I will probably meet you to-day about " Mrs. Kulp's," on the Powder Spring and Marietta road.

I am, &c.,

W. T. SHERMAN,
Major General Commanding.

General SCHOFIELD,
Commanding Army of the Ohio.

HEADQUARTERS MILITARY DIVISION OF THE MISSISSIPPI,
In the field, June 22, 1864.

GENERAL : I will start early to look at the position of McPherson, as near the north base of Kenesaw as I can safely do, and then come to Wallace's, or the house in front, and then over to Hooker. I have ordered Schofield to cross his whole command over Nose's creek and turn the head of his column up toward Marietta until he reaches Hooker ; to support and co-operate on his right, but to keep his cavalry and a part of his rear infantry on the Sandtown road, prepared to regain it in case the enemy show signs of let go. I fear we will get our commands too close, but I suppose Schofield can find room to deploy south of the Powder Spring and Marietta road. You may order Hooker to extend to that road and leave Schofield beyond. If he can get possession of the ground up to Mrs. Kulp's, I wish him to do so, and the balance of your line to conform. I will explain McPherson's orders when I meet you.

I am, &c.,

W. T. SHERMAN,
Major General Commanding.

Major General THOMAS,
Commanding Army of the Cumberland.

HEADQUARTERS MILITARY DIVISION OF THE MISSISSIPPI,
In the field, June 22, 1864.

GENERAL : I am starting for what I deem the point of most activity to-day, though the state of the roads won't admit of much activity. Yet we may gain possession of ground useful. I wish you to keep Garrard moving about, without breaking connexion with you entirely, so as to keep the enemy on his guard on his right flank ; the same of Blair's corps, operating on a circle of small radius.

The 15th corps might wheel a little to the right, gaining ground and increasing the pressure on the enemy, holding fast all it makes, while Dodge's two divisions should be disposed so as best to cover Big Shanty as against a rally from Kenesaw on the road at its base. Keep the skirmish line in motion all the time, but hold the rear masses ready to re-enforce Thomas, should he become heavily engaged.

Thomas will keep pressing up to Marietta, his right on the Powder Spring road, and his left on the Burnt Hickory, contracting his lines as he advanced.
Yours, truly,

W. T. SHERMAN,
Major General Commanding.

Major General McPHERSON,
Commanding Army of the Tennessee.

HEADQUARTERS MILITARY DIVISION OF THE MISSISSIPPI,
In the field, Big Shanty, June 22, 1864—9 p. m.

GENERAL: When on the hill in front of your centre to-day, waiting for you, I signalled to General Hooker:

" How are you getting along ?   Near what house are you ?
" W. T. SHERMAN,
" *Major General.*"

At this hour (9½) I have received this answer :

" KULP HOUSE—5.30 p. m.

"We have repulsed two heavy attacks and feel confident, our only apprehension being from our extreme right flank.   Three (3) entire corps are in front of us.

" Major General HOOKER."

I was at the Wallace house at 5.30 p. m., and the Kulp house was within two miles, and though I heard some cannonading, I had no idea of his being attacked, and General Hooker must be mistaken about three (3) entire corps being in his front.   Johnston's army has only three corps, and I know there was a very respectable force along McPherson's front, so much so that this general thought the enemy was massing against him.   I know there was some force in front of Palmer and Howard, for I was there.   Still, it is very natural the enemy should meet Hooker at that point in force, and I gave Schofield orders this morning to conduct his column from Nose's creek, on the Powder Spring road, toward Marietta, and support Hooker's right flank, sending his cavalry down the Powder Spring road toward Sweetwater, and leaving some infantry from his rear to guard the fords.   Captain Dayton says General Schofield receipted my orders, which were in writing.   If later information shows that Schofield is not up, send a staff officer and notify him of the necessity, and, if need be, call off all of Palmer's, and notify McPherson, who has his orders for this very contingency. To-morrow, if need be, we must bring things to a crisis.

Cars and telegraph now all right.   Some of John E. Smith's men are at Chattanooga, so that I think our road will be better guarded.   The cavalry of Lowe should be out on the Tennessee road, patrolling from Cartersville to Spring place.
Yours,

W. T. SHERMAN,
Major General Commanding.

Major General THOMAS,
Commanding Army of the Cumberland.

HEADQUARTERS MILITARY DIVISION OF THE MISSISSIPPI,
In the field, Big Shanty, June 22, 1864.

GENERAL: General Hooker, this p. m., advanced to the Kulp house, two and a half miles southwest of Marietta, and reports finding the enemy in as strong force as three (3) corps.   He was attacked twice, and successfully repulsed the enemy. General Thomas thinks that that will be the enemy's tactics, and that you ought to attack Marietta from that side of Kenesaw, but I judge the safer and better plan to be the one I indicated, viz: for you to leave a light force and cover that flank, and throw the remainder, rapidly and as much out of view as possible, to our right.

You may make the necessary orders, and be prepared for rapid action tomorrow. So dispose matters that the big guns of Kenesaw will do you as little mischief as possible.

Yours, &c.,

W. T. SHERMAN,
Major General.

Major General McPherson,
Commanding Army of the Tennessee.

HEADQUARTERS MILITARY DIVISION OF THE MISSISSIPPI,
In the field, Big Shanty, June 23, 1864.

GENERAL : As the question may arise, and you have a right to the support of my authority, I now decide that the use of torpedoes is justifiable in war in advance of an army, so as to make his advance up a river or over a road more dangerous and difficult. But after the adversary has gained the country by fair warlike means, then the case entirely changes. The use of torpedoes in blowing up cars and the road after they are in our possession, is simply malicious. It cannot alter the great problem, but simply makes trouble. Now, if torpedoes are found in the possession of an enemy to our rear, you may cause them to be put on the ground and tested by wagon-loads of prisoners, or, if need be, by citizens implicated in their use. In like manner, if a torpedo is suspected on any part of the railroad, order the point to be tested by a car-load of prisoners, or citizens implicated, drawn by a long rope. Of course an enemy cannot complain of his own traps.

I am, &c.,

W. T. SHERMAN,
Major General Commanding.

Major General J. B. Steedman,
Commanding District of the Etowah, Chattanooga.

[Cipher.]

HEADQUARTERS MILITARY DIVISION OF THE MISSISSIPPI,
In the field, Big Shanty, June 23, 1864.

General HALLECK, *Washington, D. C.:*

We continue to press forward, operating upon the principles of an advance against fortified positions. The whole country is one vast fort, and Johnston must have full fifty miles of connected trenches, with abatis and finished batteries. We gain ground daily, fighting all the time. On the 21st General Stanley gained a position near the south end of Kenesaw, from which the enemy attempted in vain to drive him, and the same day General T. J. Wood's division took a hill which the enemy assaulted three times at night without success, leaving more than a hundred dead on the ground. Yesterday the extreme right, Hooker and Schofield, advanced on the Powder Spring road to within three miles of Marietta. The enemy made a strong effort to drive them away, but failed signally, leaving more than two hundred dead on the field.

Our lines are now in close contact and the fighting incessant, with a good deal of artillery. As fast as we gain one position the enemy has another all ready, but I think he will soon have to let go Kenesaw, which is the key to the whole country. The weather is now better, and the roads are drying up fast.

Our losses are light, and, notwithstanding the repeated breaks in the road to our rear, supplies are ample.

W. T. SHERMAN,
Major General.

MEMPHIS, June 22, 1864.

Major General SHERMAN:

All is going well. Forrest still remains at Baldwin and Tupello in large force. Smith's force consists of nine thousand (9,000) infantry, three thousand cavalry and four (4) batteries. They will move towards Corinth and endeavor to draw Forrest as far up as possible. He will no doubt concentrate everything this side of Grenada and will leave Mobile defenceless. If while Smith is engaging them, General Canby would send from New Orleans ten thousand (10,000) men to Mobile, via Pascagoula, that city would be easily captured The force of Forrest is larger than you suppose, but should have been whipped.

C. C. WASHBURN,
Major General.

CHATTANOOGA, June 24, 1864.

Captain DAYTON:

The enemy with squads of cavalry are making desperate efforts to cut our communications. The bridges are now all guarded, and mounted force patrolling both sides of the road. Will have tops of cars protected with plank so that guards can defend them. General Jno. E. Smith is at Larkinsville this morning; can reach Stevenson to-night.

J. B. STEEDMAN,
Major General.

HEADQUARTERS MILITARY DIVISION OF THE MISSISSIPPI,
In the field, near Kenesaw, June 24, 1864.

GENERAL: I am directed by the general commanding to acknowledge the receipt through you of General Rousseau's communication in copy, the original of which also came to hand.

The general commanding thinks quite favorably of the suggestions therein, and desires you to instruct General Rousseau to gradually collect his available force of cavalry and infantry at Pulaski, Athens and Decatur, upon the representation of protecting our roads against Forrest, but really to strike as proposed, the cavalry to be well fed, and the infantry stripped for light rapid movements, and to be ready to move at telegraphic notice from us. The time to do it will be when we have forced Johnston across the Chattahoochee. The general commanding has just received telegraphic information that General A. J. Smith moves from Memphis, via Corinth, to engage Forrest, (who is now at Baldwin,) anywhere between Corinth and Tupello. Smith has nine thousand (9,000) infantry and three thousand (3,000) cavalry.

I am, general, very respectfully, yours,

L. M. DAYTON, Aide-de-Camp.

Major General G. H. THOMAS,
Commanding, &c.

[Cipher.]

HEADQUARTERS MILITARY DIVISION OF THE MISSISSIPPI,
In the field, near Kenesaw Mountain, June 25, 1864.

General HALLECK, *Washington, D. C.:*

I have nothing new to report; constant skirmishing and cannonading. I am making some changes in the disposition of our men, with a view to attack the enemy's left centre. I shall aim to make him stretch his line until he weakens it, and then break through.

Johnston has made repeated attempts to break our roads to the rear, and has succeeded in two instances, which were promptly repaired. General Steedman, at Chattanooga, reports that General Pillow approached from the south with three thousand (3,000) men, but was met at Lafayette by Colonel Watkins and repulsed; full details not yet received. I think the arrangements to protect our rear are ample against any probable danger.

W. T. SHERMAN,
Major General Commanding.

[Cipher.]

HEADQUARTERS MILITARY DIVISION OF THE MISSISSIPPI,
In the field, near Kenesaw, June 26, 1864, 10½ a. m.

General SCHOFIELD:

I don't care about Colonel Riley succeeding; let him throw up a hasty parapet for his guns and fire away, and make all dispositions as though he intended to force a passage. Same with General Cox, up where he is. It should be done to-day, to induce the enemy to strengthen that flank to-night.

W. T. SHERMAN,
Major General Commanding.

HEADQUARTERS MILITARY DIVISION OF THE MISSISSIPPI,
Near Kenesaw Mountain, June 26, 1864.

General LORENZO THOMAS, *Louisville, Kentucky:*

I was gratified at the receipt of your despatch from Chattanooga. I would have answered sooner if our telegraph had not been broken so often of late. As I wrote you, I know all the people have left north Georgia for the region of the Flint and Apalachicola, with their negroes.

The regiments of blacks now in Chattanooga and Tennessee will absorb all the recruits we can get; but if you raise new regiments, they could be well employed about Clarksville, Bowling Green, and on the Tennessee river—say at the terminus of the northwest railroad. My preference is to make this radical change with natural slowness. If negroes are taken as soldiers by undue influence or force, and compelled to leave their women in the uncertainty of their new condition, they cannot be relied on; but if they can put their families in some safe place and then earn money as soldiers or laborers, the transition will be more easy and the effect more permanent.

What my order contemplated was the eagerness of recruiting captains and lieutenants to make up their quota in order to be commissioned. They would use a species of force or undue influence, and break up our gangs of laborers, as necessary as soldiers. We find gangs of negro laborers well organized on the Mississippi, at Nashville, and along the railroads, most useful, and I have used them with great success as pioneer companies attached to divisions, and I think it would be well if a law would sanction such an organization, say, of one hundred (100) to each division of four hundred (400) men.

The first step in the liberation of the negro from bondage will be to get him and family to a place of safety, then to afford him the means of providing for his family, (for their instincts are very strong,) then gradually use a proportion, greater and greater each year, as sailors and soldiers. There will be no great difficulty in our absorbing the four millions (4,000,000) of slaves in this great industrious country of ours, and being lost to their masters, the cause of the war is gone, for this great money interest ceases to be an element in our politics and civil economy. If you divert too large a proportion of the able-bodied into the ranks, you will leave too large a class of black paupers on our hands. The great mass of our soldiery must be of the white race, and the black troops should for some years be used with caution, and with due regard to the prejudice of the races. As was to be expected, in some instances they have done well, in others badly; but on the whole the experiment is worthy a fair trial, and all I ask is that it be not forced beyond the laws of natural development. In Maryland, Missouri, and Kentucky, it may be wisely used to secure their freedom with the consent of owners.

W. T. SHERMAN,
Major General Commanding.

[Cipher.]

HEADQUARTERS MILITARY DIVISION OF THE MISSISSIPPI,
Near Kenesaw Mountain, June 26, 1864.

General SCHOFIELD:

Is the brigade across Olley's creek, above the Sandtown road, or at the road? Describe to me well the situation of that flank, that I may advise Thomas and McPherson.

W. T. SHERMAN,
Major General Commanding.

[Cipher]

HEADQUARTERS MILITARY DIVISION OF THE MISSISSIPPI,
In the field, near Kenesaw Mountain, June 26, 1864.

Major General SCHOFIELD:

All right. Be careful of a brigade so exposed, but I am willing to risk a good deal.

W. T. SHERMAN,
Major General Commanding.

[Cipher.]

HEADQUARTERS MILITARY DIVISION OF THE MISSISSIPPI,
In the field, near Kenesaw Mountain, June 26, 1864.

Major General SCHOFIELD:

Good bridge should be made to-night across Olley's creek, where the brigade is across, and operations resumed there in the morning early.

W. T. SHERMAN,
Major General Commanding.

[Cipher.]

HEADQUARTERS MILITARY DIVISION OF THE MISSISSIPPI,
Near Kenesaw Mountain, June 27, 1864.

Major General SCHOFIELD:

I will be on Signal Hill to-day, where I will have a telegraph post. Keep some orderlies at your telegraph station, that my orders may reach you during the day.

W. T. SHERMAN,
Major General Commanding.

[Cipher.]

HEADQUARTERS MILITARY DIVISION OF THE MISSISSIPPI,
Near Kenesaw Mountain, June 27, 1864.

General THOMAS:

I will be on Signal Hill to-day, where I have a telegraph station. Keep some orderlies at your telegraph office, who can reach you promptly with orders, and keep me well advised.

W. T. SHERMAN,
Major General Commanding.

[Cipher.]

HEADQUARTERS MILITARY DIVISION OF THE MISSISSIPPI,
Near Kenesaw Mountain, June 27, 1864.

Major General McPHERSON:

I will be on Signal Hill, where I have a telegraph office. Leave some orderlies at your telegraph station, that orders may reach any part of your line with despatches. Keep me well advised, as I must work the flanks according to the progress of the centre.

W. T. SHERMAN,
Major General Commanding.

[Cipher.]

HEADQUARTERS MILITARY DIVISION OF THE MISSISSIPPI,
In the field, June 27, 1864—11.45 a. m.

General SCHOFIELD:

Neither McPherson nor Thomas has succeeded in breaking through, but each has made substantial progress at some cost. Push your operations on the flank, and keep me advised.

W. T. SHERMAN,
Major General Commanding.

[Cipher.]

HEADQUARTERS MILITARY DIVISION OF THE MISSISSIPPI,
In the field, June 27, 1864—11.45 a. m.

General THOMAS:

McPherson's column marched near the top of the hill through very tangled brush, but was repulsed; it is found almost impossible to deploy, but they still hold the ground. I wish you to study well the positions, and if it be possible to break the line do it; it is easier now than it will be hereafter. I hear Leggett's guns well behind the mountain.

W. T. SHERMAN,
Major General Commanding.

[Cipher.]

HEADQUARTERS MILITARY DIVISION OF THE MISSISSIPPI,
In the field, June 27, 1864—1.30 p. m.

General THOMAS:

McPherson and Schofield are at a dead lock. Do you think you can carry any part of the enemy's main line to-day? McPherson's men are up to the abatis, and can't move without the direct assault. I will order the assault if you think you can succeed at any point. Schofield has one division close up on the Powder Spring road, and the other across Olley's creek, about two miles to his right and rear.

W. T. SHERMAN,
Major General Commanding.

[Cipher.]

HEADQUARTERS MILITARY DIVISION OF THE MISSISSIPPI,
In the field, June 27, 1864—2.25 p. m.

General THOMAS:

Secure what advantageous ground you have gained; but is there anything in the enemy's present position that if we should approach by regular saps he could not make a dozen new parapets before our saps are completed? Does the nature of the ground warrant the time necessary for regular approaches?

W. T. SHERMAN,
Major General Commanding.

[Cipher.]

HEADQUARTERS MILITARY DIVISION OF THE MISSISSIPPI,
In the field, June 27, 1864.—4.10 p. m.

General THOMAS:

Schofield has gained the crossing of Olley's creek on the Sandtown road, the only advantage of the day. You may order all ground of value gained to-day to be secured, and prepare batteries in the manner proposed by Davis. I doubt if we can resort to regular approaches.

W. T. SHERMAN,
Major General Commanding.

7 *

[Cipher.]

HEADQUARTERS MILITARY DIVISIOM OF THE MISSISSIPPI,
In the field, June 27, 1864.—4. 10 p. m.

General SCHOFIELD:

Let Cox secure well the crossing at Olley's creek on the Sandtown road, and take all advantage of that flank should we move in that direction. Otherwise hold fast all you have and remain on the defensive.

W. T. SHERMAN,
Major General Commanding.

HEADQUARTERS DEPARTMENT OF THE CUMBERLAND,
June 27, 1864.—6 p. m.

Major General SHERMAN:

The assault of the enemy's works in my front was well arranged, and the officers and men went to their work with the greatest coolness and gallantry. The failure to carry them is due only to the strength of the works, and to the fact that they were well managed, thereby enabling the enemy to hold them securely against the assault. We have lost nearly two thousand (2,000) officers and men, among them two brigade commanders—General Harker, commanding a brigade in Newton's division, and Colonel Dan McCook, commanding a brigade in Jeff. Davis's division—both reported to be mortally wounded, besides some six (6) or eight (8) field officers killed.

Both General Harker and Colonel McCook were wounded on the enemy's breastworks, and all say had they not been wounded we would have driven the enemy from his works.

Both Generals Howard and Palmer think that they can find favorable positions on their lines for placing batteries for enfilading the enemy's works. We took between ninety (90) and one hundred (100) prisoners.

Respectfully,

GEO. H. THOMAS,
Major General.

[Cipher.]

HEADQUARTERS MILITARY DIVISION OF THE MISSISSIPPI,
Near Kenesaw Mountain, June 27, 1864.

General THOMAS:

Let your troops fortify as close up to the enemy as possible; get good positions for artillery, and group your command as conveniently as you can by corps and divisions, keeping reserves. Schofield has the Sandtown road within eleven miles of the Chattahoochee, and we could move by that flank. The question of supplies will be the only one. I regret beyond measure the loss of two such young and dashing officers as Harker and Dan McCook. McPherson lost two or three of his young and dashing officers, which is apt to be the case in unsuccessful assaults. Had we broken the line to-day it would have been most decisive, but as it is our loss is small compared with some of those east; it should not in the least discourage us. At times, assaults are necessary and inevitable. At Arkansas Post we succeeded; at Vicksburg we failed. I do not think our loss to-day greater than Johnston's when he attacked Hooker and Schofield, the first day we occupied our present ground.

W. T. SHERMAN,
Major General Commanding.

[Cipher.]

HEADQUARTERS MILITARY DIVISION OF THE MISSISSIPPI,
In the field, near Kenesaw, June 27, 1864.

General HALLECK:

Pursuant to my orders of the 24th, a diversion was made on each flank of the enemy, especially on the Sandtown road, and at 8 a. m. General McPherson attacked at the southwest end of the Kenesaw, and General Thomas at a point about a mile further south; at the same time skirmishers and artillery, along the whole line, kept up a sharp fire. Neither attack succeeded, though both columns reached the enemy's works, which are very strong. General McPherson reports his loss about five hundred, and General Thomas about two thousand; the loss particularly heavy in general and field officers. General Harker is reported mortally wounded; also Colonel Dan McCook, commanding brigade, Colonel Rice, 57th Ohio, very seriously. Colonels Barnhill, 40th Illinois, and Augustine, 55th Illinois, are killed.

The facilities with which defensive works of timber and earth are constructed gives the party on the defensive great advantage.

I cannot well turn the position of the enemy without abandoning my railroad, and we are already so far from our supplies that it is as much as the road can do to feed and supply the army. There are no supplies of any kind here. I can press Johnston and keep him from re-enforcing Lee, but to assault him in position will cost us more lives than we can spare.

McPherson took to-day a hundred prisoners and Thomas about as many, but I do not suppose that we have inflicted heavy loss on the enemy, as he kept close behind his parapets.

W. T. SHERMAN,
Major General.

[Cipher.]

HEADQUARTERS MILITARY DIVISION OF THE MISSISSIPPI,
In the field, near Kenesaw, June 27, 1864.

General MCPHERSON:

Is General Blair back? Report to me fully his operations for to-day. Schofield's right division (Cox) has gained a good position on the other side of Olley's creek and at the head of Nickajack. If we had our supplies well up I would move by the right flank, but suppose we must cover our railroad for a few days.

W. T. SHERMAN,
Major General Commanding.

[Cipher.]

HEADQUARTERS MILITARY DIVISION OF THE MISSISSIPPI,
June 27, 1864.—9. p. m.

General THOMAS:

Are you willing to risk the move on Fulton, cutting loose from our railroad? It would bring matters to a crisis, and Schofield has secured the way.

W. T. SHERMAN,
Major General Commanding.

[Cipher.]

WASHINGTON, *June* 28, 1864.—4 p. m.

Major General SHERMAN:

General Grant directs me to say that the movements of your army may be made entirely independent of any desire to retain Johnston's forces where they are. He does not think that Lee will bring any more additional troops to Richmond, on account of the difficulty of feeding them.

H. W. HALLECK,
Major General.

[Cipher.]

HEADQUARTERS MILITARY DIVISION OF THE MISSISSIPPI,
In the field, near Kenesaw, June 29, 1864.

Major General HALLECK, *Washington, D. C.:*

Our loss on the 27th will not exceed fifteen hundred (1 500.) As usual, the first reports were overstated. General Harker is dead. The wounded are doing well, and most are already sent to the rear in cars. Some few of the dead and wounded were left in the enemy's hands, close to his parapet.

I am accumulating stores that will enable me to cut loose from the railroad for a time, and avoid the Kenesaw Hill, which gives the enemy too much advantage. I will aim to get to the railroad below Marietta by a circuit, or actually reach the Chattahoochee. Our right flank is now on the Sandtown road below Olley's creek.

W. T. SHERMAN,
Major General.

[Cipher.]

HEADQUARTERS MILITARY DIVISION OF THE MISSISSIPPI,
In the field, near Kenesaw, June 29, 1864.

General ROUSSEAU, *Nashville, Tennessee:*

I have yours of the 27th. Of course go on and make all the preparations, but do not start until we know something definite of General A. J. Smith, and until I have pushed Johnson across the Chattahoochee. The points of importance are Montgomery, Opelika, and Columbus, Georgia. I have had forage placed at Pensacola in case of the party having to go there. Don't move until I give specific orders.

W. T. SHERMAN,
Major General Commanding.

HEADQUARTERS MILITARY DIVISION OF THE MISSISSIPPI,
In the field, near Kenesaw, June 30, 1864.

General SCHOFIELD:

General Thomas is here. He will study his ground well and prepare to relieve Hascall's division to-night, in which event I want you with your whole force to occupy between Olley's creek and Nickajack, to drive the enemy from the forks of the road, and picket as far down the Fulton road as Nickajack creek, and as far on the Sandtown road as possible. At the same time General

Stoneman's cavalry, supported by McCook, should move across Sweetwater by Powder Springs, and down the west side of Sweetwater creek to Sweetwater town, which crossing once secure, Stoneman to hold it and McCook to return to Lost Mountain.

General McPherson's command to remain where it is until our stores are complete, when his cavalry will guard the roads from Marietta towards Alatoona, while McPherson moves with his whole command down the Sandtown road to the Chattahoochee. If Johnston holds on to the Kenesaw, then we must strike some point on the railroad between Marietta and the bridge; but if he let go of Marietta, then we will swing across the railroad to a position that gives us again the use of the railroad.

W. T. SHERMAN, Major General Commanding.

[Cipher.]

HEADQUARTERS MILITARY DIVISION OF THE MISSISSIPPI,
In the field, near Kenesaw, June 30, 1864.

General ROUSSEAU, Nashville, Tennessee:

The movement that I want you to study and be prepared for is contingent on the fact that General A. J. Smith defeats Forrest or holds him well in check and after I succeed in making Joe Johnston pass the Chattahoochee with his army, when I want you to go in person or to send some good officer with 2,500 good cavalry well armed, and a sufficient number of pack-mules loaded with ammunition, salt, sugar and coffee, and some bread or flour, depending on the country for forage, meat and corn-meal. The party might take two light Rodman guns, with orders in case of very rapid movements to cut the wheels and burn the carriages, taking sledges along to break off trunnions and wedge them into the muzzles. The expedition should start from Decatur, move slowly to Blountsville and Ashville, and if the way is clear, cross the Coosa at the Ten Islands or the railroad bridge, destroying it after their passage, then move rapidly for Talladega or Oxford, and then for the nearest ford or bridge over the Tallapoosa. That passed, the expedition should move with rapidity on the railroad between Tuskegee and Opelika, breaking up the road and twisting the bars of iron. They should work on that road night and day, doing all the damage possible, toward and including Opelika. If no serious opposition offer, they should threaten Columbus, Georgia, and then turn up the Chattahoochee to join us, between Marietta and Atlanta, doing all the mischief possible. No infantry in position should be attacked, and the party should avoid all fighting possible, bearing in mind, for their own safety, that Pensacola, Rome, the Etowah and my army, are all places of refuge. If compelled to make Pensacola, they should leave their horses, embark for New Orleans and come round to Nashville again.

Study this well and be prepared to act on orders when the time comes. Selma, though important, is more easily defended than the route I have named.

W. T. SHERMAN,
Major General Commanding.

HEADQUARTERS ARMY OF THE OHIO, June 30, 1864.

Major General SHERMAN:

It occurs to me as a question worthy of consideration whether Johnston, in anticipation of your present movement, may not bring up to Marietta two or three weeks' supplies, close the gorge of his lines in rear of Marietta, and meet you there in a strongly intrenched position and with a greater amount of supplies than you can carry.

J. M. SCHOFIELD, Major General.

HEADQUARTERS MILITARY DIVISION OF THE MISSISSIPPI,
In the field, near Kenesaw, June 30, 1864—8½ p. m.

General SCHOFIELD:

Johnston may do as you suggest, but I hardly think, even in the event you conjecture, will he be willing to have me interfere between him and the rest of the confederacy. I am not bound to attack him in his position, after getting below him, but may cross the Chattahoochee and destroy all his railroads before he can prevent it, which will be a desperate game for us both. I am aware of all the chances, but we must take the initiative and risk something, or attack him where he now is.

Our communications are now secure, and the time more favorable for making a risk than if we wait looking at each other till he gets cavalry to our rear.

W. T. SHERMAN,
Major General Commanding.

HEADQUARTERS MILITARY DIVISION OF THE MISSISSIPPI,
In the field, near Kenesaw, June 30, 1864.

General SCHOFIELD:

I think I have contemplated every move on the chess-board of war, but am always much obliged for your full views. I regard each of my three armies as able to hold in check any attempt of the enemy to mass or overwhelm a part until the others come up, and try so to manage that each army is an unit. Should Johnston hold us in the new position aimed at, we still have the Alatoona and Etowah to our rear all safe, and more secure by a division of five thousand (5,000) men that has reached Chattanooga and Kingston from Huntsville.

W. T. SHERMAN,
Major General Commanding.

HEADQUARTERS MILITARY DIVISION OF THE MISSISSIPPI,
In the field, near Kenesaw, July 1, 1864.

General STEEDMAN, *Chattanooga, Tennessee:*

To-morrow I propose to move in such a way that my communication with the railroad may be broken for some days, and great attention must be given to the line of the Etowah, especially Cartersville and Alatoona. Now that you have General John E. Smith's division, send to Alatoona and Rome the two regiments that belong there, that have been detained along the road. You will now have all of Lowe's division of cavalry for guarding off to the east; it has heretofore been tied down to Kingston, but should now be over about Adairsville and Talking Rock, scouting all the time.

W. T. SHERMAN,
Major General Commanding.

[Cipher.]

HEADQUARTERS MILITARY DIVISION OF THE MISSISSIPPI,
In the field, near Kenesaw, July 1, 1864.

Major General HALLECK, *Washington, D. C.:*

General Schofield is now south of Olley's creek and on the head of Nickajack. I have been hurrying down provisions and forage, and to-morrow night propose to move General McPherson from the left to the extreme right, back of General

Thomas. This will bring my right within three miles of Chattahoochee, and about five of the railroad. By this movement I think I can force Johnston to move his army down from Kenesaw to defend his railroad crossing and the Chattahoochee, when I will by the left flank reach the railroad below Marietta. But I cut loose from the railroad with ten (10) days' supplies in wagons. Johnston may come out of his intrenchments and attack General Thomas, which is what I want, for General Thomas is well intrenched parallel with the enemy, south of Kenesaw. I think Alatoona and the line of the Etowah are strong enough for me to venture on this move. The movement is substantially down the Sandtown road, straight for Atlanta.

W. T. SHERMAN,
Major General Commanding.

[Cipher]

HEADQUARTERS MILITARY DIVISION OF THE MISSISSIPPI,
In the field, near Kenesaw, July 2, 1864.

General ROUSSEAU, Nashville, Tennessee:

Now is the time for the raid to Opelika. Telegraph me whether you go yourself, or who will command. Forrest is in Mississippi, and Roddy has also gone there. All other rebel cavalry is here.

W. T. SHERMAN,
Major General Commanding.

HEADQUARTERS MILITARY DIVISION OF THE MISSISSIPPI,
In the field, Marietta, July 3, 1864—6¼ p. m.

General MCPHERSON:

Thomas has Hooker on the road out of Marietta, which is called an Atlanta road, but runs to the Sandtown road, crossing Nickajack at Ruff & Dunn's mill; he finds the enemy intrenched a mile this side of the mill. Howard is on the main Atlanta road, which is on the left of the railroad, and Palmer is intermediate, all finding the enemy near the line indicated by the crossroad from above Week's to the main road, about a mile and a half below Ruff's. I am convinced the enemy left Marietta in haste and confuson this morning. All the columns have taken many prisoners, and had the pursuit been vigorous we could have secured three or four thousand (3,000 or 4,000) prisoners and many wagons. Now the halt is of course to save time. If you ever worked in your life, work at daybreak to-morrow on the flank, crossing Nickajack somehow, and the moment you discover confusion pour in your fire. You know what a retreating mass across pontoon bridges means. Feel strong to-night and make feints of pursuit with artillery. I know Johnston's withdrawal is not strategic, but for good reasons, after he crosses the Chattahoochee; but his situation with that river behind him is not comfortable at all. If you can get him once started, follow up and call on Schofield. Let him read this. You both see the whole game as well as I do. Let Stoneman threaten about Baker and Howell's ferries, and you secure, if you can, the bridge and crossing at Nickajack, opposite Thomas. I will send Logan to you to-morrow, but you have as many men as can operate in that pocket. I don't confine you to any crossing, but press the enemy all the time in flank, till he is across the Chattahoochee.

W. T. SHERMAN,
Major General Commanding.

HEADQUARTERS MILITARY DIVISION OF THE MISSISSIPPI,
In the field, Marietta, July 3, 1864—6¼ p. m.

GENERAL THOMAS:

The more I reflect, the more I know Johnston's halt is to save time to cross his material and men. No general, such as he, would invite battle with the Chattahoochee behind him. I have ordered McPherson and Schofield to cross Nickajack at any cost, and work night and day to get the enemy started in confusion toward his bridges. I know you appreciate the situation. We will never have such a chance again, and I want you to impress on Hooker, Howard, and Palmer the importance of the most intense energy of attack to-night and in the morning, and to press with vehemence at any cost of life and material. Every inch of his line should be felt, and the moment there is a give, pursuit should be made by day with lines, and by night with a single head of column and section of artillery to each corps following a road. Hooker should communicate with McPherson by a circuit, if necessary, and act in concert. You know what loss would ensue to Johnston if he crosses his bridges at night in confusion, with artillery thundering at random on his rear.

I have reason to know that if our head of column had made for Ruff's instead of Marietta, we would have cut off two thousand (2,000) men and three hundred (300) wagons. But still we have now the best chance ever offered of a large army fighting at a disadvantage, with a river to his rear.

Send copies of this to Hooker, Palmer, and Howard. I have instructed McPherson, Schofield, and Garrard.

W. T. SHERMAN,
Major General Commanding.

[Cipher.]

HEADQUARTERS MILITARY DIVISION OF THE MISSISSIPPI,
Marietta, Ga., July 3, 1864—10 a. m.

General HALLECK, *Washington, D. C.:*

The movement on our right caused the enemy to evacuate. We occupied Kenesaw at daylight, and Marietta at 8½ a. m. Thomas is moving down the main road toward the Chattahoochee, McPherson toward the mouth of Nickajack, on the Sandtown road. Our cavalry is on the extreme flank. Whether the enemy will halt this side of Chattahoochee or not will soon be known. Marietta is almost entirely abandoned by its inhabitants, and more than a mile of the railroad iron is removed between the town and the foot of Kenesaw. I propose to press the enemy close till he is across the Chattahoochee river, when I must accumulate stores and better guard my rear.

W. T. SHERMAN,
Major General Commanding.

HEADQUARTERS MILITARY DIVISION OF THE MISSISSIPPI,
In the field, July 4, 1864.

GENERAL: I am satisfied the enemy will attempt with his cavalry to cross the Chattahoochee about Roswell, and make an attempt on our communications. To counteract him you will move in that direction, and watch close, taking some position in which to rally our infantry, a brigade of which is at Marietta, a strong brigade at Alatoona, and General Thomas will be instructed to hold McCook's brigade ready to go to your assistance. You may draw out at once and go to Roswell, and if you can find your way to it you may gain a secure position, from which you can watch that point.   In case the enemy's cavalry get across, you must hurry to him, wherever opposition is possible, and send couriers rapidly to me, and to the point of the railroad threatened.   In the mean time, report to me frequently, and use your cavalry as though you were preparing to cross yourself, or were only waiting for the waters to subside and make the ford practicable. You now understand the geography so well there that I have no doubt you can prevent Wheeler from doing much damage between Marietta and Alatoona.   In case he passes down by Canton to go toward Cartersville send notice, and hang on his rear.   We now have a full division of infantry at Kingston. Arrest every citizen in the country whom you find likely to prove a spy, and keep moving, so that your force cannot be computed.

I am, &c.,

W. T. SHERMAN,
Major General Commanding.

General GARRARD,
Commanding Division of Cavalry.

HEADQUARTERS MILITARY DIVISION OF THE MISSISSIPPI,
In the field, July 4, 1864.

Major General THOMAS:

I have no doubt that the enemy will attempt to molest our rear with his cavalry, and that he has reserved Roswell fortified for that very purpose.   To counteract his designs, I have ordered Garrard with his whole cavalry to proceed to Roswell, take the place if he can, otherwise hang near it, watching the river, opposing such a movement all he can, and giving us and all points of the railroad timely notice.   I wish you would so hold McCook as promptly to re-enforce Garrard if need be.   As soon as I ascertain the exact situation on the right, as to Turner's Ferry, and what progress McPherson has made, I will order Schofield round where Garrard now is.   I will go to-morrow, and in the mean time I wish you to hold strong the points now at Howard's and Palmer's head of column, and merely picket light the road by which Garrard moved, as I feel sure the enemy will not attempt a sally there.   Hooker need not hold the line from Palmer round to McPherson's, but draw in to his left, save by a line of videttes. I want you with your whole army to press steadily down on the enemy, while McPherson cuts in on his flank, Schofield to be held to re-enforce either part. Stoneman will threaten to cross the Chattahooche, and break the Atlanta and West Point road, especially if the enemy send cavalry against our line of road. Instead of occupying Ackworth, Big Shanty, and Marietta, I think we had better concentrate about the base of Kenesaw, near that water station, a point that could be defended against cavalry with great ease.

I am, &c.,

W. T. SHERMAN,
Major General Commanding.

HEADQUARTERS MILITARY DIVISION OF THE MISSISSIPPI,
In the field, three miles from railroad bridge, July 5, 1864—8 p. m.

GENERAL: I have ordered Schofield over to this road, in rear of the centre, preparatory to moving him over to about the north of Rottenwood, or Roswell factory, according to reports I may receive from General Garrard.   I was in hopes you would get control of the ridge commanding Turner's Ferry before the enemy could get across, but I think it is now too late, unless you have gained the ridge described as lying along the Chattahooche, above the mouth of Nickajack.

Do not attempt it unless it be certain of success, or unless you know that some part of Johnston's army or material is not yet across. My information is that Hood's and Polk's corps are across, and that Hardee remains on this side, occupying a line of intrenchments from the bridge down to Nickajack. I rather think the enemy will preserve this order of things until we develop our game. Stoneman will continue to threaten the river between Nickajack and Sweetwater, and you may co-operate and gain any substantial advantage you can, but be prepared to move whenever events may call. Hooker should be up nearer to Palmer. Howard's left is on the Chattahoochee, near Paice's Ferry, where the enemy had a pontoon bridge, which is cut loose and is swung to their bank. I understand he has two pontoon bridges at the railroad bridge. That bridge is still good, and was being very actively used to-day in passing trains. We have the road to within about two (2) miles of the bridge, including Vining's Station, where Johnston was last night.

I am, &c.,

W. T. SHERMAN,
Major General Commanding.

Major General McPHERSON.

HEADQUARTERS MILITARY DIVISION OF THE MISSISSIPPI,
In the field, near Chattahoochee river, July 5, 1864.

DEAR STONEMAN: I have your note, which is very satisfactory. I have heard of your general success from other quarters. I will instruct General Barry to give you a good four-gun battery if he can get one from some of the commands. Our left is now on the river above the railroad bridge. We find Hardee's corps intrenched on this side the river from the bridge down to the mouth of Nickajack; we hear the other two corps and militia are across. We can see Atlanta plain, but it will require hard fighting and science to take it. It must be done. Garrard is gone up to Roswell, and I hope to hear from him to-night. I think Johnston will send all his effective cavalry round by the north to strike our railroad, and must keep Garrard well on that flank with McCook to support him. I think you can whip anything that attempts to cross on your flank. Keep up the delusion of our crossing below Sandtown as long as possible, and I have reason to believe the enemy expects it. We have a nice game of war and must make no mistakes. We ought to have caught Johnston on his retreat, but he had prepared the way too well. We have killed and crippled a good number and have a couple thousand prisoners, some taken in fair fight and some gathered up straggling behind. He can no longer look into our camps as he did from Kenesaw. Try and pick up as many of his scouts as you can, and gather in every citizen of whom you entertain a suspicion. Schofield will move over to our left, up the Chattahoochee, about Roswell or below it. Write often. My headquarters are on the main road about three miles back from railroad bridge.

W. T. SHERMAN,
Major General Commanding.

[Cipher.]

HEADQUARTERS MILITARY DIVISION OF THE MISSISSIPPI,
In the field, near Chattahoochee river, July 5, 1864.

General HALLECK, *Washington:*

On the 3d we pursued the enemy by all the roads south till we found him in an intrenched position which had been prepared in advance; its salient on the main Marietta and Atlanta road about five miles south of Marietta, and the wings behind the Nickajack and Rottenwood creeks. During the 4th, General Thomas pressed the salient, and McPherson and Schofield moved against Nickajack. By pressing close and threatening the Chattahoochee at Sandtown and below, Johnston retreated in the night, and now has his main force and wagons across the Chattahoochee, with Hardee's corps on this side strongly intrenched in a sort of *tête-du-pont* on a ridge of hills beginning at the railroad bridge and extending down the river to the mouth of the Nickajack. We have worked hard, and now Thomas' left is on the Chattahoochee, three miles above the railroad bridge at Paice's Ferry. Stoneman has been most active with the cavalry about Sweetwater, and is now on the Chattahoochee about Sandtown, and General Garrard started this morning for Roswell Factory. I have no report from him yet. I am now far ahead of my railroad and telegraph and want them to catch up, and may be here some days. Atlanta is in plain view nine miles distant. We have had continual skirmishing, but our losses are small, while we have inflicted more to the enemy. Our prisoners taken in the last two days will not fall much short of two thousand (2,000.) The extent of the enemy's parallel already taken is wonderful, and much of the same sort confronts us yet, and is seen beyond the Chattahoochee.

W. T. SHERMAN,
Major General Commanding.

HEADQUARTERS MILITARY DIVISION OF THE MISSISSIPPI,
In the field, near Chattahoochee River, July 6, 1864.

GENERAL: I have just received your note announcing that you have possession of Roswell. This is important; watch well the crossing there, but not in force, keep your main force concealed somewhat. General McCook has just started for some point between Rottenwood and Soap creeks, where he will be near you. I intend to throw Schofield over on that flank the moment I propose to attempt a crossing. Fords are much better than bridges, and therefore have the river examined well as to fords. I am on the main road at the point where a branch goes to Vining's, on the railroad. Howard is at Vining's, and has possession of Paice's. McPherson's right is at Howell's Ferry, below Nickajack. The enemy holds this bank from the railroad bridge down to Nickajack, and seems to have it well fortified. Atlanta in plain view. Stoneman threatens the river down to Sweetwater. I will soon have a telegraph at Vining's, and you can thus communicate by Marietta. You will have rest for a few days, and should take advantage of all grain-fields.

Yours, truly,

W. T. SHERMAN,
Major General Commanding.

General GARRARD.

[Cipher.]

HEADQUARTERS MILITARY DIVISION OF THE MISSISSIPPI,
In the field, on Chattahoochee, July 6, 1864.

Major General HALLECK, *Washington, D. C.:*

I have just received Secretary Stanton's despatch, and don't understand how Semmes and crew were allowed to leave the sinking Alabama in an English yacht.

I would have preferred the President had not proclaimed martial law in Kentucky, but simply allowed the military commanders to arrest and banish all malcontents, while the honest and industrious stay-at-homes were encouraged by the increase of security. Johnston made two breaks in the railroad, one above Marietta, and one near Vining's Station. The former is already done, and Johnston's army has already heard the sound of our locomotives. The telegraph is done to Vining's, and the field wire is just at my bivouac, and will be ready to carry this to you as soon as translated into cipher.

I propose to study the crossings of the Chattahoochee, and when all is ready, to move quick. As a beginning, I keep the wagons and troops well back from the river, and display to the enemy only the picket line, with a few batteries along at random. Have moved General Schofield to a point where he can in a single march reach the Chattahoochee at a point above the railroad bridge, where there is a ford. At present the waters are turbid and swollen by the late rains, but if the present hot weather lasts, the water will run down very fast. We have pontoons enough for four (4) bridges, but, as our crossing will be resisted, we must manœuvre some. All the regular crossing-places are covered by forts apparently of long construction; but we shall cross in due time, and instead of attacking Atlanta direct, or any of its forts, propose to make a circuit, destroying all its railroads. This is a delicate movement and must be done with caution.

Our army is in good condition and full of confidence, but the weather is intensely hot, and a good many men have fallen with sun-stroke. This is a high and healthy country, and the sanitary condition of the army is good.

W. T. SHERMAN,
Major General Commanding.

[Cipher.]

HEADQUARTERS MILITARY DIVISION OF THE MISSISSIPPI,
In the field, Chattahoochee River, July 6, 1864.

General ROUSSEAU, Nashville and Decatur :

That cavalry expedition must now be off, and must proceed with the utmost energy and confidence. Everything here is favorable, and I have official information that General A. J. Smith is out from Memphis with force enough to give Forrest full occupation. Expeditions inland are also out from Vicksburg and Baton Rouge, as well as against Mobile. If managed with secrecy and rapidity the expedition cannot fail of success and will accomplish much good.

W. T. SHERMAN,
Major General Commanding.

HEADQUARTERS MILITARY DIVISION OF THE MISSISSIPPI,
In the field, near Cattahoochee, July 7, 1864—8 a. m.

DEAR GENERAL : I send Major McCoy down to see you. I did intend to ride the lines to-day, but have my mind so intent on a crossing place that I want to be near. The cars now run into Marietta and down as far as a break, that will be repaired to-day, about four miles back of the bridge.

The enemy hold, as a tête-du-pont, the hills from Nickajack to a point about two miles above the bridge. I rather prefer this should be so, as he will have less on the other side. I wish you to display as much anxiety to cross as possible and as low down, but keep your masses ready to move to the real quarter when required.

I wish you to use artillery pretty freely, and if, as I understand, you have a plunging fire on the extreme point of that range near Nickajack, get plenty of guns—say thirty—and give it thunder.

I send you a copy of an important despatch from Canby, in addition to which General Rousseau will start from Decatur for Opelika.

If you see Stoneman feel him, and see how he would like to work down the river, say thirty (30) miles, and also make a dash at Opelika, swinging back to us or to Rome for safety. A break of twenty miles from Opelika westward is perfectly practicable and would be a good blow. In the mean time, we can improve our communications and get a sure crossing at some point above.

Yours, &c.,

W. T. SHERMAN,
Major General Commanding

General McPherson.

Headquarters Military Division of the Mississippi,
In the field, near Chattahoochee, July 7, 1864.

General: Your report is received and is most acceptable. I had no idea that the factories at Roswell remained in operation, but supposed the machinery had all been removed. Their utter destruction is right and meets my entire approval; and to make the matter complete, you will arrest the owners and employes and send them under guard, charged with treason, to Marietta, and I will see as to any man in America hoisting the French flag, and then devoting his labor and capital to supplying armies in open hostility to our government, and claiming the benefit of his neutral flag. Should you, under the impulse of anger, natural at contemplating such perfidy, hang the wretch, I approve the act beforehand.

I have sent General Schofield to reconnoitre over on that flank, and I want a lodgement made on the other bank as soon as possible, anywhere from Roswell down to the vicinity of Soap's creek. I have no doubt the opposite bank is picketed, but, as you say, the main cavalry force of Wheeler has moved to the other flank, and we should take advantage of it. If you can make a lodgement on the south bank anywhere, and secure it well, do so. General Schofield will be near to follow it up and enlarge the foothold. He had just started from Ruff's Station a few minutes before I received your despatch, but I telegraphed the substance to be sent to overtake him. Keep a line of couriers back to Marietta, and telegraph me very fully and often. I now have the wires to my bivouac.

By selecting some one ford, say the second or third below the mouth of Willeyoe creek on your sketch, and holding a force there concealed, say a brigade with your battery; then have the heads of each of your other two brigades cross at night at the nearest fords, and, without firing a gun, close in front of the brigade in position ready to cross with artillery. When across with artillery, the best position on a commanding hill should be fortified. I will see that the cavalry is relieved by General Schofield at once. I merely suggest this plan, and its execution about daylight to-morrow, and I prefer you should do it.

I assure you, spite of any little disappointment I may have expressed, I feel for you personally not only respect but affection, and wish for you unmeasured success and reputation; but I do wish to inspire all cavalry with my conviction that caution and prudence should be but a very small element in their characters.

I repeat my orders that you arrest all people, male and female, connected with those factories, no matter what the clamor, and let them foot it, under guard, to Marietta, whence I will send them by cars to the north. Destroy and make the same disposition of all mills, save small flouring-mills manifestly for local use, but all saw-mills and factories dispose of effectually, and useful laborers, excused, by reason of their skill as manufacturers, from conscription, are as much prisoners as if armed. The poor women will make a howl. Let them take along their children and clothing, providing they have the means of hauling or you can spare them. We will retain them until they can reach a country where they can live in peace and security.

In your next letter give me as much information as you can as to the size and dimensions of the burned bridge at Roswell across the Chattahoochee. We have plenty of pontoon bridging, but I much prefer fords for so large an army as we have.

I am, with respect, yours truly,

W. T. SHERMAN,
Major General Commanding.

General GARRARD,
Roswell, Georgia.

[Cipher.]

HEADQUARTERS–MILITARY DIVISION OF THE MISSISSIPPI,
In the field, near Chattahoochee, July 7, 1864.

General HALLECK, *Washington, D. C.:*

General Garrard reports to me that he is in possession of Rosswell, where were several valuable cotton and wool factories in full operation, also paper-mills, all of which, by my order, he destroyed by fire. They had been for years engaged exclusively at work for the confederate government; and the owner of the woollen factory displayed the French flag, but as he failed also to show the United States flag, General Garrard burned it also. The main cotton factory was valued at a million of United States dollars. The cloth on hand is reserved for the use of United States hospitals; and I have ordered General Garrard to arrest for treason all owners and employés, foreign and native, and send them under guard to Marietta, whence I will send them north. Being exempt from conscription, they are as much governed by the rules of war as if in the ranks. The women can find employment in Indiana. This whole region was devoted to manufactories, but I will destroy every one of them. Johnston is manœuvring against my right, and I will try and pass the Chattahoochee by my left. Ask Mr. Stanton not to publish the substance of my despatches, for they reach Richmond in a day, and are telegraphed at once to Atlanta. The Atlanta papers contain later news from Washington than I get from Nashville. Absolute silence in military matters is the only safe rule. Let our public learn patience and common sense.

W. T. SHERMAN,
Major General Commanding.

NEW ORLEANS, *June 27, 1864.*

Major General SHERMAN:

General Washburn has sent me a copy of your despatch to him of the 14th instant. I had previously written to him that he should employ A. J. Smith's troops, and any others that he could reach, to pursue and, if possible, destroy Forrest's command. I have placed under his control all the militia from the northwestern States that were ordered to report to me, and several regiments of old troops from Missouri. This will enable him to give Smith an effective force of twelve (12) or fifteen (15) thousand men, and leave a reserve of five thousand (5,000) for other operations. I will start the expedition against Mobile four days later. A cavalry expedition will start at the same time from Vicksburg, for the purpose of distracting the attention of the enemy from Smith's operations and those in this neighborhood. A large cavalry force will leave the river above Baton Rouge for the purpose of cutting the Mobile and Ohio road, and Steele will also be instructed to make a demonstration in the direction of Price's force. We have labored under great disadvantages in having no resources for water transportation on the river, but this will soon be overcome.

E. R. S. CANBY
Major General.

[Cipher.]

HEADQUARTERS MILITARY DIVISION OF THE MISSISSIPPI,
In the field, near Chattahoochee, July 7, 1864.

General E. R. S. CANBY, *New Orleans:*

Your despatch of the 27th June is received and is very agreeable news. I think Generals Smith and Mower can take care of Forrest. We have fought Johnston steadily back for a hundred miles over very difficult ground fortified at immense labor. I don't think our loss exceeds that of the enemy. It has been one immense skirmish, with small battles interspersed.

This army remains strong in numbers and spirit, and has been wonderfully supplied. Though repeatedly broken, our railroad and telegraph are in good order to the rear, and I have depots of supplies accumulated at fortified points to my rear.

Atlanta is in sight, and is defended by a well-handled army and a circle of finished redoubts; yet I shall not pause. The expeditions from Memphis, Vicksburg, and Baton Rouge are most important, and will keep employed the forces of the enemy that might be most mischievous to my rear.

Also, the move on Mobile will be most opportune, no matter in what strength, even if confined to a feint.

On the 9th I start a lightly equipped cavalry force of about three thousand, (3,000,) without wagons, from Decatur, Alabama, to Opelika, to break up the single track from Montgomery eastward, the effect of which will be to separate Alabama from Georgia. This force may be compelled to go to Pensacola. Please let the commanding officer at Pensacola look out for them about the 20th to 25th of July. If they make Pensacola, they will leave horses there and come back to Tennessee by water. Major General Rousseau will command.

W. T. SHERMAN,
Major General Commanding.

[Cipher.]

HEADQUARTERS MILITARY DIVISION OF THE MISSISSIPPI,
In the field, near Chattahoochee river, July 7, 1864.

General ROUSSEAU, *Nashville and Decatur:*

I have no new instructions or information to convey to you, but expect you to leave Decatur on the 9th. If Roddy be about Tuscumbia you might send a small infantry force down to Waterloo to amuse him by threatening to cross and to burn the Bear Creek bridge, eight (8) miles back from Eastport and five (5) miles east from Iuka. You may give out that you are going to Selma, but be sure to go to Opelika and break up railroad between it and Montgomery. There is but a single road there that unites the Georgia roads with the Alabama roads. I am convinced General A. J. Smith will give full employment to Forrest, and I will keep Joe Johnston fully employed, and Canby will look out for the Mobile garrison. When you reach the roads, do your work well, burn the ties in piles, heat the iron in the middle, and when red-hot let the men pull the ends so as to give a twist to the rail. If simply bent the rails may be used again; but if the rails are twisted or wrenched they cannot be used again. In retreating, you should take the back track; and if pursued, turn for me, or for Rome, or Kingston, or Alatoona.

Be sure to take no wagons, but pack some led horses. Travel early and late in the days, but rest at midday. and midnight. Spare your horses for the first week, and keep them ready for the return trip. I think the only force in your route is Pillow's, about Oxford, or Jacksonville, or Gadsden. We are down to the Chattahoochee and will soon be across. All is well with us.

W. T. SHERMAN,
Major General Commanding.

HEADQUARTERS MILITARY DIVISION OF THE MISSISSIPPI,
In the field, near Chattahoochee, July 7, 1864.

General SCHOFIELD, *Ruff's Station:*

You may move to the neighborhood of the mouth of Soap's creek. Mask well your command, and make a lodgement across the Chattahoochee, but do not attempt it until you have a ford near by, by which to re-enforce the party first sent, or by which it may be necessary to retire. We can, after lodgement, make roads to the crossing, and may add pontoon bridges, of which we have enough for four bridges. After securing a point opposite Soap's creek, Roswell's will follow as a matter of course, and will be additional. The moment I hear that General Garrard has made a lodgement at Roswell's, I will send a division of General McPherson to hold fast all he makes. With Roswell's and mouth of Soap's creek, we have plenty of room, with Marietta as the depot.

I will go down to General McPherson's and stir them up in the morning by way of diversion.

W. T. SHERMAN,
Major General Commanding.

HEADQUARTERS MILITARY DIVISION OF THE MISSISSIPPI,
In the field, near Chattahoochee, July 8, 1864.

General SCHOFIELD, *Ruff's Station:*

It is all important I should know as soon as possible the general topography on the other side of the river, as to the practicability of the roads in every direction, especially toward Stone Mount and Decatur. If you can catch a few people who ought to know all about it send them to me.

I will go to the extreme right to-day. General Rousseau will start from Decatur for Opelika to-morrow, and General Stoneman may feign down as far as Campbelton. I think the railroad bridge was burned last night. No other news.

W. T. SHERMAN,
Major General Commanding.

DECATUR, *July* 8, 1864.

Major General SHERMAN:

I am off to-day, after all sorts of petty annoyances composing delays. I hope to accomplish fully what you desire, and shall do my best. I go sixteen (16) miles to-day, and hope to reach the point in seven (7) to eight (8) days.

L. H. ROUSSEAU,
Major General.

HEADQUARTERS MILITARY DIVISION OF THE MISSISSIPPI
In the field, near Chattahoochee, July 9, 1864.

General THOMAS:

I have an Atlanta paper of the 6th. I think its tone is changed, and it apologizes for the necessity of civilians quitting the place. By it I see that General Slocum is at Jackson, Mississippi, and have no doubt we will soon perceive the effect of General Smith's move in Mississippi, and General Canby's against Mobile.

If General Howard could get a cable over to that pontoon bridge and haul it into place, it would be a constant threat at that point.

W. T. SHERMAN,
Major General Commanding.

HEADQUARTERS MILITARY DIVISION OF THE MISSISSIPPI,
In the field, near Chattahoochee, July 8, 1864.

General THOMAS:

General Garrard will effect a lodegment to-morrow morning at Roswell, and General Schofield about the mouth of Soap's creek. The moment I hear that General Garrard is successful, I will send one of General McPherson's corps up; but he is so far off that it may become necessary to re-enforce him (General Garrard) in the night to-morrow, in which case I will call for a division of General Howard, nearest to Roswell, to be relieved by General McPherson as soon as he can get there. At daybreak to-morrow make some display to assist in covering the movements.

W. T. SHERMAN,
Major General Commanding.

ROSWELL, *July* 9, 1864—7 a. m.

Major General SHERMAN:

I have the ridge on the south bank of the river. The infantry should come up at once. I see no reason why I cannot hold it; but cannot tell what may occur before long.

I am, very respectfully, your obedient servant,

K. GARRARD,
Brigadier General U. S. V.

ROSWELL, *July* 9, 1864—9 p. m.

Major General SHERMAN:

I have to report the arrival of General Newton with his division, 4th corps. All was quiet, and he relieved me about dark. My cavalry pickets are about

8 *

two miles from the river on the Atlanta road. There has been but slight opposition to-day, though my cavalry pickets stand opposite to those of the enemy, and have had some skirmishing. No sign of large force of the enemy's infantry. The ford is very rough, and about belly-deep. Wagons might be passed over, though it would be better to have the bridge built. Dimensions of old bridge: length six hundred and forty-two (642) feet; six (6) spans; good stone piers fourteen (14) feet from water.

K. GARRARD,
Brigadier General Commanding Cavalry.

HEADQUARTERS MILITARY DIVISION OF THE MISSISSIPPI,
In the field, near Chattahoochee, July 9, 1864.

General HALLECK, *Washington, D. C.:*

I telegraph to you, and Mr. Secretary Stanton answers. Drop me a word now and then of advice and encouragement. I think I have done well to maintain such an army in this country, fighting for sixty (60) days, and yet my losses are made up by the natural increase. The assault I made was no mistake. I had to do it. The enemy, and our own army and officers, had settled down into the conviction that the assault of lines formed no part of my game, and the moment the enemy was found behind anything like a parapet, why, everybody would deploy, throw up counter-works, and take it easy, leaving it to the "Old Man" to turn the position. Had the assault been made with one-fourth more vigor, (mathematically,) I would have put the head of George Thomas's whole army right through Johnston's deployed line, on the best ground for "go ahead," while my entire forces were well in hand on roads converging to my then object, Marietta. Had Harker and McCook not been struck down so early, the assault would have succeeded, and then the battle would have all been in our favor, on account of our superiority in numbers and initiative. Even as it was, Johnston has been much more cautious since, and gives ground more freely. His next fighting line (Smyrna camp ground) he only held one day.

I have got General Schofield across the Chattahoochee with two good pontoon bridges without loss, and momentarily wait the news of my cavalry being across at "Roswell" factory, where is the best ford on the whole river; but before going ahead I will add there a good pier or trestle bridge, and will, at some point intermediate, convenient to roads, put down two more pontoon bridges, making five bridges and three fords, before I put the army across the Chattahoochee.

I call your attention to the enclosed paper in reference to the Roswell factories. They were very valuable, and were burned by my orders. They have been engaged almost exclusively in manufacturing cloth for the confederate army, and you will observe they were transferred to the English and French flags for safety; but such nonsense cannot deceive me. They were tainted with treason, and such fictitious transfer was an aggravation. I will send all the owners, agents, and employés up to Indiana to get rid of them here. I take it a neutral is no better than one of our own citizens, and we would not respect the property of one of our own citizens engaged in supplying a hostile army.

Write me a note occasionally, and suggest anything that may occur to you, as I am really in the wilderness down here; but I will fight any and all the time on anything like fair terms, and that is the best strategy; but it would not be fair to run up against such parapets as I find here.

Your friend,

W. T. SHERMAN,
Major General.

HEADQUARTERS MILITARY DIVISION OF THE MISSISSIPPI,
In the field, near Chattahoochee, July 9, 1864.

General SCHOFIELD:

General Garrard is across at Roswell, and Dodge is moving to that point with orders to fortify a *tête de pont* and to build a good trestle bridge. I want from you a minute description of your position, and all information as to roads leading from it to the east about Stone mountain. I propose to operate some to the south to accumulate stores, and then go ahead.

W. T. SHERMAN,
Major General Commanding.

[Cipher.]

HEADQUARTERS MILITARY DIVISION OF THE MISSISSIPPI,
In the field, near Chattahoochee, July 9, 1864.

General HALLECK, *Washington, D. C.:*

General Schofield effected a lodgement across the Chattahoochee, near the mouth of Soap's creek last night, and has two good pontoon bridges. He captured the single gun that guarded the passage, but the guard fled. General Garrard crossed at Roswell factory, and has a secure lodgement at the Shallow ford. General Dodge is moving to that point to take Garrard's place, and has orders to build a good bridge there. These crossings will be strongly covered with forts. I will then endeavor to break the railroad south of Atlanta by an expedition from Decatur, under General Rousseau, and another from here. In the mean time will collect supplies, and secure better my rear, and then cross over the main army and go ahead. Weather is very hot, but the country is high and healthy.

W. T. SHERMAN,
Major General Commanding.

HEADQUARTERS MILITARY DIVISION OF THE MISSISSIPPI,
In the field, near the Chattahoochee, July 9, 1864.

GENERAL: We now have a good lodgement on the other bank of the river. Schofield at the mouth of Soap's creek, and Garrard opposite Roswell. I saw General Dodge to-day en route for Roswell, and explained to him the importance of the plan, and he understands it fully. He and Garrard can hold it secure whilst we manœuvre a little more on our right, and give time to collect stores at Marietta, and for Rousseau to get a good offing. We noticed a good deal of flutter in the enemy's camps to-day, troops and wagons moving rapidly east and north. Johnston sees I threaten Decatur and Stone mountain, and now is a good time for Stoneman to strike south. I want him, if possible, to secure a point at Campbellton, or below, and strike the West Point road. I do believe he can do it, for Johnston will spread his force so much that it will be weak at all points. I have told Stoneman that if he secures both banks at Campbellton, with its ferry-boats, he may call on you for a brigade to hold it whilst he strikes the railroad.

Of course we do not intend to attack the *tête de pont* of the enemy, and unless Johnston supposes I have scattered my force too much he will not venture to sally; and if he does, our position is as strong against him as his against us, and I have no apprehensions on that score. Therefore, if Stoneman calls for a brigade send it.

Keep hammering away all the time, and the moment he lets go this bank occupy it; but if he holds on, as soon as the time comes we will let him stay on this side, and we will go over.

With Thomas things are *statu quo*. Railroad and telegraph all right.

Yours,

W. T. SHERMAN,
Major General Commanding.

General McPherson, *Army of the Tennessee.*

HEADQUARTERS MILITARY DIVISION OF THE MISSISSIPPI,
Near the Chattahoochee, July 9, 1864.

GENERAL: In pursuance of our conversation of this day, I have to request that you proceed with your command to Campbellton to-morrow night, appearing suddenly before the place, and securing, if possible, the boats there, or forcing the enemy to destroy them. If you can possibly do it, get possession of those boats, and also of the other bank. I am very anxious that an attack or demonstration be made against the railroad below Atlanta, and will instruct General McPherson to have a brigade of infantry ready to come down and hold the river, whilst you, with cavalry, strike the road. I am satisfied that the crossing of Schofield and Garrard above will draw in that direction Johnston's chief army, and that what troops are left south of Atlanta will be strung out as far as West Point, where he will keep the chief force. The point where the road would be easiest reached will be, say, half way from Atlanta to West Point, but it would not be safe for you to pass Campbellton unless the ferry is well destroyed. The bridge at Franklin is almost too far down, but still it, too, might be reached by you, and either used or destroyed. A ford but little known or used below Campbellton and this side of the Franklin bridge will be the best, if such exist, and you may incur any risk, sure of my approval, for, whether you make a break of the road, or merely cause a diversion, you will do good.

Don't be absent more than four or five days, and keep me advised on all possible occasions.

Yours, truly,

W. T. SHERMAN,
Major General Commanding,

Major General STONEMAN,
Commanding Division of Cavalry.

HEADQUARTERS MILITARY DIVISION OF THE MISSISSIPPI,
In the field, near Chattahoochee, July 10, 1864.

General THOMAS :

Signal officers report railroad and all other bridges burning; of course, if such be the case the enemy has gone across; yet I hear firing of pickets. Report to me the truth as soon as ascertained.

W. T. SHERMAN,
Major General Commanding.

HEADQUARTERS MILITARY DIVISION OF THE MISSISSIPPI,
In the field, near Chattahoochee, July 10, 1864.

General THOMAS :

Let Howard move up to supporting distance of Schofield to assist him in case the enemy attempt to dislodge him.

Detachments of Hooker and Palmer should occupy the redoubts this side, but keep your wagons and masses out of sight for the present.

W. T. SHERMAN,
Major General Commanding.

HEADQUARTERS DEPARTMENT OF THE CUMBERLAND,
July 10, 1864—4. 45 a. m.

Major General SHERMAN:

The enemy has left my front and burned the railroad and wagon bridges over the river. I have ordered the skirmishers to feel up and ascertain if they are still on this side. I presume the firing we heard is the pickets exchanging shots across the river.

GEO. H. THOMAS,
Major General.

HEADQUARTERS DEPARTMENT OF THE CUMBERLAND,
July, 10 1864.

Major General SHERMAN:

Hooker and Palmer occupy the enemy's works in their fronts, and have skirmishers on the river bank. Their camps have not been moved. Howard has been ordered to move to supporting distance of Schofield.

GEO. H. THOMAS,
Major General.

HEADQUARTERS MILITARY DIVISION OF THE MISSISSIPPI,
In the field, near Chattahoochee river, July 10, 1864.

General DODGE, *Roswell:*

I have been out all day and just back. Have received General Garrard's and your despatches. I design that General McPherson's whole army shall come to that flank, and you are to prepare the way. General Newton will stay with you till you feel all safe, when he will rejoin his corps now in support of General Schofield, eight (8) miles below you. General Garrard will picket the roads, and I want you to fortify a *tête de pont* and bridge. General McPherson will operate to the right, and then, when all is ready, will come rapidly to your flank. Therefore, make all preparations to that end. General Schofield has a secure place opposite the mouth of Soap's creek. Keep me well advised by courier to Marietta and telegraph.

W. T. SHERMAN,
Major General Commanding.

HEADQUARTERS MILITARY DIVISION OF THE MISSISSIPPI,
In the field, near Chattahoochee river, July 10, 1864.

General THOMAS:

General Schofield has a good bridge and position, but the road up the hill is narrow, crooked and steep. I think the road out from Powers's ferry is better and leads straight to the Cross Keys, the first point common to the roads out from Roswell, (McPherson,) Phillips's, (Schofield's,) and Powers's and Paice's, (yours.) General Dodge will make a good bridge at Roswell; General Schofield will make a bridge at Phillips's, and you can have your own and McPherson's pontoons at Powers's and Paice's. General Howard is close up to General Schofield, and General Newton will join him as soon as General Dodge has made his bridge and works. I think it would be well for General Howard to secure the hill at Powers's ferry, just below the crossing, and move the pontoons down as soon as General Schofield gets a trestle bridge done. I want General McPherson to feign strong at Turner's and cover General Stoneman's movements down the river, and I want you to make strong demonstrations at the railroad bridge, but keep in mind that you are to cross at Powers's and Paice's. All the roads back to Marietta are good, but the cross-roads are steep and hilly. The road from Powers's to Vining's is quite good—crosses Rottenwood at a mill-dam. All preparations should be made in three days.

W. T. SHERMAN,
Major General Commanding.

HEADQUARTERS MILITARY DIVISION OF THE MISSISSIPPI,
In the field, near Chattahoochee, July 10, 1864.

GENERAL: I have pretty much made up my mind as to the next move, but would be glad to hear any suggestion from you.

I propose that General Stoneman shall attempt to break the road below Atlanta; to accumulate stores at Marietta, and increase our guards to the rear; then suddenly to shift you to Roswell, General Dodge in the mean time to get you a good *tête de pont* and bridge. General Schofield is already at Phillips's ferry, across and fortified; he, too, will make a good trestle bridge. General Thomas will group his at Powers's and Paice's ferries.

But for the next three days, while these preparations are being made, I want you to demonstrate as though attempting to cross at Turner's or below, and General Thomas the same at the railroad bridge. When General Stoneman is back, I will give you the word to shift rapidly to Roswell and cross over, and in anticipation you can get your wagons back to Marietta, except such as you need. General Thomas will need yours and his pontoons to cross at Powers's and Paice's. At the right time I will leave Generals Stoneman and McCook to cover the front and cross all the balance of the army and advance it with its right on or near Peach Tree creek, and the left (you) to swing towards Stone mountain. Johnston will be found to occupy his redoubts about Atlanta, and also Stone mountain and Decatur. We can manœuvre so as to compel him to weaken his centre or one of his flanks, when we can act. If he neglect his right or centre, we get on his Augusta road. If he neglect Atlanta, we take it. If he assume the offensive, we cover our roads and base, and can make as good use of Peach Tree as he. If General Stoneman could break the road, so much the better; but if he cannot, I calculate that General Rousseau will do so within a week, quite as early as we can be at or near Cross Keys.

The ground opposite still continues rough, but that we cannot help. I find all the roads leading back from Roswell, Phillips's and Powers's ferries to Marietta are good, but the cross-roads are hilly and sharp.

The advantage of this plan over the one of crossing to the south is that we are all between the enemy and our base; and now that he has destroyed his own bridges, he cannot get over without fighting us. Study your maps and be ready, but in the mean time stir up the enemy all you can on that flank and make feints as though designing to cross the Chattahoochee.

W. T. SHERMAN,
Major General Commanding.

Major General MCPHERSON,
Commanding Army of the Tennessee.

HEADQUARTERS LEFT WING, 11TH ARMY CORPS,
Roswell, July 10, 1864—1.30 p. m.

Major General SHERMAN:

My troops are arriving and crossing. I have been here three hours, and in company with General Newton have thoroughly examined the country. I will occupy and fortify to-night a *tête de pont* one-half mile from the river and extending up and down one mile, covering the entire ford, bridge and roads leading to them. The ford is one-half mile or more in extent, very rough and impracticable, except for troops to bridge the stream. I will have to build over six hundred and fifty (650) feet in length. I shall use the old piers and trestle between, and we have a strong picket out three miles, covering the forks and road leading to McAfee's bridge, eight (8) miles up the river, and the road that leads to Atlanta. It is too far out to take the command until the river is easily passed by artillery and trains.

G. M. DODGE, Major General.

HEADQUARTERS MILITARY DIVISION OF THE MISSISSIPPI,
In the field, near Chattahoochee river, July 11, 1864.

General DODGE, Roswell, Georgia :

I know you have a big job, but that is nothing new for you. Tell General Newton that his corps is now up near General Schofield's crossing, and that all is quiet thereabouts. He might send down and move his camp to the proximity of his corps, but I think Roswell and Shallow Ford so important, that I prefer him to be near you until you are well fortified. If he needs rations, tell him to get his wagons up, and I think you will be able to spare him day after to-morrow. I know the bridge at Roswell is important, and you may destroy all Georgia to make it good and strong.

W. T. SHERMAN,
Major General Commanding.

HEADQUARTERS MILITARY DIVISION OF THE MISSISSIPPI,
In the field, near Chattahoochee river, July 11, 1864.

GENERAL : The importance of your command to the success of my operations is, I know, already appreciated by you; but when I suggest any additional work or experience, I beg you to consider it as resulting from my supposed large experience in the military art.

In the first place, I fear that our infantry officers suppose if cavalry comes about, they are excused from doing anything but to defend their own posts. This is not so. Infantry can always whip cavalry, and in a wooded and mountainous country can actually thwart it, and even at times capture it. Of course, as a general rule, a footman cannot catch a horseman on a fair road or country, but nothing is more awkward in a wooded and mountainous country than a command of cavalry forced to go through narrow defiles, across streams at particular fords or bridges, or up and down certain valleys which can be seen from the mountain tops and ambushes. I have not yet seen in this war a cavalry force of a thousand that was not afraid of the sight of a dozen infantry bayonets, for the reason that the cavalry, to be effective, has to have a road or smooth field; whereas the infantry man steps into the bushes and is safe, or can block a road in five minutes and laugh at the man on horseback.

The moral I wish to inculcate by these simple illustrations is, by knowing the country and thinking ahead, an infantry garrison can act against cavalry. Therefore, it is expected of the infantry guarding our road, that they are not to sit down and let cavalry prance all around them, but that they must ambush their roads, anticipate their passage at mountain passes and creek crossings, or can pursue them and catch them jammed in narrow roads or at bridges. Thus at Dalton a lookout should be kept all along Taylor's ridge to give notice of horsemen in the far off valleys, and then they should be waylaid. Rewards should be offered and paid to faithful citizens and negroes who give notice of the presence of parties of the enemy, but they should always be waylaid and pursued.

Another matter I will draw your attention to: officers and men naturally slip into houses and establish headquarters offices, &c., and are about as useless as if posted in Canada. Make a positive order that each garrison shall build *anew* a good stockade with earthwork, abattis, &c., not too strong, but to serve as a stronghold and rallying point, to hold a dash of cavalry in check, and more especially to allow a part of the garrison to hold the post while the greater portion goes forth to battle with the enemy. A fixed garrison is harmless and useless. Its only value is in its power of offence.

I think you had better embody some of these ideas, and such others as may suggest themselves to you, in a general order, and have it printed on pasteboard and hung up at every post, and then make your inspectors enforce it.

We are now in full possession of the country down to the Chattahoochee, and have two good crossings—one at Roswell, and the other at the mouth of Soap's creek, known as Phillips's, and I only await a few developments to go ahead. General Vandever telegraphs from Rome that Pillow's force has gone towards Meridian. If another attempt is made from that quarter, it should be counteracted by moving behind it from Rome and Gunter's landing.

W. T. SHERMAN,
Major General Commanding.

Major General STEEDMAN,
  Commanding District of Etowah.

[Cipher.]

HEADQUARTERS MILITARY DIVISION OF THE MISSISSIPPI,
In the field, near Chattahoochee river, July 11, 1864.

General HALLECK, *Washington, D. C.:*

The enemy is now all beyond the Chattahoochee, having destroyed all his bridges. We occupy the west bank for thirty miles, and have two heads of columns across—one at the Shallow ford, at Rossville, and the other at the mouth of Soap's creek, Phillips's. At these we are making good pier bridges. Water is shallow, rock bottom, but strong and rapid current. I propose to have another of pontoons lower down, about the mouth of Rottenwood or Island creeks.

The last works abandoned by the enemy were the strongest of all, embracing two detached redoubts, and extending along the river hills for about five miles, having in its whole extent finished abatis and parapet, with glacis obstructed with chevaux-de-frise and all manner of impediments. But the moment Johnston detected, I had ignored his fort, and secured two good lodgements above him, on the east bank, at Roswell factory and at Philips's, he drew his forces across and burned all his bridges, viz: one railroad and trestle and three (3) pontoons.

We now commence the real game for Atlanta, and I expect pretty sharp practice; but I think we have the advantage, and I propose to keep it.

W. T. SHERMAN,
Major General Commanding.

HEADQUARTERS MILITARY DIVISION OF THE MISSISSIPPI,
In the field, near Chattahoochee river, July 11, 1864.

General THOMAS:

I have ordered General McPherson to send his pontoons here to-morrow. I will order them to Powers's ferry, and I will want you to effect a lodgement there to-morrow night and next day. There is no enemy of any size to our immediate front, and General Dodge reports the enemy's cavalry alone above Peach Tree creek, at Buckhead. He says he has an Atlanta paper of the 10th; that all the wealthy people are leaving, and that a council of war was held, when it was decided to fight for Atlanta. General Rousseau telegraphs from Decatur that he started that day, and would be on the Montgomery and Opelika road in eight (8) or nine (9) days. I think we should, as soon as possible, secure the opposite bank, from Roswell down to Peach Tree creek. I think the bridge across Peach Tree, near the railroad bridge, is still standing. I watched it close to-day; I think I saw half a dozen men pass it, but, with that exception, there was no life visible. There was no danger in standing in full view in the redoubt to-day. The signal officer reports the absence of all camps from the other side to-day. I suppose Johnston will group his army about Atlanta and wait for us to develop our game. I only await news from Stoneman to put General McPherson in motion.

W. T. SHERMAN,
Major General Commanding.

HEADQUARTERS MILITARY DIVISION OF THE MISSISSIPPI,
In the field, near Chattahoochee river, July 12, 1864—2 a. m.

GENERAL: I have received your despatches of last night. You may put in motion at once the 15th corps and trains for Roswell, leaving General Blair with such artillery and wagons as he may need to await the return of General Stoneman, and to make in the mean time the necessary demonstrations about Sandtown, Howell's and Turner's. The enemy, having destroyed his bridges, cannot come back on General Blair, and therefore he can strip light so as to follow you as little encumbered as possible when General Stoneman does get back or is heard from. Instruct General Blair fully on these points, and let him report to me direct while thus established. Let your troops move in the cool of the evening and by moonlight and in the morning, sparing men and animals as much as possible. You will then proceed to Roswell in person and take control of matters on that flank, giving the necessary orders to your own troops and to General Garrard's cavalry. I want everything done that is prudent and necessary at Roswell to make it a kind of secondary base for operations against Atlanta and the roads east towards Augusta and Macon. As you know, the bridges are under progress, and the telegraph will be there as soon as you. The ford there though rough, is always practicable in case of accident to ourselves or the bridge, and constitutes one of the reasons for its use as a point of departure and the roads to and from Roswell are old and much used. The country thereabouts is also represented as abounding in grass, grain, and cornfields, all of which will come into use.

Your wagons and artillery should move by Marietta and fill up with provisions, forage and ammunition, and I think that also is the best road for the troops, though a few miles could be saved by cutting across by Smyrna camp-ground.

If convenient, you might ride by the Turner's Ferry road, along the enemy's recent works, by General Thomas's and my headquarters, to confer with me and to compare maps.

I am, with respect, yours, &c.,

W. T. SHERMAN,
Major General Commanding.

Major General McPHERSON,
Commanding Army of the Tennessee.

HEADQUARTERS MILITARY DIVISION OF THE MISSISSIPPI,
In the field, near Chattahoochee river, July 12, 1864.

DEAR GENERAL: I have written you but once since the opening of the campaign, but I report by telegraph to General Halleck daily, and he furnishes you copy. My progress was slower than I calculated, from two chief causes—an uninterrupted rain from June 2 to about the 22d, and the peculiar sub-mountainous nature of the country from the Etowah to the Chattahoochee. But we have overcome all opposition and whipped Johnston in every fight when we were on anything like fair terms, and I think the army feels that way, that we can whip the enemy in anything like a fair fight; but he has uniformly taken shelter behind parallels of strong profile, made in advance for him by negroes and militia. I regarded an assault on the 27th of June necessary for two good reasons : 1st, because the enemy, as well as my own army, had settled down into the belief that "flanking" alone was my game; and 2d, that on that day and ground, had the assault succeeded, I could have broken Johnston's centre and pushed his army back in confusion and with great loss to his bridges over the Chattahoochee. We lost nothing in morale in the assault, for I followed it up on the extreme right, and compelled him to quit the very strong lines of Kenesaw, Smyrna camp-ground, and the Chattahoochee in quick succession.

My railroad and telegraph are now up, and we are rapidly accumulating stores in Marietta and Alatoona; that will make us less timid about the roads to our rear. We have been wonderfully supplied in provisions and ammunition; not a day has a regiment been without bread and essentials. Forage has been the hardest, and we have cleaned the country, in a breadth of thirty (30) miles, of grain and grass. Now the corn is getting of a size which makes it a good fodder, and the railroad has brought us grain to the extent of four (4) pounds per animal per day. I have now fulfilled the first part of the "grand plan;" our lines are up to the Chattahoochee, and the enemy is beyond.

John Morgan failed in his Kentucky raid, and we have kept Forrest employed in Mississippi. The defeat of General Sturgis was unfortunate, still he kept Forrest away from us; and now General A. J. Smith is out from Memphis with a force amply sufficient to whip him. I hear of General Slocum at Jackson, Mississippi; and General Canby telegraphs me of a proposed raid from Baton Rouge, and another against Mobile, so that I am well satisfied that all my people are well employed. At this moment I have General Stoneman down the Chattahoochee, with orders, if possible, to cross and strike the railroad between

Montgomery and West Point, and break it good; to return to the army of the Tennessee, if possible, but if headed off, to make for Pensacola.

The moment I got Johnston to the Chattahoochee I sent General Schofield to the ford above, and he effected a crossing without the loss of a man, and has two pontoon bridges.   About the same time, General Garrard's cavalry crossed still above, at Roswell factory, and has been relieved by General Dodge's corps, so that I now cover the Chattahoochee, and have two good crossings well secured. By to-night I will have a third.   As soon as I hear from General Stoneman, I will shift all of General McPherson's army to Roswell, and cross General Thomas about three (3) miles above the railroad bridge, and move against Atlanta—my left well to the east, to get possession of the Augusta road about Decatur or Stone mountain.   I think all will be ready in three (3) days.   I will have nearly one hundred thousand (100,000) men.

I feel certain we have killed and crippled for Joe Johnston as many as we have sent of our men to the rear; have sent back about six or seven thousand prisoners; have taken eleven (11) guns of Johnston, and about ten (10) in Rome; have destroyed immense iron, cotton, and wool mills; and have possession of all the nitre country.

My operations have been rather cautious than bold, but on the whole I trust are satisfactory to you.   All of Polk's corps is still here; also Hardee's and Hood's, and the Georgia militia under G. W. Smith.

Let us persevere, trusting to the fortunes of war, leaving statesmen to work out the solution.

W. T. SHERMAN,
Major General Commanding.

Lieutenant General GRANT,
  Near Petersburg, Virginia.

[Cipher.]

HEADQUARTERS MILITARY DIVISION OF THE MISSISSIPPI,
In the field, Chattahoochee river, July 13, 1864.

General HALLECK, *Washington, D. C.:*

All is well.   I have now accumulated stores at Alatoona and Marietta, both fortified and garrisoned points.   Have also three points at which to cross the Chattahoochee in my possession, and only await General Stoneman's return from a trip down the river, to cross the army in force and move on Atlanta. Stoneman is now out two (2) days, and had orders to be back on the fourth (4th) or fifth (5th) day at farthest.   Rousseau should reach Opelika about the 17th of July.

Before regulations are made for the States to send recruiting officers into the rebel States, I must express my opinion that it is the height of folly.   I cannot permit it here.   I will not have a set of fellows hanging about on any such pretences.   We have no means to transport and feed them.   The Sanitary and Christian commissions are enough to eradicate all trace of Christianity from our minds, much less a set of unscrupulous State agents in search of recruits.   All these dodges are make-shifts that render us ridiculous in our own estimation.   I must protect my army, and say beforehand I have no means to transport recruiting parties south of Nashville, or to feed them if they come here in spite of me.

W. T. SHERMAN,
Major General Commanding.

Roswell Bridge, *July* 14, 1864.

Major General Sherman:

The bridge is finished, and the 15th army corps will cross the river this afternoon, and be in position by night on the left and a little in advance of General Dodge. Nothing new here.

J. B. McPHERSON,
Major General.

Roswell Bridge, *July* 14, 1864—5 p. m.

Major General Sherman:

Would it not be a good move for Garrard to cross his division at McAfee's bridge; push one of his brigades out towards Cross Keys, and engage the cavalry there; and send his other brigade rapidly *via* Lawrenceville down to Covington on the railroad, and burn the bridge across Yellow river and other streams in the vicinity, and do all the damage they can?

The distance is forty (40) miles.

J. B. McPHERSON,
Major General.

Headquarters Military Division of the Mississippi,
In the field, near Chattahoochee river, July 14, 1864.

General John E. Smith, *Alatoona:*

I regard Alatoona of the first importance in our future plans. It is a second Chattanooga. Its front and rear are susceptible of easy defence, and its flanks are strong. The post properly extends from the Etowah to Alatoona Depot, and its flanks the Pumpkin Vine and Alatoona creeks, embracing a space wherein can be accumulated supplies that would make a raid to our rear less to be feared, giving us the means of living till repairs could be made. I want you to study it in all its bearings. As long as our army is in front in good order, of course no enemy could threaten Alatoona; and then its garrison should scout the country for miles around, especially up the Pumpkin Vine and Euharlee creeks, and in the direction of Noonday and Canton. Everything in the nature of grain, forage, and vegetables should be collected. No suspicious citizens should be allowed near the railroad or in the country. The safety of this army must not be imperilled by citizens. If you entertain a bare suspicion against any family, send it to the north. Any loafer or suspicious person seen at any time should be imprisoned and sent off. If guerillas trouble the road or wires between Kingston and Ackworth, they should be shot without mercy. Rowland Springs, Laffing Gall, Canton, and Dallas should receive sudden and unexpected visits by night, by parties about two hundred (200) strong.

I will soon be in motion again, and will feel more confidence that I know you are at Alatoona.

W. T. SHERMAN,
Major General Commanding.

[Cipher.]

Headquarters Military Division of the Mississippi,
In the field, near Chattahoochee river, July 14, 1864.

General Halleck, *Washington:*

If State recruiting agents must come into the limits of my command under the law, I have the honor to request that the commanding officers or adjutants of regiments be constituted such agents, and that States be entitled to a credit for recruits they may enlist, who are accepted and mustered in by the regular mustering officers of their division and corps. This will obviate the difficulty I apprehend from civilian agents.

W. T. SHERMAN,
Major General Commanding.

HEADQUARTERS MILITARY DIVISION OF THE MISSISSIPPI,
In the field, near Chattahoochce river, July 15, 1864.

General THOMAS :

A man came in last night from Columbus, Georgia, with a provost marshal's pass of July 4th, who had escaped from Anderson, and was captured the time I went to Meridian. He gives but little news, and says the guards at Columbus and West Point are not over five hundred (500) each. Heard nothing from Mobile or Montgomery on his way up. A scout in from Atlanta with dates to 3 p. m., 13th, says Bragg and staff had arrived, and Kirby Smith with twenty thousand (20,000) men was expected from Meridian—all bosh, of course. All newspapers have quit Atlanta, except the Memphis Appeal; that I suppose is tired of moving and wants to be " let alone."

W. T. SHERMAN,
Major General Commanding.

HEADQUARTERS MILITARY DIVISION OF THE MISSISSIPPI,
In the field, near Chattahoochee river, July 15, 1864.

GENERAL : I have just heard from General Stoneman, who says he will be at Sweetwater town to-night. I have ordered him to hurry and relieve you. Haul out of sight all your guns to-night, ready in the morning to move to Roswell. You can save much distance by coming by my headquarters, and taking a road near the Chattahooche, but the main Marietta road is plainer and easier for wagons, and it may be is best. Choose for yourself. Don't go to Roswell town, but to the bridge, and across to where General McPherson is.

I am, sir, very respectfully, &c.,

W. T. SHERMAN,
Major General Commanding.

General BLAIR, *Commanding 17th Corps.*

HEADQUARTERS MILITARY DIVISION OF THE MISSISSIPPI,
In the field, near Chattahoochee river, July 15, 1864.

General McPHERSON, *Roswell :*

I have heard from General Stoneman. He did not break the lower railroad, but burned a bridge over the Chattahoochee, near Newman. He will be in to-night, and I have ordered General Blair to move for Roswell to-morrow. You may, therefore, make all preparation to move out towards the Stone mountain the day after to-morrow. Notify General Garrard to move in connexion with you, sending his train to yours. That Augusta road must be destroyed and occupied between Decatur and Stone mountain by you and General Garrard.

W. T. SHERMAN,
Major General Commanding.

HEADQUARTERS MILITARY DIVISION OF THE MISSISSIPPI,
In the field, near Chattahoochee river, July 16, 1864.

General THOMAS:

I am about moving camp to the vicinity of Powers, and will visit Generals Howard and Schofield, where I can be found in case of necessity.

I can't imagine what cavalry it is that General Granger reports at Clayville. What is the gunboat about? It should be at Guntersville at once. If Johnston has ordered this movement, he will not care about Huntsville or Decatur, but Stevenson and Bridgeport. The latter is of vital importance to us, and he knows it.

W. T. SHERMAN,
Major General Commanding.

HEADQUARTERS MILITARY DIVISION OF THE MISSISSIPPI,
In the field, on Chattahoochee river, July 16, 1864.

General MCPHERSON, *Roswell:*

Move in the morning according to Orders 35, but don't strike for the railroad till further orders. General Corse is here. General Blair started early to-day, and will be with you to-morrow. All well here.

W. T. SHERMAN,
Major General Commanding.

CITY POINT, VA., *July* 16, 1864—10 a. m.

Major General SHERMAN:

The attempted invasion of Maryland having failed to give the enemy a firm foothold north, they are now returning with possibly twenty-five thousand (25,000) troops. All the men they have here beyond a sufficiency to hold their string of fortifications will be an element of weakness by eating up their supplies. It is not improbable, therefore, that you will find in the next fortnight re-enforcements on your front to the number indicated above. I advise, therefore, that if you get Atlanta, you set about destroying the railroad as far to the east and south of you as possible. Collect all the stores of the country for your own use, and select a point that you can hold until help can be had. I shall make a desperate effort to get a position here which will hold the enemy without the necessity of so many men. If successful, I can detach from here for other enterprises, looking much to your assistance or anything elsewhere.

U. S. GRANT, *Lieutenant General.*

WASHINGTON, *July* 16, 1864—4. 30 p. m.

Major General SHERMAN:

Lieutenant General Grant wishes me to call your attention to the possibility of Johnston's being re-enforced from Richmond, and the importance of your having prepared a good line of defence against such an increase of rebel force. Also, the importance of getting as large an amount of supplies collected at Chattanooga as possible.

H. W. HALLECK,
Major General, Chief of Staff.

HEADQUARTERS MILITARY DIVISION OF THE MISSISSIPPI,
In the field, on Chattahoochee, July 16, 1864.

Generals THOMAS and MCPHERSON:

Despatches from Generals Grant and Halleck to-day speak of the enemy having failed in his designs in Maryland, and cautioning me that Lee may in the next fortnight re-enforce Johnston by twenty thousand (20,000) men. It behooves us therefore to hurry, so all will move to-morrow as far as Nancy's creek.

W. T. SHERMAN,
Major General Commanding.

[Cipher.]

HEADQUARTERS MILITARY DIVISION OF THE MISSISSIPPI,
In the field, Chattahoochee, July 16, 1864.

General HALLECK, *Washington, D. C.:*

I have yours and General Grant's despatches. I had anticipated all possible chances and am accumulating all the stores possible at Chattanooga and Alatoona, but I don't fear Johnston with re-enforcements of twenty thousand (20,000) if he will take the offensive, but I recognize the danger arising from my long line and the superiority of the enemy's cavalry in numbers and audacity.

I move to-morrow from the Chattahoochee towards Decatur and Stone mountain, east of Atlanta. All well. Copy of this to General Grant.

W. T. SHERMAN,
Major General Commanding.

[Cipher.]

HEADQUARTERS MILITARY DIVISION OF THE MISSISSIPPI,
In the field, east of Chattahoochee river, July 17, 1864.

General HALLECK, *Washington, D. C.:*

To-day we have moved out from the Chattahoochee to Nancy's creek. General Thomas on the right from Paice's ferry towards Atlanta, General Schofield on the centre near Cross Keys, and General McPherson on the left near General Schofield. To-morrow I propose to advance General Thomas to Peach Tree creek, about Buck Head, General Schofield on the Decatur road, and General McPherson to the vicinity of the railroad east of Decatur, and his cavalry division, under General Garrard, will break the railroad.

If we can break the railroad I propose to place the left wing across it near Decatur, and break up the railroad eastward as far as the cavalry can operate with prudence. To-day we encounter nothing but cavalry.

W. T. SHERMAN,
Major General Commanding.

HEADQUARTERS MILITARY DIVISION OF THE MISSISSIPPI,
In the field, lot No. 165 *our map, east of*
Chattahoochee river, July 17, 1864.

GENERAL: General Schofield has just been here and described his position as on Nancy's creek, his pickets on south side near Cross Keys, about lots 304, 15, and 16.

General McPherson is on the road from Roswell to Decatur; his advance about lot 326, a mile above General Schofield. General S. says that the road represented on our map, as from Roswell to Buck Head, is a broad, well travelled road, and has a branch about lot No. 94, leading to Paice's ferry. This corresponds with what General Corse tells me, that you found a large road branching to the left soon after leaving Paice's ferry. It is well to mark this road, as it may be useful to us.

General Howard can take a good road from here to Buck Head, starting at his present front, and moving southeast to the main road from Roswell to Buck Head just before it crosses Nancy's creek. Approaching Buck Head from this quarter about the same time that Generals Schofield and McPherson get to the Peach Tree from the east will, of course, relieve any pressure you may encounter on the main road.

General Schofield will move early for the Peach Tree road, in front of Cross Keys, and take post about lots 239, 247, and 272, with pickets forward as far as 196, and General McPherson will seek for position in the valley of North Fork of Peach Tree, about 267, 266, 284, and 285, and send General Garrard to break the road and telegraph.

You should leave a corps in front of Donaldson's, and have the other two as early as possible at and in front of Buck Head. Then feel down strong to Peach Tree, and see what is there. A vigorous demonstration should be made, and caution your commanders not to exhibit any of the signs of a halt or pause, as in that event too much resistance would be made on the other flank. You know the reasons for the utmost activity, and I need not repeat them. Let all your commanders have full orders to-night, and before joining General Schofield in the morning I will point out to General Howard the road by which he can reach Buck Head in five (5) miles from here.

Give orders as soon as any head of column reaches Buck Head to feel up the Peach Tree road for General Schofield, who will surely be in position before your troops can be.

   I am yours truly,

W. T. SHERMAN,
Major General Commanding.

Major General THOMAS,
  Commanding Army of the Cumberland.

HEADQUARTERS MILITARY DIVISION OF THE MISSISSIPPI,
In the field at San House, Peach Tree road,
five miles northeast of Buck Head, Ga., July 18, 1864.

GENERAL: I have reports from General McPherson to 2 p. m. He has reached the railroad at a point two (2) miles from Stone mountain and seven (7) miles from Decatur, had broken the telegraphs and road, and by five (5) p. m. will have four (4) or five (5) miles broken. To-morrow I want a bold push for Atlanta, and have made my orders, which, I think, will put us in Atlanta or very close to it. Hold on about Howell's Mill and the main road, and let your left swing across Peach Tree, about the South Fork, and connect with General Schofield, who will approach Decatur from the north, whilst General McPherson moves down from the east. It is hard to realize that Johnston will give up Atlanta without a fight, but it may be so. Let us develop the truth.

   Yours, &c.,

W. T. SHERMAN,
Major General Commanding.

Major General THOMAS, *Buck Head.*

[Cipher.]

HEADQUARTERS MILITARY DIVISION OF THE MISSISSIPPI,
In the field, near Cross Keys, Ga., July, 18, 1864.

General HALLECK, *Washington:*

We moved to-day rapidly, and General McPherson reached the Atlanta and Augusta road at a point seven (7) miles east of Decatur and four (4) miles from Stone mountain. General Garrard's cavalry at once set to work to break up the road, and was re-enforced by Brigadier General Morgan L. Smith's division of infantry, and they expect by night to have five (5) miles of road effectually destroyed. Thus far, we have encountered only cavalry, with light resistance, and to-morrow will move on Decatur and Atlanta.

I am fully aware of the necessity of making the most of time, and shall keep things moving.

W. T. SHERMAN,
Major General Commanding.

CITY POINT, VA., *July* 19, 1864—10.30 p. m.

Major General SHERMAN:

I see by Richmond papers of yesterday that Smith has left Tupelo, and is moving towards Ripley. Although they call it a retreat, I judge from S. D. Lee's despatch that Forrest has been badly whipped. Smith, however, ought to be instructed to keep a close watch on Forrest, and not permit him to gather strength and move into Middle Tennessee.

U. S. GRANT, *Lieutenant General.*

NEW ORLEANS, *July* 20, 1864.

Major General SHERMAN:

Your telegram of the 7th has been received. You have already been advised that the force intended for the operations against Mobile have been sent to the army of the Potomac. I am now preparing a smaller force to act, in co-operation with the navy, in an attack which Admiral Farragut will make on that harbor. This force will be ready in six (6) days, and, although much smaller than was contemplated originally, will, no doubt, have a good effect.

General Asboth at Pensacola has been advised of General Rousseau's expedition, and will be prepared for it. Forage and subsistence will be sent to Pensacola, and transportation held in readiness to be sent as soon as I hear of his arrival. The diversion of so large a force from this command will limit our movements very materially, but I will do whatever I can to facilitate you.

E. R. S. CANBY,
Major General Commanding.

[Cipher.]

HEADQUARTERS MILITARY DIVISION OF THE MISSISSIPPI,
In the field, near Atlanta, Ga., July 20, 1864—9 p. m.

General HALLECK, *Washington, D. C.:*

I have a despatch from General Grant. Answer him in my name that Major General A. J. Smith has the very order he suggests, viz: to hang on to Forrest, and prevent his coming to Tennessee. I will, however, renew the orders.

9*

I advanced from the Chattahoochee in force on the 17th. On the 18th General McPherson and General Garrard's cavalry reached the Augusta road, and destroyed about five (5) miles of it east of Decatur. On the 19th the whole line crossed Peach Tree creek, General McPherson occupying Decatur. To-day we moved on Atlanta, and have been fighting all day. Our line now extends from a point on the railroad two and a half (2½) miles east of Atlanta, round by north to the mouth of Peach Tree creek. We find the enemy in force, but will close in to-morrow. By the Atlanta papers we learn that Johnston is relieved, and that Hood commands; that Rousseau is on the railroad at Opelika; and that most of the newspapers and people have left Atlanta.

General Thomas is on my right, General Schofield in the centre, and General McPherson on the left; General Garrard's cavalry on the left rear of General McPherson, Generals Stoneman and McCook on the west bank guarding our right flank. The enemy still clings to his intrenchments. If General Grant can keep Lee from re-enforcing this army for a week, I think I can dispose of it. We have taken several hundred prisoners, and had some short, severe encounters; but they were partial. We have pressed the enemy back at all points, until our rifle shots can reach the town. If he strengthens his works, I will gradually swing round between him and his only source of supply—Macon.

W. T. SHERMAN,
Major General Commanding.

HEADQUARTERS MILITARY DIVISION OF THE MISSISSIPPI,
In the field, near Atlanta, Ga., July 20, 1864—*midnight.*

GENERAL: After destroying the bridge at McAfee's, which I suppose is already done, you will send to General McPherson's guard at the bridge at Roswell your wagons, led horses, and baggage, and proceed rapidly to Covington on the main wagon and railroad east—distance about thirty (30) miles from Decatur—take the road by Latimer, touching the road at or beyond Lithonia, and thence substantially along the railroad, destroying it effectually all the way, especially the Yellow river bridge this side of Covington, as well as the road bridge over Yellow river after you have passed. From Covington send detachments to destroy the rail and road bridges east of Covington over the Ulcofauhatchee. Try and capture and destroy some locomotives and cars and the depots and stores at Covington; but of private property only take what is necessary for your own use, except horses and mules, of which you will take all that are fit for service, exercising, of course, some judgment as to the animals belonging to the poor and needy. On your return select your own route, but I would suggest that by way of Sheffield, Rock bridge, and Stone mountain, or even further north if you prefer. I want you to put your whole strength at this, and do it quick and well. I know it can be done. By passing Yellow river by the road bridge, and then pushing for the railroad bridges right and left, the guards will run or even burn their own bridges. You ought to catch some trains about Covington, as there is no telegraph to give them timely warning. I believe that the cavalry is mostly withdrawn from that flank of the enemy, and that you can ride roughshod over any force there; at all events, it is a matter of vital importance, and must be attempted with great vigor. The importance of it will justify the loss of one-quarter of your command. Be prepared with axes, hatchets, and bars to tear up sections of track, and make bonfires; when the rails are red-hot, they must be twisted. Burning will do for bridges and culverts, but not for ordinary tracks. Let the work be well done.

The whole thing should be done in two days, including to-morrow.   I will notify General McPherson, that he may look out for his rear and trains.

I am, with respect, yours truly,

W. T. SHERMAN,
Major General Commanding.

General GARRARD,
Commanding Cavalry Division.

If the McAfee bridge is not already burned, you can send a messenger to the guard already there to do it, and move to Roswell.   This need not delay your departure for Covington at once.   S.

HEADQUARTERS MILITARY DIVISION OF THE MISSISSIPPI,
In the field, near Atlanta, Ga., July 21, 1864.

GENERAL: After leaving you to-day I visited General Palmer, and saw his skirmishers advance well to his right flank.   I am satisfied the enemy will not attempt to hold Atlanta and the fort at the railroad crossing of the Chattahoochee.   There is a weak place in that line, and it can best be reached by advancing General Johnson on the direct road as far as possible, and bringing Generals Baird and Davis up on his right.   I do not think the enemy will assume the offensive from the fort on the Chattahoochee, but it may be prudent to let General McCook watch him on both sides of the river.   The front of General Hooker is very narrow; but I admit it is the point where your line should be strongest. General Howard's two divisions in this direction have advanced a good distance over a complete line of the enemy's defences, and I think both Generals Wood and Stanley are up to the main line of intrenchments; that from Wood's right rifled guns can reach the town.   The enemy still holds the hill near where General Stanley's left and General Schofield's right are, and they keep up an infernal clatter; but it sounds to me like a waste of ammunition.   General McPherson to-day charged and carried a hill, losing two hundred and fifty (250) men, but killing some and taking prisoners.   From this hill he has an easy range of the town.   We will try the effect of shelling to-morrow, and during it you had better make all the ground you can.

I do not believe the enemy will repeat his assaults, as he had in that of yesterday his best troops, and failed signally.   Therefore I don't fear for your right flank; still it is well to be prudent.   Our maps are all wrong, and the quicker we can get our surveys up and published the better.   I will look to Schofield and McPherson to morrow.

Yours, truly,

W. T. SHERMAN,
Major General Commanding.

Major General THOMAS,
Army of the Cumberland.

HEADQUARTERS MILITARY DIVISION OF THE MISSISSIPPI,
In the field, near Atlanta, Ga., July 21, 1864.

His Excellency President LINCOLN, *Washington, D. C.:*

Your despatch is received.   I have the highest veneration for the law, and will respect it always, however it conflicts my opinion of its propriety.   I only telegraphed to General Halleck because I had seen no copy of the law, and supposed the War Department might have some control over its operations. When I have taken Atlanta, and can sit down in some place, I will convey by letter a fuller expression of my views in relation to this subject.*

With great respect,

W. T. SHERMAN,
Major General Commanding.

WASHINGTON, *July* 21, 1864—9 a. m.

Major General SHERMAN:

Richmond Whig of the 20th learns from Macon Confederate that but little quartermaster or commissary stores remain in Atlanta, all having been moved to safer and more secure points. It also says that it has every reason to hope that Sherman's rear will be cut in the next ten days.

Johnston has been relieved, and Hood takes his place, much to the surprise of the army and the public; also that the change indicates that there will be no more retreating, but that Atlanta will be defended at all hazards, and to the last extremity.

U. S. GRANT, *Lieutenant General.*

(Cipher.)

HEADQUARTERS MILITARY DIVISION OF THE MISSISSIPPI,
In the field, near Atlanta, Ga., July 21, 1864.

GENERAL: Yesterday, at 4 p. m., the enemy sallied from his intrenchments and fell suddenly and heavily on our line in the direction of Buck Head. The blow fell upon General Newton's division of General Howard's corps; on General Ward's, General Geary's, and General Williams's divisions of General Hooker's corps; and General Johnson, of General Palmer's corps. For two hours the fighting was close and severe, resulting in the complete repulse of the enemy, with a heavy loss in dead and wounded. He left his dead and many wounded in our posssession. We retained undisputed posession of all the ground fought over. General Newton reports he has buried two hundred (200) of the enemy's dead, and is satisfied he wounded at least twelve hundred (1,200.) His entire loss is only one hundred (100,) as his men were partially covered by a rail barricade. At the time of the attack General Hooker was in the act of advancing his lines, so that he fought his corps uncovered, in comparatively open ground, and on fair terms with the enemy. The contest was very severe. He has buried about four hundred (400) of the rebel dead, took seven (7) colors, and has collected many of the wounded and other prisoners. General Hooker thinks that the rebel wounded in his front fully equals four thousand (4,000,) but I don't like to make guesses in such matters; his own loss will be covered by fifteen hundred (1,500.) On the whole, the result is most favorable to us.

To-day we have gained important positions, so that Generals McPherson and Schofield, on the east, have batteries in position that will easily reach the heart of the city, and General Howard, on the north, also has advanced his lines about two (2) miles, being within easy cannon range of the buildings in Atlanta. He compelled the enemy to give up a long line of parapet which constituted an advance line of intrenchments. The city seems to have a line all round it, at an average distance from the heart of the town of one and a half ($1\frac{1}{2}$) mile, but our shot passing over this line will destroy the town—and I doubt if Hood will stand a

---

* Recruiting agents in rebel States.

bombardment—still he has fought hard at all points to-day. I will open on the town from the east and northeast to-morrow, and General Thomas will advance his right from the mouth of Peach Tree creek to cross the railroad to the northwest of the town. I have sent General Garrard's cavalry eastward to Covington, to break railroad and destroy the bridge on Yellow river and the Ulcofauhatchee creek.

In the action yesterday the rebel Generals O'Bannon and Stewart were reported killed, and among the dead were three colonels and many officers. Brigadier General Gresham was severely wounded yesterday, but is in no danger of life or limb.

W. T. SHERMAN,
Major General Commanding.

General HALLECK,
Washington, D. C.

HEADQUARTERS MILITARY DIVISION OF THE MISSISSIPPI,
In the field, near Atlanta, Ga., July 23, 1864.

GENERAL: I have heard of General Rousseau's return to Marietta. Please order him at once to relieve General Stoneman, on the other side of the river, and let General Stoneman come to me with his whole force. Please send the enclosed order for me at once. The attack on our left to-day has been desperate and persistent, and the losses on both sides quite heavy. I want you to relieve it to-morrow by an actual attack, or strong demonstration on the right. I will send word early in the day if it is renewed. I suppose it will be kept up as long as General Garrard is out. I want General Stoneman to move out to General Garrard's relief. You can use Generals McCook and Rousseau on your right.

I am, &c.,

W. T. SHERMAN,
Major General Commanding.

Major General THOMAS,
Army of the Cumberland.

HEADQUARTERS MILITARY DIVISION OF THE MISSISSIPPI,
In the field, near Atlanta, Ga., July 23, 1864—2 a. m.

General ROUSSEAU, *Marietta:*

Your despatch is received, and you have done well. I hate to call on you so soon for more service; but time is pressing. I want you to move down right away to the railroad bridge and relieve General Stoneman, who is watching the Chattahoochee below Turner's ferry. He will describe to you the country and what is needed. I want him relieved as soon as possible, that he may come over here. I hope to see you in a few days.

I am, &c.,

W. T. SHERMAN,
Major General Commanding.

[Cipher.]

HEADQUARTERS MILITARY DIVISION OF THE MISSISSIPPI,
In the field, near Atlanta, Ga., July 23, 1864.

General HALLECK, *Washington, D. C.:*

General Rousseau reports from Marietta yesterday his safe return from Opelika, having destroyed that depot, thirty (30) miles of railroad towards Mont_ gomery, three (3) miles towards Columbus, and two towards West Point. His entire loss twelve (12) killed and thirty (30) wounded. He brings in four hundred (400) mules and three hundred (300) horses.

W. T. SHERMAN,
Major General Commanding.

[Cipher.]

HEADQUARTERS MILITARY DIVISION OF THE MISSISSIPPI,
In the field, near Atlanta, Ga., July 23, 1864.

General HALLECK, Washington, D. C.:

Yesterday morning the enemy fell back to the intrenchments proper of the city of Atlanta, which are in a general circle of a radius of one and a half ($1\frac{1}{2}$) miles, and we closed in. While we were forming our lines and selecting positions for batteries the enemy appeared suddenly out of the dense woods in heavy masses on our extreme left, and struck the 17th corps, General Blair, in flank, and was forcing it back when the 16th corps, General Dodge, came up and checked the movement; but the enemy's cavalry got well to our rear and into Decatur, and for some hours our left flank was completely enveloped. The fighting that resulted was continuous until night, with heavy loss on both sides. The enemy took one of our batteries, (Murray's, of the regular army,) that was marching in its place in column on the road, unconscious of danger. About 4 p. m. the enemy sallied against the division of General Morgan L. Smith, which occupied an abandoned line of rifle trench near the railroad east of the city and forced it back some four hundred (400) yards, leaving in his hands for the time two (2) batteries, but the ground and batteries were immediately after recovered by the same troops re-enforced. I cannot well approximate our loss, which fell heaviest on the 15th and 17th corps, and count it three thousand (3,000,) but I know that, being on the defensive, we have inflicted equally heavy loss on the enemy. General McPherson, when arranging his troops about 11 a. m., and passing from one column to another, unconsciously rode upon an ambuscade without apprehension, at some distance ahead of his staff and orderlies, and was shot dead. His body was sent in charge of his personal staff back to Marietta and Chattanooga. His loss at that moment was most serious; but General Logan at once arranged the troops and had immediate direction of them during the rest of the day. Our left, though refused somewhat, is still within easy cannon range of Atlanta. The enemy seems to man his extensive parapets and at the same time has to spare heavy assaulting columns; but to-day we will intrench our front lines, which will give me troops to spare to meet those assaults.

I cannot hear of the loss of more than a few wagons taken by the enemy's cavalry during his temporary pause in Decatur, whence all the trains had been securely removed to the rear of the main army under cover of a brigade commanded by Colonel Sprague.

During the heavy attack on the left, the remainder of the line was not engaged.

W. T. SHERMAN,
Major General Commanding.

HEADQUARTERS MILITARY DIVISION OF THE MISSISSIPPI,
In the field, near Atlanta, Ga., July 23, 1864—8 p. m.

GENERAL: I have this moment returned from an examination of our entire line. You know your own. The balance extends in a circle at about one thousand (1,000) yards distant from the enemy's lines as far as Proctor's creek, the whole of Palmer's corps being east and south of the railroad. All have covered their fronts with parapets, so that the enemy will not attempt a sally. The question now is, what next? I will in person explain all that is necessary to produce the result aimed at as soon as General Garrard returns. You need not apprehend a renewal of the attack on the part of the enemy, but, on the contrary, you may begin to feel out with skirmishers and supports into the woods east of General Giles Smith's division and General Dodge's corps. In the morning early let General Wood's division move into Decätur, stay awhile, and return. Let details of men and pioneers begin at your very front and break up and destroy the railroad absolutely back to and including Decatur. Until we conclude upon the best manner of reducing Atlanta we cannot be better employed than in rendering the Atlanta and Augusta road useless; especially have the iron rails heated and twisted.

I want your skirmishers to feel out to-morrow early in front of General Dodge for a double purpose; to hold on that flank the cavalry of Wheeler, while we operate on General Thomas's flank and centre, a diversion for General Garrard, now on his return from his expedition.

I am, with respect,

W. T. SHERMAN,
Major General Commanding.

Major General JOHN A. LOGAN,
Commanding Army of the Tennessee.

HEADQUARTERS MILITARY DIVISION OF THE MISSISSIPPI,
In the field, near Atlanta, Ga., July 23, 1864—8 a. m.

GENERAL: I have examined the line of circumvallation and have no fear of the enemy even attempting to test its strength. But until we get our cavalry in hand and position, I will not attempt anything serious. You may therefore keep things "statu quo," and look only to your supplies of food and ammunition.

I have seen General Rousseau, and am satisfied that he has made a break that cuts off Alabama for a month, and he has brought us in pretty fair condition some twenty-five hundred additional cavalry.

I am, &c.,

W. T. SHERMAN,
Major General Commanding.

Major General SCHOFIELD,
Commanding Army of the Ohio.

HEADQUARTERS MILITARY DIVISION OF THE MISSISSIPPI,
In the field, near Atlanta, Ga., July 24, 1864.

GENERAL: It is my painful duty to report that Brigadier General James B. McPherson, United States army, major general of volunteers, and commander of the army of the Tennessee in the field, was killed by a shot from ambuscade about noon yesterday. At the time of this fatal shot he was on horseback, placing his troops in position near the city of Atlanta, and was passing by a cross-road from a moving column towards the flank of troops that had already been established on the line. He had quitted me but a few minutes before, and was on his way to see in person to the execution of my orders. About the time of this sad event the enemy had sallied from his intrenchments of Atlanta and by a circuit had got to the left and rear of this very line, and had begun an attack which resulted in serious battle; so that General McPherson fell in battle, booted and spurred, as the gallant knight and gentleman should wish. Not his the loss, but the country's; and this army will mourn his death and cherish his memory as that of one who, though comparatively young, had risen by his merit and ability to the command of one of the best armies which the nation had called into existence to vindicate its honor and integrity.

History tells us of but few who so blended the grace and gentleness of the friend with the dignity, courage, faith and manliness of the soldier. His public enemies, even the men who directed the fatal shot, ne'er spoke or wrote of him without expressions of marked respect; those whom he commanded loved him even to idolatry; and I, his associate and commander, fail in words adequate to express my opinion of his great worth. I feel assured that every patriot in America on hearing this sad news will feel a sense of personal loss, and the country generally will realize that we have lost not only an able military leader, but a man who, had he survived, was qualified to heal the national strife which has been raised by designing and ambitious men.

His body has been sent north in charge of Major Willard, Captains Steele and Gile, his personal staff.

I am, with great respect,

W. T. SHERMAN,
Major General Commanding.

General L. Thomas,
Adjutant General U. S. A.

HEADQUARTERS MILITARY DIVISION OF THE MISSISSIPPI,
In the field, near Atlanta, Ga., July 24, 1864.

GENERAL: I have pretty well surveyed the whole position, and by the aid of maps and my own observation, think I understand the case pretty well.

Our lines are now strong in front, and we compass Atlanta from the railroad on the east to the railroad west. The enemy having failed in his assault on your flank before it was covered by any defensive works, and having sustained most serious loss, will not again attempt it, but will await our action. I now enclose you a map made by General Schofield's engineer, which shows the roads to your present right rear. I sent Captain Poe to see you this morning, but from what Captain Hickenlooper says, I think I may have failed to convey to you my right meaning, which is this:

The only object in placing the army of Tennessee on that flank was, to reach and destroy the railroad from Atlanta towards Augusta. That is partially done, and the work of destruction should be continued as far as possible. I wish you to keep one division or more employed day and night in breaking and burning the road until General Garrard returns. I feel no doubt but that he has succeeded in breaking the bridges across Yellow river and the Ulcofauhatchee, but he may have to fight his way back, and to relieve him I wish you to push your skirmishers out from General Dodge's front, and from General Blair's left, as though you were going to push your way by the east of Atlanta to the Macon road. To keep up this delusion you should send a column cautiously down one of those roads or valleys southeast and engage the enemy outside his works, but not behind his trenches.

As soon as General Garrard is back you can discontinue all such demonstrations and prepare for your next move. I propose to give you timely notice to send your wagons behind General Thomas, and then to move your army behind the present line, to the extreme right, to reach, if possible, the Macon road, which you know to be the only road by which Atlanta can be supplied. This will leave General Schofield the left flank, which will be covered by the works he has constructed on his front, and he can use the abandoned trenches of the enemy to cover his left rear. You will no longer send your wagons by Roswell, but by Buck Head and Paice's ferry, and when you change you will draw from the railroad bridge to which our cars now run, and at which point we are now making a pier bridge, and also two pontoons. General Stoneman will surely be at Decatur to-day, and we will have two divisions of cavalry on our right, viz: Generals McCook's and Harrison's (General Rousseau's.)

Act with confidence; know that the enemy cannot budge you from your present ground, and act offensively to show him that you dare him to the encounter. You can understand that, being on the defensive, he cannot afford to sally, unless at great peril. General Schofield has so strengthened his front that I feel no uneasiness about that flank, and only study now to make the next move so quickly that we may reach East Point or its vicinity with as little loss as possible. My headquarters are now behind General Howard's corps, General Newton's division, on the main Marietta and Atlanta road, which crosses the Chattahoochee at Paice's ferry and passes through Buck Head. I am at a large white house near the enemy's old line of intrenchments, a prolongation of the same which passes from where I saw you yesterday, by General Schofield's position. I have just heard that General Garrard is back. Go on breaking that road good.

I am, truly, &c.,

W. T. SHERMAN,
Major General Commanding.

Major General JOHN A. LOGAN,
Commanding Army of the Tennessee.

HEADQUARTERS MILITARY DIVISION OF THE MISSISSIPPI,
In the field, near Atlanta, Ga., July 24, 1864—2 p. m.

GENERAL; I am rejoiced to hear you are back safe and successful. General Rousseau has brought me two thousand five hundred (2,500) good cavalry, having been to Opelika and destroyed thirty (30) miles of road between West Point and Montgomery. I will give you time to rest, and then we must make quick work with Atlanta. I await your report with impatience, and in the mean time tender to you the assurance of my great consideration.

Your friend,

W. T. SHERMAN,
Major General Commanding.

General GARRARD, *Decatur.*

[Cipher.]

HEADQUARTERS MILITARY DIVISION OF THE MISSISSIPPI,
In the field, near Atlanta, Ga., July 24, 1864.

General HALLECK, *Washington, D. C.:*

On making up reports and examining the field, I find the result of Hood's attack on our left more destructive than I reported. Our loss will not foot up two thousand (2,000) killed and wounded, whereas we have found over one thousand (1,000) rebel dead, which will make, with the usual proportion of wounded, a loss to the enemy of full seven thousand (7,000.) General Garrard also has returned perfectly successful, having completely destroyed the two large bridges near Covington, forty (40) miles towards Augusta, brought in two hundred prisoners and some good horses, and destroyed the public stores at Covington and Conyer's stations, including two thousand (2,000) bales of cotton, a locomotive, and train of cars. Our communications are yet all safe and the army in good condition in all respects. As soon as my cavalry rests, I propose to swing the army of the Tennessee round by the right rapidly, and interpose between Atlanta and Macon, the only line open to the enemy.

W. T. SHERMAN,
Major General Commanding.

[Telegram.]

HEADQUARTERS MILITARY DIVISION OF THE MISSISSIPPI,
In the field, near Atlanta, Ga., July 24, 1864.

General HALLECK, *Washington, D. C.:*

The sudden loss of General McPherson was a heavy blow to me. I can hardly replace him, but must have a successor. After thinking over the whole matter, I prefer that Major General O. O. Howard be ordered to command the army and department of the Tennessee. If this meets the President's approval notify me by telegraph, when I will put him in command, and name others to fill the vacancies created. General Logan, as senior, commands the army of the Tennessee for the present. After we have taken Atlanta I will name officers who merit promotion; in the mean time I request that the President will not give increased rank to any officer who has gone on leave from sickness or other cause than wounds in battle.

W. T. SHERMAN,
Major General Commanding.

HEADQUARTERS MILITARY DIVISION OF THE MISSISSIPPI,
In the field, near Atlanta, July 25, 1864.

GENERAL: I find it difficult to make prompt report of results coupled with some data or information without occasionally making some mistakes. General McPherson's sudden death and General Logan's succeeding to the command, as it were, in the midst of battle, made some confusion on our extreme left, but it soon recovered and made sad havoc with the enemy, who had practiced one of his favorite games of attacking our left when in motion and before it had time to cover its weak end.

After riding over the ground and hearing the varying statements of the actors on that flank, I directed General Logan to make an official report of the actual results, and I herewith enclose it.

Though the number of dead rebels seems excessive, I am disposed to give full credit to the report that our loss, though only three thousand five hundred and twenty-one (3,521) killed, wounded, and missing, the enemy's dead alone on the field nearly equal that number, viz, three thousand two hundred and forty (3,240.)

Happening at that point of the line when a flag of truce was sent in to ask permission for each party to bury its dead, I gave General Logan authority to permit a temporary truce on that flank alone, while our labors and fighting proceeded at all others.

I also send you a copy of General Garrard's report of the breaking of railroad toward Augusta.

Now I am grouping my command to attack the Macon road, and with that view will intrench a strong line of circumvallation and flanks, so as to have in reserve as large an infantry column as possible to co-operate with all the cavalry to swing round to the south and east and control that road at or below East Point.

I have the honor to be, your obedient servant,

W. T. SHERMAN,
Major General Commanding.

Major General HALLECK, *Washington, D. C.*

HEADQUARTERS MILITARY DIVISION OF THE MISSISSIPPI,
In the field, near Atlanta, Ga., July 25, 1864.

Colonel JAMES HARDIE,
Inspector General, Washington, D. C.:

I have your despatch of yesterday announcing the appointment of General Osterhaus as major general. I do not object to his appointment, but I wish to put on record this my emphatic opinion that it is an act of injustice to officers who stand by their posts in the day of danger to neglect them, and advance such as Generals Hovey and Osterhaus, who left us in the midst of bullets to go to the rear in search of personal advancement. If the rear be the post of honor, then we had better all change front on Washington.

W. T. SHERMAN,
Major General Commanding.

[Cipher.]

HEADQUARTERS MILITARY DIVISION OF THE MISSISSIPPI,
In the field, near Atlanta, Ga., July 25, 1864.

General WASHBURN, *Memphis:*

It was by General Grant's special order that General Smith was required after his fight to persevere and continue to follow Forrest. He must keep after him till recalled by me or General Grant, and if Forrest goes towards Tennessee, General Smith must follow him, aiming to reach the Tennessee river at Decatur.

We have had some hard fighting here, but have got the enemy in a tight place now inside of Atlanta. General Rousseau broke the road at Opelika and my cavalry has broken up the road towards Augusta for fifty (50) miles out. Only one railroad remains to the enemy, viz., that to Macon, and I am nearly ready to strike it, after which the enemy must come out of Atlanta to fight or be invested.

General Smith must keep well out after Forrest, and rather watch him closely than attempt to pursue him, but when he does fight he should keep the advantage. The railroad could supply him out as far as Grand Junction. It is of vital importance that Forrest do not go to Tennessee.

W. T. SHERMAN,
Major General Commanding.

HEADQUARTERS MILITARY DIVISION OF THE MISSISSIPPI,
In the field, near Atlanta, Ga., July 25, 1864.

GENERAL: I have your application for the services of General Corse, which I grant, because I want you to have good division commanders. But I beg you to see that no injustice is done to General Sweeney. I have noticed for some time a growing dissatisfaction on the part of General Dodge with General

Sweeney. It may be personal. See that General Dodge prefers specific charges and specifications, and you, as the army commander, must be the judge of the sufficiency of the charges. No one but the commander of an army can arrest and send away a general ; it is a high power, but I construe the power to reside with the commanders of my three armies, because each has a command other than the troops here on the spot. You, as commander of the army of the Tennessee, should judge as to the cause of arrest and see that no injustice is done a general officer. You can see how cruel it would be to a brave and sensitive gentleman and officer to be arrested, deprived of his command and sent to the rear at this time. I do not believe General Dodge would willingly do an act of injustice, but still you are the one to judge.

I fear that General Sweeney will feel that even I am influenced against him to befriend General Corse, but it is not so. I give up General Corse because the good of the service demands that, at this crisis, you should have good division commanders.

I am, with respect, your obedient servant,

W. T. SHERMAN,
Major General Commanding.

Major General JOHN A. LOGAN,
Commanding Army of the Tennessee.

[Cipher.]

HEADQUARTERS MILITARY DIVISION OF THE MISSISSIPPI,
In the field, near Atlanta, Ga., July 25, 1864—8 p. m.

Lieutenant General GRANT, *Petersburg :*

Your despatch of 21st did not come till to-day. Johnston is relieved and Hood commands. Hood has made two attempts to strike hard since we crossed Chattahoochee, and both times got more than he bargained for. No doubt he expected to cut to my rear, but I have already cut to *his* rear, having broken his Augusta road out for fifty miles and his southern road at Opelika. None remains to him but the Macon road, and I think I will have that soon. I would rather that Hood should fight it out at Atlanta than to retreat further to Macon. If you can keep away re-enforcements, all well. My army is all in hand and the rear well guarded.

W. T. SHERMAN,
Major General Commanding.

HEADQUARTERS MILITARY DIVISION OF THE MISSISSIPPI,
In the field, near Atlanta, Ga., July 26, 1864.

GENERAL : I have received your letter of July 26, asking permission, after breaking good the railroad below McDonough, to push on, release the officers there, and afterwards to go to Andersonville and release the men confined there. I see many difficulties, but, as you say, even a chance of success will warrant the effort, and I consent to it. You may, after having fulfilled my present orders, send General Garrard back to the left flank of the army, and proceed with your command proper to achieve both or either of the objects named. I will keep the enemy busy, so that you shall have nothing to contend with but the cavalry ; and if you can bring back to this army any or all those prisoners of war, it will be an achievement that will entitle you and your command to the love and admiration of the whole country. Be careful to break telegraph wire and railroad when and wherever you go, especially the telegraph, as it will prevent the enemy following your movement.

W. T. SHERMAN,
Major General Commanding.

Major General GEORGE STONEMAN.
Commanding Division of Cavalry.

HEADQUARTERS MILITARY DIVISION OF THE MISSISSIPPI,
In the field, before Atlanta, Ga., July 26, 1864.

GENTLEMEN: As a part of the movement to-morrow, I wish, whilst the cavalry is moving out, say at 6 a. m., and General Logan's troops are shifting from left to right, that you send from some point of the front of each division in our line of circumvallation a bold party, of about a regiment strong, to push back the enemy's outlying pickets and feel their position. This will have the effect of holding them, and drawing there as large a body of the enemy as possible, as he will surely do on such a display.

Inasmuch as General Jeff. C. Davis's division is placed as a strong right flank, and, therefore, will be almost entirely in reserve when the army of the Tennessee gets to the right, I wish the demonstration to his front to be still more decided, viz: a whole brigade should move on the ridge due south from the hill intrenched beyond Proctor's creek, and should push back the enemy beyond any little rifle-pits to his main line which will be found upon the main ridge which extends from Atlanta to East Point. This brigade should move toward the old village of White Hall, about two and a half miles from Atlanta. These demonstrations should proceed slowly and deliberately, and last all day, and should be as bold and provoking to the enemy as possible, tempting him to sally out and test our present lines.

I am, &c.,

W. T. SHERMAN,
Major General Commanding.

Major Generals THOMAS and SCHOFIELD.

HEADQUARTERS MILITARY DIVISION OF THE MISSISSIPPI,
In the field, near Atlanta, Ga., July 26, 1864.

General THOMAS:

General McCook represents the enemy's cavalry to his front intrenched behind good works extending from about White Hall down to the Chattahoochee, and he apprehends difficulty in breaking through. I have consented to his dropping down the west bank of the Chattahoochee to a point about Campbelltown, crossing there and striking out for the railroad. This will turn the position of the cavalry, and force them back to meet General McCook on more open ground.

W. T. SHERMAN,
Major General Commanding.

HEADQUARTERS MILITARY DIVISION OF THE MISSISSIPPI,
In the field, near Atlanta, Ga., July 26, 1864.

General THOMAS:

Major General Howard is ordered to the command of the army and department of the Tennessee. I want him in his new command at once.

W. T. SHERMAN,
Major General Commanding.

[Cipher.]

HEADQUARTERS MILITARY DIVISION OF THE MISSISSIPPI,
In the field, near Atlanta, Ga., July 26, 1864.

General HALLECK, *Washington :*

To-morrow we begin to move against Atlanta, having strongly intrenched our front from the railroad east of Atlanta to a hill south of Proctor's creek. I move the whole army of the Tennessee to the right, extending the line south, threatening East Point, and forcing, as I think, Hood to abandon Atlanta, or allow us at small cost to occupy the railroad south of the town, that to the east being well destroyed. At the same time I send by night a force of about three thousand five hundred (3,500) cavalry under General McCook, and around by the left about five thousand (5,000) cavalry under Stoneman, with orders to reach the railroad about Griffin's. I also have consented that General Stoneman, after he has executed this part of his plan, if he find it feasible, may, with his division proper, about two thousand, (2,000,) go to Macon and attempt the release of our officers and prisoners there, and then to Andersonville to release the twenty thousand (20,000) of our men prisoners there. This is probably more than he can accomplish, but it is worthy of a determined effort.

Whilst these are in progresss, I will with the main army give employment to all the rebel army still in Atlanta.

W. T. SHERMAN,
Major General Commanding.

[Cipher.]

HEADQUARTERS MILITARY DIVISION OF THE MISSISSIPPI,
In the field, near Atlanta, Ga., July 27, 1864.

General HALLECK, *Washington, D. C. :*

My two cavalry expeditions are off to make a wide circuit and reach the Macon road well to the southeast of Atlanta, and the army of the Tennessee is shifted to the extreme right, reaching well towards the railroad, so that I think to-morrow must develop something. The cavalry will have to fight the enemy's cavalry, and we can hold the infantry and artillery to Atlanta and force them to extend and choose between Atlanta and East Point. I don't think the enemy can hold both. All are well pleased with General Howard's appointment but Generals Logan and Hooker. The former thought he ought to have been allowed the command of the army in the field until the end of the campaign, but I explained to him that a permanent department commander had to be appointed at once, as discharges, furloughs, and much detailed business could alone be done by a department commander. General Hooker is offended, because he thinks he is entitled to the command. I must be honest, and say he is not qualified or suited to it. He talks of quitting. If General Thomas recommends, I shall not object. He is not indispensable to our success. He is welcome to my place, if the President awards it, but I cannot name him to such an important command as the army of the Tennessee.

All is well. The enemy to-day offered no serious opposition to the changes of to-day, and our skirmishing and artillery was just enough to make things interesting.

W. T. SHERMAN,
Major General Commanding.

HEADQUARTERS MILITARY DIVISION OF THE MISSISSIPPI,
In the field, near Atlanta, Ga., July 27, 1864.

SIR: Your despatch of yesterday is received. I beg you will not regard me as fault-finding, for I assert that I have been well sustained in every respect during my entire services. I did not suppose my despatches would go outside the offices at the War Department; I did not suppose you were troubled with such matters. ———— and ———— are both worthy men, and had they been promoted on the eve of the Vicksburg campaign it would have been natural and well accepted; but I do think you will admit that their promotion, coming to us when they had gone to the rear—the one offended because I could not unite in the same division five infantry and five cavalry regiments, and the other for temporary sickness—was enough to occasion disappointment. You can see how ambitious aspirants for military fame regard these things. They come to me and point them out as evidences that I am wrong in encouraging them to a silent, patient, discharge of duty. I assure you that every general of my army has spoken of it. and referred to it as evidence that promotion results from importunity, and not from actual service. I have refrained from recommending any thus far in the campaign, as I think we should reach some stage in the game before stopping to balance accounts or writing history. I assure you that I do think you have consistently acted throughout the war with marked skill in the matter of military appointments, and that as few mistakes have been made as could be expected. I will furnish all my army and division commanders with a copy of your despatch, that they may feel reassured.

With great respect,

W. T. SHERMAN,
Major General Commanding.

His Excellency PRESIDENT LINCOLN,
Washington.

HEADQUARTERS MILITARY DIVISION OF THE MISSISSIPPI,
In the field, near Atlanta, Ga., July 27, 1864.

General HALLECK, *Washington:*

General Hooker has applied to be relieved of the command of the 20th army corps, assigning as a reason the appointment of General Howard, his junior, to command the army of the Tennessee. General Thomas asks the following appointments:

General D. S. Stanley to command the 4th corps, vice Howard, transferred.

General H. W. Slocum to command the 20th corps, vice Hooker, relieved at his own request.

I approve these nominations, and ask orders, by telegraph, that General Slocum may be summoned from Vicksburg, where he now is.

W. T. SHERMAN,
Major General Commanding.

HEADQUARTERS MILITARY DIVISION OF THE MISSISSIPPI,
In the field, near Atlanta, Ga., July 28, 1864.

General THOMAS:

Try and thin your strong lines as much as possible to-morrow, so as to make good reserves for action. Let these reserves be ready to move at any moment. Our cavalry will surely reach the Macon road to-night, and to-morrow the enemy will do something desperate.

W. T. SHERMAN,
Major General Commanding.

HEADQUARTERS MILITARY DIVISION OF THE MISSISSIPPI,
In the field, near Atlanta, Ga., July 29, 1864.

General THOMAS:

Until the result of our cavalry movement is known, I want the utmost activity on our flanks. General Howard, by this time, must have his line strong. I wish you to take General Davis's division, and one of General Williams's, and operate from General Howard's right flank towards East Point. Don't form a line, but move so as to occupy or threaten the railroad. General Schofield will do the same on the left. I will stay at home to-day, to be convenient to the telegraph. Keep me well advised. Don't extend the line, but operate in the nature of a strong reconnoissance towards East Point, having General Howard's line as a point of departure and safety.

W. T. SHERMAN,
Major General Commanding.

HEADQUARTERS DEPARTMENT OF THE TENNESSEE,
July 29, 1864.

Major General SHERMAN:

We have counted six hundred and forty-two (642) rebel dead, and there are still others in front of our lines and not yet recovered. It is fair to presume that their wounded are five or six times that number. We may count largely on their missing, great numbers having been seen going to the rear, and many stragglers are being picked up in the woods. A just estimate of their (enemy's) loss would, I believe, be not less than five thousand (5,000.) Our loss, as far as reported, less than six hundred.

O. O. HOWARD,
Major General.

[Cipher.]

HEADQUARTERS MILITARY DIVISION OF THE MISSISSIPPI,
In the field, near Atlanta, Ga., July 29, 1864.

General HALLECK, *Washington:*

The result of the enemy's attack yesterday, chiefly on the 15th corps, is thus reported by General Howard:

We have counted six hundred and forty-two (642) rebel dead, and there are still others in front of our lines; it is fair to presume that their wounded are five or six times that of their dead. Over one hundred (100) prisoners are in hand, and others being gathered up in the woods. General Howard estimates the enemy's loss at five thousand (5,000,) and our loss at less than six hundred (600.)

General W. H. T. Walker was killed on the 22d, and it is now reported by prisoners that Wheeler was killed yesterday. We are so near the enemy's line that their intrenched artillery prevents our advancing the lines, so as to take full advantage of the battle, they gathering into the city their more remote dead.

The parapets of Atlanta present a will-filled line wherever we approach them. General Thomas is making to-day a strong reconnoissance in force towards East Point, and General Schofield on the left. Our cavalry has now been out three days, and must have done its work about Griffin.

W. T. SHERMAN,
Major General Commanding.

HEADQUARTERS DEPARTMENT OF THE CUMBERLAND,
July 29, 1864.

Major General SHERMAN:

I have just returned from the right. I have intrenched Morgan on the Howell or Green's ferry road, to the right and southwest of Logan. He has complete command of that road, and has his skirmishers out half a mile to his front. They have driven the rebels into intrenched rifle-pits, and report intrenched lines heavily manned a short distance in rear of their skirmish rifle-pits. I also directed Ward to take position on Morgan's right, and refuse his right so as to make a strong right flank. Ward fronts the Howell's ferry road, and runs along it towards the Chattahoochee for half a mile, and then falls back this way. Howard had good ground to fight on yesterday. I saw several dead rebels that Ward's men were burying. If, after intrenching, Howard will thin out and extend to his right, Morgan and Ward can move still further to the right, and might perhaps overlap the enemy.

While Morgan and Ward made their advance, I had Williams, Johnson, and Baird make strong reconnoissances to their fronts. They all report their belief that the enemy has either retired altogether or has withdrawn the greatest part of his forces, and only now has a weak skirmish line covering his fortifications around the city. I have directed them to feel strongly to-night and determine whether the enemy has retired or not.

GEO. H. THOMAS, *Major General.*

HEADQUARTERS DEPARTMENT OF THE CUMBERLAND,
July 29, 1864.

Major General SHERMAN:

I will send to General Morgan immediately for the strength of the 10th Illinois.

I take great pleasure in announcing the capture of an entire rebel regiment, one hundred and fifteen officers and men, by the first division, 20th corps, while advancing its lines in obedience to my orders of last night. The position obtained is very advantageous to us also, as it will enable me to shorten my lines considerably and have a better view of the ground in front.

G. H. THOMAS, *Major General.*

HEADQUARTERS ARMY OF THE OHIO,
July 30, 1864.

Major General SHERMAN:

I have your despatch expressing your desire that I advance my picket line in front of the distillery near the road leading to Atlanta. I tried that on the 28th, and found it impracticable, for this reason, viz: The point referred to is in a large re-entering angle of the enemy's works, and the enemy's picket line in that vicinity is enfiladed by the artillery of both the adjacent salients. Neither the enemy's picket line nor even the main curtain in rear should be held by our troops until those salients are carried. One of them is three-quarters of a mile to my left, and hence beyond my reach; the other is somewhat to my right. I will see General Stanley and ascertain what can be done about this latter salient. Perhaps we can drive in the skirmishers around it and keep down its fire with our sharpshooters.

Respectfully,

J. M. SCHOFIELD, *Major General.*

10*

HEADQUARTERS MILITARY DIVISION OF THE MISSISSIPPI,
In the field, near Atlanta, Ga., July 30, 1864.

Colonel JAMES A. HARDIE, *Inspector General, Washington, D. C.:*

Be pleased to convey my thanks to the President for his prompt bestowal of the appointments as brigadier generals on the eight (8) most worthy colonels named in your despatch to-day.

W. T. SHERMAN,
Major General Commanding.

HEADQUARTERS MILITARY DIVISION OF THE MISSISSIPPI,
In the field, near Atlanta, Ga., July 31, 1864.

Generals THOMAS and HOWARD:

I am just back from an interview with General Schofield.

General Garrard is back. He was sent by General Stoneman to Flat Rock, where he was surrounded by Wheeler's cavalry, but he remained two days expecting General Stoneman to send him orders, when he broke out to Lattimore's, where he heard General Stoneman had gone to Covington and beyond. Not having further orders, he came home *via* the Peach Tree road. His fight was a small affair, being only one (1) officer and six (6) men wounded, and riding down one brigade of the enemy. He thinks Wheeler still remains on the right of Atlanta, extending the infantry line. I think General Stoneman has gone to Macon, east of Yellow river, and that it is well. I have ordered General Garrard in on our left, and to-morrow night will let him fill with a skirmish line General Schofield's position, and move all of General Schofield's to the right of General Howard, and with the divisions of Generals Davis and Ward kept in reserve on the right to strike a blow beyond our new right flank when intrenched. Our right flank must be advanced in close and absolute contact with the enemy, and with General Schofield on that flank, I think we can make him quit Atlanta, or so weaken his line that we can break through somewhere, the same as our Kenesaw move.

Study the road, so that Generals Schofield and Howard may have a line close up to the enemy—as close as possible. I will send a regiment of cavalry down the west bank of the Chattahoochee to feel for General McCook. I must have a bolder commander for General Garrard's cavalry, and want General Thomas to name to me General Kilpatrick, or some good brigadier, for the command.

W. T. SHERMAN,
Major General Commanding.

HEADQUARTERS MILITARY DIVISION OF THE MISSISSIPPI,
In the field, near Atlanta, Ga., August 1, 1864.

SIR: I am obliged for a copy of your letter to the honorable E. M. Stanton, of date July 22, as it will enable me to reply at once.

It seems Dr. Luke Miller, a commissioner of your State, has been denied a pass on the military railroad below Nashville, for the purpose of ministering to the wants of the sick and wounded soldiers of your State here at the front, and your letter is doubtless intended as an appeal to the Secretary of War to compel me to grant such a pass. You will be amazed when on this simple statement I must accuse you of heartless cruelty to your constituents; but such is the fact. You would take the very bread and meat out of your soldiers' mouths, that a State inspector might come and supervise the acts of other medical officers here on the spot, commissioned by yourself. You would load down our cars with travellers, and limit our ability to feed our horses and transport the powder and ball necessary to carry on this war. I tell you that with the aid of the best talent our country affords, and by laboring night and day, one *single* track of railroad *cannot* supply us; and I have been compelled to lay by for days to accumulate supplies for another step in our progress. To be sure, a single passenger would be a small matter; but he is two hundred pounds avoirdupois, and his bulk and weight in bread and meat would feed one hundred men a day, or one man one hundred days; and you can make the same calculation for forage and cartridges.

Now, how many States are there with commissioners? And are medical commissioners the only ones who claim to come below Nashville? Why, sir, go to Nashville and see. Every State has one, every congressional district, and every county; then the sanitary agents and societies, and Christian Commission, with all their ramifications; and a still more numerous and appealing class—the parents, and brothers and sisters of soldiers, dead, or wounded, or sick, or refugees searching lost parents, families and children. Will you say which of these shall have preference over the very food our men eat? Now, every regiment has its colonel and field officers, its surgeon and chaplain, and all may and do write letters daily. We strain our every nerve the moment a soldier is sick or wounded to send him to the rear to the best hospitals, and you know that agents and commissioners are not essential at all, but, on the contrary, embarrass us in all the details; then, I repeat, that by trying to force me to transport your commissioners you unknowingly and unconsciously are guilty of the cruel act of taking the bread out of some poor soldier's mouth, or the corn necessary to feed our horses that they may work. Why not accord to us on the spot a credit for some good sense and feeling? Why, when we beg you for mercy's sake to allow us for the period of our brief campaign to have the exclusive use of our single track of rail, every foot of which we must guard, and every inch of which has cost us a precious life? Why do you mistrust our purpose, and appeal for compulsory process? I beg you will see how differently men regard the same state of facts from a different stand-point.

I see you regarded the refusal by General Webster of a railroad pass for your commissioner as a want of respect for your State and office. Be assured that for you personally and officially, and for the State of Minnesota, I feel the most profound respect; but if I am to be charged with this campaign, instead of relaxing my already stringent rules at Nashville, I will make them more and more severe, that I may better feed, clothe, and equip the army, whose life and success hang by that slender thread.

I am, &c.,

W. T. SHERMAN,
Major General Commanding.

To his Excellency STEPHEN MILLER,
    Governor of Minnesota, St. Paul.

HEADQUARTERS DEPARTMENT OF THE CUMBERLAND,
    August 1, 1864—9 p. m.

Colonel Brownlow reports that McCook destroyed twelve (12) miles of the Macon railroad and a bridge over the Whitewater longer than the Chattahoochee bridge. He also destroyed over five hundred (500) wagons—Hood's, Hardee's, and other headquarter wagons among them. Unfortunately, he then turned back on his old route, and commenced to destroy the West Point road, when he was attacked on the 29th, near Newman, by infantry and cavalry in overwhelming numbers, surrounded, and all who did not cut their way through were either killed or captured.

There are nearly five hundred now in Marietta, and Brownlow thinks many more will find their way in. The 1st Wisconsin was cut off near Campbellton, and returned two days ago. I will send you his report in the morning.

GEORGE H. THOMAS,
Major General.

Major General SHERMAN.

HEADQUARTERS MILITARY DIVISION OF THE MISSISSIPPI,
In the field, near Atlanta, Ga., August 2, 1864.

General WEBSTER, *Nashville:*

Too many citizens manage to come to the front. Be even more stringent than heretofore. Grant no passes beyond Chattanooga, and only the smallest possible number that far. Surgeons can fill the offices of the Sanitary Commission, and chaplains minister to the wants of the soldiers.

If any recruits are coming from the north I want them forwarded with despatch by the cars.

W. T. SHERMAN,
Major General Commanding.

THIRTEEN MILES SOUTHWEST OF DALLAS,
August 2, 1864.

Major General SHERMAN:

On the morning of the 29th I cut the West Point railroad at Palmetto, and thoroughly destroyed the Macon railroad for two (2) miles and a half. At Lovejoy's removed telegraph wire for five (5) miles and burned two trains. I also burned one hundred (100) bales of cotton, and over five hundred (500) wagons, including headquarters trains of nearly their whole army, Hardee's entire transportation and the cavalry command supply train; killed about eight hundred (800) mules and captured seventy-two (72) commissioned officers and three hundred and fifty (350) men. Wheeler was between McDonough and the road when I cut it. Fought Jackson's division near Lovejoy's and repulsed them; was forced to return by the way of Newman's, and found infantry there. I cut the railroad and telegraph, and four miles out was attacked by Jackson's, Wheeler's and Roddy's commands, and finally, by infantry, two brigades that had been stopped there on their way to Atlanta; smashed Ross's Texas brigade in trying to break through to the river, capturing General Ross, with all his horses and men. I was finally completely surrounded, and compelled to abandon everything that would impede me in order to cut my way through. I ordered Colonels Croxton and Torry to cut through with their brigades. I took Colonel Jones with me and got through twelve hundred (1,200) men by a charge in column and crossed the river below Franklin. I have not yet heard from Croxton or Torry's commands, but suppose they got out, as they made the attempt while I was fighting. Colonel Dow, Colonel Torry, Major Austin, wounded; Major Paine killed; Harrison missing, supposed a prisoner. My loss very heavy. No co-operation from Stoneman. I will be in Marietta to-morrow.

E. M. McCOOK,
Brigadier General.

HEADQUARTERS ARMY OF THE OHIO,
August 2, 1864—10 p. m.

Major General SHERMAN:

From all that I can see I judge that the enemy's infantry fire bends back opposite my left centre, and runs from that point nearly south behind a small branch of the creek in front of Howard and myself. The force in front of my right appears to be cavalry. To seriously threaten the enemy's flank and railroad communications it will be necessary to cross the creek in front of my right, and reach the Sandtown road, which is about a mile beyond the creek. If this move can be made with a sufficiently large force the result must be very decisive. Please inform me if you desire me to push forward to-morrow, and also whether Morgan's and Ward's divisions will be absolutely under my command, or only to be called on when the necessity shall arise. At present they are within easy supporting distance; but if I move they should move with me.

Respectfully,

J. M. SCHOFIELD,
Major General.

HEADQUARTERS MILITARY DIVISION OF THE MISSISSIPPI,
In the field, near Atlanta, Ga., August 3, 1864.

General THOMAS:

I am just in from the right. General Schofield has one division across Utoy, and General Baird was crossing at 6 p. m.; pretty severe skirmish, but no battle. I came by General Logan, who has been fighting with artillery and picket lines all day; he carried a line and took fifty (50) prisoners. Enemy retook the pits, but our shirmishers got in safe. General Logan again took them, with one hundred and fifty (150) prisoners; his loss very small; he was still hammering away when I left him along his line, and this relieved the pressure on Generals Schofield and Baird. I think by morning he will have a lodgement across Utoy, on or very near the Big Sandtown road, that will seriously threaten the railroad. I have heard of General McCook and am well pleased. I heard very heavy firing up your way. Tell me all about it.

W. T. SHERMAN,
Major General Commanding.

[Cipher.]

HEADQUARTERS MILITARY DIVISION OF THE MISSISSIPPI,
In the field, near Atlanta, Ga., August 3, 1864.

General HALLECK, Washington:

We have had pretty lively times to-day generally, closing in, taking some two or three hundred prisoners. Under the pressure I got two divisions across the head of Utoy creek, well towards the railroad, and to-morrow will push still more on that flank.

General McCook, after all, has got in, bringing twelve hundred (1,200) of his men; he reports that on the 29th July he broke the West Point road at Palmetto, and then crossed over the Macon road at Lovejoy's, where he took up two (2) miles of track; burned two trains and one hundred (100) bales of cotton and five (5) miles of telegraph. He fell upon the rebel wagon train and burned over five hundred (500) wagons and killed eight hundred (800) mules; he captured seventy-two (72) officers and three hundred and fifty (350) men;

but his progress eastward and north, according to the plan, was stopped by a superior force of cavalry, and he turned towards Newman, where he was completely surrounded. He ordered two of his small brigades to make their way to the Chattahoochee while he held the enemy. About five hundred (500) of them are in, but the balance, about one thousand, (1,000,) are doubtless captured or killed. He then with twelve hundred (1,200) men charged through in column, riding down Ross's Texas brigade and capturing Ross, the commander; but he had to drop all prisoners and encumbrances to save his command; he crossed the Chattahoochee below Franklin, and up by Dallas to Marietta. The plan was for him to meet General Stoneman at Lovejoy's, but he did not meet him. Prisoners report that Yankee cavalry was shelling Macon on the 1st instant; so I think General Stoneman has a chance of rescuing those prisoners. It was a bold and rash adventure, but I sanctioned it, and hoped for its success from its very rashness.

I think that all Georgia is now in my front, and Stoneman may meet with but little opposition and succeed in releasing those prisoners. The difficulty will then commence for them to reach me. My lines are very strong and cover well all our bridges across Chattahoochee. I will use my cavalry hereafter to cover the railroad, and use infantry and artillery against Atlanta. A large part of Hood's army is militia that cannot be trusted in the open field, and I think we have crippled the three fighting corps now commanded by Stewart, Stephen D. Lee, and Hardee. It is even whispered that Hardee has resigned, but this is as yet but the story of deserters.

W. T. SHERMAN,
Major General Commanding.

HEADQUARTERS 4TH ARMY CORPS,
August 3, 1864—8.30 p. m.

Major General SHERMAN:

I have the honor to report, in answer to your inquiry, that I carried the picket line on the whole corps front excepting Gibson's and Wood's divisions. Newton's men went within one hundred (100) yards of the Star fort. The rebels opened from at least twenty (20) pieces. The rebels rallied and drove back Hazen's skirmishers. We took about forty (40) prisoners. Three of Cheatham's brigades are certainly in our front. They say Cleburn is on the rebel right. We could see troops move in and deploy in the works during the fight. I send through General Thomas a "Chattanooga Rebel" of the 3d August. Stoneman was at Clinton on the 1st; he had destroyed Oconee bridge, burned cars, &c., on the Central railroad. I had thirty or forty (30 or 40) killed and wounded to-day. My belief is that the rebel force is quite strong on this front yet. Gibson met a destructive fire of musketry and canister.

D. S. STANLEY, *Major General.*

MARIETTA, *August 4, 1864.*

Major General SHERMAN:

Colonel Adams, commanding brigade of Stoneman's cavalry, is here with 1st and 11th Kentucky, about nine hundred (900) strong. He thinks that the balance of the command are prisoners, including General Stoneman. He cut the railroad south of Macon. The command was overwhelmed by the rebels between Monticello and Clinton.

SAM'L ROSS,
Colonel 20th Connecticut, Commanding.

HEADQUARTERS MILITARY DIVISION OF THE MISSISSIPPI,
In the field, near Atlanta, Ga., August 4, 1864.

General SCOFIELD:

I have notified other commanders that the attack will commence at three p. m. That will be early enough. In the mean time make all preparations, especially to look to your connexion with General Howard. I will be over. General Palmer will be ordered to report to you with his command.

W. T. SHERMAN,
Major General Commanding.

HEADQUARTERS MILITARY DIVISION OF THE MISSISSIPPI,
In the field, near Atlanta, Ga., August 4, 1864.

General PALMER:

You will during the movement against the railroad report to and receive orders from General Schofield. General Thomas will personally look to the front of Atlanta. General Howard will co-operate with General Schofield, and General Schofield, re-enforced by your corps, is charged to reach the railroad. Obey his orders and instructions. Acknowledge receipt.

W. T. SHERMAN,
Major General Commanding.

[Cipher.]

HEADQUARTERS MILITARY DIVISION OF THE MISSISSIPPI,
In the field, near Atlanta, Ga., August 4, 1864.

General GRANT, *City Point:*

General Stoneman only had two thousand three hundred (2, 300) men. Nine hundred (900) have got in. I fear the balance are captured, as related in your despatch. General Stoneman was sent to break railroad, after which I consented he should attempt the rescue of our prisoners at Andersonville.

W. T. SHERMAN,
Major General Commanding.

[Cipher.]

MEMPHIS, *August 4, 1864.*

Major General SHERMAN:

Your telegram of the first instant just received. The force of Forrest is at Montgomery, stationed below Okalona, and I am moving in that direction, while Smith is after him with five thousand (5, 000) cavalry and ten thousand (10,000) infantry. He will hardly go into Middle Tennessee. The country where Forrest's command is is full of corn and meat, and Smith can subsist there. I have ordered him to push after Forrest wherever he may be and to go as far as Columbus, Mississippi, in pursuit of him, if necessary, and have all railroads this side of there destroyed. I telegraphed you on the 2d, but if you do not approve of the plans there laid down I shall expect to hear from you by the time Smith reaches Oxford, and will move then as you may direct. If you approve of the plan there indicated, shall Smith, after penetrating as far down as Columbus, march north to Decatur or Tuscumbia, or return here?

Should he meet and effectually whip Forrest, should he not return here and be sent to Mobile?

C. C. WASHBURN,
Major General.

HEADQUARTERS MILITARY DIVISION OF THE MISSISSIPPI,
In the field, near Atlanta, Ga., August 4, 1864.

General SCHOFIELD :

That is very well as to your left, but I want to assume the offensive on the right, and I wish you to order General Palmer to advance his left division till he reaches the Sandtown road, and its right supported by General Davis's division. General Johnson's division should reach the Sandtown road more to the right and close to the left on General Davis. The connexion between you and General Howard is not important. Slash down the timber in the valley of Utoy, and a single battery with a regiment of skirmishers will hold a mile against the whole of Hood's army. I want all of your army and General Palmer's corps to turn the enemy's left, and the sooner it is done the better. I wish you to make written orders, so that Generals Palmer and Baird cannot mistake them. Their delay this afternoon was unpardonable.

If the enemy ever gets a column through our lines we will let go our breastworks and turn on his flanks, and therefore I don't care about our line being continuous and uniform. If they sally it will be quick and by some well-defined road.

W. T. SHERMAN,
Major General Commanding.

[Cipher.]

HEADQUARTERS MILITARY DIVISION OF THE MISSISSIPPI,
In the field, near Atlanta, Ga., August 4, 1864.

General GRANT, *City Point :*

I have your second despatch about General Stoneman. I have newspapers, with dates from Macon of the 1st, speaking of General Stoneman's capture as a rumor, but not as a fact. He started from here in connexion with two other parties that have got back ; he had two thousand three hundred (2,300) men, and after breaking the Macon road he was to make an effort to rescue our prisoners. Colonel Adams with nine hundred (900) of his men got back to Marietta to-day, and telegraphs me Stoneman was attacked at Clinton, Georgia, by overwhelming numbers, and they fear he is captured. It may be so, but I hope he may, like General McCook, dodge and get in.

General Washburn is moving from Holly Springs on Columbus, Mississippi. He thinks that Forrest is dead of the wound he received in his battle with General Smith.

The country in which I am operating is very difficult for a large army, and the defensive positions very strong and hard to circumvent; but perseverance will move mountains.

I ought to be better advised of your plans and movements. I hear you have blown up the outer bastion of Petersburg, but don't know how near you are to getting full possession of the place, or its bearing on Richmond.

Hood uses his militia to fill his lines, and shows a bold front wherever I get at him.

W. T. SHERMAN,
Major General Commanding.

[Copy by telegraph.]

HEADQUARTERS MILITARY DIVISION OF THE MISSISSIPPI,
In the field, near Atlanta, Ga., August 4, 1864.

General WEBSTER, *Nashville :*

As some confusion and misunderstanding has occurred relative to my orders as to newspapers and newspaper carriers, I will repeat that it is a small business for me to attend to in the midst of an active campaign, and one that ought never to reach my notice.

The military railroad is to carry supplies for the army. It cannot carry all the supplies allowed by law and usage, and therefore preference must be given to some things over others: 1st, ammunition; 2d, clothing; 3d, provisions, for men; 4th, forage for horses; and as I cannot in person supervise the bills of lading or loading of trains, I leave this to the quartermaster at Nashville, who has the best knowledge of the state of supplies forward and at the depot, as well as the capacity of the cars. Newspapers are a kind of freight, and as such I do not object to the quartermaster at Nashville shipping any number of bundles consigned to any of the posts forward, because they occupy little space, and the bulk of such newspapers cannot materially affect the quantity of provisions shipped; but newsvenders, like any other merchants, must not travel in the cars to sell their goods any more than grocers or hucksters. They may send bundles of their papers in the cars by consent of the quartermaster who loads the cars. Every army commander can send his mail messengers daily each way, and these may carry papers as a part of the army mails, and the orders of Generals Thomas, Howard and Schofield, for officers and men are military orders of transportation that quartermasters will respect the same as mine. Passes to citizens, as far as Chattanooga, in very limited numbers, may be granted by the authority of either of these army commanders, and they may send to the rear car-loads of prisoners, refugees and citizens without limit, but I have ordered that on no pretence must citizens come this side of Chattanooga, for I find them useless mouths that I cannot afford to feed.

My orders also are that officers must live on the soldier's ration; yet if the quartermaster at Nashville can keep our supplies up, and also send supplies to officers above the rations without interfering with the regular freight, he may do so. In other words, I hold the officers of the quartermaster department responsible that the army stores take precedence of all other stores, and if he send anything else he cannot allege it as a reason for a failure to keep up the regular supplies. The railroad has supplied us well, better than I expected, and I am willing to continue to trust the regular quartermasters, who thus far have managed the bussiness well.

There is and can be no conflict of orders. No one can question my orders when they are positive, but I do not choose to make orders touching freight absolutely positive, save in large articles, such as cotton and produce, that would, if attempted, soon absorb our cars, and thereby diminish the ability of our railroad to handle the vast amount of supplies on which we depend.

All I order as to newspapers is that no monopoly should be allowed, and officers can be supplied as in other mail matters, and venders may get the quartermaster at Nashville to carry their bundles, but not their carriers. These are superfluous.

W. T. SHERMAN,
Major General Commanding.

Headquarters Military Division of the Mississippi,
In the field, near Atlanta, Ga., August 4, 1864—10.45 p. m.

General PALMER:

From the statements made by yourself and General Schofield to-day, my decision is that he ranks you as major general, being of same date of commission, and by previous superior rank as brigadier general. The movements for to-morrow are so important that the orders of the superior on that flank must be regarded as military orders, and not in the nature of co-operation. I did hope that there was no necessity of making this decision, but it is better for all parties interested that no question of rank should occur during active battle.

The Sandtown road and the railroad, if possible, must be gained to-morrow if it costs half your command. I regard the loss of time this afternoon as equal to the loss of two thousand (2,000) men.

W. T. SHERMAN,
Major General Commanding.

HEADQUARTERS MILITARY DIVISION OF THE MISSISSIPPI,
In the field, near Atlanta, Ga., August 5, 1864.

General THOMAS, Army of the Cumberland :

Yesterday General Palmer raised the question of rank with General Schofield. I went in person and found that General Schofield ranked General Palmer as a brigadier, but General Palmer was appointed and confirmed major general to date November 29, 1862. General Schofield was also nominated from same date, but the Senate would not confirm. But since that session the Senate has confirmed, and General Schofield has his commission of same date as General Palmer, and ranks him, therefore, by virtue of prior commission. I have so decided, and General Palmer asks to be relieved of his command and ordered north. I declined, and ordered him emphatically to go on to-day and execute the plan prescribed for yesterday in connexion with and under command of General Schofield. I have another letter from him asking to be relieved after to-day's operation. Now, what say you ? General Davis is unwell, and General Johnson ranks him. That is the largest corps we have, and thus far has not sustained heavy loss in this campaign. It moves slowly and reluctantly, and there is something wrong. What are your plans and wishes?

General Schofield reports that General Johnson's division has reached the Sandtown road, well to the right, by a road I put it on last night. General Morgan's division also has reached it, and General Baird is swinging by a left wheel so his right flank will reach it. Generals Schofield and Palmer have both gone out to complete the movement, which involves a push towards the railroad till our right flank is near enough to the railroad to control it by short range artillery.

There was sharp firing for a few moments this morning, but it has ceased now, so that I begin to think we will succeed on that flank without the serious battle I apprehended. Still, keep your ears open, and if you hear heavy musketry over near Whitehall, either make a break into Atlanta, or so occupy the lines that the enemy may not detach too heavily against Generals Schofield and Palmer. Generals Howard and Schofield will connect by a shorter line across the head of Utoy creek. Our cavalry has scouted down to the mouth of Utoy creek.

W. T. SHERMAN,
Major General Commanding.

HEADQUARTERS MILITARY DIVISION OF THE MISSISSIPPI,
In the field, near Atlanta, Ga., August 5, 1864.

General SCHOFIELD :

Despatch received. All right. Press that attack on the right. I will judge by the sound, and if I judge you are too hard pressed, will order Generals Thomas and Howard to assault somewhere. Get some part of your command where you can reach easily the railroad with short-range guns, and then intrench a strong flank. It is worth a battle, and the closer the first advantages are followed up the better. The weakest point of the enemy must be mathematically at some point between Atlanta and East Point. Keep me often advised of your progress, and I will come over any minute you say, but can better handle the whole army from here by telegraph.

W. T. SHERMAN,
Major General Commanding.

HEADQUARTERS MILITARY DIVISION OF THE MISSISSIPPI,
In the field, near Atlanta, Ga., August 5, 1864.

General PALMER, *at the front:*

I have communicated to General Thomas the substance of our former notes and messages, and have received the following reply by telegraph : " I regret to hear that Palmer has taken the course he has, and as I know he intends to offer his resignation as soon as he can properly do so, I recommend that his application be granted."

Now, if General Schofield has a major general's commission going back to equal date with yours, though confirmed subsequently with retroactive effect, he ranks you by reason of former superior commission; and if you resign because you measure your number of men as greater than his, and your services in battle as giving you greater right to command, you commit the mistake of substituting your own individual opinion over the established law and military usage. The special assignment of General Schofield to the command of a separate army and department shows that he enjoys the confidence of the President even above his mere lineal rank. If you want to resign, wait a few days, and allege some other reason— one that will stand the test of time. Your future is too valuable to be staked on a mistake. Your case clearly falls under an old article of war : " When two or more commanders happen together, the officer highest in rank commands the whole." General Schofield ranks you by his commission, and it would not do for military men to discuss the nice question of how far back the President may give effect to a commission.

I again ask you not to disregard the friendly advice of such men as General Thomas and myself, for you cannot misconstrue our friendly feelings towards you.

I am, &c.

W. T. SHERMAN,
Major General Commanding.

HEADQUARTERS MILITARY DIVISION OF THE MISSISSIPPI,
In the field, near Atlanta, Ga., August 5, 1864.

Hon. E. M. STANTON, *Secretary of War, Washington:*

The time has now come that we must have the exclusive use of the north-western road from Nashville to Reynoldsburg. It has been substantially done for some time, but Governor Johnson retains the management of it for some reason, under your former orders; but to be of service to us in the present emergency it must be in the control of Mr. Anderson, superintendent of military roads, that trains may run continuously from the Tennessee river, at Reynoldsburg, to our camp.

This main road has been admirably managed, and has supplied this vast army, so that not a man, horse, or mule has been for a day without food, and with abundant supplies of clothing and ammunition. Our progress may be slow to you all at a distance, but if you ever cross this ground you will not accuse us of being idlers.

W. T. SHERMAN.
Major General Commanding.

HEADQUARTERS MILITARY DIVISION OF THE MISSISSIPPI,
In the field, near Atlanta, Ga., August 5, 1864.

General THOMAS:

I telegraphed to General R. S. Granger this morning that he need not send the battery along with the infantry brigade. If not needed at Decatur, order General Granger to send it to Nashville in reserve.

I know that the slowness of the troops on the right was not the fault of the men, but the want of proper direction on the part of the commanders. First, was the question of rank; and next, the course taken was too far west away from the railroad rather than towards it. To-night General Schofield will put General Johnson in the trenches, take his out, and move perpendicular to the road, and not extend to the right more than is necessary, and will have Generals Baird and Morgan in support. If we can keep the forts of Atlanta full, with four (4) divisions in hand, we can whip any force outside of rebel intrenchments, and will have General Johnson near enough for support. All our line is well developed, but is generally strengthened by good abatis and parapet, and conforms pretty close to the enemy, so that if we force the enemy to stick in his trenches, General Schofield should surely reach the railroad and overcome any force the enemy has outside. I have no doubt by our delay the enemy is better prepared than he would have been could we have moved quick, as I ordered yesterday. Last night I could see the cars, say, a mile and a quarter due southeast, whereas Generals Baird and Johnson to-day moved southwest, or nearly due west, away from the enemy. But we will try again to-morrow, and persevere to the end. I have written to General Palmer at length, and asked him to come and see me very early in the morning, and if he wants to go I will assent, and in that event will make the recommendations you suggested this morning.

I have personally examined our line from right to left, and feel no uneasiness as to the enemy making a sally. I know it will be hard to make an assaulting column, but all I want is to force the enemy to hold troops at all points, so as not to mass too heavy on our right.

W. T. SHERMAN,
Major General Commanding.

HEADQUARTERS ARMY OF THE OHIO,
August 6, 1864.

Major General SHERMAN:

In my movement this morning I made a circuit to the right far enough to strike beyond what appeared to be, and probably was yesterday, the enemy's flank, but found intrenchments of ordinary strength, with extensive entanglements in front. Reilly assaulted gallantly and energetically, and I believe with more confidence on the part of himself and men, but the obstructions were so great that it was found impossible to reach the parapet. Reilly's loss about five hundred (500) men, including many valuable officers. After this failure I made a much larger circuit to the right, for the purpose of breaching the enemy's flank on a point of his line not protected by abatis. I struck the point where the Sandtown road crosses the main Utoy creek. Here the enemy's line makes a sharp salient, bending back along the north bank of the creek. The main line was prolonged by cavalry, with artillery, toward the Chattahoochee. General Hascall sent two brigades under General Cooper to clear this flank, which he did by crossing the creek, but too late for any further operations. We are intrenching the ground we have gained, and will be ready for work in the morning.   The losses in Cox's and Hascall's divisions are probably not more than one thousand (1,000) men.   I have not thought it advisable to put in more than the 23d corps to-day, except in making demonstrations to draw the enemy from the points of attack.

General Johnson has been with me during the day, and has promptly executed all my orders.   Colonel Warner, who left me late this evening, can explain to you more fully our situation.   If you take the blue colored map of Atlanta and vicinity, the forks of the Utoy creek, southeast of the town of Utoy, is, I believe, Hascall's position.   I will determine more accurately to-night.

J. M. SCHOFIELD,

Major General.

[Cipher.]

HEADQUARTERS MILITARY DIVISION OF THE MISSISSIPPI,
In the field, near Atlanta, Ga., August 6, 1864.

General HALLECK, *Washington :*

We have now developed our lines along with the enemy from the Augusta railroad on our left to the Utoy Post Office on our right, and the enemy faces us at all points with equal force and superior works.   General Schofield tried to break through at a point near our right, with a brigade, (General, Reilly's,) but his men were caught in the entanglement and lost, probably, five hundred (500.) We have skirmished heavily along the whole line, using artillery freely, but have made no impression.   I will continue to work to the right to find the extreme flank and threaten the railroad, if possible, to draw him out of Atlanta, or force him to attack us.   But our line is already too extended and weak.   By means of his militia, of which he has the whole population of Georgia, he is enabled to use his three regular corps as reserves.   Our losses to-day will foot up one thousand (1,000.)   I will soon need re-enforcements, and if you can replace General A. J. Smith, at Memphis, with negro or fresh troops, I would order him here *via* Decatur; he must now be en route for Columbus, Mississippi.   I have called forward a brigade from Decatur.

I am now convinced that General Stoneman surrendered near Macon with seven hundred (700) of his men, ordering two small brigades to break out and get in.   One, Colonel Adams, with nine hundred (900) men, is in, but their time is out, and they will be discharged; the other brigade, Capron's, I fear was scattered and picked up in detail.   His entire loss will be about thirteen hundred (1,300;) General McCook's loss five hundred (500.)   Damage done roads, cars, and bridges was very large, but the enemy now runs cars into Atlanta from Macon.

W. T. SHERMAN,
Major General Commanding.

HEADQUARTERS MILITARY DIVISION OF THE MISSISSIPPI,
In the field, near Atlanta, Ga., August 6, 1864.

General THOMAS :

General Schofield has been at work to-day with his two divisions and holds General Johnson in support.   He has just finished working up his measurement and locates himself at the fork of Utoy creek, two (2) miles west of East Point. Though our line is extended, we cannot do better than to contract and strengthen by defences our present front and let General Schofield work so as to threaten East Point. I don't believe the enemy can defend so long a line, and he may be forced to choose between the two, Atlanta and East Point, unless he has repaired the Augusta road, of which there are no signs; or unless he can drive back General Johnson's flank, which controls that road, he will be compelled to give up Atlanta to secure East Point.

General Schofield asks for a couple of topographical engineers; he lost his only one yesterday. Can you spare him one or two? If so, order them to report to him.

He tried to break through the enemy's lines by a brigade to-day, but failed, losing five hundred (500) men. Instead of going round East Point, I would prefer the enemy to weaken so we may break through at some point, and wish you to continue to make such an effort. I will instruct General Howard to do the same about the head of Utoy creek, his right.

W. T. SHERMAN,
Major General Commanding.

HEADQUARTERS MILITARY DIVISION OF THE MISSISSIPPI,
In the field, near Atlanta, Ga., August 6, 1864.

General SCHOFIELD :

I will try to send you some more engineers to-morrow. I will have to borrow of other armies. Continue to work to-morrow in such a manner as to best threaten the railroad at or below East Point, and keep your own and the 14th corps united so as to defend yourselves against the enemy, should he let go Atlanta and shift to his communications. If you can threaten that road he is bound to choose, and you know what choice he will make. I advise you to see to-night that the right, by which the Big Sandtown road comes out from the enemy to your line, is well covered, for he will, if at all, sally by well known roads. The valleys of the two forks of the Utoy can easily be held by a thin line and an entanglement of timber. General Thomas will continue to press Atlanta up the valley of Proctor's creek, and General Howard by Utoy.

The militia by which Hood holds his long lines of intrenchments are worthless save for that purpose, but they enable him to use his good troops, distributed, doubtless, by brigades to rush to threatened points. I don't think he will mass them all unless he gives up Atlanta and throws his force at one move to East Point.

If you be at the forks of the main Utoy, two (2) miles west of East Point, your cavalry should cross the upper fork and picket the crossing at Utoy Post Office. You should also open a more direct road to where your headquarters are, which serves as a key-point.

W. T. SHERMAN,
Major General Commanding.

HEADQUARTERS MILITARY DIVISION OF THE MISSISSIPPI,
In the field, near Atlanta, Ga., August 6, 1864.

General SCHOFIELD :

I have your despatch. There is no alternative but for you to continue to work on that flank with as much caution as possible, and it is possible the enemy may attack us or draw out. He must defend that road.

W. T. SHERMAN,
Major General Commanding.

[Cipher.]

NEW ORLEANS, *August 6, 1864.*

Major General SHERMAN :

The fleet under Admiral Farragut passed the forts at the entrance of Mobile bay at 8 a. m. yesterday. The monitor Tecumseh was blown up by a rebel torpedo and lost nearly all her crew. The rebel ram Tennessee and gunboat Selma were captured after an obstinate resistance. The other gunboats took shelter under the guns of Fort Morgan. Admiral Farragut expects to capture or destroy them to-day and to secure a landing east of Fort Morgan and in the bay for our troops. Fort Powell is reported abandoned and blown up ; Fort Gaines was invested by the land troops under General Granger, and is reported to have surrendered, but this is not official. The loss in the fleet in killed, wounded, and drowned is about two hundred (200.) With the exception of the Tecumseh none of our vessels were lost, and the Hartford is the only one that is seriously injured. I am sending Granger all the forces I can collect Kirby Smith, I have no doubt, is trying to send a part of his forces east of the Mississippi, but I think we will be able to prevent it.

E. R. S. CANBY,
Major General.

HEADQUARTERS DEPARTMENT OF THE CUMBERLAND,
August 6, 1864—12 m.

Major General SHERMAN :

The enemy has been feeling our lines from Williams's right toward the left, apparently to see whether we have weakened our lines or not. The skirmishing on the left is probably for the same purpose, but it will be well to ascertain whether he intends more serious work, which Stanley can do by sending Garrard to feel his flanks. Howard thinks he is trying to get out of Atlanta clear. That may be, but Stanley must be watchful and not give ground until he can see he intends to attack him, then have him withdraw gradually to rear line, and let him come on until he becomes well entangled in the abatis before opening fire on him, but not leave present position until he thinks it absolutely necessary

GEO. H. THOMAS,
Major General.

[Cipher.]

HEADQUARTERS MILITARY DIVISION OF THE MISSISSIPPI,
In the field, near Atlanta, Ga., August 6, 1864.

General HALLECK, *Washington, D. C. :*

General Palmer has resigned his command of the 14th army corps, and General Thomas has relieved him of the command. General Thomas recommends the promotion of General Jeff. C. Davis as major general and assignment to the command of the 14th corps. In the event the President will not consent to this, General Thomas asks the promotion and assignment of General J. M. Brannan. I approve his recommendations, and ask a speedy return.

W. T. SHERMAN,
Major General Commanding.

WASHINGTON, D. C.,
August 6, 1864—1.45 p. m.

Major General SHERMAN:

An order by the President, under the act of Congress for the military possession of the northwestern railroad, has been issued, and will be forwarded you by the Adjutant General. Do not imagine that we are impatient of your progress; instead of considering it slow we regard it rapid, brilliant and successful beyond our expectations. Take your time, and do your work in your own way. This department is only anxious to afford you every assistance within its power.

E. M. STANTON,
Secretary of War.

HEADQUARTERS MILITARY DIVISION OF THE MISSISSIPPI,
In the field, near Atlanta, Ga., August 7, 1864.

General SCHOFIELD:

That's right. Go on in your own way to accomplish the end, and keep your five (5) divisions so as to hold the enemy till a battle is fought. I will look a little closer at General Howard's front to see if there is not a weak place there in the enemy's line; there should be about the head of Utoy's north fork. I will then work my way down to you on the extreme right.

W. T. SHERMAN,
Major General Commanding.

HEADQUARTERS MILITARY DIVISION OF THE MISSISSIPPI,
In the field, near Atlanta, Ga., August 7, 1864.

Generals THOMAS and HOWARD:

The line assaulted yesterday was an incomplete one. By feeling its left, Bates's division evacuated and fell back to the real line, which is near the railroad. I ordered the skirmishers to be pushed in, and the strength demonstrated, and developed heavy musketry fire and artillery. We have gained valuable ground and full possession of the real Sandtown road. Our lines are close up and by morning will be intrenched, so we will keep on working by that flank; but I want the whole line advanced wherever it be possible, and that General Thomas bring from Chattanooga two (2) 30-pounder Parrotts, or siege carriages, and batter the town. The closer we advance our line, we contract and stengthen.

General Schofield's right does not yet really threaten the railroad, though a full mile nearer East Point than last night.

W. T. SHERMAN,
Major General Commanding.

[HEADQUARTERS DEPARTMENT OF THE CUMBERLAND,
August 7, 1864.

Major General SHERMAN:

I will keep the attention of the enemy fully occupied by threatening all along my front, but I have no hopes of breaking through his lines anywhere in my front as long as he has a respectable force to defend them. My troops are so thinned out that it will be impossible to form an assaulting column sufficiently strong to make an attack sure.

GEO. H. THOMAS, *Major General.*

HEADQUARTERS MILITARY DIVISION OF THE MISSISSIPPI,
In the field, near Atlanta, Ga., August 7, 1864.

General GRANT, *Washington:*

I was gratified to learn that you were satisfied with my progress. Get the War Department to send us recruits daily as they are made, for we can teach them more war in our camp in one day than they can get at a rendezvous in a month. Also tell Mr. Lincoln that he must not make the least concession in the matter of the September draft. It is right and popular with the army, and the army is worth considering.

I am glad you have given General Sheridan the command of the forces to defend Washington. He will worry Early to death. Let us give those southern fellows all the fighting they want, and when they are tired we can tell them we are just warming to the work. Any signs of let-up on our part is sure to be falsely construed, and for this reason I always remind them that the siege of Troy lasted six years, and Atlanta is a more favorable town than Troy. We must manifest the character of dogged courage and perseverance of our race.

Don't stay in Washington longer than is necessary to give impulse to events, and get out of it. It is the centre of intrigue.

I would like to have General Mower made a major general. He is a real fighter.

W. T. SHERMAN,
Major General Commanding.

[Cipher.]

HEADQUARTERS MILITARY DIVISION OF THE MISSISSIPPI,
In the field, near Atlanta, Ga., August 7, 1864.

General HALLECK, *Washington:*

Have received to-day the despatches of the Secretary of War and General Grant, which are very satisfactory. We keep hammering away here all the time, and there is no peace inside or outside of Atlanta. To-day General Schofield got round the flank of the lines assaulted yesterday by General Reilley's brigade, turned it, and gained the ground where the assault was, with all our dead and wounded. We continued to press on that flank, and brought on a noisy but not a bloody battle. We drove the enemy behind his main breastworks, which cover the railroad from Atlanta to East Point. We captured a good many skirmishers, which are of their best troops, for the militia hug the breastworks close. I do not deem it prudent to extend more to the right, but will push forward daily by parallels, and make the inside of Atlanta too hot to be endured.

I have sent to Chattanooga for two (2) thirty (30) pounder Parrotts, with which we can pick out almost any house in the town. I am too impatient for a siege, but I don't know but here is as good a place to fight it out as further inland. One thing is certain, whether we get inside of Atlanta or not, it will be a used-up community by the time we are done with it.

W. T. SHERMAN,
Major General Commanding.

HEADQUARTERS ARMY OF THE OHIO,
August 8, 1864—8.30 p. m.

Major General SHERMAN:

Hascall only succeeded in getting one brigade across the creek and intrenched. The enemy is pretty strong in front of that brigade, and has used artillery freely

11 *

Hascall is making good roads and bridges across the creek. It seems clear that we are as near to the railroad as we can get on this side of the creek without breaking the rebel lines. To cross the creek, takes us around below East Point. Whether one division is sufficient force to make that move with seems extremely doubtful. Possibly, the demonstration may be sufficient to make Hood let go of Atlanta. I am satisfied Cox's right is not more than a mile from East Point.

J. M. SCHOFIELD,
Major General.

HEADQUARTERS DEPARTMENT OF THE CUMBERLAND,
August 8, 1864.

Major General SHERMAN :

The 4½-inch guns have not yet arrived. They are not due until to-morrow. I have selected a very good point for them on Geary's left, where you can get a fair view of the town, and half a mile nearer than any other position. It was reported that they were to leave Chattanooga at 8 a. m. to-day. The position selected enfilades Whitehall street, upon which is General Hood's headquarters, and the battery is being built to-night.

GEORGE H. THOMAS,
Major General.

HEADQUARTERS MILITARY DIVISION OF THE MISSISSIPPI,
In the field, near Atlanta, Ga., August 8, 1864.

General SCHOFIELD :

I have your despatch. Continue to press by the right. It is impossible for the enemy to extend much further. Generals Thomas and Howard will continue to press forward if Colonel Garrard watches all the passes of Utoy creek. I have no fears of that flank. If General Cox has a view of the railroad over clear ground to his right, distant only a mile, our rifle guns will reach it. Still, General Hascall should move straight towards it, and intrench as close as he can get. I think that open ground is below East Point, and the railroad you see is the East Point road, which the enemy does not use. I have your despatch of 8.30. See in person to the point occupied by General Hascall. Let good bridges and roads be prepared, and intrench the point as a flank to threaten below East Point. Strengthen the main line as much as possible, so that if the enemy will fight on that flank you may have as much force as possible to support ; but explain to General Hascall, if they allow him to intrench, they will not attack him, but feign for the purpose of breaking out somewhere else.

W. T. SHERMAN,
Major General Commanding.

HEADQUARTERS ARMY OF THE OHIO,
August 10, 1864.

Major General SHERMAN :

Either our maps or surveys, or both, are so evidently erroneous that I am very uncertain about the distance from Hascall's present position to the West Point railroad. But I have no doubt he can reach it without assaulting parapets, and by moving nearly in a southeasterly direction from his present position. The distance may be a little more than a mile, and it may be three miles. I think it probable that another corps on this flank would be able to prolong the line to the Macon railroad ; or better, that one corps in addition to mine could swing loose from the flank of the 14th, strike in the rear of East Point, and get a position crossing the railroad, from which we could not be driven.

The country south of Utoy appears less broken and much more cultivated than north of it. Hascall is on the main Campbellton road. There is said to be a big road a short distance in his front leading to East Point. I have not been able to learn of any others in that vicinity. Can you not take Proctor's creek for your left flank, bring supplies by Turner's ferry, and thus throw even two corps yet to the right? It appears to me that such a move, if made rapidly, ought to bring success.

J. M. SCHOFIELD,
Major General.

[Cipher.]

HEADQUARTERS MILITARY DIVISION OF THE MISSISSIPPI,
In the field, near Atlanta, Ga., August 9, 1864.

General HALLECK, *Washington:*

General Schofield developed the enemy's position to below East Point. His line is well fortified, embracing Atlanta and East Point, and his redoubts and lines seem well filled. Cavalry is on his flanks. Our forces, too, are spread for ten (10) miles. So Hood intends to stand his ground. I threw into Atlanta about three thousand (3,000) solid shot and shells to-day, and have got from Chattanooga four $4\frac{1}{2}$-inch rifled guns and will try their effect. Our right is below Utoy creek. I will intrench it and the flanks, and study the ground a little more before adopting a new plan. We have had considerable rain, but, on the whole, the weather is healthy. Colonel Caperton, of General Stoneman's command, with several squads of men, are at Marietta, and will reduce his loss below a thousand.

W. T. SHERMAN,
Major General Commanding.

[Cipher.]

HEADQUARTERS MILITARY DIVISION OF THE MISSISSIPPI,
In the field, near Atlanta, Ga., August 10, 1864.

General U. S. GRANT, *Washington:*

Your despatch of 9th is received. It is to replace our daily losses that I propose that all recruits made daily in the western States, instead of accumulating at depots, should at once come to Nashville, and be sent here on the cars, which can bring four hundred (400) a day without interfering with freights. I have ordered General Washburn, at Memphis, to have General A. J. Smith, who is now marching on Columbus, Mississippi, come to Decatur, Alabama, whence I can bring to this army certain regiments and fragments that properly belong here, and a division that I originally designed to form a part of this army. The balance of infantry and cavalry I would send back *via* Savannah and Jackson. Tennessee. My lines are now ten (10) miles long, extending from the Augusta road on the left, round to East Point on the south. I cannot extend more without making my lines too weak. We are in close contact, and skirmishing all the time. I have just got up four $4\frac{1}{2}$-inch rifled guns, with ammunition, and propose to expend about four thousand rifled shot in the heart of Atlanta. We have already commenced it with our lighter ordnance. Since July 28 General Hood has not attempted to meet us outside his parapets.

In order to possess and destroy effectually his communications, I may have to leave a corps at the railroad bridge well intrenched, and cut loose with the balance and make a desolating circle around Atlanta. I do not propose to assault the enemy's works, which are too strong, or to proceed by regular approaches. I have lost a good many regiments, and will lose more by the expiration of service, and this is the only reason why I want re-enforcements. I have killed, crippled, and captured more of the enemy than we have lost by his acts.

W. T. SHERMAN,
Major General Commanding.

HEADQUARTERS MILITARY DIVISION OF THE MISSISSIPPI,
In the field, near Atlanta, Ga., August 10, 1864.

General THOMAS:

I have your last despatch. I hear the guns and shells also. The enemy's battery of 32-pounders rifled are firing on us here from the White Hall fort to draw off or divert our fire. Keep up a steady, persistent fire on Atlanta with the $4\frac{1}{2}$-inch guns and 20-pounder Parrott's, and order them to pay no attention to the side firing by which the enemy may attempt to divert their attention. I think those guns will make Atlanta of less value to them as a large machine shop and depot of supplies. The inhabitants have, of course, got out.

W. T. SHERMAN,
Major General Commanding.

HEADQUARTERS MILITARY DIVISION OF THE MISSISSIPPI,
In the field, near Atlanta, Ga., August 10, 1864.

General THOMAS:

I hear General Brannan's guns at General Geary's battery, and hear the shells burst in Atlanta. Send word to the battery to work all night and not limit themselves to five (5) minute guns, but to fire slowly and steadily each gun as it is ready. Also order the guns at General Williams's front to be got ready and put to work with similar orders to-night. General Howard will get his 20-pounders near the same point, which he pronounces much better than that at General Geary's, which he visited with me to-day. General Williams's right and General Howard's left are on Proctor's creek, from which you look up the valley to what seems to be the heart of Atlanta; the ridge on which are the railroad and White Hall being plainly visibe, as also that by which the Marietta road enters the town, the intervening angle being cleared ground, giving a fine field of fire. I think the $4\frac{1}{2}$-inch guns on General Williams's right can demolish the big engine-house.

W. T. SHERMAN,
Major General Commanding.

HEADQUARTERS MILITARY DIVISION OF THE MISSISSIPPI,
In the field, near Atlanta, Ga., August 10, 1864.

General SCHOFIELD:

Your report is received. Do you think General Hascall can reach West Point railroad from his position without assaulting parapets?

Do you think a further prolongation would enable us to reach the Macon road without cutting loose from our base?

How are the roads south of Utoy?

Do you observe any change in the character of the country?

We are now cannonading with 4½-inch rifle bolts, and have four thousand (4, 000) of them on hand.

W. T. SHERMAN,
Major General Commanding.

HEADQUARTERS MILITARY DIVISION OF THE MISSISSIPPI,
In the field, near Atlanta, Ga., August 10, 1864.

General HOWARD:

I thank you for the suggestion. I am studying all the combinations possible, and beg you to think also and communicate to me; but be careful to keep your own confidence. I spoke of the same thing to-day to General Thomas, and he goes to look at the railroad bridge to see to a proper cover there for the wagons and a corps. I want to expend four thousand (4,000) heavy rifle shots on the town before doing anything new, and then will be prepared to act quick. General Schofield has been reconnoitring the right all day, and after he has answered a few more of my questions, I will give you the substance of his report.

W. T. SHERMAN,
Major General Commanding.

HEADQUARTERS MILITARY DIVISION OF THE MISSISSIPPI,
In the field, near Atlanta, Ga., August 10, 1864.

Generals THOMAS and HOWARD:

General Schofield has examined closely his whole line, which lies south, a little east, parallel with the enemy, one brigade being on the Campbelltown road, south of Utoy. He is not absolutely certain that his right is near the West Point railroad, and yet urges that another corps can reach the Macon road, and wants to make Proctor's creek our left flank, draw our supplies from Turner's ferry, and keep on extending. My own experience is, the enemy can build parapets faster than we march, and it would be the same thing by extending right or left. In a single night we would find ourselves confronted with parapets which we would fear to attack in the morning. He describes the country south of Utoy as more open and better cultivated. I want the 4½-inch and 20-pounder guns to hammer away, and I will think of the next move.

W. T. SHERMAN,
Major General Commanding.

HEADQUARTERS MILITARY DIVISION OF THE MISSISSIPPI,
In the field, near Atlanta, Ga., August 11, 1864.

General SCHOFIELD:

I have read and considered your despatch. It is a physical impossibility for the enemy to ascertain the force which moves against the railroad, and to act against it with any more than one-third of his reserves. The other two-thirds will be from four (4) to eight (8) miles off. Colonel Garrard's cavalry passed along the flank to-day unopposed, and I do not think the West Point road more than two (2) miles from General Hascall's present flank. You will, therefore, make the expedition with one division, the other either placed intermediate or ready to act; of course without abandoning our present base, or dividing our force into two (2) equal parts. I have no other corps to give you. You may consider it a reconnoissance in force not to go over three (3) miles from General Cox's present right. I know a full proportion of the enemy is on our left and centre, and if any change occurs in the night I will be sure to advise you. Our heavy ordnance, playing for the past thirty (30) hours from the Buck Head road into Atlanta, has kept to the parapets a full proportion of the enemy all the way round to your old position and beyond, and if I am to give weight to the testimony from official sources, the enemy at this moment exhibits most force on his present right. I have no idea that he can throw on you even a third of his reserve force, because he will look upon the movement as a decoy to weaken his line somewhat that we may break in. Besides, we know his line as well as ours is so stretched out that his reserves are not over one thousand (1,000) men per mile, for his infantry three (3) miles east of the Howard House, round to the main road below East Point, is full fifteen miles long, requiring at his parapets forty thousand (40,000) men, leaving him no reserve on that flank that can disturb two divisions. We must act. We cannot sit down and do nothing, because it involves risk. Being on the offensive, we must risk, and that is the flank on which we calculate to make the risk—indeed have been manœuvering to that end ever since the army of the Tennessee shifted from left to right.

W. T. SHERMAN,
Major General Commanding.

[Cipher.]

HOLLY SPRINGS, MISSISSIPPI,
August 11, 1864.

Major General SHERMAN:

Yesterday General Hatch attacked a force from Forrest's command, two thousand (2,000) strong, under General Chalmers, at Oxford, and drove him pell-mell towards Grenada, capturing three cannons. A large portion of A. J. Smith's forces are south of the Tallahatchee at Abbeville, but, owing to the very heavy rains for the last few days washing the railroad badly, there has been some delay in getting supplies forward. I hope that two days more may place everything on the south side of the Tallahatchee. There is reason to believe that they mean to fight us on this line between here and Grenada. As soon as they can be brought to bay and whipped effectually, General Smith will move to Decatur. In addition to his own force proper, ten thousand (10,000) strong, he has three thousand colored troops from Memphis, three Minnesota regiments sent me from St. Louis, and four thousand (4,000) cavalry. When he takes up his line of march for Decatur, shall he not send back to Memphis all but his own forces, as it will be perfectly safe to do so? My forces now at Memphis are all "hundred-days" men, whose time will expire on the thirtieth.

General Canby orders me at all times to keep a force on hand to assist General Steele, should he heed help. When your orders and General Canby's conflict, whom am I to obey? I have been embarrassed by conflicting orders heretofore. To have obeyed General Canby would have defeated General Smith's last expedition. General Forrest is not dead, but was in Pontotoc four (4) days ago.

C. C. WASHBURNE, Major General.

GENERAL STANLEY'S HEADQUARTERS,
August 11, 1864.

Major General SHERMAN:

General Garrard just reports as follows:

Please tell General Sherman that men from Stoneman's command are daily coming in; that they came along the railroad, and that on Sunday nothing had been done towards repairing the road. A large part of their cavalry is now in the neighborhood of Covington, and it is generally believed that they will soon make a grand raid to Tennessee or Kentucky. An officer who has just got in staid in that neighborhood three days, as he could not get out of way of their cavalry. He says he has never seen so much cavalry in one body. Persons from near Atlanta also report the rebel cavalry moving over towards Covington.

D. S. STANLEY, Major General.

[Cipher.]

HEADQUARTERS MILITARY DIVISION OF THE MISSISSIPPI,
In the field, near Atlanta, Ga., August 13, 1864—8 p. m.

General HALLECK, Washington, D. C.:

We have now pressed the enemy's lines from the east around to East Point on the south. The nature of ground, with its artificial defences, makes it too, difficult to assault, and to reach the Macon road by a further extension will be extra hazardous. I have ordered army commanders to prepare for the following plan: Leave one corps strongly intrenched at the Chattahoochee bridge in charge of our surplus wagons and artillery; with sixty thousand (60,000) men, reduced to fighting trim, to make circuit of devastation around the town, with a radius of fifteen or twenty miles.

To do this, I go on the faith that the militia in Atlanta are only good for the defence of its parapets, and will not come out.

I would like the utmost activity to be kept up in Mobile bay, and, if possible, about the mouth of Appalachicola; also to be assured that no material re-enforcements have come here from Virginia.

If I should ever be cut off from my base, look out for me about St. Mark's, Florida, or Savannah, Georgia.

W. T. SHERMAN,
Major General.

[Cipher.]

HEADQUARTERS MILITARY DIVISION OF THE MISSISSIPPI,
In the field, near Atlanta, Ga., August 13, 1864.

General Halleck, Washington, D. C.:

In making the circuit of Atlanta, as proposed in my despatch of to-day, I necessarily run some risk. If there be any possibility of Admiral Farragut and the land forces of Gordon Granger taking Mobile (which rebel prisoners now report, but the report is not confirmed by Macon papers of the 11th which I have seen,) and further of pushing up to Montgomery, my best plan would be to wait awhile, as now, and at the proper time move down to West Point, and operate into the heart of Georgia from there.

Before cutting loose as proposed, I would like to know the chances of our getting the use of the Alabama river this campaign. I could easily break up the railroads back to Chattanooga, and shift my whole army down to West Point and Columbus, a country rich in corn, and make my fall campaign from there.

I know Fort Morgan must succumb in time.

W. T. SHERMAN,
Major General.

HEADQUARTERS ARMY OF THE OHIO,
August 14, 1864.

Major General SHERMAN:

The officer I sent to the right reports three strong batteries along the edge of the woods near East Point, all looking down the valley towards Hascall's position. The one most to our right is where you saw the enemy working day before yesterday. The others are visible from a point on the Campbellton road, a few hundred yards west of where you were. The batteries are connected by infantry parapet, which, however, is not visible south or west of the left battery. Probably the line there bends southeast through the woods. A large force is working on each battery, but very few men are seen elsewhere. There has been no indication of movement of troops there to-day.

J. M. SCOHIELD,
Major General.

HEADQUARTERS MILITARY DIVISION OF THE MISSISSIPPI,
In the field, near Atlanta, Ga., August 14, 1864.

General SCHOFIELD:

There is no doubt Wheeler is up about Dalton with a large cavalry force. I want our cavalry now to feel the enemy's flanks strong, and will order General Kilpatrick to cross at Sandtown and make a bold push for Fairburn, and General Garrard, in like manner, to feel well around the enemy's right flank. Let your cavalry go down in the morning to Sandtown and report for the expedition to General Kilpatrick.

W. T. SHERMAN,
Major General Commanding.

RESACA, *August* 15, 1864—9.45 p. m.

Major General SHERMAN:

I can now give you the particulars of the Dalton affair. The town was seized about 6 p. m. yesterday. Colonel Leibold occupied the fort and declined to surrender. Early this morning General Steedman arrived there with one New York, and one Ohio, and six companies of negro regiments, and immediately attacked the enemy, and after four hours' fighting, drove them toward Spring Place. The enemy's loss heavy. We are collecting the dead and wounded. Colonel Leibold expects another attack. The enemy supposed to be six thousand (6,000) strong, with two batteries. I had two companies at the Water Tank, $1\frac{3}{4}$ mile south of Dalton. They were attacked at daylight this morning, and after four hours' fighting, surrendered. The railroad is destroyed from the Tank north to Dalton. The enemy still in the neighborhood of Tilton.

General Smith, with two thousand (2,000) men, is due here at 11 o'clock. The cavalry at Calhoun, I think, should be ordered to this place to-night.

G. B. RAUM,
Colonel Commanding Brigade.

HEADQUARTERS MILITARY DIVISION OF THE MISSISSIPPI,
In the field, near Atlanta, Ga., August 15, 1864.

Generals THOMAS, HOWARD, and SCHOFIELD:

Colonel Raum, at Resaca, reports the enemy's cavalry on the railroad near Tilton, tearing up track. Give orders that will insure great economy in provisions and forage, until we can estimate the time required to repair damages. I have nothing from beyond Resaca. General John E. Smith, at Cartersville, will collect all the infantry that can be spared from the defence of material points about Alatoona, and go up the road.

W. T. SHERMAN,
Major General Commanding.

CARTERSVILLE, *August* 15, 1864.

Major General SHERMAN:

I am just starting up the road with about two thousand (2,000) men. Despatch received from Resaca says the rebel force is moving northeast from Dalton, burned a bridge below Dalton, and tore up the track. My cavalry not heard from.

JNO. E. SMITH, *Brigadier General.*

HEADQUARTERS MILITARY DIVISION OF THE MISSISSIPPI,
In the field, near Atlanta, Ga., August 15, 1864.

Generals THOMAS, SCHOFIELD, and HOWARD:

General John E. Smith has gone up the road with two thousand (2,000) men in cars. Wheeler failed to take Dalton, and has gone northeast, where he cannot do us much harm. I will order that he be kept in that direction. He may disturb some of General Schofield's garrisons; but if he could not take Tilton or Dalton, he will not venture much, and all above will be on their guard, and prepared. As soon as this news is confirmed and ratified, I will put in execution our plans. So get ready. I want to hear of Generals Kilpatrick's and Garrard's explorations before making orders.

W. T. SHERMAN,
Major General Commanding.

HEADQUARTERS MILITARY DIVISION OF THE MISSISSIPPI,
In the field, near Atlanta, Ga., August 15, 1864.

General SCHOFIELD:

There will be plenty of time to dispose of wagons after my orders are issued. I want to hear of Generals Kilpatrick and Garrard before making my orders, but I am more and more satisfied the movement we contemplate is the true one to be made. I think Generals Steedman and John E. Smith will drive Wheeler far away, and repair our road in two days. Give me the earliest news of the cavalry on your flank.

W. T. SHERMAN,
Major General Commanding.

HEADQUARTERS ARMY OF THE OHIO,
August 16, 1864—1.45 p. m.

Major General SHERMAN:

I have just heard from Kilpatrick through Colonel Garrard. His despatch is dated 12 m. Kilpatrick had moved up the Campbellton road toward the right of our infantry, to a cross-road leading to Mount Gilead church, where the rebel cavalry is encamped, with the intention of moving out and attacking them. My troops are ready to move at once, if the enemy send infantry against our cavalry.

J. M. SCHOFIELD, *Major General.*

HEADQUARTERS DEPARTMENT OF THE CUMBERLAND,
August 16, 1864.

Major General SHERMAN:

General Kilpatrick reports that he forced the enemy back into his camp near the railroad, five miles above Fairburn station; destroyed the station and public buildings, telegraph, and railroad, for about three miles. Jackson's division has thus far refused to give him battle. He anticipates an attempt will be made to prevent his return this morning, and feels·confident he can destroy Jackson, provided cavalry alone meets him.

GEO. H. THOMAS, *Major General.*

HEADQUARTERS MILITARY DIVISION OF THE MISSISSIPPI,
In the field, near Atlanta, Ga., August 16, 1864.

General THOMAS:

The news from General Kilpatrick is first-rate; he has acted so as to show the enemy that he will fight. I do believe he, with his own and General Garrard's cavalry, could ride right around Atlanta and smash the Macon road all to pieces. But I don't want to risk our cavalry; I don't fear the enemy's trying to cut off his return. General Schofield's position is such that infantry will not leave their lines to go down to Camp creek.

W. T. SHERMAN,
Major General Commanding.

HEADQUARTERS MILITARY DIVISION OF THE MISSISSIPPI,
In the field, near Atlanta, Ga., August 16, 1864.

GENERAL: It occurs to me that preliminary to a future report of the history of the campaign, I should record certain facts of great personal interest to officers of this command.

General McPherson was killed by the musketry fire at the beginning of the battle of July 22. He had in person selected the ground for his troops, constituting the left wing of the army, I being in person with the centre, General Schofield. The moment the information reached me, I sent one of my staff to announce the fact to General John A. Logan, the senior officer present with the army of the Tennessee, with general instructions to maintain the ground chosen by General McPherson, if possible, but if pressed too hard to refuse his left flank, but at all events to hold the railroad and main Decatur road; that I did not propose to move or gain ground by that flank, but rather by the right, and that I wanted the army of the Tennessee to fight it out unaided. General Logan admirably conceived my orders and executed them, and if he gave ground on the left of the 17th corps it was properly done by my orders; but he held a certain hill by the right division of the 17th corps, the only ground on that line, the possession of which by an enemy would have damaged us, by giving a reverse fire on the remainder of the troops. General Logan fought that battle out as required, unaided, save by a small brigade sent by my orders from General Schofield to the Decatur road, well to the rear, where it was reported the enemy's cavalry had got into the town of Decatur, and was operating directly on the rear of Logan; but that brigade was not disturbed, and was replaced that night by a part of the 15th corps, next to General Schofield, and General Schofield's brigade brought back so as to be kept together on its own line.

General Logan managed the army of the Tennessee well during his command, and it may be that an unfair inference might be drawn to his prejudice because he did not succeed to the permanent command. I am forced to choose a commander, not only for the army in the field, but of the department of the Tennessee, covering a vast extent of country with troops much dispersed. It was a delicate and difficult task, and I gave preference to Major General O. O. Howard, then in command of the 4th army corps in the department of the Cumberland. Instead of giving my reasons, I prefer that the wisdom of the choice be left to the test of time. The President kindly ratified my choice, and I am willing to assume the responsibility. I meant no disrespect to any officer, and hereby declare that General Logan submitted with the grace and dignity of a soldier, gentleman, and patriot, resumed the command of his corps proper, (15th,) and enjoys the love and respect of his army and of his commanders. It so happened that on the 28th of July I had again thrown the same army to the extreme right, the exposed flank, where the enemy repeated the same manœuvre, striking in mass; the extreme corps deployed in line, and refused as a flank the 15th, Major General Logan; and he commanded in person, General Howard and myself being near, and that corps, as heretofore reported, repulsed the rebel army completely, and next day advanced and occupied the ground fought over and the road the enemy sought to cover. General Howard, who had that very day assumed his new command, unequivocably gave General Logan all the credit possible: and I also beg to add my unqualified admiration of the bravery, skill, and, more yet, good sense that influenced him to bear a natural disappointment and do his whole duty like a man. If I could bestow on him substantial reward it would afford me unalloyed satisfaction; but I do believe, in the consciousness of acts done from noble impulses and gracefully admitted by his superiors in authority, he will be contented. He already holds the highest commission known in the army, and it is hard to say how we can better manifest our applause.

At the time of General Howard's selection, Major General Hooker commanded the 20th army corps in the army of the Cumberland, made up for his special accommodation out of the old 11th and 12th corps, whereby Major General Slocum was deprived of his corps command. Both the law and practice are and have been to fill the higher army commands by selection. Rank or dates of commission have not controlled, nor am I aware that any reflection can be inferred unless the junior be placed immediately over the senior; but in this case General Hooker's command was in no manner disturbed. General Howard was not put over him, but in charge of a distinct and separate army. No indignity was offered or intended, and I must say that General Hooker was not justified in retiring. At all events, had he spoken or written to me I would have made every explanation and concession he could have expected, but could not have changed my course, because then, as now, I believe it right and for the good of our country and cause.

As a matter of justice, General Slocum, having been displaced by the consolidation, was deemed by General Thomas as entitled to the vacancy created by General Hooker's voluntary withdrawal, and has received it.

With great respect,

W. T. SHERMAN,
Major General Commanding.

Major General HALLECK,
Chief of Staff, Washington, D. C.

HEADQUARTERS MILITARY DIVISION OF THE MISSISSIPPI,
In the field, near Atlanta, Ga., August 16, 1864.

Generals THOMAS, HOWARD, and SCHOFIELD:

We will commence the movement against the railroad about Jonesboro' Thursday night, unless something occurs in the mean-time to mar the plan. I will make my orders, and the preliminary preparations may be begun.

If Wheeler interrupts our supplies we can surely cut off those of Hood, and see who can stand it best.

W. T. SHERMAN, *Major General.*

HEADQUARTERS MILITARY DIVISION OF THE MISSISSIPPI,
In the field, near Allatoona, August 16, 1864.

General THOMAS :

General Schofield reports that General Kilpatrick did not find the enemy's cavalry at his old camp at Mount Gilead church, but I don't know where that church is. It is manifest that all the efficient cavalry of the enemy is to our rear. They will tear up the road beyond Cartersville; but I think Wheeler has been driven off towards East Tennessee, and trust that General John E. Smith will return to Cartersville; he has cars enough. There are three (3) regiments and eight (8) guns at Allatoona and Etowah bridge, and I have ordered General McArthur to send any re-enforcements he can spare, and call on us to replace them at Marietta. I do think our cavalry should now break the Macon road good. If we can save our rations at Marietta and Allatoona, and break the Macon road for many miles, we can wait as long as Hood.

What say you to letting General Kilpatrick have two of General Garrard's brigades, and then to strike across to the Macon road and tear it up good. He has scouted the country now, and knows it, and can act with confidence and due caution. General Schofield is well on that flank and makes a good cover. I like this plan better than to send General Garrard up to Cartersville, for the enemy will simply run off; but General Kilpatrick with two good brigades can reach across to the Macon road about Rough and Ready and tear up six or eight miles by to-morrow night or next day.

W. T. SHERMAN,
Major General Commanding.

HEADQUARTERS MILITARY DIVISION OF THE MISSISSIPPI,
In the field, near Atlanta, Ga., August 17, 1864.

General SCHOFIELD :

I think I will defer the grand movement for a day or so, and precede it by a cavalry movement on the Macon road, between Rough and Ready and Jonesboro' I propose to give General Kilpatrick his whole division and two of General Gararrd's brigades, to move quietly down to Camp Creek, and then, by a rapid movement, strike and break thoroughly the Macon road ; your infantry to co-operate and divert attention. We know that Wheeler is well to the north with a large part of the cavalry, and now is the time. I expect General Kilpatrick up. Any preparations for the infantry move will be all right, and we need only postpone the time of execution.

W. T. SHERMAN,
Major General Commanding.

HEADQUARTERS MILITARY DIVISION OF THE MISSISSIPPI,
In the field, near Atlanta, Ga., August 17, 1864.

Major General THOMAS :

I have a message from General Kilpatrick, enclosing a copy of his report to General Elliot. He thinks it not only possible, but comparatively easy, to break the railroad to Macon effectually. I do not want to move this vast army and its paraphernalia around Atlanta unless forced to do so, and it does seem the enemy has offered us the very opportunity we seek.

We know positively that Wheeler is above Dalton, and that he must have taken the very flower of his cavalry. He has and may do us harm, but that we cannot help. I do not think he can carry any point of our road that he can maintain, and his own necessities will force him back soon, with jaded and worn-out horses. Now, ours can be quietly moved to Sandtown at a walk, and, according to General Kilpatrick, reach Red Oak, or any point below the enemy's infantry, and by a single dash can beat the remaining cavalry of the enemy, and break up many miles of that railroad. General Garrard, with one brigade, can amuse those on the east, and General Kilpatrick, with his own and the two brigades of General Garrard, under Colonel Long, could make in a single move a break that would disturb Hood seriously. The risk will be comparatively small, as General Schofield can act in support with his whole command. I am perfectly alive to the fact that the loss of our cavalry would be most serious, but I do think such an opportunity, if neglected, will never again appear. In this combination I would merely suspend the final execution of the movement of the whole army till the result of this move is reached. I think we could give General Kilpatrick such orders that he would not be rash, and General Schofield could move to his right a couple of miles, and make it certain that Hood would not attempt to use infantry to interpose to the return of our cavalry. Don't make any orders till you and I have perfectly agreed on this plan. In the mean time anything done towards the movement of the whole army will not be lost, as it simply amounts to sending to the bridge all the loose ends.

I have sent for General Kilpatrick to come up.

W. T. SHERMAN,
Major General Commanding.

HEADQUARTERS DEPARTMENT OF THE CUMBERLAND,
August 17, 1864.

Major General SHERMAN:

Information from all sources seem to confirm the report that Wheeler has taken off the greater part of his cavalry. I therefore think this will be as good a time as could be taken to make another raid on the Macon railroad; but if you send Kilpatrick, I would insist on his taking the most practicable route, and avoid the enemy's infantry as much as possible.

GEO. H. THOMAS,
Major General.

HEADQUARTERS ARMY OF THE OHIO,
August 17, 1864.

Major General SHERMAN:

The following is just received. The messenger will wait for your orders.

J. M. SCHOFIELD,
Major General.

" HEADQUARTERS CAVALRY DIVISION, D. C.,
"August 17, 1864.

" To Major General SCHOFIELD:

" I send you the report of my operations yesterday by one of my aides to make certain that you get it. I am satisfied that, with two of General Garrard's brigades and my own division, I can break the Macon road effectually at any point the major general commanding may be pleased to indicate. Such an opportunity to strike the enemy a terrible blow has never been offered. If it is desirable to make the attempt, I should wish to see you, and will visit your headquarters for that purpose.

" Very respectfully, your obedient servant,

"J. KILPATRICK,
"Brigadier General Volunteers."

HEADQUARTERS MILITARY DIVISION OF THE MISSISSIPPI,
In the field, near Atlanta, Ga., August 17, 1864.

General THOMAS:

General Kilpatrick is here, and gives me a description of his position at Sandtown, that convinces me he can, in connexion with General Schofield, so effectually destroy the Macon railroad that it cannot be used in two weeks, and that, too, without risking his cavalry.

You will, therefore, order General Garrard to send to Sandtown, *via* Paice's ferry and the west bank, the two brigades of cavalry heretofore notified, with a battery of artillery to move to night and report on arrival to General Kilpatrick, at Sandtown. The horses should be well fed, and could take some wagons of shelled corn as far as Sandtown, when the wagons may return. Men provided with full ammunition, five (5) days' bread, sugar, coffee, and plenty of salt.

General Kilpatrick will keep his command concealed all day to-morrow, and move to-morrow night, cross the West Point road above Fairburn, reach the Macon railroad near Jonesboro', face towards East Point, and break road to the south.

The despatch I sent you an hour ago is conclusive that Wheeler is away, and but little rebel cavalry is left here.

General Kilpatrick will want a diversion day after to-morrow, and I will see that General Schofield makes one; and I wish you to have General Garrard's remaining brigade and General Stanley's division give full occupation to that flank. I will risk the other.

Instruct General Garrard to be sure to send the pioneers along with the cavalry, provided with tools to break up railroad.

General Kilpatrick represents forage abundant down there.

General Kilpatrick ranks General Garrard, and the latter may go along if you prefer.

W. T. SHERMAN,
Major General Commanding.

HEADQUARTERS MILITARY DIVISION OF THE MISSISSIPPI,
In the field, near Atlanta, Ga., August 17, 1864.

Generals THOMAS, SCHOFIELD, and HOWARD:

I now have positive and official information that General Wheeler has gone up into East Tennessee, beyond Spring Place. We will repair all damages to railroad and telegraph to-night. I will not move our infantry now, but break the Macon road all to pieces with our cavalry to-morrow night. Therefore, be active and demonstrate against Atlanta to occupy the entire front, and make them believe we will attack them in their trenches during to-morrow and next day.

W. T. SHERMAN,
Major General Commanding.

HEADQUARTERS MILITARY DIVISION OF THE MISSISSIPPI,
In the field, near Atlanta, Ga., August 17, 1864.

GENERAL: I beg you will convey the following orders to govern General Kilpatrick in his movement on the Macon road. It is not a raid, but a deliberate attack for the purpose of so disabling that road that the enemy will be unable to supply his army in Atlanta. He will have his own division of cavalry and two good brigades from General Garrard's division. With these he will move

to-morrow night, aiming to cross the West Point road between Red Oak and
Fairburn. If he has time he should remove a small section of the road without
using fire, simply to lessen the chances of an infantry force being sent to intercept his return. He should then move in force to the nearest point of the Macon
road about Jonesboro', and should destroy as much of that road as he possibly
can, working steadily until forced to take to his arms and horses for battle. He
should avoid battle with infantry or artillery, but may safely fight any cavalry
he encounters, because we know that the enemy has sent Wheeler with full six
thousand (6,000) cavalry up into East Tennessee. I leave the extent of the
break to General Kilpatrick, but will only say that he cannot destroy too much.
Having fulfilled his task, he will return and resume his post on the right flank
of the army, and send General Garrard's brigades back to their division on the
left. General Schofield will be instructed to move to his right as far as prudent
the day after to-morrow, and all the army should so engage the attention of the
enemy that he cannot detach infantry as against General Kilpatrick.

Instruct the general to advise us at the earliest possible moment of his success.

I am, with respect, yours truly,

W. T. SHERMAN,
Major General Commanding.

Major General THOMAS,
    Commanding Army of the Cumberland.

HEADQUARTERS MILITARY DIVISION OF THE MISSISSIPPI,
In the field, near Atlanta, Ga., August 17, 1864.

General HALLECK, *Washington:*

Your despatch of yesterday is received. We must have the Alabama river,
and if I remember the bay, the best river channel is on the Tensas side ; but,
of course, I must trust to Admiral Farragut and General Canby. I have a tight
grip on Atlanta, and was on the point of swinging round to the southeast when
Wheeler went to my rear with six thousand (6,000) cavalry ; he has passed into
East Tennessee, having damaged us but little. I will avail myself of his absence to
reciprocate the compliment, and to-morrow night the Macon road must be broken
good. General Kilpatrick will undertake it. Wheeler cannot disturb Knoxville
or Loudon. He may hurt some of the minor points, but, on the whole, East
Tennessee is a good place for him to break down his horses, and steal new ones.
All well.

W. T. SHERMAN,
Major General Commanding.

HEADQUARTERS MILITARY DIVISION OF THE MISSISSIPPI,
In the field, near Atlanta, August 17, 1864.

General CANBY, *New Orleans:*

Despatch of 6th received. Convey to Admiral Farragut my admiration of
the bold and successful passage of Mobile fort. I am familiar with Fort Morgan,
and would advise that a single gun-boat lay above Pilot Cove and prevent supplies going to Fort Morgan, and time will work its fall. To reduce Mobile I
would pass a force up the Tensas and across to old Fort Stoddart, and operate
in the direction of Citronelle. The Mobile and Ohio road broken and the river
occupied, Mobile would be untenable to the rebels. If possible the Alabama

river should be possessed by us in connexion with my movements. I could easily open communication with Montgomery, but I doubt if you will have troops enough till the September draft. I am pressing Atlanta hard, but don't want Kirby Smith here. I can beat Hood in the open field, but not intrenched. I have repeatedly disabled his roads, but he manages to patch them up.

W. T. SHERMAN,
Major General Commanding.

HEADQUARTERS MILITARY DIVISION OF THE MISSISSIPPI,
In the field, near Atlanta, Ga., August 18, 1864—7 a. m.

Major General SCHOFIELD:

I wanted to come down to the extreme right to-day, and may still, but I must watch matters to our rear. Hood no doubt supposes he has put Wheeler on our line, and is demonstrating accordingly; he has small parties to cut our wires nightly. We cannot now get Marietta. Nevertheless, unless something very extraordinary takes place to-day, I want General Kilpatrick to start and break up that Macon road all to pieces. Keep your own cavalry as videttes on your right flank, and to-morrow they might venture as close East Point as possible, and break up some more of that railroad, whilst General Kilpatrick draws their cavalry towards Jonesboro', as they will be sure to watch if they don't fight him. Use your troops to-day as though investing and feeling their left flank, but to-morrow venture out a little. Keep me well advised of all facts that will enable me to divine Hood's scheme.

W. T. SHERMAN,
Major General Commanding.

HEADQUARTERS MILITARY DIVISION OF THE MISSISSIPPI,
In the field, near Atlanta, Ga., August, 18, 1864—11.30 a. m.

General SCHOFIELD:

Our telegraph now works to Chattanooga. The conclusion my mind has arrived at is that Hood sent Wheeler's cavalry to occupy our road at Dalton; that he had re-enforced East Point with a division of his old corps, which last night was brought back, on the supposition that Wheeler had succeeded and we would begin to detach to our rear.

Now, of all times, this is the time for our cavalry to do its work well, and if you hear nothing of me before three o'clock, send a messenger to General Kilpatrick, with a note stating that all things are most favorable for his work; to break as much of the Macon road as he possibly can, and as he swings back, to rest on the West Point road at some point below Fairburn and make another big tear up. If he feels master of the situation on the road he cannot tear up too much track or twist too much iron. It may save this army making a long and hazardous flank march.

Tell him what you will do to-morrow to occupy the enemy's infantry on their flank, and assure him I will cause the same along our whole line, especially on our extreme left. I will see that General Garrard risks all he can to amuse what cavalry the enemy has about Decatur and Stone mountain.

W. T. SHERMAN,
Major General Commanding.

[Cipher.]

HEADQUARTERS MILITARY DIVISION OF THE MISSISSIPPI,
In the field, near Atlanta, Ga., August 18, 1864—6 p. m.

General HALLECK, *Washington:*

We have been hammering away at Atlanta; and I was going to put a corps intrenched at the railroad 'bridge, and with the balance swing round by the south and east, but Hood has sent off his cavalry, which touched our road at two or three points, which are already repaired, and that cavalry has gone up into East Tennessee, leaving me now superior in cavalry; and I hope the opportunity thus given me will save me the risk and excessive labor of making a wide circuit in this hot weather.   To-night General Kilpatrick will start for the Macon road with five (5) brigades of cavalry, which can whip all the enemy's cavalry present, and to-morrow I will demonstrate along my whole line to give General Kilpatrick time to make a good break in that road so vital to Hood.   We all feel confident that we can succeed, and for that reason I do not regret that Wheeler has gone up into East Tennessee.   I think we have force enough at Knoxville, the gap, and Kingston to hold vital points till necessity will force Wheeler to come back; but I will leave him to be attended to by those in my rear.

W. T. SHERMAN,
Major General Commanding.

HEADQUARTERS ARMY OF THE OHIO,
August 18, 1864—6.45 p. m.

Major General SHERMAN:

I have extended my line more than a mile, substantially parallel to that of the enemy, and have a pretty good flank.   The enemy's works appear to be occupied only in moderate force.   They have shown no movement during the day. I propose to-night to draw out two brigades of each division of the 14th corps, leaving one brigade of each division, including Hascall's, to hold the present lines. This will give me a movable force of about eighteen thousand (18,000) men with which to make my movement against the enemy's left.   This will, of course, make our lines very weak, but I reckon strong enough against any probable attack.

J. M. SCHOFIELD,
Major General.

HEADQUARTERS DEPARTMENT OF THE TENNESSEE,
August 18, 1864.

Major General SHERMAN:

I have been along my entire line this a. m.   Considerable artillery was developed by the demonstration, and a strong skirmish throughout.   Not many men can be seen in the main works in front of General Logan, but I do not think they have been removed.   The division previously reported consisted of seven regiments of infantry.   When last seen they were moving opposite the left of the 15th corps, going towards our left.   There were a great many stragglers.

O. O. HOWARD,
Major General.

12*

CITY POINT, VIRGINIA, *August* 18, 1864.

Major General SHERMAN:

Richmond papers of the 17th give it as the opinion of military men that Atlanta can hold out one month yet. In the mean time, like us, they expect something to turn up. If you can hold tight as you are now, and prevent raids upon your rear, you will destroy most of that army. I never would advise going backward, even if your roads are cut so as to preclude the possibility of receiving supplies from the north, but would work to command the accumulation of ordnance stores and supplies while you can; if it comes to the worst, move south, as you suggest.

I have forced the enemy to move a large force north of the James, and am now moving one corps by our left around Petersburg. I expect no great results, but will probably cut the Weldon road again, and will also demonstrate to the enemy that he has now the minimum garrison possible to hold his present lines with, and that to hold his roads he must re-enforce.

U. S. GRANT,
Lieutenant General.

[Cipher.]

HEADQUARTERS MILITARY DIVISION OF THE MISSISSIPPI,
In the field, near Atlanta, Ga., August 19, 1864—10.45 a. m.

General GRANT, *City Point:*

I have your two despatches of 14th and 16th, also that of 18th. I will never take a step backwards, and have no fears of Hood. I can whip him outside of his trenches, and think in time I can compel him to come out. I think at this moment I have a fine cavalry force on the only road which can feed him, and, if necessary, will swing my whole army across it also.

W. T. SHERMAN,
Major General Commanding.

HEADQUARTERS DEPARTMENT OF THE TENNESSEE,
August 19, 1864.

Major General SHERMAN:

The skirmishing you hear is apparently between me and the 14th corps. Have not heard from my right yet.

O. O. HOWARD,
Major General.

HEADQUARTERS DEPARTMENT OF THE TENNESSEE,
August 19, 1864.

Major General SHERMAN:

General Dodge is wounded in the side of the head by a musket ball; not seriously.

O. O. HOWARD,
Major General.

HEADQUARTERS DEPARTMENT OF THE TENNESSEE,
August 19, 1864.

Major General SHERMAN :

The firing to-night occurred in front of the right of the 15th corps. The enemy attempted to capture our working parties. They failed. General Lightburn was wounded in De Grass's battery, in a similar manner to General Dodge. The officers and men on the right of the 15th corps have observed fires in the direction of Macon since 6 o'clock. One of my staff just returned reports he saw the fires still burning.

O. O. HOWARD, *Major General.*

[Cipher.]

HEADQUARTERS MILITARY DIVISION OF THE MISSISSIPPI,
In the field, near Atlanta, August 19, 1864—7 p. m.

General HALLECK, *Washington :*

I have Secretary Stanton's despatch announcing the promotion of Colonel Long, a hard-working and worthy cavalry officer. We have made heavy demonstrations all day, especially on our flanks, to hold the enemy while our cavalry is out after the Macon road. I hope this time the work will be better done than before. We control all other railroads.

General Dodge received a ball wound in his forehead, but it is pronounced not serious. All well.

W. T. SHERMAN,
Major General Commanding.

HEADQUARTERS DEPARTMENT OF THE CUMBERLAND,
August 20, 1864—7.30 p. m.

Major General SHERMAN :

I forwarded General Stanley's report of operations since 3 a. m., about 1 o'clock to-day. He has kept the enemy fully occupied ever since yesterday noon. So has Garrard's brigade. We have made three captures of rebel scouts, and from papers found on one of them I infer Hood is exceedingly anxious to know where our left flank is and its strength.

Geary's signal officer reports having observed the light of a large fire last night in the direction of Rough and Ready station just before the storm came on.

GEO. H. THOMAS,
Major General.

HEADQUARTERS ARMY OF THE OHIO,
August 21, 1864.

Major General SHERMAN :

Prisoners captured by General Cox last evening report that Kilpatrick struck the railroad at Jonesboro' the morning after he started. Very distant artillery firing was heard in the direction of Macon from our right last evening. I have heard nothing further indicative of Kilpatrick's movements. Cox is making a demonstration on the right to aid him on his return. Enemy is using artillery quite freely in front of 14th corps this morning.

J. M. SCHOFIELD,
Major General.

[Cipher.]

HEADQUARTERS MILITARY DIVISION OF THE MISSISSIPPI,
In the field, near Atlanta, Georgia, August 21, 1864—10 a. m.

General HALLECK, *Washington:*

General Howard and I have talked over the affairs of the department of the Tennessee, and admit the wisdom of General Canby exercising command of all the troops on the Mississippi. To preserve organizations already existing, without materially diminishing the military force on the Mississippi, we ask that certain fragments of regiments and brigades, not exceeding in the aggregate twenty-five hundred (2,500) men, be allowed to come to their organization here. Also, if possible, that a division of the 17th corps, originally designated as part of General McPherson's column, but detained up Red river, be also allowed to come by any route deemed advisable by General Washburne. To accomplish these results General Howard sends to-day a staff officer to Louisville to confer with you by telegraph, and then to go to Memphis and accomplish whatever you may conclude. Be assured that General Howard and I both cheerfully concede anything that will produce good results. I think it would be well not to change the limits of the departments, but to have all troops now belonging to the department of the Tennessee still make returns to General Howard, but be subject to the military orders of General Canby, to whom they could make reports of effective force that would satisfy his purposes. All well. Expect to hear of General Kilpatrick every hour. Nothing further of Wheeler.

W. T. SHERMAN,
Major General Commanding.

HEADQUARTERS MILITARY DIVISION OF THE MISSISSIPPI,
In the field, near Atlanta, August 21, 1864—8 p. m.

General STEEDMAN, *Chattanooga:*

I have your despatch of to-day, and if a gun-boat can get up to Kingston it would be well to send it. Wheeler cannot do us serious harm up there, and cavalry has not the industry to damage railroads seriously. General Schofield thinks Knoxville has provisions for three (3) months, and is very strongly fortified. So you need not bother Wheeler there further than to keep him watched by scouts and citizens, and let me know his future course. I don't want him to come back by way of the Oostonaula. Now is the time to get all your forces in good position to move rapidly against his flank if he comes back anywhere between Spring Place and Talking Rock. Dalton is the best point from which to watch him, and I think it would be well to make a bridge across the Connasauga, near the mouth of Cuoyehuttie, on the road from Dalton to Spring Place, and build a small, but strong, redoubt between the forks at the bridge, as a threat to that flank. I don't know the ground at Dalton or Spring Place, but by the maps. I know if you have a respectable force at Dalton and the Spring Place road, fortified as I describe, Wheeler will not dare to pass down this way. If he go into Kentucky by Cumberland gap or Somerset, there are forces enough to attend to him there. I feel confident General Grant will give Lee enough to do, so he cannot detach any considerable force towards Knoxville.

W. T. SHERMAN,
Major General Commanding.

HEADQUARTERS DEPARTMENT OF THE CUMBERLAND,
August 22, 1864—7.30 p. m.

Major General SHERMAN:

General Kilpatrick is about to start for your headquarters. He reports having torn up four miles connectedly of railroad between Rough and Ready and Jonesboro', and ten (10) miles at intervals, and destroyed two trains, including the one destroyed by Kline. He virtually captured Ross's brigade, but could not bring the men away. He was attacked by Jackson's cavalry and a division of infantry, but effected his escape before the enemy could surround him, and brought off his own artillery, and one piece of the four captured. Two pieces and nine caissons were destroyed by him. He brought in about seventy (70) prisoners and three battle flags and all his own wounded; has ninety-seven (97) killed and missing. Among the missing four officers. Brigadier General Long was wounded in two places. He speaks in high terms of the behavior of his whole command. Captain Bartlett is well and on the road with him to your headquarters.

GEO. H. THOMAS,
Major General.

CHATTANOOGA, *August* 22, 1864.

Major General SHERMAN:

Wheeler is now between the Hiawassee and Little Tennessee rivers, both too high to ford. I think I can force him back through the mountains toward North Carolina by concentrating force at Charleston, and moving on him from that place. I have force enough and can concentrate them in time. I await your orders; concentrating at Dalton as you directed.

Respectfully,

JAMES B. STEEDMAN,
Major General.

[Cipher.]

HEADQUARTERS MILITARY DIVISION OF THE MISSISSIPPI,
In the field, near Atlanta, Ga., August 22, 1864—10 p. m.

General HALLECK:

General Kilpatrick is back. He had pretty hard fighting with a division of infantry and three (3) brigades of cavalry. He broke the cavalry into disorder and captured a battery which he destroyed, except one (1) gun which he brought in, in addition to all his own. He also brought in three captured flags and seventy (70) prisoners. He had possession of a large part of Ross's brigade, but could not encumber himself with them. He destroyed three (3) miles of the road about Jonesboro', and broke pieces for about ten (10) miles more, enough to disable the road for ten days.

I expect I will have to swing across to that road in force to make the matter certain. General Kilpatrick destroyed two (2) locomotives and trains.

It has been very quiet with us here. Wheeler is about Athens, Tennessee, and General Steedman will move out against him from Chattanooga.

W. T. SHERMAN,
Major General Commanding.

HEADQUARTERS MILITARY DIVISION OF THE MISSISSIPPI,
In the field, near Atlanta, Ga., August 23, 1864—1.30 p. m.

General BURBRIDGE, *Louisville:*

I don't believe Wheeler and Morgan are going into Kentucky; but should they, you should be prepared for them. Of course I cannot turn back for a cavalry raid. If Colonel Laibold held Wheeler at bay with four hundred (400) men at Dalton in a redoubt, you surely can hold him in Kentucky with General Ammen and General Tillson at Cumberland gap and Knoxville.

Get your people well in hand, and in no event allow alarm to spread in Kentucky. The enemy cannot spare a large force now to invade Kentucky. It is a raid designed to make clamor, and nothing more.

W. T. SHERMAN,
Major General Commanding.

HEADQUARTERS ARMY OF THE OHIO,
August 23, 1864.

Major General SHERMAN:

I have on hand supplies for the grand movement, and only need long enough notice to send my baggage wagons to the rear. I will have the maps about Utoy, Red Oak, &c., completed this evening.

J. M. SCHOFIELD, *Major General.*

HEADQUARTERS DEPARTMENT OF THE CUMBERLAND,
August 23, 1864.

Major General SHERMAN:

The teams of my command have only five (5) days' forage on hand; otherwise my command will be ready to commence the movement to-morrow. Colonel McKay tells me that in three days the whole army could be supplied with ten (10) days' forage.

GEO. H. THOMAS, *Major General.*

HEADQUARTERS DEPARTMENT OF THE CUMBERLAND,
August 23, 1864.

Major General SHERMAN:

I would like to commence the movement without being hurried, and can do so by Thursday night. I think the cavalry ought to have a little rest and time to shoe up. I will be perfectly prepared by Thursday with provisions, and can arrange to get forage by Sandtown the day after, if forage comes down.

GEO. H. THOMAS, *Major General.*

[Cipher.]

HEADQUARTERS MILITARY DIVISION OF THE MISSISSIPPI,
In the field, near Atlanta, Ga., August 23, 1864—11.30 p. m.

General HALLECK, *Washington:*

All well. Give currency to the idea that I am to remain quiet till events transpire in other quarters, and let the idea be printed, so as to reach Richmond in three (3) days. You understand the effect.

W. T. SHERMAN,
Major General Commanding.

HEADQUARTERS MILITARY DIVISION OF THE MISSISSIPPI,
In the field, near Atlanta, Ga., August 24, 1864—8 a. m.

Generals THOMAS, SCHOFIELD and HOWARD:

I will ride down to the bridge to-day to see the lay of ground and the character of the redoubts there. Go on and make all the preparations possible, so that our movement when begun may proceed rapidly and safely. Our maps should be compiled, and as many roads laid down between Red Oak and Jonesboro' as we can be sure of existence.

W. T. SHERMAN,
Major General Commanding.

HEADQUARTERS MILITARY DIVISION OF THE MISSISSIPPI,
August 24, 1864.

Major General SHERMAN:

A fire seems to be raging in Atlanta, direction ten (10) degrees south of east from my tree. Can see heated air rising in dense columns; seems to be spreading. Town is filled with smoke.

I have directed my heavy guns to fire on the town.

O. O. HOWARD,
Major General.

[Cipher.]

HEADQUARTERS MILITARY DIVISION OF THE MISSISSIPPI,
In the field, near Atlanta, Ga., August 24, 1864—7.15 p. m.

General HALLECK, *Washington:*

Heavy fires in Atlanta all day, caused by our artillery. I will be all ready and will commence the movement round Atlanta by the south to-morrow night, and for some time you will hear little of me. I will keep open courier line with Chattahoochee bridge by way of Sandtown. 20th corps will hold the bridge, and I will move with the balance of the army provisioned for twenty (20) days.

W. T. SHERMAN,
Major General Commanding.

[Cipher.]

HEADQUARTERS MILITARY DIVISION OF THE MISSISSIPPI,
In the field, near Atlanta, Ga., August 24, 1864—8 p. m.

General R. S. GRANGER, *Decatur, Alabama:*

I am satisfied the enemy designs to make desperate attempts on our road. I have your despatch, and think it probable Roddy is over there; also Clanton. Do the best you can and keep General Rousseau advised. Cavalry usually do so little damage to a road that it can be repaired faster than they damage it. Guard well the vital points, such as bridges and tunnels, and when the enemy scatters, as he is sure to do, pitch into his detachments.

W. T. SHERMAN,
Major General Commanding.

[Cipher.]

HEADQUARTERS MILITARY DIVISION OF THE MISSISSIPPI,
In the field, near East Point, Ga., August 26, 1864—6.45 p. m.
General HALLECK, *Washington:*

I have moved the 20th corps to the Chattahoochee bridge, where it is intrenched, and with the balance of the army am moving for Jonesboro', on the Macon road. Last night we made the first move without trouble; to-night we make the second; and the third will place the army massed near Fairburn. If Hood attacks he must come out, which is all we ask. All well thus far.

W. T. SHERMAN,
Major General Commanding.

HEADQUARTERS MILITARY DIVISION OF THE MISSISSIPPI,
In the field, Red Oak, Georgia, August 28, 1864—6.45 p. m.

GENERAL: We will remain here to-morrow. I wish the railroad thoroughly destroyed as far forward as possible, and to the rear until you meet General Howard's troops. Let the destruction be so thorough that not a rail or tie can be used again. My own experience demonstrates the proper method to be to march a regiment to the road, stack arms, loosen two (2) rails opposite the right and two (2) opposite the left of the regiment, then to heave the whole track, rails and ties, over, breaking it all to pieces; then pile the ties in the nature of crib-work, and lay the rails over them; then by means of fence-rails make a bon-fire, and when the rails are red-hot let men give the rail a twist, which cannot be straightened without machinery. Also fill up some of the cuts with heavy logs and trunks of trees and branches, and cover up and fill with dirt. Please give minute instructions on this subject to-night, and have the work commenced as early in the morning as possible, taking proper precautions also to guard against attack on either of the working parties or the general position.

General Howard has received similar instructions, and General Schofield will be moved to your left front.

W. T. SHERMAN,
Major General Commanding.

Major General THOMAS, *Commanding.*

HEADQUARTERS MILITARY DIVISION OF THE MISSISSIPPI,
In the field, Red Oak, Ga., August 28, 1864—6.45 p. m.

GENERAL: Colonel Wilson is here. I wrote you by Captain Knox. Our movement has been slower on the left, on account of the proximity to the enemy and a necessity for greater caution. General Thomas is in position; his two corps crossing the railroad and facing Atlanta. General Schofield still remains about Mount Gilead church. We will remain on the road to-morrow and break it in the most thorough manner possible. General Thomas will work forward and break to you. I want you to do the best job of railroad destruction on record, using General Kilpatrick to cover you while at work, and to explore roads to the east, and make such reconnoissance towards Campbellton as will be useful to us in the future. Also fill up some cuts in the railroad with logs and trees, and cover with dirt, so we may rest perfectly satisfied as regards the use of this railroad during the remainder of this campaign.

It is more important that each bar of iron should be heated and twisted than that a great amount of imperfect work be done; for if the iron can be used again in this wooded country, ties can be easily supplied.

Yours, &c.,

W. T. SHERMAN,
Major General.

Major General HOWARD, *Commanding, &c.*

HEADQUARTERS MILITARY DIVISION OF THE MISSISSIPPI,
In the field, Red Oak, Ga., August 29, 1864—8 p. m.

Major General THOMAS, *Commanding Army Cumberland*:

I have seen General Howard. You will move to-morrow for Shoal Creek church and on to the road leading from Decatur to Fayetteville, half way from Morrow's mill and the Renfro place (Couch's.) Move the head of your column by Mrs. Long's place, taking care to leave room for General Schofield to pass the same point up towards Morrow's mill. Please report to me if Generals Davis or Stanley moved towards East Point far enough to secure the road by which I design General Schofield to move, viz: from D. Mim's, up along the railroad to the road represented as leading down to Mrs. Long's. General Howard starts at 7 a. m. I would like you to reach Shoal Creek church as early as 10 a. m. at farthest, to cover General Howard's movement, who will, if possible, reach Jonesboro' to-morrow.

Yours, &c.,

W. T. SHERMAN,
Major General Commanding.

HEADQUARTERS MILITARY DIVISION OF THE MISSISSIPPI,
In the field, near Red Oak, August 29, 1864—8 p. m.

Major General SCHOFIELD:

I have been down to General Howard. The railroad is well broken down two and a half (2½) miles below Fairburn, which is six (6) miles from here. Several cuts are also filled with trees, rocks, and earth.

We will move to-morrow for our next objective. General Howard will move for Jonesboro'; General Thomas by way of Shoal Creek church, Mrs. Long's, and Couch's, on the road from Morrow's mill, towards Fayetteville. I want you to cover the movement with your two (2) divisions and the cavalry of General Garrard. It may be best for you to occupy the parapets made by Generals Stanley and Davis until your trains are well towards Shoal Creek church, and then move towards any strong position south and west of Morrow's mill, covering the Decatur road and in communication with General Thomas at Couch's. I don't know how far towards East Point Generals Stanley and Davis went to-day, but if you can I want you to gain your position *via* D. Mim's and the road across by Mrs. Long's. If you find this difficult, maintain a defensive position till the trains are well out, and then follow General Thomas's movement as far as Long's, and thence to the one described.

W. T. SHERMAN,
Major General Commanding.

[Cipher.]

HEADQUARTERS MILITARY DIVISION OF THE MISSISSIPPI,
In the field, Couch's House, August, 31, 1864—8 a. m.

General HALLECK:

At this time I would not suggest a change in the geographical lines of the departments of Ohio and Cumberland, because Generals Thomas and Schofield are now in actual battle and cannot give their attention to the necessary details. I will see both of them to-day, and will then communicate my opinion.

We reached the West Point road and broke up twelve miles of it thoroughly, then marched on a big left wheel for the Macon road; General Schofield, on the left, aiming for Rough and Ready; General Thomas's centre and General Howard's right aiming for Jonesboro'. The left and centre, as yet, have met with little or no opposition, but General Howard has fought two brigades of cavalry all the way from Fairburn. Last night darkness overtook him within a mile of Jonesboro', having pushed the cavalry so close that he secured the Flint river bridge.

To-day I press at all points, but expect to make a lodgement on the road at or below Jonesboro', when I propose to swing the whole army upon it, and break it all to pieces. I expect and am prepared for hard fighting, and have the army well in hand.

W. T. SHERMAN,
Major General Commanding.

HEADQUARTERS MILITARY DIVISION OF THE MISSISSIPPI,
In the field, near Jonesboro', Ga., August 31, 1864—11 p. m.

GENERAL: I wish you would instruct General Slocum at the bridge to feel forward to Atlanta as boldly as he can by the direct road leading from the bridge, and to send any cavalry force he can raise over towards Decatur, to watch the movements of the enemy in that quarter. Advise him fully of the situation of affairs here, and assure him that we will fully occupy the attention of the rebel army outside of Atlanta.

Yours, truly,

W. T. SHERMAN,
Major General Commanding.

Major General THOMAS,
Commanding Army of the Cumberland.

HEADQUARTERS MILITARY DIVISION OF THE MISSISSIPPI,
In the field, near Jonesboro', September 1, 1864.

GENERAL: In order that no doubt may exist as to future operations, I wish your army to press directly after the enemy, southward, with all the speed and vigor possible, till we reach Griffin, where I will make new orders. I regret to learn that General Stanley remained to-day for hours on the railroad awaiting orders when he heard firing heavy to his front and right. I may be in error, but such is reported to me by Captain Audenreid and Captain Poe. I knew you had given him orders, and think we should not overlook it. I don't know why Stanley could not have pushed along the railroad whilst General Davis was heavily engaged, and absolutely enveloped the enemy in Jonesboro'. Now he has time to fortify, and we may be compelled to modify all our plans. If General Stanley lost a minute of time when he should have been in action, I beg you will not overlook it, as it concerns the lives of our men and the success of our arms.

General Davis's attack, though some hours later than I expected, was still spirited and good, and was measurably successful.

I suppose now the rebel General Stewart has made his junction, which improves our chances at Atlanta, but gives us harder work out here.

Please renew your orders to General Slocum to make a dash at Atlanta before the enemy has time to haul off the artillery and stores.

Yours, truly,

W. T. SHERMAN,
Major General Commanding.

Major General THOMAS,
Commanding Army of the Cumberland.

HEADQUARTERS MILITARY DIVISION OF THE MISSISSIPPI,
In the field, near Jonesboro', Ga., September 1, 1864.

GENERAL : From reports of my staff I think enough of the railroad has been broken, until we have conquered the army now lying at Jonesboro'. We had pretty hard fighting with them this afternoon, and I think had all our force been engaged we would have beaten them, but now Stewart's corps will effect its junction, and the enemy will fortify. Yet he may underrate our strength, and I wish you, to-morrow early, to get over to the northeast of Jonesboro' and approach from that quarter; and should the enemy retreat, follow him with energy, hanging on his left flank; follow roads east of the railroad as far as Griffin.

General Thomas will follow the railroad substantially, and Howard will keep to the right. I don't see why the enemy should elect to hold Jonesboro' defensively, as we have broken his road; so if you find him intrenched don't assault, but feel below the town. General Howard has General Blair's corps with Kilpatrick's cavalry across Flint river feeling out for the railroad below Jonesboro'. If you think Stewart's corps has passed round by the east from Atlanta and joined Hood at Jonesboro', you may order Garrard up to act with you around to the south of Jonesboro'; but if there be anything to our rear, keep him holding all roads by which Hardee or Hood (both are now represented as present) can receive re-enforcements from the rear. At all events, call Garrard close up, that he may be within reach, if needed, which will be the case if the enemy retreat to-morrow. His movements are so slow that you had better send to him to-night specific orders.

Now that the army is united, you are, of course, subject to no one's orders but mine. But if fighting occurs, or you have a chance to attack, the orders are always to attack. We don't care about Jonesboro', but we want to destroy our enemy.

Yours, truly,

W. T. SHERMAN,
Major General Commanding.

Major General SCHOFIELD,
Commanding Army of the Ohio.

HEADQUARTERS MILITARY DIVISION OF THE MISSISSIPPI,
In the field, near Jonesboro', Ga., September 1, 1864—8 p. m.

GENERAL : In order that you may act advisedly, I will merely state that Jonesboro' is of no value to us, but we are now trying to cripple and destroy the army now there. General Thomas will push him in the direction of the railroad south, General Schofield will operate on the east, and you on the west of the railroad.   If he retreats, we will follow without halt or delay, if possible, to Griffin.   If he remains in Jonesboro', we must envelop him and destroy his communications south, as they are already destroyed north.   Your troops are now well disposed, and General Blair can do good service by feeling out and reaching the railroad, if possible.   He should not be content with a cavalry break, but one of some extent, and well done.   Send word to Osterhaus to have his artillery officers listen for the cars to-night, and if heard, to open artillery on them at random.

If the enemy retreats, I think you could make best progress by marching rapidly to Fayetteville, and then toward Griffin, following on the flanks of the enemy.   I suppose the bridge is destroyed, but General Thomas has a pontoon train that could reach there in a day.   This train is at Renfrew's, (Renfro's,) eight (8) miles from Fayetteville, from which there are several roads across Flint river, the one fulfilling most conditions being the one towards Fayetteville station. Still, if you can learn of roads east of Flint river that will be available, and yet not bring you in contact with General Thomas's troops, it would be the safer, as all the army will then be together, and no part separated by an impassable stream.   Should the enemy remain in Jonesboro' to-morrow hold your line as now, and give to General Blair's movements all the force you can.

   Yours, truly,

W. T. SHERMAN,
Major General Commanding.

Major General HOWARD,
  Commanding Army of the Tennessee.

HEADQUARTERS MILITARY DIVISION OF THE MISSISSIPPI,
  In the field, near Lovejoy's, September 2, 1864—8 p. m.

Major General SCHOFIELD :

I have strong evidence that the enemy blew up his magazines and abandoned the place of Atlanta to General Slocum.   If this be so, it is unnecessary for us to go further at this stage.   I have parties breaking up the railroad from Jonesboro' to our lines, and to-morrow wish you to feel for the McDonough road, so as to command it if possible, but keep up strong connexion with General Stanley, and do not assault works of the enemy.   If he gives you a fair chance punish him.   I have couriers back to ascertain the exact state of affairs in Atlanta, and will be governed by what I hear.

W. T. SHERMAN,
Major General Commanding.

HEADQUARTERS MILITARY DIVISION OF THE MISSISSIPPI,
  In the field, near Lovejoy's, September 2, 1864—8 p. m.

Major General HOWARD :

You know that General Garrard reports General Slocum in possession of Atlanta.   I have sent couriers to learn the exact truth.   If it be so, we do not care about pushing the enemy any further at this time.

Had we prevented him making intrenchments it would have been well, but as he has a strong line I do not wish to waste lives by an assault.   You may, therefore, order the skirmishers close up, but hold your lines so as not to suffer much.   If the enemy be gone in the morning, occupy his lines to your front, and await orders.

   Yours, &c.,

W. T. SHERMAN,
Major General Commanding.

HEADQUARTERS MILITARY DIVISION OF THE MISSISSIPPI,
In the field, near Lovejoy's, Ga., September 2, 1864—8 p. m.

Major General THOMAS:

Until we hear from Atlanta the exact truth, I do not care about your pushing your men against breastworks. Destroy the railroad well up to your lines, keep skirmishers well up, and hold your troops in hand for anything that may turn up As soon as I know positively that our troops are in Atlanta I will determine what to do.

I have ordered General Schofield to feel for the McDonough road, to prevent re-enforcements coming to the enemy from that direction.

Yours, &c.,

W. T. SHERMAN,
Major General Commanding.

[Cipher—By courier to Atlanta.]

HEADQUARTERS MILITARY DIVISION OF THE MISSISSIPPI,
In the field, near Lovejoy's Station, 26 miles
south of Atlanta, September 3, 1864.

Major General HALLECK, *Washington, D. C.:*

As already reported, the army drew from about Atlanta, and on the 30th had made a good break of the West Point railroad, and reached a good position from which to strike the Macon railroad—the right, General Howard, near Jonesboro'; the left, General Schofield, near Rough and Ready; and centre, General Thomas, at Couch's. General Howard found the enemy in force at Jonesboro; intrenched his troops, the salient within a half a mile of the railroad. The enemy attacked him at 3 p. m., and was easily repulsed, leaving his dead and wounded. Finding strong opposition on the right, I advanced the left and centre rapidly to the railroad; made a good lodgement, and broke it all the way from Rough and Ready down to Howard's left, near Jonesboro', and by the same movement I interposed my whole army between Atlanta and the part of the enemy intrenched in and around Jonesboro'. We made a general attack on the enemy at Jonesboro' on the 1st of September, the 14th corps, General Jeff. C. Davis, carrying the works handsomely with ten (10) guns, and about a thousand prisoners. In the night the enemy retreated south, and we have followed him to another of his well-chosen and hastily constructed lines, near Lovejoy's. Hood, at Atlanta, finding me on his road, the only one that could supply him, and between him and a considerable part of his army, blew up his magazines in Atlanta, and left in the night time, when the 20th corps, General Slocum, took possession of the place. So Atlanta is ours, and fairly won.

I shall not push much further on this raid, but in a day or so will move back to Atlanta, and give my men some rest.

Since the 5th of May we have been in one constant battle or skirmish, and need rest. Our losses will not exceed twelve hundred, (1,200,) and we have possession of over three hundred (300) rebel dead, two hundred and fifty (250) wounded, and over fifteen hundred (1,500) well prisoners.

W. T. SHERMAN,
Major General Commanding.

[Cipher.]

HEADQUARTERS MILITARY DIVISION OF THE MISSISSIPPI,
In the field, near Lovejoy's Station, September 3, 1864.

Major General SLOCUM, *Atlanta, Georgia:*

Have all the stores moved forward from Allatoona and Marietta to Atlanta, take possession of all good buildings for government purposes, and see they are not used as quarters. Advise the people to quit now. There can be no trade or commerce until the war is over. Let Union families go to the north with their effects, and "secesh" families move on. Cotton must all go to Nashville as United States property, and pretended claimants may collect testimony for the pursuit of the proceeds of sale after they reach the United States treasury in money.

W. T. SHERMAN,
Major General Commanding.

[Cipher.]

HEADQUARTERS MILITARY DIVISION OF THE MISSISSIPPI,
In the field, near Lovejoy's, Ga., September 4, 1864.

General HALLECK, *Washington:*

The 20th corps now occupies Atlanta and the Chattahoochee bridges. The main army is now here, grouped below Jonesboro'. The enemy hold a line facing us, with front well covered by parapets, and flanks covered by Walnut creek on the right, and a confluent of Flint river on his left. His position is too strong to attack in front, and to turn it would carry me too far from our base at this time; besides, there is no commensurate object, as there is no valuable point to his rear till we reach Macon, one hundred and three (103) miles from Atlanta. We are not prepared for that, and I will gradually fall back and occupy Atlanta, which was, and is, our grand objective point already secure.

For the future, I propose that of the drafted men I receive my due share, say fifty thousand (50,000.) That an equal or greater number go to General Canby, who should now proceed with all energy to get Montgomery, and the reach of the Alabama river, above Selma, that when I know he can move on Columbus, Georgia, I move on La Grange and West Point, keeping to the east of the Chattahoochee; that we form a junction; repair roads to Montgomery, and open up the Appalachicola and Chattahochee rivers to Columbus, and move from it as a base straight on Macon. This campaign can be made in the winter, and we can safely rely on the corn of the Flint and Chattahoochee to supply forage.

If the Tensas channel of the Alabama river can be used, General Gardner, with his rebel garrison, could continue to hold Mobile for our use when we want it. I propose to move all the inhabitants of Atlanta, sending those committed to our cause to the rear, and the rebel families to the front. I will allow no trade, manufactories, or any citizen there at all, so that we will have the entire use of the railroad back, as also such corn and forage as may be reached by our troops.

If the people raise a howl against my barbarity and cruelty, I will answer that war is war, and not popularity-seeking. If they want peace, they and their relatives must stop the war.

W. T. SHERMAN,
Major General Commanding.

CITY POINT, VA., *September* 4, 1864—9 p. m.

Major General SHERMAN:

I have just received your despatch announcing the capture of Atlanta. In honor of your great victory, I have ordered a salute to be fired with shotted guns from every battery bearing upon the enemy. The salute will be fired within an hour, amidst great rejoicing.

U. S. GRANT,
Lieutenant General.

WASHINGTON, D. C., *September* 5, 1864—10.55 a. m.

Major General SHERMAN:

I have the pleasure of transmitting to you the following orders which were made Saturday by the President on receipt of the news of the capture of Atlanta.

E. M. STANTON,
Secretary of War.

EXECUTIVE MANSION, *September* 3, 1864.

The national thanks are tendered by the President to Major General W. T. Sherman and the gallant officers and soldiers of his command, before Atlanta, for the distinguished ability, courage, and perseverance displayed in the campaign in Georgia, which, under Divine favor, has resulted in the capture of Atlanta. The marches, battles, sieges, and other military operations that have signalized the campaign must render it famous in the annals of war, and have entitled those who have participated therein to the applause and thanks of the nation.

ABRAHAM LINCOLN,
President of the United States.

EXECUTIVE MANSION,
Washington, D. C., September 3, 1864.

Ordered—1. That on Monday, the 5th day of September, commencing at the hour of 12 o'clock noon, there shall be given a salute of one hundred (100) guns at the arsenal and navy yard, Washington; and on Tuesday, the 6th of September, or on the day after the receipt of this order, at each arsenal and navy yard in the United States, for the recent brilliant achievements of the fleet and land forces of the United States in the harbor of Mobile, and in the reduction of Fort Powell, Fort Gaines, and Fort Morgan. The Secretary of War and the Secretary of the Navy will issue the necessary directions in their respective departments for the execution of this order.

2. That on Wednesday, the 7th of September, commencing at the hour of 12 o'clock noon, there shall be fired a salute of one hundred guns at the arsenal at Washington, and at New York, Boston, Philadelphia, Baltimore, Pittsburg, Newport, Kentucky, and St. Louis, and New Orleans, Mobile and Pensacola, Hilton Head and Newbern, the day after the receipt of this order, for the brilliant achievements of the army under command of Major General Sherman, in the State of Georgia, and for the capture of Atlanta. The Secretary of War will issue directions for the execution of this order.

ABRAHAM LINCOLN,
President of the United States.

[Cipher.]

HEADQUARTERS MILITARY DIVISION OF THE MISSISSIPPI,
In the field, near Jonesboro', Ga., September 6, 1864.

General GRANT, *City Point, Virginia:*

I have received your despatch, and will communicate it to the troops in general orders. We are gradually falling back to Atlanta, feeding high on the cornfields of the confederacy. I will be in Atlanta in a day or two, and will communicate fully with you. I have always felt that you would personally take more pleasure in my success than in your own, and I reciprocate the feeling in its fullest extent.

W. T. SHERMAN,
Major General Commanding.

[Cipher.]

HEADQUARTERS MILITARY DIVISION OF THE MISSISSIPPI,
In the field, near Jonesboro', September 6, 1864.

Hon. E. M. STANTON, *Washington, D. C.:*

I have just received your telegram, and shall announce it to the whole army, preceded by the expression: "The general commanding announces to the army with pride and satisfaction," and followed by "all corps, regiments, and batteries may, without further notice, inscribe 'Atlanta' on their colors." We are moving back to Atlanta slowly, making good use of the cornfields, which our animals needed, and to prevent a boast of the enemy that we were in a hurry. I have burned a good deal of cotton, but will save enough to pay the expense of the salute.

W. T. SHERMAN,
Major General Commanding.

[Cipher.]

HEADQUARTERS MILITARY DIVISION OF THE MISSISSIPPI,
In the field, Atlanta, Ga., September 8, 1864.

General HALLECK, *Washington:*

General Thomas is in, and his troops are now grouping about Atlanta. General Schofield has also arrived, and has gone to place his troops in Decatur. I have not yet heard from General Howard, but suppose him to be at East Point. I have just ridden to see a portion of the enemy's lines, which are very strong, and demonstrate the wisdom of our mode and manner of attack.

I have but little news of Wheeler, except that last night General Steedman was at Athens, Alabama, and Wheeler was supposed to be crossing the Tennessee, towards the south, about Lamb's ferry. Generals Rousseau, Granger, and Steedman have enough troops to handle Wheeler, and I suppose the railroad will soon be repaired. We have enough stores for a month, and I feel no uneasiness on that score; yet if necessary I can send some troops to the rear. I telegraphed you yesterday that you could use General A. J. Smith, as proposed, to act against Price in Missouri. We are well, and have no doubt, after a short rest, will be impatient again to sally forth in search of adventure.

W. T. SHERMAN,
Major General Commanding.

[Cipher.]

HEADQUARTERS MILITARY DIVISION OF THE MISSISSIPPI,
In the field, Atlanta, Ga., September 8, 1864.

General WEBSTER, *Nashville* :

Don't let any citizens come to Atlanta, not one. I won't allow trade or manufactures of any kind, but will remove all the present population, and make Atlanta a pure military town. Give public notice to this effect.

General Thomas's army is now in and around Atlanta; General Howard at East Point, and General Schofield at Decatur. I want Wheeler cleaned out, the roads repaired, and everything to the rear made right. Send forward paymasters. If the Sanitary Commission have stores, let them be sent to the agent at Chattanooga, whence we can draw as fast as we need.

Hood's army retreated towards Macon, but will, I suppose, halt about Griffin. I was unprepared to follow below Lovejoy's, twenty-eight (28) miles south of Atlanta, for we have been fighting constantly since about the 7th of May, and the men need rest and quiet. Our last move was beautiful and perfectly successful, as you observe from our occupation of the famous Atlanta. We have already found nineteen (19) guns, and others are being found daily. At Jonesboro', at the battle, we took two four (4) gun batteries, and in the whole move have near three thousand (3,000) prisoners. We killed about five hundred (500) at Jonesboro', and wounded about twenty-five hundred (2,500.) Our entire loss since beginning the movement will not exceed fifteen hundred (1,500.)

W. T. SHERMAN,
Major General Commanding.

[Cipher.]

HEADQUARTERS MILITARY DIVISION OF THE MISSISSIPPI,
In the field, Atlanta, Ga., September 9, 1864.

General HALLECK, *Washington* :

All our troops are now in position, comfortable and well. In a day or two I will have telegraphic communication from Roswell round to Sandtown, and can act promptly. A few of the enemy's cavalry followed us from Rough and Ready, and last evening General Hood sent in a flag of truce, asking to exchange prisoners. I have about two thousand (2,000) in hand, and will exchange if he will make a fair deal. I have sent out my inspector general to confer and agree and to make arrangements for the exodus of citizens. I am not willing to have Atlanta encumbered by the families of our enemies; I want it a pure Gibraltar, and will have it so by the first of October.

I think Generals Rousseau and Steedman are stirring Wheeler up pretty well, and I hope they will make an end of him, as Gillen has of Morgan. I have ordered renewed activity, and to show no mercy to guerillas or railroad breakers. It makes a world of difference if "my bull gores your ox or your's mine." Weather beautiful, and all things seem bright.

W. T. SHERMAN,
Major General Commanding.

[Cipher.]

HEADQUARTERS MILITARY DIVISION OF THE MISSISSIPPI,
In the field, Atlanta, Ga., September 10, 1864.

General CANBY, *New Orleans* :

Despatch of 29th received. I got Atlanta by a couple of good moves. You succeeded at Fort Morgan sooner than I expected. We must have the Alabama

13 *

river now and also the Appalachicola at the old arsenal, and up to Columbus. My line is so long now that it is impossible to protect it against cavalry raids; but if we can get Montgomery and Columbus, Georgia, as bases in connexion with Atlanta, we have Georgia and Alabama at our feet. You ought to have more men, and it is a burning shame that at this epoch we should need men, for the north is full of them. They can raise a political convention any time of fifty to one hundred thousand (50,000 to 100,000) men, and yet they pretend they cannot give us what we want. But keep at it, and I only want to express my idea that I would not bother with the city of Mobile, which will simply absorb a garrison for you, but would use the Tensas channel, and notify General Gardner, of the rebel army, to maintain good order, &c., in the now useless streets of Mobile.

I will be ready to sally forth again in October, but ought to have some assurance that, in case of necessity, I can swing into Appalachicola or Montgomery and find friends.

W. T. SHERMAN,
Major General Commanding.

[Cipher.]

CITY POINT, VIRGINIA,
September 10, 1864.

Major General SHERMAN :

As soon as your men are properly rested and preparations can be made, it is desirable that another campaign should be commenced.

We want to keep the enemy continually pressed to the end of the war. If we give him no peace while the war lasts, the end cannot be far distant. Now that we have all of Mobile bay that is valuable, I do not know but it will be the best move for Major General Canby's troops to act upon Savannah, whilst you move on Augusta. I should like to hear from you, however, on this matter.

U. S. GRANT, *Lieutenant General.*

[Cipher.]

HEADQUARTERS MILITARY DIVISION OF THE MISSISSIPPI,
In the field, Atlanta, September 10 1864—8 p. m.

General GRANT, *City Point :*

I have your despatch of to-day. My command need some rest and pay. Our roads are also broken back near Nashville, and Wheeler is not yet disposed of. Still, I am perfectly alive to the importance of pushing our advantage to the utmost. I do not think we can afford to operate further, dependent on the railroad, it takes so many men to guard it, and even then it is nightly broken by the enemy's cavalry that swarms about us. Macon is distant one hundred and three miles (103) miles, and Augusta one hundred and seventy-five (175) miles. If I could be sure of finding provisions and ammunition at Augusta or Columbus, Georgia, I can march to Milledgeville and compel Hood to give up Augusta or Macon, and could then turn on the other. The country will afford forage and many supplies, but not enough in any one place to admit of a delay. In scattering for forage we have a great many men picked up by the enemy's cavalry. If you can manage to take the Savannah river as high as Augusta, or the Chattahooche as far up as Columbus, I can sweep the whole State of Georgia ; otherwise I would risk our whole army by going too far from Atlanta.

W. T. SHERMAN, *Major General.*

HEADQUARTERS MILITARY DIVISION OF THE MISSISSIPPI,
In the field, Atlanta, September 12, 1864.

General A. J. SMITH, *Cairo, Illinois :*

I have been trying for three months to get you and Mower to me, but am headed off at every turn. General Halleck asks for you to clean out Price. Can't you make a quick job of it and then get to me ? Your command belongs to me and is only loaned to help our neighbors, but I fear they make you do the lion's share. However, do as General Halleck orders, and as soon as possible come to me. All well.

W. T. SHERMAN,
Major General Commanding.

[Cipher.]

In the field, Atlanta, September 12, 1864.

General GRANT, *City Point, Virginia :*

I have Macon papers of the 10th and 11th. Dick Taylor is in command of the department, including Mobile ; Forrest and his men have reached Mobile. All well here. The exodus of people is progressing, and matters coming into shape. I will have all official reports of the campaign in and off for Washington by the 15th.

I don't understand whether you propose to act against Savannah direct from Fort Pulaski, or by way of Florida, or from the direction of Mobile. If you can take Savannah by a sudden *coup-de-main*, it would be valuable. The enemy is evidently concentrating all his Mississippi force at Mobile, and Hood is about Lovejoy's Station watching me, apprehensive of big raids.

W. T. SHERMAN,
Major General.

HEADQUARTERS MILITARY DIVISION OF THE MISSISSIPPI,
In the field, Atlanta, September 12, 1864.

General HALLECK, *Washington, D. C. :*

I do not think I need at this time cavalry horses in undue proportion ; I have lost faith in cavalry raids, and our men take bad care of their animals. There is a large abundance of forage in Alabama and Georgia, and independent columns of cavalry might operate by a circuit from one army to another and destroy the enemy's cavalry, which is more to be feared by us than their infantry. As soon as General Grant determines for me the next move on the chess-board, I will estimate the number I will want, and in the mean time would not ask more than a fair proportion for remount. Wheeler might have been utterly destroyed if we had had more cavalry in Tennessee, but that is now too late. In the future we will have to use cavalry offensively, and trust to the enemy's corn-fields for forage. Our road is repaired and bringing forward supplies, but I doubt its capacity to do much more than feed our teams and artillery horses. All well.

W. T. SHERMAN,
Major General Commanding.

HEADQUARTERS MILITARY DIVISION OF THE MISSISSIPPI,
In the field, Atlanta, September 12, 1864.

GENERAL : I have yours of to-day. You asked to exchange prisoners, and I consented as far as those which remained in my hands and this side of Chattanooga. These I will exchange in the manner stated, and not otherwise. As you could not know those of our men whose terms of service have expired, I authorized Colonel Warner to say I would receive any number taken of this army between certain dates—say the last two thousand—or in any other single period ; but as a matter of business I offered terms that could not be misunderstood.

You have not answered my proposition as to the men " captured in Atlanta who are soldiers of the confederate army, detailed on extra duty" in the shops.

I think I understand the laws of civilized nations, and the " customs of war ;" but if at a loss at any time, I know where to seek for information to refresh my memory.

If you will give our prisoners at Andersonville a little more elbow-room, and liberty to make, out of the abundant timber, shelter for themselves, as also a fair allowance of food to enable them to live in health, they will ask nothing more until such time as we will provide for them.

I am, with respect, your obedient servant,

W. T. SHERMAN,
Major General Commanding.

General J. B. HOOD,
Commanding Army of the Tennessee, Confederate Army.

HEADQUARTERS MILITARY DIVISION OF THE MISSISSIPPI,
In the field, Atlanta, Georgia, September 13, 1865.

GENERAL : I enclose you a couple of rebel papers of September 9th and 13th, which contain articles I would have you and Mr. Stanton to read. In the latter you will find General Hood has published my letter about moving the people of Atlanta and his answer. You will observe he characterizes this removal in somewhat harsh terms, and I feel sure he has made his answer public before it went to the Richmond government, as is required by their official usage. He has therefore appealed to the public as a demagogue, and hopes to make capital. Of course he is welcome, for the more he arouses the indignation of the southern masses, the bigger will be the pill of bitterness they will have to swallow. The people of Atlanta are going, and we will have the place for military uses, and not have to engage in a ceaseless wrangle every time we need a house or site for a battery. The present rebel line would require a garrison of thirty thousand (30,000) men, whereas we must contract it to the vital points, viz., the railroad and necessary storehouses, all of which can be embraced in a circle of quarter the radius ; and requiring less than a sixth part of that number. I can't use this line of reasoning to a people who have no right to gain such a clue to our future plans and purposes. At some future time I will submit to you the entire correspondence between General Hood and myself on this subject, as also of the special exchange of prisoners, not yet concluded ; and at the present I send you only my reply to his insinuations of unprecedented cruelty towards the families of a " brave people," which I hardly expect he will publish. If his is widely circulated it might also be well to let the southern papers get mine through northern channels.

I will have all my official reports in by the 15th, which will dispose of the past and leave us free to think of and prepare for the future ; and now I will only renew the expression of the hope that our ranks will soon be replenished by a liberal supply of recruits.

Yours truly,

W. T. SHERMAN,
Major General Commanding.

Major General HALLECK, *Washington.*

HEADQUARTERS MILITARY DIVISION OF THE MISSISSIPPI,
In the field, Atlanta, Ga., September 15, 1864.

General HALLECK, *Washington, D. C.:*

My report is done, and will be forwarded as soon as I get a few more of the subordinate reports. I am awaiting a courier from General Grant. All well, and troops in fine, healthy camps, and supplies coming forward finely.

Governor Brown has disbanded his militia to gather the corn and sorghum of the State. I have reason to believe that he and Stevens want to visit me, and I have sent them a hearty invitation.

I will exchange two thousand (2,000) prisoners with Hood, but no more.

W. T. SHERMAN,
Major General Commanding.

[Cipher.]

NEW ORLEANS, LOUISIANA,
September 17, 1864.

Major General SHERMAN:

Your despatch of the 10th has just been received. The operations you suggest have been in contemplation, and preparations are now in progress. I think I can give you the assurance that you will find friends in Mobile. If the trouble in Arkansas river should be soon ended, how far east of that will depend upon the re-enforcements that can be spared for this command.

E. R. S. CANBY.
Major General.

[Cipher.]

HEADQUARTERS MILITARY DIVISION OF THE MISSISSIPPI,
In the field, Atlanta, Ga., September 17, 1864.

President LINCOLN, *Washington, D. C.:*

I will keep the department fully advised of all developments as connected with the subject in which you feel interested.

A Mr. Wright, former member of Congress from Rome, Georgia, and a Mr. King, of Marietta, are now going between Governor Brown and myself. I have said that some of the people of Georgia are now engaged in rebellion, begun in error and perpetuated in pride, but that Georgia can now save herself from the devastation of war preparing for her only by withdrawing her quota out of the confederate army, and aiding me to expel Hood from the borders of the State; in which event, instead of desolating the land as we progress, I will keep our men to the high roads and commons, and pay for the corn and meat we need and take.

I am fully conscious of the delicate nature of such assertions, but it would be a magnificent stroke of policy if I could, without surrendering a foot of ground or of principle, arouse the latent enmity to Davis of Georgia.

The people do not hesitate to say that Mr. Stevens was and is a Union man at heart, and they feel that Jeff. Davis will not trust him, or let him have a share in his government.

W. T. SHERMAN,
Major General.

[Cipher.]

HEADQUARTERS MILITARY DIVISION OF THE MISSISSIPPI,
In the field, Atlanta, Ga., September 19, 1864.

GENERAL: Your messenger has not yet arrived. Things remain *statu quo.* Most of the inhabitants are gone, and I am exchanging two thousand (2,000) prisoners with Hood on a special exchange, with the understanding that I get an equal number of my own men back, whom I can put right away to duty. He raised the question of humanity, but I am not to be moved by such tricks of the enemy. I have taken high ground with Hood on purpose. A deserter just in says Stewart's corps is moving back to Macon with a view of going to Virginia. I have ordered one of my female scouts from New Orleans to Augusta, and will send some out from here, and give you prompt notice of any of Hood's army going east. I can quickly bounce him out of Lovejoy's, but think him better there, where I can watch him, than further off. I await the arrival of your messenger with impatience. All well, but large numbers of our men and officers are being discharged, time out, and we must have recruits.

W. T. SHERMAN, *Major General.*

Lieutenant General U. S. GRANT,
City Point, Virginia.

HEADQUARTERS MILITARY DIVISION OF THE MISSISSIPPI,
Atlanta, Georgia, September 20, 1864.

Major General O. O. HOWARD, *East Point:*

General Thomas will send two of Garrard's brigades to Kilpatrick, and order him to feel well down toward Fayetteville and Lovejoy's. Support him, if necessary, only so far as is consistent with the truce and to discover what Hood is about. I will have spies to-night at Macon to watch which way he goes. I think he will move back to Macon and send some men to Richmond.

W. T. SHERMAN, *Major General.*

[Cipher.]

HEADQUARTERS MILITARY DIVISION OF THE MISSISSIPPI,
Atlanta, Georgia, September 20, 1864.

General GRANT, *City Point:*

Colonel Porter is just come, and I have read your letter with much interest. I will send east my official reports, and write more fully by Colonel Porter. In the mean time all is well, and I can watch your movements with interest. I hear that General Sheridan is now fighting.

W. T. SHERMAN, *Major General.*

[Cipher.]

HEADQUARTERS MILITARY DIVISION OF THE MISSISSIPPI,
In the field, Atlanta, Ga., September 20, 1864.

Hon. E. M. STANTON, *Secretary of War:*

Thank you for the appointment of Captain Coverdale. I hope General Sheridan will give Early a good, hard fight.

I think Hood is moving from Lovejoy's, but cannot yet form an intelligent guess as to the direction he will take. I will have some spies in his camp to-night, and have ordered Kilpatrick to feel his flanks about Fayetteville.

Everything continues well with us.

W. T. SHERMAN, *Major General.*

HEADQUARTERS MILITARY DIVISION OF THE MISSISSIPPI,
In the field, Atlanta, Ga., September 21, 1864.

GENERAL: Yours of the 20th instant, asking me to treat as a prisoner of war W. C. Glover, company H, fourth Tennessee regiment of cavalry, employed as a scout by your authority, and who is said to have been captured by me, and is about to be executed at Chattanooga as a spy or bushwhacker is received.

I confess I know nothing about the matter at all, but I will at once proceed to find out the facts and communicate them to you as early as possible; but I can relieve any undue anxiety on the part of the friends of Glover by assuring them that no one can be executed by us without a full and fair record trial by a sworn tribunal, at which the prisoner is always allowed to have his witnesses and counsel.

Since you left our service some few changes have been made in the laws of Congress and the powers of reviewing officers of courts-martial. The act of April 10, 1806, defining spies and their punishment, is materially modified by that of February 13, 1862. Also, by an act of Congress approved December 24, 1861, the commanding general of a division, or separate (detached) brigade, can assemble a general court-martial; but in case of the sentence of death, the case must be reviewed, and the necessary order be given by the officer commanding the army in the field or department to which the division or brigade belongs.

General George H. Thomas commands the department in which Chattanooga lies, and has the review of all such cases, and you must know that he would never order the execution of an innocent man.

I have no doubt, however, that a scout regularly detailed may push his operations so as to make him a spy. If found lurking around the "fortifications, encampments, posts, quarters, or headquarters of the armies of the United States, or any of them," he would clearly fall within the meaning of the laws and be liable to the penalty of death.

I have the honor to be your obedient servant,

W. T. SHERMAN, *Major General.*

General J. B. HOOD,
Commanding Confederate Forces.

HEADQUARTERS MILITARY DIVISION OF THE MISSISSIPPI,
In the field, Atlanta, Georgia, September 20, 1864.

GENERAL: I have the honor to acknowledge, at the hands of Lieutenant Colonel Porter, of your staff, your letter of September 12, and accept with thanks the honorable and kindly mention of the services of this army in the great cause in which we are all engaged.

I send by Colonel Porter all official reports which are completed, and will in a few days submit a list of names which I deem worthy of promotion.

I think we owe it to the President, to save him the invidious task of election among a vast number of worthy applicants, and have ordered my army commanders to prepare their lists with great care, and to express their preferences, based upon claims of actual capacity and services rendered. These I will consolidate and submit in such a form that if mistakes are made they will at least be sanctioned by the best contemporaneous evidence of merit, for I know that vacancies do not exist equal in number to that of the officers that really deserve promotion.

As to the future, I am pleased to know your army is being steadily re-enforced by a good class of men, and I hope it will go on until you have a force that is numerically double that of your antagonist, so that with one part you can watch him, and with the other you can push out boldly from your left flank, occupy the South-Side railroad, compel him to attack you in position, or accept battle on your own terms.

We ought to ask our country for the largest possible armies that can be raised, as so important a thing as the self-existence of a great nation should not be left to the fickle chances of war.

Now that Mobile is shut out to the commerce of our enemy, it calls for no further effort on our part unless the capture of the city can be followed by the occupation of the Alabama river and the railroad down to Columbus, Georgia, when that place would be a magnificent auxiliary to my further progress into Georgia; but until General Canby is much re-enforced, and until he can more thoroughly subdue the scattered armies west of the Mississippi, I suppose that much cannot be attempted as against the Alabama river and Columbus, Georgia.

The utter destruction of Wilmington, North Carolina, is of importance only in connexion with the necessity of cutting off all foreign trade to our enemy, and if Farragut can get across the bar, and the move can be made quick, I suppose it will succeed. From my knowledge of the mouth of Cape Fear river, I anticipate more difficulty in getting the heavy ships across the bar than in reaching the town of Wilmington; but of course the soundings of the channel are well known at Washington, as well as the draught of his iron-clads, so that it must be demonstrated as feasible, or else it would not be attempted. If successful, I suppose that Fort Caswell will be occupied and the fleet at once sent to the Savannah river. Then the reduction of the city is the only question. It once in our possession, and the river open to us, I would not hesitate to cross the State of Georgia with sixty thousand (60,000) men, hauling some stores and depending on the country for the balance. Where a million of people find subsistence my army won't starve; but, as you know, in a country like Georgia, with few roads and innumerable streams, an inferior force could so delay an army and harass it, that it would not be a formidable object, but if the enemy knew that we had our boats on the Savannah I could rapidly move to Milledgeville, where there is abundance of corn and meat, and I could so threaten Macon and Augusta that he would give up Macon for Augusta; then I would move to interpose between Augusta and Savannah, and force him to give me Augusta, with the only powder mills and factories remaining in the south, or let us have the Savannah river. Either horn of the dilemma would be worth a battle. I would prefer his holding Augusta, as the probabilities are, for then, with the Savannah river in our possession, the taking of Augusta would be a mere matter of time. This campaign would be made in winter.

But the more I study the game the more am I convinced that it would be wrong for me to penetrate much further into Georgia without an objective beyond. It would not be productive of much good. I can start east and make a circuit south and back, doing vast damage to the State, but resulting in no permanent good; but by mere threatening to do so I hold a rod over the Georgians, who are not over-loyal to the south. I will therefore give my opinion that your army and Canby's should be re-enforced to the maximum; that after you get Wilmington you strike for Savannah and the river; that General Canby be instructed to hold the Mississippi river, and send a force to get Columbus, Georgia, either by way of the Alabama or Appalachicola; and that I keep Hood employed and put my army in fine order for a march on Augusta, Columbus, and Charleston; so be ready as soon as Wilmington is sealed as to commerce, and the city of Savannah is in our possession.   I think it will be found that the movements of Price and Shelby west of the Mississippi are mere diversions.   They cannot hope to enter Missouri save as raiders, and the truth is, General Rosecrans should be ashamed to take my troops for such a purpose.   If you will secure Wilmington and the city of Savannah from your centre, and let General Canby have the Mississippi river and west of it, I will send a force to the Alabama and Appalachicola, provided you give me one hundred thousand (100,000) of the drafted men to fill up my old regiments; and if you will fix a day to be in Savannah, I will insure our possession of Macon and a point on the river below Augusta.   The possession of the Savannah river is more than fatal to the possibility of a southern independence. They may stand the fall of Richmond, but not of all Georgia.

I will have a long talk with Colonel Porter, and tell him everything that may occur to me of interest to you.

In the mean time know that I admire your dogged perseverance and pluck more than ever.   If you can whip Lee and I can march to the Atlantic, I think Uncle Abe will give us a twenty days' leave of absence to see the young folks.

Yours as ever,
W. T. SHERMAN, Major General.

Lieutenant General U. S. GRANT,
    Commander-in-chief, City Point, Va.

[By telegraph.]

HEADQUARTERS MILITARY DIVISION OF THE MISSISSIPPI,
In the field, Atlanta, Ga., September 21, 1864.

Lieutenant General GRANT, *City Point, Virginia:*

Lieutenant Colonel Porter will start back in the morning and will bring you full answer to your letter, also all my official reports of the past.   I prefer that General Canby and a part of Farragut's fleet should continue to threaten Mobile city, but not attempt its capture; that a small force with gunboats ascend the Appalachicola to the arsenal, and up to Columbus if possible; that you take the city of Savannah by a *coup-de-main*, at the same time or soon after your active movements about Petersburg and the mouth of Cape Fear river.   Savannah in our possession and boats at liberty to work up the Savannah river, I am willing to start for Augusta in the manner I propose in my letter of last night, which Colonel Porter will bring.   I beg you to give my personal congratulations to Sheridan, and my earnest hope that he will push Early back on Lynchburg. We can't do much up the Tennessee and Virginia valley.   It is too long. Burbridge will attempt the capture and destruction of the salt-works about Abingdon, from Kentucky and Knoxville.   Schofield has gone to Knoxville to make the arrangements.   All well.

W. T. SHERMAN, Major General.

HEADQUARTERS MILITARY DIVISION OF THE MISSISSIPPI,
In the field, Atlanta, Ga., September 21, 1864.

Major General O. O. HOWARD, *East Point:*

The general wishes, if possible, that you put some persons on the track of Hood and find out where he is going.   He has been trying to get out persons from here, but does not succeed in finding any person that is worth much or reliable.

L. M. DAYTON, Aide-de Camp.

[Cipher.]

HEADQUARTERS MILITARY DIVISION OF THE MISSISSIPPI,
In the field, Atlanta, Ga., September 21, 1864.

Hon. E. M. STANTON, *Washington, D. C.:*

Magnificent from General Sheridan, and his success will have an effect all over the country.

Hood is falling back from Lovejoy's, but I will not follow him now, but will watch his motions with my cavalry. I write very fully to General Grant by a special aide to-day. He will bring my report to Washington. My information from the interior of Georgia is all favorable to our cause. I send copies of your despatch about Sheridan to General Hood with my compliments, but I know it does not afford "comfort to the enemy."

W. T. SHERMAN, *Major General.*

[Cipher.]

HEADQUARTERS MILITARY DIVISION OF THE MISSISSIPPI,
In the field, Atlanta, Ga., September 21, 1864.

Hon. E. M. STANTON, *Washington, D. C.:*

In my despatch of to-day I reported that Hood was falling back. Reports just in seem to indicate that he has shifted from the Macon road, at Lovejoy's, over to the West Point road, about Palmetto station, where his men are intrenching. I will watch him, as I do not see what he designs by this movement.

W. T. SHERMAN, *Major General.*

HEADQUARTERS MILITARY DIVISION OF THE MISSISSIPPI,
In the field, Atlanta, Ga., September 22, 1864.

GENERAL: My latest authentic information from Andersonville is to the 12th, and from what I learn, our prisoners of war confined there, and being removed to Savannah, Charleston, and Millen, need many articles which we possess in superfluity, and can easily supply with your consent and assistance, such as shirts and drawers, socks, shoes, soap, candles, combs, scissors, &c.

If you will permit me to send a train of wagons, with a single officer to go along under a flag of truce, I will send down to Lovejoy's or Palmetto a train of wagons loaded exclusively with ten thousand (10,000) or fifteen thousand (15,000) of each of these articles, and a due proportion of soap, candles, &c., under such restrictions as you may think prudent to name.

I would like to have my officer go along to issue these things, but will have no hesitation in sending them if you will simply promise to have them conveyed to the places where our prisoners are and have them fairly distributed.

I have the honor to be your obedient servant,

W. T. SHERMAN,
Major General Commanding.

General J. B. HOOD,
Commanding Confederate Army, Palmetto Station.

HEADQUARTERS MILITARY DIVISION OF THE MISSISSIPPI,
Atlanta, Ga., September 22, 1864.

DEAR SIR: Yours of September 14 is received, and I assure you the compliments you have lavished on me makes me fear that my services and abilities are overrated. I don't want to be elevated an inch more than I can sustain myself, for pride will have its fall.

The condition of the prisoners at Andersonville has always been present to my mind, and could I have released them I would have felt more real satisfaction than to have won another battle. General Stoneman's trip was partly for that purpose, and I fear it failed partially because the general took a road east of Ocmulgee, instead of west, as I contemplated and ordered. I have frequent messages from them, and have sent word to the men to be of good cheer, that the day of their deliverance was approaching; but I now think that Jeff. Davis is removing them to Charleston, Savannah, and a point on the Macon and Savannah road, at Millen, where a branch puts off for Augusta. My last escaped prisoner left Andersonville on the 12th, at which date many train-loads had gone off eastward, and this reduction of the number will improve the condition of the balance.

I am now engaged in exchanging, with General Hood, a couple thousand of prisoners, but this is confined to the last two thousand captured from my army, who, of course, are not in as bad condition as those who have been longer confined. During the few days that must expire before the papers are completed, I will have occasion to write to General Hood, and will offer to send down some fifty or sixty tons of clothing and other necessaries; but I doubt if he will consent. These confederates are as proud as the devil, and hate to confess poverty, but I know they are really unable to supply socks, drawers, undershirts, scissors, combs, &c., which our men need more than anything else to preserve cleanliness and health. Should, however, he assent, I will telegraph you to send me such articles as we do not have on hand, and will give credit to your commission for all I obtain. This appears to me the best manner in which I can carry out your humane, patriotic, and most worthy object.

With sentiments of great respect, your friend,

W. T. SHERMAN,
Major General Commanding.

JAMES E. YATEMAN,
President Western Sanitary Commission, St. Louis, Mo.

HEADQUARTERS MILITARY DIVISION OF THE MISSISSIPPI,
In the field, Atlanta, Ga., September 24, 1864.

General HOWARD, *East Point:*

I have no doubt Hood has resolved to throw himself on our flanks to prevent our accumulating stores, &c., here, trusting to our not advancing into Georgia. Some cavalry got possession of Athens yesterday. I think I will send a division from Thomas to Bridgeport, and the balance of the one you have at Rome, viz: Corse, so as to act in case the enemy puts himself up west of the Coosa. Let Corse get all ready.

W. T. SHERMAN, *Major General.*

HEADQUARTERS MILITARY DIVISION OF THE MISSISSIPPI,
In the field, Atlanta, Ga., September 24, 1864.

General HOWARD, *East Point:*

You may order General Corse to proceed to Rome by cars, and there unite his division against any force that may attempt to threaten Bridgeport from the direction of Gadsden. Let them march up to-morrow and take cars in the evening. The whole division will rejoin us before we take the field.

W. T. SHERMAN,
Major General Commanding,

[Cipher.]

HEADQUARTERS MILITARY DIVISION OF THE MISSISSIPPI,
In the field, Atlanta, Ga., September 25, 1864.

GENERAL : Hood seems to be moving as it were to the Alabama line, leaving open to me the road to Macon as also to Augusta, but his cavalry is busy on our roads. A force, number estimated as high as eight thousand, (8,000,) are reported to have captured Athens, Alabama, as also a regiment of three hundred and fifty (350) sent to their relief. I have sent Newton's division up to Chattanooga in cars, and will send another division to Rome. If I was sure that Savannah would soon be in our possession, I would be tempted to make for Milledgeville and Augusta, but I must secure what I have.

Jeff. Davis is at Macon.

W. T. SHERMAN,
Major General.

General HALLECK, *Washington, D. C.*

[Cipher.]

HEADQUARTERS MILITARY DIVISION OF THE MISSISSIPPI,
In the field, Atlanta, Ga., September 26, 1864.

GENERAL : I have re-enforced my line back as far as Chattanooga, but in Middle Tennessee we are weak, on account of the number of regiments out of time. I would like to have any regiments in Indiana or Ohio sent to Nashville, or recruits would do.

Jeff. Davis is on a visit to Hood at Palmetto.

W. T. SHERMAN,
Major General.

Major General H. W. HALLECK, *Washington, D. C.*

[Cipher.]

CITY POINT,
September 26, 1864—10 a. m.

Major General SHERMAN :

It will be better to drive Forrest from Middle Tennessee as a first step, and do anything else that you may feel your force sufficient for. When a movement is made on any part of the sea-coast, I will advise you. If Hood goes to the Alabama line, will it not be impossible for him to subsist his army ?

U. S. GRANT,
Lieutenant General.

[Cipher.]

HEADQUARTERS MILITARY DIVISION OF THE MISSISSIPPI.
In the field, Atlanta, Georgia, September 26, 1864.

GENERAL : I have your despatch of to-day. I have already sent one division (General Newton) to Chattanooga, and another (Corse) to Rome. Our armies are much reduced ; and if I send back much more, I will not be able to threaten Georgia much. There are men enough to the rear to whip Forrest, but they are necessarily scattered to defend the road.

Can you expedite the sending to Nashville of the recruits that are in Indiana and Ohio? They could occupy the forts. Hood is now on the West Point road, twenty-four miles south of this, and draws his supplies by that road. Jeff. Davis is there to-day, and superhuman efforts will be made to break my road. Forrest is now lieutenant general, and commands all the enemy's cavalry.

W. T. SHERMAN, *Major General.*

Lieut. General U. S. GRANT, *City Point.*

[Cipher.]

HEADQUARTERS MILITARY DIVISION OF THE MISSISSIPPI,
In the field, Atlanta, Georgia, September 26, 1864.

GENERAL: General Newton's division is now at Chattanooga, and General Corse at Rome. We can defend our roads below Bridgeport, and General Granger and the gunboats can protect those from Decatur to Stevenson. Rousseau should collect all the force he can and move straight for Pulaski and Florence. Call forward from Kentucky any troops that can be spared there, and hold all that come from the rear till Forrest is disposed of. Caution Rousseau to unite his movable force, and not let it be picked up in detail. Recruits should now be coming forward fast. Ask Rosecrans for me if he cannot spare A. J. Smith, and explain to him that he may be needed. I wanted him for this very contingency, which I foresaw. Use my name and concentrate at Nashville all the men you can. Recall Generals Steedman and Schofield if you know where they are.

The policy should be, small but well-commanded bodies in the block-houses and a movable force to act straight against Forrest, who must scatter for forage.

W. T. SHERMAN, *Major General.*

General J. D. WEBSTER, *Nashville.*

[Cipher.]

CITY POINT,
September 26, 1864—6 30 p. m.

Major General SHERMAN:

Jeff. Davis was at Richmond on last Thursday. This I think is beyond doubt. I have evidence that General Sheridan's victory has created the greatest consternation and alarm for the safety of the city. I will give them another shake before the end of the week.

U. S. GRANT, *Lieutenant General.*

[Cipher.]

HEADQUARTERS MILITARY DIVISION OF THE MISSISSIPPI,
In the field, Atlanta, Ga., September 27, 1864.

GENERAL: Jeff. Davis was certainly at Macon on the 23d, for he made a very significant speech, which is given at length, and which I ordered to be telegraphed as far as Louisville.

Forrest has burnt the bridges over Elk, near Athens, but I think General Rousseau can keep him off the Chattanooga road. Still all recruits should be sent to Nashville with despatch.

W. T. SHERMAN, *Major General.*

Lieut. General U. S. GRANT, *City Point.*

[Cipher.]

WASHINGTON, D. C.,
September 27, 1864—9 a. m.

Major General SHERMAN:

You say Jeff. Davis is on a visit to General Hood.   I judge that Brown and Stephens are the objects of his visit.

A. LINCOLN,
President United States.

[Cipher.]

CITY POINT, VIRGINIA,
September 27, 1864—8.30 a. m.

Major General SHERMAN:

It is evident from the tone of the Richmond press, and all other sources, that the enemy intend making a desperate effort to drive you from where you are. I have directed all new troops from the west, and from the east, too, if necessary, if none are ready in the west, to be sent to you. If General Burbridge is not too far on the way towards Abingdon, I think he had better be recalled, and his surplus troops sent into Tennessee.

U. S. GRANT, *Lieutenant General.*

[Cipher.]

CITY POINT, VIRGINIA,
September 27, 1864—10.30 a. m.

Major General SHERMAN :

I have directed all recruits and new troops from all the western States to be sent to Nashville to receive their further orders from you.   I was mistaken about Jeff. Davis being in Richmond on Thursday last ; he was then on his way to Macon.

U. S. GRANT, *Lieutenant General.*

[Cipher.]

HEADQUARTERS MILITARY DIVISION OF THE MISSISSIPPI,
In the field, Atlanta, Ga., September 28, 1864.

GENERAL : I will send up the road to-night another division, and want you to call forward from the rear all you can get, so as to make a movable column. Ask General Tower to take charge of the forts, and distribute the men.

Bring close in all the camps, especially those of the 13th regulars, and assign each detachment to its post.   I will send General Thomas to Stevenson to operate on Forrest's rear.

W. T. SHERMAN, *Major General.*

General J. D. WEBSTER,
Nashville, Tennessee.

HEADQUARTERS MILITARY DIVISION OF THE MISSISSIPPI,
In the field, Atlanta, Ga., September 28, 1864.

GENERAL : I have just returned from General Howard. I think that a movement of all our cavalry not actually on picket should be made rapidly on

Carrollton, to interrupt any communication from Hood's army, at Palmetto, with his cavalry over about the Tennessee. After striking Carrollton, it should move boldly up towards Hood's army, and then draw back to Sandtown.

W. T. SHERMAN,
Major General.

Major General G. H. Thomas,
 Commanding Department of the Cumberland.

[Cipher.]

Headquarters Military Division of the Mississippi,
In the field, Atlanta, Ga., September 28, 1864.

President Lincoln, *Washington, D. C.:*

I have positive knowledge that Mr. Davis made a speech at Macon on the 22d, which I mailed to General Halleck yesterday. It was bitter against Johnson and Governor Brown. The militia is on furlough. Brown is at Milledgeville, trying to get a legislature to meet next month, but he is afraid to act unless in concert with other governors. Judge Wright, of Rome, has been here, and Messrs. Hill and Nelson, former members of Congress, are also here now, and will go to meet Wright at Rome, and then go back to Madison and Milledgeville. Great efforts are being made to re-enforce Hood's army and to break up my railroad, and I should have at once a good reserve force at Nashville. It would have a bad effect if I am to be forced to send back any material part of my army to guard roads, so as to weaken me to an extent that I could not act offensively if the occasion calls for it.

W. T. SHERMAM,
Major General.

Headquarters Military Division of the Mississippi,
In the field, Atlanta, Ga., September 28, 1864.

General: Your despatch is just received. I send back to Stevenson and Decherd General Thomas to look to Tennessee, and have ordered a brigade of the army of the Tennessee up to Eastport, and the cavalry across to that place from Memphis, to operate against the flank of any force going into Tennessee by any of the fords near Florence. I want Appalachicola arsenal taken, also Savannah; and if the enemy does succeed in breaking up my roads, I can fight my way across to one or the other place; but I think it better to hold on to Atlanta and strengthen to my rear, and therefore am glad you have ordered troops to Nashville. Forrest has got into Middle Tennessee, and will, I feel certain, get on my main road to-night or to-morrow; but I will guard well from this back to Chattanooga, and trust to troops coming up from Kentucky to hold Nashville and forward to Chattanooga.

W. T. SHERMAN,
Major General.

Lieut. General U. S. Grant, *City Point.*

Headquarters Military Division of the Mississippi,
In the field, Atlanta, Ga., September 29, 1864.

General: I have your letter of September 27, and have telegraphed to St. Louis for combs, scissors, &c., and as soon as received, I will make up a train for Griffin, loaded with articles for our prisoners of war, and send it in charge of an officer, to be turned over to one of yours, with invoices complete and blank rolls for issue. I will give you notice prior to starting the train. I will see the prisoners who are in, and learn from them more minutely the wants of our men, and make the invoice accordingly, but it will not exceed the quantity before stated.

I am, with respect, &c.,

W. T. SHERMAN,
Major General.

General J. B. HOOD,
Commanding Confederate Army, Palmetto.

HEADQUARTERS MILITARY DIVISION OF THE MISSISSIPPI,
In the field, Atlanta, Ga., September 27, 1864.

SIR: Send me all the shirts, fine combs, and scissors for cutting hair, you can spare for our prisoners south. I will, on their receipt, send them out under an agreement with General Hood. I would like to get twelve hundred (1,200) fine combs and four hundred (400) scissors. Our commissary can supply soap and candles, and the quartermaster has shoes, socks, and under-clothing.

W. T. SHERMAN,
Major General.

Mr. JAMES E. YATEMAN,
Sanitary Commission, St. Louis.

HEADQUARTERS DEPARTMENT OF THE TENNESSEE,
September 29, 1864.

Major General SHERMAN:

The indications are that Hood is moving across the Chattahoochee.

O. O. HOWARD,
Major General.

HEADQUARTERS MILITARY DIVISION OF THE MISSISSIPPI,
In the field, Atlanta, Ga., September 28, 1864.

GENERAL: You cannot be too particular about Allatoona and about the Pumpkin Vine. It is reported Hood is about passing the Chattahoochee to the west, and I will watch him, and see if he will cross over to the Selma road, or try to get on to our road.

W. T. SHERMAN,
Major General.

General JOHN E. SMITH, *Cartersville.*

NEW ORLEANS,
August 29, 1864, *via Cairo, September* 9, 1864.

Major General SHERMAN:

Your despatch of the 17th has just reached me. The reduction of Fort Morgan was necessary in order to secure the ingress and egress of heavy vessels. It was handsomely done, but the fort is greatly injured. I have a reserve of twelve thousand men up the river to watch Kirby Smith. I do not think he can cross in any force without being discovered in time to prevent it, but I cannot use this force against Mobile and prevent the passage. The route you suggest has been considered, and with twenty thousand men we could control the Alabama river from Mobile to Montgomery. Major General Frederick Steele is losing a good many men by expiration of service, and I cannot draw any from him. I asked some time ago that all the troops that could be spared from the west, and were not required for your army, should be sent to Memphis. I will keep the army about Mobile uneasy, and will act against the city and river the moment I can gather a sufficient force.

E. R. S. CANBY,
Major General.

[Cipher.]

HEADQUARTERS MILITARY DIVISION OF THE MISSISSIPPI,
In the field, Atlanta, Ga., September 29, 1864.

General H. W. HALLECK, Washington, D. C. :

I have now effected the actual exchange of two thousand (2,000) prisoners of my own army. General Stoneman will be here to-morrow, and Colonel Harrison is already in. Our prisoners have been moved from Andersonville to Savannah, Millen, and Charleston; any change will be for the better. I have agreed with Hood to send to Griffin, to be forwarded to our prisoners, a supply of clothing, soap, combs, &c.; the latter will be furnished by the Sanitary Commission, and the former by the quartermaster. I take it for granted Forrest will cut our road, and I think we can prevent his making a serious lodgement; his cavalry will travel a hundred miles in less time than ours will ten. I have sent two divisions up to Chattanooga, and one to Rome, and General Thomas started to-day to clear out Tennessee, but our road should be watched from the rear, and I am glad General Grant has ordered reserves for me to Nashville. I prefer for the future to make the movement on Milledgeville, Millen, and Savannah river. Hood now rests twenty-four miles south, his left on the Chattahoochee, and his right on the West Point road. He is removing the iron of the Macon road. I can whip his infantry, but his cavalry is to be feared.

W. T. SHERMAN, Major General.

HEADQUARTERS MILITARY DIVISION OF THE MISSISSIPPI,
In the field, Atlanta, Ga., September 30, 1864.

GENERAL: I have pretty clear information that Hood has a part of his infantry across the Chattahoochee, twenty-four miles south of us, and it may be all. I know that desperate efforts will be made to render our roads useless. Forrest is in Middle Tennessee, but I think will have his hands full, for I have sent up two divisions of Thomas, and Thomas went up himself yesterday. I may have to make some quick counter moves east and southeast. Keep your folks ready to send baggage into Atlanta and to start on short notice. Make your preparations quietly without attracting any notice. There are fine corn and potato fields about Covington and the Ocmulgee bottoms. We are well supplied with bread, meat, &c., but forage is scarce and may force us to strike out. If we make a counter move I will go out myself with a large force, and take such a route as will supply us, and, at the same time, make Hood recall the whole or part of his army.

Yours, &c.,

W. T. SHERMAN,
Major General.

General Cox, Decatur, Georgia.
14 *

ROME, *September 30, 1864.*

Major General SHERMAN:

The judge is here, waiting for the two gentlemen. He reports Hood's army across the Chattahoochee—a portion at Villa Rica; all moving on Blue mountain. Their cavalry at Carrollton.

JNO. M. CORSE, *Brigadier General.*

[Cipher.]

HEADQUARTERS MILITARY DIVISION OF THE MISSISSIPPI,
In the field, Atlanta, Ga., September 30, 1864.

Major General G. H. THOMAS, *Chattanooga:*

Your despatch is received. I have notified all army commanders to stop furloughs. Give orders to keep the telegraph line *via* Knoxville and Cumberland Gap in good order. There is no doubt some of Hood's infantry is across the Chattahoochee, but I don't think his whole army is across. If he moves his whole force to Blue mountain, you watch him from the direction of Stevenson, and I will do the same from Rome, and as soon as all things are ready I will take advantage of his opening to me all of Georgia.

W. T. SHERMAN, *Major General.*

MARIETTA, *September 30, 1864.*

Major General SHERMAN:

Deserters and citizens report the following: Hood with his army in three columns crossed the Chattahoochee on Sunday last at Campbellton, and above and below. Citizens on their line of march told them that the soldiers (rebel) said they were going to Rome. I have sent scouts in that direction, and will soon hear from there. All quiet here.

J. McARTHUR, *Brigadier General.*

[Cipher.]

CHATTANOOGA, *September 30, 1864.*

Major General SHERMAN:

My latest news up to 10 a. m. is, that Forrest was at Lynchburg, and Milroy's scouts reported that they heard some of Forrest's officers say that they would attack the Nashville and Chattanooga railroad to-day, and destroy it north as they did the other. I am getting Morgan's troops arranged, and hope he will reach there to-night. If Forrest does not break the road to-day, I hope it will be secure by to-night. Granger's information confirms Milroy's as to Forrest's position last night. I have heard from Rousseau at Wartrace; his cavalry to his front and right observing Forrest's movements. He also reports Forrest at Lynchburg, (Lynville.)

GEO. H. THOMAS, *Major General.*

[Cipher.]

HEADQUARTERS MILITARY DIVISION OF THE MISSISSIPPI,
In the field, Atlanta, Ga., September 30, 1864.

GENERAL: I have yours and Rousseau's despatches. Try and make a junction with Rousseau. I suppose Forrest will manage to break the road to-night; but leave defensive garrisons, and push right at him with as heavy a force as you can get, and as soon as possible. He won't fight, but infantry can dog him. Take provisions and forage of the towns and people, and replace them after the work is done. If you can turn him towards Lamb's Ferry, Granger should make a redoubt, covering the ford, and hold him in check until the infantry can get up. We will never have a better chance at him than now. I will watch Hood here.

W. T. SHERMAN,
Major General.

General G. H. THOMAS,
 Chattanooga, Tennessee.

HEADQUARTERS DEPARTMENT OF THE TENNESSEE,
October 1, 1864.

Major General SHERMAN:
 The following just received.

O. O. HOWARD,
Major General.

" MEMPHIS, September 28, 1864.

" Forrest made a speech at Tupelo on the 16th instant, and told his men he was going to Middle Tennessee to operate on Sherman's communications, and promised that he would compel Sherman to evacuate Georgia within sixty days; also promised all the horses they wanted. On the 20th he was at Cherokee, near the Tennessee, with most of his command. He probably has about five thousand (5,000) men. A small force has crossed the Tennessee lower down. Staff officer from you has not arrived. The information in regard to Forrest is entirely reliable. You are aware, I suppose, that I am now weak. All the 16th corps has gone, the one-hundred-day-men gone, and nearly half of my cavalry sent after Price and Shelby, and one regiment to St. Louis.

" C. C. WASHBURNE,
" Major General."

[Cipher.]

HEADQUARTERS MILITARY DIVISION OF THE MISSISSIPPI,
In the field, Atlanta, Ga., October 1, 1864.

General G. H. THOMAS, *Chattanooga:*

Hood has evidently crossed the Chattahoochee to the west, but has not gone to Blue mountain. Kilpatrick, on the Sweetwater, reports he could hear drums at reveille. There is too much ostentation in this move of Hood's, and he may attemp to swing his cavalry on our road. I have ordered General Garrard over to Powder Springs. I will watch him close. Make as quick work with Forrest as you can, and get back to co-operate with me.

W. T. SHERMAN,
Major General.

[Cipher.]

CHATTANOOGA, October 1, 1864—12 m.

Major General SHERMAN:
 General Granger reported last evening from Huntsville that the enemy had appeared before Huntsville, and had demanded the surrender of the town. He had no doubt but that he could hold the place, but asked for re-enforcements, as he

did not have force enough to assume the offensive. I have sent General Morgan's division to him this morning. I hear from General Rousseau, who says he has sent General Milroy with Calver's brigade to Decherd with instructions to send out cavalry scouts, and to report promptly anything of interest. Main cavalry force has been ordered to Winchester, with instructions to push out scouting parties on all roads west of railroad. From the best information, he does not believe the enemy is in the vicinity of Tullahoma or Decherd. The operator at Decherd reports an engine in from the tunnel, and all is quiet there. No excitement and no signs of the enemy. The indications are that the road is clear to Nashville. I am just about sending out a construction train for Nashville to test the road, and see if all is right. I will start the trains through again.

GEORGE H. THOMAS, Major General.

[Cipher.]

HEADQUARTERS MILITARY DIVISION OF THE MISSISSIPPI,
In the field, Atlanta, Ga., October 1, 1864.

Lieutenant General U. S. GRANT, City Point:

Hood is evidently on the west side of Chattahoochee, below Sweetwater. If he tries to get on my road this side of the Etowah I shall attack him; but if he goes on to the Selma and Talladega road, why would it not do for me to leave Tennessee to the forces which Thomas has, and the reserves soon to come to Nashville, and for me to destroy Atlanta, and then march across Georgia to Savannah or Charleston, breaking roads and doing irreparable damage? We cannot remain on the defensive.

W. T. SHERMAN, Major General.

[Cipher.]

HEADQUARTRES MILITARY DIVISION OF THE MISSISSIPPI,
In the field, Atlanta, Ga., October 1, 1864.

Generals HOWARD and COX:

I have not yet heard from General Grant as to my proposed campaign; but it is well for you to bear in mind that if Hood swings over to the Alabama road, and thence tries to get into Tennessee, I may throw back to Chattanooga all of General Thomas's men as far down as Kingston, and draw forward all else, send back all cars and locomotives, destroy Atlanta, and make for Savannah or Charleston, via Milledgeville and Millen. If Hood aims at our road this side of Kingston, and in no manner threatens Tennessee, I will have to turn on him.

Keep these things to yourselves. The march I propose is less by two hundred (200) miles than I made last fall, and less than I accomplished in February, and we could make Georgia a break in the confederacy by ruining both east and west roads, and not running against a single fort until we get to the sea-shore and in communication with our ships.

W. T. SHERMAN,
Major General Commanding.

[Cipher.]

HEADQUARTERS MILITARY DIVISION OF THE MISSISSIPPI,
In the field, Atlanta, Ga., October 1, 1864—2 p. m.

General G. H. THOMAS, Chattanooga:

I have your despatch of noon. Use your own discretion as to the matters north of the Tennessee river. If I can induce Hood to swing across to Blue mountian, I shall feel tempted to start for Milledgeville, Millen, and Savannah or Charleston, absolutely destroying all Georgia, and taking either Savannah or Charleston. In that event I would order back to Chattanooga everything the other side of Kingston, and bring forward all else, destroy Atlanta and the bridge, and absolutely scour the southern confederacy. In that event Hood would be puzzled, and would follow me; or if he entered Tennessee, he could make no permanent stay. But if he attempts the road this side of Kingston or Rome, I will turn against him. Forrest will not attack our forts—that is manifest—but will try and get possession of Decatur. All the infantry and cavalry not in forts or block-houses should be directed against him by roads— say the Shelbyville pike and Fayetteville.

W. T. SHERMAN,
Major General.

HEADQUARTERS MILITARY DIVISION OF THE MISSISSIPPI,
In the field, Atlanta, Ga., October 1, 1864.

General CORSE, Rome:

General Hood has evidently crossed a part, if not the whole, of his army across to the west bank of the Chattahoochee, below Sweetwater. His soldiers think he is going for Blue mountain; I think not. He may attempt to get on our road this side of Allatoona or near Cassville. If at the latter, hold fast. If you hear of him this side of Allatoona, leave a small force to guard the bridge across Oostanaula, and join your forces to General John E. Smith's, and act against Hood from Allatoona. I will employ him from this quarter. He cannot tarry long, and will expose his flanks and trains, which should be harassed. We have more than a month's provisions, and a large well-appointed army, and can operate from this point. General Grant has ordered large reserves to Nashville, and General Thomas is there to manage them.

W. T. SHERMAN,
Major General Commanding.

HEADQUARTERS MILITARY DIVISION OF THE MISSISSIPPI,
In the field, Atlanta, Ga., October 2, 1864.

Major General HOWARD:

To-morrow General Garrard will feel well out beyond Powder Springs, and I want Ransom to develop the nature of the force at Shadna. Tell him to use his skirmish line and supports in front, and feel the flank towards the west as though interposing between Shadna and the river. General Cox will have a division down to Flat Rock. General Thomas reported to-day that Forrest had made his appearance at Huntsville, and he had sent General Morgan's division there. The road and telegraph to Nashville in good order yet.

W. T. SHERMAN,
Major General.

HEADQUARTERS MILITARY DIVISION OF THE MISSISSIPPI,
In the field, Atlanta, Ga., October 2, 1864.

Major General HOWARD, Commanding Army of the Tennessee:

There is a flood in the Chattahoochee, which has damaged our railroad bridge, and will of course carry away any of Hood's bridges. I want that reconnoissance pushed out boldly. As soon as it reaches Fairburn let me know, as I may push it on to the rear of their bridge. All the valuable part of the enemy's cavalry is over beyond Sweetwater, and we can do them damage on this side now. The same cause which produced the rise in the Chattahoochee will affect the Tennessee, and Forrest will be in danger with a swollen river to his rear.

W. T. SHERMAN, Major General.

MARIETTA, October 2, 1864—4 p. m.

Major General SHERMAN :

Rebels driven off and quiet restored ; have three cars burned ; road being repaired ; casualties not yet reported. Citizens, coming in for protection, report that Hood was to encamp near Grey's mills to-night. They also report that an attack will be made on Ackworth or Allatoona ; afterwards Rome. In the event of a repulse they will report by Blue mountain, Jacksonville, and Selma.

J. McARTHUR,
Brigadier General.

HEADQUARTERS MILITARY DIVISION OF THE MISSISSIPPI,
In the field, Atlanta, Ga., October 2, 1864.

General HOWARD, Present :

Let Ransom come in slowly; and if the enemy approach, sally out and attack him fiercely.

General Davis will be in close support. I will then throw General Stanley across the Chattahoochee, and be prepared to put our whole force in motion, to interpose between Hood (who may attempt to mash our road about Marietta) and his bridges at Campbellton. Be prepared to send in all your trains to Atlanta, and to follow General Stanley. I would attack this corps in position, but presume it is strongly intrenched.

I am, &c.,

W .T. SHERMAN, Major General.

HEADQUARTERS MILITARY DIVISION OF THE MISSISSIPPI,
In the field, Atlanta, Ga., October 2, 1864.

General D. S. STANLEY :

Move your command, with orders for your wagons to follow with ten (10) days' rations, to Chattahoochee bridge, and in the direction of Marietta as far as the rebel intrenchments about Smyrna camp-ground. Open communication with General Elliott, who is over towards the Sweetwater and Nose's creek, and communicate with me promptly all matters of importance by telegraph from the bridge.

W. T. SHERMAN, Major General.

HEADQUARTERS MILITARY DIVISION OF THE MISSISSIPPI,
In the field, Atlanta, Ga., October 2, 1864.

General Cox, Decatur, Georgia :

Make all preparations to send into Atlanta tents and baggage and to start for Chattahoochee bridge on short notice. Send word and recall that division at Flat Rock. Hood has evidently crossed the Chattahoochee with two corps, and left one on this side of the Chattahoochee river, near Campbellton. I propose to attack the force on the other side.

W. T. SHERMAN, Major General.

HEADQUARTERS MILITARY DIVISION OF THE MISSISSIPPI,
In the field, Atlanta, Ga., October 3, 1864.

Major Gen. JEFF. C. DAVIS, *Comm'dg 14th Corps, near Atlanta:*

Move your two (2) divisions by the nearest practicable route to the railroad bridge, cross above, and move on the left of General Stanley, about the old rebel line at Smyrna camp-ground, or Ruff's Station, looking to the west. If the reconnoissance in progress to-day confirms present appearances, we will have to strike the enemy over between that point and Dallas. Have your wagons to follow you only to the old rebel lines west of the bridge. Cross your men ahead of General Stanley's wagons, but his wagons will have precedence of yours. General Stanley passed here about 7 a. m.

W. T. SHERMAN,
Major General.

HEADQUARTERS MILITARY DIVISION OF THE MISSISSIPPI,
In the field, Atlanta, Ga., October 3, 1864.

General CORSE, *Rome:*

Hood is meditating some plan on a large scale. One corps is intrenched below Cambellton and two corps are across below Sweetwater, about Powder Springs. I send Generals Stanley and Davis over to-day, and may follow to-morrow myself with a heavy force. I am willing he should go to Blue mountain, or to strike our road at Ackworth or Cassville.

W. T. SHERMAN,
Major General.

HEADQUARTERS MILITARY DIVISION OF THE MISSISSPPI,
In the field, Atlanta, Ga., October 3, 1864.

Major General O. O. HOWARD, *East Point:*

March your command to-morrow to Ruff's Station, towards Marietta. Do you know if Kilpatrick's dismounted men have come in from Sandtown? If not, send them word to come into Atlanta. Please answer.

W. T. SHERMAN,
Major General.

[Cipher.]

NASHVILLE, *October 3, 1864.*

Major General SHERMAN:

I reached this place at 2 p. m. to-day, and found that Rousseau had organized and despatched his troops down the Alabama road as far as Franklin, and will continue after Forrest until he overtakes him, if Forrest does not cross the river before he reaches him. Major General Washburne is coming up the Tennessee river with ten thousand (10,000) cavalry and fifteen hundred (1,500) infantry. He was directed by Webster, before my arrival, to land his infantry at Johnsonville, to aid in the protection of the depot there, and to proceed up the river to Clifton (Fort Valley) with his cavalry, and move towards Athens for the purpose of striking Forrest's flank or cutting off his communication with Burbridge. General Morgan, as I despatched you last night, is moving from Athens upon Bainbridge; so it appears to me there is a fair chance of hemming Forrest in and destroying his command. The river is not fordable, and if we seize his means of crossing at Bainbridge he will be unable to cross anywhere else, and I think

Rousseau ought certainly to destroy him. Two Ohio and three Kentucky regiments of the re-enforcemenets have arrived and are being distributed along the railroad.

GEORGE H. THOMAS,
Major General.

HEADQUARTERS MILITARY DIVISION OF THE MISSISSIPPI,
In the field, Atlanta, Ga., October 3, 1864.

COMMANDING OFFICER, Allatoona:

Hood has some infantry and cavalry about Powder Springs. I am watching him close. He might deceive us by his cavalry along Nose's creek, and slip up to Ackworth and Allatoona. I want the utmost vigilance there. If he go for Allatoona, I want him delayed only long enough for me to reach his rear. Of course, his cavalry can only run across the road and bother us, but his infantry would try to capture stores, without which Hood cannot stay where he is. If he moves up toward Allatoona I will surely come in force.

W. T. SHERMAN,
Major General.

[Cipher.]
CITY POINT, VA., October 4, 1864—11.30 a. m.

Major General SHERMAN:

General Wilson has been ordered to report to you; and that he may have rank to command your cavalry, I have asked that he be brevetted a major general and assigned with that rank. I believe Wilson will add fifty (50) per cent. to the effectiveness of your cavalry.

U. S. GRANT,
Lieutenant General.

HEADQUARTERS MILITARY DIVISION OF THE MISSISSIPPI,
In the field, Smyrna Camp Ground, October 4, 1864.

General SLOCUM, Atlanta:

I have reason to believe Wheeler is on our road above Resaca. Hood's main army is between me and Allatoona. I shall attack the latter in force, but advise you to work night and day in perfecting those intrenchments and in economizing provisions; but if I live, you may count upon my coming to your rescue. The point of greatest danger is the bridge; therefore, look to it. Please answer.

W. T. SHERMAN,
Major General.

NEAR KENESAW, October, 4, 1864.

Major General SHERMAN:

Just received the following:

" MARIETTA AND DALLAS ROAD,
"On branch to Big Shanty, October 4, 1864.

" General VAN DEVER:

"I found the enemy occupying our old line of works to the railroad in more force than dismounted cavalry can dislodge from them. I cover the Dallas road. All my information leads me to believe that there is a large force of infantry with cavalry. Please communicate this to Generals Sherman and Stanley.

"W. L. ELLIOTT."

WM. VAN DEVER,
Brigadier General.

NEAR KENESAW, *October 4, 1864.*

Major General SHERMAN:

Stanley at Marietta. The enemy in strong force in my front all the morning. This afternoon he moved off to Allatoona. General Elliott reports him in too strong force for dismounted cavalry. Prisoners say the force in my front was French's division. From top of Kenesaw heavy bodies of infantry, artillery, and cavalry could be seen going north. The movement to my right was a feint. My headquarters at foot of Kenesaw; a part of the command occupying the ridge north.

WM. VAN DEVER,
Brigadier General.

LITTLE KENESAW MOUNTAIN,
October 4, 1864.

Major General SHERMAN:

We arrived here at 3.30 p. m., and have camped in the old rebel works in the vicinlty and south of Little Kenesaw. From top of the mountain I could see the rebel troops burning the road, all of which has been reported to you from other sources. Prisoners sent in by General Elliott report that they still have six (6) days' rations. They say Stewart's corps is burning the road, and Hardee and Lee's corps are in the vicinity of Pine mountain.

D. S. STANLEY,
Major General.

KENESAW MOUNTAIN, *October 5, 1864.*

Official to Major General SHERMAN:

The enemy in heavy force have moved north to Allatoona—infantry, cavalry, and artillery. Our cavalry advance is two (2) miles in his rear.

WM. VAN DEVER,
Brigadier General.

Received Signal Station, Vining's hill.

A. S. COLE, *Captain and A. S. O.*

HEADQUARTERS MILITARY DIVISION OF THE MISSISSIPPI,
In the field, near Marietta, October 5, 1864.

General ELLIOTT:

I have heard from Allatoona. All right. General Corse is there, but wounded. You need not send all of General Garrard's cavalry, but send a squadron. Let them make a circuit, and they will find nothing there.

W. T. SHERMAN,
Major General.

WIDOW ORR'S, ON ACKWORTH ROAD,
October 6, 1864—2 p. m.

Major General SHERMAN:

Your despatch is received. I have information, which seems reliable, that the enemy went back yesterday. We find no signs of them, except that a few scouts were here this morning. My advance, near Mount Olivet church, finds nothing more than here. The roads this side of Pine mountain are in places almost impassable, having evidently grown no better since we left in June. This has delayed me, as the artillery can scarcely get forward at all. I leave a brigade with the weak teams, and push on with the rest. Will observe your directions as to signals. Please send me word whether I shall endeavor to get my teams up as far as I go, or whether we shall calculate upon returning by same route.

J. D. COX, Brigadier General.

[Signal.]

HEADQUARTERS MILITARY DIVISION OF THE MISSISSIPPI,
In the field, Kenesaw, October 6, 1864.

General CORSE, Allatoona:

Let the Rome force return at once to Rome and protect the road. I will cover Allatoona.

W. T. SHERMAN, Major General.

ALLATOONA, GA., October 6, 1864—2 p. m.

Captain L. M. DAYTON, A. D. C.:

I am short a cheek-bone and one ear, but am able to whip all hell yet. My losses are very heavy. A force moving from Stilesboro' on Kingston gives me some anxiety. Tell me where Sherman is.

JOHN M. CORSE,
Brigadier General.

[Signal.]

HEADQUARTERS MILITARY DIVISION OF THE MISSISSIPPI,
In the field, Kenesaw, October 6, 1864.

General CORSE, Allatoona:

Am just in. Am very sorry at your wound, but all is right with you. If possible keep the enemy off your lines, and let me know at once what force you have, and what is at Kingston and Rome; also signal some account of your fight. Hood has retreated to Dallas.

W. T. SHERMAN, Major General.

NEAR NEW HOPE CHURCH, October 7, 1864.

Major General SHERMAN:

General Garrard near New Hope church 11.30 a. m., skirmishing with rear. Armstrong camped where he then was, and French's division at church. Can't tell route taken; rumor says Dallas; citizens tell conflicting stories. Can't determine anything. Captured General Steele and a colonel wounded. A few prisoners.

W. L. ELLIOTT,
Brigadier General, &c.

HEADQUARTERS MILITARY DIVISION OF THE MISSISSIPPI,
In the field, Kenesaw, October 7, 1864.

General CORSE, *Allatoona :*

I received your report. I have so high an appreciation of your services and those of your command, as also that of Colonel Tourtellotte and garrison, that I shall make the defence of Allatoona the subject of a general order.

I will move my army one step north to-morrow, and want you to exercise a general care over the operations from Allatoona as far as Kingston. I will so place my command that in one day's work they will replace all the ties burned between Allatoona and Kenesaw, and leave the laying of the iron to the construction party. We have two million seven hundred thousand (2,700,000) rations of bread in Allatoona, and can afford to await repairs. My infantry is now near Dallas, and cavalry must be below it. General Garrard passed New Hope before noon, and General Kilpatrick at Powder Springs at 11½ a. m. Both are ordered to push the enemy and develop his route of movement. He is already too far south to make the Etowah bridge *via* Stilesboro'. Still too much care cannot be exercised. General John E. Smith should be down, and I will be much obliged if you can send to Generals Thomas and Webster notice that Allatoona is safe in our possession, the new and contracted line finished and ready for defence, so that General Slocum can hold it against Hood's whole army. The bridge across the Chattahoochee, which was carried away by the freshet, will be done by to-morrow, and I will put ten thousand (10,000) men at work at once to replace the ties burned by the enemy, thirty-five thousand (35,000,) and have the road ready for the iron by the time the construction train comes from the north. I almost share the pain of your wound with you, but you know for quick work I cannot get along without you, and ask you, spite of pain, to keep your head clear and leave others to do your bidding. Your presence alone saved to us Allatoona the day before yesterday, but this does not detract from the merit of the others. Keep me well advised, for I now think Hood will rather swing against Atlanta and the Chattahoochee bridge than against Kingston and the Etowah bridge ; but he is eccentric, and I cannot guess his movements as I could those of Johnston, who was a sensible man and only did sensible things. If Hood does not mind I will catch him in a worse snap than he has been in yet. Rome is of no value at all save as a flank. Destroy its bridges and factories on the slightest provocation, and cover the vital points of our road.

W. T. SHERMAN.
Major General Commanding.

HEADQUARTERS MILITARY DIVISION OF THE MISSISSIPPI,
In the field, Kenesaw, October 7, 1864.

General COX :

Call in all your detachments, save the one at Allatoona, and be prepared for a march. When all reports are in, say about midnight, will send you orders.

W. T. SHERMAN,
Major General Commanding.

HEADQUARTERS MILITARY DIVISION OF THE MISSISSIPPI,
In the field, Kenesaw, October 7, 1864.

General HOWARD :

Don't move until further orders. I await further information from our cavalry.

W. T. SHERMAN,
Major General Commanding.

ATLANTA, *October 7, 1864.*

Major General SHERMAN :

Everything is perfectly quiet here ; the bridge will be finished to night.   Are you willing I should send a strong foraging party northeast ?   I think it can be safely done.

H. W. SLOCUM,
Major General.

ROME, GA., *October 9, 1864.*

Major General SHERMAN :

Your despatch to General Raum and myself, signed Dayton, is just received· The bridges across the Etowah have been effectually destroyed yesterday evening.   All intelligence I have indicates that Hood has not gone to Cedartown.

I have just finished a new pontoon bridge over the Etowah, and have sent a cavalry force to reconnoitre towards Cedartown   I have my flanks and front well patrolled, and can give you more information to-morrow.

JOHN M. CORSE,
Brigadier General.

[Cipher.]

HEADQUARTERS MILITARY DIVISION OF THE MISSISSIPPI,
In the field, Allatoona, October 9, 1864.

Major General HALLECK :

General Hood crossed the Chattahoochee, and before I was convinced of his designs he had got across to Powder Spring.   I immediately resolved to leave the 20th corps, General Slocum's, at Atlanta, and push for Marietta.   I reached the Kenesaw mountain October 6, just in time to witness at a distance the attack on Allatoona.   I had anticipated this attack, and had ordered from Rome General Corse, with re-enforcements, and the attack was met and handsomely repulsed, the enemy losing some two hundred (200) dead, and more than one thousand (1,000) wounded and prisoners.   Our loss about seven hundred (700) in the aggregate.   The enemy captured the small garrison at Big Shanty and Ackworth, and burned about seven (7) miles of our railroad, but we have at Allatoona and Atlanta an abundance of provisions.   Hood observing our approach, has moved rapidly back to Dallas and Van Wert, and I am watching him in case he tries to reach Kingston or Rome.   Atlanta is perfectly secure to us, and the army is better off out here than in camp.

W. T. SHERMAN,
Major General.

CARTERSVILLE, GA., *October 9, 1864.*

Captain L. M. DAYTON, *A. D. C.:*

A despatch just received from Resaca states that one thousand (1,000) rebel cavalry are between Villanow and Snake Creek Gap, and one hundred (100) guarding the Gap. Information received from citizens.   A train was run off track near Dalton to-night—I suppose a construction train sent down to convey crossties to Ackworth.

G. B. RAUM,
Brevet Brigadier General.

HEADQUARTERS MILITARY DIVISION OF THE MISSISSIPPI,
In the field, Allatoona, October, 9, 1864.

General CORSE, *Rome:*

I am now here, and have troops so disposed that I can move them rapidly to Rome or Kingston, if needed, but I do not wish to move them further to the rear. We have plenty of forage and provisions, and can repair the road long before our necessities call for more supplies.

Keep scouts and spies well out about Cedartown and Centre, and give me notice of Hood's movements. If he goes to Blue mountain, let him go.

W. T. SHERMAN,
Major General Commanding.

ROME, *October 9, 1864—7.30 p. m.*

Major General SHERMAN :

Your despatch received. The only indication of an enemy since my arrival here being the appearance of a cavalry force at Reynolds's ford, near Kingston. I am ready to fly there in case they should attempt a crossing. I promise to keep you advised of anything transpiring west of Kingston ; I can hardly say so much of the country around Canton.

JOHN M. CORSE,
Brigadier General.

[Cipher.]

HEADQUARTERS MILITARY DIVISION OF THE MISSISSIPPI,
In the field, Allatoona, October 9, 1864.

Major General THOMAS, *Nashville:*

I came up here to relieve our road. 20th corps at Atlanta. Hood reached our road and broke it up between Big Shanty and Ackworth, and attacked Allatoona, but was repulsed. We have plenty of bread and meat, but forage scarcer. I want to destroy all the road below Chattanooga, including Atlanta, and make for the sea-coast. We cannot defend this long line of road. Replace all the guards on the road down as far as Chattanooga, and have a reserve force for the defence of Tennessee, and bring back your divisions of Newton and Morgan. We can have the road repaired in a week, and have plenty of grub in the mean time, but I expect Hood will make a break at Kingston, Rome, or some other point soon. Sorry that Forrest escaped. I doubt the necessity of repairing the road about Elk river and Athens, and suggest that you wait before giving orders for repairs.

W. T. SHERMAN,
Major General Commanding.

[Cipher.]

HEADQUARTERS MILITARY DIVISION OF THE MISSISSIPPI,
In the field, Allatoona, Ga., October 9, 1864.

Lieut. General GRANT, *City Point, Va.:*

It will be a physical impossibility to protect the roads, now that Hood, Forrest, Wheeler, and the whole batch of devils, are turned loose without home or habitation. I think Hood's movements indicate a diversion to the end of the Selma and Talladega railroad, at Blue mountain, about sixty (60) miles southwest of Rome, from which he will threaten Kingston, Bridgeport, and Decatur, Alabama.

I propose that we break up the railroad from Chattanooga, and strike out with wagons for Milledgeville, Millen, and Savannah. Until we can repopulate Georgia it is useless to occupy it, but the utter destruction of its roads, houses, and people will cripple their military resources. By attempting to hold the roads we will lose a thousand men monthly, and will gain no result. I can make the march and make Georgia howl. We have over eight thousand (8,000) cattle and three million rations of bread, but no corn, but we can forage in the interior of the State.

W. T. SHERMAN,
Major General Commanding.

ROME, GA., October 10, 1864.

Major General SHERMAN:

I have two (2) pontoon bridges—one across the Etowah, leading south, and one across the Oostanaula, leading west. I use the one across the Oostanaula to pass my infantry and cavalry pickets and patrols. I will push my cavalry out west and feel for the enemy strong. Upon their return I will have the bridge taken up at midnight and move it up into town, unless you think otherwise and order to the contrary. Then I will destroy it at once. Further information by an escaped prisoner indicates that Hood is crossing the Coosa with his whole army. Hood's headquarters at present are at Cave Springs.

JOHN M. CORSE,
Brigadier General.

HEADQUARTERS MILITARY DIVISION OF THE MISSISSIPPI,
In the field, Allatoona, October 10, 1864.

GENERAL: My last accounts put the enemy about Cedartown, and it is prudent we should be near him. You may march your army, embracing all detachments and wagons, to and beyond Cartersville, and in case of Kingston being threatened you will hasten to that place, but not beyond without other orders. The other armies will follow provided we get intelligence that makes it proper and necessary.

Yours, &c.,

W. T. SHERMAN,
Major General Commanding.

General Cox, Com'dg Army of the Ohio.

[Cipher.]

HEADQUARTERS MILITARY DIVISION OF THE MISSISSIPPI,
In the field, Allatoona, October 10, 1864.

General J. D. WEBSTER, Nashville:

I want all the recruits that arrive to be distributed to the three (3) armies in just proportion—say one-half to the Cumberland and one-quarter to each of the Tennessee and Ohio. New regiments may guard roads, but should be kept near Nashville—that is, above the post of Stevenson and Pulaski—so as to be easily united into a good reserve force in case I leave Tennessee to itself and push for the sea. I have now beef and bread enough, but want to repair roads so as to send my sick and wounded back. Hood is near Cedartown, south of Rome, and my impression is he will rendezvous at Blue mountain, the end of the Selma and Talladega road. He may strike at Kingston or Rome, or even go up towards Bridgeport or Stevenson, but I rather think he will hang on our flanks as a threat. I will stay about here and Kingston till our road is finished or until Hood develops his game.

W. T. SHERMAN,
Major General.

HEADQUARTERS MILITARY DIVISION OF THE MISSISSIPPI,
In the field, Cartersville, October 10, 1864.

General CORSE, *Rome:*

Get your men into the strongest forts and hold them. All my army is marching hard, straight for Rome. The 23d corps is now near Cassville, and I will make the others march to-night. Is not the Oostanaula too deep to be forded? I doubt if Hood will put his army on this side the Oostanaula.

W. T. SHERMAN,
Major General Commanding.

CARTERSVILLE, *October* 10, 1864.

Captain L. M. DAYTON, *A. D. C.:*

Order the armies of the Cumberland and Tennessee to Kingston with trains; the former to leave the details to repair the railroad, and the latter to bring along fifteen hundred (1,500) head of cattle, to march well into the night, and aim to reach Kingston to-morrow. If any column on the march overtakes the rear of either, to take a road so as to pass round. Bring our headquarters to this place. Also order the cavalry to move to Kingston or Rome.

W. T. SHERMAN,
Major General.

ROME, GA., *October* 10, 1864—6.25 a. m.

Major General SHERMAN:

Negro just from Coosaville reports Hood crossing his army by pontoon bridges to west bank of Coosa. His pontoon trains arrived there last night about dark. Negro says infantry, artillery, and cavalry have all passed over it during the night. He thinks from what he can learn that they are coming to Rome. The prisoners captured say they are going to Kentucky, smashing our road as they go.

JOHN M. CORSE,
Brigadier General.

ROME, GA., *October* 10, 1864.

Major General SHERMAN:

My spies and deserters report the following, which is corroborated in different ways: Hood arrived at Cedartown yesterday morning early, and remained till 12 m., cooking two days' rations. Commenced crossing on two pontoon bridges at Coosaville at daylight this morning. Wheeler crossed one-half his forces first, followed by Lee's corps and Hardee, leaving Stewart's and the balance of Wheeler's to cross to-morrow morning. Their destination is Huntsville, &c. They are to attack Rome at daylight, squelch me and get the stores; then continue the journey. I have had men and women in and through their camps to-day. They have various reports, some of which I will report. All headquarters transportation was sent to Blue mountain. The object of the trip is recruits from Tennessee. They number ten thousand (10,000) cavalry and thirty thousand (30,000) infantry. They had twenty (20) days' rations when they left the Chattahoochee. I will hold them as long as men can stand and guns can shoot. They have pushed their forces up against my pickets to night and are quite close. I will look to you for help and keep you advised. Have sent a few men to guide Garrard through.

JOHN M. CORSE,
Brigadier General.

HEADQUARTERS MILITARY DIVISION OF THE MISSISSIPPI,
In the field, Cartersville, Ga., October 10, 1864.

General CORSE, Rome:

Forrest has been driven out of Tennessee by way of Florence. Hood will hear of this and will not venture to attack you or to push up towards Lafayette. Still be all ready, and I will hurry up my men as fast as they can march.

W. T. SHERMAN,
Major General Commanding.

[Cipher.]

HEADQUARTERS MILITARY DIVISION OF THE MISSISSIPPI,
In the field, Cartersville, October 10, 1864.

General GRANT, City Point:

Despatch about Wilson just received. Hood is now crossing Coosa twelve (12) miles below Rome, bound west. If he passes over to the Mobile and Ohio road, had I not better execute the plan of my letter sent by Colonel Porter, and leave General Thomas with the troops now in Tennessee to defend the State? He will have an ample force when the re-enforcements ordered reach Nashville.

W. T. SHERMAN,
Major General Commanding.

[Cipher.]

HEADQUARTERS MILITARY DIVISION OF THE MISSISSIPPI,
In the field, Cartersville, October 10, 1864.

General THOMAS, Nashville:

Hood has crossed the Coosa below Rome, and is now threatening that place. I am also marching for it. Collect all your command at some converging place, say Stevenson, and be prepared for anything. If he turns to Chattanooga, I will follow; but if he shoots off towards Tuscumbia, I will act according to my information of your strength. Call in all troops within your reach.

W. T. SHERMAN,
Major General.

[Cipher.]

NASHVILLE, October 10, 1864—12.30 p. m.

Major General SHERMAN:

Your despatches of 12 m. and 5 p. m. have been received. I cannot say positively that I can hold Hood with the present force I have and the re-enforcements expected, because I do not know how many re-enforcements are coming.

I will do my best, however, and, as you direct, will concentrate the infantry force about Stevenson and Huntsville, leaving a portion of the cavalry to watch the river between Decatur and Eastport. Have you given orders to Washburne, or am I to issue orders to him; and if under my command, where would you prefer that I should place his troops ?

GEO. H. THOMAS,
Major General.

HEADQUARTERS MILITARY DIVISION OF THE MISSISSIPPI,
In the field, Cartersville, Ga., October 10, 1864—4.5 p. m.

General CORSE, *Rome:*

I am glad you have two bridges. Take up the one over the Oostanaula at the last moment of safety, and keep it, for I will want to use it. Hood would have attacked you before this if he intended to, for he must know I am near you. His cavalry at the Pumpkin Vine knew we were marching through the Pass. Watch his movements close, and I think he will only throw a force towards Rome, to cover his movement either over towards the Tennessee or back to Georgia. Look out for our cavalry south of the Etowah at daylight. To get at Rome he must cross the Oostanaula again, and that will take him a whole day, and that will give me all the time I ask. I do not think he will attack Rome.

W. T. SHERMAN,
Major General.

[Cipher.]

HEADQUARTERS MILITARY DIVISION OF THE MISSISSIPPI,
In the field, Kingston, October 11, 1864—9.30 a. m.

General THOMAS, *Nashville:*

Your despatch is just received. General Corse telegraphs that all is quiet at Rome, and he thinks the enemy gone, but don't know where. I will find out. If he goes back, of course I will also. If he goes to Blue mountain, I will remain here a short time. If he sends up towards Resaca or Lafayette, I will cut in behind from Rome. The bridges from Resaca to Atlanta are all down, and we can repair the break at Big Shanty in four (4) days.

W. T. SHERMAN,
Major General.

HEADQUARTERS MILITARY DIVISION OF THE MISSISSIPPI,
In the field, Kingston, October 11, 1864—10 a. m.

COMMANDING OFFICER, *Resaca :*

In case you are threatened you should concentrate your force at the forts at the bridge. Have abatis made at once on the land side. Keep a strong cavalry picket at Snake Creek Gap. As long as the Oostanaula is high, the troops at Adairsville and Calhoun should go to Resaca.

W. T. SHERMAN,
Major General.

15*

[Cipher.]

HEADQUARTERS MILITARY DIVISION OF THE MISSISSIPPI,
In the field, Kingston, October 11, 1864—10 a. m.

Lieut. General GRANT, *City Point, Va.:*

Hood moved his army from Pametto Station across by Dallas and Cedartown, and is now on the Coosa river south of Rome. He threw one corps on my road at Ackworth, and I was forced to follow. I hold Atlanta with the 20th corps, and have strong detachments along my line. These reduce my active force to a comparative small army. We cannot remain now on the defensive. With twenty-five thousand (25,000) men and the bold cavalry he has, he can constantly break my road. I would infinitely prefer to make a wreck of the road and of the country from Chattanooga to Atlanta, including the latter city, send back all my wounded and worthless, and with my effective army move through Georgia, smashing things to the sea. Hood may turn into Tennessee and Kentucky, but I believe he will be forced to follow me. Instead of being on the defensive, I would be on the offensive. Instead of guessing at what he means to do, he would have to guess at my plans. The difference in war is full twenty-five (25) per cent. I can make Savannah, Charleston, or the mouth of the Chattahoochee, (Appalachicola.) Answer quick, as I know we will not have the telegraph long.

W. T. SHERMAN,
Major General Commanding.

HEADQUARTERS MILITARY DIVISION OF THE MISSISSIPPI,
In the field, Kingston, October 11, 1864—12 m.

General J. E. SMITH, *Cartersville :*

Look at the condition of your trains, for I may pick up your division entire and make a move on a larger scale than my Meridian trip. I think Hood has gone or will go to Blue mountain. Don't accumulate much baggage or provision at your posts. As a rule, keep on hand only what you can haul.

W. T. SHERMAN, *Major General.*

ROME, GA., *October* 11, 1864—11.30 p. m.

Major General SHERMAN :

A scout has just arrived who was fourteen (14) miles out on Summerville road. He reports Martin's division as camping last night about 7 o'clock at Farmer's bridge, over the Armuchee river. Could hear of no other troops, but citizens say Hardee crossed the Coosa river at Coosaville, and that the movement on this place was merely a feint to cover other movements. A small party crossed the Oostanaula this morning inquiring for Calhoun. He knows of no force about Snake Creek Gap nor Villanow. Things are mixed. Take these reports for what they are worth and draw your own conclusions. As soon as I get further information, will advise you.

JNO. M. CORSE,
Brigadier General.

KINGSTON, *October* 12, 1864—11.30 p. m.

Major General SHERMAN :

Resaca was attacked to-day by the enemy's infantry. Colonel Watkins evacuated Calhoun and crossed his men to Resaca, leaving horses on this side. At 10 o'clock to-night musketry was still heard. I started from Calhoun to-day and found road broke above Adairsville, and repaired it. Left Colonel Raum with three hundred and fifty (350) infantry at Calhoun to try to communicate. Loaded up all the abandoned commissary stores and brought them here with three locomotives and trains, that are now ready to take troops up the road if you desire to send any. I also placed garrisons in the block-houses that had been abandoned.

The summons to surrender is signed, "J. B. Hood, Gen'l," and closes by saying, "If the place is carried by assault no prisoners will be taken." Our men did not see it. If I hear anything more I will send you word. One regiment of enemy's infantry passed through Calhoun an hour before I got there.

E. M. McCOOK,
Brigadier General.

HEADQUARTERS MILITARY DIVISION OF THE MISSISSIPPI,
In the field, Rome, Ga., October 13, 1864.

Colonel DEAN, Kingston:

Hold fast all supplies and guard them well until we know exactly what course things take. Don't send the cars until you give time for the troops to reach Adairsville. It will be morning, I suppose, before they reach there, though I will order General Howard to push a division to-night. Keep me well advised, and ask General Raum to do the same. I have already caused their cavalry to be driven below Coosaville, capturing two guns, and have no doubt the columns now out will disturb Hood. I want him to be held at Resaca until I get there, though I suppose he will succeed or be off.

W. T. SHERMAN,
Major General.

RESACA, October 13, 1864.

Major General SHERMAN:

The enemy in heavy force are now around this place, their right resting on the river west, and their left on the river east. I have made such disposition as I feel sure will result in the defeat of the enemy. Instead of a brigade having been left by the 17th army corps to re-enforce this place, one regiment, the 10th Illinois, is with me. I trust that re-enforcements will be hurried here as soon as possible. I think, by placing a battery on the left bank of the river, opposite the right of the enemy, that his position will be enfiladed. A pontoon bridge is now over the stream. I have sent the cavalry horses, train and cars, under the protection of two hundred (200) cavalry.

G. B. RAUM,
Brevet Brigadier General.

HEADQUARTERS MILITARY DIVISION OF THE MISSISSIPPI,
In the field, Rome, Ga., October 13, 1864.

General HOWARD:

Start at once for Resaca. I have word from General Raum that he still holds the place, but needs help. He says you did not leave a brigade at Kingston, in consequence of which he has not been re-enforced.

W. T. SHERMAN,
Major General.

HEADQUARTERS MILITARY DIVISION OF THE MISSISSIPPI,
In the field, Rome, Ga., October 13, 1864.

General STANLEY :

March for Resaca at once, taking the road by Maguire's.   I have word from Colonel Raum that he holds the place.

W. T. SHERMAN,
Major General.

HEADQUARTERS MILITARY DIVISION OF THE MISSISSIPPI,
In the field, Rome, Ga., October 13, 1864.

General COX :

I have word from Resaca.   General Raum holds the place, but needs help. We must start at once.   I suppose by the time you get this you will know if that bridge is gone.   If so come, at once, and follow General Stanley, who marches by the Calhoun road.

Yours,

W. T. SHERMAN,
Major General.

HEADQUARTERS MILITARY DIVISION OF THE MISSISSIPPI,
In the field, Rome, Ga., October 13, 1864.

General RAUM, *Resaca :*

Have as many bridges finished for our use as you can by to-morrow morning. Also gain all possible intelligence of the movements of the enemy.   Ascertain if Snake Creek Gap be held in force or not, and, generally, everything that will enable me to arrive at a correct judgment.

Try and get a messenger through the mountains with as much verbal intelligence as possible of our movements.   I will try and get through to-day.

W. T. SHERMAN,
Major General.

ATLANTA, *October* 13, 1864—4.15 p. m.

Major General SHERMAN :

I am convinced Hood has taken all his troops from our front except a small cavalry force left near Sandtown.   I have sent four hundred (400) wagons for forage to South river, expect them in this evening; they are well guarded.   If they come in safely, I shall send again at once.   Our new line is well advanced and very strong.   The cattle are here.

H. W. SLOCUM,
Major General.

RESACA, *October* 13, 1864.

Major General SHERMAN :

I got those men into Resaca, and the railway and telegraph all right.   I think all the enemy will have left here by dayight, and that they have gone north along the road, burning and destroying it as they go.   All my cavalry will follow at daybreak to watch their movements.

General Raum is satisfied Hood was here in person with two corps.

E. M. McCOOK,
Brigadier General.

HEADQUARTERS MILITARY DIVISION OF THE MISSISSIPPI,
In the field, Resaca, Ga., October 14, 1864.

Colonel DEAN, *Kingston :*

Yours to Colonel Ewing received. Enemy have left here, and are moving north, on the railroad, and are also in Snake Creek Gap. Cavalry has pursued them beyond Dalton. It is Hood's whole army.

L. M. DAYTON, *Aide-de-Camp.*

RESACA, *October* 14, 1864—6.50 p. m.

Major General SHERMAN :

Just received despatch from Dalton. Cavalry dashed in there and captured ten (10) prisoners. Stewart's corps one and a half (1½) miles from there. Hood has divided his forces, one-half going towards the tunnel, tearing up the road, the other going towards Dug Gap.

E. M. McCOOK,
Brigadier General.

RESACA, *October* 14, 1864.

Major General SHERMAN :

I am here and collecting my troops. Stanley has passed towards Tilton. Reconnoissance of infantry and cavalry has gone to Snake Creek Gap.

O. O. HOWARD, *Major General.*

CHATTANOOGA, *October* 14, 1864—9 p. m.

Major General SHERMAN :

I went to Dalton yesterday, but could get no further, and found the enemy advancing on that place. I returned to Cleveland, bringing the trains and public property. General Thomas then ordered me to concentrate at Chattanooga the troops of Cleveland, Ringgold, and intermediate posts, and to take command here. I am now acting under his orders. It is reported that Dalton was captured yesterday, but I doubt the truth of the report. The enemy does not appear to be advancing on this place. I will push out to-morrow and try to develop his strength and movements. There are now troops enough here to make the place secure, and more are expected to-night.

I forward despatches from General Grant.

J. M. SCHOFIELD,
Major General.

[Cipher.]

HEADQUARTERS MILITARY DIVISION OF THE MISSISSIPPI,
In the field, near Villanow, October 15, 1864.

General SCHOFIELD, *Chattanooga :*

Despatch received. I am pushing straight for Hood, wherever he may be. Do the same with whatever force you have, and let us run him down. I am now on his trail, and will follow it. We pushed Lee's corps through Snaek Creek Gap to-day, and at Villanow I will find out where he is going to, and will follow him, no matter where.

Get in communication with me as soon as possible. We hold Atlanta and the road up to Resaca. The break at Big Shanty must be nearly done.

W. T. SHERMAN,
Major General.

ROME, *October* 15, 1864.

Major General SHERMAN:

I sent two brigades, one section of artillery, and one regiment of cavalry towards Summerville, as directed. Struck the enemy three miles above there, at the bridge where they showed artillery and strong line. Captured General Allen, inspector general, who says there are three brigades of cavalry at the bridge, and Wheeler's command near Dirttown. Citizens report Hood is now coming back, and that there is infantry near Summerville. Will advise you further.

JNO. M. CORSE,
Brigadier General.

CHATTANOOGA, *October* 15, 1864—12 midnight.

Major General SHERMAN:

I have information that the enemy, a corps of infantry and Wheeler's cavalry, moved west from Dalton yesterday. The railroad is destroyed to near Tunnell hill. Colonel Wright will start parties to repair it in the morning. I am disposing the troops to protect the road from this place to Bridgeport, and reopen the way to Resaca.

J. M. SCHOFIELD,
Major General.

[Cipher.]

HEADQUARTERS MILITARY DIVISION OF THE MISSISSIPPI,
In the field, near Villanow, Ga., October 16, 1864.

General SCHOFIELD:

We took Ship's Gap to-day, capturing a part of the 24th South Carolina· Two corps are represented at Lafayette, and one went south from Villanow· They obstructed Snake Creek pass to delay our trains, but by to-morrow I can move in any direction. I want the first positive fact that Hood contemplates an invasion of Tennessee. Invite him to do so. Send him a free pass in. Reoccupy the railroad, and put the construction corps to work to repair the break from the Tennessee to Resaca. I will get my trains up here and move according to the best information I can get.

W. T. SHERMAN,
Major General.

[Cipher.]

HEADQUARTERS MILITARY DIVISION OF THE MISSISSIPPI,
In the field, Ship's Gap, Ga., October 16, 1864.

General THOMAS, *Nashville:*

Send me Davis and Newton's old divisions. Re-establish the road, and I will follow Hood wherever he may go. I think he will move to Blue mountain. We can maintain our men and animals on the country.

W. T. SHERMAN,
Major General.

[Cipher.]

HEADQUARTERS MILITARY DIVISION OF THE MISSISSIPPI,
In the field, Ship's Gap, Ga., October 16, 1864.

Major General H. W. HALLECK, *Washington, D. C.:*

I got the despatch in cipher about providing me a place to come out on salt water, but the cipher is imperfect, and I cannot make out whether Savannah or Mobile be preferred; but I also want to know if you are willing that I should destroy Atlanta and the railroad. Hood broke eight (8) miles of road at Big Shanty, and about fifteen (15) from Resaca to the tunnel. The break at Big Shanty is repaired, but the other will take some time. I now have a position where I don't care which way he moves. I think the rebels will now go back south.

W. T. SHERMAN,
Major General.

ATLANTA, *October* 17, 1864.

Major General SHERMAN:

I have a Montgomery paper of the 12th. The despatches from Hood, as well as the editiorials, state that Beauregard is with Hood, and that the army is going to cross the Tennessee river.

H. W. SLOCUM,
Major General.

NASHVILLE, *October* 17, 1864—10.30 a. m.

Major General SHERMAN:

Your despatch from Ship's Gap, 5 p. m., just received. Schofield, whom I placed in command of the two divisions, Wagner's and Morgan's, was to move up Lookout valley this a. m. to intercept Hood should he be marching for Bridgeport. I will order him to join you with the two divisions and reconstruct the road as soon as possible. Will also re-organize the guards for posts and blockhouses. The latter is a difficult undertaking, as several of the regiments on that duty are clamorous to be sent home to be mustered out of service, and new regiments and recruits don't arrive rapidly enough to relieve them. I am accomplishing the work, however, as fast as possible.

Mower and Wilson have arrived and are on their way to join you. I hope you will adopt Grant's idea of turning Wilson loose rather than undertake the plan of a march with the whole force through Georgia to the sea, inasmuch as General Grant cannot co-operate with you as at first arranged.

GEO. H. THOMAS,
Major General.

[Cipher.]

HEADQUARTERS MILITARY DIVISION OF THE MISSISSIPPI,
In the field, Ship's Gap, Ga., October 17, 1864.

General SCHOFIELD:

Your despatch is received. Hood is not at Deer Head Cove. We occupy Ship's Gap and Lafayette. Hood is moving south *via* Summerville, Alpine, and Gadsden. If he enters Tennessee it will be to the left of Huntsville, but I think he has given up all such idea. I want the road repaired to Atlanta, the sick and wounded sent north of the Tennessee, my army recomposed, and I will make the interior of Georgia feel the weight of war. It is folly for us to be moving our armies on the reports of scouts and citizens. We must maintain the offensive. Your first move on Trenton and Valley Head was right; the move to defend Caperton's Ferry is wrong. Notify General Thomas of these my views. We must follow Hood till he is beyond reach of mischief, and then resume the offensive.

W. T. SHERMAN,
Major General.

HEADQUARTERS MILITARY DIVISION OF THE MISSISSIPPI,
In the field, Ship's Gap, Ga., October 17, 1864.

General CORSE, *Rome:*

We occupy Ship's Gap and Lafayette, and will move to-morrow on Summerville. General Garrard is sent to Dirttown. I want you to show your cavalry and some infantry about Coosaville, and to keep up communication with General Garrard, and if a chance offers to your small force, to hit some part of Hood's army in flank. I think he will move *via* Summerville and Alpine on Gadsden.

At Chattanooga they expect him at Caperton's Ferry, which is absurd.

W. T. SHERMAN,
Major General.

[Cipher.]

HEADQUARTERS MILITARY DIVISION OF THE MISSISSIPPI,
In the field, Ship's Gap, Ga., October 17, 1864.

General THOMAS, *Nashville:*

Hood won't dare go into Tennessee. I hope he will. We now occupy Ship's Gap and Lafayette, and Hood is retreating towards Alpine and Gadsden. I am moving General Garrard to-day to Dirttown, and will move General Corse out to Coosaville, and with the main army move on Summerville.

If Hood wants to go into Tennessee, west of Huntsville, let him go, and then we can all turn on him, and he cannot escape. The gunboats can break any bridge he may attempt above Decatur. If he attempts to cross, let him do so in part, and then let a gunboat break through his bridge. I will follow him to Gadsden, and then want my whole army united for the grand move into Georgia.

W. T. SHERMAN,
Major General.

[Cipher.]

HEADQUARTERS MILITARY DIVISION OF THE MISSISSIPPI,
In the field, Ship's Gap, Ga., October, 17, 1864.

General THOMAS, *Nashville:*

To-morrow I move on Summerville. Hood is not going to enter Tennessee. Keep up enough force to watch the river below and at the shoals, and let all the rest march towards me, or to re-enforce the railroad. Order, in my name, the renewal of the attempt to get Eastport, and ask Admiral Porter, if necessary, to send up an iron-clad.

We should command the Tennessee river up to Muscle shoals perfectly. I will follow Hood to and below Gadsden. He cannot maintain an army north of the Tennessee, especially if we hold Eastport, and thereby control or threaten the railroad from Corinth to Decatur, which I am told has been partially restored by Forrest, who is not now with Hood.

W. T. SHERMAN,
Major General.

[Cipher.]

CHATTANOOGA, October 17, 1864—11 p. m.

Major General SHERMAN:

Unless I receive further orders from you, or such information as renders it unwise, I will march to-morrow with Morgan's and Wagner's division, via Rossville and Gordon's mills, and join you as soon as practicable. I will bring as many beef cattle as the troops can take care of. My scouts report no enemy west of Lookout mountain to-day. They report Bird and Dug Gaps held by rebel cavalry. Colonel Warner is here. I have no later information from you than what he brought.

J. M. SCHOFIELD,
Major General.

[Cipher.]

NEW ORLEANS, October 18, 1864.

Major General SHERMAN:

I learn by intercepted despatch from Jeff. Davis to Kirby Smith, dated at Montgomery on the 30th, that the orders to cross the Mississippi had been received. I presume that duplicate of this despatch has reached Kirby Smith, as Magruder's force, about eighteen or twenty thousand (18,000 or 20,000) men, suddenly left General Steele's front and moved in the direction of the Washita river. I have sent a fast boat to communicate this intelligence to the troops and gunboats on the river, and, as I have now about eight thousand (8,000) troops afloat, and will at once increase the number, I think the crossing can be prevented. The crossing will probably be attempted in the neighborhood of Gaines's landing.

ED. R. S. CANBY,
Major General.

[Cipher.]

NASHVILLE, October 18, 1864—1 p. m.

Major General SHERMAN:

I have received your despatch from Ship's Gap of yesterday noon. Am ready to carry out your orders should Hood attempt to come into Tennessee. General Wilson will take a duplicate of this to you, and will explain my views on your plan of operations. Telegraphed to General Grant and his replies and suggestions to you. There is one thing, however, I don't wish—to be in command of the defence of Tennessee, unless you and the authorities in Washington deem it absolutely necessary.

Major General Mower has arrived and has reported for orders. I have advised him to remain here until he hears from you, not knowing but that you may still wish to place him at Eastport. I heard from Generals Granger and Croxton last night, who report nothing new of the movements of the enemy. Morgan's and Wagner's divisions leave Chattanooga to-day to report to you, escorting about eight thousand (8,000) beef cattle for the army. The necessary orders have been given for the repairs of the railroad. It will be completed as rapidly as possible. I have arranged with Lieutenant Green, commanding gunboat fleet on the lower Tennessee, to patrol the river as far up as Eastport. Lieutenant Grassford, commanding between Bridgeport and Decatur, patrols that portion of the river daily, and co-operates with me very cordially. I believe affairs north of the Tennessee river are getting into much better shape, and I hope to join you again very soon.

GEO. H. THOMAS,
Major General.

[Cipher.]

HEADQUARTERS MILITARY DIVISION OF THE MISSISSIPPI,
In the field, Summerville, Ga., October 19, 1864—12 m.

Major General HALLECK, Washington, D. C.:

Hood has retreated rapidly by all roads leading south. Our advance columns are now at Alpine and Mellville Post Office. I shall pursue him as far as Gaylesville. The enemy will not venture towards Tennessee, except around by Decatur. I propose to send the 4th corps back to General Thomas, and leave him with that corps, the garrisons and new troops to defend the line of the Tennessee, and with the rest to push into the heart of Georgia and come out at Savannah, destroying all the railroads of the State.

The break at Big Shanty is repaired, and that about Dalton should be in ten (10) days. We find abundance of forage in the country.

W. T. SHERMAN,
Major General Commanding.

[Cipher.]

HEADQUARTERS MILITARY DIVISION OF THE MISSISSIPPI,
In the field, Summerville, Ga., October 19, 1864.

General G. H. THOMAS, Nashville, Tennessee:

Make a report to me as soon as possible of what troops you now have in Tennessee; what are expected, and how disposed. I propose, with the armies of the Tennessee, the Ohio, and two corps of yours, to sally forth and make a hole in Georgia and Alabama that will be hard to mend. Hood has little or no baggage, and will escape me. He cannot invade Tennessee, except to the west of Huntsville. I want the gunboats and what troops are on the Tennessee to be most active up at the head of navigation. I want General Wilson and General Mower with me, and would like General McCook's division made up to twenty-five hundred (2,500) men mounted. I will send back into Tennessee the 4th corps, all dismounted cavalry, all sick and wounded, and all incumbrances whatever, except what I can haul in our wagons, and will, probably, about November 1, break up the railroad and bridges, destroy Atlanta, and make a break for Mobile, Savannah, or Charleston. I want you to remain in Tennessee and take command of all my division not actually present with me. Hood's army may be set down at forty thousand, (40,000,) of all arms, fit for duty; he may follow me or turn against you. If you can defend the line of the Tennessee in my absence of three (3) months, is all I ask.

W. T. SHERMAM,
Major General.

[Cipher.]

HEADQUARTERS MILITARY DIVISION OF THE MISSISSIPPI,
In the field, Summerville, Ga., October 19, 1864.

Colonel L. C. EASTON, *Chief Quartermaster, Chattanooga:*

Go in person to superintend the repairs of the railroad, and make all orders in my name that will expedite its completion. I want it finished to bring back to Chattanooga the sick, wounded, and surplus trash. On the 1st of November I want nothing in front of Chattanooga save what we can use as food and clothing and haul in our wagons. There is plenty of corn in the country, and we only want forage for the posts. I allow ten (10) days to do all this, by which time I expect to be near Atlanta.

W. T. SHERMAN,
Major General Commanding.

[Cipher.]

HEADQUARTERS MILITARY DIVISION OF THE MISSISSIPPI,
In the field, Summerville, Ga, October 19, 1864.

Colonel A. BECKWITH, *Chief Com. Sub. and Act'g Q. M., Atlanta, Ga.:*

Hood will escape me. I want to prepare for my big raid. On the 1st of November I want nothing in Atlanta but what is necessary to war. Send all trash to the rear at once and have on hand thirty (30) days' food and but little forage. I propose to abandon Atlanta and the railroad back to Chattanooga, and sally forth to ruin Georgia and bring up on the sea-shore. Make all dispositions accordingly. I will go down the Coosa until sure that Hood has gone to Blue mountain.

W. T. SHERMAN,
Major General Commanding.

HEADQUARTERS MILITARY DIVISION OF THE MISSISSIPPI,
In the field, Summerville, Ga., October 19, 1864.

GENERAL: At some more leisure time I will record the facts relating to Hood's attack on my communications. He has partially succeeded, from the superior mobility of his columns, moving without food or wagons. I now have him turned back, and am pushing him until he will not dare turn up Will's valley without having me at his rear, and the Tennessee at his front. My opinion is he will go to Blue mountain, the terminus of the Selma and Talladega road, where he and Beauregard will concoct new mischief.

We must not be on the defensive, and I now consider myself authorized to execute my plan to destroy the railroad from Chattanooga to Atlanta, including the latter city, (modified by General Grant from Dalton, &c.,) strike out into the heart of Georgia, and make for Charleston, Savannah, or the mouth of Appalachicola. General Grant prefers the middle one, Savannah, and I understand you to prefer Selma and the Alabama. I must have alternatives, else, being confined to one route, the enemy might so oppose that delay and want would trouble me; but, having alternatives, I can take so eccentric a course that no general can guess at my objective. Therefore, when you hear I am off have lookouts at Morris island, South Carolina, Ossabaw sound, Georgia, Pensacola and Mobile bays. I will turn up somewhere, and believe I can take Macon, Milledgeville, Augusta, and Savannah, Georgia, and wind up with closing the neck back of

Charleston, so that they will starve out.   This movement is not purely military or strategic, but it will illustrate the vulnerability of the south.   They don't know what war means; but when the rich planters of the Oconee and Savannah see their fences, and corn, and hogs, and sheep vanish before their eyes, they will have something more than a mean opinion of the "Yanks."   Even now our poor mules laugh at the fine cornfields, and our soldiers riot on chestnuts, sweet potatoes, pigs, chickens, &c.   The poor people come to me and beg us for their lives; but my customary answer is, "Your friends have broken our railroads which supplied us bountifully, and you cannot suppose our soldiers will suffer when there is abundance within reach."

It will take ten (10) days to finish up our roads, during which I will eat out this flank and along down the Coosa, and then will rapidly put into execution "the plan."   In the mean time I ask that you give to General Thomas all the troops you can spare of the new levies, that he may hold the line of the Tennessee during my absence of say ninety (90) days.

I am, &c.,

W. T. SHERMAN,
Major General.

Major General H. W. HALLECK,
Washington, D. C.

[Cipher.]

HEADQUARTERS MILITARY DIVISION OF THE MISSISSIPPI,
In the field, Summerville, Ga., October 19, 1864.

General WILSON, *Chief of Cavalry, Nashville:*

General Garrard has about twenty-five hundred (2,500) cavalry, General Kilpatrick fifteen hundred, (1,500,) General McCook six hundred, (600;) there may be about one thousand (1,000) other cavalry with my army.   These embrace all the cavalry ready for battle.   I wish you would see Generals Johnston and Thomas, bring to me about twenty-five hundred (2,500) new cavalry, and then go to work to make up three divisions, each of twenty-five hundred, (2,500,) for the hardest fighting of the war.   I am going into the very bowels of the Confederacy, and propose to leave a trail that will be recognized fifty years hence.

W. T. SHERMAN,
Major General Commanding.

HEADQUARTERS MILITARY DIVISION OF THE MISSISSIPPI,
In the field, Summerville, Ga., October 20, 1864.

GENERAL: I think I have thought over the whole field of the future, and being now authorized to act, I want all things bent to the following general plan of action for the next three months:

Out of the forces now here and at Atlanta I propose to organize an efficient army of sixty to sixty-five thousand (60,000 to 65,000) men, with which I propose to destroy Macon, Augusta, and it maybe Savannah and Charleston; but I will always keep open the alternatives of the mouth of the Appalachicola and Mobile.   By this I propose to demonstrate the vulnerability of the south, and make its inhabitants feel that war and individual ruin are synonymous terms.   To pursue Hood is folly, for he can twist and turn like a fox and wear out any army in pursuit; to continue to occupy long lines of railroads simply exposes our small detachments to be picked up in detail, and forces me to make counter-marches to protect lines of communication. I know I am right in this, and shall proceed to its maturity. As to details, I propose to take General Howard and his army, General Schofield and his, and two of your corps, ziz: Generals Davis's and Slocum's. I propose to remain along the Coosa watching Hood until all my preparations are made, viz : until I have repaired the railroad, sent back all surplus men and material, and stripped for the work. Then I will send General Stanley, with the 4th corps, across by Wills' valley and Caperton's to Stevenson, to report to you. If you send me five or six thousand (5,000 or 6,000) new conscripts, I may also send back one of General Slocum's or Davis's divisions, but I prefer to maintain organizations. I want you to retain command in Tennessee, and before starting I will give you delegated authority over Kentucky, and Mississippi, Alabama, &c., whereby there will be unity of action behind me. I will want you to hold Chattanooga and Decatur in force, and on the occasion of my departure, of which you will have ample notice, to watch Hood close. I think he will follow me, at least with his cavalry, in which event I want you to push south from Decatur and the head of the Tennessee for Columbus, Mississippi, and Selma, not absolutely to reach those points, but to divert or pursue according to the state of facts. If, however, Hood turns on you, you must act defensively on the line of the Tennessee. I will ask, and you may also urge, that at the same time General Canby act vigorously up the Alabama river.

I do not fear that the southern army will again make a lodgement on the Mississippi, for past events demonstrate how rapidly armies can be raised in the northwest on that question, and how easily handled and supplied. The only hope of a southern success is in the remote regions difficult of access. We have now a good entering wedge, and should drive it home. It will take some time to complete these details, and I hope to hear from you in the mean time. We must preserve a large amount of secrecy, and I may actually change the ultimate point of arrival, but not the main object.

I am, &c.,

W. T. SHERMAN,
Major General Commanding.

Major General THOMAS,
Commanding Department of the Cumberland.

HEADQUARTERS MILITARY DIVISION OF THE MISSISSIPPI,
In the field, Gaylesville, Ala., October 21, 1864.

General CORSE :

I have received your note, and am glad of the fair prospect of things both at home and with us. Hood retreated with more precipitancy than I had first supposed, and I learn that the day you and General Cox moved out of Rome we stampeded the train back to Blue mountain. I now have my infantry up to Little river and at Cedartown, and the mass about here. I will push cavalry well down towards Gadsden, and want a pontoon bridge at Cedartown. Send your spare one down with the knowledge that it will be destroyed when we are done with it. Inasmuch as the boats may be fired on, I want you to send your cavalry and one or two brigades of infantry down by Van's valley, Cave spring, and the Centre road, to cover the movement. As soon as I get the bridge I will occupy Centre, after eating out this Chattanooga valley, which we find rich in forage, and some potatoes, hogs, chickens, &c. I explain to the people that we have abundance of provision at the north ; that we have good roads to our rear, and that we design to supply our own wants ; but Hood has broken our road, and we must make it off the country. I think we can save enough forage to pay for the repairs. I don't want too much accumulation at

Rome or anywhere, for I design something else ; but we will send our trains into and through Rome to meet us elsewhere in a few days. Telegraph to Chattanooga to send all mails and express matter to this army *via* Rome. I have ordered a courier line back. I want you to establish one forward, say to Coosaville. Order the boats in descending to destroy or bring along all boats, canoes, floats, &c., &c. Let them be armed and ordered to proceed with caution. Find for me, if you can, where the steamboats that are above the Ten Islands are now sunk. I may get them up or further destroy them. Continue to give daily budgets of news, and keep all the posts advised of our whereabouts.

W. T. SHERMAN,
Major General Commanding.

[Cipher.]

HEADQUARTERS MILITARY DIVISION OF THE MISSISSIPPI,
In the field, Gaylesville, Ala., October 20, 1864.

General SLOCUM, *Atlanta, Ga.:*

I have your despatch of the 18th. Use all your energies to send to the rear everything not needed for the grand march. I will take your corps along. We will need one and a half million rations of bread, coffee, sugar, and salt, half a million rations of salt meat, and all else should be shipped away. All sick and wounded should be sent to Resaca and Chattanooga as soon as the road is open. General Thomas and staff will remain in Tennessee. I will take two of the corps of the army of the Cumberland and send General Stanley's back. I want to be near Atlanta, and ready by November 1. Keep out strong foraging parties and keep the bridges well secured. Have the lightest pontoon bridges and trains ready. All else will be sent to the rear or destroyed. The enemy has retreated rapidly before us down the Coosa towards Gadsden.

W. T. SHERMAN,
Major General Commanding.

[Cipher.]

HEADQUARTERS MILITARY DIVISION OF THE MISSISSIPPI,
In the field, Gaylesville, Ala., October 22, 1864.

General GRANT, *City Point, Va.:*

I feel perfectly master of the situation here. I still hold Atlanta, and the road with all bridges and vital points well guarded, and I have in hand an army before which Hood has retreated precipitately down the valley of the Coosa. It is hard to divine his future plans, but by abandoning Georgia, and taking position with his rear to Selma, he threatens the road from Chattanooga to Atlanta, and may move up to Tennessee by Decatur. He cannot cross the Tennessee except at Muscle shoals, for all other points are patrolled by our gunboats.

I am now perfecting arrangements to put into Tennessee a force able to hold the line of the Tennessee whilst I break up the railroad in front of Dalton, including the city of Atlanta, and push into Georgia and break up all its railroads and depots, capture its horses and negroes, make desolation everywhere ; destroy the factories at Macon, Milledgeville, and Augusta, and bring up with sixty thousand (60,000) men on the sea-shore about Savannah or Charleston. I think this far better than defending a long line of railroad. I will leave General George H. Thomas to command all my military division behind me, and take with me only the best fighting material. Of course I will subsist on the bountiful cornfields and potato patches, as I am now doing, luxuriously.   I have now all your despatches, and there will be time to give me further instruction.

Canby should be most active as against Selma from the direction of Mobile, and I will order similar movements from the Mississippi river and Decatur, provided Beauregard follows me, as he will be forced to do by public clamor.

W. T. SHERMAN,
Major General U. S. A.

[Cipher.]

HEADQUARTERS MILITARY DIVISION OF THE MISSISSIPPI,
In the field, Gaylesville, Ala., October 23, 1864.

General SLOCUM, Atlanta, Ga.:

Your despatch of the 20th received.   Am delighted at your success in foraging. Go on, pile up the forage, corn, and potatoes, and keep your artillery horses fat; send back all unserviceable artillery, and, at the last moment, we can count up our horses and see what we can haul, and send back all else.   One gun per thousand men will be plenty to take along.   Hood is doubtless now at Blue mountain, and Forrest over about Corinth and Tuscumbia, hoping by threatening Tennessee to make me quit Georgia.   We are piling up men in Tennessee enough to attend to them, and to leave me free to go ahead.   The railroad will be done in a day or two.   We find abundance of corn and potatoes out here, and we enjoy them much.   They cost nothing a bushel.   If Georgia can afford to break our railroad, she can afford to feed us.   Please preach this doctrine to men who go forth and are likely to spread it.   All well.

W. T. SHERMAN,
Major General Commanding.

[Cipher.]

HEADQUARTERS MILITARY DIVISION OF THE MISSISSIPPI,
In the field, Gaylesville, Ala., October 23, 1864.

General THOMAS, Nashville, Tenn.:

Despatch of 18th received.   I wrote you in great detail by Colonel Warner.   Hood is now at Blue mountain, and Forrest is evidently over about Tuscumbia.   No doubt they will endeavor conjointly to make me come out of Georgia, but I don't want them to succeed.   All Georgia is now open to me, and I do believe you are the man best qualified to manage the affairs of Tennessee and north Mississippi.

I want approximate returns of all troops subject to your orders, and, as I wrote you, I can spare you the 4th corps and about five thousand (5,000) men not fit for my purposes, but which will be well enough for garrison at Chattanooga, Murfreesburo', and Nashville.   What you need is a few points fortified and stocked with provisions, and a good movable column of twenty-five thousand (25,000) men that can strike in any direction.

I await further reports from you before doing anything, but am making all preparations necessary.   We find abundance of forage and stores down here, and have not the most distant fears of want or starvation.   All my animals are improving, and General Slocum, at Atlanta, reports foraging most successful; four hundred (400) wagons on one occasion, seven hundred (700) on another, and six hundred (600) now out.   If Hood breaks our road, Georgia must pay for it.

W. T. SHERMAN,
Major General Commanding

[Cipher.]

HEADQUARTERS MILITARY DIVISION OF THE MISSISSIPPI,
In the field, Gaylesville, Ala., October 24, 1864.

General H. W. HALLECK, *Washington:*

We have heard of General Sheridan's victory at Cedar creek. We can't afford to burn gunpowder, but our men can make up in yelling, which is just as good. We have pushed the enemy to Gadsden, and are now living on the country until the road is repaired, which will be done by Thursday, the 27th. I will send back all sick, wounded, and surplus property, ready to take up our baggage and march wherever it may seem best. General Wilson is here, and asks for time to make up a good cavalry force, but I will be governed by the movements of Beauregard. I send an order made by Beauregard on assuming command, which seems to be of enough importance to telegraph. General Slocum reports all well at Atlanta; he has gathered near two thousand (2,000) wagon-loads of corn and forage. All my animals here are improving on the cornfields of the Coosa; and you will observe my position at Gaylesville, Blue Pond, and a pontoon laid at Cedar Bluff, with a division at Alpine and Will's Valley Head, is very good to watch the enemy about Gadsden and Blue mountain.

Beauregard announces his theorem to be to drive Sherman out of Atlanta, which he still holds defiantly and dares him to the encounter, but is not willing to chase him all over creation.

W. T. SHERMAN,
Major General Commanding.

HEADQUARTERS MILITARY DIVISION OF THE MISSISSIPPI,
In the field, Gaylesville, Ala., October 25, 1864.

SIR : I do not wish to be considered as in any way adverse to the organization of negro regiments, further than as to its effects on the white race. I do wish the fine race of men that people our northern States should rule and determine the future destiny of America; but if they prefer trade and gain, and leave to bought substitutes and negroes the fighting, (the actual conflict,) of course the question is settled, for those who hold the swords and muskets at the end of this war (which is but fairly begun) will have something to say. If negroes are to fight, they, too, will not be content with sliding back into the status of slave or free negro. I much prefer to keep negroes yet, for some time to come, in a subordinate state; for our prejudices, yours as well as mine, are not yet schooled for absolute equality.

Jeff. Davis has succeeded perfectly in inspiring his people with the truth that liberty and government are worth fighting for; that pay and pensions are silly nothings compared to the prize fought for. Now, I would aim to inspire our own people also with the same idea—that it is not right to pay one thousand (1,000) dollars to some fellow, who will run away, to do his fighting, or to some poor negro who is thinking of the day of jubilee; but that every young and middle-aged man should be proud of the chance to fight for the stability of his country without profit and without price; and I would like to see all trade and manufactures *absolutely* cease until this fight is over; and I have no hesitation or concealment in saying that there is not, and should not be, the remotest chance of peace again on this continent till all this is realized, save the peace which would result from the base and cowardly submittal to Jeff. Davis's terms. I would use negroes as surplus, but not spare a single white man, not one. Any white man who don't and won't fight *now* should be killed, banished, or denationalized, and then we would discriminate among the noisy patriots and see who really should vote.

If the negroes fight and the whites don't, of course the negroes will govern. They won't ask you or me for the privilege, but will simply take it, and probably reverse the relation hitherto existing, and they would do right.

If, however, the government has determined to push the policy to the end, it is both my duty and pleasure to assist, and in that event I should like to have Colonel Bowman, now commanding the district of Wilmington, Delaware, to organize and equip such as may fall into the custody of the army I command.

I am, with respect, your obedient servant,

W. T. SHERMAN,
Major General Commanding.

Hon. E. M. STANTON,
Secretary of War, Washington, D. C.

[Cipher.]

NASHVILLE, *October* 25, 1864—8.30 p. m.

Major General SHERMAN :

I have reports this evening from General Granger that Hood, with his army is moving down the Tennessee river, by the way of Guntersville and Summerville Have you any information tending to confirm my reports received ?

GEO. H. THOMAS,
Major General.

[Cipher.]

HEADQUARTERS MILITARY DIVISION OF THE MISSISSIPPI,
In the field, Gaylesville, Ala., October 26, 1864.

Major General THOMAS, *Nashville, Tennessee :*

A reconnoissance pushed down to Gadsden to-day reveals the fact that the rebel army is not there, and the chances are it has moved west. If it turns up at Guntersville I will be after it; but if it goes, as I believe, to Decatur and beyond, I must leave it to you at present, and push for the heart of Georgia. All I want is to get my sick and wounded back to a safe place. I start the 4th corps back to morrow, *via* Winston's and Valley Head, ordering it to Bridgeport or Chattanooga, according to what orders Stanley may have from you. Stanley will have about fifteen thousand (15,000) men. Beauregard may attempt Tennessee from the direction of Muscle shoals, but when he finds me pushing for Macon, Milledgeville, &c., he will turn back. I send you a copy of my order giving you supreme command in my absence.

W. T. SHERMAN,
Major General Commanding.

[Cipher.]

NASHVILLE, *October* 26, 1864—2 p. m.

Major General SHERMAN :

General Granger telegraphs me again to-day that Hood's army is threatening to cross the Tennessee river at various places between Guntersville and Decatur. I have sent down to him all the re-enforcements I have to spare at this time. Have you any information that Hood has moved with his army in the direction indicated in these reports ?

GEO. H. THOMAS,
Major General.

16*

[Cipher.]

NASHVILLE, TENN., *October* 26, 1864—10.30 p. m.

Major General SHERMAN :

General Granger reports that the enemy appeared in force in front of Decatur to-day about 3 p. m.   His pickets were driven in, but no serious attack was made on him by the enemy.   Have sent him all the re-enforcements I can get. From his report it would seem that Hood intends to attempt the crossing of the Tennessee river.

GEO. H. THOMAS,
Major General.

[Cipher.]

NASHVILLE, *October* 27, 1864—9 a. m.

Major General SHERMAN :

Your despatch of 9 a. m. yesterday is received.   I telegraphed you last night that the enemy had appeared in force in front of Decatur and drove in our pickets.   Have ordered him to defend Decatur to the last extremity, and have ordered gunboats to patrol the river from Bridgeport to Decatur as well as they are able.   I have also a small force at Whiteside, with artillery, and at Claysville. Have only been able to send Granger three new regiments, the others being necessary to place guards for block-houses on the railroad to Chattanooga and Pulaski.   I have ordered forward the new regiments as fast as possible, but as yet there are eight regiments behind.   Granger believes Hood's army is near Decatur for the purpose of crossing the Tennessee river.   I would like to get the 4th corps as soon as you can spare it.

GEO. H. THOMAS,
Major General.

[Cipher.]

HEADQUARTERS MILITARY DIVISION OF THE MISSISSIPPI,
In the field, Gaylesville, Ala., October 27, 1864.

GENERAL : I have sent the 4th corps, General Stanley's, back to Stevenson. This corps is about fifteen thousand (15,000) strong.   I will also send all the men not suited to our long march, but they will answer for defending posts. These, with what General Thomas has, will enable him to hold Tennessee ; and in a few days I hope to be all ready to carry into effect my original plan.

No doubt Hood has gone off toward the west about Decatur, and may attempt and succeed in crossing the Tennessee, although that river is high and patrolled by gunboats.   If he attacks fortified places he will soon cripple his army so that Thomas can dispose of him.   I will wait a few days to hear what headway he makes about Decatur, and may yet turn to Tennessee ; but it would be a great pity to take a step backwards.   I think it would be better even to let him ravage the State of Tennessee, provided he does not gobble up too many of our troops.

General Thomas is well alive to the occasion, and better suited to the emergency than any man I have.   He should be strengthened as soon as possible, as the successful defence of Tennessee should not be left to chance.

W. T. SHERMAN,
Major General Commanding.

Major General HALLECK,
Washington, D. C.

[Cipher.]

HEADQUARTERS MILITARY DIVISION OF THE MISSISSIPPI,
In the field, Gaylesville, Ala., October 28 1864.

General THOMAS, *Nashville, Tennessee:*

I have your despatches of the 26th and 27th, announcing that Hood's force has appeared before Decatur. I have already sent the 4th corps, which should reach Wauhatchee to-morrow; use it freely, and if I see that Hood crosses the Tennessee, I will send Schofield. On these two corps you can engraft all the new troops; with the balance I will go south. Hood has little ammunition and cannot afford to attack fortified places. Caution all posts to defend themselves manfully, and Hood will soon exhaust himself. The greatest danger is of garrisons being cut off. Instruct them, and see that each has provisions to last until relief comes. If Hood crosses, it will be about Lamb's ferry or Bainbridge. Wilson is now well down toward Jacksonville, and appearances are that Hood has shifted his stores on to the Mobile and Ohio railroad. I will go to Rome to-morrow. Keep me well advised.

W. T. SHERMAN,
Major General Commanding.

[Cipher.]

HEADQUARTERS MILITARY DIVISION OF THE MISSISSIPPI,
In the field, Rome, Ga., October 28, 1864.

General STEEDMAN, *Chattanooga, Tennessee:*

Telegraph to General Granger he must hold on to the death. Hood has no ammunition to spare, and cannot afford to assault. Send Granger some ammunition, if you can safely do so, by a boat. The gunboats ought all to be there.

Movements will occur elsewhere that will make Hood quit Decatur. Tell Granger to delay Hood there as long as he can. Stanley's corps will reach Wauhatchee to-morrow, and I will also send up Schofield's corps. Let General Thomas re-enforce Granger, if necessary; but he don't want too many men.

W. T. SHERMAN,
Major General Commanding.

[Cipher.]

HEADQUARTERS MILITARY DIVISION OF THE MISSISSIPPI,
In the field, Rome, Ga., October 28, 1864.

Major General THOMAS, *Nashville, Tennessee:*

General Granger must hold as long as he can. Hood won't assault. Both Allatoona and Resaca beat him off, and neither was as strong as Decatur. General Granger don't want too many men; they would be in his way. The gunboats should be near him. Hood cannot spare ammunition to bombard. General Stanley will be at Wauhatchee to-morrow, and I may also send Schofield up from here. Notify all commanders of fortified places that numbers are nothing; they must hold their posts against a million. Let them get provisions and ammunition in now. If troops come from Missouri, Eastport would be a good place, unless Hood succeeds in crossing the Tennessee.

W. T. SHERMAN,
Major General Commanding.

WARRENSBURG, *Mo., October* 29, 1864.

Major General SHERMAN:

Your despatch received. General Halleck says, in a despatch of to-day, General Grant thinks I can and ought to send you re-enforcements. I have looked upon General A. J. Smith's command as a loan from you. They are now near Kansas border, and will march toward St. Louis with all practicable speed, scouting the country. They will be provided with everything needful, and sent to you as soon as they can reach the Mississippi. I have no cavalry available. I would like very much to know your exact wants and situation.

W. S. ROSECRANS,
Major General.

[Cipher.]

HEADQUARTERS MILITARY DIVISION OF THE MISSISSIPPI,
In the field, Rome, Ga., October 29, 1864.

Major General THOMAS, *Nashville, Tennessee:*

General Stanley should reach Wauhatchee to-day. Schofield will be here to-night, and I will push him right away for Resaca, to go to Chattanooga if events call for it. Order all recruits and drafted men accordingly, viz: those for 14th, 15th, 17th and 20th corps to come to the front. Appoint some good man to organize and arm the convalescents I send back. I repeat, should the enemy cross the Tennessee in force, abandon all minor points and concentrate your forces at some point where you cover the road from Murfreesboro' to Stevenson.

Engraft on Stanley and Schofield all the new troops. Give Schofield a division of new troops. Give General Tower all the men you can to finish the forts at Nashville, and urge on the navy to pile up gunboats in the Tennessee.

W. T. SHERMAN,
Major General Commanding.

[Cipher.]

HEADQUARTERS MILITARY DIVISION OF THE MISSISSIPPI,
In the field, Rome, Ga., October 29, 1864.

Major General THOMAS, *Nashville, Tennessee:*

We have reconnoitred well down to Gadsdon and Jacksonville. Hood took with him all his infantry and a good deal of cavalry. He started for Bridgeport and Guntersville, but my movements have thrown him clear across to the Mobile and Ohio railroad. If he do not attack Decatur to-day he will not at all; but he will go to Tuscumbia and depend on the Mobile road. Now, I want you to be all ready for him if he enters Tennessee. He will work as fast as possible, for winter is coming; but he cannot have supplies, and will be dependent on the country. I have sent General Stanley back; give him as many conscripts as possible, and use him as the nucleus. I will send also Schofield back, who will relieve you of all that Knoxville branch; but, if necessary, break up all minor posts, and get about Columbia as big an army as you can, and go at him. You may hold all the cavalry and new troops, except new artillery assigned to the corps with me. I would like Dalton held, but leave that to you; Chattanooga, of course, and Decatur, in connexion with the boats. If, to make up a force adequate, it be necessary, abandon Huntsville, and that line, and the Nashville and the Decatur road, except so far as it facilitates an army operating toward Florence. Already the papers in Georgia begin to howl at being abandoned, and will howl still more before they are done. Get, if you can, Generals A. J. Smith's and Mower's divisions, belonging to my army, from Missouri, and let them come to you *via* Clifton. Get the gunboats to fill the Tennessee river, and that will bother the enemy much; and if you can make a good lodgement at Eastport, Hood could not use the Corinth and Decatur road, for there are only seven (7) miles of good road from Eastport to Iuka. Schofield has not got in yet, but I will push him right on to Resaca. I will give you notice when I start. All preparations are now progressing, but I want to know Hood's movements, and how well you are prepared, before I start.

W. T. SHERMAN,
Major General Commanding.

WARRENSBURG, Mo., *October* 29, 1864.

Major General SHERMAN:

I forgot to say that Winslow's cavalry, that came with General Mower, will be sent to Memphis as soon as it can be done. It is now on the Kansas border, has had a hard campaign, and must be remounted, which will be done as speedily as possible.

W. S. ROSECRANS,
Major General.

[Cipher.]

HEADQUARTERS MILITARY DIVISION OF THE MISSISSIPPI,
In the field, Rome, Ga., October 29, 1864.

Major General ROSECRANS, *Warrensburg, Mo.:*

I have your despatches to-day. I have pushed Beauregard to the west of Decatur, but I know he is pledged to invade Tennessee and Kentucky, having his base on the old Mobile and Ohio road. I have put Thomas in Tennessee, and given him as many troops as he thinks necessary, but I don't want to leave it to chance, and therefore would like to have Smith's and Mower's divisions up the Tennessee river as soon as possible. Could you get them on board of boats at Booneville, or higher up, and let the boats run to Paducah, where orders would meet them?

I propose, myself, to push straight down into the heart of Georgia, smashing things generally.

W. T. SHERMAN,
Major General.

[Cipher.]

HEADQUARTERS MILITARY DIVISION OF THE MISSISSIPPI,
In the field, Rome, Ga., October 29, 1864.

General THOMAS, *Nashville, Tennessee:*

I have your despatch. General Stanley has reached Chattanooga, and can, with the assistance of the cars, reach Athens in less than four days. I hear that the enemy has passed to the west of Decatur, and therefore will cross about Florence. I don't see how Beauregard can support his army, but Jeff. Davis is desperate, and his men will undertake anything possible. If necessary, draw heavy on Chattanooga, depending on Schofield to replace them. Schofield is not yet up, but I will push him right along to Resaca. With Decatur held, and a good gunboat force up at the head of navigation, the enemy will be bold to enter Tennessee; but we must expect anything. If they wait to get supplies about Tuscumbia you will get the Missouri troops. Have your orders to meet them at Paducah.

W. T. SHERMAN,
Major General.

CHATTANOOGA, October 29, 1864—8 p. m.

Major General SHERMAN:

The following has just been received from Decatur, dated October 24—4.40 p. m.:

"I told you we drove the rebs out of their rifle-pits yesterday, capturing one hundred and twenty, (120.) In the evening we made another sortie, spiking a couple of guns, and making fourteen (14) more prisoners. In this skirmish we lost forty (40) killed and wounded. Our loss altogether, up to this time, amounts to eighty (80.) We blew up four (4) caissons, and dismounted two (2) pieces of artillery. We killed and wounded a very large number of the enemy, full five hundred (500.) About four (4) o'clock this a. m., they began to leave in direction of Courtland. I have been probing them at different points all day, finding them in force until 4 o'clock this evening, when our forces carried their last line of rifle-pits; enemy evidently believing us to be in very strong force here, judging from what their prisoners have stated. I have endeavored to keep up this impression. I am picketing the river with all the cavalry in my possession, down to the mouth of Elk river. If gunboat returns, now some miles up river, I will send a regiment down the river to Brown's ferry. Negroes who escaped from them, and prisoners, say that Hood and Beauregard are both with them. Received a despatch from Athens; stated that two couriers from Florence reported that the enemy had crossed below Cypress creek in large force. I think this information is to the same effect as that forwarded by General Croxton.

"It will hardly be necessary now to report, any how. I will send you, however, all the information I can obtain.

"R. S. GRANGER,
"Brigadier General."

Respectfully,

JAS. B. STEEDMAN,
Major General.

CHATTANOOGA, October 29, 1864.

Major General SHERMAN:

Just received the following:

"DECATUR, 29—9.30 p. m.

"I have conversed with a number of deserters, prisoners, and escaped negroes, and from their information I am led to believe it is the impression among the officers and men of Hood's army that they are bound to get into Middle Tennessee. The deserter who has just left me says that their first aim was to take this place, and fully expected to do so. He thought now they would certainly attempt to cross above or below. I am convinced their infantry forces left in the direction of Courtland, and they may send some cavalry to cross above. My guide, Harris, a sharp fellow, says, from what he has heard above, that they will try to cross above, near Whitesburg. I have sent him up there on the gunboat Thomas. I have also ordered, in addition to the force there already, five (5) companies of 181st Ohio, about four hundred and twenty (420) men. I have sent to Brown's ferry one hundred and fifty of the 10th Indiana, and will send the Stone River down there with one hundred (100) men of 181st Ohio. I think Hood will, if he intends to cross, make the effort between Elk River and Eastport. Instructed Colonel Lyon to guard all passes from mouth of Flint river to Triana, and scout river with cavalry.

"R. S. GRANGER,
" *Brigadier General.*"

—

"29th—11 p. m.

" In my last telegram I omitted to mention another reason why I think Hood will go to Tuscumbia before crossing. He was evidently out of supplies; his men were all grumbling; the first thing the prisoners asked for was something to eat. Hood could not get anything if he should cross this side of Rogersville.

"R. S. GRANGER,
" *Brigadier General.*"

JAS. B. STEEDMAN,
Major General.

[Cipher.]

NASHVILLE, TENNESSEE,
October 30, 1864—2 p. m.

Major General SHERMAN:

Your two despatches, of 12 p. m. (midnight) yesterday, received. One division of Stanley's troops has already left Chattanooga for Athens, and Tindall promises to have them all off by to-morrow. Have despatch from Croxton at 9 p. m. last night. He says nothing further of the crossing of the enemy at Florence, but he learns from a source he cannot doubt that Hood's whole army reached Town creek last night, and would cross there. Have already directed him to oppose Hood with his whole available force, reporting directly to Stanley, at Athens, and to me here *via* Pulaski. Ordered Hatch last night to re-enforce Croxton at once. Granger believes Hood has gone towards Tuscumbia, but thinks he will be compelled to wait a day or two to get provisions, as his troops were almost mutinous at not having food when he was before Decatur. If he delays two days he will have no chance to get across. Think General Schofield better remain at Resaca for a day or two, or until we get further information. Have directed General Steedman to push forward all recruits and drafted men belonging to regiments with you. Have repeated my application to Commander Pennock for gunboats to go up Tennessee river. Have telegraphed General Rosecrans at St. Louis to send A. J. Smith's and Mower's divisions to Eastport; cavalry to Memphis. I doubt if Rosecrans will send them.

GEO. H. THOMAS,
Major General.

[Cipher.]

HEADQUARTERS MILITARY DIVISION OF THE MISSISSIPPI,
In the field, Rome, Ga., October 30, 1864.

Major General THOMAS, *Nashville, Tennessee:*

Despatch of to-day received. I agree with Granger that Hood must delay for provisions. He cannot ford the Tennessee, and must pass his artillery by a pontoon bridge, which can only be laid, in the reach about Florence, between Colbut's and Muscle shoals. Schofield is here, and moves to-morrow for Resaca to report to you. Jeff. Davis will move to Kingston and Howard to Marietta, *via* Vanwert and Dallas. I will keep all the horses, and will send Wilson with all the dismounted cavalry back to Tennessee, where he can make up a very heavy cavalry force, subject to your orders, in case I depart for the south. Hood must have seen Stanley moving to you, and has heard the result of affairs in Missouri and the Shenandoah, and will hesitate to put his army in Middle Tennessee at this season of the year, with the Tennessee river at his back ; but I want you to keep me advised up to the last moment.

It may take five (5) days yet to get everything back, and during that time he may turn towards me, thinking I have divided my forces. General Rosecrans telegraphs me that he has ordered General Mower and Smith's divisions, to Tennessee, and I have asked him to embark them at Boonville or Lexington and send them in boats to the Tennessee river, reporting to you from Puducah'

W. T. SHERMAN,
Major General.

[Cipher.]

NASHVILLE, October 30, 1864—9 p. m.

Major General SHERMAN :

General Granger reports enemy gone from his front, moving off towards Tuscumbia. He sent out force to follow up the rear of the enemy as he moved off, capturing some prisoners. He reports prisoners admit Hood's loss, killed and wounded, at Decatur, numbered in the neighborhood of one thousand, (1,000.) Colonels Doolittle and Morgan, who had just returned from the reconnoissance, report heavy firing down the river, at about the rate of eight shots per minute, continuing for about fifteen (15) minutes. It is probably General Croxton opposing the enemy at Bainbridge, as he reported last night that he had learned from a reliable source that the enemy intended crossing at that place. Have not heard from Croxton to-day. The whole of General T. J. Wood's division, 4th corps, left Chattanooga, on cars, at 10 a. m. to-day, for Athens, and General Stanley expects to have his other two divisions en route by to-morrow morning. I believe they will reach Athens in time to prevent the enemy from making further progress into the country. Have ordered an additional brigade of cavalry to scout from this place to-morrow morning to re-enforce Croxton.

GEO. H. THOMAS,
Major General.

[Cipher.]

WARRENSBURG, MO., October 30, 1864—11 p. m.
(through HEADQUARTERS DEPARTMENT OF MISSOURI,
St. Louis, Missouri, October 30, 1864—12 p. m.)

Major General SHERMAN :

Your telegram of 29th, 12 p. m., received. The river is so low that General A. J. Smith can reach the Mississippi river sooner by marching. He leaves in the morning. It will require ten (10) days to reach the Mississippi river, where boats and complete supplies will await him. Whatever is possible will be done to enable you to make a sure thing against Beauregard. I hope you will be able to give that army a thorough defeat.

W. S. ROSECRANS,
Major General

[Cipher.]

HEADQUARTERS MILITARY DIVISION OF THE MISSISSIPPI,
In the field, Rome, Ga., October 31, 1864.

Major General THOMAS, *Nashville, Tennessee:*

You must unite all your men into one army, and abandon all minor points, if you expect to defeat Hood. He will not attack posts, but march around them. Schofield is marching to-day from here to Resaca, where he will report to you for orders. His advance will be at Resaca to-night.

W. T. SHERMAN,
Major General.

[Cipher.]

NASHVILLE, *October* 31, 1864—9.30 a. m.

Major General SHERMAN:

General Croxton reports enemy crossed Tennessee river, four miles above Florence. He reports, also, that he was unable to prevent enemy's crossing, but will resist their further progress as long as possible. Have ordered General Hatch to move to Lawrenceburg, between Hood and Columbia, and to co-operate with General Croxton in resisting enemy's progress. Have ordered Stanley's corps to Pulaski to hold that place. Can you send me General Schofield to take post at Columbia at once? I make this application because the force at Chattanooga is not sufficiently large or well organized to do more than defend that place.

GEORGE H. THOMAS,
Major General.

ATLANTA, *October* 31, 1864.

Major General SHERMAN:

Your despatch received. It will take more than one-half the available cars between here and Chattanooga to move the 23d corps. The removal of stores to the rear will have to stop in a great measure. The railroad has been open but two (2) days. Much has been done, but there is still more to do than can be done in seven days, with the usual rate of accidents. If the 23d corps move by cars it will take eleven (11) days to complete everything. We still require some hundreds of cars of stores to complete your supplies and outfit. Under the circumstances, shall cars be sent at once to move the 23d corps? Answer.

L. C. EASTON.
A. BECKWITH.

[Cipher.]

NASHVILLE, *October* 31, 1864—12 m.

Major General SHERMAN:

Have telegraphed to General Rosecrans at Saint Louis, and also to commanding officer at Paducah, but can hear nothing from them. Now that Hood has undoubtedly crossed the river, I think it important that General Schofield should be sent to Columbia as soon as possible, as I have no certainty of getting any other troops. There are still six regiments due from the north. If you approve this, please order General Schoffeld to proceed at once by rail to Columbia.

GEORGE H. THOMAS,
Major General

[Cipher.]
NASHVILLE, *October* 31, 1864—6.30 p. m.

Major General SHERMAN:

Am endeavoring to concentrate my troops as much as possible, and trying to place them at Pulaski—Decatur being held by Granger's forces—and shall therefore order General Schofield to come with all his corps, except one brigade, by rail, as speedily as possible. I am sure Stanley's force will not be large enough to drive Hood's whole army back. He has a large cavalry force. I can hear nothing of the troops from Missouri, and cannot, therefore, rely upon their reaching me. Neither can I hear anything of the new regiments expected.

I consider it absolutely necessary for General Schofield to come. There is no doubt but there is a large force of the enemy in West Tennessee, and now crossing the Tennessee, near Florence. I learn by telegram from Johnsonville that one gunboat and five transports were captured last night below Johnsonville. Commanding officer at Johnsonville expects to be attacked daily, and I have no troops to re-enforce him, unless the Missouri troops should accidentally get there in time to do so. The water in the Tennessee river having fallen very low, the enemy was expected to cross at three or four points, in spite of Croxton's efforts to prevent them.

If General Hatch does not disregard my orders for him to halt at Pulaski, he and Croxton, with Stanley, may be able to hold Hood at Pulaski until General Schofield can get up.

GEORGE H. THOMAS,
Major General.

[Cipher.]

HEADQUARTERS MILITARY DIVISION OF THE MISSISSIPPI,
In the field, Rome, Ga., November 1, 1864.

Major General GEORGE H. THOMAS, *Nashville, Tenn.:*

Despatch received. The fact that Forrest is down about Johnsonville, while Hood with his infantry is still about Florence and Tuscumbia, gives you time for concentration. The supplies about Chattanooga are immense, and I will soon be independent of them; therefore I would not risk supplies coming in transitu from Nashville to Chattanooga. In like manner, we have large supplies in Nashville, and if they be well guarded, and Hood can't get our supplies, he can't stay in Tennessee long.

General Schofield will go to you as rapidly as cars can take him, and I have no doubt, after the emergency is passed, and the enemy has done us considerable damage, re-enforcements will pour to you, more than can be provided for or taken care of. In the mean time do your best.

I will leave here to-morrow for Kingston, and keep things moving towards the south. Therefore hold fast all new troops coming to you, excepting such as are now at Chattanooga, to whom I will give orders.

W. T. SHERMAN,
Major General.

[Cipher.]

HEADQUARTERS MILITARY DIVISION OF THE MISSISSIPPI,
In the field, Rome, Ga., November 1, 1864.

Lieut. General U. S. GRANT, *City Point, Va.:*

As you foresaw, and as Jeff. Davis threatened, the enemy is now in the full tide of execution of his grand plan to destroy my communications and defeat this army. His infantry, about thirty thousand, (30,000,) with Wheeler and Roddy's cavalry, from seven to ten thousand, (7,000 to 10,000,) are now in the neighborhood of Tuscumbia and Florence, and the water being low, are able to cross at will. Forrest seems to be scattered from Eastport to Jackson, Paris, and the lower Tennessee, and General Thomas reports the capture by him of a gunboat and five transports. General Thomas has near Athens and Pulaski Stanley's corps, about fifteen thousand (15,000) strong, and Schofield's corps, ten thousand, (10,000,) en route by rail, and has at least twenty to twenty-five thousand (20,000 to 25,000) men, with new regiments and conscripts arriving all the time, also. General Rosecrans promises the two divisions of Smith and Mower, belonging to me, but I doubt if they can reach Tennessee in less than ten (10) days. If I were to let go Atlanta and North Georgia and make for Hood he would, as he did here, retreat to the southwest, leaving his militia, now assembling at Macon and Griffin, to occupy our conquests, and the work of last summer would be lost. I have retained about fifty thousand (50,000) good troops, and have sent back full twenty-five thousand, (25,000,) and have instructed General Thomas to hold defensively Nashville, Chattanooga, and Decatur, all strongly fortified and provisioned for a long siege. I will destroy all the railroads of Georgia, and do as much substantial damage as is possible, reaching the sea-coast near one of the points hitherto indicated, trusting that Thomas with his present troops, and the influx of new troops promised, will be able in a very few days to assume the offensive.

Hood's cavalry may do a good deal of damage, and I have sent Wilson back with all dismounted cavalry, retaining only about four thousand five hundred (4,500.) This is the best I can do, and shall, therefore, when I get to Atlanta the necessary stores, move south as soon as possible.

W. T. SHERMAN,
Major General.

[Cipher.]

CITY POINT, *November* 1, 1864—6 p. m.

Major General SHERMAN:

Do you not think it advisable, now that Hood has gone so far north, to entirely ruin him before starting on your proposed campaign? With Hood's army destroyed, you can go where you please with impunity. I believed, and still believe, if you had started south while Hood was in the neighborhood of you, he would have been forced to go after you. Now that he is so far away, he might look upon the chase as useless, and he will go in one direction while you are pushing the other. If you can see the chance for destroying Hood's army, attend to that first, and make your other move secondary.

U. S. GRANT,
Lieutenant General.

[Cipher.]

HEADQUARTERS MILITARY DIVISION OF THE MISSISSIPPI,
In the field, Rome, Ga., November 2, 1864.

Major General THOMAS, *Nashville, Tennessee:*

Despatch of 7 p. m., 1st, received. I sent you yesterday copies of General Rosecrans's despatches, showing that Smith's and Mower's divisions are en route; but it will take ten (10) days for them to reach Paducah. It is now raining, and Beauregard will be very cautious in going north of the Tennessee at this season of the year. Schofield is on the railroad, and can be moved rapidly to any point you indicate. Have you any positive knowledge that any part of Beauregard's infantry has passed the Tennessee? Wilson is also coming to you with Garrard's dismounted cavalry, and it would be well to have horses and equipments awaiting them. According to Wilson's account, you will have in ten (10) days full twelve thousand (12,000) cavalry, and I estimate your infantry force, independent of railroad guards, full forty thousand (40,000) men, which is a force superior to the enemy.

W. T. SHERMAN,
Major General.

[Cipher.]

HEADQUARTERS MILITARY DIVISION OF THE MISSISSIPPI,
In the field, Rome, Ga., November 2, 1864.

Lieut. General U. S. GRANT, City Point, Va.:

Your despatch is received. If I could hope to overhaul Hood, I would turn against him with my whole force; then he would retreat to the southwest, drawing me as a decoy from Georgia, which is his chief object. If he ventures north of the Tennessee, I may turn in that direction and endeavor to get between him and his line of retreat; but, thus far, he has not gone above the Tennessee. Thomas will have a force strong enough to prevent his reaching any country in which we have an interest, and he has orders, if Hood turns to follow me, to push for Selma. No single army can catch him, and I am convinced the best results will follow from our defeating Jeff. Davis's cherished plan of making me leave Georgia by manœuvring. Thus far I have confined my efforts to thwart his plans, and have reduced my baggage so that I can pick up and start in any direction; but I would regard a pursuit of Hood as useless. Still, if he attempts to invade Middle Tennessee, I will hold Decatur, and be prepared to move in that direction; but, unless I let go Atlanta, my force will not be equal to his.

W. T. SHERMAN,
Major General.

[Cipher.]

HEADQUARTERS MILITARY DIVISION OF THE MISSISSIPPI,
In the field, Kingston, Ga., November 2, 1864.

Lieut. General U. S. GRANT, City Point, Va.:

If I turn back, the whole effect of my campaign will be lost. By my movements I have thrown Beauregard well to the west, and Thomas will have ample time and sufficient troops to hold him until re-enforcements meet him from Missouri, and recruits. We have now ample supplies at Chattanooga and Atlanta to stand a month's interruption to our communications, and I don't believe the confederate army can reach our lines save by cavalry raids, and Wilson will have cavalry enough to checkmate that. I am clearly of opinion that the best results will follow me in my contemplated movement through Georgia.

W. T. SHERMAN,
Major General.

[Cipher.]

CITY POINT, VA., November 2, 1864—11.30 a. m.

Major General SHERMAN:

Your despatch of 9 a. m. yesterday is just received. I despatched you the same date advising that Hood's army, now that it had worked so far north, ought to be looked upon more as the object. With the force, however, you have left with General Thomas, he must be able to take care of Hood and destroy him. I really do not see that you can withdraw from where you are to follow Hood, without giving up all we have gained in territory. I say, then, go on as you propose.

U. S. GRANT,
Lieutenant General.

[Cipher.]

HEADQUARTERS MILITARY DIVISION OF THE MISSISSIPPI,
In the field, Kingston, Ga., November 2, 1864.

Captain PENNOCK, *United States Navy, Mound City:*

I don't know what boats you have up the Tennessee now, but hear that Number Fifty-five has been captured by Forrest. I trust you will keep that river well patrolled, increasing the capacity of the boats according to the draught of water. If the present rains continue, one or two iron-clads would do most important service. In a few days I will be off for salt-water, and hope to meet my old friend Admiral Porter again. Will you be kind enough to write to him, and tell him to look out for me about Christmas from Hilton Head to Savannah? During my absence, please confer freely with General Thomas, who commands in my stead.

W. T. SHERMAN,
Major General.

[Cipher.]

NASHVILLE, *November 2, 1864—1.30 p. m.*

Major General SHERMAN:

Your despatch of 8 a. m. to-day just received. I this morning received the first telegram from Rosecrans. Contents similar to the one you sent me. I have just heard from General Croxton, who despatched to me at 7 p. m. yesterday, who says he has been within two miles of Florence on the Huntsville side, and three miles on the Lawrenceburg side. The enemy is there with a large force intrenched. They have laid pontoons at Florence, and are reported still crossing. He finds no cavalry, but Forrest is reported crossing below Florence. I think he must be mistaken about Forrest crossing below Florence. It may be Wheeler. General Hatch should be with Croxton by this time, and, although the rain may have made the roads bad, I am in hopes that the balance of Stanley's troops will reach Pulaski to-day. It will not be possible for me to raise within the next ten days more than Stanley's and Schofield's corps, and Croxton's and Hatch's cavalry, unless I should withdraw railroad guards immediately, which should not be done so long as we must operate the road. The convalescents will, of course, only be fit to garrison Chattanooga, Whitesides, and Bridgeport. It will need all the troops Granger has to hold Decatur. General Steedman's troops, belonging to my army, are almost dwindled away by expiration of service. Eventually General Wilson can organize twelve thousand (12,000) cavalry from dismounted men now in Tennessee and coming from the front; but he can't do this in ten (10) days. We will all do the best we can. If Beauregard halts to fortify, I hope we shall be ready for him. It has rained some, but not a great deal, here.

GEO. H. THOMAS,
Major General.

[Cipher.]

HEADQUARTERS MILITARY DIVISION OF THE MISSISSIPPI,
In the field, Kingston, Ga., November 2, 1864.

Major General THOMAS, *Nashville:*

I have your despatch of to-day. If Granger will continue to demonstrate on the Moulton road with as strong a force as he can take out of Decatur, he will compel Beauregard to leave a similar force in observation. In like manner, Grierson at Memphis should be instructed to demonstrate out in the direction of Ripley or Corinth, to threaten the Mobile and Ohio railroad, on which he manifestly must depend. Then, having united Schofield and Stanley, and filled them as much as you can with your new troops, Beauregard will be checkmated; but if he advances from Florence, fight him cautiously, taking every advantage of your fortifications and the natural obstructions of the coun ry. I think he will aim for Fayetteville and Shelbyville, but you know the country better than I do. General A. J. Smith reports himself en route from Warrensburg, Missouri. To make things sure, you can call on the governors of Kentucky and Indiana for some militia, cautioning them against a stampede, no matter what occurs. Try and avoid, as I know you will, all false alarms. I am pushing my arrangements, and will soon be off.

W. T. SHERMAN,
Major General.

[Cipher.]

HEADQUARTERS MILITARY DIVISION OF THE MISSISSIPPI,
In the field, Kingston, Ga., November 2, 1864.

Lieut. General GRANT, *City Point, Va.:*

Despatch of 11.30 a. m. received. I will go on and complete my arrangements, and in a few days notify you of the day of my departure.

General Thomas reports to-day that his cavalry reconnoitred within three (3) miles of Florence yesterday, and found Beauregard intrenching. I have ordered him to hold Nashville, Chattanooga, and Decatur, all well supplied for a siege; all the rest of his army to assemble about Pulaski, and to fight Beauregard cautiously and carefully; at the same time for A. J. Smith and all re-enforcements to get up to enable him to assume a bold offensive, and to enable Wilson 'to get a good mount of cavalry. I think Jeff. Davis will change his tune when he finds me advancing into the heart of Georgia instead of retreating, and I think it will have an immediate effect on your operations at Richmond.

W. T. SHERMAN,
Major General.

WARRENSBURG, MO., *November 2, 1864.*

Major General SHERMAN:

I am now under orders to join you with my command, and will lose no time in reaching St. Louis and embarking for destination en route. I have about five hundred (500) men in Memphis belonging to the first and third divisions, 16th army corps. They are in detachments, and in occupation of the forts in Memphis. I now most earnestly request that you will order all men belonging to the first and third divisions to be relieved from duty at once and sent to Cairo, Illinois, and to report to me by telegraph at St. Louis.

A. J. SMITH, *Major General.*

ROME, *November 2, 1864.*

Major General SHERMAN:

General Howard reports last night at 6.30 at Cedartown, and nicely in camp. Says Hood took much, but left plenty of corn, and some pigs are left. Some scouting and observing parties of the enemy's cavalry about him. A captured letter from a citizen to Governor Brown complains bitterly of Hood's army and its lawlessness, and begs him to get orders from Jeff. Davis to stop it.

L. M. DAYTON, *A. D. C.*

[Cipher.]

NASHVILLE, *November 2, 1864—11.30 p. m.*

Major General SHERMAN:

Can't learn yet that Beauregard has started in any direction. He is across the river at Florence, but as yet has not moved from his intrenchments.

GEO. H. THOMAS,
Major General.

[Cipher.]

HEADQUARTERS MILITARY DIVISION OF THE MISSISSIPPI,
In the field, Kingston, Ga., November 3, 1864.

Major General THOMAS, *Nashville, Tennessee:*

Your despatch received. Glad to learn the Venus was recaptured, and have no doubt gunboat 55 will be recaptured or destroyed. Don't fail to give me the earliest notice of Beauregard's starting north, for he is watching us and will be influenced by our movements. Now that Forrest is scattered is a good time for your cavalry to pitch into Wheeler if he ventures out from Florence.

W. T. SHERMAN,
Major General.

[Cipher.]

HEADQUARTERS MILITARY DIVISION OF THE MISSISSIPPI,
In the field, Kingston, Ga., November 3, 1864.

Maj. Gen. H. W. HALLECK, *Headquarters Army, Washington, D. C.:*

The situation of affairs now is as follows: Beauregard, with Hood's army, is at Florence with a pontoon bridge, protected from our gunboats from below by the Colbert shoals, from above by the Muscle shoals. He has with him Wheeler's and Roddy's cavalry. Forrest's cavalry is down about Fort Herman. The country round about Florence has been again and again devastated during the past three years, and Beauregard must be dependent on the Mobile and Ohio railroad, which also has been broken and patched up in its whole extent. He purposes and promises his men to invade Middle Tennessee for the purpose of making me let go Georgia. The moment I detected that he had passed Gadsden, I detached the 4th corps, General Stanley, fifteen thousand (15,000) strong, who is now at Pulaski; and subsequently the 23d corps, General Schofield, ten thousand, (10,000,) who is now on cars moving to Nashville. This gives General Thomas two full corps and about five thousand cavalry, besides ten thousand (10,000) dismounted cavalry and all the new troops recently sent to Tennessee, with the railroad guards, with which to encounter

Beauregard, should he advance further. Besides which, General Thomas will have the active co-operation of the gunboats, both above and below the shoals, and the two divisions of Smith and Mower en route from Missouri. I therefore feel no uneasiness as to Tennessee, and have ordered General Thomas to assume the offensive in the direction of Selma, Alabama. With myself I have the 20th corps at Atlanta, the 15th and 17th near Kenesaw, and the 14th here. I am sending to the rear, as fast as cars will move, the vast accumulation of stuff that in spite of my endeavors has been got over the road, and am sending forward just enough bread and meat to enable me to load my wagons, destroy everything of value to the enemy, and start on my contemplated trip. I can be ready in five (5) days, but am waiting to be more certain that Thomas will be prepared for any contingency that may arise. It is now raining, which is favorable to us, and unfavorable to the enemy. Davis has utterly failed in his threat to force me to leave in thirty (30) days, for my railroad is in good order from Nashville to Atlanta, and his army is further from my communications now than it was twenty (20) days ago. I would advise the accumulation of all troops available up the Tennessee river (now in good boating stage) about Clifton, subject to General Thomas's orders, and that Canby leave the Mississippi river, to be watched by gunboats and local garrisons, and push, with about fifteen thousand (15,000) men, for the Alabama river and Selma. These co-operating movements would completely bewilder Beauregard, and he would burst with French despair. I propose to adhere, as near as possible, to my original plan, and on reaching the sea-coast will be available for re-enforcing the army in Virginia, leaving behind a track of desolation as well as a sufficient force to hold fast all that is of permanent value to our cause. When I leave Atlanta it will contain little that will be of use or comfort to the enemy.

W. T. SHERMAN,
Major General.

[Cipher.]

NASHVILLE, November 3, 1864—2.30 p. m.

Major General SHERMAN:

Your message, 9.30 a. m. yesterday, received. Will give instructions to Granger to continue his demonstrations between Decatur and Moulton. General Croxton still holds the two fords of Shoal creek, mentioned to you in a former despatch. I heard from him yesterday at 3 p. m. He reports he drove in the enemy's cavalry pickets. A scout had just returned from Town river, who reported that they were waiting for Hardee's corps and cavalry. Croxton intended to attempt to destroy their pontoon bridge last night. Have not yet heard result. If I can get Grierson's cavalry at Memphis, I will have it pushed out toward Mobile and Ohio railroad, and threaten Beauregard's communications. I propose to place General A. J. Smith's command, with the assistance of the gunboats, as near Eastport as possible, unless Beauregard gets start of me. But if he don't move before Sunday, I will have Generals Schofield and Stanley together at Pulaski, and he can then move wherever he pleases. Will fill up Stanley's and Schofield's corps as soon as possible, but at present almost entire transportation of the road is taken up by conscripts and recruits for commands at the front. Six of the new regiments are still due, and not heard from since starting. If it is not necessary for Generals Schofield and Stanley to move from Pulaski before I can get General A. J. Smith well up the Tennessee river, Beauregard will have to leave his present position, or be cut off from his railroad communications. I have six gunboats on Tennessee river now coming up. Lieutenant Shirk has no doubt but he can open river and raise blockade. Am afraid it will take longer for Wilson to reorganize and mount his cavalry than he thinks. When he does complete it, we will be strong enough to restore quiet all along borders and undertake the expedition into Alabama. Have made great exertions to prevent stampeding, and so far have succeeded measurably well, but I find it hard work. Have just heard from General Schofield at Chattanooga. A portion of his troops have started on cars, and he has strong hopes of getting them all off by rail to-morrow evening.

GEORGE H. THOMAS,
Major General.

[Cipher.]

HEADQUARTERS MILITARY DIVISION OF THE MISSISSIPPI,
In the field, Kingston, Ga, November 4, 1864.

Major General STEEDMAN, Chattanooga, Tennessee:

Your despatch of to-day is received, indicating that Beauregard has moved toward Corinth. I do not wish him in a better place. The trains on our railroad are not working to my satisfaction. Tell the superintendent I want him to stop running cars for the accommodation of travellers, but to make up a gang of three or four hundred cars to carry to Atlanta in one trip all we need, and take back all that is necessary. I want this done at once, as I propose to start as soon as the present storm clears away. The whole army is now distributed along the road so as to cover it perfectly. I would like to have you meet me here to confer and superintend the removal back to Chattanooga of all railroad stock and garrisons on the breaking up of the road. Answer.

W. T. SHERMAN,
Major General.

SMYRNA CAMP-GROUND, November 5, 1864.

Major General SHERMAN :

My command is at this place.

O. O. HOWARD, Major General.

ATLANTA, November 4, 1864.

Major General SHERMAN :

I am much disappointed in the working of the road. I have urged everybody and everything, but have been able to get in here only seventy-seven (77) cars in the last twenty-four (24) hours, all of which have been properly unloaded, reloaded, and started back. I am sorry to disappoint you, but am doing my very best. They have accumulated more plunder in the last two months than I supposed could have been got here in six. We have an abundant supply of grain, which I wish you would send animals here to eat up.

L. C. EASTON, C. Q. M.

[Cipher.]

CHATTANOOGA, November 4, 1864.

Major General SHERMAN :

By 12 noon to-morrow there will be on the route to Atlanta and in that place three hundred and seventy (370) freight cars, two hospital trains, and two wrecking trains, loaded with all freight that has been ordered. There will be

17*

one hundred (100) cars in to-night, which can be returned to-morrow if wanted. The storms have interfered very materially with the running of trains. I will come down to-morrow.

 JAMES B. STEEDMAN,
Major General.

ATLANTA, November 5, 1864.

Major General SHERMAN:

I believe that I have now in the commissary depots at Atlanta everything we will require for the trip.

 A. BECKWITH,
Chief Commissary of Subsistence.

[Cipher.]

ATLANTA, November 5, 1864—10 a. m.

Major General SHERMAN:

The superintendent, Mr. Taylor, reports this morning two hundred and fifty (250) cars between Chattanooga and Kingston, bound south, detained by small accidents. These cars should be detained in Atlanta till a sufficient number arrive, say five hundred in round numbers, to make everything perfectly safe and sure to clean up the entire road to Chattanooga. General Steedman should be directed to come with his troops and the balance of the stores immediately, bringing two hundred and fifty (250) cars. We propose that the whole five hundred (500) cars reach Atlanta before any trains be started back to Chattanooga. Our superintendent, Mr. Taylor, thinks he can work out your idea. Answer, if this meets your views, in order that there may be concert of action

 L. C. EASTON, B. G., &c.
A. BECKWITH, Colonel and C. S.

HEADQUARTERS MILITARY DIVISION OF THE MISSISSIPPI,
In the field, Kingston, Ga., November 6, 1864.

COMMANDING OFFICERS of all the posts and stations:

Beauregard with Hood's army is at Florence and Tuscumbia, a country already devasted and stripped of provisions. Forrest is opposite Johnsonville, on the Tennessee river, and has done considerable damage to gunboats and transports, but has captured no provisions, and, as that is but one of three of our lines of supply, the temporary interruption will not be felt. I want the preparations heretofore ordered for this army to go on with as much speed as possible, but the possibilities are, time will be allowed in our present camp for the complete payment of all our troops, the sending back the soldiers' money, and the presidential election of Tuesday next. Also attention must be paid to getting the conscripts to their proper companies and have them properly armed and clothed.

 W. T. SHERMAN,
Major General.

[Cipher.]

NASHVILLE, *November* 6, 1864—12.30 p. m.

Major General SHERMAN:

I received from General Croxton this a. m., at 10 o'clock, despatches to effect that enemy had attacked him in strong force, and had driven him across Shoal creek, on p. m. 4th instant, compelling him to fall back to Four-Mile creek. The following telegram, just received from him, I forward for your information:

"FOUR-MILE CREEK, *November* 6, 1864—12.30 p. m.

"Major General SHERMAN:

"Enemy recrossed Shoal creek last night. I had scouts on road twelve miles above Florence at 8 p. m,, and at that time no rebels had appeared at that point except two, who returned to Baugh's mills at sundown, reporting cavalry force there. General Hatch was at Sugar creek at 3 p. m. yesterday morning, moving to Lexington, to which point I sent him full despatches last night. Have not heard from him, but as soon as do, will advise that we move down and occupy line of Shoal creek. I doubt if enemy meditates immediate advance. Think their cavalry are operating elsewhere, and they are waiting for it. Prisoner who belongs to 3d Virginia regiment, who helped to build their bridge, reports that Hardee's corps crossed Tuesday, and that they have no other force this side. They had about a division at the fight yesterday.

"JNO. M. CROXTON,
"*Brigadier General.*"

I forward also following, just received from General Schofield:

"JOHNSONVILLE, *November* 6, 1864—7 p. m.

"Major General THOMAS:

"Have just arrived here. Colonel Gallop's scouts have returned. Report only small cavalry force enemy this side river. There appears also only to be small force and no artillery opposite here. Think Colonel Gallop's brigade will be sufficient for this place, but will examine ground in morning and report definitely. Think it would be well to detain all troops at Nashville except those which belong to Colonel Gallop's brigade.

"J. M. SCHOFIELD,
"*Major General.*"

I shall concentrate all General Schofield's troops at Pulaski, with exception of Colonel Gallop's brigade, which, for present, will leave at Johnsonville. General Wilson has just arrived here and arranged with me this evening for a complete remount and thorough organizing of the cavalry. Think we shall have no further trouble with the cavalry excepting that attending getting horses to the front. Have just heard from General Granger at Decatur, who reports a reconnoissance from his post had just returned from within eight (8) miles of Courtland. Met eight hundred (800) enemy's cavalry, all Texas troops, at Fox's creek, drove them a mile beyond, but could obtain no information in addition to that heretofore reported. The outpost at Brown's ferry reports only few rebel cavalry on opposite shore, who made no attempt to cross. All of General Stanley's troops are now at Pulaski in position for enemy should he attempt to advance. The cavalry is well up to enemy's position, and will be able to give the earliest information of his movements north.

GEO. H. THOMAS,
Major General.

HEADQUARTERS MILITARY DIVISION OF THE MISSISSIPPI,
In the field, Kingston, Ga., November 6, 1864.

DEAR GENERAL: I have heretofore telegraphed and written you pretty fully, but I still have some thoughts in my busy brain that should be confided to you as a key to future developments.

The taking of Atlanta broke upon Jeff. Davis so suddenly as to disturb the equilibrium of his usually well-balanced temper, so that at Augusta, Macon, Montgomery, and Columbia, South Carolina, he let out some of his thoughts which otherwise he would have kept to himself. As he is not only the President of the southern confederacy, but also its commander-in-chief, we are bound to attach more importance to his words than we would to those of a mere civil chief magistrate.

The whole burden of his song consists in the statement that Sherman's communications *must* be broken and his army destroyed. Now, it is a well settled principle that if we can prevent his succeeding in his threat we defeat him, and derive all the moral advantages of a victory. Thus far Hood and Beauregard conjointly have utterly failed to interrupt my supplies or communications. My railroad and telegraph are now in good order from Atlanta back to the Ohio river. His losses in men at Allatoona, Resaca, Ship's Gap, and Decatur, exceed in number ours at the block-houses at Big Shanty, Allatoona creek, and Dalton; and the rapidity of his flight from Dalton to Gadsden takes from him all the merit or advantage claimed for his skilful and rapid lodgement on my railroad. The only question in my mind is, whether I ought not to have dogged him far over into Mississippi, trusting to some happy accident to bring him to bay and to battle; but I then thought that by so doing I would play into his hands, by being drawn or decoyed too far away from our original line of advance. Besides, I had left at Atlanta a corps and guards along the railroad back to Chattanooga, which might have fallen an easy prey to his superior cavalry. I felt compelled, therefore, to do what is usually a mistake in war—divide my forces—send a part back into Tennessee, retaining the balance here.

As I have before informed you, I sent Stanley back directly from Gaylesville and Schofield from Rome, both of whom have reached their destination; and thus far Hood, who has brought up at Florence, is further from my communications than when he started; and I have in Tennessee a force numerically greater than his, well commanded and well organized; so that I feel no uneasiness on the score of Hood reaching my main communications.

My last accounts from General Thomas are to 9.30 last night, when Hood's army was about Florence in great distress about provisions, as it well must be, and that Devil Forrest was down about Johnsonville, making havoc among the gunboats and transports. But Schofield's troops were arriving at Johnsonville and a fleet of gunboats was reported coming up from below, able to repair that trouble. You know that that line of supplies was only opened for summer's use, when the Cumberland is not to be depended upon. We now have abundant supplies at Atlanta, Chattanooga, and Nashville, with the Louisville and Nashville railroad and the Cumberland river unmolested; so that I regard Davis's threat to get his army on my rear, or on my communications, as a miserable failure.

Now, as to the second branch of my proposition: I admit that the first object should be the destruction of that army; and if Beauregard moves his infantry and artillery up into the pocket about Jackson and Paris, I will feel strongly tempted to move Thomas directly against him, and myself move rapidly by Decatur and Purdy, to cut off his retreat. But this would involve the abandonment of Atlanta, and a retrograde movement which would be very doubtful of expediency or success; for, as a matter of course, Beauregard, who watched me with his cavalry and his friendly citizens, would have timely notice, and would slip out and escape, to regain what we have earned at so much cost. I am more than satisfied that Beauregard has not the nerve to attack fortifications, or to meet me in open battle; and it would be a great achievement for him to make me abandoned Atlanta by mere threats and manœuvres.

These are the reasons which have determined my former movements.

I have employed the last ten (10) days in running to the rear the sick and wounded and worthless, and all the vast amount of stores accumulated by our army in the advance—aiming to organize this branch of my army into four well-commanded corps, encumbered by only one (1) gun to a thousand men, and provisions and ammunition which can be loaded up in our mule wagons, so that we can pick up and start on the shortest notice. I reckon that by the 10th instant this end will be reached, and by that date I also will have the troops all paid; the presidential election over and out of our way; and I hope the early storms of November, now prevailing, will also give us the chance of a long period of fine healthy weather for campaigning. Then the question presents itself: "What shall be done?" On the supposition, always, that Thomas can hold the line of the Tennessee, and very shortly be able to assume the offensive, as against Beauregard, I propose to act in such manner against the material resources of the south as utterly to negative Davis's boasted threat and promises of protection. If we can march a well-appointed army right through his territory, it is a demonstration to the world—foreign and domestic—that we have a power which Davis cannot resist. This may not be war, but rather statesmanship; nevertheless, it is overwhelming to my mind that there are thousands of people abroad and in the south who will reason thus: If the north can march an army right through the south, it is proof positive that the north can prevail in this contest, leaving only open the question of its willingness to use that power. Now, Mr. Lincoln's election, (which is assured,) coupled with the conclusion thus reached, makes a complete logical whole. Even without a battle, the results, operating upon the minds of sensible men, would produce fruits more than compensating for the expense, trouble, and risk.

Admitting this reasoning to be good, that such a movement *per se* be right, still there may be reasons why one route would be better than another. There are three from Atlanta—southeast, south, and southwest—all open, with no serious enemy to oppose at present.

The first would carry me across the only east and west railroad remaining to the confederacy, which would be destroyed, and thereby the communications between the armies of Lee and Beauregard severed. Incidentally, I might destroy the enemy's depots at Macon and Augusta, and reach the sea-shore at Charleston, or Savannah; from either of which points I could re-enforce our armies in Virginia.

The second and easiest route would be due south, following, substantially, the valley of Flint river, which is very fertile and well supplied, and fetching up on the navigable waters of the Appalachicola, destroying *en route* the same railroad, taking up the prisoners of war still at Andersonville, and destroying about four hundred thousand (400,000) bales of cotton near Albany and Fort Gaines. This, however, would leave the army in a bad position for future movements.

The third, down the Chattahoochee to Opelika and Montgomery, thence to Pensacola or Tensas bayou, in communication with Fort Morgan. This latter route would enable me at once to co-operate with General Canby in the reduction of Mobile, and occupation of the line of the Alabama.

In my judgment, the first would have a material effect upon your campaign in Virginia; the second would be the safest of execution; but the third would more properly fall within the sphere of my own command, and have a direct bearing upon my own enemy, "Beauregard." If, therefore, I should start before I hear further from you, or before further developments turn my course, you may take it for granted that I have moved *via* Griffin to Barnsville; that I break up the road between Columbus and Macon *good*, and then, if I feign on Columbus, will move *via* Macon and Millen to Savannah, or if I feign on Macon you may take it for granted I have shot off towards Opelika, Montgomery, and Mobile bay or Pensacola.

I will not attempt to send couriers back, but trust to the Richmond papers to keep you well advised. I will give you notice by telegraph of the exact time of my departure.

General Steedman is here to clear the railroad back to Chattanooga, and I will see that the road is broken completely between the Etowah and the Chattahoochee, including their bridges, and that Atlanta itself is utterly destroyed.

I am, with respect,

W. T. SHERMAN, *Major General.*

Lieut. General U. S. GRANT,
Commander-in-Chief, City Point, Virginia.

[Cipher.]

HEADQUARTERS MILITARY DIVISION OF THE MISSISSIPPI,
In the field, Kingston, Ga., November 7, 1864.

Major General HALLECK, *Washington, D. C.:*

By the 10th the election will be over, the troops all paid, and all our surplus property will be back to Chattanooga. On that day or the following, if affairs should remain as now in Tennessee, I propose to begin the movement which I have hitherto fully described.

I can hear of no large force to our front, and, according to General Thomas, Hood remains about Tuscumbia, and he feels perfectly confident of his ability to take care of him.

You can safely communicate with me for the next three (3) days.

W. T. SHERMAN,
Major General.

HEADQUARTERS MILITARY DIVISION OF THE MISSISSIPPI,
In the field, Kingston, Ga., November 7, 1864.

Major General G. H. THOMAS, *Nashville, Tennessee:*

Your despatch of to-day just received. I think Beauregard is checkmated. I will be all ready by the 10th, but will give you more positive notice in a day or two. Glad that A. J. Smith is heard from. All men belonging to his two divisions that are not in hospital you will order in my name from Memphis. I would like to know, if possible, if Hood's whole army is at Tuscumbia, or has gone towards Corinth.

W. T. SHERMAN, *Major General.*

HEADQUARTERS MILITARY DIVISION OF THE MISSISSIPPI,
In the field, Kingston, Ga., November 8, 1864.

COMMANDING OFFICERS *of all posts:*

This is the rain I have been waiting for, and as soon as it is over we will be off.

W. T. SHERMAN, *Major General.*

HEADQUARTERS MILITARY DIVISION OF THE MISSISSIPPI,
In the field, Kingston, Ga., November 8, 1864.

Major General H. W. HALLECK, *Washington, D. C.:*

Despatch of to-day received. All my preparations will be completed by the 10th. It is now raining, which is favorable, as the chances are, after it clears away, we will have a long spell of fine weather for marching. General Thomas has been instructed to assume the offensive as soon as possible, and I will send him a copy of your despatch, that he may know of the contemplated movement on the river by Hurlbut.

W. T. SHERMAN,
Major General.

CITY POINT, *Virginia*, 10½ p. m., 7th.

Major General SHERMAN:

Your despatch of this evening received. I see no present reason for changing your plan; should any arise you will see it; or if I do, I will inform you. I think everything here favorable now.

Great good fortune attend you. I believe you will be eminently successful, and at worst can only make a march less fruitful of results than hoped for.

U. S. GRANT,
Lieutenant General.

HEADQUARTERS MILITARY DIVISION OF THE MISSISSIPPI.
In the field, Kingston, Ga., November 8, 1864.

TYLER, *Louisville, Kentucky :*

Despatch me to-morrow night and the next night a summary of all news, especially of elections, that I may report them to Governor Brown, at Milledgeville, where I expect a friendly interview in a few days.

Keep this very secret, for the world will lose sight of me shortly, and you will hear worse stories than when I went to Meridian. Jeff. Davis's thirty (30) days are up for wiping us out, and we are not wiped out yet by a good deal. Ewing reached here to-day. All well.

W. T. SHERMAN,
Major General.

[Cipher.]

NASHVILLE, *November* 9, 1864—9 p. m.

Major General SHERMAN:

Your two despatches of 6 p. m., 8 and 9 a. m., to-day, are received. General Croxton, from Four-Mile creek, reports yesterday, 8 p. m., that river has risen more than two feet on shoals, enough to make six (6) feet below them. A scout from over the river reports the bulk of Hood's army still on that side; and have also a report from General Granger, who says Elk river is still up, and that two couriers crossed in skiff last evening, who communicated with Rogersville. General Croxton still holds east bank of Shoal creek, but enemy have a heavy force on west bank, supposed to be one corps. The enemy is reported to have one at Florence, and one corps on south side of the river opposite Florence. It is also reported that Roddy has gone to Corinth. The contradictory nature of these reports indicate, plainly, however, that the entire infantry force of the enemy is in and about Florence and Tuscumbia. General Hatch reports yesterday from Taylor's Spring, Alabama, that he intended attacking enemy this morning along the entire line, to ascertain where the enemy is and the position he holds. Your despatch for Lieutenant General Grant, City Point, marked immediately and important, will go forward by special messenger by first train in the morning.

GEO. H. THOMAS,
Major General.

MILITARY DIVISION OF THE MISSISSIPPI,
In the field, Kingston, Ga., November 10, 1864.

Brigadier General JOHN M. CORSE, *Rome, Georgia :*

In the execution of sealed orders No. 115, you will destroy to-night all public property not needed by your command, all foundries, mills, work-shops, warehouses, railroad depots, and other storehouses convenient to the railroad, together with all wagon shops, tanneries or other factories useful to our enemy. Destroy the bridges completely, and then move your command to-morrow to Kingston and beyond, passing General Davis's command, after which proceed by easy marches till you overtake your corps and report to its commander.

W. T. SHERMAN,
Major General.

MILITARY DIVISION OF THE MISSISSPPI,
In the field, Kingston, Ga., November 10, 1864.

C. A. DANA, *Assistant Secretary of War, Washington :*

If indiscreet newspaper men publish information too near the truth, counter-act its effect by publishing other paragraphs calculated to mislead the enemy—such as Sherman's army has been much re-enforced, especially in the cavalry, and he will soon move in several columns in a circuit so as to catch Hood's army.   Sherman's destination is not Charleston, but Selma, where he will meet an army from the Gulf, &c., &c.

W. T. SHERMAN,
Major General.

HEADQUARTERS MILITARY DIVISION OF THE MISSISSIPPI,
In the field, Kingston, Ga., November 10, 1864.

General THOMAS, *Nashville :*

Your despatch of 5 p. m. is received.   All will be ready to start from here the day after to-morrow.   Keep me well advised.   I think you will find Hood marching off, and you should be ready to follow him.   Decatur, Tuscaloosa, Columbus and Selma are all good points to forage and feed an army.   Let me keep Beauregard busy, and the people of the south will realize his inability to protect them.

W. T. SHERMAN,
Major General.

HEADQUARTERS MILITARY DIVISION OF THE MISSISSIPPI,
In the field, Kingston, Ga., November 11, 1864.

Major General H. W. HALLECK,
Headquarters United States Army, Washington, D. C.:

My arrangements are now all complete, and the railroad cars are being sent to the rear.   Last night we burned all foundries, mills, and shops of every kind in Rome, and to-morrow I leave Kingston, with the rear guard, for Atlanta, which I propose to dispose of in a similar manner, and to start on the 16th on the projected grand raid.   All appearances still indicate that Beauregard has got back to his old hole at Corinth, and I hope he will enjoy it.   My army prefers to enjoy the fresh sweet potato fields of the Ocmulgee.   I have balanced all the figures well, and am satisfied that General Thomas has in Tennessee a force sufficient for all probabilities, and I have urged him, the moment Beauregard turns south, to cross the Tennessee at Decatur and push straight for Selma. To-morrow our wires will be broken, and this is probably my last despatch. I would like to have Foster to break the Savannah and Charleston road about Pocotaligo about the 1st of December. All other preparations are to my entire satisfaction.

W. T. SHERMAN,
Major Gneeral.

MARIETTA, *November 11, 1864.*

Captain L. M. DAYTON, *Aide-de-Camp:*

Four deserters came in this morning; left Montgomery on 2d; came to Opelika on cars; left that place on 4th; passed Carrollton on 9th. Hood was at Corinth. All convalescent soldiers now being sent to that point. Some infantry and fifteen hundred (1,500) cavalry at Opelika. Three brigades of cavalry at Carrollton, and five regiments at Villa Rica. Small force at West Point and Newnan. Cars run to Newnan. No information regarding Atlanta and Macon railroad. Citizens from Carrollton, and other points in that direction, think we are retreating from Atlanta.

J. KILPATRICK,
Brigadier General.

ATLANTA, *November 11, 1864.*

Major General SHERMAN:

The army of Tennessee have obtained and have got in their wagons all they can haul and all they want. Same of 20th army corps. There is great plenty of salt, coffee, salt meat, pepper and soap here. The 14th army corps may want a little more bread, and, perhaps, a little more sugar. I have about one hundred thousand (100,000) rations bread for 14th army corps; twenty-two thousand(22,000) rations sugar. I do not know how much General Davis may have on hand, but presume he has two hundred thousand (200,000) rations of bread. Everything is loaded in Atlanta save what is held for the 14th army corps. There are at least one million two hundred thousand (1,200,000) rations of the principal rations in hands of troops and available.

A. BECKWITH, *Colonel, &c.*

ATLANTA, GA., *November 11, 1864.*

Major General SHERMAN:

With what the army now has in its (provision) wagons, what is between here and Kingston, and what I have here in store, I think I can make out five (5) days' grain, commencing with to-morrow.

L. C. EASTON, *Chief Quartermaster.*

[Cipher.]

NASHVILLE, *November 11, 1864—9 p. m.*

Major General SHERMAN:

Following from Granger received to-day. It confirms previously reported position of the enemy:

DECATUR, 11*th*—10 a. m.

Two men from tenth Tennessee, made prisoners at Florence, escaped Saturday night from the rebels. They confirm report of two corps having crossed. One corps still on south bank.

They assert that enemy are still very badly off for clothing, many being barefoot, but they are expecting clothing by train. They say railroad is not completed to Tuscumbia, but only to Cherokee, fifteen (15) miles from there. They have train of wagons from Cherokee, and one pontoon bridge at the foot of the island above old railroad bridge. They say enemy are fortifying. Talk in their camps is, they are going to advance on Nashville.

R. S. GRANGER, *Brigadier General.*

Stanley from Pulaski reports nothing new. Water still very high. It is hoped the rise would carry off the enemy's bridge. They say it is trestled at both ends, with pontoons in the middle. Deserters say Georgia troops are disgusted and are deserting. Received despatch from General Washburne to-day, dated Memphis, 8th. He says advices from Corinth that but few troops there then; that cavalry had brought up a lot of conscripts, absentees from Hood's army, who went towards Tuscumbia. Also reports enemy repairing road from Cherokee to Tuscumbia. About 29th ultimo four thousand (4,000) rebel soldiers came down Blue Mountain railroad to Selma, and were sent to Hood by the way of Meridian and Corinth; also, ten (10) car-loads ammunition from Selma. The impression is that Beauregard intends to make Corinth his base, supplies being sent up constantly on the Mobile and Ohio railroad. He was to send out cavalry reconnoissance 9th, but says his force not strong enough to threaten Mobile and Ohio railroad much. Have not heard from General A. J. Smith's troops since last report, but daily expecting him here. No reports from Hatch or Croxton to-day. Rear-Admiral Lee informs me he is pushing to put one iron-clad on Tennessee river; one on Cumberland, with a third convenient to be placed on either, according to necessity of the case.

GEO. H. THOMAS,
Major General.

HEADQUARTERS MILITARY DIVISION OF THE MISSISSIPPI,
In the field, Kingston, Ga., November 11, 1864

Major General THOMAS, *Nashville, Tennessee:*

Despatch of to-night received. All right. I can hardly believe Beauregard would attempt to work against Nashville from Corinth as a base at this stage of the war, but all information seems to point that way. If he does, you will whip him out of his boots. But I rather think you will find commotion in his camp in a day or two. Last night we burned Rome, and in two more days will burn Atlanta, and he must discover that I am not retreating, but, on the contrary, fighting for the very heart of Georgia. About a division of rebel cavalry made its appearance this morning south of the Coosa river, opposite Rome, and fired on the rear guard as it withdrew. Also, two days ago some of Iverson's cavalry, about eight hundred, (800,) approached Atlanta from the direction of Decatur with a section of guns and swept round towards Whitehall, and disappeared in the direction of Rough and Ready. These also seem to indicate that Beauregard expected us to retreat. I hear of about fifteen hundred (1,500) infantry down at Carrollton, and also some infantry at Jonesboro,' but what numbers I cannot estimate. These are all the enemy I know to be in this neighborhood, though a rumor is that Breckinridge has arrived with some from West Virginia. To-morrow I begin the movement laid down in my Special Field Order 115, and shall keep things moving thereafter. By to-morrow morning all trains will be at or north of Kingston, and you can have the exclusive use of all the rolling stock. By using detachments of recruits and dismounted cavalry in your fortifications, you will have Schofield, and Stanley, and A. J. Smith, strengthened by eight or ten new regiments, and all of Wilson's cavalry, you could safely invite Beauregard across the Tennessee, and prevent his ever returning. I still believe, however, that the public clamor will force him to turn and follow me, in which event you should cross at Decatur and move directly towards Selma as far as you can transport supplies. The probabilities are, the wires will be broken to-morrow, and that all communication will cease between us; but I have directed the main wire to be left, and will use it if possible, and wish you to do the same. You may act, however, on the certainty that I sally from Atlanta on the 16th with about sixty thousand (60,000) men, well provisioned, but expecting to live liberally on the country.

W. T. SHERMAN,
Major General.

HEADQUARTERS MILITARY DIVISION OF THE MISSISSIPPI,
In the field, Kingston, November 12, 1864.

General HOWARD, *Smyrna:*

I start this morning. As soon as all the trains have passed north you may begin the work on the railroad. I want your army across the Chattahoochee on the third day. J. E. Smith and Corse are marching to-day. Davis will leave here in a few hours.

W. T. SHERMAN,
Major General.

HEADQUARTERS MILITARY DIVISION OF THE MISSISSIPPI,
In the field, Kingston, November 12, 1864.

General STEEDMAN, *Chattanooga:*

I start this morning. All the trains are here, and will be despatched north. As soon as the last one has passed Adairsville, draw in the garrisons and begin the work prescribed in order one hundred and fifteen (115.) Telegraph me to-night at Allatoona all information, and keep General Thomas well advised of your actions.

W. T. SHERMAN,
Major General.

[Cipher.]

NASHVILLE, *November* 12, 1864—8.30 a. m.

Major General SHERMAN:

Your despatch of 12 o'clock last night received. I have no fears that Beauregard can do us any harm now, and if he attempts to follow you I will follow him as far as possible. If he does not follow you, I will then thoroughly organize my troops, and, I believe, shall have men enough to ruin him unless he gets out of the way very rapidly. The country of middle Alabama, I learn, is teeming with supplies this year, which will be greatly to our advantage. I have no additional news to report from the direction of Florence. I am now convinced that the greater part of Beauregard's army is near Florence and Tuscumbia, and that you will at least have a clear road before you for several days, and that your success will fully equal your expectations.

GEORGE H. THOMAS,
Major General.

(This was the last despatch received before cutting communications and starting for Savannah.)

HEADQUARTERS MILITARY DIVISION OF THE MISSISSIPPI,
In the field, Cartersville, November 12, 1864.

Major General THOMAS, *Nashville:*

Despatch received.   All right.

W. T. SHERMAN,
Major General.

(Here wires were cut and all communication ceased.)

HEADQUARTERS MILITARY DIVISION OF THE MISSISSIPPI,
In the field, Atlanta, Ga., November 15, 1864.

GENERAL: The general-in-chief directs me to say that, upon your arrival at Madison, he desires that you will, if it can be done without too much delay, send eastward to the Oconee river and destroy the railroad bridge. By looking at the map you will see that a force sufficient to do this work can be sent from Madison, and afterwards join you further on. It is important the bridge should be destroyed.

I am, general, respectfully, your obedient servant,

L. M. DAYTON, *Aide-de-Camp.*

Major General SLOCUM,
Commanding Left Wing, &c.

HEADQUARTERS MILITARY DIVISION OF THE MISSISSIPPI,
In the field, near Yellow River, Ga., November 18, 1864.

Despatch received. All is well with this column, which will be to-night on the east side of the Ulcofauhachee, and to-morrow will take the Milledgeville road, leaving you the Eatonton road. Don't be in a hurry, but break up that railroad as far as the Oconee, in the most thorough manner, so that every rail will be disabled; better do that work well now when there is no opposition and you will have to give it your personal attention, else it will be slighted by your officers; impress on them its great importance, and that if done well now, it will not have to be done over at some future time under less favorable circumstances. I had every man of Davis's command at work yesterday all day and into the night, and yet they slighted some of their work, but I will set them at work again to-day between the Yellow and Alcovy (Ulcofauhachee) rivers, about Covington. Our own experience shows how easily roads may be relaid if we have iron; therefore I want each bar of iron actually twisted either around a tree or with one of the hooks.

One division will be amply sufficient to go down to the bridge on Oconee.   If you reach Eatonton by Monday it will be early enough.   Keep your men fresh, and devour large quantities of potatoes and corn along the route.

W. T. SHERMAN,
Major General.

Major General SLOCUM,
Commanding Left Wing, &c.

HEADQUARTERS MILITARY DIVISION OF THE MISSISSIPPI,
In the field, Cobb's Plantation, November 22, 1864.

GENERAL : I am directed by the general-in-chief to write you as follows: The march of this wing has been since leaving Atlanta in two columns, and very successful up to this time. The 14th corps is now on the Hillsboro' road, ten (10) miles west of Milledgeville, and the 20th corps must now be in the capital, having marched by the Eatonton road. The Georgia railroad, from and including the Oconee bridge, west to Lithonia, is well destroyed. Troops in fine condition, having fed high on sweet potatoes and poultry. Stock is also doing well, though the roads have been very heavy. The general desires you will report to him at Milledgeville to-morrow, (where he will go early,) in detail, your operations since leaving Atlanta, and also the position of your command in view of his making further orders. In the mean time you cannot do too much permanent damage to that railroad east of Macon and about Gordon.

You will also notify General Kilpatrick a similar report is desired of him.

I am, general, respectfully yours, &c.,

L. M. DAYTON, *Aide-de-Camp.*

General Howard,
Commanding Army of the Tennessee.

HEADQUARTERS MILITARY DIVISION OF THE MISSISSIPPI,
In the field, Milledgeville, Ga., November 23, 1864.

Major General Howard,
Commanding Army of the Tennessee:

By instructions of the general-in-chief, I give you the following directions: continue to destroy the railroad eastward to the Oconee in the most complete and thorough manner, burning and twisting every rail, and the same for a distance to the west towards Macon; also destroy the Oconee bridge. You may lay your pontoon over the Oconee, but do not cross any of your command until further orders. Hardee has probably swung around via Albany for Savannah, which the general says is all right, and he don't care particularly. Kilpatrick will be moved here or in this vicinity for the present. The probability is, we will concentrate at or near Sandersville. Prosecute the railroad destruction in the most thorough manner and communicate with the general-in-chief frequently.

I am, general, respectfully yours, &c.,

L. M. DAYTON, *Aide-de-Camp.*

HEADQUARTERS MILITARY DIVISION OF THE MISSISSIPPI,
In the field, Tennille Station, Ga., November 27, 1864—10.15 a. m.

General: The general commanding is now at this point and has put in motion two (2) divisions of the 14th corps without wagons from Sandersville, by Fenn's bridge, to Louisville. The 20th corps with all the trains of the left wing will move to Louisville by the road passing through Davisboro'. He wishes you to move your two corps eastward on the two roads, starting from Irwin's Cross-roads, as follows: the right column crossing Ohoopee river, straight for Johnson's; thence along the main Savannah road to the first point where it intersects the road from Swainsboro', through Canoochee, Bark Camp, and Rocky Creek church, to Waynesboro'. At that point the commanding officer should have instructions to turn towards Station No. 9, in the absence of other orders. The left column to take the road from Irwin's Cross-roads direct towards Louisville until it intersects the road from Sandersville, next south of the railroad and south of Williamson's Swamp creek until abreast of Station No. 10, (or Sebastopol,) where it is probable we will cross the Ogeechee. The general proposes to attend this latter column himself.

Please renew your instructions to the detail breaking up the railroad from

Oconee to Tennille not to be in too great a hurry, but to do their work well. From this point it can join its proper corps on either of the above named routes. The general finds it difficult to get information of roads, but those described exist on all our maps.

Very respectfully, your obedient servant,

HENRY HITCHCOCK,
Major and Assistant Adjutant General.

Major General O. O. HOWARD,
Commanding Army of the Tennessee.

HEADQUARTERS MILITARY DIVISION OF THE MISSISSIPPI,
In the field, Ga., Station 9½, November 30, 1864—3 p. m.

Major General SLOCUM, *Commanding Left Wing, &c.:*

Your despatch of 7 p. m., 29th, just received, and the general-in-chief directs that you move your whole command by all practicable roads in the direction of Millen, keeping well to the north in the neighborhood of Bark Camp, Birdsville and Buck Head church, making a lodgement on the railroad north of Millen, destroying a section of track in the direction of Augusta, and turning on Millen in case your hear the sounds of battle.

We are at station 9½, marked Burton on our maps, and will finish the railroad up to Millen.

As we are a day ahead, you will have to march pretty briskly.

L. M. DAYTON, *Aide-de-Camp.*

HEADQUARTERS MILITARY DIVISION OF THE MISSISSIPPI,
In the field, Station 9, Georgia, December 1, 1864.

GENERAL: Yours of this date from opposite No. 8 is at hand, which I acknowledge by direction of the general-in-chief.

He has read your order to General Blair, and says " all right." He does not wish you to move to-morrow further than abreast of No. 7.

General Slocum is now abreast of us here, and to-morrow will reach the vicinity of Buck Head church, where there will be some delay to us, while Slocum is swinging around, and you may calculate on staying at No. 7 a day or two for us to get up even. At present Wheeler is very active, and Kilpatrick is operating in connexion with General Slocum. You will make disposition to cross at No. 7, but whether it will be necessary to do so will depend on the dispositions of the enemy.

I am, general, yours, &c.,

L. M. DAYTON, *Aide-de-Camp.*

Major General HOWARD,
Commanding Army of the Tennessee.

HEADQUARTERS MILITARY DIVISION OF THE MISSISSIPPI,
In the field, Station 9, December 1, 1864.

GENERAL: Your despatch of 12 m. yesterday just received, and Captain Audenreid has also returned. Your operations have been entirely satisfactory to the general-in-chief. He wishes you to move on the flank of the left wing, holding your command well in hand for further work, but always giving the enemy all he wants when he offers you battle. As regards retaliation, you must be very careful as to the correctness of any information you may receive about the enemy murdering or mutilating our men. You may keep the prisoners you have or turn any portion of them over to General Slocum's infantry to guard, and keep such as you may wish to retain for your own object. You may communicate with Wheeler by flag of truce, and notify him of the conduct of his command toward our men; and that you shall retaliate, which you may do until you feel satisfied. When our men are found and you are fully convinced the enemy have killed them after surrender in fair battle, or have mutilated their bodies after having been killed in fair battle, you may hang and mutilate man for man without regard to rank.

I am, general, respectfully yours, &c.,

L. M. DAYTON, *Aide-de-Camp.*

Brig. Gen. J. KILPATRICK,
Commanding Cavalry Division.

HEADQUARTERS MILITARY DIVISION OF THE MISSISSIPPI,
In the field, near Millen, Ga., December 2, 1864.

GENERAL: The general-in-chief has made camp near the mouth of Buck Head creek and the troops are passing over into Millen. He wishes you tomorrow to make a good break of the railroad from Millen towards Augusta, to the right and left of the points crossed by the 14th and 20th corps, after which to move out and continue the march toward Savannah by two roads, leaving the one along the railroad for General Blair. The two roads indicated on our maps, the one passing near Millen and Hunters mills, and the other sweeping around by Sharpe's and Buck Creek post office, will answer; but if one can be found leading from the upper road through Sylvania towards Halley's ferry, on the Savannah river, it would answer our purpose better for your left corps. General Kilpatrick will be instructed to confer with you and cover your rear. Dress to the right on the 17th corps, whose progress you can rate by the smoke. General Blair will continue to burn the railroad as he marches, as far as Ogeechee church. The general wishes all the heads of columns to be on the road leading from Millroy to Halley's ferry on the fourth day, including to-morrow.

Communicate as often as possible with him; but failing to hear from him, always act in concert with General Blair's column, which alone is expected to meet opposition. General Howard, with the 15th corps, will continue on the south bank of the Ogeechee, ready to turn any position of the enemy in case he offer opposition to our progress.

I am, general, very respectfully, &c.,

L. M. DAYTON, *Aide-de-Camp.*

Major General H. W. SLOCUM,
Commanding Right Wing.

HEADQUARTERS MILITARY DIVISION OF THE MISSISSIPPI,
In the field, near Millen, Ga., December 2, 1864.

GENERAL: The army will move on Savannah, delaying only to continue the destruction of the railroad from Millen as far as Ogeechee church. General Howard will continue to move along the south bank of the Ogeechee, General Blair along the railroad, and General Slocum by the two roads lying north of the railroad, between it and the Savannah river. The general wishes you to confer with General Slocum, to make a strong feint up in the direction of

Waynesboro, and then to cover his rear from molestation by dashes of cavalry. I send you copies of two letters from members of Wheeler's staff, which will interest you; after reading, please return them for file in this office.

I am, general, respectfully yours, &c.,

L. M. DAYTON, *Aide-de-Camp.*

General KILPATRICK,
Commanding Cavalry Division.

HEADQUARTERS MILITARY DIVISION OF THE MISSISSIPPI,
In the field, near Millen, Ga., December 2, 1864.

GENERAL: The next movement will be on Savannah; your two corps moving along down the Ogeechee; General Blair to destroy the railroad as far as Ogeechee church; and the 15th corps keeping on the south and west bank, ready to cross over in case of opposition to General Blair; otherwise it will not cross until near Eden No. 2. General Slocum will take the two roads north of the railroad and between it and the Savannah river. As he will have to make a wide detour, we must allow him until the fourth day to reach the road from Millroy to Halley's ferry, on the Savannah river; this will make slow marching for you, but, as a general rule, the rear of the 15th corps should be about abreast of General Blair's head of column. The general has a Savannah paper of yesterday, from which he notices the enemy still remain in doubt as to our intentions, being divided between Macon, Augusta, and Savannah; and also that an expedition of gunboats has passed up the Broad river toward Coosawahatchee.

If at any time during your progress you judge it feasible, you might despatch a small, bold party of scouts down towards Hinesville to burn some culverts, and tear up some track, and cut the telegraph wires in several places on the Savannah and Gulf railroad, over which the city of Savannah is now chiefly supplied. The fewer the men, and the sooner such a party start, the better. The country is very sparsely settled, and very favorable for such an expedition.

I am, general, &c.,

L. M. DAYTON, *Aid-de-Camp.*

Major General O. O. HOWARD,
Commanding Army of the Tennessee.

HEADQUARTERS MILITARY DIVISION OF THE MISSISSIPPI,
In the field, No. 5½, C. R. R., December 4, 1864—¾ p. m.

GENERAL: Your note of 10 a. m. has been received. The day has been so good that General Blair has got to the point on our map indicated by the intersection of the main road with that leading through Sylvania, Hunter's Mills, and Paris Academy, viz: four (4) miles west of Halcyon Dale. He keeps three brigades breaking railroad abreast of him. His advance, on arrival here, was fired on, but by parties who took good care to fire at long range and take to their heels. My judgment is, that if any opposition is made to us this side of Savannah, it will occur near Ogeechee church; but Howard's movement south of Ogeechee, by Millroy, will turn that position.

You have nothing to apprehend on your front, but should look to your rear, especially on General Davis's flank, until you get in the neck between Ogeechee church and Halley's ferry. I want you to report to me frequently, but, in the absence of orders, to move your entire wing, with Kilpatrick's cavalry, in the direction of Springfield and Monteith, getting your left flank on the

Savannah and Charleston railroad about Saint Augustine creek. General Blair will continue to move along the railroad, and the 15th corps will continue on the west side of the Ogeechee until abreast of Eden No. 2.

We continue to find abundance of forage, and all our animals are in first-rate condition. Nevertheless, I want to impress upon all the importance of filling all empty wagons; for it may be to our interest to act rapidly, without waiting to draw supplies from our new base.

If our marching on this flank is too fast for you, please notify me, and I will check it, as I am aware you are moving on a large circle.

We heard the firing to-day which you report, which, from its rate of fire, I inferred to be from Kilpatrick, who is fond of using artillery.

I do not know that I reported to you that at Millen we got a despatch that Bragg proposed to follow us with ten thousand (10,000) men from Augusta. If we can draw him down towards Savannah, we can turn on him and send him off at a tangent.

I am, general, &c.

W. T. SHERMAN.
Major General.

Major General SLOCUM, Commanding Left Wing, &c.

HEADQUARTERS MILITARY DIVISION OF THE MISSISSIPPI,
In the field, Ogeechee Church, Ga., December 5, 1864.

GENERAL: Since sending the messenger to you this morning, General Blair has entered this place almost unopposed. Some field-works are fresh, and, so far as I have examined, would be such as would be thrown up by five thousand (5,000) inexperienced hands.

General Slocum reports he will be to-night at the point where his road next north of this intersects the one from here to Poor Robin; but he has not heard from Generals Davis and Kilpatrick since he heard their firing yesterday morning. Davis has orders to move from the point where he separated from Slocum, viz: Buckhead church to Halley's ferry, abreast of this on the Savannah, via Sylvania. I have sent a courier to General Slocum to communicate with Davis at once, and report to me at what moment he will be ready to move on.

You will observe that with Davis at Halley's, we threaten South Carolina, and to that extent will confuse our enemy; but I will not lose a moment, only we must move in concert, or else will get lost. You may make all the dispositions to cross at No. 3, but the point No. 2 is the true one, unless modified by local geography.

I will disturb the railroad but little south of this, as we may have use for it out this far; still, Blair can burn the bridges and culverts, and burn enough barns to mark the progress of his head of column. I don't want him to start until I know Davis is abreast.

Yours, &c.,

W. T. SHERMAN, Major General.

Major General HOWARD,
Commanding Army of the Tennessee.

HEADQUARTERS MILITARY DIVISION OF THE MISSISSIPPI,
In the field, No. 4½ Ogeechee Church, December 6, 1864.

GENERAL: Your report of December 5 has been received, and gives the general-in-chief great satisfaction. He begs you to convey to your command his thanks for their gallant and valuable services in driving the enemy in confusion beyond Brier creek, and in destroying those bridges so useful to the enemy.

At your suggestion he has ordered each army corps commander to select from his command one hundred cavalry horses, with a sufficient number of negroes to lead them, and to conduct them for your use to General Slocum's column, which is now on the middle Savannah road where it crosses the Statesboro' and Halley's ferry road. A copy of that order is enclosed, and you can adopt your own course to secure them. You may always rely upon the general for cavalry horses, as, in order to keep you well mounted, he will dismount every person connected with the infantry not necessary for its efficient service, and take team horses, even if the wagons and contents have to be burned.

On this flank matters have moved smoothly, and as we are a good distance in advance, are lying by for General Davis and yourself to get up abreast. General Howard is now near Brannan's store, west of the Ogeechee, abreast of Springfield. General Blair is here at Ogeechee church, where McLaws, with about five thousand (5,000) men, had prepared quite an extensive line of intrenchments; but Howard's movement outflanked him and he quit without a fight, and is now supposed to be at Eden No. 2. General Slocum is about six miles north of Ogeechee church, waiting for General Davis to get up abreast on the Halley's Ferry road. As soon as all are up we will move on Savannah by the four main roads from Brannan's store, Ogeechee church, Springfield, and the Savannah river road. As Wheeler is disposed of, you might, for the sake of forage, divide your command, coming together say about Monteith. We find a great deal of forage, but presume our infantry trains consume it all; still they do not seem to know that rice in the straw, fed in moderation, is most excellent forage; and you can take advantage of it, as you will find an abundance along the Savannah and Ogeechee rivers. As you come down, make a good deal of smoke and fuss about Halley's (now Hutchinson's) ferry and Sister's ferry, as though threatening to cross into South Carolina; and should Ebenezer creek be up, send word to General Davis to leave his brigade down until you are across.

No news from the outside world of any interest, but the fleet is known to be watching for us, as the citizens report it sending up rockets every night.

I am, general, with much regard,

L. M. DAYTON, *Aide-de-Camp.*

General KILPATRICK,
   Commanding Cavalry.

HEADQUARTERS MILITARY DIVISION OF THE MISSISSIPPI,
   In the field, Ogeechee Church, December 6, 1864—3½ p. m.

GENERAL: Your despatch of 1.30 p. m. is just received, as also yours of 7 a. m., which was answered. The general is pleased at the progress of General Davis, but not knowing where he was, it compelled the halting of this column here to close up. To-morrow the general-in-chief expects General Howard to be at Eden No. 2, General Blair at Guyton, and if General Davis's head of column reaches Ebenezer, and can lay a bridge over that creek, it will answer. He wishes you not to pass Springfield, but from there to communicate with him at Guyton; but in the absence of orders the movement for the day following should be such as to place General Davis at or in advance of St. Augustine creek; and the column you are with, at or near Monteith. General Blair will be at Eden No. 2, and Howard will cross the river (Ogeechee.)

I am, general, yours respectfully,

L. M. DAYTON, *Aide-de-Camp.*

Major General H. W. SLOCUM,
   Commanding Left Wing.

HEADQUARTERS MILITARY DIVISION OF THE MISSISSIPPI,
In the field, Ogeechee Church, December 6, 1864—3.45 p. m.

GENERAL: Your despatch of to-day is just received. Reports from General Slocum and General Kilpatrick have also been received; the former will camp to-night on Turkey creek, in advance of this column, with his command well closed up. The latter attacked Wheeler near Thomas's station, and drove him through Waynesboro' and across Brier creek in confusion, killing and wounding a number, and capturing a hundred of his men; he also burned all the bridges on Brier creek, including (for good) the railroad bridge. To-morrow the entire army will move, General Slocum's left corps reaching Ebenezer, himself Springfield, and the 17th corps Guyton. The general-in-chief desires you in conjunction to reach Eden, opposite No. 2, and while General Blair threatens No. 2 by moving on No. 3, (Guyton,) to effect a crossing at or below No. 2.

I am, general, yours with regard,

L. M. DAYTON, Aide-de-Camp.

Major General HOWARD,
Commanding Army of the Tennessee.

HEADQUARTERS MILITARY DIVISION OF THE MISSISSIPPI,
In the field, 2½ miles from No. 3, December 7, 1864.

GENERAL: Owing to the rain General Blair did not reach Guyton to-day, but is at the point about two and a half (2½) miles northwest of Guyton. The bridge over the small stream, without name, is burned, and some obstructions there are now being removed, so that early in the morning his column will move right forward on the road which passes about two (2) miles west of Guyton, and about the same distance east of Eden, where your road and ours come together. It will be well if you can find a road passing from Springfield to Monteith and Pooler's, and General Davis should be instructed to reach St. Augustine and the vicinity of Cherokee Hill. We must first secure the road indicated from Cherokee Hill to Silk Hope and Litchfield. We hear that the enemy is fortifying in a semicircle around Savannah and about four miles from it.

I am, general, respectfully yours,

W. T. SHERMAN, Major General.

Major General SLOCUM,
Commanding Left Wing.

HEADQUARTERS MILITARY DIVISION OF THE MISSISSIPPI,
In the field, December 8, 1864—7 p. m.

GENERAL: We are at a point on the road from Millen to Savannah, about two (2) miles north of No. 2, called Mount Zion church.

General Slocum is but a short distance from us, and will move, to-morrow, on a road which branches off from this road and comes into the Augusta road ten (10) miles north of Savannah, where he will effect a junction with General Davis, destroy that railroad, drive the enemy within his intrenchments, and then work to the right and form a junction with us on this road as near Savannah as we may get. General Blair will move on this road by Pooler's, and so on until we drive the enemy within the intrenchments of Savannah, wherever they may be.

The general wishes you to get down in the neighborhood of Beverly, Silk Hope, or Litchfield, so as to advance in the direction of the plank road until we come together or communicate by the road which leads from Silk Hope to Chero kee Hill. He aims to push the enemy far enough into Savannah to have the use of the shell road as a route of supply. If you can possibly do so, he wishes you to send a note by a canoe down the Ogeechee, pass the railroad bridge in the night, and inform the naval commander that we have arrived in fine condition, and are moving directly against Savannah, but for the present do not risk giving any details.

      I am, general, with respect, &c.,

L. M. DAYTON, Aide-de-Camp.

Major General HOWARD,
      Commanding Army of the Tennessee.

HEADQUARTERS MILITARY DIVISION OF THE MISSISSIPPI,
In the field, Pooler's No. 1, December 9, 1864.

GENERAL: Your despatch from the canal bridge just received. The 17th corps moved at the usual hour to-day and found the enemy defending the position covered by the swamp, about fifteen miles from Savannah. There was some skirmish fighting and use of artillery on both sides, but General Mower, who was in advance, handsomely drove the enemy from his positions and works, and we reached this point in good season.

The 17th corps will move as usual to-morrow morning, and will proceed until it reaches the main line of the enemy's works, supposed to be about four (4) miles from Savannah, when it will work to the right and connect with you. The general-in-chief desires you to move on the direct road on Savannah as usual, making progress until the enemy's main line is developed. He also wishes you to communicate with the fleet if possible. General Kilpatrick's command is divided, covering this and General Davis's column, and reports positively that Wheeler is on the east side of the Savannah river.

If the Mr. Cuyler you have as a prisoner be R. R. Cuyler, brother of Surgeon Cuyler of the old army, or his son George, the general-in-chief wishes you to send him to us when practicable, and in the mean time treat him as well as possible. Present the general's best wishes to Mr. King, and say he regrets Brown had not the good sense to follow his advice.

The general thinks best for you to leave a brigade at the bridge at Fort Argyle, to hold and guard it, as we may need it. We have not heard from General Slocum direct, but the sound of his guns would place him at Cherokee Hill, or near there; we heard them at sundown.

      I am, general, yours, &c.,

L. M. DAYTON, Aide-de-Camp.

Major General HOWARD,
      Commanding Army of the Tennessee.

HEADQUARTERS MILITARY DIVISION OF THE MISSISSIPPI,
In the field, Poolers, No. 1, December 9, 1864.

GENERAL: As yet we have heard nothing from you to-day except your guns, nearly due north from us, at three to five p. m. General Howard has reported, and is in possession of the Gulf railroad; captured one piece of artillery and some prisoners and a train of cars. Both corps have met opposition, but have overcome it, and Howard will move the 15th via the plank road, and the 17th via this, the main road, on Savannah, in the morning. The general wishes you to continue along the Savannah river in your movement on the city, making as much progress as you can, until the enemy's main line is developed.

I am, general, very respectfully, yours, &c.,

L. M. DAYTON, *Aide-de-Camp.*

Major General SLOCUM,
Commanding Left Wing.

HEADQUARTERS MILITARY DIVISION OF THE MISSISSIPPI,
In the field, near Savannah, December 11, 1864—2 a. m.

GENERAL: Your despatch of December 10, and also Special Field Order 191, are just received. The general-in-chief wishes you to secure the trains cut off on the Gulf road, and also describe to him what is the position of King's bridge and Dillon's ferry—neither are on the map. I have had couriers looking for you since five p. m., 10th, with orders, but they are unable to find your headquarters. I send enclosed another copy. The general understands the trains to be between Way's and Fleming's stations.

I am, general, very respectfully, &c.,

L. M. DAYTON, *Aide-de-Camp.*

Major General O. O. HOWARD,
Commanding Army of the Tennessee.

HEADQUARTERS MILITARY DIVISION OF THE MISSISSIPPI,
In the field, near Savannah, Ga., (General Howard's Headquarters,)
December 15, 1864—2 p. m.

GENERAL: The general-in-chief has just returned from a visit to Ossabaw and Wassaw sounds, and directs me to inform you in full terms of the result. After having opened communication by signal with the gunboats, and got possession of Fort McAllister, he went in person to the gunboat below Fort McAllister, which proved to be a messenger boat from the flag-ship lying at the mouth of Ossabaw sound. After making communications to Washington, &c., he returned to Fort McAllister, and was overtaken by a messenger from General Foster, just from Port Royal. The general went on board General Foster's boat, and proceeded with him down the bay in hope to meet the admiral, but did not find him till after running around into Wassaw sound. General Foster then proceeded to Port Royal at 12 m. yesterday, to return with a fleet of transports loaded with six hundred thousand (600,000) rations and ten (10) days' forage for forty thousand (40,000) animals, and promised to be here by to-night. He will also bring with him six 20-lb. Parrott guns and six 30-lb. Parrotts, with three hundred rounds of ammunition per gun. The general then transferred to the admiral's vessel and returned to Fort McAllister, whence the admiral accompanied him as far up as the rice mill, where he had left his horse. He is now at General Howard's headquarters, and has sent for his camp to be transferred to a point near this, which is not far from the seven (7) mile post on the main road leading west from Savannah to the Ogeechee, marked on our map as a plank road. This point is about five (5) miles from his present headquarters, on the Louisville road. General Foster has five thousand (5,000) men near the Charleston railroad, north of Broad river, and near enough to the railroad to command it, so that he feels sure that cars cannot pass either way, but he has been unable to reach the railroad itself with his men, on account of the enemy's force. The gunboats and General Howard occupy all other avenues of approach to Savannah, connecting with your right. Now, if you can close the Savannah river to navigation, and also get a force over the Savannah river to threaten in flank any dirt road leading out of Savannah, between the city and Coosahatchie, the investment of the city will be complete, and the enemy will have no escape. The general wants to place the batteries expected from General Foster in position as near the heart of Savannah as possible, ready to bombard it as soon as possible. You may therefore send horses to the Ogeechee river, at King's bridge, ready to haul those guns to your right front, and as soon as they are well in position, ready to open on the city, he proposes to demand its surrender. In the mean time our stores of all kinds will come up Ossabaw sound and the Ogeechee river to King's bridge, and thence be hauled to the camps. The canal is admirably adapted to your use, and the general suggests that you send some competent staff officer over to the Ogeechee, and, in concert with General Easton, chief quartermaster, collect as many boats as possible to transport your stores from King's bridge through the canal up to your very camp. At Dr. Cheves' plantation, ten (10) miles from King's bridge, the general himself saw at least half a dozen fine large flats, built expressly to transport rice through the canal to Savannah—the very thing wanted—and he has no doubt on other plantations at least twenty or twenty-five (20 or 25) boats could be collected, each capable of transporting twenty (20) tons. In dry weather wagons will be best, but in case of rainy weather these boats would be admirable. As soon as possible the general wants your batteries which are nearest the city prepared to execute the foregoing plans, and he wants you to write to him in full to-night any ideas that may have been suggested by your closer observation of the ground in your immediate front, and you may at once give orders for hauling provisions and forage from King's bridge, as Admiral Dahlgren assured him this morning that he would have all torpedoes and obstructions removed in the course of to-day. There is also a steamboat load of mail for your army, Colonel A. H. Markland in charge, which will be at King's bridge the instant torpedoes are removed. Captain Merritt brings this to you, and can satisfy all your inquiries, as he has been with the general.

I have the honor to be, general, very respectfully, your obedient servant,

HENRY HITCHCOCK,
Major and Aide-de-Camp.

Major General H. W. Slocum,
   Commanding Left Wing.

Headquarters Armies of the United States,
City Point, Va., December 3, 1864.

General : The little information gleaned from the southern press indicating no great obstacle to your progress, I have directed your mails, which previously had been collected in Baltimore by Colonel Markland, special agent of the Post Office Department, to be sent as far as the blockading squadron off Savannah, to be forwarded to you as soon as heard from on the coast. Not liking to rejoice before the victory is assured, I abstain from congratulating you and those under your command until bottom has been struck. I have never had a fear, however, for the result.

Since you left Atlanta no very great progress has been made here. The enemy has been closely watched, though, and prevented from detaching against you. I think not one man has gone from here except some twelve or fifteen hundred dismounted cavalry. Bragg has gone from Wilmington. I am trying to take advantage of his absence to get possession of that place. Owing to some preparations Admiral Porter and General Butler are making to blow up Fort Fisher, and which, while I hope for the best, do not believe a particle in, there is a delay in getting this expedition off. I hope they will be ready to start by the 7th, and that Bragg will not have started back by that time.

In this letter I do not intend to give you anything like directions for future action, but will state a general idea I have, and will get your views after you have established yourself on the sea-coast. With your veteran army I hope to get control of the only two through routes, from east to west, possessed by the enemy before the fall of Atlanta. This condition will be filled by holding Savannah and Augusta, or by holding any other post to the east of Savannah and Branchville. If Wilmington falls, a force from there can co-operate with you.

Thomas has got back into the defences of Nashville, with Hood close upon him. Decatur has been abandoned, and so have all the roads except the main one leading to Chattanooga.

* * * * * * * *

I hope Hood will be badly crippled or destroyed. After all becomes quiet, and the roads up here so bad that there is likely to be a week or two that nothing can be done, I will run down the coast and see you.

Yours, truly,

U. S. GRANT, *Lieutenant General.*

Major General W. T. SHERMAN,
Commanding Armies near Savannah.

HEADQUARTERS ARMIES OF THE UNITED STATES,
City Point, Va., December 6, 1864.

GENERAL: On reflection, since sending my letter by the hands of Lieutenant Dunn, I have concluded that the most important operation toward closing out the rebellion will be to close out Lee and his army. You have now destroyed the roads of the south, so that it will probably take them months, without interruption, to re-establish a through line from east to west. In that time, I think, the job here will be effectually completed. My idea now is that you establish a base on the coast, fortify, and leave in it all your artillery and cavalry, and enough infantry to protect them, and, at the same time, so threaten the interior that the militia of the south will have to be kept at home. With the balance of your command come here by water with all despatch. Select yourself the officer to leave in command, but you I want in person. Unless you see objections to this plan which I cannot see, use every vessel going to you, for the purpose of transportation.

Very respectfully, your obedient servant,

U. S. GRANT, *Lieutenant General.*

Major General W. T. SHERMAN,
Commanding Military Division of the Mississippi.

HEADQUARTERS MILITARY DIVISION OF THE MISSISSIPPI
In the field, near Savannah, December 16, 1864.

GENERAL: I received day before yesterday, at the hands of Lieutenant Dunn, your letter of December 3, and last night, at the hands of Colonel Babcock, that of December 6. I had previously made you a hasty scrawl from the tugboat Dandelion in Ogeechee river, advising you that the army had reached the sea-coast, destroying all railroads across the State of Georgia, and investing closely the city of Savannah, and had made connexion with the fleet.

Since writing that note, I have in person met and conferred with General Foster and Admiral Dahlgren, and made all the arrangements which I deemed essential to reduce the city of Savannah to our possession; but since the receipt of yours of the 6th I have initiated measures looking principally to coming to you with fifty thousand or sixty thousand (50,000 or 60,000) infantry, and incidentally to take Savannah, if time will allow. At the time we carried Fort McAllister so handsomely by assault, with twenty-two (22) guns and its entire garrison, I was hardly aware of its importance; but since passing down the river with General Foster, and up with Admiral Dahlgren, I realize how admirably adapted are Ossabaw sound and Ogeechee river to supply an army operating against Savannah. Sea-going vessels can easily come to King's bridge, a point on Ogeechee river fourteen and a half (14½) miles due west of Savannah, from which point we have roads leading to all our camps. The country is low and sandy, and cut up with marshes, which in wet weather will be very bad; but we have been so favored with weather that they are all now comparatively good, and heavy details are constantly employed in double corduroying the marshes, so that I have no fear even of a bad spell of weather. Fortunately, also, by liberal and judicious foraging, we reached the sea-coast abundantly supplied with forage and provisions, needing nothing on arrival except bread. Of this we started from Atlanta with from eight to twenty (8 to 20) days' supply for corps, and some of the troops only had one (1) day's issue of bread during the trip of thirty (30) days; and yet they did not want, for sweet potatoes were very abundant as well as corn-meal, and our soldiers took to them naturally. We started with about five thousand (5,000) head of cattle, and arrived with over ten thousand (10,000,) of course consuming mostly turkeys, chickens, sheep, hogs, and the cattle of the country. As to our mules and horses, we left Atlanta with about two thousand five hundred (2,500) wagons, many of which were drawn by mules which had not recovered from the Chattanooga starvation, all of which were replaced, the poor mules shot, and our transportation is now in superb condition. I have no doubt the State of Georgia has lost by our operations fifteen thousand (15,000) first-rate mules. As to horses, Kilpatrick collected all his remounts, and it looks to me, in riding along our columns, as though every officer has three or four led horses, and each regiment seems to be followed by at least fifty (50) negroes and foot-sore soldiers riding on horses and mules. The custom was for each brigade to send out daily a foraging party of about fifty (50) men on foot, who invariably returned mounted, with several wagons loaded with poultry, potatoes, &c., and, as the army is composed of about forty (40) brigades, you can estimate approximately the quantity of horses collected. Great numbers of these were shot by my orders, because of the disorganizing effect on our infantry of having too many idlers mounted. General Easton is now engaged in collecting statistics on this subject; but I know the government will never receive full accounts of our captures, although the result aimed at was fully attained, viz: to deprive our enemy of them. All these animals I will have sent to Port Royal, or collected behind Fort McAllister, to be used by General Saxton in his farming operations or by the quartermaster's department, after they are systematically accounted for.

While General Easton is collecting transportation for my troops to James river, I will throw to Port Royal island all our means of transportation I can, and collect the balance near Fort McAllister, covered by the Ogeechee river and intrenchments to be erected, and for which Captain Poe, my chief engineer, is now reconnoitring the grounds; but, in the mean time, I will act as I have begun, as though Savannah city were my only objective, namely: the troops will continue to invest Savannah closely, making attacks and feints wherever we have firm ground to stand upon, and I will place some thirty (30) pounder Parrots, which I have got from General Foster, in position near enough to reach the centre of the city, and then will demand its surrender. If General Hardee is alarmed or fears starvation, he may surrender; otherwise, I will bombard the city, but not risk the lives of my own men by assaults across the narrow causeways by which alone we can reach it. If I had time, Savannah, with all its dependent fortifications, is already ours, for we hold all its avenues of supply. The enemy has made two desperate efforts to get boats from above to the city, in both of which he has been foiled; General Slocum, whose left flank rests on the river, capturing and burning the first boat, and in the second instance driving back two gunboats, and capturing the steamer Resolute, with seven naval officers and a crew of twenty-five seamen. General Slocum occupies Argyle island and the upper end of Hutchinson island, and has a brigade on the South Carolina shore opposite, and he is very urgent to pass one of his corps over to that shore. But in view of the change of plan made necessary by your orders of the 6th, I will maintain things *in statu quo* till I have got all my transportation to the rear and out of the way, and until I have sea-transportation for the troops you require at James river, which I will accompany and command in person. Of course, I will leave Kilpatrick with his cavalry, say five thousand three hundred (5,300,) and it may be a division of the 15th corps; but, before determining this, I must see General Foster, and may arrange to shift his force (now over about the Charleston railroad, at the head of Broad river) to the Ogeechee, where, in co-operation with Kilpatrick's cavalry, he can better threaten the State of Georgia than from the direction of Port Royal. Besides, I would much prefer not to detach from my regular corps any of its veteran divisions, and would even prefer that other less valuable troops should be sent to re-enforce Foster from some other quarter. My four (4) corps, full of experience and full of ardor, coming to you en masse, equal to sixty thousand (60,000) fighting men, will be a re-enforcement that Lee cannot disregard. Indeed, with my present command I had expected, after reducing Savannah, instantly to march to Columbia, South Carolina, thence to Raleigh, and thence to report to you. But this would consume, it may be, six weeks' time after the fall of Savannah, whereas by sea I can probably reach you with my men and arms before the middle of January.

As to matters in the southeast, I think Hardee in Savannah has good artillerists, some five thousand (5,000) or six thousand (6,000) good infantry, and, it may be, a mongrel mass of eight thousand or ten thousand (8,000 or 10,000) militia and fragments. In all our marching through Georgia, he has not forced me to use anything but a skirmish line, though at several points he had erected fortifications, and made bombastic threats. In Savannah he has taken refuge in a line constructed behind swamps and overflowed rice-fields, extending from a point on the Savannah river, about three miles above the city, around to a branch of the Little Ogeechee, which stream is impassable from its salt marshes and boggy swamps, crossed only by narrow causeways or common corduroy roads. There must be twenty-five thousand (25,000) citizens, men, women, and children, in Savannah, that must also be fed, and how he is to feed them beyond a few days I cannot imagine, as I know that his requisitions for corn on the interior counties of Georgia were not filled, and we are in possession of the rice-fields and mills which could alone be of service to him in this neighborhood. He can draw nothing from South Carolina, save from a small corner down in the southeast, and that by a disused wagon road.. I could easily get possession of this, but hardly deem it worth the risk of making a detachment which would be in danger by its isolation from the main army.

Our whole army is in fine condition as to health, and the weather is splendid. For that reason alone, I feel a personal dislike to turning northward.

I will keep Lieutenant Dunn here until I know the result of my demand for the surrender of Savannah, but, whether successful or not, shall not delay my execution of your orders of the 6th, which will depend alone upon the time it will require to obtain transportation by sea.

I am, with respect, &c., your obedient servant,

W. T. SHERMAN,
Major General United States Army.

Lieutenant General U. S. GRANT,
Commander-in-Chief, City Point, Virginia.

HEADQUARTERS MILITARY DIVISION OF THE MISSISSIPPI,
In the field, near Savannah, Ga., December 17, 1864.

GENERAL: You have doubtless observed, from your station at Rosedew, that sea-going vessels now come through Ossabaw sound and up Ogeechee, to the rear of my army, giving me abundant supplies of all kinds, and more especially of heavy ordnance necessary to the reduction of Savannah. I have already received guns that can cast heavy and destructive shot as far as the heart of your city. Also, I have for some days held and controlled every avenue by which the people and garrison of Savannah can be supplied, and I am therefore justified in demanding the surrender of the city of Savannah and its dependent forts, and shall await a reasonable time your answer before opening with heavy ordnance. Should you entertain the proposition, I am prepared to grant liberal terms to the inhabitants and garrison; but should I be forced to resort to assault or the slower and surer process of starvation, I shall then feel justified in resorting to the harshest measures, and shall make little effort to restrain my army, burning to avenge the great national wrong they attach to Savannah and other large cities, which have been so prominent in dragging our country into civil war.

I enclose you a copy of General Hood's demand for the surrender of the town of Resaca, to be used by you for what it is worth.

I have the honor to be, your obedient servant,

W. T. SHERMAN,
Major General.

General WILLIAM J. HARDEE,
Commanding Confederate Forces in Savannah.

HEADQUARTERS MILITARY DIVISION OF THE MISSISSIPPI,
In the field, near Savannah, Ga., December 18, 1864—8 p. m.

GENERAL: In compliance with the plan I indicated to you some days since, I made a demand during yesterday on General Hardee for the surrender of the city of Savannah and its dependent forts, and to-day received his answer declining to accede. You are aware I am ordered to carry this army to Virginia by sea, but I hope still to get possession of Savannah before sufficient transportation can be had to enable me to comply with General Grant's order. The thirty (30) pounder Parrotts which you sent me are now being hauled to batteries prepared for them, and in about two days' time, if we can possibly get the ground to stand upon, we shall assault the enemy's lines at four or more points. It is all-important that the railroad and telegraph wire should be broken between Savannah and Charleston, and the very best point is where your forces are represented to be, viz., near the Tullafinny. It seems to me that our operations here, especially along the Savannah river, must have drawn away every man from that quarter that they could possibly spare, and a bold rush on the railroad would probably develop a weaker force there than is supposed to be, or it may be that you could diminish that force, and use the balance in a small handy detachment east of Tullafinny, over about Old Pocotaligo. I merely throw out these ideas, and reiterate that it would aid us very much in this quarter if that force of yours be kept most active, more especially if you succeed in breaking the railroad and the telegraph wire, the further toward Charleston the better. Even if nothing better can be done, let them whale away with their thirty (30) pounder Parrotts, and break the road with cannon balls. It is possible, as a part of the general movement, that I may send a force in co-operation with the navy toward the Union plank-road from the direction of Bluffton. I will go over and see the admiral again to-morrow, and it may be that I will see you, as in your last note you said that you would return again.

I have the honor to be, your obedient servant,

W. T. SHERMAN,
Major General Commanding.

Major General J. G. FOSTER,
Commanding Department of the South, Hilton Head.

HEADQUARTERS MILITARY DIVISION OF THE MISSISSIPPI,
In the field, near Savannah, Ga., December 18, 1864.

GENERAL: I wrote you at length by Colonel Babcock on the 16th instant. As I therein explained my purpose, yesterday I made a demand on General Hardee for the surrender of the city of Savannah, and to-day received his answer refusing. Copies of both letters are herewith enclosed. You will notice that I claim that my lines are within easy cannon range of the heart of Savannah, but General Hardee claims we are four and a half miles distant. But I myself have been to the intersection of the Charleston and Georgia Central railroad, and the three (3) mile post is but a few yards beyond, within the line of our pickets. The enemy has no pickets outside of his fortified line, which is a full quarter of a mile within the three (3) mile post; and I have the evidence of Mr. R. R. Cuyler, president of the Georgia Central railroad, who was a prisoner in our hands, that the mile-posts are measured from the Exchange, which is but two squares back from the river. But by to-morrow morning I will have six (6) 30-pounder Parrott's in position, and General Hardee will learn whether I am right or not. From the left of our line, which is on the Savannah river, the spires can be plainly seen, but the country is so densely wooded with pine and live-oak, and lies so flat, that we can see nothing from any other part of our lines. General Slocum feels confident that he can make a successful assault at one or two points in front of the 20th corps, and one or two in front of General Davis's (14th) corps. But all of General Howard's troops, the right wing, lie behind the Little Ogeechee, and I doubt if it can be passed by troops in the face of an enemy; still we can make strong feints, and if I can get a sufficient number of boats I shall make a co-operative demonstration up Vernon river or Wassaw sound. I should like very much, indeed, to take Savannah before coming to you; but, as I wrote to you before, I will do nothing rash or hasty, and will embark for the James river as soon as General Easton, who is gone to Port Royal for that purpose, reports to me that he has an approximate number of vessels for transportation of the contemplated force. I fear even this will cost more delay than you anticipate, for already the movement of our transports and the gunboats has required more time than I had expected. We have had dense fogs, and there are more mud banks in the Ogeechee than were reported, and there are no pilots whatever.

Admiral Dahlgren promises to have the channel buoyed and staked; but it is not done yet. We find only six (6) feet water up to King's bridge at low tide, about ten (10) up to the rice-mills, and sixteen (16) to Fort McAllister. All these points may be used by us, and we have a good strong bridge across Ogeechee at King's, by which our wagons can go to Fort McAllister, to which point I am sending the wagons not absolutely necessary for daily use, the negroes, prisoners of war, sick, &c., en route for Port Royal.

In relation to Savannah, you will remark that General Hardee refers to his still being in communication with his war department. This language he thought would deceive me, but I am confirmed in the belief that the route to which he refers, namely, the Union plank road, on the South Carolina shore, is inadequate to feed his army and the people of Savannah, for General Foster assures me that he has his force on that very road near the head of Broad river, and that his guns command the railroad, so that cars no longer run between Charleston and Savannah. We hold this end of the Charleston road, and have destroyed it from the three (3) mile post back to the bridge about twelve (12) miles above.

In anticipation of leaving this country, I am continuing the destruction of their railroads, and at this moment have two divisions and the cavalry at work breaking up the Gulf railroad from the Ogeechee to the Altamaha, so that even I do not take Savannah, I will leave it in a bad way. But I still hope that events will give me time to take Savannah, even if I have to assault with some loss. I am satisfied that unless we take it, the gunboats never will, for they can make no impression upon the batteries which guard every approach from the sea. And I have also a faint belief that when Colonel Babcock reaches you, you will delay operations long enough to enable me to succeed here. With Savannah in our possession, at some future time, if not now, we can punish South Carolina as she deserves, and as thousands of people in Georgia hope we will do.

I do sincerely believe that the whole United States, north and south, would rejoice to have this army turned loose on South Carolina, to devastate that State in the manner we have done in Georgia, and it would have a direct and im-mediate bearing on your campaign in Virginia.

I have the honor to be, your obedient servant,

. W. T. SHERMAN,
Major General Commanding.

Lieut. General U. S. GRANT,
 City Point, Virginia.

HEADQUARTERS MILITARY DIVISION OF THE MISSISSIPPI,
In the field, near Savannah, Ga., December 19, 1864.

GENERAL: The general-in-chief has gone to the bay. He directs me to further instruct you to push the preparations for the attack on the defences of Savannah as rapidly as possible, and then await further directions before doing more.

He will endeavor to get co-operations from Admiral Dahlgren and General Foster, with whom he will confer before returning. If in the mean time any-thing should occur that you would wish to communicate to him, please to send to me and I will forward.

I am, genenral, with respect,

L. M. DAYTON, *Aide-de-Camp.*

Major General SLOCUM, *Commanding Left Wing.*

HEADQUARTERS MILITARY DIVISION OF THE MISSISSIPP
In the field, near Savannah, Ga., December 19, 1864.

GENERAL : The general-in-chief has gone to the bay. He wishes you to push the preparations for attacking Savannah with all possible speed, but to await orders for the attack. He will see General Foster and the admiral before returning, and will get co-operation from both if possible. Should anything occur that you would like to communicate to the general, I will forward for you.

I am, general, with respect,

L. M. DAYTON, *Aide-de-Camp.*

Major General O. O. HOWARD,
 Commanding Army of the Tennessee.

HEADQUARTERS MILITARY DIVISION OF THE MISSISSIPPI,
In the field, near Savannah, Ga., December 22, 1864—5 a. m.

GENERAL : The general-in-chief has just returned to his headquarters, having been somewhat delayed on his way back from Port Royal by high winds. You are no doubt already aware that the enemy has evacuated Savannah, and our troops are in full possession of the city. For the present, however, supplies will continue to be received *via* Ogeechee river and the King's bridge road. The general directs me to say that he wishes you, until further orders, to continue to guard the depot of supplies at King's bridge with your cavalry, on the west side of the river, in connexion with the brigade of infantry still remaining between Big and Little Ogeechee. He is anxious to hear as soon as possible from General Mower's force sent down the Gulf railroad, also from your cavalry sent towards the Altamaha, and desires that you will at once send him all information you have or may obtain respecting them. He will himself go into Savannah this morning, and remove his headquarters thither, and will send you further orders after going there.

I am, general, respectfully, your obedient servant,

HENRY HITCHCOCK,
Major and A. A. G.

Brigadier General KILPATRICK,
Commanding Cavalry Division, Army of Georgia.

HEADQUARTERS MILITARY DIVISION OF THE MISSISSIPPI,
In the field, Savannah, Ga., December 22, 1864.

DEAR GENERAL : I take great satisfaction in reporting that we are in possession of Savannah and all its forts. At first I proposed to extend across the river above the city from Slocum's left, but the enemy had a gunboat and ram heavily armed that would have made the step extra-hazardous; also the submerged rice-fields on the northeast bank were impracticable. I then went to Hilton Head to arrange with General Foster to re-enforce his movement from Broad river, but before I had completed the move Hardee got his garrison across and off on the Union plank-road. Our troops entered at daylight yesterday, took about eight hundred (800) prisoners, over one hundred (100) guns, some of the heaviest calibre, and a perfect string of forts from Savannah around to McAllister; also twelve thousand (12,000) bales of cotton, one hundred and ninety (190) cars, thirteen (13) locomotives, three (3) steamboats, and an immense supply of shells, shot, and all kinds of ammunition. There is a complete arsenal here, and much valuable machinery. The citizens mostly remain, and the city is very quiet. The river below is much obstructed, but I parted with Admiral Dahlgren yesterday at 4 p. m., and he will at once set about removing them and opening a way. The enemy blew up an iron-clad, the Savannah, a good ram, and three tenders, (small steamers.) As yet we have made but a partial inventory, but the above falls far short of our conquests. I have not a particle of doubt but that we have secured one hundred and fifty (150) fine guns with plenty of ammunition.

I have now completed my first step, and should like to go on to you *via* Columbia and Raleigh, but will prepare to embark as soon as vessels come. Colonel Babcock will have told you all, and you know better than anybody else how much better troops arrive by a land march than when carried by transports. I will turn over to Foster Savannah and all its out-posts, with, say, one division of infantry, Kilpatrick's cavalry, and plenty of artillery. Hardee has, of course, moved into South Carolina, but I do not believe his Georgia troops, militia and fancy companies, will work in South Carolina. His force is reported by citizens at from fifteen to twenty thousand (15 to 20,000.)

The capture of Savannah, with the incidental use of the rivers, gives us a magnificent position in this quarter, and if you can hold Lee, and if Thomas can continue as he did on the 18th, I could go on and smash South Carolina all to pieces, and also break up roads as far as the Roanoke. But, as I before re-marked, I will now look to coming to you as soon as transports are ready. We all well and as confident as ever.

Yours truly,

W. T. SHERMAN,
Major General Commanding.

Lieut. General U. S. GRANT,
Com'dg Armies of the United States, City Point, Va.

HEADQUARTERS OF THE ARMY,
Washington, December 16, 1864.

GENERAL: Lieutenant General Grant informs me that in his last despatch sent to you, he suggested the transfer of your infantry to Richmond. He now wishes me to say that you will retain your entire force, at least for the present, and, with such assistance as may be given you by General Foster and Admiral Dahlgren, operate from such base as you may establish on the coast. General Foster will obey such instructions as may be given by you. Should you have captured Savannah, it is thought that by transferring the water-batteries to the land side, that place may be made a good depot, and base for operations on Augusta, Branchville, or Charleston. If Savannah should not be captured, or if captured and not deemed suitable for this purpose, perhaps Beaufort would serve as a depot. As the rebels have probably removed their most valuable property from Augusta, perhaps Branchville would be the most important point at which to strike, in order to sever all connexions between the Virginia and the Northwestern railroads. General Grant's wishes, however, are that this whole matter of your future actions should be left entirely to your discretion.

We can send you from here a number of complete batteries of field artillery, with or without horses, as you may desire. Also, as soon as General Thomas can spare them, all the fragments, convalescents and furloughed men of your army. It is reported that Thomas defeated Hood yesterday, near Nashville, but we have no particulars, nor official reports, telegraphic communications being interrupted by a heavy storm. Our last advices from you were in General Howard's note, announcing his approach to Savannah.

Yours, truly,

H. W. HALLECK,
Major General, Chief of Staff.

Major General SHERMAN,
Via Hilton Head.

HEADQUARTERS OF THE ARMY,
Washington, December 18, 1864.

MY DEAR GENERAL: Yours of the 13th, by Major Anderson, is just received. I congratulate you on your splendid success, and shall very soon expect to hear of the crowning work of your new campaign, in the capture of Savannah. Your march will stand out prominently as the great one of this great war. When Savannah falls, then for another wide swath through the centre of the confederacy. But I will not anticipate. General Grant is expected here this morning, and will probably write you his own views.

I do not learn from your letter, or Major Anderson, that you are in want of anything which we have not provided at Hilton Head. Thinking it probable that you might want more field artillery, I had prepared several batteries, but the great difficulty of foraging horses on the coast will prevent our sending any, unless you actually need them. The hay crop this year is short, and the quartermaster's department has great difficulty in procuring a supply for our animals.

General Thomas has defeated Hood, near Nashville, and it is hoped that he will completely crush his army. Breckinridge, at last accounts, was trying to form a junction near Murfreesboro', but as Thomas is between them, Breckinridge must either retreat or be defeated.

*   *   *   *   *   *   *   *

Orders have been issued for all officers and detachments, having three months or more to serve, to rejoin your army, *via* Savannah. Those having less than three months to serve will be retained by General Thomas. Should you capture Charleston, I hope that by *some* accident the place may be destroyed; and if a little salt should be sown upon its site, it may prevent the growth of future crops of nullification and secession.

Yours, truly,

H. W. HALLECK,
Major General, Chief of Staff.

Major General W. T. SHERMAN, *Savannah.*

HEADQUARTERS ARMIES OF THE UNITED STATES,
Washington, D. C., December 18, 1864.

MY DEAR GENERAL: I have just received and read, I need not tell you with how much gratification, your letter to General Halleck. I congratulate you and the brave officers and men under your command on the successful termination of your most brilliant campaign. I never had a doubt of the result. When apprehensions for your safety were expressed by the President, I assured him, with the army you had, and you in command of it, there was no danger, but you would *strike* bottom on salt water some place. That I would not feel the same security, in fact would not have intrusted the expedition to any other living commander.

*   *   *   *   *   *   *   *

Breckinridge is said to be making for Murfreesboro'. If so, he is in a most excellent place. Stoneman has nearly wiped out John Morgan's old command, and five days ago entered Bristol. I did think the best thing to do was to bring the greater part of your army here and wipe out Lee. The turn affairs now seem to be taking has shaken me in that opinion. I doubt whether you may not accomplish more toward that result where you are than if brought here, especially as I am informed since my arrival in the city that it would take about two months to get you here, with all the other calls there are for ocean transportation.

I want to get your views on what ought to be done and what can be done. If you capture the garrison of Savannah, it certainly will compel Lee to detach from Richmond, or give us nearly the whole south. My own opinion is, Lee is averse to going out of Virginia; and if the cause of the south is lost, he wants Richmond to be the last place surrendered. If he has such views, it may be well to indulge him until we get everything else in our hands.

Congratulating you and the army again upon the splendid results of your campaign, the like of which is not read of in past history, I subscribe myself, more than ever, if possible, your friend,

U. S. GRANT, *Lieutenant General.*

Major General W. T. SHERMAN,
Commanding Military Division of the Mississippi.

HEADQUARTERS MILITARY DIVISION OF THE MISSISSIPPI,
In the field, Savannah, Ga., December 23, 1864.

DEAR GENERAL: Major Dixon arrived last night, bringing your letter of the 10th December, for which I am very much obliged, as it gives me a clear and distinct view of the situation of affairs at Nashville up to that date. I have also from the War Department a copy of General Thomas's despatch, giving an account of the attack on Hood on the 15th, which was successful, but not complete. I await further accounts with anxiety, as Thomas's complete success is necessary to vindicate my plans for this campaign, and I have no doubt that my calculations that Thomas had in hand (including A. J. Smith's troops) a force large enough to whip Hood in fair fight was correct. I approve of Thomas's allowing Hood to come north far enough to enable him to concentrate his own men, though I would have preferred that Hood should have been checked about Columbia. Still, if Thomas followed up his success of the 15th, and gave Hood a good whaling, and is at this moment following him closely, the whole compaign in my division will be even more perfect than the Atlanta campaign, for at this end of the line I have realized all I had reason to hope for, except in the release of our prisoners, which was simply an impossibility.

December 24.—I have just received a letter from General Grant, giving a detail of General Thomas's operations up to the 18th, and I am gratified beyond measure at the result

Show this letter to General Thomas, and tell him to consider it addressed to him, as I have not time to write more now. I want General Thomas to follow Hood to and beyond the Tennessee, and not to hesitate to go on as far as Columbus, Mississippi, or Selma, Alabama, as I know that he will have no trouble whatever in subsisting his army anywhere below Sand mountain and along the Black Warrior. In the poorest part of Georgia I found no trouble in subsisting my army and animals, some of my corps not issuing but one (1) day's bread from Atlanta to Savannah.

Keep me fully advised by telegraph, *via* New York, of the situation of affairs in Tennessee. I will be here probably ten (10) days longer, and in communication for a longer time.

I am, very truly, yours,

W. T. SHERMAN, *Major General.*

General J. D. WEBSTER,
Nashville, Tennessee.

HEADQUARTERS MILITARY DIVISION OF THE MISSISSIPPI,
Savannah, Ga., December 24, 1864.

GENERAL: Your letter of December 18th is just received. I feel very much gratified at receiving the handsome commendation you pay my army. I will, in general orders, convey to the officers and men the substance of your note.

I am also gratified that you have modified your former orders, as I feared that the transportation by sea would very much disturb the unity and *morale* of my army, now so perfect.

The occupation of Savannah, which I have heretofore reported, completes the first part of our game and fulfils a great part of your instructions; and I am now engaged in dismantling the rebel forts, which bear upon the sea and channels, and transferring the heavy ordnance and ammunition to Fort Pulaski and Hilton Head, where they can be more easily guarded than if left in the city.

The rebel inner lines are well adapted to our purpose, and, with slight modifications, can be held by a comparatively small force, and in about ten (10) days I expect to be ready to sally forth again. I feel no doubt whatever as to our future plans. I have thought them over so long and well that they appear as clear as daylight. I left Augusta untouched on purpose, because the enemy will be in doubt as to my objective point, after crossing the Savannah river, whether it be Augusta or Charleston, and will naturally divide his forces. I will then move either on Branchville or Columbia, by any curved line that gives me the best supplies, breaking up in my course as much railroad as possible, then ignoring Charleston and Augusta both. I would occupy Columbia and Camden, pausing there long enough to observe the effect. I would then strike for the Charleston and Wilmington railroad, somewhere between the Santee and Cape Fear rivers, and, if possible, communicate with the fleet under Admiral Dahlgren (whom I find a most agreeable gentleman, in every way accommodating himself to our wishes and plans.) Then I would favor Wilmington, in the belief that Porter and Butler will fail in their present undertaking. Charleston is now a mere desolated wreck, and is hardly worth the time it would take to starve it out. Still, I am aware that, historically and politically, much importance is attached to the place, and it may be that, apart from its military importance, both you and the administration would prefer I should give it more attention; and it would be well for you to give me some general idea on that subject, as otherwise I would treat it, as I have expressed, as a point of little importance, after all its railroads leading into the interior are destroyed or occupied by us. But on the hypothesis of ignoring Charleston and taking Wilmington, I would then favor a movement direct on Raleigh. The game is then up with Lee, unless he comes out of Richmond, avoids you and fights me, in which case I should reckon on your being on his heels.

Now that Hood is used up by Thomas, I feel disposed to bring the matter to an issue as quick as possible. I feel confident that I can break up the whole railroad system of South Carolina and North Carolina, and be on the Roanoke, either at Raleigh or Weldon, by the time the spring fairly opens; and if you feel confident that you can whip Lee outside of his intrenchments, I feel equally confident that I can handle him in the open country.

One reason why I would ignore Charleston is this: That I believe they will reduce the garrison to a small force, with plenty of provisions, and I know that the neck back of Charleston can be made impregnable to assault, and we will hardly have time for siege operations.

I will have to leave in Savannah a garrison, and, if Thomas can spare them, I would like to have all detachments, convalescents, &c., belonging to these four corps sent forward at once. I don't want to cripple Thomas, because I regard his operations as all important, and I have ordered him to pursue Hood down into Alabama, trusting to the country for supplies.

I reviewed one of my corps to-day, and shall continue to review the whole army. I don't like to boast, but I believe this army has a confidence in itself that makes it almost invincible. I wish you would run down and see us; it would have a good effect, and would show to both armies that they are acting on a common plan. The weather is now cool and pleasent, and the general health very good.

Your true friend,

W. T. SHERMAN, *Major General.*

Lieut. General U. S. GRANT,
  City Point, Virginia.

HEADQUARTERS MILITARY DIVISION OF THE MISSISSIPPI,
In the field, Savannah, December 24, 1864.

GENERAL: I had the pleasure of receiving your two letters of the 16th and 18th instant to-day, and I feel more than usually flattered by the high encomiums you have passed on our recent campaign, which is now complete by the occupation of Savannah.

19 *

I am also very glad that General Grant has changed his mind about embarking my troops for James river, leaving me free to make the broad swath you describe through South and North Carolina, and still more gratified at the news from Thomas in Tennessee, because it fulfils my plans which contemplated his being fully able to dispose of Hood in case he ventured north of the Tennessee river. So I think, on the whole, I can chuckle over Jeff. Davis's disappointment in not turning my Atlanta campaign into a "Moscow disaster."

I have just finished a long letter to General Grant, and have explained to him that we are engaged in shifting our base from the Ogeechee over to the Savannah river, dismantling all the forts made by the enemy to bear upon the salt-water channels, and transferring the heavy ordnance, &c., to Fort Pulaski and Hilton Head, and in remodelling the enemy's interior lines to suit our future plans and purposes. I have also laid down the programme of a campaign which I can make this winter, which will put me in the spring on the Roanoke in direct communication with him on the James river. In general terms, my plan is to turn over to General Foster the city of Savannah and to sally forth with my army re-supplied, cross the Savannah, feign on Charleston and Augusta, but strike between, breaking en route the Charleston and Augusta railroad, also a large part of that from Branchville and Camden toward North Carolina, and then rapidly move to some point of the railroad from Charleston to Wilmington, between the Santee and Cape Fear rivers; then communicating with the fleet in the neighborhood of Georgetown, I would turn upon Wilmington or Charleston, according to the importance of either; I rather prefer Wilmington, as a live place, over Charleston, which is dead and unimportant when its railroad communications are broken. I take it for granted the present movement on Wilmington will fail. If I should determine to take Charleston I would turn across the country, (which I have hunted over many a time, from Santee to Mount Pleasant,) throwing one wing on the peninsula between Ashley and Cooper. After accomplishing one or the other of these ends, I would make a bee-line for Raleigh, or Weldon, when Lee would be forced to come out of Richmond or acknowledge himself beaten. He would, I think, by the use of the Danville railroad, throw himself rapidly between me and Grant, leaving Richmond in the hands of the latter. This would not alarm me, for I have an army which I think can manœuvre, and I would force him to attack me at a disadvantage, always under the supposition that Grant would be on his heels; and if the worst come to the worst, I could fight my way down to Albemarle sound or Newbern.

I think the time has come now when we should attempt the boldest moves, and my experience is that they are easier of execution than more timid ones, because the enemy is disconcerted by them—as, for instance, my recent campaign.

I also doubt the wisdom of concentration beyond a certain point, as the roads of this country limit the amount of men that can be brought to bear in any one battle; and I don't believe that any one general can handle more than sixty thousand (60,000) men in battle.

I think my campaign of the last month, as well as every step I take from this point northward, is as much a direct attack upon Lee's army as though I were operating within the sound of his artillery.

I am very anxious that Thomas should follow up his success to the very uttermost point. My orders to him before I left Kingston were, after beating Hood, to follow him as far as Columbus, Mississippi, or Selma, Alabama, both of which lie in districts of country which I know to be rich in corn and meat.

I attach more importance to these deep incisions into the enemy's country, because this war differs from European wars in this particular—we are not only fighting hostile armies but a hostile people, and must make old and young, rich and poor, feel the hard hand of war, as well as their organized armies. I know that this recent movement of mine through Georgia has had a wonderful effect in this respect. Thousands who had been deceived by their lying papers into the belief that we were being whipped all the time, realized the truth, and have no appetite for a repetition of the same experience. To be sure, Jeff. Davis has his people under a pretty good shape of dicipline, but I think faith in him is much shaken in Georgia, and I think before we are done South Carolina will not be quite so tempestuous.

I will bear in mind your hint as to Charleston, and don't think "salt" will be necessary. When I move the 15th corps will be on the right of the right wing, and their position will bring them naturally into Charleston first; and if you have watched the history of that corps, you will have remarked that they generally do their work up pretty well. The truth is, the whole army is burning with an insatiable desire to wreak vengeance upon South Carolina. I almost tremble at her fate, but feel that she deserves all that seems in store for her. Many and many a person in Georgia asked me why we did not go to South Carolina; and when I answered that I was *en route* for that State, the invariable reply was, " Well, if you will make those people feel the severities of war, we will pardon you for your desolation of Georgia."

I look upon Columbia as quite as bad as Charleston, and I doubt if we shall spare the public buildings there as we did at Milledgeville.

I have been so busy lately that I have not yet made my official report, and think I had better wait until I get my subordinate reports before attempting it, as I am anxious to explain clearly not only the reasons for every step, but the amount of execution done, and this I cannot do until I get the subordinate reports; for we marched the whole distance in four or more columns, and of course I could only be present with one, and generally that one engaged in destroying railroads. This work of destruction was performed better than usual, because I had an engineer regiment provided with claws to *twist the bars* after being heated. Such bars can never be used again; and the only way in which a railroad line can be reconstructed across Georgia is to make a new road from Fairburn station, twenty-four (24) miles southwest of Atlanta, to Madison, a distance of one hundred (100) miles, and before that can be done I propose to be on the road from Augusta to Charleston, which is a continuation of the same.

I felt somewhat disappointed at Hardee's escape from me, but really am not to blame. I moved as quick as possible to close up the " Union causeway," but intervening obstacles were such that before I could get my troops on the road Hardee had slipped out. Still, I know that the men that were in Savannah will be lost, in a measure, to Jeff. Davis, for the Georgia troops under G. W. Smith declared they would not fight in South Carolina, and they have gone north, en route for Augusta; and I have reason to believe the North Carolina troops have gone to Wilmington; in other words, they are scattered. I have reason to believe that Beauregard was present in Savannah at the time of its evacuation, and I think that he and Hardee are now in Charleston, doubtless making preparations for what they suppose will be my next step.

Please say to the President that I received his kind message through Colonel Markland, and feel thankful for his high favor. If I disappoint him in the future, it shall not be from want of zeal or love to the cause.

Of you I expect a full and frank criticism of my plans for the future, which may enable me to correct errors before it is too late. I do not wish to be rash, but want to give my rebel friends no chance to accuse us of want of enterprise or courage.

Assuring you of my high personal respect, I remain, as ever, your friend,

W. T. SHERMAN,
Major General.

Major General H. W. HALLECK,
 Chief of Staff, Washington, D. C

HEADQUARTERS MILITARY DIVISION OF THE MISSISSIPPI,
In the field, Savannah, Ga., December 28, 1864.

GENTLEMEN: I have a copy of the resolutions adopted by you. They are surely strong enough and patriotic enough. I will aid you all that is possible, and do all in my power to encourage you and to defend you in your course. I do think we have been at war long enough for truth to reveal itself. We are fellow-countrymen, and bound by every principle of honor and honesty to maintain and defend the "Union" given us by Washington, and that is all I aim at; and the moment Georgia resumes her place in the Union, and sends her representatives to Congress, she is at once at peace, and all the laws, both national and State, are revived. If you will stay at home quietly and call back your sons and neighbors to resume their peaceful pursuits, I will promise you ammunition to protect yourselves and property. If rebel soldiers do any of you violence I will retaliate; and if you will bring your produce to Savannah I will cause it to be protected in transitu and allow it to be sold in market to the highest bidder, and our commissary will buy your cattle, hogs, sheep, &c.

It would be well to form a league and to adopt some common certificate, so that our officers and soldiers may distinguish between you and open rebels. I will be glad to confer with any of your people, and will do all that is fair to encourage you to recover the peace and prosperity you enjoyed before the war.

I am, with respect,

W. T. SHERMAN,
Major General.

Messrs. P. J. STANFIELD, A. J. PAGITT, AND OTHERS,
of Liberty and Tatnall Counties, Georgia.

HEADQUARTERS MILITARY DIVISION OF THE MISSISSIPPI,
In the field, Savannah, Ga., December 29, 1864.

GENERAL: I have read with pleasure your report just received, as well as those of your brigade commanders.

I beg to assure you that the operations of the cavalry under your command have been skilful and eminently successful. As you correctly state in your report, you handsomely feigned on Forsyth and Macon, afterwards did all that was possible towards the rescue of our prisoners at Millen, which failed simply because the prisoners were not there; and I will here state (that you may have it over my signature) that you acted wisely and well in drawing back from Wheeler to Louisville, as I had instructed you not to risk your cavalry command. And subsequently, at Thomas's station, Waynesboro', and Brier creek, you whipped a superior cavalry force, and took from Wheeler all chance of boasting over you. But the fact that to you, in a great measure, we owe the march of four strong columns of infantry, with heavy trains and wagons, over three hundred (300) miles through an enemy's country, without the loss of a single wagon, and without the annoyance of cavalry dashes on our flanks, is honor enough for any cavalry commander.

I will retain your report for a few days that I may, in my report, use some of your statistics, and then will forward it to the War Department, when I will indorse your recommendations, and make such others as I may consider necessary and proper.

I am, truly, your friend,

W. T. SHERMAN,
Major General Commanding.

Brigadier General JUDSON KILPATRICK,
Commanding Cavalry Division, Army of Georgia.

HEADQUARTERS MILITARY DIVISION OF THE MISSISSIPPI,
In the field, Savannah, Ga., December 31, 1864.

GENERAL: The steamer leaves with the mail this afternoon at 5 p. m. I write only to say that since my last to you there is nothing of importance to communicate. The city is perfectly quiet and orderly. The enemy appear to be making preparations to receive us over in South Carolina. As soon as I can accumulate a sufficient surplus of forage and provisions to load my wagons I shall be ready to start. We find the Savannah river more obstructed than we expected. It is filled with crib-works loaded with paving-stones, making mud islands, with narrow, tortuous and difficult channels. All our stores have to be lightered up from the ship's anchorage about Tybee.

I have been engaged in reviewing my troops, and feel a just pride in their fine soldierly condition and perfect equipment.

I propose at once to make lodgements in South Carolina about Port Royal, opposite this city, and up about Sister's ferry. When all is ready, I can feign at one or more places and cross at the other; after which my movements will be governed by those of the enemy, and such instructions as I may receive from Lieutenant General Grant before starting. I do not think I can employ better strategy than I have hitherto done, namely, make a good ready, and then move rapidly to my objective, avoiding a battle at points where I would be encumbered by wounded, but striking boldly and quickly when my objective is reached.

I will give due heed and encouragements to all peace movements, but conduct war as though it could only terminate with the destruction of the enemy and the occupation of all his strategic points.

The weather is fine, the air cool and bracing, and my experience in this latitude convinces me that I may safely depend on two good months for field work.

I await your and General Grant's answer to my proposed plan of operations before taking any steps indicative of future movements. I should like to receive, before starting, the detachments left behind in Tennessee belonging to these four corps; and it would be eminently proper that General Foster should be re-enforced by about five thousand (5,000) men, to enable him to hold Savannah without calling upon me to leave him one of my old divisions, which is too valuable in the field to be left behind in garrison.

I would also deem it wise so far to respect the prejudices of the people of Savannah as not to garrison the place with negro troops. It seems a perfect bugbear to them, and I know that all people are more influenced by prejudice than by reason.

The army continues in the best of health and spirits, and, notwithstanding the habits begotten during our rather vandalic march, its behavior in Savannah has excited the wonder and admiration of all.

I am, with great respect, very truly yours,

W. T. SHERMAN,
Major General Commanding.

Major General H. W. HALLECK,
Chief of Staff, Washington, D. C.

HEADQUARTERS MILITARY DIVISION OF THE MISSISSIPPI,
In the field, Savannah, Ga., December 31, 1864.

GENERAL: Your note enclosing Mr. Cohen's of this date is received, and I answer frankly through you his inquiries.

First. No one can practice law as an attorney in the United States without acknowledging the supremacy of our government. If I am not in error, an attorney is as much an officer of the court as the clerk, and it would be a novel thing in a government to have a court to administer law that denied the supremacy of the government itself.

Second. No one will be allowed the privileges of a merchant; or, rather, to trade is a privilege which no one should seek of the government without in like manner acknowledging its supremacy.

Third. If Mr. Cohen remains in Savannah as a denizen, his property, real and personal, will not be disturbed, unless its temporary use be necessary for the military authorities of the city. The title to property will not be disturbed in any event until adjudicated by the courts of the United States.

Fourth. If Mr. Cohen leaves Savannah under my Special Order No. 143, it is a public acknowledgment that he "adheres to the enemies of the United States," and all his property becomes forfeited to the United States. But, as a matter of favor, he will be allowed to carry with him clothing and furniture for the use of himself, his family, and servants, and will be transported within the enemy's lines, but not by way of Port Royal.

These rules will apply to all people, and from them no exceptions will be made.

I have the honor to be, general, your obedient servant,

W. T. SHERMAN, *Major General.*

Major General F. P. BLAIR,
Commanding 17th Army Corps.

HEADQUARTERS MILITARY DIVISION OF THE MISSISSIPPI,
In the field, Savannah, Ga., December 31, 1864.

DEAR ADMIRAL: Captain Breese has this moment arrived with your letter of December 29, and I assure you it does my heart good to feel that I am once more near you. I hope soon we will meet again in person.

I have already submitted to Generals Halleck and Grant a plan for a campaign which will bring my whole army to Wilmington, which I know I can take as easily, if not more so, than Savannah. I do not think you can take those shore-batteries with your gunboats, or do more than drive the gunners to the cover of their bomb-proofs. I have examined carefully many of the forts about Savannah, and find them so well covered by traverses and bomb-proof shelters that you might blaze away at them for a month, from the direction of the sea channels, without materially harming them. I have no doubt, however, from what you say, that Butler's men ought to have taken Fort Fisher in about three minutes, for its bomb-proofs cannot possibly shelter more than two hundred men, who would be, as you say, crouching in a defenceless position as against an attacking force. But even after you have got Fisher, then comes Caswell, Fort Johnson, and, I suppose, a string of forts all the way back to Wilmington. Now, I propose to march my whole army through South Carolina, tearing up railroads and smashing things generally; feign on Charleston, and rapidly come down on Wilmington from the rear, taking all their works in reverse. I submitted this plan to General Grant on the 24th, and shall expect his answer very soon, and will be ready to start the moment I can replenish my wagons with bread, sugar, coffee, &c.

At present the Savannah river is badly obstructed by heavy cribs filled with cobblestones, which have served to make islands of mud and sand, leaving narrow, difficult, and tortuous channels between. Through these channels all our stores have to be brought in launches and light-draught boats, of which we have an inadequate number, so that thus far we barely get enough for daily consumption. But all hands are hard at work, and I hope by the 10th of January to get enough ahead to load our wagons and be ready to start. It will take some time for me to reach Wilmington, but I am certain that mine is the only mode by which the place can be taken effectually.

My army is a good one, but not large enough to make detachments from. I had to leave with Thomas enough men to whip Hood, and have written to General Grant to send to Foster enough men to hold Savannah while I move with my entire force.

It is very important that I should have two or more points along the coast where I can communicate with you, and where I could have some spare ammunition and provisions in reserve, say Bull's bay, Georgetown, and Masonboro.'

I think, when you come to consider my position, you will agree with me that my proposition is better than to undertake to reduce, in detail, the forts about Wilmington; and you can so manœuvre as to hold a large portion of the enemy to the sea-coast while I ravage the interior; and when I do make my appearance on the coast we will make short work of them all.

I have shown to Captain Breese my letters to Grant and Halleck, and will explain to him fully everything that will interest you, and as soon as I can hear from General Grant, will send a steamer to you advising you of the time of starting.   I rather fear, however, that the President's anxiety to take Charleston may induce Grant to order me to operate against Charleston rather than Wilmington, though I much prefer the latter.—Charleston being a dead cock in the pit altogether.

I am, most truly, your friend,

W. T. SHERMAN, *Major General.*

Admiral D. D. PORTER,
Commanding North Atlantic Blockading Squadron.

HEADQUARTERS ARMIES OF THE UNITED STATES,
City Point, Va., December 26, 1864.

GENERAL: Your very interesting letter of the 22d instant, brought by the hands of Major Gray, of General Foster's staff, is just at hand.

As the major starts back at once, I can do no more at present than simply acknowledge its receipt.   The capture of Savannah, with its immense stores, must tell upon the people of the south.   All well here.

Yours, truly,

U. S. GRANT, *Lieutenant General.*

Major General W. T. SHERMAN,
Savannah, Georgia.

HEADQUARTERS ARMIES OF THE UNITED STATES,
City Point, Va., December 27, 1864.

GENERAL: Before writing you definite instructions for the next campaign I wanted to receive your answer to my letter written from Washington.   Your confidence in being able to march up and join this army pleases me, and I believe it can be done.   The effect of such a campaign will be to disorganize the South, and prevent the organization of new armies from their broken fragments. Hood is now retreating with his army broken and demoralized.   His loss in men has probably not been far from 20,000 besides deserters.   If time is given, the fragments may be collected together, and many of the deserters reassembled.   If we can we should act to prevent this.   Your spare army, as it were, moving as proposed, will do this.

In addition to holding Savannah, it looks to me that an intrenched camp ought to be held on the railroad between Savannah and Charleston.   Your movements towards Branchville will probably enable Foster to reach this with his own force. This will give us a position in the south from which we can threaten the interior without marching over long, narrow causeways, easily defended, as we have heretofore been compelled to do. Could not such a camp be established about Pocotaligo or Coosawhatchie?

I have thought that, Hood being so completely wiped out for present harm, I might bring A. J. Smith here with from ten thousand to fifteen thousand. With this increase I could hold my lines, and move out with a greater force than Lee has. It would compel him to retain all his present force in the defences of Richmond or abandon them entirely. This latter contingency is probably the only danger to the easy success of your expedition. In the event you should meet Lee's army you would be compelled to beat it or find the sea-coast. Of course I shall not let Lee's army escape if I can help it, and will not let it go without following it to the best of my ability.

Without waiting further directions, then, you may make preparations to start on your northern expedition without delay. Break up the railroads in South and North Carolina, and join the armies operating against Richmond as soon as you can.

I will leave out all suggestions about the route you should take, knowing that your information, gained daily in the progress of events, will be better than any that can be obtained now. It may not be possible for you to march to the rear of Petersburg; but failing in this, you could strike either of the sea-coast ports in North Carolina held by us. From there you could easily take shipping. It would be decidedly preferable, however, if you could march the whole distance. From the best information I have you will find no difficulty in supplying your army until you cross the Roanoke. From there here is but a few days' march, and supplies could be collected south of the river to bring you through. I shall establish communication with you there by steamboat and gunboat. By this means your wants can be partially supplied.

I shall hope to hear from you soon, and to hear your plan, and about the time of starting.

Please instruct Foster to hold on to all the property captured in Savannah, and especially the cotton. Do not turn it over to citizens or treasury agents without orders of the War Department.

Very respectfully, your obedient servant,

U. S. GRANT, *Lieutenant General.*

Major General W. T. SHERMAN,
Commanding Military Division of the Mississippi.

HEADQUARTERS MILITARY DIVISION OF THE MISSISSIPPI,
In the field, Savannah, Ga., January 2, 1865.

GENERAL: I have received by the hands of General Barnard your note of 26th, and letter of 27th December.

I herewith enclose to you a copy of a projet which I have this morning, in strict confidence, discussed with my immediate commanders. I shall need, however, larger supplies of stores, especially grain. I will enclose to you with this letters from General Easton, quartermaster, and Colonel Beckwith, commissary of subsistence, setting forth what will be required, and trust you will forward them to Washington, with your sanction, so that the necessary steps may be taken at once to enable me to carry out this plan on time. I wrote you very fully on the 24th, and have nothing to add to that. Everything here is quiet, and if I can get the necessary supplies in my wagons I shall be ready to start at the time indicated in my projet, (January 15.) But until those supplies are in hand I can do nothing; after they are I shall be ready to move with great rapidity. I have heard of the affair at Cape Fear; it has turned out as you will remember I expected. I have furnished General Easton a copy of the despatch from the Secretary of War. He will retain possession of all cotton here, and ship it as fast as vessels can be had to New York. I shall immediately send the 17th corps over to Port Royal, by boats furnished by Admiral Dahlgren and General Foster, without interfering with General Easton's vessels, to make a lodgement on the railroad at Pocotaligo.

General Barnard will remain with me a few days, and I shall send this by a staff officer, who can return on one of the vessels of the supply fleet. I suppose that now General Butler has got through with them, you can spare them to us.

My report of recent operations is nearly ready, and will be sent on in a day or two, as soon as some further subordinate reports come in.

I am, with great respect, very truly, your friend,

W. T. SHERMAN, *Major General.*

Lieut. General U. S. GRANT, *City Point.*

EXECUTIVE MANSION,
Washington, December 26, 1864.

MY DEAR GENERAL SHERMAN: Many, many thanks for your Christmas gift, the capture of Savannah. When you were about leaving Atlanta for the Atlantic coast, I was anxious, if not fearful; but feeling that you were the better judge, and remembering that "nothing risked, nothing gained," I did not interfere. Now, the undertaking being a success, the honor is all yours; for I believe none of us went further than to acquiesce. And taking the work of General Thomas into the count, as it should be taken, it is indeed a great success. Not only does it afford the obvious and immediate military advantages, but, in showing to the world that your army could be divided, putting the stronger part to an important new service, and yet leaving enough to vanquish the old opposing force of the whole—Hood's army—it brings those who sat in darkness to see a great light. But what next? I suppose it will be safer if I leave General Grant and yourself to decide.

Please make my grateful acknowledgments to your whole army, officers and men.

Yours, very truly,

A. LINCOLN.

HEADQUARTERS MILITARY DIVISION OF THE MISSISSIPPI,
In the field, Savannah, January 6, 1865.

DEAR SIR: I am gratified at the receipt of your letter of December 26, at the hands of General Logan, especially to observe that you appreciate the division I made of my army, and that each part was duly proportioned to its work.

The motto, "Nothing venture, nothing win," which you refer to, is most appropriate, and should I venture too much, and happen to lose, I shall bespeak your charitable inference.

I am ready for the "great next" as soon as I can complete certain preliminaries, and learn of General Grant his and your preferences of intermediate "objectives."

With great respect, your servant,

W. T. SHERMAN, *Major General.*

His Excellency President LINCOLN, *Washington.*

HEADQUARTERS MILITARY DIVISION OF THE MISSISSIPPI,
In the field, Savannah, January 16, 1865.

GENERAL: I have your reports of Saturday and yesterday, and am glad you got the position of Pocotaligo so cheaply. It is of great value to us in the future, and I wish you to have it thoroughly strengthened, and all water channels to its south and east reconnoitred. Don't seem to feel up the peninsula, but rather towards the Salkehatchie. Go on and accumulate supplies and stores, and get ready, as soon as possible, to sally forth with your whole wing, supplied as well as possible. I have ordered Slocum to push one division to Hardeeville and Purysburg, and to open up communication with you. I will try and get Davis started by Wednesday, but cannot hear of the troops from Baltimore, to relieve Geary here. I will not move from Pocotaligo till we get a good supply in our wagons, as that is the great point.

Truly yours,

W. T. SHERMAN,
Major General.

Major General HOWARD,
Commanding Right Wing, Beaufort.

HEADQUARTERS MILITARY DIVISION OF THE MISSISSIPPI,
In the field, Savannah, Ga., January 16, 1865.

GENERAL: Since my letter of this morning, I have official reports from General Howard, commanding right wing. He crossed from Beaufort island on Saturday, the 14th, by Port Royal ferry, to the main land, with the 17th corps, General Blair, and marched for Pocotaligo. They encountered the enemy near Garden's corner, but soon outflanked him and followed, dislodging him from position to position, till he took refuge in a strong fort at Pocotaligo. This is described as a well-constructed enclosed work, pierced for twenty-four (24) guns, and the approaches covered by the peculiar salt-marsh points that guard this coast. Night overtook the command there, and Sunday morning the enemy was gone. Howard expresses great satisfaction thereat, as it was Sunday, and it saved him an assault which might have cost him some valuable lives. As it was, he lost Lieutenant Chandler, of General Leggett's staff, killed, and Captain Kellogg, of General Giles A. Smith's staff, wounded. He writes that eight or ten will cover his loss. He reports three guns captured at Garden's corner. We are therefore now in possession of good high ground on the railroad at Pocotaligo, with a good road back twenty-five (25) miles to Beaufort.

I will order Howard to forage toward Charleston, but proceed to get my army and trains across, and can start north the moment I can get my wagons loaded.

The weather at sea has been so stormy that vessels are behind, and it has been touch and go to get daily food. I have ordered Slocum to push a division up to Hardeeville and Purysburg, and think I can use the Savannah river up to that point. We are hard at work corduroying the roads across the rice-fields by the Union causeway.

The Secretary told me I would surely receive four thousand (4,000) men from Baltimore, to garrison Savannah. They are not heard of here yet.

Yours, truly,

W. T. SHERMAN,
Major General.

Lieut. General U. S. GRANT,
City Point, Virginia.

HEADQUARTERS MILITARY DIVISION OF THE MISSISSIPPI,
In the field, Savannah, Ga., January 17, 1865.

DEAR ADMIRAL: I am this moment in receipt of your letter of January 12, with the roll of maps, for which I am much obliged, and I hope you will succeed at Fisher, as it will set free much of your fleet for other purposes; but if Terry does not assault, he should occupy the peninsula at the narrow neck represented on the map, about four miles north of Fisher, with a strong line looking to the rear, and a battery of 20-pounder Parrotts commanding the channel of Cape Fear river. I know that the enemy would not naturally keep in Fort Fisher to exceed five or six hundred (500 or 600) men, and they could be held there; still, if he takes it, it settles that matter, and the majority of his troops could return to Grant, or re-enforce Newbern, and work out towards Kingston.

I will send my railroad man, W. W. Wright, up to Newbern, and can send any number of cars and locomotives, so that we can use that road back to Kingston and Goldsboro'. We have here also a good deal of railroad iron.

Pursuant to my plan, the 17th corps got Pocotaligo and the railroad on the 15th, and I would now be in motion for Branchville and Orangeburg, only stores have been delayed by the storms of the past month. But the possession of Pocotaligo and road back to Beaufort, as also from here forward to Hardeeville, gives us a clear start, and I will be off as soon as I can get bread enough to load my wagons.

The division of Grover, sent by Grant to hold Savannah, has begun to arrive, so I can take with me my entire army.

I have studied the maps well, and like the appearance of Newbern and Goldsboro', and would like Newbern held with all tenacity. If Lee sees the points, he may try to checkmate me there; and if you have anything to do with it, hold fast to Newbern with the tenacity of life. I explained, in person, its importance to the Secretary of War, who promised to run in there and attend to it.

I will make a good ready, and then stand from under. I shall account it a happy day if I stand once more on your deck. The world shall not be grieved at little jealousies, for we feel a just pride in the pure courage and patriotism of each other.

I will write you again before I again drive out of sight and hearing.

Very truly, your friend,

W. T. SHERMAN, *Major General.*

Admiral D. D. PORTER,
Commanding North Atlantic Squadron, off Wilmington.

HEADQUARTERS MILITARY DIVISION OF THE MISSISSIPPI,
In the field, Savannah, Ga., January 17, 1865.

DEAR ADMIRAL: I have this moment received your note of the 16th instant, with the letter and roll of charts from Admiral Porter. I send you, herewith, letter to Admiral Porter, which I beg you will send him at your earliest convenience, but it is not of enough importance to detach a ship.

I regret exceedingly the loss of the monitor Patapsco, especially that she carried down so many valuable lives.

Admiral Porter thinks he and General Terry can take Fort Fisher, or, at all events, occupy the peninsula above it, and cut it off from Wilmington. Of this we shall hear soon, as he proposes to renew the attack on the 13th or 14th; and in case of taking Fort Fisher he would send to Charleston all his fleet, save enough to blockade Wilmington, and keep up communication for the troops on shore; otherwise, he could hold on there to engage the attention of the enemy about there, to keep them from me.

You will have heard that we took Pocotaligo on the 15th according to my plans, and we now have the 17th corps, General Blair, strongly intrenched on the railroad. I would by this time also have had my left wing at Sister's ferry, but have been and still am delayed by the non-arrival of our stores necessary to fill our wagons.

The first instalment of General Grover's division, which is to garrison Savannah, has just arrived, and all will be in to-morrow.

I would prefer you should run no risk at all. When we are known to be in rear of Charleston, about Branchville and Orangeburg, it will be well to watch if the enemy lets go of Charleston, in which case Foster will occupy it; otherwise the feint should be about Bull's bay.

We will need no cover about Port Royal, nothing but the usual guard-ships. I think you will concur with me that, in anticipation of the movement of my army to the rear of the coast, it will be unwise to subject your ships to the heavy artillery of the enemy or his sunken torpedoes.

I will instruct Foster, when he knows I have got near Branchville, to make a landing of a small force at Bull's bay, to threaten, and it may be occupy the road from Mount Pleasant to Georgetown. This will make the enemy believe I design to turn down against Charleston, and give me a good offing for Wilmington. I will write you again, fully, on the eve of starting in person.

Your friend,

W. T. SHERMAN, Major General.

Admiral J. A. DAHLGREN,
  Commanding South Atlantic Squadron, off Charleston.

HEADQUARTERS MILITARY DIVISION OF THE MISSISSIPPI,
In the field, Savannah, Ga., January 18, 1865.

DEAR GENERAL: Your note of January 17, with enclosures, is received. It is best that all the 15th corps not yet off should march, and that you get your whole command in the neighborhood of Pocotaligo and Coosawhatchie, and make as many wharves as possible, that you may accumulate stores in your wagons.

Slocum has two (2) divisions at Hardeeville and Purysburg, and to-day a gunboat and two transports move up to that point, and it will be five days before Slocum can have Sister's ferry and Robertsville.

The division of Cuvier Grover is now arriving, and will occupy Savannah; this will relieve Geary's division.

Davis will start to-morrow for Sister's ferry, on the west bank of Savannah, with Kilpatrick's cavalry. I now have official notice that Terry carried Fort Fisher by assault, capturing seventy-two (72) guns and one thousand seven hundred and eighty (1,780) prisoners. This closes up Cape Fear river and helps us. I want them also to strengthen Newbern and work out the railroad towards Goldsboro'.

Get your command so as to move north as soon as possible, and get all the bread and forage accumulated you can.

As soon as possible we will cast off, and then for another cruise that will, in my judgment, do more to bring matters to a crisis than the last.

Choose the best points you can find to land stores for Pocotaligo. Don't cross the Salkehatchie, but hold all the ground up to it as though we intended to break across. The next movement I want the enemy to feel is from the left flank. Purysburg is reported a fine point, with deep river and a good bluff.

Yours, truly,

W. T. SHERMAN,
Major General Commanding.

General HOWARD.

HEADQUARTERS MILITARY DIVISION OF THE MISSISSIPPI,
In the field, Savannah, Ga., January 19, 1865.

GENERAL: At my suggestion your command has been re-enforced by the troops serving in North Carolina and a division under command of Major General Grover. I have also turned over to you the city of Savannah and forts dependent, and beg now to indicate, in general terms, the course which I propose to pursue, and your share of the undertaking.

I propose to march, as soon as my wagons are loaded with forage and provisions, to the railroad leading from Augusta to Charleston, striking it to the west of Branchville, breaking up that road effectually. I will then move in compact order, and occupy that space of country lying in the triangle formed by Kingston, Columbia, and Camden. There I propose to devote some attention to Columbia and the railroads in that neighborhood. If I find sufficient forage and subsistence for my army, and meet with no reverse, I may move with rapidity to Florence, South Carolina, in hopes to rescue some ten thousand (10,000) prisoners confined there; at all events, breaking up the road there. I will move direct for Smithland, at the mouth of Cape Fear river, or to Newbern, North Carolina, according to the condition of my army at that time.

When you hear of our being in motion about Coosawhatchie, towards Barnwell, I want a diversion created at Bull's bay, against the Mount Pleasant and Georgetown road, about the twenty-four (24) mile post, to create the impression that my purpose is to swing down against Charleston by the peninsula between the Ashley and Cooper. I think one thousand (1,000) men, with the co-operation of the navy, will be sufficient to accomplish that end. At the same time the command at Morris's island should feel the forces on James's island, either to detect the diminution of the enemy's forces there, or to compel the enemy to keep as many troops there as possible. I regard any attempt to enter Charleston harbor by its direct channel, or to carry it by storm, or James's island, as too hazardous to warrant the attempt. Therefore, any demonstration in that quarter should be merely diversions, or to take advantage of anything they may neglect by reason of my appearance in their rear.

After I have passed the Santee, similar diversions should be made about Georgetown, and, if the opportunity presents itself, the fort there might be carried and dismantled; and I would like to have a good lookout kept by the navy for any boat or message I might send down the Santee or Peedee with a cipher despatch. I have already furnished Admiral Dahlgren with the key, which is the same used by our telegraphic operators, a copy of which you had better procure at once through the War Department from Washington.

In whatever you may do to aid me along the coast by diversions, I must leave you in a great measure to be guided by such information as reaches you from sources controlled by the enemy, of which you must be duly suspicious; but bearing in mind the foregoing, and knowing the strength and temper of my army, you can arrive at a pretty fair conclusion.

I take it for granted that Forts Fisher and Macon, on the North Carolina coast, will be held secure, and it would be well that you give to each commanding officer, from time to time, such instructions as will make them co-operate with the general movement to the extent of their power. I attach great importance to the point at Newbern, and think you had better send to that point an inspector general. Notify the commanding officer of the importance of the position, and if need be re-enforce him. Notify him, further, that the railroad from Morehead City to Newbern must be looked to with great care. I propose to send to Newbern an officer in whom I have great confidence, Colonel W. W. Wright, to examine the railroad, to ascertain the quantity of rolling stock, and to convey there, by the time I can arrive, increased stock and iron, with the necessary operatives to extend the road to Kingston and Goldsboro'. But, as a matter of course, these preliminary preparations should be made so as to attract as little attention as possible. In this connexion, I would caution you, and by you to caution others, against the mischievous newspaper men who would sacrifice the whole army for a little personal notoriety. If any of them are about and likely to divulge so important a secret, don't risk them, but imprison them till the time is past. At this moment we have learned the capture of Wilmington, which may modify matters somewhat, but the general principles above indicated will be still applicable and sufficient for your guidance.

I would like to have you confer frequently with Admirals Dahlgren and Porter, apprise them of all movements, and call upon them for any assistance in the way of gunboats, &c.

I am, with respect, your obedient servant,

W. T. SHERMAN,
Major General Commanding.

Major General J. G. FOSTER,
Commanding Department of the South.

HEADQUARTERS MILITARY DIVISION OF THE MISSISSIPPI,
In the field Savannah, Ga., January 21, 1865.

GENERAL : In fulfilment of my project, General Howard moved the 17th corps, General Blair, from Thunderbolt to Beaufort, South Carolina, and on the 14th, by a rapid movement, secured the Port Royal ferry and moved against Pocotaligo, which he gained on the 15th, the day appointed. By that course he secured the use of the ground in South Carolina up to the Salkehatchie, (Saltketcher,) and General Slocum was ordered, in like manner, to get his wing up about Robertsville, by the way of the Savannah river and the Union causeway.

The transfer of men, animals, and wagons by steamers is a very slow process, and on the 19th General Slocum had only two divisions of the 20th at Purysburg and Hardeeville, with open communications with Howard. John E. Smith crossed by the Union causeway, on which Slocum had put ten days' hard work, but the hard rains had raised the Savannah river, so that the whole country was under water, and the corduroy road, on the Union causeway, was carried away, cutting off one brigade of John E. Smith, one division of the 15th corps, (Corse's,) and all of the 14th corps, (General Davis's.) All were ordered to move up the west bank of the Savannah, to cross at Sister's ferry, but the rains have so flooded the country that we have been brought to a standstill; but I will persevere and get the army, as soon as possible, up to the line from Sister's ferry to Pocotaligo, where we will have *terra firma* to work on. Our supplies have come daily, that is, we have never had four days' forage ahead ; but I will depend on enough coming to get me out to the neighborhood of Barnwell, where we will find some.

General Grover's division now occupies Savannah, which I had re-fortified, and I have turned over everything to General Foster, so that nothing now hinders me but water. I rather think the heavy rains in January will give us good weather in February and March. You cannot do much in Virginia till April or May ; and when I am at Goldsboro', and move against Raleigh, Lee will be forced to divide his command or give up Richmond.

As soon as possible, if I were in your place, I would break up the department of the James. Make the Richmond army one ; then when I get to Goldsboro' you will have a force to watch Lee, and I can be directed to gradually close in, cutting all communications. In the mean time Thomas's army should not be reduced too much, but he should hold Chattanooga, Decatur, and Eastport, collect supplies, and in all February and March move on Tuscaloosa, Selma, Montgomery, and back to Rome, Georgia, when he could be met from Chattanooga. I take it for granted that Beauregard will bring, as fast as he can, such part of Hood's army as can be moved over to Augusta, to hit me in flank as I swing round Charleston. To cover the withdrawal, Forrest will be left in Mississippi and West Tennessee to divert attention by threatening the boats on the Mississippi and Tennessee rivers. This should be disregarded, and Thomas should break through the shell, expose the trick, and prevent the planting of corn this spring in middle Alabama.

The people of Georgia, like those of Mississippi, are worn out with care; but they are so afraid of their own leaders that they fear to organize positive resistance. Their motives of honor and fair play are that, by abandoning the cause now, they would be construed as mean for leaving their comrades in the scrape. I have met the overtures of the people frankly, and given them the best advice I know how.

I enclose copies of orders issued for the guidance of General Foster and other officers on this coast. These orders are made in conference with the Secretary of War.

I have been told that Congress meditates a bill to make another Lieutenant General for me. I have writen to John Sherman to stop it, if it is designed for me. It would be mischievous, for there are enough rascals who would try to sow differences between us, whereas you and I now are in perfect understanding. I would rather have you in command than anybody else, for you are fair, honest, and have at heart the same purpose that should animate all I should emphatically decline any commission calculated to bring us into rivalry, and I ask you to advise all your friends in Congress to this effect, especially Mr. Washburne. I doubt if men in Congress fully realize that you and I are honest in our professions of want of ambition. I know I feel none, and to-day will gladly surrender my position and influence to any other who is better able to wield the power. The flurry attending my recent success will soon blow over and give place to new developments.

I enclose a letter of general instructions to General Thomas, which I beg you to revise and endorse or modify.

I am truly yours,

W. T. SHERMAN, Major General.

Lieut. General U. S. Grant,
    City Point, Virginia.

Headquarters Military Division of the Mississippi,
In the field, Savannah, January 21, 1865.

General: Before I again dive into the interior and disappear from view, I must give you in general terms such instructions as fall within my province, as commander of the division.

I take it for granted that you now reoccupy in strength the line of the Tennessee from Chattanooga to Eastport. I suppose Hood to be down about Tuscaloosa and Selma, and that Forrest is again scattered to get horses and men, and to divert attention. You should have a small cavalry force, say two thousand (2,000) men, to operate from Knoxville through the mountain pass along the French Broad into North Carolina, to keep up the belief that it is to be followed by a considerable force of infantry. Stoneman could do this while Gillem merely watches up the Holston.

At Chattanooga should be held a good reserve of provisions and forage, and in addition to its garrison a small force that could on short notice relay the railroad to Resaca. Prepare to throw provisions down to Rome on the Coosa. You remember I left the railroad track from Resaca to Kingston and Rome with such a view. Then with an army of twenty-five thousand (25,000) infantry and all the cavalry you can get, under Wilson, you should move from Decatur and Eastport to some point of concentration about Columbus, Mississippi, and then march to Tuscaloosa and Selma, Alabama, destroying fences, gathering horses and mules and wagons, to be burned, and doing all the damage possible, burning up Selma, that is the navy yard, the railroad back towards the Tombigbee, all iron foundries, mills, or factories. If no considerable army opposes you, you might reach Montgomery and deal with it in like manner, and then, at leisure, work back along the Selma and Rome road *via* Talladega and Blue mountain, to the valley of Chattanooga to Rome, or Lafayette. I believe such a raid perfectly practicable and easy, and that it would have an excellent effect.

It is nonsense to suppose that the people of the south are enraged or united by such movements. They reason very differently. They see in them the sure and inevitable destruction of all their property ; they realize that the confederate armies cannot protect them, and they see in the repetition of such raids the inevitable result of starvation and misery. You should not go south of Selma and Montgomery, because south of that line the country is barren and unproductive.

I would like to have Forrest hunted down and killed, but doubt if we can do that yet. While you are thus employed I expect to pass through the centre of South and North Carolina, and I suppose Canby will also keep all his forces active and busy. I have already secured Pocotaligo and Grahamsville, from which I have firm roads into the interior. We are all well.

                    Yours, truly,

                                        W. T. SHERMAN,
                                        Major General Commanding.

Major General GEORGE H. THOMAS,
        Commanding army in the field, North Alabama, via Nashville.

HEADQUARTERS MILITARY DIVISION OF THE MISSISSIPPI,
        In the field, Savannah, Ga., January 21, 1865.

DEAR GENERAL : I have this moment received your letter of the 17th, enclosing the very full and complete returns, which give me all the data save only the gauge of your railroad, of which we are in doubt; one of my charts represents the gauge as 4 feet 10 inches, and the other at 5 feet. I shall send up my principal railroad man, Colonel W. W. Wright, to look at it and accumulate at Morehead City and Newbern iron and cars ready for use when the time comes. We can supply all those of the five-feet gauge out of captured stock. I don't want you to risk Newbern or Morehead City, and to take Kingston now would attract attention, and lengthen your line too much to be held with any degree of security. Therefore, don't attempt to hold more than you now have, until you know I am near at hand, and you can discover the effect of my approach.

I shall aim to reach Goldsborough, the effect of which will be threefold :

1st. With my army at Goldsborough the enemy could not remain at Wilmington.

2d. I would have two railroads to the coast for supplies, viz : Morehead City and Wilmington.

3d. Goldsborough is the point from which to strike Raleigh.

If my army can fight its way across South Carolina and reach Goldsborough, these results will be certain.

I have already secured Pocotaligo, and am moving my army into position on a line from Sister's ferry, on the Savannah, across to Pocotaligo, whence I will move around Charleston and across the country to Fayetteville and Goldsborough or Wilmington, according to the supplies I find. General Foster will hold Savannah, &c., and will have a small force in hand to take advantage of any let-go the enemy may venture to make. I would have been off before this, but am delayed by the rains, which have flooded the whole country. Don't attract attention, but hold Newbern and Morehead City (Fort Macon) secure as points for me to depend on. Don't risk anything; let me run the risk, but stand prepared to aid me as I approach. I leave my chief quartermaster and commissary here to follow me up with boats and supplies.

I do not think Grant will spare you any more men, nor do I think them necessary for the simple defensive position you should maintain. As I approach you I may aim for the railroad near where it crosses the Neuse, near Kingston. As I suppose there the enemy will oppose me, it may be prudent to open communication with you before I cross and attack the position at Kingston or Goldsborough. But Goldsborough is the strategic point I shall aim to secure in North Carolina.

I am, with respect, your obedient servant,

W. T. SHERMAN, *Major General.*

General INNIS N. PALMER,
Commanding District of North Carolina, Newbern.

HEADQUARTERS MILITARY DIVISION OF THE MISSISSIPPI,
In the field, Beaufort, S. C., January 24, 1865.

DEAR ADMIRAL: Weather now fine and promises us dry land. I will go to-day to Pocotaligo and Coosawhatchie; to-morrow will demonstrate on Salkehatchie, and would be obliged if you would feel up Edisto or Stono, just to make the enemy uneasy on that flank, and to develop if he intends to hold fast to Charleston and Columbia, or both. It will take five days for Slocum to get out of the savannas of Savannah, and during that time I will keep Howard seemingly moving direct on Charleston, though with no purpose of going beyond the Salkehatchie.

Yours,

W. T. SHERMAN,
Major General.

Admiral DAHLGREN.

HEADQUARTERS MILITARY DIVISION OF THE MISSISSIPPI,
In the field, Beaufort, S. C., January 24, 1865.

GENERAL: I was directed this morning by General Sherman to write you by steamer Arago as follows:

He reached here yesterday from Savannah, and this morning went up to Pocotaligo to look to matters in person, and proposes to-morrow to secure Salkehatchie bridge as a demonstration, and also to reconnoitre until Slocum gets out to high ground from Sister's ferry. The storm has been severe and continuous for several days, delaying movements by bad roads; but now it is clear, the roads are improving rapidly, and it bids fair for good weather. I may hear from the general during the night, and will then despatch you further.

I am, with respect,

L. M. DAYTON,
Assistant Adjutant General.

Lieut. General GRANT,
City Point, Va.

20 *

HEADQUARTERS MILITARY DIVISION OF THE MISSISSIPPI,
In the field, Pocotaligo, S. C., January 27, 1865.

DEAR ADMIRAL: I have now reconnoitred all the country from the Salke-hatchie bridge back to and including Coosawhatchie. The enemy had fortified every path leading from the various landings to the railroad, and could have bothered us a good deal had we not got Pocotaligo in the way we did, by the several diversions and the quick, prompt attack. From here we will find no trouble in getting an offing. I have official reports that Slocum got off for Sister's ferry on the 25th, and he should be there to-morrow. It will take him till Monday or Tuesday to cross over, load his wagons, and rendezvous at Robertsville, when we will be off. I hope this cold, clear weather will last for that time, as the roads here would cut to the hub after an hour's rain.

I have been feeling the Combahee ferry, and also at the bridge, but the river is over its banks and fills the swamps for a mile back—too deep at points to wade, and too shallow at others to use boats. I can only see a few rebels on the other bank, but a prisoner captured says there is a brigade back a short distance, and a considerable force about Green Pond, ten (10) miles east of this. We find no enemy this side of the Salkehatchie except cavalry, which is simply watch-ing us, but I will clear it away in a hurry when we are ready to move. I will be sure to let you know the moment we are off, and will leave Hatch's division of Foster's command here to cover our movement.

I am, with respect, yours truly

W. T. SHERMAN,
Major General.

Admiral DAHLGREN,
Commanding South Atlantic Squadron.

HEADQUARTERS MILITARY DIVISION OF THE MISSISSIPPI,
In the field, Pocotaligo, S. C., January 27, 1865.

GENERAL: We had heavy and continuous rains up to and including the 24th instant, causing all the rivers, the Savannah included, to outflow their banks, and making the roads simply impassable. I came up to this point on the 25th, and with the troops here, the 17th corps, have been demonstrating against the Salkehatchie, but that stream is out of its banks, and we cannot cross. I only aim to drive the enemy over towards Edisto, a little further from our flank, when I move against the Charleston and Augusta road. I have in person reconnoi-tred the ground from the Salkehatchie bridge back to Coosawhatchie, and find the country very low and intersected by creeks and points of salt marsh, making roads very bad, but I am pushing to get the right wing here, and have official notice from General Slocum that he had the 20th corps, General Williams, on this side the Savannah, at Purysburg, and on the 25th the 14th corps, General Davis, would resume his march from Cherokee Hill, ten (10) miles out of Savan-nah, where he was caught by the rain-storm, so that I expect to hear of the left wing and cavalry marching to Sister's ferry to-morrow. A gunboat and fleet of transports will attend the left wing up the Savannah river, and General Slocum is ordered to replenish his wagons, rendezvous at Robertsville, and report his readiness to me.

I expect on Monday or Tuesday next, viz: February 1, to be all ready, when I will move rapidly up towards Barnwell, and wheel to the right on the railroad at Midway, leaving Branchville to the right; after destroying that road, I will move on Orangeburg, and so on to Columbia, avoiding any works the enemy may construct in my path, and forcing him to fight me in open ground if he risk battle. I will use Hatch's division, of Foster's command, four thousand, (4,000,) to cover my movement, by posting it between this and Salkehatchie bridge. You will note that our position is now nearer Branchville than Charleston. I get a few deserters and have made some prisoners who report cavalry only between me and Barnwell, and infantry between us and Charleston. Of course I shall keep up the delusion of an attack on Charleston always, and have instructed General Foster to watch the harbor close from Morris island, and when he hears of my firing on the railroad near Branchville, to make a landing at Bull's bay, and occupy the Georgetown road, twenty-four (24) miles east of Charleston; Admiral Dahlgren will also keep up the demonstration on Charleston.

My chief difficulties will be to supply my army, but on this point I must risk a good deal, based upon the idea that where other people live we can, even if they have to starve or move away. Weather is cold and clear. I will write again.

W. T. SHERMAN,
Major General Commanding.

Major General H. W. Halleck,
Chief of Staff, Washington, D. C.

Headquarters Military Division of the Mississippi,
In the field, Pocotaligo, S. C., January 28, 1865.

General: Yours of the 27th is received, and I am pushing my efforts to secure a departure by Monday or Tuesday next. I have in person reconnoitred the country from Salkehatchie bridge to Coosawhatchie. The country is very low and swampy, and impassable, save by the roads marked on our maps. I have no doubt this whole belt of land once formed the sea-coast, with its sound, islands and marsh, which, by the progress seaward of the beach, is left inland, but still possessing its character of sound islands, surrounded by fresh-water marsh. This is the first point of terra firma, and has better connexions inland. As near as I can learn, Gillisonville, on the south of Coosawhatchie, is a corresponding point of the main land, and Robertsville, of course.

Therefore, until I am surely between Augusta and Charleston it would be imprudent to let go this point. I have ordered General Hatch to move to a camp between this place (which is near Pocotaligo depot) and Salkehatchie bridge, and to picket Coosawhatchie fort and the fort back at Pocotaligo bridge. The latter is the key point for "defence," but for offence the line of the railroad is the proper one. I would, therefore, not reduce Hatch's force here till you have ascertained the effect on Charleston by my appearance west of Branchville. All Salkehatchie is under water for a mile on either side of the regular bed, and it is almost impossible to get to it.

The bridges have been burned by the enemy, who seems to occupy the opposite bank, but his force, if amounting to anything, is kept well back.

I could see a few men at the railroad bank, and what seemed a gun en embrasure, but it was not fired, although our men stood in tempting groups on the railroad bank this side in easy 6-pounder range.

We find cavalry to our front towards Barnwell, and hear of some infantry, but I suppose the enemy simply is watching me, and keeps his main force where it can be thrown rapidly on exposed points.

Your demonstration on Willeton is right, but should not be more than a demonstration—that is, a lodgement seemingly to cover the disembarcation of a large body. The admiral's feeling up the Edisto and Stono is well, but my movement to the rear of Charleston is the principal, and all others should be accessory, merely to take advantage of any "let go."

Try and keep me well advised of Slocum's progress; he reports that Davis would move on the 25th, and he should be at Sister's ferry to-day. I shall cause him to be felt for to-morrow.

Yours, truly,

W. T. SHERMAN, *Major General.*

Major General J. G. FOSTER,
Commanding Department of the South, Hilton Head.

HEADQUARTERS MILITARY DIVISION OF THE MISSISSIPPI,
In the field, Pocotaligo, S. C., January 28, 1865.

GENERAL: Yours of yesterday came at night. If Easton did not give vessels to carry Logan's mules, it was for a most excellent reason, that he did not have them. Slocum reports that he had ordered Davis to move on the 25th, and he should reach Sister's ferry to-day; the rear can close on him while he lays his bridge. Slocum was to go by river, so as to meet Davis and Williams there. I confide in his energy and judgment to get his command across by Monday. You may now let Foster's troops occupy the old fort at Pocotaligo bridge, where the Charleston and Savannah turnpike road crosses; they will also hold Coosawhatchie fort, but the main body move to-day to a camp covering the Salkehatchie bridges, prepared to fall back on Pocotaligo fort, and the works at the depot now occupied by Mower and Leggett. You may now move your two corps to points in front, north of the railroad, and be ready to march by all the roads leading north, between the Coosawhatchie and Salkehatchie, with your wagons to close up the moment they are loaded. Roads are now comparatively good. Giles Smith's division should make room for Hatch, but Mower and Leggett can start from their present camps. The 15th corps should take position to the left or right front, according to your intention of giving one or the other the right of your movement. We will have to get nearly up to Barnwell before turning toward Midway. The point marked Heywardsville looks like a good point for the 15th corps, and could be reached from the position of John E. Smith's camp. Giles Smith could move to the point about four (4) miles north and west of the Salkehatchie bridge, when you would have your two corps already to move by separate roads, viz: one following substantially the Salkehatchie, and the other the Coosawhatchie, leaving Corse to make his junction as arranged at Hickory Hill. Hatch can supply his command by boats altogether, so as not to occupy our roads at all. You had better begin this movement to-morrow.

I am, &c.,

W. T. SHERMAN,
Major General Commanding.

Major General HOWARD,
Commanding Right Wing.

HEADQUARTERS MILITARY DIVISION OF THE MISSISSIPPI,
In the field, Pocotaligo, S. C., January 28, 1865.

GENERAL: The modifications you suggest in my general directions are approved, and the movements ordered for to-morrow will be deferred to Monday, provided the weather does not change. You should push matters now that the weather is fair, and better leave behind those who are not ready, as, do what you may, some will not be ready.

You cannot count on crossing Salkehatchie till you are in Barnwell district, nor is it practicable. Your right flank should aim for Midway and Columbia.

Yours, &c.,

W. T. SHERMAN,
Major General Commanding.

Major General O. O. HOWARD,
Commanding Right Wing.

HEADQUARTERS MILITARY DIVISION OF THE MISSISSIPPI,
In the field, Pocotaligo Depot, January 28, 1865.

GENERAL: General Williams reports to me to-day, from Purysburg, that you have passed up the Savannah river to Sister's ferry, and, therefore, I infer you will be there, and that Davis can get out to Robertsville by Monday. On that day Howard will have the 15th corps at McPhersonville, and the 17th at a point north of the Salkehatchie bridge, ready to start the moment you are ready. Remember that every day's delay takes away one day's rations from Howard, and, if possible, be all ready to start on Tuesday from Robertsville. The 15th corps will keep along the east of Coosawhatchie, the 17th along the Salkehatchie, and will cross it at River's bridge, in Barnwell district; the order of march and general orders will be the same as on the Georgia march. Until we reach the Charleston and Augusta road, I want the most rapid possible movement, Kilpatrick to keep to your left front. Corse should cross to your rear to Hickory Hill, and fall in with his corps there. Work hard to load your wagons, and report to me here at Pocotaligo Depot your readiness to move on Tuesday, if possible. I think you can find two or more good roads, and these will improve as we go north unless the weather changes. It is very important that we hurry to our first point before Hood gets across and makes a junction about Columbia.

If you are all ready on Tuesday you may act on the supposition that Howard is equally so. Let Kilpatrick see this letter. I will shift over to see you up about the edge of Barnwell district.

I am, &c.,

W. T. SHERMAN,
Major General Commanding.

Major General SLOCUM,
Commanding Right Wing.

HEADQUARTERS MILITARY DIVISION OF THE MISSISSIPPI,
In the field, Pocotaligo, S. C., January 29, 1865.

GENERAL: I have your letter of yesterday. Tell Admiral Dahlgren I regret the loss of the Dia-Ching, but can quote Admiral Porter, who told me once, that "ships were made to be lost." Your movement, by Edisto, is good; but understand me as of opinion, that if the enemy mans his works facing the sea, you cannot gain them, save at a disadvantage, but by demonstrating at points of land from which troops can move against the railroad by a rapid, quick march, you compel him to keep the entire railroad guarded from Charleston to Salkehatchie; but I don't care about the road being actually broken until the latter part of next week. If you know that the enemy falls behind the Edisto, you should break the railroad anywhere this side of him, and then you could reduce Hatch's command here to the number you calculated, viz: one thousand (1,000) men; but so long as McLaws (rebel) has the railroad, by which he can handle four or five thousand (4,000 or 5,000) men rapidly, it will be imprudent to leave Hatch too weak. There is no use in a force here at all unless it is on the railroad. This point, Pocotaligo, is the most salient, and therefore best; but, if deemed unsafe at any time, the fort at Coosawhatchie would fulfil the same conditions, and its river is deeper and better. I have no doubt a steamboat could work up to the Coosawhatchie fort at high tide; flats drawn by barges could, certainly. I merely want a point of security here till I am surely beyond the Santee, and by a force here you better cover your island and the Savannah river than by any other disposition of your troops.

I expect from Tennessee a force of some five to eight thousand (5,000 to 8,000) men belonging to the four (4) corps with me here. Stop them at Hilton Head, and use them, unless they get there in time to reach me, which is very improbable. Out of them you can make up a good command to demonstrate on Charleston, Georgetown, and from Smithville, Cape Fear river, as I progress, aiming to join their respective commands when we touch the seaboard. If I break the railroad to Augusta and Columbia, it will be well to strike that to Wilmington, unless Wilmington, in the mean time, be taken by Terry. The easiest point to reach that railroad will be from Cape Fear river, to the south and west of Wilmington.

Make as much display on Edisto and about Stono, next Wednesday and Thursday, as possible, and cause the troops at Morris island to make a lodgement on James island, if possible. That is the vital part of Charleston harbor.

I am, &c.,

W. T. SHERMAN,
Major General Commanding.

Major General J. G. FOSTER,
Commanding Department of the South.

HEADQUARTERS ARMIES OF THE UNITED STATES,
Washington, D. C., January 21, 1865.

GENERAL: Your letters brought by General Barnard were received at City Point and read with interest. Not having them with me, however, I cannot say that in this I will be able to satisfy you on all points of recommendation, as I arrived here at 1 p. m. and must leave at 6 p. m., having in the mean time spent over three hours with the Secretary and General Halleck. I must be brief.

Before your last request to have Thomas make a campaign into the heart of Alabama, I had ordered Schofield to Annapolis, Maryland, with his corps. The advance, 6,000 will reach the seaboard by the 23d, the remainder following as rapidly as railroad transportation can be procured from Cincinnati. The corps numbers over 21,000 men.

*　　*　　*　　*　　*　　*　　*　　*

Thomas is still left with a sufficient force (surplus) to go to Selma under an energetic leader. He has been telegraphed to to know whether he could go; and if so, by which of several routes he would select. No reply is yet received. Canby has been ordered to act offensively from the sea-coast to the interior towards Montgomery and Selma. Thomas's forces will move from the north at an early day, or some of his troops will be sent to Canby. Without further re-enforcements, Canby will have a moving column of 20,000 men.

Fort Fisher, you are aware, has been captured. We have a force there of 8,000 effective; at Newbern about half that number. It is rumored through deserters that Wilmington also has fallen. I am inclined to believe the rumor, because, on the 17th, we know the enemy were blowing up their works about Fort Caswell, and that on the 18th Terry moved on Wilmington.

If Wilmington is captured, Schofield will go there; if it is not, he will be sent to Newbern. In either event all the surplus forces at the two points will move to the interior, towards Goldsboro', in co-operation with your movements. From either point railroad communication can be run out, there being here abundance of rolling stock, suited to the gauge of those roads. There have been about 16,000 men sent from Lee's army south; of these you will have 14,000 against you if Wilmington is not held by the enemy, casualties at Fort Fisher having overtaken about 2,000.

All these troops are subject to your orders as you come in communication with them. They will be so instructed. From about Richmond I will watch Lee closely, and if he detaches much more, or attempts to evacuate, will pitch in. In the mean time should you be brought to a halt anywhere, I can send two corps of 30,000 effective men to your support from the troops about Richmond.

To resume: Canby is ordered to operate to the interior from the gulf; A. J. Smith may go from the north, but I think it doubtful. A force of 28,000 or 30,000 will co-operate with you from Newbern or Wilmington, or both; you can call for re-enforcements.

This will be handed to you by Captain Hudson, of my staff, who will return with any message you may have for me. If there is anything I can do for you in the way of having supplies on shipboard, at any point on the sea-coast ready for you, let me know it.

Yours, truly,

U. S. GRANT, *Lieutenant General.*

Major General W. T. SHERMAN,
Commanding Military Division of the Mississippi.

HEADQUARTERS MILITARY DIVISION OF THE MISSISSIPPI,
In the field, Pocotaligo, S. C., January 29, 1865.

DEAR GENERAL: Captain Hudson has this moment arrived with your letter of January 21, which I have read with interest.

The capture of Fort Fisher has a most important bearing on my campaign, and I rejoice in it for many reasons, because of its intrinsic importance, and because it gives me another point of security on the seaboard. I hope General Terry will follow it up by the capture of Wilmington, although I do not look for it from Admiral Porter's despatch to me. I rejoice that Terry was not a West Pointer, that he belonged to your army, and that he had the same troops with which Butler feared to make the attempt.

Admiral Dahlgren, whose fleet is re-enforced by some more iron-clads, wants to make an assault *à la* Fisher on Fort Moultrie, but I withhold my consent for the reason that the capture of all Sullivan's island is not conclusive as to Charleston; the capture of James island would be, but all pronounce that impossible at this time. Therefore I am moving, as hitherto designed, for the railroad west of Branchville, then will swing across to Orangeburg, which will interpose my army between Charleston and the interior. Contemporaneous with this, Foster will demonstrate up the Edisto, and afterwards make a lodgement at Bull's bay, and occupy the common road which leads from Mount Pleasant toward Georgetown. When I get to Columbia, I think I shall move straight for Goldsboro' *via* Fayetteville. By this circuit I cut all roads and devastate the land, and the forces along the coast commanded by Foster will follow my movement, taking anything the enemy lets go, or so occupy his attention that he cannot detach all his forces against me. I feel sure of getting Wilmington, and maybe Charleston, and being at Goldsboro', with its railroads finished back to Morehead City and Wilmington, I can easily take Raleigh, when it seems that Lee must come out of his trenches or allow his army to be absolutely invested. If Schofield comes to Beaufort he should be pushed out to Kingston, on the Neuse, and maybe Goldsboro', or rather a point on the Wilmington road south of Goldsboro'. It is not necessary to storm Goldsboro', because it is in a distant region, of no importance in itself; and if its garrison is forced to draw supplies from its north, it will be eating up the same stores on which Lee depends for his command.

I have no doubt Hood will bring his army to Augusta, and Canby and Thomas should penetrate Alabama as far as possible, to keep employed at least a part of Hood's army; or, what would accomplish the same thing, Thomas might re-occupy the railroad from Chattanooga forward to the Etowah, viz: Rome, Kingston, and Allatoona, thereby threatening Georgia. I know that the Georgia troops are disaffected. At Savannah I met delegates from the several counties of the southwest that manifested a decidedly hostile spirit to the confederate cause. I nursed it along as far as possible and instructed Grover to keep it up.

My left wing must now be at Sister's ferry, crossing the Savannah river to the east bank. Slocum has orders to be at Robertsville to-morrow, prepared to move on Barnwell. Howard is here, all ready to start for the Augusta railroad at Midway.

We find the enemy on the east side of the Salkehatchie, and cavalry in our front, but all give ground on our approach and seem to be merely watching us. If I start on Tuesday, in one week I will be near Orangeburg, having broken up the Augusta road from the Edisto westward twenty or twenty-five miles. I will be sure that every rail is twisted. Should I encounter too much opposition near Orangeburg, then I will for a time neglect that branch and rapidly move on Columbia and fill up the triangle formed by the Congaree and Wateree, tributaries of the Santee, breaking up that great centre of the Carolina roads, Up to that point I feel full confidence, but from there I may have to manœuvre some, and will be guided by the questions of weather and supplies. You remember I had fine weather all February for my Meridian trip, and my memory of the weather at Charleston is that February is usually a fine month. Before the March storms come I should be within striking distance of the coast. The months of April and May will be the best for operations from Goldsboro' to Raleigh and the Roanoake. You may rest assured that I will keep my troops well in hand, and if I get worsted will aim to make the enemy pay so dearly that you will have less to do. I know this trip is necessary to the war. It must be made sooner or later, and I am on time and in the right position for it. My army is large enough for the purpose, and I ask no re-enforcement, but simply wish the utmost activity at all other points, so that concentration against me may not be universal. I expect Davis will move heaven and earth to catch me, for success to my column is fatal to his dream of empire. Richmond is not more vital to his cause than Columbia and the heart of South Carolina.

If Thomas will not move on Selma, order him to occupy Rome, Kingston, and Allatoona, and again threaten Georgia in the direction of Athens.

I think the poor white trash of the south are falling out of their ranks, by sickness, desertion, and every available means, but there is a large class of vindictive southerners who will fight to the last. The squabbles in Richmond, the howls in Charleston, and the disintegration elsewhere, are all good omens to us; but we must not relax one iota, but, on the contrary, pile up our efforts.

I would ere this have been off, but we had terrific rains which caught me in motion, and nearly drowned some of my columns in the rice-fields of the Savannah, swept away our causeway which had been carefully corduroyed, and made the swamps hereabout mere lakes of slimy mud; but the weather is now good, and I have my army on *terra firma*. Supplies, too, came for a long time by daily driblets instead of in bulk, but this is now all remedied, and I hope to start on Tuesday.

I will issue instructions to Foster based on the re-enforcement of North Carolina; and if Schofield come, you had better relieve Foster, who cannot take the field and needs an operation on his leg; and let Schofield take command, with headquarters at Beaufort, North Carolina, and with orders to secure, if possible, Goldsboro', with its railroad communication back to Beaufort and Wilmington. If Lee lets us get that position he is gone up.

I will start with my Atlanta army, sixty thousand, (60,000,) supplied as before, and depending on the country for all excess of thirty (30) days. I will have less cattle on the hoof, but I hear of hogs, cows, and calves in Barnwell and the Columbia districts. Even here we found some forage. Of course the enemy will carry off and destroy some forage, but I will burn the houses where the people burn forage, and they will get tired of that.

I must risk Hood, and trust to you to hold Lee or be on his heels if he comes south. I observe that the enemy has some respect for my name, for they gave up Pocotaligo quick when they heard that the attacking force belonged to me. I will try and keep up that feeling, which is a real power.

With respect, your friend,

W. T. SHERMAN,
Major General Commanding.

Lieut. General U. S. GRANT,
  City Point, Virginia.

I leave my chief quartermaster and commissary behind to follow coastwise.

HEADQUARTERS MILITARY DIVISION OF THE MISSISSIPPI,
In the field, Pocotaligo, S. C., January 29, 1865.

GENERAL: I have just received despatches from General Grant, stating that Schofield's corps, the 23d, twenty-one thousand (21,000) strong, is ordered east from Tennessee and will be sent to Beaufort, North Carolina. That is well; I want that force to secure a point on the railroad about Goldsboro', and then to build the road out to that point. If Goldsboro' be too strong to carry by a rapid movement, then a point near the Neuse, south of Goldsboro', but holding the bridge and position about Kingston, and fortify it strong. The movement should be masked by the troops already at Newbern. Please notify General Palmer that these troops are coming, and for him to prepare to receive them. Major General Schofield will command them in person, and is admirably adapted for the work. If it is possible I want him to secure Goldsboro' with the railroad back to Morehead City and Wilmington. As soon as General Schofield reaches Fort Macon, have him to meet some one of your staff to explain in full the detail of the situation of affairs with me, and you can give him chief command of all troops at Cape Fear and in North Carolina. If he finds the enemy has all turned south against me, he need not follow, but turn his attention against Raleigh; but if he can secure Goldsboro' and Wilmington, it will be as much as I expect before I have passed the Santee. Send him all detachments of men that have come to join my army. They can be so organized and officered as to be more efficient, for they are nearly all old soldiers who have been detached or on furlough. Until I pass the Santee you can better use these detachments at Bull's bay, Georgetown, &c.

I will instruct General McCallum, of the railroad department, to take his men up to Beaufort, North Carolina, and use them on the road out. I do not know that he can employ them on any road here. I did instruct him, while awaiting information from North Carolina, to employ them in building a good trestle bridge across Port Royal ferry, but I now suppose the pontoon bridge will do. If you move the pontoons be sure to make a good road out to Garden's corner and mark it with sign-boards, obstructing the old road, so that should I send back any detachments they would not be misled.

I prefer that Hatch's force hereabouts should not be materially weakened until I am near Columbia, when you may be governed by the situation of affairs about Charleston. If you can break the railroad between this and Charleston, then this force could be reduced.

I am, with respect, &c.,

W. T. SHERMAN,
Major General Commanding.

Major General J. G. FOSTER,
Commanding Department of the South.

HEADQUARTERS MILITARY DIVISION OF THE MISSISSIPPI,
In the field, Pocotaligo, S. C., January 29, 1865.

GENERAL: I have well reconnoitred hereabouts, and am satisfied that it is not to our interest to reconstruct, at this time, any of the railroads out of Savannah. After securing all the property there, I wish you to transfer your men and tools to North Carolina, (Newbern,) unless Wilmington should fall into our possession, and prepare to make railroad communication to Goldsboro' by the middle of March. You need not build the bridge over Port Royal, which I requested of you at Savannah; that can be done by Foster's command.

General Grant advises me of heavy re-enforcements being sent to North Carolina. You may therefore at once transport Colonel Wright and his operators to Newbern or Wilmington, if that place be in our possession, and prepare timber, iron, cars and locomotives adapted to the roads of North Carolina, enough to build out to Goldsboro' when you can get possession of the road.

Let Colonel Wright report to General Schofield or other commanding officer he may find, who, on presenting this letter will furnish all aid.

General Easton will furnish the necessary transportation.

I have the honor to be your obedient servant,

W. T. SHERMAN,
Major General Commanding.

General McCALLUM,
Railroad Department, Savannah,
In his absence, Colonel W. W. Wright.

HEADQUARTERS MILITARY DIVISION OF THE MISSISSIPPI,
In the field, Pocotaligo, S. C., January 29, 1865.

GENERAL: I wish you to-morrow to send a detachment to the forks of the road this side of the Salkehatchie, and then make demonstrations as though preparatory to cross over to the east side. Try and make a pathway of fallen timber through the swamp so as to enable skirmishers to appear near the river bank at the railroad and wagon road bridges; also, if possible, let one or more horsemen try to pass through the water along the wagon road. I think the water must have subsided enough for this. Also let a party take tools and prepare, on the railroad causeway, a place (countersunk) for two guns en embrasure.

Report to me what is seen by night. I will remain here until I hear from General Slocum about Robertsville, when the whole army will move north, leaving you to cover this point. I deem it important to hold the position on the railroad for some time, say ten (10) days after I leave, and during that time to feel across the Salkehatchie in the direction of Charleston, so as to destroy the railroad as far towards the Edisto as possible. As long as the railroad is intact up to Salkehatchie you will see an enemy may rapidly interpose between here and Port Royal, which might incommode us. At the same time General Foster will try and cut the road between this and Charleston, the effect of which will be to make the enemy guard the road in its whole length. After I have reached the Augusta road I do not think this road will be of much use to the enemy.

I am, with respect,

W. T. SHERMAN,
Major General Commanding.

General HATCH, *Commanding Division.*

HEADQUARTERS MILITARY DIVISION OF THE MISSISSIPPI,
In the field, Pocotaligo, S. C., January 30, 1865.

GENERAL: The general-in-chief desires me to say that he is waiting anxiously to hear from General Slocum, that he may know all is ready, and will then give the order for moving. General Slocum has orders to report his readiness. He (General Sherman) wishes you to hold your command in readiness and prepared to reach Hickory Hill Post Office the next march; also to have General Blair reconnoitre with a view of learning if there be a practicable road for communication and marching from McPhersonville to Robertsville.

There is a lot of recruits, &c., here that will report to you to-night; the general says if you have arms you may put them to duty, but if not, and can't make good use of them, you may send them to Beaufort if you wish.

The general does not wish you to move beyond your present position until all are ready and orders made.

I am, with respect,

L. M. DAYTON, *A. A. G.*

Major General O. O. HOWARD,
Commanding Army of the Tennessee.

HEADQUARTERS MILITARY DIVISION OF THE MISSISSIPPI,
In the field, Pocotaligo, S. C., January 31, 1865.

GENERAL: Howard moves Wednesday morning *via* Hickory Hill and River's bridge. Communicate with me at Hickory Hill, and follow us as rapidly as possible by the old Orangeburg road, by Lawtonville, Duck Branch Post Office, and Beaufort bridge. Let Kilpatrick's cavalry keep on your left front.

I have not heard of your crossing the Savannah yet, but negroes report your pushing the enemy through Lawtonville.

Make the most possible of this fine weather.

W. T. SHERMAN,
Major General.

Major General SLOCUM, *Sister's Ferry.*

HEADQUARTERS MILITARY DIVISION OF THE MISSISSIPPI,
In the field, 4 miles from Hickory Hill, February 1, 1865—1 p. m.

GENERAL: Your letters of January 31 are received. I cannot modify my orders relative to General Saxton having the charge of recruiting blacks. The Secretary made that point. I think the impression at Washington is that both you and I are inimical to the policy of arming negroes, and all know that Saxton is not, and his appointment reconciles that difficulty.

If anything serious occurs correspond directly with Mr. Stanton, and mak your points. Let Grant know I am in motion, and telegraph to Easton that i Slocum has to wait for provisions it will be dead loss, as we are eating up ours

Let Hatch continually feel the Salkehatchie, and the moment the enemy lets go, get the railroad broken back to the Edisto.

Yours,

W. T. SHERMAN, *Major General.*

Major General J. G. FOSTER,
Commanding Department of the South.

HEADQUARTERS MILITARY DIVISION OF THE MISSISSIPPI,
In the field, near Hickory Hill, February 1, 1865.

GENERAL: Your note of this morning is received. All right; get word over to Slocum that I have started and will be opposite River's bridge to-morrow. I may await him there, or go on to the railroad about Midway. He should push cavalry first, and corps by corps, as fast as ready. Keep feeling at the Salkehatchie bridge and the ferry, and if the enemy lets go, follow up to the Edisto. Let's coop him in Charleston, close. Foster will demonstrate about Edisto island.

Roads are very fair, obstructed at the swamps, but we cut away about as fast as a column marches. We find some hogs, bacon, and corn, but much has been carried off by Wheeler, who is ahead.

Open communication to-night with Slocum from Coosawhatchie to Robertsville.

Yours,

W. T. SHERMAN, *Major General.*

Brigadier General JOHN P. HATCH,
Commanding Coast Division.

HEADQUARTERS MILITARY DIVISION OF THE MISSISSIPPI,
In the field, Hickory Hill, S. C., February 1, 1865—5 p. m.

GENERAL: I have a letter from General Williams detailing your difficulties. I think you had better despatch Williams with his two divisions, and Kilpatrick's cavalry, by the road leading through Duck Branch Post Office, to Beaufort bridge, and overtake us and fol ow as soon as possible with the balance. I deem it important to get on the railroad as soon as possible. We will march slowly, say ten or twelve miles a day, towards Midway, and I want you to come up on our left, say at Blackville or Graham's. You will find some meat and forage. We have already found some.

Wheeler had a division of cavalry here, but they ran; they had obstructed the roads, but these were cleared out without delay. Tell Corse he may come by Hickory Hill or Duck Branch, as he finds most convenient. You might occupy roads to the left for convenience.

Yours,

W. T. SHERMAN, *Major General.*

Major General H. W. SLOCUM,
Commanding Left Wing.

HEADQUARTERS MILITARY DIVISION OF THE MISSISSIPPI,
Hickory Hill Post Office, S. C., February 2, 1865—3¾ a. m.

GENERAL: I have just read your despatch. You may go on with two divisions and secure, if possible, Rivers's bridge. Let one division keep to Anglesey's post office by the south of Whippy.   Logan will move so as to get his head of column on the road leading from Duck Branch post office to Anglesey's. That road (the old Orangeburg) is supposed to be on good, firm ground, and is an old road leading to Beaufort's bridge, which is the one I expect to use.

Wheeler's cavalry is mostly to our left.   At Rivers's you will find rebel infantry and artillery in position.

Slocum is unable to cross the Savannah by reason of water over the banks; will have to bridge three-quarters of a mile, from four to six feet of water. We may have to go to the railroad without him.   I have a cipher despatch from him, the contents of which, when translated, I will tell the bearer of this.

Yours,

W. T. SHERMAN,
Major General.

Major General O. O. Howard,
Commanding Army of the Tennessee.

Headquarters Military Division of the Mississippi,
In the field, 2½ miles north of Duck Branch Post Office,
31½ from Pocotaligo February 2, 1865—7 p. m.

General: I wrote you on the road yesterday touching the matter of General Saxton, and gave you my reasons for not changing my orders.   I still adhere to that conclusion, but have no objection whatever that you should apply to the Secretary of War direct, and leave him to judge.   But as to military discipline, I decide that General Saxton cannot go to a military post, and do anything which, in the judgment of its commander, is calculated to produce confusion and disorder.   The commanding officer of a post is the proper person to see that it does not become encumbered with idle or worthless vagabonds of any color, sex, or kind.   You may sustain General Grover in anything he may do as to maintaining good order and government at Savannah.

The Secretary of War is charged by Congress with the administration of the war policy, and we are bound to respect his authority and wishes, and these are contained in my orders.   If General Saxton presumes on any special influences, let him alone and he will commit some breach of military propriety, when you will take action.

I consider he has no more control over organizations of colored troops after they are mustered and paid than the superintendent of the general recruiting service for white troops.   During the inchoate existence of a regiment or company he may use it about his rendezvous for guard and police; but after troops are organized as companies, battalions, or regiments, mustered in and paid by the United States, they at once become, like any other part of your command, subject to your orders and details.   Indeed, were I in your place I would prefer this disposition, as it relieves you of all the details of organization.   As to Littlefield's duties, you can put him subject to Saxton, or you can give him the details of any other officers and men of your command at your own option.   You may require him to apply for such details as he wants, and you can make them just as you would for the quartermaster.

As to the nomination of officers for negro regiments, that purely belongs to the appointing power, the President, who may delegate it to whom he sees fit. As to steamboats, I don't think General Easton has any feeling as to you, but I think he has an idea that Major Thomas, much his junior, is left to judge.   If he knows that you give the subject your personal attention he will be content. It would be well for you to confer with him, for I have given him "*carte blanche,*" and hold him accountable as to my immediate army.

My movements now will depend for a day or two on Slocum, but you had better be all ready for the steps I indicated. We find a good deal of cavalry on all the roads, but they do not delay our march. The infantry is behind the Salkehatchie, which is a swampy, ugly stream, all the way up to Barnwell. I am much obliged for the paper. All well.
  Yours truly,

             W. T. SHERMAN,
             Major General Commanding.

General J. G. FOSTER,
  Commanding Department of the South.

HEADQUARTERS MILITARY DIVISION OF THE MISSISSIPPI,
      In the field, February 3, 1865—5 p. m.

General HOWARD :

Your note and orders of last night were not received until a few moments ago. General Logan got here last night, and to-day drove the enemy from a position on the other side of Duck creek. General Williams brought up five brigades of Slocum's troops, but no later news of Slocum ; thinks he will have a hard time to get across Savannah river at all.

I ordered Wood's division to Anglesey's post office, and John E. Smith is between. To-morrow the 15th corps will move on Beaufort's bridge, which is also strongly defended, and I will order Williams toward Barnwell, to the point marked " Hayes."

I will myself stop at Anglesey's post office till I hear what progress is made to effect a lodgment across the Salkehatchie. General Wood's is now at Anglesey's, and will lead to Beaufort's to-morrow. If Slocum were up I would move him to Barnwell at once, but can use Williams to produce the same effect.
  Yours,

             W. T. SHERMAN,
             Major General.

HEADQUARTERS MILITARY DIVISION OF THE MISSISSIPPI,
   In the field, Duck Branch Post Office, February 3, 1865.

GENERAL : Move your command to-morrow ; two divisions to Beaufort's bridge, and one to Anglesey's post office. Better pursue the same order as now, and let all march—say at 6 a. m. That will bring the divisions of Wood and John E. Smith at Beaufort's, and Hazen's at Anglesey's. I will move Williams by our left rear around to Arnold church and Hayes.
  Yours,

             W. T. SHERMAN,
             Major General Commanding.

General LOGAN,
  Commanding 15th Corps.

HEADQUARTERS MILITARY DIVISION OF THE MISSISSIPPI,
  In the field, Duck Branch Post Office, S. C., February 4, 1865—3 a. m.

GENERAL : Enclosed I send you copy of report just received from Major General Howard, his operations giving full possession of the Salkehatchie.

General Sherman desires that you will move your command slowly to the point indicated in the instructions sent yesterday p. m., these operations giving you, probably, a clear road ; it is reported that Wheeler has passed around our front across the Salkehatchie.

Please communicate with General Slocum the progress made and our present situation, and the fact of our being in possession of the Salkehatchie, given by Mower's assault to-day ; also such other items as will be of information to him. We will move as indicated.

I am, general, with respect,

L. M. DAYTON,
Assistant Adjutant General.

Brevet Major General WILLIAMS,
Commanding 20th Corps.

P. S.—Send substance of this to Slocum. I think you had better send the bulk of your train, under small escort, by the direct road to Beaufort's bridge, to which point you may conduct your command around by Allendale post office and Arnold church, making as much display as possible. Take enough wagons and artillery with you to forage *good*, and try and be at Beaufort's bridge to-morrow night, so you can pass the Salkehatchie there without fail. Then, probably, we shall move without waiting for Slocum, though I want Kilpatrick up as quick as possible; but he should swing round to Barnwell, but not further west without orders.

Yours,

W. T. SHERMAN,
Major General.

HEADQUARTERS MILITARY DIVISION OF THE MISSISSIPPI,
In the field, Beaufort's Bridge, S. C., February 5, 1865.

GENERAL : General Kilpatrick is now up to Allendale post office, and will move to-morrow on Barnwell, and thence to join us about Bamburg.

I wish your wing to move now with all expedition consistent with due caution, and make a strong lodgement on the South Carolina railroad anywhere from Graham's to the Edisto.

I will instruct General Williams to cross here, and move four miles towards Barnwell, and thence follow cross-roads in the direction of Graham's station.

I suppose you will move the 17th corps direct on Midway, and the 15th corps on Bamburg. I will attend the 15th corps.

I am yours, &c.,

W. T. SHERMAN,
Major General Commanding.

General HOWARD,
Commanding Army of the Tennessee.

HEADQUARTERS MILITARY DIVISION OF THE MISSISSIPPI,
In the field, Beaufort's Bridge, S. C., February 5, 1865.

GENERAL : Captain Newton has just arrived, and I am glad you are up. The enemy is all in the mist as to our movements, save they think Slocum's command has gone up to Augusta, and that I am moving on Branchville. We carried the position at Rivers's yesterday, and to-day have passed both corps across— 17th at Rivers's, and 15th here at Beaufort's. I sent Williams round by Allendale to make a feint on Barnwell. To-morrow the 17th corps will move rapidly on Midway, and the 15th on Bamburg ; Williams will follow in reserve.

The enemy intended to defend the line of Salkehatchie, but are now falling back to the Edisto. Presuming you get to-day to Allendale Post Office, I want you to-morrow to move rapidly on Barnwell, keeping up any feint you may please in the direction of Augusta. Next day strike the railroad where you please, from Blackville to Lowry's. If you can, get and destroy cars, locomotives, and depots, but don't delay long, but effectually destroy some piece of the track, enough to cut communication, and then turn to us about Duncanville or Bamburg. You will find plenty of corn and bacon. I think Wheeler's forces are scattered, and he has no idea where you are up to this moment, so you can act with a rush. Some cavalry retreated before General Williams to the northwest, towards Augusta, and other parts across the bridges of Salkehatchie. I don't care about your going into Barnwell, and only refer to it as the point where you will likely find cleared roads across the swamp. The bridges amount to nothing; the swamp is the worst, and you may cross it wherever you please. I expect to hear from you the night of February 7, or morning of the 8th, when I will be with the 15th corps not far from Duncanville or Bamburg.

On this side the Salkehatchie we find the roads fine, with farms and abundance of forage. None has been destroyed.

The farmers west of Salkehatckie were ordered to move their forage and stock to the east of Salkehatchie, the rebels expecting to hold that line.

Mystify the enemy all you can, but break that road while I move straight on it about Lowry's.

    Yours,

W. T. SHERMAN, Major General.

General KILPATRICK,
    Commanding Cavalry, Allendale.

HEADQUARTERS MILITARY DIVISION OF THE MISSISSIPPI,
In the field, Beaufort's Bridge, S. C., February 5, 1865.

GENERAL: The right wing of the army will move early to-morrow against the South Carolina railroad in the neighborhood of Bamburg.

I wish you to cross the Salkehatchie and move for the same point, but for convenience of movement suggest you take the Barnwell road to Ayer's, where a road leads to Blackville which intersects one coming into the direct Bamburg road from here, at the Little Salkehatchie. As you approach the Little Salkehatchie I think you can find some road to Bamburg, without coming into collision with the 15th corps, that will occupy ten miles of that road; I think such a road will be found from Nimmon's to Duncanville, crossing Little Salkehatchie, above or at Dowling's mill. I will be near the leading division of the 15th corps. Kilpatrick will be about Barnwell to-morrow night, and will strike the railroad next day between Blackville and Graham's.

If you can find any other road than the one I suggest, which is nearly parallel with the one travelled by the 15th corps, and not more than six or seven miles off, you can take it; always sending me word, and in case of hearing the sound of serious battle, change your course towards it.

    I am, yours, &c.,

W. T. SHERMAN,
Major General Commanding.

General A. S. WILLIAMS, Commanding 20th Corps.

HEADQUARTERS MILITARY DIVISION OF THE MISSISSIPPI,
In the field, Beaufort's Bridge, S. C., February 5, 1865.

GENERAL: I have instructed General Howard to move the right wing, and make a lodgement on the South Carolina railroad, in the neighborhood of Bamburg. You may, therefore, in anticipation of the movement, make orders for the 15th corps to take the direct road to Duncanville.   Kilpatrick will move by Barnwell, and I have ordered General Williams to cross the Big Salkehatchie by this bridge ; thence to take the Barnwell road out as far as Ayer's, where a road branches to Blackville.   He will follow that to about Nimmon's, trusting to find some road leading up to Graham's or Duncanville.

I would like, if possible, that Hazen should be on the north side of the Barnwell road by eight o'clock, so that Williams can pass him, and that the two armies should not get mixed at the place where Hazen's camp now is.

I am, yours, &c.,

W. T. SHERMAN, *Major General.*

Major General J. A. LOGAN,
Commanding 15th Corps.

HEADQUARTERS MILITARY DIVISION OF THE MISSISSIPPI,
In the field, five miles from Bamburg, February 6, 1865.

GENERAL : You may make your orders, and march to-morrow on Lowry's Station, South Carolina railroad, and make a strong lodgement and break up the road.   Inasmuch as the enemy must, by this time, have detected our plan, you should be prepared for battle.   You know that the 17th corps is approaching Midway by the road from Rivers's bridge, and should now be within eight miles. You have only five miles to Bamburg, and one more to Lowry's.   Williams is just behind you, and Kilpatrick is supposed to be at Barnwell, and has orders to strike the railroad about Blackville and turn to Bamburg.   Williams is ordered to move straight on Graham's Station, unless he hears you engaged, when he will turn to your left flank.

You had better march with two divisions, disencumbered of all wagons save a few with cartridges, and the ambulances, and let your train follow to any point you may select, about Bamburg or Lowry's, to be parked.   As soon as you reach the railroad set to work to destroy it effectually, viz : every rail must be twisted.

Your advance should push out a mile or so beyond the railroad, towards South Edisto, on the Cannon's Bridge road.   If you hear Howard engaged lean towards Midway, but get the road broken anyhow.   I will be with you, but want you to fight your own battle, as I am a non-combatant.   The enemy ought to fight us, but I don't believe he will.

Yours, &c.,

W. T. SHERMAN, *Major General.*

Major General J. A. LOGAN,
Commanding 15th Corps.

Have the left-hand road at the church clear for Williams by 8 a. m.

S.

[Cipher despatch.]

HEADQUARTERS MILITARY DIVISION OF THE MISSISSIPPI,
Armies in the field, Lowry's Station, February 7, 1865.

General FOSTER, *Hilton Head, S. C.:*

We are on the railroad at Midway.   Weather bad ; water high, and roads bad.   These may force me to turn against Charleston before crossing the Santee.   Enemy has retreated east and north across the Edisto.   We will break up fifty miles of this road towards Augusta, and then move over towards Columbia.

21*

Watch Charleston close, and threaten Bull's bay.   Hatch's force should now get across to Edisto, about Jacksonboro' and Willstown.   Slocum is not yet up.

W. T. SHERMAN,
Major General Commanding.

[Cipher despatch.]

HEADQUARTERS MILITARY DIVISION OF THE MISSISSIPPI,
Army in the field, February 7, 1865.

Admiral DAHLGREN :

We are on the South Carolina road at Midway, and will break fifty miles from Edisto towards Augusta ; I then cross towards Columbia.   Weather is bad and country full of water.   This cause may force me to turn against Charleston.   I have ordered Foster to move Hatch up to the Edisto about Jacksonboro' and Willstown, also to make that lodgement at Bull's bay.

Watch Charleston close ; I think Davis will order it to be abandoned lest he lose its garrison as well as guns.   We are all well, and the enemy retreats before us.   Send word to Newbern that you have heard from me, and the probabilities are that high waters may force me to the coast before I reach North Carolina, but to keep Wilmington busy.

W. T. SHERMAN,
Major General.

HEADQUARTERS MILITARY DIVISION OF THE MISSISSPPI,
In the field, Lowry's, February 7, 1865.

GENERAL : We are on the railroad and the enemy has retreated across the Edisto.   I propose to break up the road westward, so you may let Geary join Williams about Graham's, and let Davis take any road you may prefer to the left to reach the neighborhood of Blackville.   You may send that corps (14th) through Barnwell for the sake of forage.   We find plenty, but I fear we leave but little behind us.   Weather is villanous, but we can't help it and must do the best we can.

Send back to Coosawhatchie fort, or any other point you may think best, the enclosed cipher messages to General Foster and Admiral Dahlgren.   Send by several messengers and by secure roads.

Yours, &c.,

W. T. SHERMAN,
Major General.

Major General SLOCUM, *on the Road.*

HEADQUARTERS MILITARY DIVISION OF THE MISSISSIPPI,
In the field, Lowry's Station, S. C., Railroad, February 7, 1865.

GENERAL : Your note of 2 p. m. is received.   We are all on the road, and will break road to-morrow and then move up towards Augusta.   You can remain where you are and try and secure the bridge at the head of Young's island.   I will pass the Edisto, above that point, and as high as Guignard's bridge.   Make a good break while you are about it.   If you feel confident you may move up the road, making occasional breaks, and meet us on your return about White

Pond in two days after to-morrow. I will order Davis's corps to come round through Barnwell to White Pond or Windsor's. Don't risk much, but keep your horses and men well in hand.

Yours,

W. T. SHERMAN, *Major General.*

General KILPATRICK, *Commanding Cavalry.*

HEADQUARTERS MILITARY DIVISION OF THE MISSISSIPPI,
In the field, Lowry's Station, S. C., February 8, 1865.

GENERAL: Yours of this date is received. Burn all cotton. The confederate congress has appropriated all cotton to its own use. It is the only cash article left to the enemy. I send you a letter to Wheeler in answer to his, which you can leave with the lady to be sent to Wheeler as best she can.

Destroy the railroad and its attachments, tanks, sheds, everything that facilitates its use. I will send you orders for to-morrow, which amount to moving up to Blackville. If you hear of Geary to-day in reach, turn him at once to Blackville; Slocum should move the 14th corps towards Williston. I think the left wing will cross the Edisto about Guignard's and Pine Log bridges. I want to get the left wing on the Orangeburg and Edgefield road as soon as possible. We are twisting the iron here beautiful. I will send the engineers up to you to-morrow, they do the work best.

W T. SHERMAN
Major General.

General A. S. WILLIAMS, *Graham's.*

HEADQUARTERS MILITARY DIVISION OF THE MISSISSIPPI,
In the field, February 8, 1865.

GENERAL: Yours addressed to General Howard is received by me. I hope you will burn all cotton and save us the trouble. We don't want it, and it has proven a curse to our country. All you don't burn, I will. As to private houses occupied by peaceful families, my orders are not to molest or disturb them, and I think my orders are obeyed. Vacant houses, being of no use to anybody, I care little about, as the owners have thought them of no use to themselves. I don't want them destroyed, but do not take much care to preserve them.

I am, with respect, yours, truly,

W. T. SHERMAN, *Major General.*

Major General J. WHEELER,
Commanding Cavalry Corps, Confederate Army.

HEADQUARTERS MILITARY DIVISION OF THE MISSISSIPPI,
In the field, Lowry's, February 8, 1865.

GENERAL: I have just received your note in cipher. I send you a copy of orders for the next move which will give you the key to the whole. Wheeler writes to General Howard, offering not to burn cotton if we don't burn houses. I assured him that he would oblige me by burning cotton, as it saves us the trouble; that we don't burn occupied houses; but if people vacate their own houses, I don't think they should expect us to protect them.

You may burn all cotton. Spare dwelling-houses that are occupied, and teach your men to be courteous to women—it goes a great ways—but take all provisions and forage you need. Act as though you are, or are to be, followed by infantry.

I expect Hood's army will try and join the South Carolina army about Columbia, and I will try and interpose again at Orangeburg. I will order the 14th corps to Williston and Guignard's bridge or Pine Log bridge. Edisto is narrow and easily crossed up there. The Orangeburg and Edgefield road is the key line of South Carolina.

   Yours,

           W. T. SHERMAN, *Major General.*

General KILPATRICK, *Blackville.*

HEADQUARTERS MILITARY DIVISION OF THE MISSISSIPPI,
   In the field, Graham's Station, February 9, 1865.

DEAR GENERAL: Your note of this morning is received. Williams moved hence for Blackville this morning. The Michigan engineers have been ordered to your flank to twist railroad iron. Tell Williams I have inspected his work here, and the bars are not twisted. Better do half the work and do it thoroughly; unless there be a warp the bar can be straightened again. All the cavalry is now, and has been, on your flank. Kilpatrick was last night up at Williston, where he whipped a division of cavalry, and is moving to break up railroad, partially, as far as Aiken.

I was in hopes you would turn Davis off below Coosawhatchie swamp through Barnwell to Williston or White pond. Get him as soon as possible at work on the railroad from Williston west, and in the mean time have the bridge at Guignard's and Pine Log examined so as to cross there, or at the head of Young's island. My orders of yesterday give the next movement.

To-day, Howard, with the 17th corps, is moving to Binnaker's bridge. Two divisions of the 15th corps are at the forks of the roads west of this, and the other at Holman's bridge.

Don't take any of Kilpatrick's cavalry to make escorts or orderlies, for he has to fight and contend now with double and nearly treble his numbers. For courier duty and orderlies pick up horses and mount drummers and non-combatants. If necessary to get horses break up teams and use mules for ambulances, burning up the empty wagons. Howard has no cavalry save one fragment of mounted infantry. By keeping on our left you will have, henceforth, good forage.

Pine Log ford will be the place for Kilpatrick to cross over the South Edisto. Your best points will be the head of Young's island and Guignard's.

We must all turn amphibious, for the country is half under water. Mower had to fight at the Salkehatchie with his men up to their arm-pits, he setting the example.

I think we can spend all of to-morrow on railroad-breaking, but next day we must be across Edisto. You can gain time on Howard as he swings against Orangeburg. Your wing will move on Columbia.

   Yours,

           W. T. SHERMAN, *Major General.*

Major General SLOCUM, *Blackville.*

HEADQUARTERS MILITARY DIVISION OF THE MISSISSIPPI,
   In the field, Walker's House, near S. C. Railroad,
        February 9, 1865—2¼ p. m.

GENERAL: An officer has just left me for Blackville, where Slocum will arrive with Geary's division, which completes the 20th corps at Blackville. Davis is moving for Barnwell, and will come up to the west of Blackville about Williston. I have ordered Slocum to put in to-morrow good on the railroad, and then look to crossing the Edisto at the head of Young's island and at Guignard's.

I want you to effect a crossing at or between Binnaker's and Holman's bridges. Do it in your own way, using all the 17th corps and one division of the 15th corps, sent by Logan to Holman's bridge. If you can secure a lodgement to-morrow and get to work on a bridge at Binnaker's, it will be time enough to cross day after to-morrow. All accounts appear that the road from Binnaker's to Orangeburg is better than from Holman's.

I am seven miles from Binnaker's, five from Holman's, and six from Blackville. I will probably go up to Blackville to-morrow to see Slocum.

Keep me well advised of your purposes. As soon as Logan completes the destruction of the railroad to Blackville he can move his two other divisions down to Holman's, or where you need them.

It is, to me, patent that the enemy has only cavalry at the Edisto, and we must keep it busy, that Kilpatrick may encounter less about Aiken. His movement on Aiken, besides the substantial damage, will disconcert the part of S. D. Lee's corps that did not get over the railroad.

Proceed to effect a lodgement on the north of the Edisto by cautious, but persistent, efforts ; once across, the enemy will fall behind the Santee.

Yours,

W. T. SHERMAN, *Major General.*

Major General HOWARD,
    Commanding Right Wing.

HEADQUARTERS MILITARY DIVISION OF THE MISSISSIPPI,
    In the field, near Graham's, South Carolina Railroad,
        February 10, 1865.

GENERAL : I have just returned from Blackville, where I saw General Slocum. The 20th corps is all up and at work destroying railroad. The 14th corps, General Slocum thinks, will reach Williston to-night. I also learn that General Corse is close at hand. So all things are in readiness for the move on Orangeburg. General Slocum will have his two corps on the Orangeburg and Edgefield road, opposite the new bridge at the head of Fair's island and Guignard's, by the day after to-morrow. You had better move the 17th corps straight on Orangeburg, aiming to get within two or three miles, ready the next day to cross by pontoons above Orangeburg and make a lodgement on the road. The 15th corps should move to-morrow to Bull-fight pond, and next day to North Edisto, at the mouth of Mill Branch creek, or Caw Caw, according to the appearance about Orangeburg. I will accompany the 15th corps and camp with it to-morrow night.

I want to have the railroad broken good from about Orangeburg up above the State road, (Matthew's Post Office,) but would prefer that one corps should do the work, leaving the 15th corps to follow a course more to the west, in support of the left wing, in the event of Dick Taylor having got to Augusta with Hood's old army.

Slocum's orders will take him by the most direct road possible to Columbia, but making to the left about the Sand Hills in case he comes in contact with one of your columns. I have nothing from Kilpatrick to-day.

If to morrow, or next day, we observe a concentration of force about Orangeburg, I can draw from Slocum by the Edgefield road.

I will notify General Logan to put his corps in motion to-morrow for Bull-fight pond.

Yours, truly,

W. T. SHERMAN, *Major General.*

General O. O. HOWARD,
    Commanding Right Wing.

HEADQUARTERS MILITARY DIVISION OF THE MISSISSIPPI,
In the field, Walker's House, February 10, 1865.

GENERAL: I have this moment written General Howard that he may begin his movement on Orangeburg. You may, therefore, in the morning early put your corps in motion for Bull-fight pond, on the Edgefield and Orangeburg road, and there await orders from General Howard or myself. I will accompany you, going from here direct to Holman's bridge.

I am, &c., yours, truly,

W. T. SHERMAN.

Major General JNO. A. LOGAN,
Commanding 15th Corps.

HEADQUARTERS MILITARY DIVISION OF THE MISSISSIPPI,
In the field, February 10, 1865.

GENERAL: Your note from Johnston's is just received. I cannot change my plans now, as they are in progress. I don't care about Aiken, unless you can take it with a dash, and, as Wheeler's attention is drawn to that quarter, you can let it work.

To-morrow the right wing moves on Orangeburg, and after breaking that railroad good, we will proceed as heretofore indicated. Davis should be at Williston to-night, or early to-morrow. Keep in communication with him, and conform to his movements.

It won't pay to have infantry chasing Wheeler's cavalry; it is always a bad plan, and is injurious to detach infantry, save for a day or a single occasion. You can see Davis when he comes up, and he can spare a brigade for a day or so; but I don't want a brigade of infantry to go off to the flank, when the whole army would have to wait for it, or it would be marched to death to catch up.

Wheeler or a part of his command was on the north side of South Edisto yesterday, and the concentration of the enemy is being made at Columbia, though I have no doubt that attention has been drawn towards Augusta; but I will not delay the main move an hour, and, therefore, want Davis to move on as soon as he can repair the bridge. Slocum will give him his orders, and I wish you to conform to the movements of the left corps, give it notice of danger from the direction of Augusta, and only attack Wheeler when he exposes himself. When operating near General Davis's corps, he will doubtless let you have a brigade of infantry, from time to time, but not as a permanent thing.

Yours, truly,

W. T. SHERMAN,
Major General.

General KILPATRICK,
Commanding Cavalry.

HEADQUARTERS MILITARY DIVISION OF THE MISSISSIPPI,
In the field, 21 miles from Columbia, February 13, 1865.

GENERAL: Yours of this date is received. I would like to have Blair try and stampede the guard at the Congaree bridge by a semblance of attack, for which purpose one division to the rear of his trains, and leaving one to advance on the bridge, burning only the trestles, while the other confines its attention to twisting bars.

Corse's and Wood's are now within five or six miles of Sandy creek. I think you can put all the 15th corps across Sandy creek to-morrow, and Blair's trains and division to Sandy Creek Post Office, where the Orangeburg and State roads meet.   One march, viz: the day after to-morrow, will bring us easily up abreast of Columbia.

Captain Audenreid, in riding ahead to-day, captured a rebel lieutenant just out of Columbia, and passing himself off as a rebel, extracted from him much information.

The force now at Columbia is small, and the people are not expecting us now, thinking that Augusta or Charleston is our objective.   I think Slocum will be abreast of Columbia to-morrow.   I will keep with the leading division of this corps.

Yours,

W. T. SHERMAN,
Major General.

General Howard,
Commanding Right Wing.

P. S.—If you want more roads beyond Sandy creek you can depend on any number to the left.   The country is of poor pine lands, and is full of farm roads. To-day the road was perfect, and there seemed any number running to every point of the compass.

S.

Headquarters Military Division of the Mississippi,
In the field, opposite Columbia, February 16, 1865.

General: General Howard has to pass Saluda and Broad rivers at the same time, requiring more bridging than he has.   I send this through him, that he may note on it how many boats he wants.   I suppose you can spare ten, as you will be able to remove that over the Saluda before you pass the Broad.

In case Howard calls for any pontoons, he will conduct them to the point where he needs them.

Yours, truly,

W. T. SHERMAN,
Major General Commanding.

Major General Slocum,
Commanding, &c.

Headquarters Military Division of the Mississippi,
In the field, opposite Columbia, S. C., February 16, 1865.

Dear General: I see the bridge over Broad burning.   It is very important that you effect a crossing to-night.   If necessary get over the Saluda the bulk of the 15th corps, then take up enough pontoons to finish one across the Broad.

Send an officer with the enclosed note to General Slocum, who can send you ten boats before daylight.   Slocum can pass Broad river as high up as Alston, and thereby use his bridges at one day's interval.

Yours,

W. T. SHERMAN,
Major General Commanding.

Major General Howard,
Commanding Right Wing.

Send the enclosed by an officer to conduct the pontoons.

HEADQUARTERS MILITARY DIVISION OF THE MISSISSIPPI,
In the field, Winnsboro', S. C., February 21, 1865—6 p. m.

DEAR GENERAL: Generals Slocum and Davis are here. Slocum sends his wagons and pontoons to-morrow straight for the ferry at Rocky Mount post office, by Gladden's grove; he will keep four divisions breaking up road as far as the Chester district line, and aim to cross his whole command day after to-morrow. Let Blair finish up the road good to this point, and then assemble at Poplar spring and effect a crossing of the Wateree, prepared to get all across the day after to-morrow. Slocum will assemble his command at Gladden's. Communicate with me there or at Rocky Mount. After crossing, Slocum will have the road from Lancaster to Chesterfield, and you from your ferry straight for Cheraw, dipping a little south to get on the Camden road. I will keep with the 20th corps, which is General Slocum's right.

Yours, &c.,

W. T. SHERMAN,
Major General Commanding.

Major General HOWARD.

HEADQUARTERS MILITARY DIVISION OF THE MISSISSIPPI,
In the field, Winnsboro', February 21, 1865.

GENERAL: I presume you to be now about Lemon's or Buck-Head post office, and base my present calculations on that supposition. I would like you to move with your whole force to the neighborhood of Blackstock depot, or Springwell post office, taking position and manœuvring so as to seem to be the advance of the whole army, in the direction of Chesterville and Charlotte, and to cover General Davis's operations in breaking up the railroad as far as he can during to-morrow and next day. As soon as Davis withdraws to cross the Catawba, move with him and cross to the east bank of the Catawba (or Wateree) on Slocum's pontoons, which will be laid at Rocky Mount post office. I would like to have you all across during the night of the 23d, so you can move next day on Lancaster. I would like to have the railroad bridge across Broad river at the mouth of Tiger burned, and I think the enemy himself will burn it if you approach it or send a small party to threaten it; also several of the bridges and trestles on the same railroad below where it crosses Broad river about Ashford's ferry and about Dawkins's. I hope you have already damaged that road considerably. I wish, as a rule, whenever you are near a railroad, you will, unless cautioned otherwise, have your men burn bridges, depots and water-tanks, and break switches; also, all saw-mills should be destroyed—not only burned, but their engines and boilers disabled. Davis will be near you and be on hand in case of need, but I don't want you to be drawn off so that you cannot have your trains and men ready to pass the pontoons during the night of the 23d. Better caution your commanders so as to keep in your foragers, else they will be left behind, as some were about Columbia.

I will be with this wing some days and would like to see you either here, or, better, at the bridge in crossing the Catawba.

I enclose you General Slocum's orders for to-morrow and next day. General Howard will be at Poplar spring and Peay's ferry.

Yours, truly,

W. T. SHERMAN, *Major General.*

Major General KILPATRICK,
Commanding Cavalry.

HEADQUARTERS MILITARY DIVISION OF THE MISSISSIPPI,
In the field, Rocky Mount Post Office, February 22, 1865—9 p. m.

GENERAL : Yours of to-day from Peay's ferry, has just been received. General Sherman desires me to say that he would like to have you put your whole command over the river with due expedition, and suggests it would be well to move out in the direction intended, some ten or twelve miles, say Russell Place, until the high or table land may be reached. He also wishes you to reconnoitre for roads towards Cheraw well, and towards Camden.

Two divisions of the 20th corps, with the entire train of this wing, have reached this point, and are mostly in camp; the bridge is completed ready for crossing; the balance of the command is destroying railroad.

Yours, with respect,

L. M. DAYTON,
Assistant Adjutant General.

Major General HOWARD,
Commanding Right Wing.

HEADQUARTERS MILITARY DIVISION OF THE MISSISSIPPI,
In the field, Rocky Mount, S. C., February 23, 1865.

GENERAL : Yours of last night is received; your disposition of matters is all right. The bridge is laid and troops are crossing. I am anxious to get the wagons across and up on high ground before the rain comes. I wish you would keep your cavalry on roads to the north of the direct one by Gladden's grove, as that will be needed all day for infantry and wagons. You shall have the bridge as fast as your brigades arrive.

I regret the matter you report that eighteen of your men have been murdered after surrender, and marked that the enemy intended to kill all foragers. It leaves no alternative; you must retaliate man for man, and mark them in the like manner. Let it be done at once. We have a perfect war-right to the products of the country we overrun, and may collect them by foragers or otherwise. Let the whole people know the war is now against them because their armies flee before us and do not defend their country or frontier as they should. It is pretty nonsense for Wheeler, and Beauregard, and such vain heroes, to talk of our warring against women and children. If they claim to be men they should defend their women and children and prevent us reaching their homes. Instead of maintaining their armies let them turn their attention to their families, or we will follow them to the death ; they should know that we will use the produce of the country as we please.

I want the foragers to be regulated and systematized, so as not to degenerate into common robbers ; but foragers, as such, to collect corn, bacon, beef, and such other products as we need, are as much entitled to our protection as our skirmishers and flankers.

You will, therefore, at once shoot, and leave by the road-side, an equal number of their prisoners, and append a label to their bodies stating that man for man shall be killed for every one of our men they kill. If our foragers commit excesses punish them yourself, but never let an enemy judge between our men and the law. For my part I want the people of the south to realize the fact that they shall not dictate laws of war or peace to us. If there is to be any dictation we want our full share.

Yours, truly,

W. T. SHERMAN,
Major General Commanding.

Major General KILPATRICK,
Commanding Cavalry.

HEADQUARTERS MILITARY DIVISION OF THE MISSISSIPPI,
In the field, Rocky Mount Post Office, February 23, 1865—10 a. m.

GENERAL: I have just been down to the bridge. It will take all of to-day and to-morrow to get this wing across and out. You may go ahead, but keep communication with me.

I expect Kilpatrick here this p. m., and will send him well to the left. He reports that two of his foraging parties were murdered by the enemy after capture, and labelled "death to all foragers." Now, it is clearly our right to subsist our army on the enemy. Napoleon always did it; but could avail himself of the civil power he found in existence to collect forage and provisions by regular impressments. We cannot do that here, and I contend, if the enemy fails to defend his country, we may rightfully appropriate what we want. If our foragers are out under mine, yours, or other proper authority, they must be protected. I have ordered Kilpatrick to select of his prisoners man for man, shoot them, and leave them by the road-side labelled, so that our enemy will see that for every man he executes he takes the life of one of his own.

I want the foragers, however, to be kept within reasonable bounds for the sake of discipline. I will not protect them when they enter dwellings and commit wanton waste—as women's apparel, jewelry, and such things as are not needed by our army; but they may destroy cotton and tobacco, because these are assumed by the rebel government to belong to it, and are used as a valueable source of revenue. Nor will I consent to our enemy taking the lives of our men on their judgment. They have lost all title to property, and can lose nothing not already forfeited, but we should punish our own soldiers for a departure from our orders, and if the people resist our foragers I will not deem it wrong, but the confederate army must not be supposed to be the champions of any people.

I lay down these general rules, and wish you to be governed by them. If any of your foragers are murdered, take life for life, leaving a record of each.

I am, with respect,

W. T. SHERMAN,
Major General Commanding.

Major General HOWARD, *Commanding Right Wing.*

HEADQUARTERS MILITARY DIVISION OF THE MISSISSIPPI,
In the field, Rocky Mount, February 23, 1865.

GENERAL: Your note of to-day is received. I don't see that we can do better than to follow the roads you have indicated, although they carry you too far south. General Davis will cross to-morrow and get on the road from Lancaster to Cheraw, *via* Chesterfield. General Williams is now at Colonel Ballard's, but his trains are not yet across. Kilpatrick will cross at 7 p. m., move out five miles, and to-morrow move to Lancaster, and there await General Davis's coming. I will accompany General Williams, and expect to be about Hanging Rock to-morrow night; thence will find a road across to Chesterfield. I fear much the present rain will make the roads very bad. You will have better roads and should move slower. If circumstances warrant, you might send a small cavalry force into Camden and get more positive news of Charleston; it might save your being troubled by cavalry to burn the bridge. If you should calculate that you will reach Cheraw much in advance of us, you may threaten Florence, or actually break the railroad near there to divert attention from our real course.

Yours, truly,

W. T. SHERMAN, *Major General.*

General HOWARD, *Commanding Right Wing.*

HEADQUARTERS MILITARY DIVISION OF THE MISSISSIPPI,
In the field, 1 *mile north of Warrenton,*
15 *miles south of Lancaster, February* 24, 1865.

GENERAL: General Davis is not yet across, and the roads are so very bad that I think it will take him all day and to-morrow to get well over and up on high land. The 20th corps is here. We can see the 17th corps passing eastward, about one mile south.

General Davis is ordered to take roads that will bring him into the direct road from Lancaster to Chesterfield, and the 20th corps will move by Hanging Rock, and thence by roads to the south of Davis. Unless the rain cease we will have a hard time. Don't push too fast, but gather as much food as you can *en route.* I think you could send into Camden with safety, but there is no object. When you get to Lynch's creek you might pass the 9th Illinois cavalry across, and push them toward Florence, with orders to break two or three bridges about Timmonsville, and then to rejoin you at Cheraw. I don't believe there is any cavalry of the enemy down there, and ours might pick up some good horses. The only object would be to prevent the shipment, by cars, of the garrison of Charleston to Fayetteville or Wilmington to oppose us. If, at the time, you suppose all of the Charleston garrison is east of Florence, the expedition would not be advisable.

I believe Foster is in possession of Charleston, because of the general belief to that effect, and the reports of the negroes you sent me. I have also just released a prisoner, captured yesterday by the 20th corps, who was a bright lad, sixteen (16) years old, son of Richard Bacot, who was at West Point with me, and whom I knew well at Charleston. This boy left Charleston last Thursday at 12 m., at which time he says our troops had been shelling the city for twenty-four hours from James's island. He was a hospital attendant, and was sent along with the sick from the hospitals to Florence, thence to be conveyed to the hospital at Cheraw. He said the orders for the evacuation had been published, and the garrison were to be rendezvoused along the Florence road at Porcher's and Bonneau's; they were removing the powder and ammunition, but would leave the heavy guns. The gunboats were to be blown up. He says the first orders were to go to Columbia, but they were changed.

If you can possibly employ a negro to go through to Charleston, make a cipher despatch, telling our general position and destination, and an order of liberal payment.

I think you will have good roads, and that there is no danger in our spreading out this side of Cheraw, thence to Fayetteville roads favor us, as also from Fayetteville to our destination. At both Cheraw and Fayetteville are bridges that can be secured by holding the towns responsible.

We find no enemy hereabouts, and suppose them all to be about Charleston and Salisbury. General Kilpatrick must now be at Lancaster; he crossed last night and was off this morning.

　　　　　Yours, truly,

　　　　　　　　　　　　　　W. T. SHERMAN,
　　　　　　　　　　　　　　　　Major General.

Major General HOWARD,
　　Commanding Right Wing.

HEADQUARTERS MILITARY DIVISION OF THE MISSISSIPPI,
In the field, February 24, 1865.

GENERAL: It is officially reported to me that our foraging parties are murdered after captured, and labelled "death to all foragers;" one instance of a lieutenant and seven men near Chesterville, and another of twenty "near a ravine eighty rods from the main road," about three miles from Feasterville. I have ordered a similar number of prisoners in our hands to be disposed of in like manner.

I hold about one thousand prisoners captured in various ways, and can stand it as long as you, but I hardly think these murders are committed with your knowledge, and would suggest that you give notice to the people at large that every life taken by them results in the death of one of your confederates.

Of course you cannot question my right to "forage on the country." It is a war right as old as history. The manner of exercising it varies with circumstances, and if the civil authorities will supply my requisitions I will forbid all foraging. But I find no civil authorities who can respond to calls for forage and provisions, therefore must collect directly of the people. I have no doubt this is the occasion of much misbehavior on the part of our men, but I cannot permit an enemy to judge, and punish with wholesale murder.

Personally I regret the bitter feelings engendered by this war, but they were to be expected, and I simply allege that those who struck the first blow and made war inevitable ought not in fairness to reproach us for the natural consequences. I merely assert our "war right" to forage, and my resolve to protect my foragers to the extent of life for life.

Your obedient servant,

W. T. SHERMAN,
Major General United States Army.

Lieut. General WADE HAMPTON,
Commanding Cavalry forces, C. S. A.

HEADQUARTERS MILITARY DIVISION OF THE MISSISSIPPI,
In the field, Hanging Rock, February 27, 1865.

GENERAL : Your letter is just received. It is all important that you keep me advised. Davis was slow in using the bridge, and it was carried away and was not mended until to-day. He will be all over to-night. The movement you describe is the proper one—to keep on the left rear of the left infantry corps.

I have word from Howard that will put him near Cheraw to-morrow night, and I will push to meet him, but must wait till General Davis gets along ; probably will be about Horton's tavern to-morrow night. Keep feeling the different roads towards Charlotte till you hear. General Davis is well towards the head of Lynch's creek and then draw off.

General Howard captured a good many horses and mules and some militia ; he will send a division light to Florence simply to break that road, and prevent the removal of any more railroad stock.

There is little doubt our troops are in Charleston, and General Howard reports that a despatch reached Camden yesterday that we also had taken Wilmington. In that event the enemy will collect all his force about Raleigh as soon as he sees I am not coming to Charlotte.

Keep me advised daily. A despatch sent to the nearest corps to be forwarded will answer the purpose, but I think Hampton will draw off as soon as he feels General Howard's approach to Cheraw. General Howard is moving on the two roads from Young's and Tillersville.

General Slocum's 20th corps will probably pass at Blakeney's, and General Davis's at MacManus's. You will have no trouble with Lynch's creek, as it is passable anywhere above MacManus's.

Yours, truly,

W. T. SHERMAN, Major General.

Major General KILPATRICK, Lancaster.

HEADQUARTERS MILITARY DIVISION OF THE MISSISSIPPI,
In the field, Finley's Bridge, Lynch's Creek, March 1, 1865.

GENERAL : General Slocum has the 20th corps across Lynch's creek and a good bridge. General Davis is across the Catawba, and ought to be about fifteen miles behind us. To-morrow all will move forward fifteen miles, which will bring us near Chesterfield, next day at Cheraw ; General Davis, in the mean time, closing his gap. Push General Blair straight on Cheraw. With the 15th corps move on the same point, careful to reach the railroad below Cheraw and break it ; then on Cheraw. We will cross to the north of Cheraw. The enemy cannot hold Cheraw against us, because it is on a branch road, and we can insulate it. Johnston, if there, will not fight with a bridge behind him. We may have to cross the Pedee with a serious enemy in front, but we must not allow the confederates time to fortify Cheraw.

I know Hampton was, in person, above Lancaster, also Wheeler. I had an original communication from Wade Hampton yesterday, and he is still watching Kilpatrick, who is at Lancaster, till Davis gets past. Push with all energy straight on Cheraw, cutting its roads below, and I will be up on the 3d instant.

Yours, truly,

W. T. SHERMAN,
Major General Commanding.

General O. O. HOWARD,
Commanding Right Wing.

———

HEADQUARTERS MILITARY DIVISION OF THE MISSISSIPPI,
In the field, March 2, 1865.

GENERAL : The 20th corps is now starting from Big Lynch's creek for Chesterfield, twenty miles distant. The 14th corps is now at Little Lynch's creek, behind us, and will march by MacManus's bridge towards Chesterfield.

General Howard was, on the 28th February, across Lynch's creek, at Tiller's, and General Blair within sixteen miles of Cheraw. All move on Cheraw, where it is said the Charleston and Wilmington garrison are expecting to meet us. I don't believe they will fight on this side the Pedee, but you may move on General Davis's left, near Chesterfield, and by the time you get there I can select the points of crossing ; but if there be any enemy at Cheraw he will, of course, break the bridge there, and force us to use pontoons, in which case we will probably use Cheraw and Sneedsboro'.

General Howard sent his company of scouts from Tiller's towards the Charleston and Wilmington road, but they met two brigades of cavalry near Mount Elon Post Office, and were driven back. General Howard reports Hampton's headquarters at Darlington, but I doubt it. I don't think the enemy would leave his cavalry or any material part of it between us and the sea. Doubtless he is watching and using the railroad east and south of us, but to what extent I cannot conjecture until I know whether our people have Wilmington. I suppose that Schofield, by this time, must be on the railroad north of Wilmington at or near Goldsboro'.

Keep near General Davis's left, and act defensively till we know about Cheraw. I will be with the 20th corps, near Chesterfield, where the Lancaster road meets this, about four miles this side of Chesterfield. I will send infantry to Chesterfield to secure, if possible, the bridges across Thompson's creek, near that place. To-morrow at Cheraw.

You should be to-night on Lynch's creek, and to-morrow near Chesterfield.

Roads are sandy and good. Enemy leaves us good bridges, and thus far we find not even pickets. General Blair found some cavalry on his road, who gave ground easily.

Yours, &c.,

W. T. SHERMAN,
Major General Commanding.

General KILPATRICK, *near Lancaster.*

HEADQUARTERS MILITARY DIVISION OF THE MISSISSIPPI,
In the field, Chesterfield, S. C., March 3, 1865—6 a. m.

GENERAL : I got your despatch from Blakeney's last night. I want you to interpose between Charlotte and Cheraw until we are across. General Blair's head of column was thirteen miles southwest of Cheraw last night. General Jackson's division of the 20th corps pushed Butler's cavalry at a run through Chesterfield and across the bridges of Thompson's creek, saving the one on the Wadesboro' road, excepting one post, which the enemy had time to cut. The other bridge on the Cheraw road was burned. The balance of the corps is pretty well strung out by reason of the roads. I don't know exactly where General Davis is, but will direct him on Sneedsboro', and would like you to report to me the nature of the roads, especially the one from Mount Croghan, by Sinclair. By the way, what is your true position, and you should get a party over on the plank road on the line of Jones's creek, and cut off any courier line from Wadesboro'. I think Hardee will try and escape towards Wadesboro', and in that event you will strike his flank ; anyhow I want you to let go everything and cut his column, reporting to me that I may throw infantry across ; but until I hear the exact state of matters at Cheraw, will move the right wing on Cheraw and left wing on Sneedsboro'. I don't much care now what Beauregard does. He has no railroad now to circulate on, and must foot it, as we do ; but he has not the trains that we have, and he can move more rapidly than we. I want, of course, to get across Pedee, and will then fight him where he pleases, and don't care for his Virginia re-enforcements ; we have to meet them some time, and now as well as later. Only let me know in advance as much as possible the route or routes on which his infantry moves. His cavalry gives no clue by which I can judge. My belief, however, is, that Beauregard is tied to a railroad, and that railroad will be from Charlotte to Danville. I have no doubt that Wilmington is, or soon will be, in our hands, and, moreover, that Schofield will, or has, made a lodgement on the Goldsboro' road. A mere strong picket of observation towards Monroe to give General Davis notice of the approach of danger will suffice. The bulk of your force should be north of Thompson's creek from Burche's up towards Jones's creek. Reconnoitring parties should examine Pedee from Jones's creek down, but do nothing to show a purpose to cross.

Yours, truly,

W. T. SHERMAN,
Major General.

Major General KILPATRICK,
Commanding Cavalry.

HEADQUARTERS MILITARY DIVISION OF THE MISSISSIPPI,
In the field, Chesterfield, S. C., March 3, 1865—7 a. m.

GENERAL : General Kilpatrick reports that he is near Blakeney's, and will move to-day around the head of Thompson's creek, to the neighborhood of Sinclair, and reconnoitre well across to the Pedee. General Blair also reports from his position thirteen miles from Cheraw, on the Camden road. General Howard halted him there until the 15th corps got up in supporting distance. The 15th corps has been delayed by all sorts of mishaps occasioned by high water, but General Blair, pursuant to my orders, is moving straight on Cheraw. I want you to finish up the two bridges here; get up your troops from the rear, and move the 20th corps towards Cheraw, north of Thompson's creek, until you know General Blair is in Cheraw, when it will work across to the plank road and up to Sneedsboro', where I design your wing and the cavalry to cross over. You may instruct General Davis to move on Sneedsboro' at once, but I don't see as he can do better than to come here and use your upper bridge, unless he gets better roads and more forage by Mount Croghan, Sinclair, MacQuaig's, &c.

I believe that Hardee is at Cheraw with his Charleston garrison, and it may be part of the Wilmington force, but I rather think these latter will be used to meet Schofield about Goldsboro', but I want Hardee attacked rapidly and boldly, if in any position this side of the Pedee. If he makes the mistake to fight on this side, we ought to catch him. I have instructed General Kilpatrick to get a brigade of cavalry across to the plank road at once, to observe and attack any force moving on that road from any direction. If Hardee tries to escape towards Wadesboro', we must let go our trains and attack him in flank. I think Beauregard without many wagons is tied to his Charlotte and Danville railroad. He would not dare depend on the coast road, held as it is and threatened at Goldsboro'. Let us get across the Pedee at all hazards, as soon as possible, and then we are all right with Fayetteville as our objective, and the Cape Fear river as an alternate base of operations.

Yours,

W. T. SHERMAN, *Major General.*

Major General SLOCUM.
Commanding Left Wing.

Headquarters Military Division of the Mississippi,
In the field, Chesterfield, S. C., March 3, 1865—2½ p. m.

GENERAL: Your despatch of 3.30 p. m. yesterday from Black creek is just received. I wrote this a. m. to General Blair a letter to be sent to you, which may reach you before this, but will repeat.

General Slocum took Chesterfield yesterday, driving Butler's cavalry to and through the town, but the enemy broke one of the bridges and burned the other. Both are now repaired, and General Slocum will push one division down on the north bank so as to uncover your crossing; but send me word as soon as you are over that the 20th corps may cross over to the Pedee towards Sneedsboro', where I want his wing and the cavalry to cross. Of course I am a little impatient to get across Pedee before Beauregard can swing around from Charlotte and Salisbury and oppose our crossing. Once across the Pedee I don't fear the whole confederate army, for, if need be, we can swing in against the right bank of Cape Fear, and work down until we meet our people; but I shall aim to reach Fayetteville and Goldsboro', where I know Schofield must now be.

I have ordered General Davis from MacManus' bridge *via* Mount Croghan to Sneedsboro', and Kilpatrick is above him towards Wadesboro'. Roads are very bad up here, either quick-sand or red clay. The country is also poor; still, thus far we find forage, bacon, and corn-meal.

I met at Winnsboro' Mrs. Aiken, wife of the very Colonel Aiken you report as killed in the fight with Duncan. She was a Miss Gayle, of Mobile, sister of Mrs. General Gorgas, of the rebel ordnance department. In her conversation with me she said she supposed her husband would have to "submit" or get killed, and I answered her that "such was the case," but I hardly thought so soon to be a prophet.

I will send your letter to General Slocum with instructions to read it, and push one or two divisions down towards Cheraw as fast as possible, leaving his wagons near the Sneedsboro' road.   I will stay here to-night, and to-morrow go down in hopes to go into Cheraw.   I don't believe Hardee will fight on this side the river, and it is now too late for him to slip out by way of Wadesboro'.

Your rear division will have plenty of time to close up while you are getting your crossing secured and bridged.   I take it all the bridges across Thompson's creek are gone, unless it be the railroad bridge, which may have been spared for the sake of the rebel wounded that must still be there.   I also feel confident that Wilmington is in our possession, and that none of its garrison is at Cheraw.

Yours, truly,

W. T. SHERMAN,
Major General.

Major General HOWARD,
Commanding Right Wing.

HEADQUARTERS MILITARY DIVISION OF THE MISSISSIPPI,
In the field, Chesterfield, S. C., March 3, 1865—5.45 p. m.

GENERAL: Your despatch from Cheraw to the general-in chief is received. He has written you twice to-day, viz., once direct, and once through General Blair; and he desires me to say those letters contain his views and wishes as regards immediate operations, *i. e.*, for you to concentrate your command at Cheraw, and make a crossing of, and lodgement beyond the Pedee with all possible despatch, as it is all-important that we at once hold its left bank.

If you think you will have time, the general would like to have you send any kind of a force from the rear portion of your command, (probably mounted would be the best,) down to Florence, with directions to destroy everything of public property there.   We will come into Cheraw to-morrow morning.

It is not probable there is much of an enemy at Florence.

I am, general, with respect, &c.,

L. M. DAYTON,
Assistant Adjutant General.

Major General HOWARD,
Commanding Army of the Tennessee.

HEADQUARTERS MILITARY DIVISION OF THE MISSISSIPPI,
In the field, Chesterfield, S. C., March 3, 1865.

GENERAL: To-morrow the general-in-chief will move into Cheraw and join the army of the Tennessee.   He wishes you to proceed and cross the Pedee with your command at Sneedsboro', as soon as possible, and also directs me to say he will make full orders at Cheraw for the next movement.

I am, general, with respect, &c.,

L. M. DAYTON,
Assistant Adjutant General.

Major General H. W. SLOCUM,
Commanding Left Wing.

HEADQUARTERS MILITARY DIVISION OF THE MISSISSIPPI,
In the field, Cheraw, S. C., March 4, 1865—8 p. m.

GENERAL: I got here at 10 a. m., and found the 17th corps in town, and laying a pontoon bridge across the Pedee. The 15th corps is also here, and their trains are coming in all safe. The bridge is down; one division (Mower's) is across, and is skirmishing about two miles out.

Hardee commanded here, and had, it is said, about fifteen thousand men, but I doubt if he had more than the Charleston garrison and S. D. Lee's corps, in all ten thousand. There was a gunboat here that had come up when the Yankees got Georgetown, but it was blown up to-day, about six miles down the river. There is a good deal of property here, such as guns, (25,) ammunition, &c., and more of a town than I expected to find.

General Howard has sent a mounted force to destroy property at and near Florence, which cannot return before the day after to-morrow, by which time I think he can have all his command across. Of course, the sooner we reach Fayetteville the better, but we must move in compact masses, as either column may encounter the whole of Hardee's command, and it may be re-enforced by some from Charleston. I have no doubt that Schofield is at work in North Carolina. I feel assured he is fully possessed of my views, and will have Goldsboro', with both the Wilmington and Newbern roads, done by the 15th instant, the day appointed. Still, it is but prudent to continue, as heretofore, to collect all the food possible, in case we are delayed thereabouts. There is a story afloat that six thousand of Schofield's men are already at Fayetteville, which will be a great success, better than we expected; but I know General Grant will spare no efforts to second us; he is fully alive to the importance of our movements.

Get your bridge down, and cross over as fast as possible, and stretch out on the roads you want, and I will order General Howard to conform to you. If you can get out ten miles during all Tuesday, it will be as much as I expect.

Yours, truly,

W. T. SHERMAN,
Major General Commanding.

Major General SLOCUM, *Commanding Left Wing.*

HEADQUARTERS MILITARY DIVISION OF THE MISSISSIPPI,
In the field, Cheraw, S. C., March 4, 1865—8 p. m.

GENERAL: I have just received your note, and the copy of your orders. I would not be surprised if it were true that some of Schofield's command were at Fayetteville. I know General Grant's anxiety for us, and he will move heaven and earth to co-operate. Your orders are all right. I have written to General Slocum, who is at Sneedsboro', and he will use the roads by Mark's creek and McFarland's bridge, and all roads north of it. It may be well for you to let General Slocum have a day's start, that the column may assume an echelon towards the north. General Slocum can hardly have all across earlier than Tuesday, and I have intimated that I would like him to be ten miles out during all Tuesday. The river with him seems to be wider than with you.

Get a good scout or two ready for me to send a message to Wilmington as soon as any of your heads of columns are across Lumber river.

Yours, truly,

W. T. SHERMAN,
Major General Commanding

Major General HOWARD,
Commanding Right Wing.

22*

HEADQUARTERS MILITARY DIVISION OF THE MISSISSIPPI,
In the field, Cheraw, S. C., March 5, 1865.

GENERAL: I was on the point of making an order for the next movement, but on looking over my last, No. 16, I find it covers the ground up to our next objective. You have the choice of roads, and I understand from Captain Ludlow that you want McFarland's and Love's bridges. All right. Let General Davis lead into Fayetteville, holding the 20th corps in support, with the cavalry on his left rear. I will hold General Howard back, but close enough to come up if Johnston wants to fight. I will now fight him if he dare, and, therefore, wish you to act on that idea, keeping each corps ready to hold the enemy if he appears in force on your left, but his strength must be developed before other corps are called from their roads. I have notified General Howard of this order, and he has simply asked, instead of holding on here to make slow marches, to gather forage and meal. I send you a copy of his orders of march. I also send you an open letter for General Kilpatrick, which read and forward to him. Major Audenreid, of my staff, left him yesterday ten miles this side of Wadesboro', and my orders to him were to hold his command, covering all roads, especially the plank road between Wadesboro' and your troops. After you have got a covering force across the Pedee, let Kilpatrick have the bridge, and move out to your left front—say Rockingham. We have been badly treated by the weather, but I hope for a better spell henceforth.

I will get messages through to Wilmington the moment any head of column is across Lumber creek, and feel sure that Schofield will meet us in force at Goldsboro'. I will draw from Savannah, Charleston, and Wilmington at least twenty-five thousand men to re-enforce our army at Goldsboro', and will put them under Schofield, as the centre or reserve, restoring the organization of the Atlanta campaign. With that army replenished and refreshed we can make things move. Indeed, I feel confident that nothing can now stand before us. I find here additional signs of discomfiture; three thousand six hundred barrels of powder are among our spoils, and the surgeons of the confederate hospitals admit that Hardee left them without supplies, or even orders. Keep me well advised of progress, and I will make things conform to your movements.

I am, &c.,

W. T. SHERMAN,
Major General Commanding.

Major General SLOCUM,
Commanding Left Wing.

HEADQUARTERS MILITARY DIVISION OF THE MISSISSIPPI,
In the field, Cheraw, S. C., March 5, 1865.

GENERAL: I was on the point of making a new general order of movement, but on examining my last, No. 16, I find it provides for the next stage. General Howard has crossed here, and is now passing trains and troops, but I will hold him back to allow General Slocum to lead to Fayetteville.

General Howard has sent some mounted infantry down to Florence to damage things there, and they cannot return until to-morrow. In the mean time General Slocum will pass over and move out on roads leading to McFarland's and Love's bridges. I will hold the right wing back, and in reserve, keeping on roads to the south of General Slocum. As soon as he has a covering force across the Peedee he will notify you and give you his bridge, when move out to Rockingham, and thence conform to his movements, getting up to Solemn Grove, and thence along down south of Little river to the roads coming into Fayetteville from Manchester.

There is a rumor here that General Schofield is already at Fayetteville.   It is certain he took Wilmington not by the evacuation of the place, but by force, capturing Haygood's brigade.   This simplifies our work very much, and will give me large re-enforcements as soon as I need them.

Hardee left here in haste and confusion, going across Pedee and burning the bridge, but we have already a pontoon bridge across, and two divisions out a couple miles.   Butler's division of cavalry is with him.   The enemy left here valuable stores, twenty-four good guns, three thousand six hundred barrels powder, two thousand muskets, the hospitals, and much ammunition and stores.

I don't think Joe Johnston will try to concentrate his forces this side of Raleigh.

Your, truly,

W. T. SHERMAN,
Major General Commanding.

General KILPATRICK,
Commanding Cavalry.

HEADQUARTERS MILITARY DIVISION OF THE MISSISSIPPI,
In the field, Cheraw, S. C., March 6, 1865.

GENERAL: I shall, in person, to-day cross the Pedee, and go out on the main Fayetteville road about five miles, to the point of Phill's creek where are encamped two divisions of the 15th corps.   There I shall await the fact that you are all across and off for Fayetteville, and will try and hold the right wing ready to turn to you in case Johnston attempts to strike you in flank, or to move on towards Fayetteville, aiming to arrive there at or near about the same time with your rear.   I propose your command should first enter and occupy Fayetteville, and secure the bridge, if possible; otherwise to make a lodgement across with pontoons.   En route break the railroad which is known as the Wilmington and Charlotte; but it is only partially down to Rockingham.   It is of little importance, but being on it, we might as well use up some of its iron.   At its depots you may find some corn and meal.

On approaching Fayetteville you may give out that if the bridge is destroyed we will deal harshly by the town; but if there be no positive resistance, and if the enemy spare the bridge, I wish the town to be dealt with generously.   Of course we will dispose of all public stores and property, but will spare private houses.   Use wheat, corn, meal, bacon, animals, wagons, &c., needed by your command, but try and keep the foragers from insulting families, by word or rudeness.   It might be well to instruct your brigade commanders that we are now out of South Carolina, and that a little moderation may be of political consequence to us in North Carolina.

At Fayetteville, if we can secure boats of any kind, even coal-flats, I will send down Cape Fear river the bulk of the refugees, white and black, which swells our numbers and consumes the food necessary for our combatants.   I have no doubt of having daily intercourse with you by courier or in person, and only name these points that you may initiate measures to accomplish these ends.

The enemy has abandoned many caissons loaded with ammunition, on his route of retreat, and if you can push or threaten him about Rockingham I doubt not he will drop more.   The moment General Davis strikes the plank road he should push with all possible speed into Fayetteville.

Yours, truly,

W. T. SHERMAN,
Major General Commanding.

Major General SLOCUM,
Commanding Left Wing, Sneedsboro'.

HEADQUARTERS MILITARY DIVISION OF THE MISSISSIPPI,
In the field, near Cheraw, S. C., March 6, 1865.

GENERAL: A copy of your orders, issued at Easterling's for to-morrow's movement, enclosed to the general-in-chief, has been received. The general desires me to say the order is satisfactory to him, and in modification has only instructed General Logan to remain in his present camp until such time as the 20th corps, now passing, can get by him on to the left-hand road *via* Clark's creek.

I am, general, yours with respect,

L. M. DAYTON,
Assistant Adjutant General.

Major General HOWARD,
Commanding Right Wing.

HEADQUARTERS MILITARY DIVISION OF THE MISSISSIPPI,
In the field, Camp on Fayetteville Road,
13 *miles from Cheraw, March* 7, 1865.

GENERAL: Yours of this date, 11 a. m., is just received. I am well pleased to learn that Hardee is making well north. Though willing to fight Joe Johnston, who now commands in chief, I would prefer to work over to the new base, to clear our columns of the impediments and make junction with Schofield, who is, doubtless, working up towards Goldsboro'. If I can get that point secure, with both railroads down to Wilmington and Newbern, you will perceive what a base I will have. Raleigh will be easy of conquest, and we can drive all Carolina north of the Roanoke, where the concentrated armies of the Confederacy will have contracted foraging ground. But of that hereafter. Now I will make for Fayetteville, and only ask you to keep up the seeming appearance of pushing after Hardee, but really keep your command well in hand and the horses and men in the best possible order as to food and forage.

To-morrow night I will send messengers with my orders for Schofield, but shall aim to reach Goldsboro'. I don't want to make southing. Our infantry columns are doing well. I will let Davis enter Fayetteville first, and if the people will spare the bridge, I want all to be easy on the citizens; but if they burn bridges or bother us, we must go the whole figure. In conversation with people evince a determination to maintain the Union, but treat all other matters as beneath a soldier's notice. Give us a whole country with a government, and leave details to the lawyers.

Deal as moderately and fairly by the North Carolinians as possible, and fan the flame of discord already subsisting between them and their proud cousins of South Carolina. There never was much love between them. Touch upon the chivalry running away, always leaving their families for us to feed and protect, and then on purpose accusing us of all sorts of rudeness.

I expect to reach Fayetteville by Saturday, and I will determine as quick as possible what is next for you, but I don't see as you can do better than hold on that flank. There is a body of infantry and cavalry left down in the pocket about Florence that might be caught, but it won't pay to chase them. Horse flesh is too precious. Keep your horses in the best order for the day when we must have a big fight; not, however, on this turn.

Yours,

W. T. SHERMAN,
Major General Commanding.

General KILPATRICK,
Commanding Cavalry, Rockingham.

[Cipher.]

HEADQUARTERS MILITARY DIVISION OF THE MISSISSIPPI,
In the field, Laurel Hill, N. C., Wednesday, March 8, 1865.
COMMANDING OFFICER, *Wilmington, N. C.:*

We are marching on Fayetteville; will be there Saturday, Sunday, and Monday, and then will march for Goldsboro'.

If possible, send a boat up Cape Fear river, and have word conveyed to General Schofield that I expect to meet him about Goldsboro'. We are all well and have done finely. The rain makes our roads difficult and may delay me about Fayetteville, in which case I would like to have some bread, sugar, and coffee; we have abundance of all else. I expect to reach Goldsboro' by the 20th instant.

W. T. SHERMAN,
Major General.

HEADQUARTERS MILITARY DIVISION OF THE MISSISSIPPI,
In the field, Bethel Church, 26 miles from Fayetteville, N. C.,
March 10, 1865—2 p. m.

GENERAL: Yours of 11.20 is just received. The heavy rain last night caught Hazen's train in a swamp, and he has had to corduroy five miles, and his train is not up yet. General Corse is behind him, just on this side of Lumber river. I will come on in the morning as fast as possible, but you may go on, ready to support General Slocum, who reports, that he will be ready to enter Fayetteville to-morrow. I have no doubt Johnston will try and get some troops to oppose, and it is well for us to anticipate his preparations, and therefore you may push so as to threaten the town on the southwest. Let General Blair take from the plank road to the river the two divisions of the 15th corps on the direct road communicating with Williams on the left, but let Slocum break into town.

I will send a staff officer to him at daylight with orders to shove right in and push for the bridge.

I think if the enemy fights us with a bridge to his rear, he commits a mistake, of which we must take immediate advantage.

If any cause delay me have preparations made at once to cross over to the east bank of Cape Fear, below the town, but we will pause thereabouts until we can get some real news from Wilmington. You may send any number of messengers to convey the intelligence that we are hereabouts, all well, and bound for Goldsboro,' unless necessity force us toward Wilmington.

I regret that this column has lost this day, but it seems inevitable.

Yours,

W. T. SHERMAN,
Major General Commanding.

Major General HOWARD,
Commanding Right Wing.

HEADQUARTERS MILITARY DIVISION OF THE MISSISSIPPI,
In the field, Raft Swamp, N. C., March 10, 1865.

GENERAL: The heavy rain of last night caught the column with which I am in the swamp, which is bottomless, and has to be cleared and corduroyed for miles to let the trains and artillery pass.

The 17th corps is now at Rockfish creek, and will have time to repair the bridges and push into Fayetteville to-morrow, Saturday. I want you to go in first ; this you can do in your own way, but General Howard will have the 17th corps and two divisions of the 15th corps near enough to support. Do all that is possible to secure the bridge across Cape Fear; but if, as I suppose will be the case, the enemy burn it, effect a lodgement at once across, and make a pontoon bridge with a brigade across intrenched. We will wait there some days. Destroy nothing until I meet you unless there be special reason that you know I will approve. I will try and be near you at sunset.

Should it be that Johnston has resolved to defend Fayetteville with a large force, it is to our interest, and you can engage his attention on the north and northwest, while General Howard closes in to the southwest. Avoid intrenchments, but make haste to prevent the making of them.

I send you this message, which may seem superfluous, but I am with troops delayed by the swamp, and cannot afford to leave anything to chance. I have sent messengers and orders to Wilmington.

I set much store on a lodgement east of Cape Fear river, and would advise your having the pontoons convenient.

The weather is now clearing away, and will give us, I hope, some days of sunshine. Our roads here are swampy in the extreme, but yours, I hope, have proven better.

Yours, &c.,

W. T. SHERMAN,
Major General Commanding.

Major General SLOCUM,
Commanding Left Wing.

HEADQUARTERS MILITARY DIVISION OF THE MISSISSIPPI,
In the field, Fayetteville, N. C., March 11, 1865.

GENERAL : I have just received your report, and read it with great satisfaction. I feared it was more, as the enemy claims from two to four hundred prisoners, which were conducted through Fayetteville. You may rest a couple of days, and then be ready to cross the river. I think there are some of the enemy that failed to escape across the bridge. You might send a strong foraging party up to the Little river bridge, and burn the railroad bridge. The enemy have sent a good deal of ordnance up towards the coal mines on the railroad. I would like to have it and the cars and the locomotives destroyed, but can hardly spare time. We will lay the pontoons to-morrow and cross on Monday. I am at the arsenal. I did not get a despatch from you at Solemn Grove.

Yours, &c.,

W. T. SHERMAN,
Major General Commanding.

General KILPATRICK,
Commanding Cavalry.

HEADQUARTERS MILITARY DIVISION OF THE MISSISSIPPI,
In the field, Fayetteville, N. C., March 11, 1865.

Major General TERRY, *Wilmington :*

I have just received your despatch of the 7th. We entered Fayetteville to-day, Hardee retreating eastward with twenty thousand men, and burning the bridge across Cape Fear river. We will cross the river to-morrow and start for Goldsboro' on Tuesday. You can calculate the time of my arrival by the weather. I will strike the Wilmington railroad about Faison's. We are all well, and have destroyed a vast amount of stores, and done the enemy irreparable damage. I will destroy the arsenal utterly. I want everything concentrated at or as near Goldsboro' as possible, with the railroad finished as near as possible.

We have a large number of negroes and refugees that I may send to Wilmington.

W. T. SHERMAN,
Major General.

[By scout.]

Headquarters Military Division of the Mississippi,
In the field, Fayetteville, N. C., March 11, 1865.

General Terry, Wilmington, N. C.:

I may send a train of wagons down the road along Cape Fear river to convey refugees and negroes that have followed my army from South Carolina.

Please ask Admiral Porter to have some gunboats feel up Cape Fear river as high as Elizabeth City, or at all events as high up as the wreck of the Chicamauga, at Indian Wells. The rebels burned their steamboats here.

W. T. SHERMAN,
Major General.

Headquarters Military Division of the Mississippi,
In the field, Fayetteville, N. C., March 12, 1865.

General: I have just received your message by the tug which left Wilmington at 2 p. m. yesterday, and arrived here without trouble. The scout who brought me your cipher message started back last night with my answers, which are superseded by the fact of your opening the river.

General Howard just reports that he has secured one of the enemy's steamboats below the city, and General Slocum will try to secure two known to be above, and we will load them with refugees, white and black, which have clung to our skirts, impeded our movements, and consumed our food.

We have swept the country well from Savannah here, and my men and animals are in fine condition. Had it not been for the foul weather, I would have caught Hardee at Cheraw, or here; but at Columbia, Cheraw, and here, we got immense stores, and have destroyed machinery, guns, ammunition, and property, of inestimable value to our enemy. At all points he has fled from us, " standing not on the order of his going."

The people of South Carolina, instead of feeding Lee's army, will now call on Lee to feed them.

I want you to send me all the shoes, stockings, drawers, sugar, coffee, and flour, you can spare; finish the loads with oats or corn. Have the boats escorted and let them run at nights at any risk. We must not lose time for Joe Johnston to concentrate at Goldsboro'. We cannot prevent his concentrating at Raleigh, but he shall have no rest. I want General Schofield to go on with his railroad from Newbern as far as he can, and you do the same from Wilmington. If we can get the roads to, and secure Goldsboro' by April 10, it will be soon enough, but every day now is worth a million of dollars. I can whip Joe Johnston provided he don't catch one of my corps in flank, and I will see that my army marches hence to Goldsboro' in compact form.

I must rid my army of from twenty to thirty thousand useless mouths; as many to go down Cape Fear as possible, and balance to go in the vehicles and on captured horses *via* Clinton to Wilmington.

I thank you for the energetic action that has marked your course, and shall be most happy to meet you.

I am truly your friend,

W. T. SHERMAN,
Major General.

Major General TERRY,
Commanding U. S. Forces, Wilmington, N. C.

HEADQUARTERS MILITARY DIVISION OF THE MISSISSIPPI,
In the field, Fayetteville, N. C., March 12, 1865.

DEAR GENERAL: We reached this place yesterday at noon—Hardee, as usual, retreating across the Cape Fear, burning his bridge but our pontoons will be up to-day, and with as little delay as possible I will be after him towards Goldsboro'.

A tug has just come up from Wilmington, and before I get off from here I hope to get up from Wilmington some shoes and stockings, sugar, coffee, and flour. We are abundantly supplied in all else, having in a measure lived off the country.

The army is in splendid health, condition, and spirit, though we have had foul weather and roads that would have stopped travel to almost any other body of men I ever heard of.

Our march was substantially what I designed—straight on Columbia, feigning on Branchville and Augusta. We destroyed, in passing, the railroad from the Edisto nearly up to Aiken; again from Orangeburg to the Congaree; again from Columbia down to Kingsville and the Wateree, and up towards Charlotte as far as the Chester line; thence I turned east on Cheraw, and thence to Fayetteville. At Columbia we destroyed immense arsenals and railroad establishments, among which were forty-three cannon. At Cheraw we found also machinery and material of war from Charleston, among which twenty-five guns and three thousand six hundred barrels of powder, and here we find about twenty guns and a magnificent United States arsenal.

We cannot afford to leave detachments, and I shall, therefore, destroy this valuable arsenal, for the enemy shall not have its use; and the United States should never again confide such valuable property to a people who have betrayed a trust.

I could leave here to-morrow, but want to clean my columns of the vast crowd of refugees and negroes that encumber me; some I will send down the river in boats, and the balance I will send to Wilmington by land under small escort as soon as we are across Cape Fear river.

I hope you have not been uneasy about us, and that the fruits of this march will be appreciated. It had to be made not only to secure the valuable depots by the way, but its incidents, in the necessary fall of Charleston, Georgetown, and Wilmington. If I can now add Goldsboro' without too much cost, I will be in position to aid you materially in the spring campaign.

Joe Johntson may try to interpose between me here and Schofield about New-bern; but I think he will not try that, but concentrate his scattered armies at Raleigh, and I will go straight at him as soon as I get my men reclothed and our wagons reloaded.

Keep everybody busy and let Stoneman push towards Greensboro' or Charlotte from Knoxville; even a feint in that quarter will be most important.

The railroad from Charlotte to Danville is all that is left the enemy, and it won't do for me to go there on account of the red clay hills, that are impassable to wheels in wet weather.

I expect to make a junction with General Schofield in ten days.

Yours, truly,

W. T. SHERMAN, *Major General.*

Lieut. General U. S. GRANT,
Commanding United States Army, City Point.

HEADQUARTERS MILITARY DIVISION OF THE MISSISSIPPI,
In the field, Fayetteville, N. C., March 12, 1865.

GENERAL : We reached this place yesterday without opposition. Our march was exactly as I expected, and its fruits all I could have asked for. We have destroyed vast magazines at Columbia, Cheraw, and here, and have destroyed effectually the railroad system of South Carolina.

From Cheraw I sent a small cavalry force to Florence, but it found a force of infantry and cavalry more than it could match, and had to return, breaking only the railroad trestles down as far as Darlington. The enemy still has much railroad stock and munitions on the track about Sumterville and Florence, and if you can make up a force of two thousand five hundred men out of your Charleston and Savannah garrisons, I want you to reach that road and destroy everything possible, and exhaust the country of supplies. The best points of departure are Georgetown and the Santee bridge. I think Admiral Dahlgren could send some light gunboats up the Santee, but don't know enough about the bar. The distance from Georgetown does not exceed sixty miles, and we look on sixty miles as a pleasant excursion. As soon as you accomplish this, reduce your garrisons at Savannah and Charleston to the minimum, and re-enforce the movement on Goldsboro', which is the real objective now. I expect to be there in ten days.

My army is in splendid health and condition, and we have had no battle involving more than a single brigade or division at a time. Our foragers have had plenty of fighting on a limited scale, and have gathered more bacon, chickens, turkeys, and corn-meal than I believed were in the country. We are now only short of bread, sugar, and coffee, and our men have been so much in the mud and water that shoes and stockings are scarce. Send to Goldsboro', *via* Newbern, all the clothing you can spare.

I am truly your friend,

W. T. SHERMAN,
Major General Commanding.

Major General FOSTER,
Commanding Department of the South, Charleston, S. C.

HEADQUARTERS MILITARY DIVISION OF THE MISSISSIPPI,
In the field, Fayetteville, N. C., Sunday, March 12, 1865.

GENTLEMEN : We need, very much, shoes, stockings, drawers, and pants ; also flour, bread, sugar, and coffee; all else we have in abundance. I cannot afford to stay here longer than Wednesday. The river is now high, and if you, or either of you, are in Wilmington, send from there what you can of such articles as I have mentioned, to the capacity of the boats you have at disposal. Do not draw from Newbern, but collect there the great depot, especially, of forage and clothing. My command will need an entire equipment of clothing. We have been in water half the time since leaving Savannah, and consequently the clothing is worn out. We have not lost a wagon, and our animals are in good condition; but I take it for granted we shall find little or no forage about Goldsboro'.

The moment you hear I am approaching Goldsboro' forward to meet me with clothing and bread, sugar and coffee, and empty wagons will meet them.

We have made a hard and extraordinary march, and achieved all I could expect. We are in good health and fighting condition.

Yours, truly,

W. T. SHERMAN,
Major General Commanding.

Generals EASTON and BECKWITH, or either,
at *Wilmington, North Carolina.*

HEADQUARTERS MILITARY DIVISION OF THE MISSISSIPPI,
In the field, Fayetteville, N. C., Sunday, March 12, 1865.

GENERAL: We reached here yesterday, and will be delayed until Tuesday or Wednesday putting down pontoons. I will destroy utterly the arsenal and other public property, and I hope to get up some shoes and small stores from Wilmington before we leave. I will then march in compact order straight for the bridge across Neuse river, south of Goldsboro'. I expect to make junction with you thereabouts. If I don't find you there I will feel towards Kinston and Newbern. I will need clothing and provisions. We have gathered plenty of cattle and bacon, and a good deal of cornmeal and molasses. We have also found plenty of corn and fodder, and my animals are all in good order. I will have trains enough for you. I have plenty wagons and mules for one hundred thousand men, so you need not bring any from the north.

On making junction with you, I want you to make your command twenty-five thousand, and will call it the centre, thus restoring our old Atlanta organization. Go on repairing the railroad towards Goldsboro', and let Terry repair the Wilmington road northward as far as he can—if possible, to the Neuse. I will get the navy to patrol Cape Fear river, so as to make the Wilmington and Goldsboro' road safe. You must judge as to the mode and manner of covering the railroad from Goldsboro' to Newbern.

I have ordered General Foster to diminish his garrison of Savannah, Charleston, and Wilmington to the minimum, and re-enforce the movement from Newbern on Goldsboro'. I really do not know if any change has been made in the command on the seaboard; but whether you or Foster command, I want the foregoing policy to be adopted. If I find that holding Savannah, Charleston, and Wilmington cost us too many men, I would not hesitate to destroy them, and use the garrisons in the field. It will be time enough to build up the country when war is over.

Keep your command well concentrated, on the defensive, advancing as fast as the road is built; but reach Goldsboro', if possible, and fortify.

Hardee crossed here with a force represented at twenty thousand, but I don't see the signs of that many; he has six batteries of four guns each. I suppose Johnston may have up about Greensboro', now moving to Raleigh, ten thousand, and I estimate Hokes's command at eight thousand. All told, he may concentrate at Raleigh forty to forty-five thousand men. I can whip that number with my present force, and with yours and Terry's added we can go wherever we can live. We can live where the people do, and if anybody has to suffer let them suffer.

Collect all the forage you can at Newbern; also provisions and clothing. We will need an immense supply of clothing, for we have been working from knee to waist deep in water for four hundred miles, and our men will need reclothing throughout.

Organize your command into divisions of about five thousand men each, but don't embrace any men rightfully belonging to the organizations now with me, but order them at once to join their proper brigades and divisions on our arrival at your neighborhood.

We have had so much bad weather in February and March that I hope we may now count on a change for the better.

Hoping to meet you in person in ten days, I am your friend,

W. T. SHERMAN,
Major General Commanding.

Major General SCHOFIELD,
Commanding at Newbern, North Carolina.

HEADQUARTERS MILITARY DIVISION OF THE MISSISSIPPI,
In the field, Fayetteville, N. C., Sunday, March 12, 1865.

DEAR SIR: I know you will be pleased to hear that my army has reached this point and have opened communication with Wilmington. A tug-boat came up this morning and will start back at 6 p. m.

I have written a letter to General Grant, the substance of which he will doubtless communicate, and it must suffice for me to tell you what I know will give you pleasure; that I have done all I proposed, and the fruits seem to me ample for the time employed. Charleston, Georgetown, and Wilmington are incidents, while the utter demolition of the railroad system of South Carolina, and the utter destruction of the enemy's arsenals of Columbia, Cheraw, and Fayetteville, are the principals of the movement. These points were regarded as inaccessible to us, and now no place in the confederacy is safe against the army of the west. Let Lee hold on to Richmond, and we will destroy his country; and then of what use is Richmond? He must come out and fight us on open ground, and for that we must ever be ready. Let him stick behind his parapets and he will perish.

I remember well what you asked me, and think I am on the right road, though a long one. My army is as united and cheerful as ever, and as full of confidence in themselves and their leaders as ever. It is utterly impossible for me to enumerate what we have done, but enclose a slip just handed me, which is but partial.* At Columbia and Cheraw we destroyed nearly all the gunpowder and cartridges the confederacy had in this part of the country.

This arsenal is in fine order and much enlarged. I cannot leave a detachment to hold it, and therefore shall burn it; blow it up with gunpowder, and then with rams knock down its walls. I take it for granted the United States will never again trust Carolina with an arsenal to appropriate at her pleasure.

Hoping that good forture may still attend my army, I remain your servant,

W. T. SHERMAN,
Major General.

Hon. E. M. STANTON, *Secretary of War.*

HEADQUARTERS MILITARY DIVISION OF THE MISSISSIPPI,
In the field, Fayetteville, N. C., Sunday, March 12, 1865.

SIR: My army is here, the enemy having fled eastward across the river, burning his bridge, but I will have pontoons down to-day. I will be here probably till Wednesday, and would like some of your boats to come up for effect,

---

*43 guns at Columbia; 25 guns at Cheraw; 17 guns at Fayetteville; total 85, of which four-fifths are field guns, and all are serviceable, 50 field and seige gun carriages, 30 caissons, 5 battery wagons, 5 travelling forges.—(Memorandum of General Barry, chief of artillery.)

and, if agreeable, can give you a load of refugees or cotton, at pleasure. I would like to produce the effect of a design to establish a base, which, of course, I do not propose to do. Water will continue high some time.

Yours, truly,

W. T. SHERMAN,
Major General

The COMMANDING OFFICER GUNBOAT FLEET,
Cape Fear River.

HEADQUARTERS MILITARY DIVISION OF THE MISSISSIPPI,
In the field, Fayetteville, N. C., Sunday, March 12, 1865—5 p. m.

GENERAL: I have this moment received, at the hands of the two officers of the navy who came from Wilmington by canoes and land, your cipher despatch of March 4. I am marching for Goldsboro', and will start Wednesday. I wrote you fully to-day, and send by this same opportunity, viz: the tug-boat Davidson that came from Wilmington last night.

Yours, truly,

W. T. SHERMAN,
Major General Commanding.

Major General SCHOFIELD,
Newbern, N. C.

HEADQUARTERS MILITARY DIVISION OF THE MISSISSIPPI,
In the field, Fayetteville, N. C., Monday, March 13, 1865.

GENERAL: Colonel Kerwin reports from Elizabeth, where he has halted his regiment, having despatched two officers and fifty men through with your cipher despatch, which is now being unravelled. I wish you would send a boat up to Elizabeth with forage and rations for Colonel Kerwin's command, and order him to ferry his command across, and to push to the railroad, and up it until he encounters me about Faison's. Your own command should also move at once up towards Goldsboro', leaving the railroad construction party to follow, as the whole country south of Goldsboro', between the Cape Fear river and the sea, will be covered by our armies. You may be short of wagons. If you can manage to reach me I can supply you with, say, two hundred (200.) I will have enough wagons for General Schofield also. I want to concentrate all my available force about Goldsboro' as soon as possible. The single road from Newbern to Goldsboro' may not have a capacity sufficient for mine, and yours, and General Schofield's armies, and I wish you to advise General Schofield that I expect him to get boats, as quick as possible, that will enable us to use the Neuse river as auxilliary, as high up as possible, when our wagons can haul forage and stores.

I have with me, say, three thousand (3,000) wagons and near forty thousand (40,000) animals, about sixty-five thousand (65,000) fighting men.

Yours, truly,

W. T. SHERMAN,
Major General Commanding.

General TERRY, *Commanding, Wilmington.*

P. S.—If General Schofield wants you at Newbern, I do not object to your re-enforcing him, but I want all the troops not absolutely necessary for garrisons to be at or near Goldsboro' in seven (7) days, viz: by Monday or Tuesday of next week.

SHERMAN, *M. G.*

HEADQUARTERS MILITARY DIVISION OF THE MISSISSIPPI,
In the field, opposite Fayetteville, Tuesday, March 14, 1865.

DEAR GENERAL: I am now across Cape Fear river with nearly all my army save a division, with orders to cross at daylight to-morrow. I shall then draw out ten miles and begin my manœuvres for the possession of Goldsboro', which is all-important for our future purposes.

I was in hopes that I could get some shoes and stockings at Wilmington, but the tug Davidson has returned with Brigadier General Dodge, chief quartermaster, with word that there is no clothing there, but he brings us some forage, sugar, and coffee. I can get along for ten days, having forced the army to collect plenty of beef, and a good deal of corn-meal.

I shall to-night move my cavalry (5,000) straight towards Raleigh, and follow it with four divisions infantry, without trains, and keep the trains off toward the right rear I will hold another four divisions in close support, and move toward Smithfield, or to strike the railroad half-way between Goldsboro' and Raleigh; then, when my trains are well across towards the Neuse, will move rapidly to Bentonville, and afterwards, at leisure, move opposite Goldsboro', and open direct communication with General Schofield, who is ordered to push against Kinston and Goldsboro'. I may cross Neuse about Cox's bridge, and move into Goldsboro', but will not attempt it till within close communication with General Schofield. I have sent full orders to Schofield. It will not do to build any determinate plan from there until I am in full possession of Goldsboro'. I have ordered Generals Schofield and Terry to push towards Goldsboro' as hard as possible from the east as I advance from the southwest. The enemy is superior to me in cavalry, but I can beat his infantry, man for man, and I don't think he can bring forty thousand (40,000) men for battle. I will force him to guard Raleigh until I have interposed between it and Goldsboro'.

Weather is now good, but threatens rain. We are all well; keep all parts busy, and I will give the enemy no rest.

Yours, truly,

W. T. SHERMAN,
Major General.

Lieut. General U. S. GRANT,
City Point.

HEADQUARTERS MILITARY DIVISION OF THE MISSISSIPPI,
In the field, opposite Fayetteville, Tuesday, March 14, 1865.

GENERAL: Quartermaster General Dodge is now with me, and I have explained many things to him. I want your nine thousand (9,000) infantry up at Goldsboro' as soon as possible. I begin my movement to-morrow, and if the weather is at all favorable will be opposite Goldsboro' in five days. I think your best plan is to move up as light as possible by the best road. When you effect a junction I can supply you two hundred (200) wagons. Until we get Goldsboro' reduced to possession, and its railroads down, we will not have much marching. General Schofield should push his railroad from Newbern, and your branch should be kept moving as fast as possible. Colonel Wright has but a limited force, but I will write to General Schofield to send some of Colonel Wright's foremen, and also one or two regiments of negro troops, as laborers. As I approach the road the enemy will doubtless remove as much of the iron as he can.

I have asked Captain Young, of the navy, to keep up an active movement along Cape Fear river, to make Joe Johnston believe I have re-supplied my wagons, and can stand a thirty days' campaign.

I shall feign strong on Raleigh, but actually approach Goldsboro', and will not attempt Goldsboro' until I have Kinston and the railroad bridge across the Neuse, so that I can draw supplies from Newbern, on the north bank of the Neuse; that once done, I think I can get Goldsboro' quick. I may do so, however, at once, according to appearances as I approach the place.

I am much obliged for the supplies, but would suggest that you estimate to keep on hand always a million of rations, independent of your own wants. I feel confident that Generals Easton and Beckwith have full supplies for me about Newbern.

I am truly yours,

W. T. SHERMAN,
Major General Commanding.

Major General TERRY,
    Commanding, &c., Wilmington.

HEADQUARTERS MILITARY DIVISION OF THE MISSISSIPPI,
In the field, opposite Fayetteville, Tuesday, March 14, 1865.

GENERAL: I am now across Cape Fear river, and to-morrow shall draw out ten miles, and next day, if weather is favorable, will begin to manœuvre on Goldsboro'. I shall feign strong on Raleigh by approaching, and it may be striking the railroad half way between Goldsboro' and Raleigh; then, as soon as the wagons are well towards Faison's, will swing rapidly in front of Goldsboro', but will not cross the Neuse till I hear from you. You must push vigorously towards Kinston and Goldsboro', with the absolute certainty that I will engage the attention of Joe Johnston's army to the west and southwest of Goldsboro'. Let the railroad construction party push their work at least as far Kinston. I want you to draw up Terry's force also, either by water or by a land march; the latter will be best. On making a junction I can spare Terry two hundred, and you three hundred wagons. I think we have transportation enough for a hundred thousand men. Be sure to accumulate food for my army, and especially clothing. Tell General Easton we will need at least one hundred thousand (100,000) suits of clothing. Our animals are in good condition, and have been accustomed to a full ration of fodder. They will wail piteously if put on a mere grain ration. If not delayed much at Goldsboro' we can soon gain a good fodder country.

You must now push as boldly as possible straight on Goldsboro', and I will do the same. Joe Johnston may try to interpose, in which case we must strike him as near at the same time as possible. If he crosses the Neuse to the south you must do the same, but I think he will await me at Goldsboro' and Raleigh, tnd I hope at both. Consolidate your command at once into an army, the centre of this. General Howard has the right wing, General Slocum the left. You can have Terry's troops, but I want the detachments that belong to this army to join their respective brigades as quick as possible. I understand that Meagher's division is composed wholly of detachments that belong to the corps now with me, viz: 15th, 17th, 14th, and 20th. I will want to give Kilpatrick as much cavalry as possible, as he has a heavy load to carry. He has to look out for Hampton, Wheeler, and Butler, all accounted as first-class men.

I take it for granted Joe Johnston now has S. D. Lee's corps, four thousand, (4,000;) Cheatham's, five thousand, (5,000;) Hoke's, eight thousand, (8,000;) Hardee's, ten thousand, (10,000;) and detachments, about ten thousand, (10,000;) making thirty-seven thousand (37,000,) with near eight thousand (8,000) cavalry.

Our duty is to effect a junction south of the Neuse; but if you can get Kinston whilst Joe Johnston is engaged with me, do so, and push on towards Goldsboro'. I will attack the Raleigh road.

Get your supplies as far forward as possible, that I may quickly replenish.

I am yours, truly,

W. T. SHERMAN,
Major General Commanding.

Major General SCHOFIELD,
Commanding at Newbern.

HEADQUARTERS MILITARY DIVISION OF THE MISSISSIPPI,
In the field, opposite Fayetteville, March 14, 1865—7 p. m.

GENERAL : I think I have studied the problem of the next move, and will give you in confidence its analysis.

We must make a strong feint on Raleigh, and strike with cavalry, if possible, the railroad near Smithfield. I take it for granted the bridge will be too strongly guarded for General Kilpatrick to surprise, and therefore I will leave him to disable that road, of course only partially, between the Neuse and Eureka. To this end the cavalry will move to-night across the bridge, beginning at 3 a. m., and will push to-morrow up the plank road to about Averysboro'; General Slocum following up with four disencumbered divisions to near the forks of the road, moving his trains by a cross-road towards Bentonville. The next move will be the cavalry to " Elevation," and General Slocum will cross Black river. The next move will bring General Slocum to Bentonville, and Kilpatrick, supported by a division of infantry, will make a dash for the railroad. This is as far as I will now determine.

I want you to be as near in support as possible. I do think it is Johnston's only chance to meet this army before an easy junction can be effected with General Schofield.

I would like you to have four (4) divisions free to move rapidly to the sound of battle in the direction of Mingo creek and Elevation, and at any event to make a junction by head of column with General Slocum at Bentonville. The weather looks bad, and I fear we may have swamps about South river. I think it would be well for you to have four divisions to get ahead of General Slocum's trains on the direct road from Fayetteville to Bentonville, and keeping ahead of him about five or six miles, so as, in case of action, to come up on his "right." I will keep near General Slocum, and wish you to keep me thoroughly advised of the position of your troops and trains, and, instead of aiming towards Faison's, rather look towards Dead Field and Everettsville.

I think Colonel Garber can give you another boat, in which case you had better send down another load of prisoners of war. Do not fail to clear your columns of the dead-weights, by sending them, *via* Clinton, to Wilmington.

I do not expect your heads of columns to be more than ten miles distant from Fayetteville to-morrow night, but it would be well for a brigade to secure the bridge across South river if not already done.

Generals Schofield and Terry are now fully advised of our whereabouts, and have my orders. Their movements will directly co-operate with ours, and I propose to make an actual junction before crossing the Neuse, unless events and weather favor a different course.

Yours, truly,

W. T. SHERMAN,
Major General Commanding.

Major General O. O. HOWARD,
Commanding Right Wing.

HEADQUARTERS MILITARY DIVISION OF THE MISSISSIPPI,
In the field, opposite Fayetteville, N. C., March 14, 1865.

GENERAL: I have notified General Howard that to-morrow night your head of column would be near the crossroads, above Kyle's landing; the next day across Black river, near Mingo; and third day near Bentonville, and have instructed him to have four (4) divisions in easy support, and a little in advance of you, say, five or six miles, so that on receiving orders or hearing battle he may come promptly up on your right.

I think Colonel Garber can promise you another boat, in which case it would be well to send to Wilmington your prisoners of war. You might leave them to-morrow where the gunboat lies, two (2) miles below General Howard's bridge, and the guard, if unable to overtake you the day after to-morrow, could follow direct to Bentonville. I want the three first marches to be made with prudence and deliberation. I am willing to accept battle with Johnston's concentrated force, but would not attack him in position until I make junction with General Schofield.

I am truly yours,

W. T. SHERMAN,
Major General Commanding.

Major General SLOCUM,
Commanding Left Wing.

HEADQUARTERS MILITARY DIVISION OF THE MISSISSIPPI,
In the field, 12 *miles from Fayetteville, N. C.,*
on Raleigh road, March 15, 1865.

GENERAL: I got a file of northern papers yesterday from Wilmington, in which I observe you are in command of the Department of the South. I have had no official communication from the War Department or General Grant since my departure from Savannah, and am compelled to pick up information the best way I can. I wrote to General Foster from Fayetteville, supposing him to be in command of the department, and hope you got the letter, and it is a fear its contents may not reach you promptly which induces me to write this.

When at Columbia I had the railroad broken down to Kingsville and the Wateree bridge; subsequently from Cheraw I aimed to strike Florence, but sent too weak a party, but the enemy himself has destroyed the Pedee bridge, and has on the railroad at Sumterville and between it and Florence a vast amount of rolling stock, the destruction of which is all important, and it should be done before any repairs can be made whereby they can be removed. I want it done at once, and leave you to devise the way. I think twenty-five hundred (2,500) men lightly equipped, with pack mules only, could reach the road either from Georgetown or the Santee bridge. I think also that you can easily make up that force from Charleston and Savannah. As to the garrisons of those places I don't feel disposed to be over-generous, and should not hesitate to burn Savannah, Charleston and Wilmington, or either of them, if the garrisons were needed. Savannah and Wilmington are the only really useful ports, because of their inland rivers. Still, I suppose you can always get garrisons of sick, disabled, or indifferent troops. All real good soldiers must now be marching. Do not let your command rest on its oars, but keep them going all the time, even if for no other purpose than to exhaust the enemy's country or compel him to defend it. The simple fact that a man's home has been visited by an enemy makes a soldier in Lee's and Johnston's army very anxious to get home to look after his family and property. But the expedition I have indicated to Sumterville and Florence has even higher aims. Those cars and locomotives should be destroyed, if to do it cost you five hundred (500) men. I know you can get there all the bacon, beef, meat, &c., your command may want, and a good deal of corn-meal.   The men could march without knapsacks, with a single blanket, and carry eight (8) days' provisions, which, with what is in the country, will feed your command two weeks.   Let it be done at once, and select your own point of departure.   After destroying those cars and engines, (not merely damaging them, but an absolute destruction of boilers, steam chambers, connecting rods, flanges, &c., &c., powder can be used to good advantage in blowing up boilers and engines, but we use cold-chisels and crowbars,) you may reduce your garrisons to the minimum and send every man to Newbern and Goldsboro'.   I want to collect an army that can whip Lee in open fight if he lets go Richmond, which I think he will soon be forced to do.

Yours, truly,

> W. T. SHERMAN,
> *Major General Commanding.*

Major General Q. A. GILLMORE,
Commanding Department of the South, Charleston, S. C.

HEADQUARTERS MILITARY DIVISION OF THE MISSISSIPPI,
In the field, Kyle's Landing, N. C., March 16, 1865—2 a. m.

GENERAL : Yours is just received ; your orders are all right.   I fear the present rain will make the roads utterly impracticable.   Hardee's whole force is in our front, near the forks of the road, and I have ordered General Slocum to go at him in the morning in good shape, but vigorously, and push him beyond Averysboro'.   General Kilpatrick is ahead, across the branch marked Taylor's Hole creek, about two miles this side the forks.

Your courier brings me good news from Generals Schofield and Terry.   General Schofield reports he whipped Bragg handsomely at Kinston, and undertakes to have supplies for us there, and probably further along.   General Terry says he can reach Faison's with his 9,000 men by Sunday or Monday, and that the rest of General Schofield's troops that had left Wilmington had made junction with General Schofield at Kinston.   Also that General Sheridan is coming to us by land with 8,000 cavalry.   So all is working well around us, and we must not scatter, but aim to converge about Bentonville, and afterwards Goldsboro'.   The rain is as bad for our opponents as for us, and I doubt if they have as good supplies or transportation as we.

General Terry has sent up 3,900 pairs of shoes, and 2,400 pairs of pants. Divide them with General Slocum.

We took Colonel Alfred Rhett, of Fort Sumter, prisoner yesterday.   He was commanding a brigade in Hardee's troops ahead, and from drop expressions I think Hardee will try and fight us at the crossroads.

Yours, truly,

> W. T. SHERMAN,
> *Major General Commanding.*

Major General HOWARD,
Commanding Right Wing.

HEADQUARTERS MILITARY DIVISION OF THE MISSISSIPPI,
In the field, 13 miles on the Raleigh Road, out of
Fayetteville, March 16, 1865—2 a. m.

GENERAL : Thank you kindly for the shoes and pants, and still more for the certain knowledge that General Schofield is in possession of Kinston.   That

23 *

is of great importance; for thence to Goldsboro' there are no bridges. I will, in consequence, move straight on Goldsboro'.

It is now raining hard, and the bottom has fallen out, and we will have to corduroy every foot of the way. Hardee is ahead of me and shows fight. I will go at him in the morning with four divisions, and push him as far as Averysboro' before turning towards Bentonville and Cox's bridge. My extreme right will aim for Everettsville and Faison's. I am delighted that General Sheridan is slashing away with his column of cavalry. He will be a disturbing element in the grand and beautiful game of war, and if he reaches me I'll make all North Carolina howl. I will make him a deed of gift of every horse in the State, to be settled for at the day of judgment. I cannot, of course, reach General Sheridan with any suggestions, but he should march for Danville, Greensboro' and Raleigh, or rather near those points, making some detours to mislead.

Tell General Dodge to keep boats running up Cape Fear, until he knows I am at my new base. This rain, so damaging to my land transportation, is a good thing for the river, which had fallen very much. He can use the rebel captured boats, which if lost are of no account. Each of these boats should be supplied a good barge, that can hold all the crew, in case the boat is caught by a fall in the river. Captain Young agreed to keep his gunboats running busy, and as high up as possible. I want to keep up the impression that I am using the Cape Fear river for supplies, for our foolish northern journals have published the fact that I am aiming for Newbern, a fact that I had concealed from everybody not necessarily in my confidence. These fellows discovered it by the course taken by the supply boats from Port Royal.

Hoping to meet you soon, I am, &c.,

W. T. SHERMAN,
Major General Commanding.

Major General TERRY, Wilmington, N. C.

P. S.—We took some prisoners to-day, among them Colonel Alfred Rhett, of Fort Sumter, who commands a brigade in Hardee's army.

SHERMAN.

HEADQUARTERS MILITARY DIVISION OF THE MISSISSIPPI,
In the field, 18 miles N. E. Fayetteville, March 17, 1865—7 a. m.

GENERAL: General Slocum found the enemy covering the narrow neck from Taylor's Hole creek up to the Goldsboro' road. He drove them from two successive positions, taking three guns, some prisoners, wounded, but losing himself pretty severely—I think as many as 300 in all; but the enemy lost heavily also, from appearances. At night the enemy still held the forks, but it is just reported that he is gone—I suppose up to Averysboro', where the Raleigh and Smithfield roads fork. Your scout Duncan is just in, having escaped from McLaw's guard, he thinks about twelve miles out on the Smithfield road. So Hardee is retreating on Smithfield.

General Slocum will feel out towards Averysboro', but move his column on the Goldsboro' road, which is that which crosses Black and Mingo creeks, just ahead of where we are. Our true tactics would be to push all our columns to Smithfield, but I will only follow Hardee far enough to give him impulse, when we must resume our course.

I want you to-day to get to where the Goldsboro' road crosses Mingo, and have that bridge well repaired. You need not come on to General Slocum, unless you hear him engaged. We might cut his column at Elevation, but it will be time enough to think of that to-night.

General Blair is getting too far off; better draw him and all your trains towards Troublefield's store.

Weather having cleared off, we may count on better roads.

Have a road for your column reconnoitred from Mingo bridge to that point north of Troublefield's where three roads meet.

I expect to be to-night somewhere between the Black river and Mingo bridge.

Yours, &c.,

W. T. SHERMAN,
Major General Commanding.

Major General O. O. HOWARD,
Commanding Right Wing.

HEADQUARTERS MILITARY DIVISION OF THE MISSISSIPPI,
In the field, March 17, 1865.

GENERAL: The enemy is gone from our front, and I take it he is up at the forks of the Raleigh and Smithfield roads—Averysboro'.

General Slocum will feel up that road, but be prepared to use the Goldsboro' road which crosses Black and Mingo. I have ordered General Howard to be at Mingo to-night, but I want your cavalry on the road which leads from Black river bridge towards Elevation. Captain Duncan, of General Howard's scouts, is here, having escaped. He reports Hardee and Wheeler ahead of us, on the Smithfield road. Wade Hampton and Butler are off in front of General Howard.

You can forage from the Goldsboro' road northward, between Black and Mingo.

Yours truly,

W. T. SHERMAN,
Major General Commanding.

Major General KILPATRICK,
Black River Mill.

HEADQUARTERS MILITARY DIVISION OF THE MISSISSIPPI,
In the field, Camp between N. river and Mingo creek, March 17, 1865.

GENERAL: North river had to be bridged and has delayed us to-day. General Davis is on the Mingo, and Williams on North river. General Kilpatrick is up the road in the direction of Elevation. We still threaten Smithfield, but to-morrow will move rapidly towards Cox's bridge and Goldsboro'. If the enemy fail to fight for Goldsboro', of course we go right in—General Slocum by Cox's bridge, and you by the south, as General Schofield comes from the east, (Kinston.) But if the enemy oppose, I propose to throw our empty wagons down to Kinston for forage and supplies, whilst we proceed to reduce Goldsboro'. To this end General Slocum will break the railroad west of Cox's bridge, and you will cross the Neuse in front, as General Schofield comes from the east, and swings against the railroad north of the town. I doubt if there be any fortifications at Goldsboro' capable of holding anything more than a railroad guard.

I have examined your order and it will do, only get on a right-hand road as soon as possible, that you may not delay General Slocum's troops, who will necessarily all be forced on the one road. Try and keep around the head of Falling Water creek, viz., to the south. I will push General Slocum to-morrow and next day, and think by day after to-morrow we will be in position, viz., you directly in front of Goldsboro', and General Slocum at Cox's bridge.

At the time I sent Colonel Ewing to you yesterday, the enemy had brought General Slocum up all standing, and it was on the theory that he would hold

General Slocum there that I wanted you at Mingo bridge. But the enemy retreated in the night on Smithfield, and we are again on the march, feigning to the left, but moving trains and troops as rapidly as the roads admit on Goldsboro'. You may do the same.

The enemy yesterday had a strong intrenched line in front of the cross-roads, and had posted the Charleston brigade about $\frac{1}{3}$ mile in front, also intrenched. The 20th corps struck the first line, turned it handsomely, and used the Charleston brigade up completely, killing about 40, and gathering about 35 wounded and a hundred well prisoners, capturing three (3) guns, but on advancing further encountered the larger line, which they did not carry, but it was abandoned at night.

This morning a division of Williams's followed as far as Averysboro', whilst the rest turned to the right, as I have heretofore stated. General Slocum lost in killed and wounded about 300. He is somewhat heavily burdened by his wounded, which must be hauled. We left the confederate wounded in a house by the road-side.

The route of retreat of the enemy shows signs of considerable panic, and I have no doubt he got decidedly the worst of it.

Yours truly,

W. T. SHERMAN, Major General.

Major General HOWARD,
Commanding Right Wing.

HEADQUARTERS MILITARY DIVISION OF THE MISSISSIPPI,
In the field, 27 miles from Goldsboro', N. C., March 18, 1865.

GENERAL: The 14th corps is here, but the 20th is well back. It started rom Averysboro' and North river, with General Kilpatrick to the north of the road. We heard some musketry and artillery in that direction, but Colonel Poe left Mingo creek, which he bridged, at 11 a. m., at which time the 20th corps was a half a mile behind.

We cannot get any further to-day. General Davis may go a couple of miles further to the forks of the road. I think this road, the Averysboro' and Goldsboro' road, will lead to Cox's bridge, though it is represented as passing three (3) miles south of Bentonville.

Get on to the right-hand road, so that General Geary and his trains may take that to Goldsboro', *via* Cox's bridge.

I think the enemy is concentrated about Smithfield, and I cannot make out whether Goldsboro' is held in force or not. I think it probable that Joe Johnston will try to prevent our getting Goldsboro'.

We find a good deal of forage to-day, but the roads still cut deep. I hope the sun will dry them up good.

Our map is evidently faulty. Can't you send me to-night a sketch of the country towards Dead Fields, Everettsville, and Faison's? I fear General Slocum will be jammed with all his trains in a narrow space, but at the same time I don't want to push you too far till this flank is better covered by the Neuse. General Slocum is back with the 20th corps, and as soon as I hear from him I will send over to you.

General Morgan's division found a couple of Hampton's regiments here, but they cleared out towards the north as soon as he deployed skirmishers.

I am, general, very respectfully, &c.,

W. T. SHERMAN,
Major General Commanding.

Major General O. O. HOWARD,
Commanding Right Wing.

HEADQUARTERS MILITARY DIVISION OF THE MISSISSIPPI,
In the field, March 18, 1865.

GENERAL: General Slocum is up. The firing you heard was General Kilpatrick, who found parties picketing the roads to the north. He reports Hardee retreating on Smithfield and Joe Johnston collecting his old Georgia army this side of Raleigh. I know that he will call in all minor posts, which embraces Goldsboro'. You may, therefore, move straight for Goldsboro', leaving General Slocum the river road, and, if possible, the one from Lee's store toward Falling Waters. Make a break into Goldsboro' from the south, and let your scouts strike out for General Schofield, at Kinston, though I hope to meet him at Goldsboro'.

Our roads are very bad, but I think the 14th corps will be at Cox's bridge to-morrow night, and will aim to strike the railroad to the northwest of Goldsboro'. If any change occurs I will notify you to-night.

Yours,

W. T. SHERMAN,
Major General.

Major General HOWARD, *Present.*

[Cipher.]

HEADQUARTERS MILITARY DIVISION OF THE MISSISSIPPI,
In the field, 10 *miles southwest of Goldsboro',*
Sunday, March 19, 1865—2 p. m.

Major General SCHOFIELD, *Kinston:*

To-night my left wing will be at Cox's bridge, and my right wing within 10, miles of Goldsboro'. To-morrow we will cross the Neuse river at Cox's bridge and be near Goldsboro', to prevent the enemy reoccupying Goldsboro' in force.

The scout Pike has arrived with your despatch of the 17th. Continue to extend the road as fast as possible, and I expect you to move towards Goldsboro', even if it be unnecessary, as I don't want to lose men in a direct attack, when it can be avoided.

Don't depend altogether on your depot, but collect forage and provisions of the people. Tell Generals Easton and Beckwith to estimate for one hundred thousand men. I must give my men and animals some rest.

We whipped Hardee easily about Averysboro'. All retreated on Smithfield and Raleigh.

W. T. SHERMAN,
Major General.

[Cipher.]

HEADQUARTERS MILITARY DIVISION OF THE MISSISSIPPI,
In the field, March 19, 1865—5 p. m.

General SCHOFIELD:

Since making my despatch to-day, General Slocum reports the enemy in force between him and Cox's bridge; thinks it is the main army of the enemy. I can hardly suppose the enemy will attempt to fight us this side the Neuse, but will direct all my columns on Cox's bridge to-morrow. You must secure Goldsboro' and fortify.

W. T. SHERMAN,
Major General.

HEADQUARTERS MILITARY DIVISION OF THE MISSISSIPPI,
In the field, Falling Creek Church, March 19, 1865—2 p. m.

GENERAL : General Howard, with one division, is now at this point, which is just three miles south of Cox's bridge and ten from Goldsboro'. A scout is just in from General Schofield, who writes that he will leave Kinston for Goldsboro' to-day or to-morrow. I have sent him a courier with orders to march straight for Goldsboro'. General Howard's four (4) divisions are strung out, but he will push them through to-night. We occupy a position dangerous to the enemy, if he thinks he is in front of the whole army. You may strengthen your position, but feel the enemy all night. If he is there at daylight, we will move straight for Cox's bridge, and then turn towards you. I think you will find him gone in the morning. General Howard has sent a regiment to Cox's bridge. It has not reported yet. He has the bridge across Falling creek, two miles east of this, towards Goldsboro', and has also some mounted men opposite Goldsboro', where they find a tête de pont occupied by the enemy. General Blair is about five miles south of this with the trains.

I will order General Kilpatrick to remain with you. Get up your trains between Lee's store and your camp, and keep the enemy busy until we can get up the 4th division of the 15th corps.

If you hear firing to your front, not explained by your own acts, you must assault or turn the enemy, for it will not do to let him fight us separately.

Yours,

W. T. SHERMAN,
Major General.

Major General SLOCUM,
Commanding Left Wing.

P. S.—Your note of 2 p. m. is just received. General Howard's regiment drove the picket from the crossroads, one mile this side of Cox's bridge; that will disturb the force to your front. General Howard can better help you from this quarter than by returning by Lee's store.

SHERMAN.

HEADQUARTERS MILITARY DIVISION OF THE MISSISSIPPI,
In the field, Falling Creek Church, March 19, 1865—5 p. m.

GENERAL : Your report of to-day is received. General Slocum thinks the whole rebel army is to his front. I cannot think Johnston would fight us with the Neuse to his rear. You may remain with General Slocum until further orders, or until the two wings come together.

If that force remain in General Slocum's front to-morrow, I will move straight on its rear.

Yours, truly,

W. T. SHERMAN, *Major General.*

General KILPATRICK,
Commanding Cavalry.

HEADQUARTERS MILITARY DIVISION OF THE MISSISSIPPI,
In the field, March 20, 1865—2 a. m.

GENERAL : Yours of 8 p. m., 19th, is just received, and I acknowledge receipt by direction of the general-in-chief, who instructed me also to say that the whole army is moving to your assistance as rapidly as possible. Upon its approach he wishes you to be prepared to assume the offensive against the enemy.

Colonel Asmussen has directions for you.   All ambulances will be given you that can.

I am, with respect,

L. M. DAYTON, *A. A. G.*

Major General SLOCUM,
Commanding Left Wing.

HEADQUARTERS MILITARY DIVISION OF THE MISSISSIPPI,
In the field, Falling Creek Church, March 20, 1865—4 a. m.

GENERAL: I got a despatch from General Schofield yesterday, saying he would start from Kinston for Goldsboro' yesterday or to-day.

I have just received information that General Terry camped his troops five (5) miles south of Faison's yesterday, and that he, in person, reached Faison's on a train last night.

I have ordered him to feel into Goldsboro' for General Schofield, and up to Cox's bridge for me.

We all move at five (5) a. m. toward you; hold fast to your position, which I take for granted is now well fortified, but be ready to attack the enemy the moment you see signs of let go; follow him as far as Mill creek, and take position covering the movement of your trains on the direct Goldsboro' road.

If it be true that General Terry has reached Faison's on a train, we will be able to send your wounded down to Wilmington from Neuse river bridge.   You shall have the use of every ambulance in the army not absolutely needed in the other corps and divisions.

Yours,

W. T. SHERMAN, *Major General.*

Major General SLOCUM,
Commanding Left Wing.

[Cipher.]

HEADQUARTERS MILITARY DIVISION OF THE MISSISSIPPI,
In the field, Falling Creek Church, March 20, 1865—4 a. m.

GENERAL: I have just learned through your cavalry of your arrival at Faison's.

Johnston, with his concentrated force, made an unsuccessful attack on my left wing yesterday, near Bentonville.   I am just starting with my right wing to attack him.

Feel into Goldsboro' for General Schofield, and up the Falling creek and Cox's bridge, for me.   We have cavalry pickets south of Goldsboro'.   The Neuse bridges are burned.

W. T. SHERMAN, *Major General.*

Major General A. H. TERRY, *Commanding, &c.*

HEADQUARTERS MILITARY DIVISION OF THE MISSISSIPPI,
In the field, Falling Creek Church, March 20, 1865—6 a. m.

GENERAL: I have this moment received your despatch of yesterday.   I had just sent off a cipher despatch to you, but as yours is plain, I infer you have no cipher clerk.

Yesterday Johnston, with his force concentrated, struck my left wing near Bentonville, and they had a severe battle, lasting until night. General Slocum beat them off, but was uneasy. I am now turning the right wing on Bentonville.

I want you to move to Mount Olive station and communicate with General Schofield, who ought to be at Goldsboro' to-night, and then feel up for me on the south of the Neuse towards Bentonville.

Get the railroad from Northeast branch to the Neuse in running order to the capacity of the captured stock.

The railroad and road bridges near Goldsboro' were burned yesterday, on being threatened by some of our cavalry parties. If General Schofield gets to Goldsboro', the road bridges should be rebuilt at once. If you need pontoons, I can send you some of canvas.

Half our trains are with General Slocum, near Bentonville, and the other half about eight miles south of this, on the road from Cox's bridge to Wilmington.

By to-night I will know if Joe Johnston intends to fight me in force, when I will communicate further. Until you know the result, you and General Schofield should work up to my support south of the Neuse.

Send that cavalry regiment through to me *via* the Bentonville road. We hold the bridge over Falling creek.

W. T. SHERMAN,
Major General.

Major General TERRY,
Faison's Depot.

HEADQUARTERS MILITARY DIVISION OF THE MISSISSIPPI,
In the field, near Bentonville, March 20, 1865—2 p. m.

GENERAL SCHOFIELD: Your despach of yesterday is received. You can march into Goldsboro' without opposition. General Terry is at Faison's, and I have ordered him to Cox's bridge till the present action is over. I am now within two miles of Slocum, but Johnston is between us. We are now skirmishing.

After occupying Goldsboro', if you hear nothing to the contrary, join a part of your force with General Terry's, and come to me, wherever I may be.

W. T. SHERMAN,
Major General.

HEADQUARTERS MILITARY DIVISION OF THE MISSISSIPPI,
In the field, March 20, 1865—8 p. m.

GENERAL: I find the topography of the country different from what I expected. The road from Falling creek church will be very bad in wet weather as far as Cox's bridge; thence for eight miles very good, with sandy ground and open fields hence about ten miles from Cox's bridge. We are on flat pine land, such as makes bad roads in wet weather.

We struck the enemy on his left rear about noon, and have pressed him very hard, and have dislodged him from all his barricades, except the line constructed as against you, which may be double, or enclosed; for our men find parapets from the road well down to Mill creek. Johnston hoped to overcome your wing before I could come to your relief; having failed in that, I cannot see why he remains, and still think he will avail himself of night to get back to Smithfield. I would rather avoid a general battle, if possible; but if he insists on it, we must accommodate him. In that event, if he be in position to-morrow, I want you to make a good road around his flank into this, and to-morrow night pass your trains and dispose your troops, so that we have our back towards Faison's and Goldsboro'. General Schofield was to leave Kinston for Goldsboro' to-day, and General Terry has arrived with 9,000 infantry at Faison's, and I have ordered him to Cox's bridge, to be drawn up here if we need him. I can also draw on General Schofield, in a few days, for 10,000 men; but I think we have enough.

First, in case of being forced to fight the enemy here, we must send our trains to Kinston for supplies, and therefore get a road at once around the flank of the enemy; the rest is in our possession—retain ordnance, and all wagons with food; all else should go down.

Make no orders as yet, till to-morrow reveals the purpose of our enemy ; but think the problem over.

Post General Hazen to your right, so as to join his own corps—the 15th. Keep General Kilpatrick on your left rear; feel the enemy at several points to-night, and if he retreats, try and get some prisoners. Make me a report of to-day's operations with you, and describe more fully the topography.

Yours,

W. T. SHERMAN, Major General.

Major General SLOCUM,
 Commanding Left Wing.

HEADQUARTERS MILITARY DIVISION OF THE MISSISSIPPI,
In the field, near Bentonville, N. C., March 20, 1865—9 p. m.

GENERAL : We struck Johnston on his left rear to-day, and have been skirmishing pretty hard all day. We have opened communication with General Slocum, who had a hard fight yesterday. We are now ready for battle, if Johnston desires it, to-morrow ; but as he has failed to overcome one wing, he will hardly invite battle with both. I don't want to fight now, or here, and therefore won't object to his drawing off to-night towards Smithfield, as he should. General Schofield moves to-day from Kinston for Goldsboro', and I wish you to go to Cox's, to which point I will send a pontoon train, if I conclude to lay a bridge there. The north side of the Neuse will afford us good foraging ground, and will be a direct threat to Smithfield, and the rear of Johnston's army, now to my front. I may have to send all my empty wagons to Kinston for clothing and supplies, but you would do well to have the railroad from Wilmington repaired up to the Neuse, and you can draw supplies up that road.

If Johnston insists on fighting us here, I may call you up ; but if he goes I will drop down to Goldsboro', put you about Faison's or Mount Olive, and General Schofield at Kinston, until we are re-supplied and equipped for the next campaign. This will take us a couple of weeks.

I suppose you will be put to your wits to feed your men until the roads are equipped, but it is wonderful how necessity develops the searching qualities of soldiers. My men seem to keep fat and healthy on parched corn and bacon.

Have both bridges over Falling Water put in good order, and tell General Schofield to repair at once the road bridge across the Neuse at Goldsboro'. The railroad bridge will be built by Colonel Wright, with his railroad gang.

I do hope we shall have some fine weather, as rain makes these roads terrible.

Yours, truly,

W. T. SHERMAN,
Major General.

Major General TERRY, *Mount Olive.*

HEADQUARTERS MILITARY DIVISION OF THE MISSISSIPPI
In the field, near Bentonville, N. C., March 21, 1865.

GENERAL: Captain Twining is here, and I send by him an order that, you will perceive, looks to staying here some days.

I thought Johnston, having failed as he attempted to crush one of my wings, finding he had not succeeded, but that I was present with my whole force, would withdraw, but he has not, and I must fight him here. He is twenty (20) miles from Smithfield, with a bad road to his rear, but his position is in the swamps, difficult of approach, and I don't like to assail his parapets, which are of the old kind.

As soon as you get Goldsboro' leave a small garrison; break the bridge across Little river, above the railroad, but use the one near its mouth, at old Waynesboro', and advance to Millard, where you can effect a junction with Terry. He need leave a very small picket at Cox's bridge. Make up a force of about 25,000 men, leaving at Goldsboro' Carter's division, if, as I understand, it is composed of troops properly belonging to this army. Let me know the moment these combinations are made, when we can act.

I would like to have your pontoon bridge across Neuse, about Jericho, so that our trains to and from Kinston can use it. General Howard will bridge at or near Goldsboro', and General Slocum at Cox's. The roads are now comparatively good, and I want to make the most of the good weather, but the moment Johnston gives ground I propose to fall back on Goldsboro', and await the completion of our railroad and the re-equipment of my army. I will probably post you at Kinston, General Terry about Faison's, and this army at Goldsboro'.

You will probably find plenty of corn, bacon, and corn-meal in the country, from Waynesboro' to Millard. The road near the Neuse is also better than the one back, as it is better drained. All the heads of creeks in this region are swampy, and level pine lands that afford bad roads.

I expect you surely at Goldsboro' to-day, and that you have at once secured the bridge across Little river. I don't think you will find anything over there but cavalry. Hoke is to our front; we took prisoners from his command yesterday.

Yours, truly,

W. T. SHERMAN, *Major General.*

Major General SCHOFIELD,
Commanding Army of the Ohio.

HEADQUARTERS MILITARY DIVISION OF THE MISSISSIPPI,
In the field, near Bentonville, N. C., March 21, 1865—6 p. m.

GENERAL: It is manifest that we are not to be favored with weather. After raining six weeks, it has, apparently, set in for another six weeks. I wish, while waiting for the pontoon train, you would keep strong details corduroying the roads at the low places, especially in the bottoms of Falling creek, at both bridges, or at the bridges on both roads, viz: the one from Cox's to Goldsboro,' and the one from Falling Creek School House to Goldsboro'. Better keep a thousand men on detail for such work. We will corduroy back towards you and you towards Goldsboro'. Rails are pretty good, but pine saplings, ten inches through, the cut split in two, the flat side laid down, make a better road.

We have had some pretty hard skirmishing all round the line, but nothing material either way. If I could get the railroad done to Goldsboro' I would be better off than Johnston, as he has the same weather, and, I think, a worse road to his base at Smithfield, both distances twenty miles.

I am very anxious to hear of General Schofield, at Goldsboro', and especially that the railroad is done to that point. It should have been completed before I got here.

Yours, truly,

W. T. SHERMAN,
Major General Commanding.

Major General TERRY, *Commanding Bridge.*

HEADQUARTERS MILITARY DIVISION OF THE MISSISSIPPI,
In the field, near Bentonville, N. C., March 22, 1865—6½ a. m.

GENERAL : I am directed by the general-in-chief to write you.

The effect of the operations of our skirmishers yesterday and last night has been that the enemy has left his position and retreated towards or beyond Mill creek. The general desires you to use all possible expedition in effecting a crossing at Cox's bridge, over the Neuse, getting the bridge down at the earliest practicable moment. If the bridge-train has not reached you, he wishes that you send couriers to it to hurry up.

Communicate these facts to Major General Schofield, and that General Sherman expects him to occupy Goldsboro' at once. Johnston may attempt sending a force there from Smithfield, and therefore it is important for General Schofield to occupy Goldsboro'.

Let your despatch bearer go at a gallop.

I am, with respect, &c.,

L. M. DAYTON,
Assistant Adjutant General.

Major General A. H. TERRY, *Commanding, &c.*

HEADQUARTERS MILITARY DIVISION OF THE MISSISSIPPI,
In the field, near Bentonville, N. C., March 22, 1865.

I have just been at the front. Johnston retreated last night on Smithfield in some confusion, leaving dead and wounded. We have pursued two miles beyond Mill creek, but are not in a condition as to our supplies to follow up our advantage, which amounts to a substantial victory, and accordingly I have ordered the army to move towards Goldsboro'. I can't imagine why I don't hear from General Schofield. Until I know he has Goldsboro', I must direct my attention on that point.

I commend highly your promptness in securing the crossing at Cox's. If you observe any of the enemy's force on the north side, move across a whole division and intrench it, so as to command all the outlet roads, and so that if I choose I can cross General Slocum's wing there, and move out against the railroad between Goldsboro' and Smithfield.

I will probably come down to-day and stay with you.

Yours, truly,

W. T. SHERMAN,
Major General Commanding.

Major General TERRY,
Commanding at Cox's Bridge.

HEADQUARTERS MILITARY DIVISION OF THE MISSISSIPPI,
In the field, near Bentonville, N. C., March 22, 1865—10 a. m.

GENERAL : The enemy having retreated precipitately and in disorder from our front, and we not being in a condition as to supplies to follow up, will move on Goldsboro', from which place I have nothing definite. General Terry reports that he has crossed the Neuse to the north bank, where he has a brigade intrenched. From that position I can take Goldsboro' without delay or trouble. I shall go there to-night. General Slocum's wing will also be at or near Cox's, but General Howard will remain till morning. To-morrow morning, unless nothing happens in the interval, move your cavalry slowly and in order by a circuit to the south, to Mount Olive Station, on the Wilmington and Goldsboro' road, and report to me from there by letter. General Terry, on his way up, secured two locomotives and a few old cars, and found the road in good order from Northeast Branch, near Wilmington, to Mount Olive, so that I hope to be able to supply you food and forage from that quarter, which will relieve the Newbern road, which, for some reason, was more damaged by the enemy.

Nevertheless, continue, as heretofore, to gather all the food and forage of the country you can. I claim, of course, the absolute right to all property lying south of our route of march, and care not how close you pinch the inhabitants, if it be done without pillage of the mere household goods and apparel of women.

General Schofield reports this morning from Goldsboro'. So our campaign is an *eminent success.*

Yours, truly,

W. T. SHERMAN,
Major General Commanding.

Major General KILPATRICK,
Commanding Cavalry Forces.

HEADQUARTERS MILITARY DIVISION OF THE MISSISSIPPI,
In the field, near Bentonville, N. C., March 22, 1865—10 a. m.

GENERAL : Your despatch of yesterday is just received. We whipped all of Joe Johnston's army yesterday, and he retreated in disorder in the night. We are in possession of the field, and our skirmishers are after his rear guard, two miles north of Mill creek. We are not in a condition as to supplies to follow up, but will gradually draw back to Goldsboro' and refit.

Push the repairs of the railroad back to Newbern. You need not advance to Millard, but secure all the bridges across Little river, and lay your pontoons across Neuse near the main road south, unless in the mean time you have used it on Little river.

We have many prisoners, and I think we can get along till our wagons get back from Kinston. General Slocum will move to-day to Cox's bridge, but General Howard will remain till morning and follow us to Goldsboro'. I will go to Cox's to-day, and if you have gone to Millard's, will communicate with you. If this finds you at Millard's, draw back to the Little river, on the Goldsboro' side.

I will not move against Raleigh till we are resupplied.

Yours, truly,

W. T. SHERMAN,
Major General Commanding.

Major General SCHOFIELD, *Goldsboro'.*

HEADQUARTERS MILITARY DIVISION OF THE MISSISSIPPI,
In the field, near Bentonville, N. C., March 22, 1865.

GENERAL : General Schofield reports from Goldsboro', which he occupied with little opposition, so that our campaign is an *eminent success.* Let General Slocum have the roads to-day, and to-morrow move at your leisure to your new position on the right of Goldsboro', facing north, first south of the Neuse and next north. I will promise that no pains or efforts on my part shall be spared to supply your command in the most thorough manner before calling on them for new efforts.

Yours, truly,

W. T. SHERMAN, *Major General.*

Major General HOWARD,
Commanding Right Wing.

HEADQUARTERS MILITARY DIVISION OF THE MISSISSIPPI,
In the field, Cox's Bridge, Neuse River, N. C., March 22, 1865.

GENERAL: I wrote you from Fayetteville, North Carolina, on Tuesday, the 14th instant, that I was all ready to start for Goldsboro', to which point I had also ordered General Schofield from Newbern and General Terry from Wilmington. I knew that General Joe Johnston was supreme in command against me, and that he would have time to concentrate a respectable army to oppose the last stage of this march. Accordingly General Slocum was ordered to send his main supply train, under escort of two divisions, straight for Bentonville, while he, with his other four divisions, disencumbered of all unnecessary wagons, should march towards Raleigh, by way of threat, as far as Averysboro'. General Howard, in like manner, sent his trains with the 17th corps well to the right, and with the four divisions of the 15th corps took roads which would enable him to come promptly to the exposed left flank. We started on the 15th; but again the rains set in, and the roads, already bad enough, became horrible.

On Tuesday, the 15th, General Slocum found Hardee's army from Charleston, which had retreated before us from Cheraw, in position across the narrow swampy neck between Cape Fear and South river, where the road branches off to Goldsboro'. There a pretty severe fight occurred, in which General Slocum's troops carried handsomely the advanced line held by a South Carolina brigade, commanded by a Colonel Butler. Its commander, Colonel Rhett, of Fort Sumter notoriety, with one of his staff, had the night before been captured by Kilpatrick's scouts, from his very skirmish line. The next morning Hardee was found gone, and was pursued through and beyond Averysboro'. General Slocum buried one hundred and eight dead rebels, and captured and destroyed three guns. Some eighty wounded rebels were left in our hands, and, after dressing their wounds, we left them in a house attended by a confederate officer and four privates, detailed out of our prisoners and paroled for the purpose.

We resumed the march towards Goldsboro'. I was with the left wing until I supposed all danger was passed; but when General Slocum's head of column was within four miles of Bentonville, after skirmishing as usual with cavalry, he became aware that there was infantry at his front. He deployed a couple of brigades, which, on advancing, sustained a partial repulse, but soon rallied; and he formed a line of the two leading divisions, Morgan's and Carlin's, of Jeff. C. Davis's corps. The enemy attacked these with violence, but was repulsed. This was in the forenoon of Sunday, the 19th. General Slocum brought forward the two divisions of the 20th corps, and hastily disposed of them for defence, and General Kilpatrick massed his cavalry on the left.

General Joe Johnston had the night before marched his whole army, Bragg, Cheatham, S. D. Lee, Hardee, and all the troops he had drawn from every quarter, determined, as he told his men, to crush one of our corps, and then defeat us in detail. He attacked General Slocum in position from 3 p. m. on the 19th till dark, but was everywhere repulsed and lost fearfully. At the time, I was with the 15th corps, marching on a road more to the right, but on hearing of General Slocum's danger directed that corps towards Cox's bridge, and that night brought Blair's corps over and on the 20th marched rapidly on Johnston's flank and rear. We struck him about noon, and forced him to assume the defensive and to fortify. Yesterday we pushed him hard, and came very near crushing him. The right division of the 17th corps, Mower's, having broken in to within a hundred yards of where Johnston himself was, at the bridge across Mill creek, last night he retreated, leaving us in possession of the field, dead, and wounded. We have over two thousand (2,000) prisoners from this affair and the one at Aveyrsboro', and I am satisfied that Johnston's army was so roughly handled yesterday that we could march right on to Raleigh; but we have now been out six weeks, living precariously upon the collections of our foragers, our men "dirty, ragged, and saucy," and we must rest and fix up a little. Our entire losses thus far, killed, wounded, and prisoners, will be covered by two thousand five hundred (2,500,) a great part of which are, as usual, slight wounds. The enemy has lost more than double as many, and we have in prisoners alone full two thousand (2,000.)

I limited the pursuit this morning to Mill creek, and will forthwith march the army to Goldsboro' to rest, re-clothe, and get some rations.

Our combinations were such that General Schofield entered Goldsboro' from Newbern; General Terry got Cox's bridge, with pontoons laid, and a brigade across intrenched; and we whipped Joe Johnston—all on the same day.

After riding over the field of battle to-day, near Bentonville, and making the necessary orders, I have ridden down to this place, Cox's bridge, to see General Terry, and to-morrow shall ride into Goldsboro'.

I propose to collect there my army proper; shall put General Terry about Faison's depot, and General Schofield about Kinston, partly to protect the road, but more to collect such food and forage as the country affords until the railroads are repaired leading into Goldsboro'.

I fear these have not been pushed with the vigor I expected, but I will soon have them both going. I shall proceed at once to organize three armies of twenty-five thousand (25,000) men each, and will try and be all ready to march to Raleigh or Weldon, as we may determine, by or before April 10.

I enclose you a copy of my orders of to-day. I would like to be more specific, but have not the data. We have lost no general officers or no organization General Slocum took three guns at Averysboro', and lost three at the first dash on him at Bentonville. We have all our wagons and trains in good order.

Yours, truly,

W. T. SHERMAN, *Major General.*

Lieut. General U. S. GRANT,
 Commander-in-Chief, City Point, Va.

HEADQUARTERS MILITARY DIVISION OF THE MISSISSIPPI,
In the field, Cox's Bridge, N. C., March 22, 1865.

GENERAL: We whipped Johnston yesterday at Bentonville. The army will march for Goldsboro'. Be prepared to feed this army, sixty-thousand (60,000,) at Goldsboro'; General Schofield's, twenty thousand (20,000,) at Kinston; General Terry's, ten thousand (10,000,) at Faison's depot; and General Kilpatrick's, five thousand (5,000), at Mount Olive station. The two former will draw up by the Newbern road; the two latter by the Wilmington road. Show this to General Easton. I will be at Goldsboro' to-morrow, and will advise you more fully.

Yours, truly,

W. T. SHERMAN,
Major General.

Brevet Brig. General BECKWITH, *Newbern.*

HEADQUARTERS MILITARY DIVISION OF THE MISSISSIPPI,
In the field, Goldsboro', N. C., March 23, 1865.

GENERAL: On reaching Goldsboro' this morning, I found Lieutenant Dunn awaiting me with your letter of March 16 and despatch of 17th. I wrote you fully from Bentonville yesterday, and since reaching Goldsboro' have learned that my letter was sent punctually down to Newbern, where it will be despatched to you.

I am very glad to hear that General Sheridan did such good service between Richmond and Lynchburg, and hope he will keep the ball moving. I know these raids and dashes disconcert our enemy and discourage him.

General Slocum's two corps, 14th and 20th, are now coming in, and I will dispose of them north of Goldsboro', between the Weldon road and Little river. General Howard to-day is marching south of the Neuse, and to-morrow will come in and occupy ground north of Goldsboro', and extending from the Weldon railroad to that leading to Kinston.

I have ordered all the provisional divisions, made up of troops belonging to other corps, to be broken up, and the men to join their proper regiments and organizations; and have ordered General Schofield to guard the railroad back to Newbern and Wilmington, and to make up a movable column equal to twenty-five thousand (25,000) men, with which to take the field. He will be my centre, as on the Atlanta campaign. I don't think I want any more troops, other than absentees and recruits to fill up the present regiments; but that I can make up an army of eighty thousand (80,000) men by April 10. I will put General Kilpatrick out at Mount Olive station on the Wilmington road, and then allow the army some rest.

We have sent all our empty wagons under escort, with the proper staff officers, to bring up from Kingston clothing and provisions. As long as we move we can gather food and forage; but the moment we stop, trouble begins.

I feel sadly disappointed that our railroads are not done. I don't like to say there has been any neglect until I make inquiries; but it does seem to me the repairs should have been made and the road properly stocked. I can only hear of one locomotive, beside the four old ones, on the Newbern road, and two damaged locomotives found by Terry on the Wilmington road. I left Generals Easton and Beckwith purposely to make arrangements in anticipation of my arrival, and I have heard from neither, though I suppose them both to be at Morehead City.

At all events, we have now made a junction of all the armies, and if we can maintain them, will, in a short time, be in position to march against Raleigh, or Gaston, or Weldon, or even Richmond, as you may determine.

If I get the troops all well placed, and the supplies working well, I might run up to see you for a day or two before diving again into the bowels of the country.

I will make in a very short time accurate reports of our operations for the past two months.

Yours, truly,

W. T. SHERMAN,
Major General Commanding.

Lieut. General U. S. GRANT,
Commanding the Armies of the United States, City Point, Va.

HEADQUARTERS MILITARY DIVISION OF THE MISSISSIPPI,
In the field, Goldsboro', March 23, 1865.

Colonel WRIGHT, *Morehead City:*

Report to me the condition of the railroad. Employ at any cost laborers to put both the Wilmington and Newbern branches in order. Hire three gangs at each point to work each eight hours, calling it a day, so that you may do three days' work in twenty-four hours. My army is now coming in, and all will be here to-day and to-morrow. I was much disappointed that this was not already done. Cars must carry into Kinston at once supplies. I will put an engineer regiment at once to work from this end. You can have as many details as you want. Expedition is the thing.

W. T. SHERMAN,
Major General.

HEADQUARTERS MILITARY DIVISION OF THE MISSISSIPPI,
In the field, Goldsboro', N. C., March 24, 1865.

GENERAL: I have kept Lieutenant Dunn over to-day that I might report further. All the army is now in save the cavalry, which I have posted at Mount Olive Station, south of the Neuse, and General Terry's command, which to-morrow will move from Cox's ferry to Faison's depot, also on the Wilmington road. I send you a copy of my orders of this morning, the operations of which will, I think, soon complete our roads. The telegraph is now done to Morehead City, and by it I learn that stores have been sent to Kinston in boats, and our wagons are there loading with rations and clothing. By using the Neuse as high up as Kinston, and hauling from there twenty-six (26) miles, and by equipping the two roads to Morehead City and Wilmington, I feel certain I can not only feed and equip the army, but in a short time fill our wagons for another start. I feel certain, from the character of the fighting, that we have got Johnston's army afraid of us. He himself acts with timidity and caution. His cavalry alone manifests spirit, but limits its operations to our stragglers and foraging parties. My marching columns of infantry don't pay the cavalry any attention, but walk right through it.

I think I see pretty clearly how, in one more move, we can checkmate Lee, forcing him to unite Johnston with him in the defence of Richmond or abandon the cause. I feel certain if he leaves Richmond, Virginia leaves the confederacy. I will study my maps a little more before giving my clear views. I want all possible information of the Roanoke as to navigability, how far up, and with what draught.

We find the country here sandy, dry, and with good roads, and more corn and forage than I expected. The families remain, but I will gradually push them all out to Raleigh or Wilmington. We will need every house in the town. Lieutenant Dunn can tell you of many things of which I need not write.

Yours, truly,

W. T. SHERMAN,
Major General.

Lieut. General U. S. GRANT, City Point, Va.

HEADQUARTERS MILITARY DIVISION OF THE MISSISSIPPI,
In the field, Goldsboro', N. C., March 24, 1865.

GENERAL: Yours of this date to the general-in-chief is received, and he is much gratified that your command is in such good condition as to forage; secure all you can.

General Terry's command will be posted at Faison's, and must have the use of the railroad to supply it. All arrangements possible are being made to the end that all troops shall be well supplied. I enclose an order of this date which will give you a complete understanding of the matter.

At present there is a good supply of subsistence, clothing, &c., at Kinston, and if you will send your spare wagons there with the proper staff officers, Colonel Garber, acting chief quartermaster, will give you loads and all supplies that can be furnished.

There is also a quantity of mail for the army there.

I am, with respect, &c.,

L. M. DAYTON,
Assistant Adjutant General.

General KILPATRICK,
Commanding Cavalry.

HEADQUARTERS MILITARY DIVISION OF THE MISSISSIPPI,
In the field, March 24, 1865.

GENERAL: A despatch from Colonel Garber states that the trains of the 15th and 17th corps sent to Kinston are returning loaded with subsistence and some clothing, &c. He says if trains are kept moving with regularity from the command to that point he can keep the army supplied from the stores that are arriving there by water. The general-in-chief suggests that you keep your spare wagons moving accordingly. Colonel Garber will need some four hundred contrabands for loading trains and unloading vessels, and with the next train you send down you should send some to him.

Respectfully, &c.,

L. M. DAYTON,
Assistant Adjutant General.

Major General HOWARD,
Commanding Right Wing.

HEADQUARTERS MILITARY DIVISION OF THE MISSSISIPPI,
In the field, Goldsboro', N. C., March 24, 1865.

General EASTON, *Chief Quartermaster, Morehead City:*

Our field transportation is in excellent condition, and if you can place, by water, fifteen hundred tons of freight per week at Kinston, independent of the railroad, it can be brought from there by the wagons when the roads are good. The teams will be the better for being out of camp. The general suggests that you aim to accomplish this. It is desirable to relieve the railroad as much as possible.

L. M. DAYTON,
Assistant Adjutant General.

[Telegram.]

HEADQUARTERS MILITARY DIVISION OF THE MISSISSIPPI,
In the field, March 24, 1865.

General DODGE, *Quartermaster, Morehead City:*

Your despatch received. Tell General Easton to unload and despatch vessels north as fast as possible, and you proceed with all speed to General Grant, and he will order the cars and locomotives we want from Norfolk and elsewhere. Lieutenant Dunn will be down to-night, before daylight, with despatches for General Grant. Wait and take him along with you. Remember how valuable time is. We can bring up daily supplies enough, but to move, I must have enough ahead to fill my wagons.

W. T. SHERMAN,
Major General.

24 *

[Telegram.]

HEADQUARTERS MILITARY DIVISION OF THE MISSISSIPPI,
In the field, Goldsboro', March 25, 1865.

General EASTON, *Morehead City :*

I will come down with Colonel Wright. Have a steamer to take me to City Point; only four in the party. If the navy has a good gunboat doing nothing I would ask for it. I want to see General Grant and return at once; to be absent not to exceed five days.

W. T. SHERMAN,
Major General.

[Telegram.]

HEADQUARTERS MILITARY DIVISION OF THE MISSISSIPPI,
In the field, March 25, 1865.

Colonel GARBER, *Kinston :*

I think 2,000 tons a week should come by water to Kinston, and then be hauled in wagons to our camps. This will help the railroad till we get it stocked, and our mules can make one round trip a week and thrive; so keep that line moving while Colonel Wright pushes his railroad from Morehead City and Wilmington. We are doing finely now.

W. T. SHERMAN,
Major General.

[Telegram.]

HEADQUARTERS MILITARY DIVISION OF THE MISSISSIPPI,
In the field, Newbern, N. C., March 30, 1865.

General SCHOFIELD, *Goldsboro' :*

Have just arrived from City Point—all well. Have completed arrangements for twenty-five additional barges and five tugs. General McCallum, of railroad department, is with me; we will be up to-night. Telegraph me any news, if there be any. General Grant with his whole army marched out of their lines towards Dinwiddie Court House, and Lee must attack him or the force left intrenched at City Point. General Sheridan is on General Grant's left. I saw him and the President, and have a full understanding. Everything seems most favorable. I want to be all ready by April 10. Please send this message to Generals Slocum and Howard. Tell General Slocum the orders were made he asked for; also, your two corps and commanders are as requested. We must hold on to Kinston till the last moment, and then throw everything round by water to Halifax, Winton, and Norfolk.

W. T. SHERMAN,
Major General.

[Telegram.]

HEADQUARTERS MILITARY DIVISION OF THE MISSISSIPPI,
In the field, Newbern, N. C., March 30, 1865.

General EASTON, *Chief Quartermaster, Goldsboro' :*

General McCallum is with me, and will be here in an hour. We came from City Point in the naval steamer Bat, through Hatteras inlet, but she broke down ten miles below, and I came up in a small row-boat, and have sent a tug down for the rest. I got at Norfolk twenty-five barges of 150 tons, and five (5) tugs. The best we can do will be to bring up to Kinston in barges three thousand (3,000) tons of supplies and load up our supply trains there, about the 6th of April. In the mean time the railroad can supply clothing, and immediate wants. Make your calculations to have all our men provided and equipped ready to start for our next objective by or before April 10. General Grant's army is in motion; it started yesterday, and I don't see how Lee can refuse to accept battle at once. We must be ready as soon as possible. Take a minute account of transportation, so as to divide it out according to effective strength. When we start I want you and General Beckwith to move by water to another point on the coast which I will designate.

W. T. SHERMAN,
Major General.

HEADQUARTERS MILITARY DIVISION OF THE MISSISSIPPI,
In the field, Goldsboro', N. C., March 31, 1865.

GENERAL: I reached Goldsboro' last night, and find all things working well. The enemy has manifested no activity hereabouts, and has only some cavalry, seemingly, moving across our front from west to east. The railroad to the seacoast at Morehead City is working well, and is doing good work, but the Wilmington branch is not yet done. I have concluded arrangements for the barges to be loaded and brought to Kinston, where our wagons will meet them; afterwards, they can be reloaded and moved up to the Chowan to await our arrival north of the Roanoke.

I shall keep things moving, and be all ready by the date fixed, April 10. In the mean time I expect to hear the result of your moving by the left flank. I will keep you daily advised of our progress.

I must now set to work to make a report of our march from Savannah to Goldsboro' before it fades from memory, or gets lost in the rush of events. John Sherman came with me here, and will return with this to Old Point. I think Lee will unite his and Johnston's army. I cannot think he will coop himself in Richmond. If he do, he is not the general he is reputed to be; but we must go straight for him and fight him in open ground, or coop him up, when starvation will tame him.

If General Sheridan swings off and is likely to come down toward me, get me word that I may meet him. I doubt if he can cross the Roanoke for a month yet, unless he has pontoons with him; but he cannot be better employed than in raiding the road about Burkesville.

Yours, truly,

W. T. SHERMAN,
Major General.

Lieut. General U. S. GRANT, City Point.

HEADQUARTERS MILITARY DIVISION OF THE MISSISSIPPI,
In the field, Goldsboro', N. C., March 31, 1865.

DEAR SIR: I had the honor and satisfaction to receive your letter and telegram of welcome when at City Point and Old Point Comfort.

I am back again at my post, possessed of the wishes and plans of the general-in-chief, and think in due time I can play my part in the coming campaign. All things are working well, and I have troops enough to accomplish the part assigned me, and only await the loading our wagons, patching up and mending made necessary by the wear and tear of the past winter.

Feeling as I do the responsibilities that rest on me, I shall spare no labor of body or mind to deserve the success and consequent blessings that you so heartily call down on me. Others must tell you of the continued harmony and confidence that pervade this army, to which qualities the country owes more than to any mere ability that I possess.

Your son is now here, and will return to Washington with John Sherman.

With great respect,

W. T. SHERMAN, *Major General.*

Hon. E. M. STANTON,
    Secretary of War.

[Telegram.]

HEADQUARTERS MILITARY DIVISION OF THE MISSISSIPPI,
In the field, Goldsboro', N. C., March 31, 1865.

General TERRY, *Commanding at Faison's Station:*

Send orders to the depot commissary of subsistence at Wilmington to send forward coffee, sugar, and hard bread with all possible despatch. Let them come up the river to the bridge, and thence by rail to this place. We greatly need these stores. Two additional locomotives and about twenty cars are now at Wilmington, ready for your branch of the road, as soon as the bridge is done. Answer.

W. T. SHERMAN,
Major General.

HEADQUARTERS MILITARY DIVISION OF THE MISSISSIPPI,
Goldsboro', N. C., April 5, 1865.

General HAWLEY, *Wilmington:*

We will be all ready here on the 10th. The Newbern road has worked admirably, and brought us full supplies already. Your road can be used for sending up the troops destined for this army. See that General Dodge understands this, and uses the road up to Monday next to bring up men, as also such forage and stores as are still needed by Generals Terry and Schofield.

W. T. SHERMAN,
Major General.

Headquarters incumbrances can remain; forward only good men for battle.

HEADQUARTERS MILITARY DIVISION OF THE MISSISSIPPI,
In the field, Goldsboro', N. C., April 5, 1865.

DEAR GENERAL: I can hardly help smiling when I contemplate my command. It is decidedly mixed. I believe, but am not certain, that you are in my jurisdiction, but I certainly cannot help you in the way of orders or men, nor do I think you need either. General Cruft has just arrived with his provisional division, which will at once be broken up and the men sent to their proper regiments, as that of Meagher was on my arrival. You may have some feeling about my asking that General Slocum should have command of the two corps that properly belonged to you, viz: 14th and 20th; but you can recall that he was but a corps commander, and could not legally make orders of discharge, transfer, &c., which was imperatively necessary. I therefore asked that General Slocum be assigned to command "an army in the field," called the " Army of Georgia," composed of the 14th corps and 20th. The order is not yet made by the President, though I have recognized it, because both General Grant and the President sanctioned it, and promised to have the order made.

My army is now here, pretty well clad and provided; divided into three parts of two corps each—much as our old Atlanta army. I expect to move on in a few days, and propose, if Lee remains in Richmond, to pass the Roanoke and open communication with the Chowan and Norfolk. This will bring me in direct communication with General Grant.

This is an admirable point—country open, and the two railroads in good order back to Wilmington and Beaufort. We have already brought up enough to fill our wagons, and only await some few articles and the arrival of some men marching up from the coast, to be off.

General Grant explained to me his orders to you, which, of course, are all right. You can make reports direct to Washington or to General Grant, but keep me advised occasionally of the general state of affairs, that I may know what is transpiring. I must give my undivided attention to matters here. You will hear from a thousand sources pretty fair accounts of our next march.

Yours, truly,

W. T. SHERMAN, *Major General.*

Major General GEORGE H. THOMAS,
Commanding Department of Cumberland.

HEADQUARTERS MILITARY DIVISION OF THE MISSISSIPPI,
In the field, Goldsboro', N. C., April 5, 1865.

GENERAL: I now enclose you a copy of my orders prescribing the movement hence for a position on the Roanoke. The movement begins on the 10th, as I promised, and by the 12th we will be fairly under way. Our railroads have worked double what I calculated, because the track is so level that a locomotive can haul twenty-five cars instead of ten or twelve, as in upper Georgia. We now have enough of bread and small stores for our wagons, and I am hurrying up Cruft's provisional division from Tennessee; also the men who belong to this army, who had been sent to Savannah and Charleston. We can use the railroad to bring up the last; the others are marching.

I get nothing from you—nothing since I left you, and am, of course, impatient to know what Lee proposes to do. I hear nothing satisfactory from Johnston. We find Wade Hampton's cavalry on the roads to Weldon and Raleigh, but evidently only watching us. They have made no efforts to strike our railroads anywhere.

I shall expect to hear the effect of your move on Dinwiddie before I get off, but shall not wait.

Yours, truly,

W. T. SHERMAN, *Major General.*

Lieut. General U. S. GRANT, *City Point.*

HEADQUARTERS MILITARY DIVISION OF THE MISSISSIPPI,
In the field, Goldsboro', N. C., April 6, 1865.

GENERAL: I wrote you very fully from Fayetteville, since which time I have joined my own immediate army with those of Terry and Schofield, and now have at this point a splendid base, with roads finished back to Newbern and Wilmington. I have also been up to see General Grant, and am ready to march again.

It is all important that the work I did in South Carolina be kept unrepaired, and more especially that the locomotives and cars penned up about Sumterville and Florence be either destroyed or brought in. I believe that Johnston has brought up to Raleigh every man that can be brought out of South Carolina and Georgia. Therefore, now is your time to do the work. The enemy should not in any event be allowed to repair the roads about Columbia, but railroads are of less importance than locomotives and cars. It is not sufficient to burn cars. The driving wheels and trucks should *all* be broken, and axles bent, boilers punctured, cylinder heads broken and cast into deep water, and connecting rods bent and hid away. I don't know what force you have left, but I judge 2,500 men, lightly equipped, can reach Sumterville and Florence from Georgetown or the Santee bridge.

We have this minute received news that our troops are in possession of Richmond and Petersburg, with twenty-five thousand prisoners, five hundred guns, General A. P. Hill killed, Lee in full retreat on Danville, with Generals Grant and Sheridan in full pursuit. Joe Johnston is between me and Raleigh, and I will be after him as soon as I get my wagons loaded. Time is now the thing. Don't exaggerate the difficulty, but go right at it and the difficulties will disappear.

Truly, your friend,

W. T. SHERMAN,
Major General Commanding.

Major General Q. A. GILLMORE,
    Commanding Department of the South, Charleston.

HEADQUARTERS MILITARY DIVISION OF THE MISSISSIPPI,
In the field, Goldsboro', April 7, 1865.

GENERAL: The success of our armies about Richmond changes the whole plan of our campaign. We have now to watch the enemy, who is adroit, and may turn up suddenly at unexpected points. Therefore don't commit yourself to any system other than to perfect the details of our present base of supplies—Goldsboro', with its two railroads. The army is so much interested in mails and small parcels that we will need such a line as, connected with others already established, will connect our army with the mail and express system of the United States. Please send a quartermaster's inspector through to Old Point by Newbern, Roanoke island, the canal, Norfolk, &c., and on his return let him make or suggest any improvements that will increase the certainty and regularity of such a line. At present some confusion may exist, caused by the change in the lines of departments, but I think this army, which includes the department of North Carolina, has so much more interest in the line than the few about Norfolk, that you could establish a new connexion from the channel straight for Old Point. Coming this way, preference should be given to mails, couriers, and general officers travelling on duty; afterwards it could carry such quartermaster or ordnance stores as might be ordered. But in no event do I want a line of government vessels to be usurped or monopolized by a set of peddlers and traders.

The bulk of supplies should come, of course, as heretofore, by sea to Morehead City, and by schooners and light draught vessels to Newbern and Wilmington.

Yours,

W. T. SHERMAN, *Major General.*

General EASTON,
    Chief Quartermaster—Present.

HEADQUARTERS MILITARY DIVISION OF THE MISSISSIPPI,
In the field, Goldsboro', N. C., April 7, 1865.

GENERAL : The capture of Richmond, and the retreat of Lee's army to the west, (Danville and Lynchburg,) necessitates a change in our plans. We will hold fast to Goldsboro' and its lines, and move rapidly on Raleigh. I want you to be all ready to move early on Monday straight on Smithfield and Raleigh by the most direct road. General Schofield will support you with the 23d corps, following you, and the 10th and cavalry will move from Mount Olive and Faison's by Bentonville and Turner's bridge; the right wing by Pikesville and Whiteley's mill, with a division around by Nahunta and Folk's bridge. If the enemy declines to fight this side of the Neuse, I will, of course, throw the right wing up to Hinton's bridge.
Yours,

W. T. SHERMAN,
Major General Commanding.

Major General SLOCUM,
Commanding Army of Georgia.

HEADQUARTERS MILITARY DIVISION OF THE MISSISSIPPI,
In the field, Goldsboro', April 6, 1865.

I have reports from Newbern, brought by General Carl Schurz, that General Grant took Petersburg last Monday ; that General Weitzel then took Richmond, with 500 guns and 25,000 prisoners; that Generals Grant and Sheridan are pursuing Lee towards Danville. This will alter our plans. We must move on Raleigh. Be all ready. I think Johnston is still near Smithfield. We must hit him hard.
Yours,

W. T. SHERMAN,
Major General.

General KILPATRICK, *Mount Olive.*

HEADQUARTERS MILITARY DIVISION OF THE MISSISSIPPI,
In the field, Goldsboro', N. C., April 7, 1865.

GENERAL : The capture of Richmond makes a change in our plans necessary. We will move early on Monday rapidly on Raleigh, holding on to the roads from Goldsboro' back and repairing forward to Raleigh.

General Slocum will move straight on Smithfield and Raleigh ; General Schofield in support, with the 10th corps and cavalry, keeping south and west of the Neuse, by Bentonville and Turner's bridge.

I want you to start early by Pikesville, Whiteley's, and Pine level, prepared to join to General Schofield's right in case the enemy fights about Smithfield ; otherwise to swing up along the Neuse, to cross over at some point, to be determined, it may be, as high up as Hinton's bridge. Send one division light, with all the mounted men you can spare, up as high as Nahunta station, thence to join your wing *via* Folk's bridge.
I am, &c.,

W. T. SHERMAN,
Major General Commanding.

Major General HOWARD,
Commanding Right Wing.

HEADQUARTERS MILITARY DIVISION OF THE MISSISSIPPI,
In the field, Goldsboro', N. C., April 7, 1865.

GENERAL: The capture of Richmond makes unnecessary our move against the Roanoke. We will move, and that with rapidity, on Raleigh, repairing and holding the railroad to that point.

General Slocum will move Monday at daybreak straight for Smithfield and Raleigh; the right wing by Pikesville and Whiteley's mill, with a division swinging round by Nahunta and Beulah.

I want you to support General Slocum with the 23d corps, keeping a pontoon bridge here at Goldsboro' and laying another at Cox's, and let the 10th corps move straight from Faison's to Bentonville and Turner's bridge. The cavalry will also be on that flank, and will strike the enemy in flank, and break the railroad *partially* about Gulley's, provided the enemy awaits our attack this side of the Neuse. You may depend on General Slocum's bridges for the 23d corps to cross the Neuse about Smithfield. Dispose your troops detailed for the railroad guards to cover the roads from Goldsboro' back, giving most care to that from Goldsboro' to Morehead city. Winton and Murfreesboro' are now no longer needed, and you can recall any force sent there.

I am yours, truly,

W. T. SHERMAN,
Major General Commanding.

Major General SCHOFIELD,
    Commanding Centre.

HEADQUARTERS MILITARY DIVISION OF THE MISSISSIPPI,
In the field, Goldsboro', N. C., April 7, 1865.

GENERAL: We will move straight on Raleigh on Monday next. General Terry's infantry will move from Faison's to Bentonville and Turner's bridge. I want you to move on his left front, and if possible reach the railroad between Smithfield and Raleigh, disable it slightly, enough to prevent its use for a day or so, and then act against the flanks of the enemy, should he retreat to Raleigh. I think the bulk of the enemy's cavalry is between us and Weldon. As soon as you cut the railroad you should keep up a communication with Terry's left, but you may act boldly and even rashly now, for this is the time to strike quick and strong. We must get possession of Raleigh before Lee and Johnston have time to confer and make new combinations, forced on them by the loss of their capital, and the defeat of their principal army about Petersburg. You can send your wagons to the nearest infantry column. I think you had better move by Troublefield's, Lees, and Elevation, crossing Middle creek as high up as the Gulley Station road.

Yours, truly,

W. T. SHERMAN, Major General.

Major General KILPATRICK,
    Commanding Cavalry, Mt. Olive.

HEADQUARTERS MILITARY DIVISION OF THE MISSISSIPPI,
In the field, Goldsboro', N. C., April 7, 1865.

GENERAL: I have the honor herewith to send you the report of Major General Kilpatrick and of Lieutenant Colonel T. G. Baylor, chief of ordnance, which I wish you to file with my report of the recent campaign. Events progress so rapidly that we have scarce time to report them fully, but I will endeavor to

get in the full reports of my army commanders before we start for Raleigh. I
I have not yet received General Grant's orders consequent on the capture of
Richmond, and defeat of Lee's army before Petersburg, but I am so confident
that I know his wishes, that my orders are all out for my entire army to move
at daylight on Monday next, the 10th, for Raleigh. Before the capture of Richmond, of which I only heard yesterday, I was preparing to feign on Raleigh,
and move across the Roanoake above Gaston, but now I shall move straight on
Raleigh, repairing the railroad to that place. From Raleigh I can reach the
Danville and Charlotte road, about Greensboro', but I expect definite orders be
fore getting off. I want my mails to come to Old Point, Dismal Swamp Canal,
Newbern, Goldsboro', &c., and have ordered General Easton to complete arrangements to that end.

It is now important that I should have more rapid communication with headquarters than heretofore.

General Meigs is now here and will start for Washington to-night.

I am, with respect, yours, truly,

W. T. SHERMAN,
Major General Commanding.

Major General H. W. HALLECK,
Chief of Staff, Washington, D. C.

HEADQUARTERS ARMIES OF THE UNITED STATES,
Wilson's Station, April 5, 1865.

Major General SHERMAN :

All indications now are that Lee will attempt to reach Danville with the rem-
nant of his force. Sheridan, who was up with him last night, reports all that
is left, horse, foot and dragoons, at twenty thousand (20,000,) much demoralized.
We hope to reduce this number one-half. I shall push on to Burkesville, and if
a stand is made at Danville, will in a very few days go there. If you can possibly do so, push on from where you are and let us see if we cannot finish the
job with Lee's and Johnston's armies. Whether it will be better for you to
strike for Greensboro' or nearer to Danville, you will be better able to judge
when you receive this. Rebel armies now are the only strategic points to
strike at.

U. S. GRANT,
Lieutenant General.

Official :

T. S. BOWERS,
Assistant Adjutant General.

HEADQUARTERS MILITARY DIVISION OF THE MISSISSIPPI,
In the field, Goldsboro', N. C., April 8, 1865.

GENERAL : I have just received your letter of the 5th from Wilson's station,
and although I have written you several letters lately, will repeat.

On Monday at daylight all my army will move straight on Joe Johnston, supposed to be between me and Raleigh, and I will follow him wherever he may
go. If he retreats on Danville to make junction with Lee, I will do the same,
though I may take a course round him, bending towards Greensboro', for the
purpose of turning him North. I will bear in mind your plain and unmistaka-
ble point that " the rebel armies are now the strategic points to strike at." I
will follow Johnston, presuming that you are after Lee, or all that you have left
of him, and if they come together, we will also. I think I will be at Raleigh

on Thursday, the 13th, and shall pursue Johnston towards Greensboro', unless it be manifest that Lee has gone towards Danville. I shall encourage him to come to bay or to move towards Danville. as I don't want to race all the way back through South Carolina and Georgia. It is to our interest to let Lee and Johnston come together, just as a billiard-player would nurse the balls when he has them in a nice place. I am delighted and amazed at the result of your move to the south of Petersburg, and Lee has lost in one day the reputation of three years. and you have established a reputation for perseverance and pluck that would make Wellington jump out of his coffin. I wish you could have waited a few days, or that I could have been here a week sooner, but it is not too late yet, and you may rely, with absolute certainty, that I will be after Johnston with about 80,000 men, provided for twenty full days, which will last me forty, and I will leave a small force here at Goldsboro' and repair the railroad up to Raleigh. If you have a spare division you might send it to General Schofield to help him hold this line of railroad out from Morehead City to Goldsboro', but I will not hesitate to let go railroad and everything, if I can get at Joe Johnston in an open field. If General Sheridan don't run his horses off their legs, and you can spare him for a week or so, let him feel down for me, and I think he can make a big haul of horses. Tell him I make him a free gift of all the blooded stock of North Carolina, including Wade Hampton's, whose pedigree and stud are of high repute.

Don't fail to have Stoneman break through the mountains of west North Carolina. He will find plenty of Union men who will aid him to reach either your army or mine, and Canby should, if he takes Mobile, get up the Alabama river about Selma, from which place he can catch all fragments passing towards Texas. I have an idea that he can get up the Alabama river even if he do not take Mobile. I have a report from General Wilson, who will, I think, break up all rail-road lines in Alabama.

  Yours, truly,

W. T. SHERMAN,
Major General Commanding.

Lieut. General U. S. Grant,
   City Point, Va.

Headquarters Military Division of the Mississippi,
In the field, Goldsboro', April 8, 1865—12 m.

General Kilpatrick, *Mt. Olive:*

I now have official intelligence from General Grant of the defeat of Lee's army, and occupation of Petersburg and Richmond. He is pursuing the fragments, represented at 20,000, towards Danville. We move on Monday rapidly on Johnston towards Raleigh. I sent you orders last night, and now repeat the substance. Move early on Monday by Troublefield's store, Lee's and Elevation, to strike the railroad between Smithfield and Raleigh. General Terry will move *via* Bentonville and Turner's bridge. The main army takes the main road, crossing the Neuse at Smithfield. Now is the time for your cavalry to work on the flanks and rear of Johnston. I think Wheeler is between this and Weldon. I think Butler's division has been sent back to South Carolina; I hear of them between Wilmington and Florence. Wade Hampton is about Smithfield, where I also suppose Johnston to be, though he may have moved back towards Raleigh. Answer.

W. T. SHERMAN,
Major General.

HEADQUARTERS MILITARY DIVISION OF THE MISSISSIPPI,

In the field, April 7, 1865.

General KILPATRICK:

Spencer can have his leave. You can communicate with me here till Monday. I will then keep with General Slocum's left corps near Cox's bridge, and be near Smithfield Tuesday. Afterwards, on the main road to Raleigh, not far from the head of column. General Sheridan has done great service against the retreating infantry, cutting off and capturing whole brigades of infantry, artillery and wagon trains. Of course I would like you to have new saddles, but time won't wait. I will have the telegraph and railroad keep up with me, and shall habitually camp near the wires to communicate back. We will keep a bridge here and at Cox's. Terry's command will be your support, until we are all across the Neuse at Smithfield, when General Slocum will be the left, General Schofield with General Terry the centre, and General Howard the right. I intend to push to Greensboro' as fast as I can do so, consistent with ordinary prudence.

W. T. SHERMAN,
Major General Commanding.

HEADQUARTERS MILITARY DIVISION OF THE MISSISSIPPI,

In the field, Goldsboro', N. C., April 8, 1865.

Dear MACOMB: You have of course heard of the defeat by General Grant of Lee's army at Petersburg, and consequent occupation of Richmond and Petersburg. I have letters from General Grant of the 5th from Wilson's station, on the road towards Burkesville, stating that he is pushing the pursuit after the retreating army. This changes our whole plans, and I will move straight for Raleigh instead of marching for the Roanoake. We will not, in consequence, have any use for Winton or Murfreesboro', and if General Schofield has sent any troops up to Winton, he will recall them, and use them to cover our railroads. I expect to march on Monday, 10th, on Raleigh and maybe Greensboro', and I give you this notice that you may not be disappointed in the recall of troops from the Chowan. So far as my operations are concerned for the next month, all I ask is that the sounds and channels leading up to Newbern and Kinston be patrolled by the gunboats. Hoping to meet you again soon,

I am, with respect, yours, truly,

W. T. SHERMAN,
Major General.

Captain W. N. MACOMB, *U. S. N.*,
Commanding Squadron, Albemarle Sound.

HEADQUARTERS MILITARY DIVISION OF THE MISSISSIPPI,

In the field, Goldsboro', April 8, 1865—7 p. m.

General MEIGS, *Morehead City:*

Am just in receipt of a cipher despatch from General Grant, at Burkesville, of 6th. He is pressing Lee hard, and expects to scatter his whole army. Davis and cabinet are at Danville. Tell Major Leet, who comes down to-day, to get to Old Point as quick as possible, and get a message to General Grant, at any cost, that I will push Joe Johnston to the death.

W. T. SHERMAN,
Major General.

[Cipher telegram.]

BURKESVILLE, *Va., April* 6, 1865.

Major General W. T. SHERMAN :

We have Lee's army pressed hard; his men scattering and going to their homes by the thousand.

He is endeavoring to reach Danville, where Jeff. Davis and his cabinet have gone. I shall press the pursuit to the end. Push Johnston at the same time, and let us finish up this job at once.

U. S. GRANT,
Lieutenant General.

HEADQUARTERS MILITARY DIVISION OF THE MISSISSIPPI,
In the field, Smithfield, N. C., April 11, 1865.

GENERAL : Your note is received. You need not have the Lowell·factory destroyed. I will wait our reception at Raleigh to shape our general policy. You may instruct General Logan to exact bonds that the factory shall not be used for the confederacy. Of course, the bond is not worth a cent; but if the factory owners do not abide by the conditions, they cannot expect any mercy the next time.

Until we get to Raleigh I propose to keep up connexion back with Goldsboro'. I shall await your coming to-morrow morning. I send you a Raleigh paper of the 10th.

Yours,

W. T. SHERMAN,
Major General Commanding.

Major General O. O. HOWARD,
Commanding Right Wing.

HEADQUARTERS MILITARY DIVISION OF THE MISSISSIPPI,
In the field, Smithfield, N. C., April 11, 1865.—10.30.

GENERAL : General Slocum has two bridges done, and will cross early and go to the point on the railroad, twelve miles out, known as Stalling's, (Gulley's on our map.) We have questioned the doctors and preachers, who all agree that our map is substantially correct, and that there is but one road between Swift creek and the Neuse, until abreast of Gulley's.

General Kilpatrick reported from Moore's house, on Middle creek, (not on our map,) which must be up near Leachburg; he reports bridges burned. If in your progress you judge Johnston to be beyond Raleigh and no fight, you can go as far to the westward as you please, aiming towards Chapel Hill and Hillsboro'. You are safe in leaving your wagons under small escort to follow until we are sure of Raleigh.

General Howard's two corps are at Pine Level and Lowell factory, and will keep well up on this side the Neuse, unless wanted.

I would give you the middle or direct road, but judge time important, to save fortifying by the enemy, but will give you *the centre* as soon as you get Cox and Terry together. In reporting your position use names on my map though incorrect.

Yours,

W. T. SHERMAN,
Major General Commanding.

Gen. SCHOFIELD, *near Fennon's bridge.*

HEADQUARTERS MILITARY DIVISION OF THE MISSISSIPPI,
In the field, Smithfield, N. C., April 11, 1865—10.30 p. m.

GENERAL : Please hereafter, in reporting your position, to use names on our map. "Moore's," on Middle creek, is not down. I suppose you to be about the mill without name. You may count on my being near Gulley's store to-morow night, and you may go as near Raleigh as you can. I have Raleigh papers of the 10th; Stoneman is raiding *strong* near Greensboro', and Wheeler is after him. A portion of Wade Hampton's cavalry is cut off over towards Weldon (Nahunta swamp.) I don't think Hampton has 2,000 cavalry with him, and this is your chance. I will push all the columns straight on Raleigh. I don't care about Raleigh now, but want to defeat and destroy the confederate army. Therefore you may run any risk. Of course don't break the railroad, except to the rear (west) of Johnston, as we want the railroad up to Raleigh.

General Wilson has taken Selma, and is threatening Montgomery. He had whipped Red Jackson, 27 miles from Selma, and at Selma knocked Forrest all to pieces. Rebel papers report Forrest wounded in three places. Abe Buford to defend Montgomery with citizens. Dick Taylor ran westward from Selma. Maury cooped up in Mobile. General Grant is between Johnston and Lee. They cannot communicate. Davis is at Danville.

Yours,

W. T. SHERMAN, *Major General.*

Gen. KILPATRICK, *Commanding Cavalry.*

HEADQUARTERS MILITARY DIVISION OF THE MISSISSIPPI,
In the field, Smithfield, N. C., April 12, 1865—5 a. m.

GENERAL : I have this moment received your telegram announcing the surrender of Lee's army. I hardly know how to express my feelings, but you can imagine them. The terms you have given Lee are magnanimous and liberal. Should Johnston follow Lee's example, I shall, of course, grant the same. He is retreating before me on Raleigh, and I shall be there to-morrow. Roads are heavy, but under the inspiration of the news from you, we can march twenty-five miles a day. I am twenty-seven miles from Raleigh, but some of my army is eight miles behind. If Johnston retreat south, I will follow him to insure the scattering his force, and capture of the locomotives and cars at Charlotte. But I take it, he will surrender at Raleigh. General Kilpatrick's cavalry is ten miles to the south and west of me, viz: on Middle creek, and I have sent Major Audenreid with orders for him to make for the south and west of Raleigh by five different roads. The railroad is being repaired from Goldsboro' to Raleigh, but I will not aim to carry it further. I shall expect to hear of General Sheridan, in case Johnston does not surrender at Raleigh ; with a little more cavalry, I would be sure to capture the whole army.

Yours, truly,

W. T. SHERMAN,
Major General Commanding.

Lieut. Gen. U. S. GRANT,
Commanding Armies of the United States, Virginia.

HEADQUARTERS MILITARY DIVISION OF THE MISSISSIPPI,
In the field, near Gulley's, 12, 1865—7 p. m.

General KILPATRICK :

Your note is received. Certainly you may go into Raleigh to-night and press Johnston's *rear.* I want him to go towards Greensboro', and I will cut across to Charlotte via Ashboro'. Cut across the rear of his column, right and left. I will come to Raleigh early. Keep me advised of the direction of Johnston's retreat as often as possible.

Yours, in haste,

W. T. SHERMAN, *Major General.*

HEADQUARTERS MILITARY DIVISION OF THE MISSISSIPPI,
In the field, Raleigh, N. C., April 13, 1865.

Lieut. Gen. U. S. GRANT,
City Point, Virginia:

We entered Raleigh this morning. Johnston has retreated westward. I shall move to Ashville and Salisbury or Charlotte. I hope General Sheridan is coming this way with his cavalry. If I can bring Johnston to a stand, I shall soon fix him. The people here have not heard of the surrender of Lee and hardly credit it. All well.

W. T. SHERMAN,
Major General.

HEADQUARTERS MILITARY DIVISION OF THE MISSISSIPPI,
In the field, Raleigh, April 13, 1865.

GENERAL: Yours of 11.50 a. m. is received and quite satisfactory, and the general wishes you to keep pushing the enemy. To-night the general will inform you of the coming move. The columns are closing up here now. Have you captured any railroad stock? No further news.

I am, &c.,

L. M. DAYTON,
Assistant Adjutant General.

General KILPATRICK, *Commanding.*

HEADQUARTERS MILITARY DIVISION OF THE MISSISSIPPI,
In the field, Raleigh, N. C., April 13, 1865.

GENERAL: I have been out and am just back, and hasten to answer yours of to-day. I have two locomotives here, and will send one up the road to bring back the cars you have captured. Please have pickets along the road so as to advise the conductor where to stop.

It will take all day to-morrow to close up our trains and to draw out on the new lines of operations, of which I will fully advise you to-morrow. Rest your animals to-morrow, or confine your operations to mere feints, and be ready for work the next day. I think we may expect General Sheridan down soon. I think I can force Johnston to disperse his army or accept battle in a few days, and will proceed as fast as I can get troops into position. We will hold Raleigh, and repair roads and telegraph back to Goldsboro',

Yours, truly,

W. T. SHERMAN,
Major General Commanding.

General KILPATRICK,
Commanding Cavalry.

HEADQUARTERS MILITARY DIVISION OF THE MISSISSIPPI,
In the field, Raleigh, N. C., April 14, 1865.

General EASTON, *Newbern :*

I want the road repaired up to Raleigh and put in order, but no stores sent up till you hear we need them. I suppose Johnston to be about Greensboro' and Salisbury, and I must go there, and will endeavor to capture his army and materials. Of course he cannot fight me now, and all I fear he may scatter his men and escape. We will take vast amounts of railroad stock and other property, because it cannot escape us, but it will take time to run it down to the seacoast. Governor Vance sought an interview with me, but before I got his messenger back our cavalry approached Raleigh, and he went off for fear of arrest. I have sent out for him to come and see me, with a promise of safety. Keep General Grant advised of my whereabouts, by all chances. The troops are now moving, but I will not go till to-morrow. I will garrison Goldsboro' and Raleigh. Send me any news that may reach you. Trains all up and in good condition. I think I will find forage enough, but, in any event, the grass and wheat fields begin to give us pasturage.

W. T. SHERMAN,
Major General Commanding.

HEADQUARTERS MILITARY DIVISION OF THE MISSISSIPPI,
In the field, Raleigh, N. C., April 14, 1865.

GENERAL: I sent you orders to-day, but now enclose you a copy. You see I am to put my army where, if Johnston tries to pass out by Charlotte, I can strike him in flank, but if he remains at Greensboro' I shall capture the whole. All I expect of you is to keep up a delusion, viz: that we are following him *via* the University and Hillsboro', until I get my infantry heads of column across the Haw river, when I want you to cross also, and feel out towards Greensboro', till I get to Ashboro', when, if he remains at Greensboro', I can approach him from the south and force him to battle, to surrender, or disperse. You will perceive that we save a couple of days by cutting across the bend in the direction of Salisbury. I am very anxious to prevent his escape towards Georgia. If he does go to Georgia we can capture all the rolling stock and vast amounts of property on the road from Salisbury back to Greensboro'. The governor asks me to suspend hostilities and to confer with him. I am willing to confer with him, but not to suspend hostilities. I will not suspend hostilities till Johnston's army is captured or scattered.

General Howard to-morrow will have one corps at Jones's station, and one at Morrison's station. Next day all move by separate roads for Ashboro'. My army is very large, and cannot move as fast as Johnston, who has the assistance of the railroads. I am in hopes that General Sheridan will come down, when he, with the aid of your cavalry, can get ahead of him, and hold him until we get up, when we can make short work of him.

The people here manifest more signs of subjugation than I have yet seen, but Jeff. Davis has more lives than a cat, and we must not trust him. If you reach the University do not disturb its libraries, buildings, or specific property.

Yours, truly,

W. T. SHERMAN,
Major General Commanding

General KILPATRICK, *Commanding Cavalry.*

HEADQUARTERS MILITARY DIVISION OF THE MISSISSIPPI,
In the field, Raleigh, N. C., April 14, 1865.

GENERAL : The letter by flag of truce is from General Johnston, which is the beginning of the end. Send my answer at once, and to-morrow do not advance your cavalry beyond the University, or to a point abreast of it on the railroad. I will be up to Morrisville to-morrow to receive the answer, and it may be to confer with General Johnston. The infantry will come to Morrisville.

Yours, truly,

W. T. SHERMAN, *Major General.*

General KILPATRICK,
Commanding Cavalry.

HEADQUARTERS MILITARY DIVISION OF THE MISSISSIPPI,
In the field, Raleigh, N. C., April 14, 1865—12 m.

GENERAL : The general-in-chief is just in receipt of a communication from General Johnston, C. S. A., which is the forerunner to events that may obviate our contemplated long march. You will, therefore, by his direction, to-morrow (15th) place one corps of your command at Holly Springs, and the other just outside of Raleigh, in the direction of the proposed march, and there await further directions from him.

I have the honor to be, general, yours, &c.,

L. M. DAYTON,
Assistant Adjutant General.

Major General J. M. SCHOFIELD,
Commanding Army of Ohio.

HEADQUARTERS MILITARY DIVISION OF THE MISSISSIPPI,
In the field, Raleigh, N. C., April 14, 1865—12 m. d.

GENERAL : The general-in-chief is just in receipt of despatches from General Johnston, C. S. A., which are tending to the end of making unnecessary our contemplated long march. You will, therefore, by his direction, to-morrow place one corps of your command at Morrisville, and the other at Jones's station, and there await further directions from him before continuing the march. The general will go to Morrisville for further communication.

I have the honor to be, with respect, yours, &c.,

L. M. DAYTON,
Assistant Adjutant General.

Major General O. O. HOWARD,
Commanding Army of the Tennessee.

HEADQUARTERS MILITARY DIVISION OF THE MISSISSIPPI,
In the field, Raleigh, N. C., April 14, 1865.

General EASTON, *Newbern :*

The capture of Selma is also announced in rebel papers. I expect every hour an answer from General Johnston, but shall start to-morrow towards Ashboro', unless he makes clear and satisfactory terms. You had better hold yourself prepared to give us forage here when the railroad is done, as we have enough provision on hand; but send nothing this side of Goldsboro' until ordered by myself or some army commander.

W. T. SHERMAN, *Major General.*

HEADQUARTERS MILITARY DIVISION OF THE MISSISSIPPI,
In the field, Raleigh, April 14, 1865.

GENERAL : I have faith in General Johnston's personal sincerity, and do not believe he would use a subterfuge to cover his movements. He could not stop the movement of his troops till he got my letter, which I hear was delayed all day yesterday by your adjutant's not sending it forward. If he gains on us by the time lost, we will make it up at the expense of North Carolina. Major McCoy will be with you, and will receive Johnston's letter, and I will instruct him to open it and send me contents. My orders are for all to be ready to move. Yesterday the roads were impassable to trains, but if the weather be favorable they will be good to-morrow.

W. T. SHERMAN,
Major General.

General KILPATRICK, *Durham's.*

HEADQUARTERS MILITARY DIVISION OF THE MISSISSIPPI,
In the field, Raleigh, April 14, 1865.

GENERAL : The general-in-chief has arranged for a meeting with General J. E. Johnston, near Durham's station, North Carolina railroad, at 12 m., April 17, and to accomplish it will leave here at 8 a. m. to-morrow, by railroad. Until further orders he directs that all troops will remain as they are at this time. The movements as directed in Special Field Orders No. 55 being for the time suspended.

I am, general, with respect,

L. M. DAYTON,
Assistant Adjutant General.

General H. W. SLOCUM,
Commanding Army of Georgia.

HEADQUARTERS MILITARY DIVISION OF THE MISSISSIPPI,
In the field, April 18, 1865—9.30 p. m.

General EASTON, *Morehead :*

Major Hitchcock leaves here in an hour for Washington with despatches of great importance. Have the most fleet steamer you can obtain ready on his arrival to take him direct to Washington, and return subject to his orders. He will telegraph you from Goldsboro' and Newbern, and you can calculate the time you will have, but he must not be delayed a minute.

By order of Major General W. T. Sherman.

L. M. DAYTON,
Assistant Adjutant General.

[By telegraph to Morehead City, steamer to Old Point, and telegraph to Lieutenant General Grant, Washington.]

HEADQUARTERS MILITARY DIVISION OF THE MISSISSIPPI,
In the field, Raleigh, N. C., April 22, 1865.

General Wilson held Macon on the 20th, with Howell Cobb, G. W. Smith, and others as prisoners; but they claim the benefit of my armistice, and he has telegraphed to me, through the rebel lines, for orders. I have answered him that he may draw out of Macon, and hold his command for further orders, unless he has reason to believe that rebels are changing the status to our prejudice.

A brigade of rebels offered to surrender to me yesterday, but I prefer to make one grand *finale*, which I believe to be perfectly practicable. There will be no trouble in adjusting matters in North Carolina, Georgia, and Alabama, and I think South Carolina ought to be satisfied with Charleston and Columbia in ruins. All we await is an answer from you and the President. Weather fine and roads good. Troops ready for fight or home.

W. T. SHERMAN,
Major General.

HEADQUARTERS MILITARY DIVISION OF THE MISSISSIPPI,
In the field, April 24, 1865.

General KILPATRICK:

Send the enclosed notice to General Johnston immediately by an officer, who will obtain a receipt for it, and send the same to me. It is a notice that the truce will end forty-eight hours after the notice reaches the rebel lines.

W. T. SHERMAN,
Major General Commanding.

HEADQUARTERS MILITARY DIVISION OF THE MISSISSIPPI,
In the field, Raleigh, N. C., April 24, 1865—6 a. m.

General JOHNSTON, *Commanding Confederate Army, Greensboro':*

You will take notice that the truce or suspension of hostilities agreed to between us will cease in forty-eight hours after this is received at your lines, under first of the articles of our agreement.

W. T. SHERMAN,
Major General.

HEADQUARTERS MILITARY DIVISION OF THE MISSISSIPPI,
In the field, Raleigh, April 24, 1865.

General JOHNSTON, *Commanding Confederate Armies:*

I have replies from Washington to my communications of April 18. I am instructed to limit my operations to your immediate command, and not to attempt civil negotiations. I therefore demand the surrender of your army on the same terms as were given General Lee, at Appomattox, of April 9th, instant, purely and simply.

W. T. SHERMAN,
Major General Commanding.

HEADQUARTERS MILITARY DIVISION OF THE MISSISSIPPI,
In the field, Raleigh, N. C., April 24, 1865.

General GILLMORE, *Hilton Head, S. C.:*

Send several couriers by different routes by land from Savannah to General Wilson, at Macon, that the truce is at an end and hostilities are resumed, and that he will go on and act according to original orders. You will also do the same.

W. T. SHERMAN,
Major General Commanding.

HEADQUARTERS MILITARY DIVISION OF THE MISSISSIPPI,
In the field, N. C., April 25, 1865.

GENERAL: You may make your orders to start to-morrow towards the enemy wherever we may find him, and instead of following the route prescribed in Special Field Orders No. 55, you may cover the railroad and cover it substantially in the direction of Greensboro' and Salisbury. Colonel Wright will be ordered to repair it behind us as far as the company's shops in Alamance county.

I am, &c.,

W. T. SHERMAN,
Major General Commanding.

Major General SCHOFIELD,
Commanding Department of North Carolina.

HEADQUARTERS MILITARY DIVISION OF THE MISSISSIPPI,
In the field, Raleigh, April 26, 1865.

General KILPATRICK, *Durham's:*

No orders further than to hold your command well in hand, ready to move on notice; but no movements will be made until after the interview between Generals Johnston and Sherman has terminated. Please have about 20 horses ready, as Generals Howard, Schofield, and probably Blair, will go up with the general.

The dismounted men will go up with your train in the morning, as the locomotives cannot haul sufficient number of cars to accommodate them.

L. M. DAYTON,
Assistant Adjutant General.

HEADQUARTERS MILITARY DIVISION OF THE MISSISSIPPI,
In the field, Raleigh, April 26, 1865.

GENERAL: The general-in-chief will again meet General J. E. Johnston, C. S. A., on same conditions of armistice as on the 18th instant. He directs that you hold your command at rest, but well in hand, ready for further move on notice from him.

I am, general, with respect,

L. M. DAYTON,
Major and Assistant Adjutant General.

Major General H. W. SLOCUM,
Commanding Army of Georgia.

HEADQUARTERS MILITARY DIVISION OF THE MISSISSIPPI,
In the field, Fort Monroe, May 8, 1865.

General SCHOFIELD, *Raleigh:*

Have arrived at Fortress Monroe, and will go to City Point to-morrow. Telegraph to General Wilson to act in all matters according to his own good sense, and in a day or so I will hear from General Grant whether I am to command my own subordinates or not. Generals Howard and Slocum have reached Petersburg.

W. T. SHERMAN,
Major General.

HEADQUARTERS MILITARY DIVISION OF THE MISSISSIPPI,
In the field, Fortress Monroe, May 8, 1865—12 p. m.

General GRANT, *Washington:*

I have full despatches from General Wilson of the 6th. One boat has arrived at Augusta all right. He is after Davis, who cannot escape, save in disguise; but he is reported in Georgia, escorted by about 70 officers, as a special body-guard, and about 3,000 cavalry.

Does Mr. Stanton's newspaper order take General Wilson from my command, or shall I continue to order him? If I have proven incompetent to manage my own command, let me know it.

W. T. SHERMAN,
Major General.

HEADQUARTERS MILITARY DIVISION OF THE MISSISSIPPI,
In the field, Manchester, Va., May 9, 1865.

General SCHOFIELD, *Raleigh:*

Your despatch is received. Notify General Wilson that he must get forage in Georgia for the present. I will notify General Grant of his wants, by telegraph, and await his instructions.

W. T. SHERMAN,
Major General.

HEADQUARTERS MILITARY DIVISION OF THE MISSISSIPPI,
In the field, Manchester, Va., May 9, 1865.

GENERAL: I have joined my army at Manchester, opposite Richmond, and await your orders. General Wilson telegraphs through General Schofield for hay and forage for 20,000 animals, to be sent up the Savannah river to Augusta. Under Secretary Stanton's newspaper orders, taking Wilson substantially from my command, I wish you would give the orders necessary for the case.

W. T. SHERMAN,
Major General Commanding.

Lieut. General U. S. GRANT,
Commander-in-Chief.

[Cipher.]

HEADQUARTERS MILITARY DIVISION OF THE MISSISSIPPI,
In the field, City Point, Va., May 9, 1865.

GENERAL: I have the honor to report my arrival at City Point, pursuant to your orders, and my army is reported by General Easton, quartermaster, to be at Manchester, opposite Richmond. I have, as yet, seen no orders for me to come to Alexandria, although that was contemplated by you at Raleigh. Will you please telegraph me orders at Manchester, where I will forthwith join the army. I have nothing from you since you left Raleigh.

W. T. SHERMAN,
Major General.

Lieut. General U. S. GRANT,
Washington, D. C.

HEADQUARTERS MILITARY DIVISION OF THE MISSISSIPPI,
In the field, Manchester, Va., May 10, 1865.

Lieut. General GRANT, *Washington, D. C.:*

Your despatch, directing me to march my command to Alexandria, just received. I have ordered the army of Georgia to move to-morrow, and the army of the Tennessee to follow next day.

W. T. SHERMAN,
Major General.

———

HEADQUARTERS MILITARY DIVISION OF THE MISSISSIPPI,
On the road, Concord Church, 25 *miles from*
Richmond, Va., May 12, 1865—4 p. m.

Lieutenant General GRANT, *Washington:*

The following despatch from General Wilson is just received and sent for your information.

W. T. SHERMAN,
Major General.

———

[By telegraph from Macon Ga., *May* 10, 1865—3 p. m.]

Major General SHERMAN, *through General Schofield:*

Captain Abraham, of General Upton's division, yesterday received surrender of two brigades rebel cavalry, two thousand strong, at Washington, Georgia, including Generals Vaughn, Dibbrell, Elzey, Williams, Loomis, Gilmer, and Lawton. General Croxton is now engaged in paroling Ferguson's brigade at Forsyth. Balance of the rebel cavalry, which started as Jeff. Davis's escort, has either been surrendered or gone home. General Vaughn told General Upton that he had received positive orders to escort Davis to Mississippi river, but on his arrival at Washington determined to go no further. The money Davis had with him (doubtless over-estimated) has been paid his troops, and scattered through the country around Washington. Lieutenant Youman, a very energetic and capable officer, reports Davis on night of the 7th tried to cross Chattahoochee at Warsaw, but lost his trail. Youman himself crossed Chattahoochee at Vining's late same night. Since then he has not been heard from. General Winslow seems to think his report probable, though he favors now the idea that he may have turned south. Alexander's brigade is in the neighborhood of Marietta. Will strike trail if there is one. My troops are all over North Georgia, at Warrenton, Athens, Madison, Warsaw, Lawrenceville, and other places, with scouts on every road. The country southward, eastward, and west is also thoroughly patrolled.

J. H. WILSON,
Brevet Major General.

———

HEADQUARTERS MILITARY DIVISION OF THE MISSISSIPPI,
In the field, Fredericksburg, Va., May 15, 1865.

GENERAL: I have to report my arrival here. I left General Slocum at noon at Chancellorsville, and he will cross the 14th at Raccoon ford, and 20th at U. S. Ford to-morrow. General Logan is not yet in, and I suspect he has found his roads badly cut up by the troops that preceded him.

W. T. SHERMAN, *Major General.*

General U. S. GRANT,
Washington, D. C.

HEADQUARTERS MILITARY DIVISION OF THE MISSISSIPPI,
In the field, Alexandria, Va., May 19, 1865.

GENERAL: I have the honor to report my arrival at camp near the Washington road, three miles north of Alexandria. All my army should be in camp near by to-day.

The 15th corps, the last to leave Richmond, camped last night at the Occoquan.

I have seen the orders for the review in the papers, but Colonel Sawyer says it is not here in official form. I am old-fashioned, and prefer to see orders through some other channels, but if that be the new fashion, so be it. I will be all ready by Wednesday, though in the rough. Troops have not been paid for eight or ten months, and clothing may be bad, but a better set of legs and arms cannot be displayed on this continent.

Send me all orders and letters you may have for me, and let some one newspaper know that the vandal Sherman is encamped near the canal bridge, half-way between the Long bridge and Alexandria, to the west of the road, where his friends, if any, can find him.

As ever, your friend,

W. T. SHERMAN,
Major General.

General RAWLINS,
Chief of Staff, Washington, D. C.

HEADQUARTERS MILITARY DIVISION OF THE MISSISSIPPI,
In the field, camp near Washington, May 28, 1865.

GENERAL: I see no public business that calls for my further stay at Washington. I have made my full testimony before the "Committee on the Conduct of the War," as ordered; and the four corps, under my command here, are in good camps, and the company and field officers are busy upon the muster-rolls and papers needed for the payment of the troops, and for disbanding of such as are entitled to discharge under existing orders. You remember that the commanders of military divisions have nothing to do with such matters, so that my longer presence is unnecessary. I will therefore ask for an order, or for instructions to return to the west—say Louisville, Kentucky, or wherever the general thinks I should take post. If the territory north of the Ohio river is to be included in the military division of the Mississippi, I would prefer, for the sake of economy, to reside in Cincinnati. I would like to take New York and Chicago in my route west, to keep appointments made by my family before my arrival here. I will be ready to leave Washington on Wednesday.

I am, with great respect,

W. T. SHERMAN,
Major General Commanding.

Colonel T. S. BOWERS,
Assistant Adjutant General, Headquarters Armies United States.

LANCASTER, OHIO, *June 30, 1865.*

General E. D. TOWNSEND,
Assistant Adjutant General U. S. Army, Washington, D. C.:

Despatch received. Assignment to St. Louis perfectly satisfactory.

W. T. SHERMAN,
Major General.

LANCASTER, OHIO, *June* 30, 1865.

Lieut. General U. S. GRANT,
Washington, D. C.:

My assignment to St. Louis is perfectly satisfactory. I go to Cincinnati to-day, and will go to Louisville, and it may be to St. Louis, before I come back.

W. T. SHERMAN,
Major General.

All of which is respectfully submitted, by your obedient servant,

W. T. SHERMAN,
Major General United States Army.

HEADQUARTERS MILITARY DIVISION OF THE MISSISSIPPI,
St. Louis, Missouri, November 21, 1865.